George S. Kaufman

GEORGE S. KAUFMAN

His Life, His Theater

MALCOLM GOLDSTEIN

New York Oxford

OXFORD UNIVERSITY PRESS

1979

Copyright © 1979 by Oxford University Press, Inc.

Library of Congress Cataloging in Publication Data
Goldstein, Malcolm.
George S. Kaufman: his life, his theater.
1. Kaufman, George Simon, 1889-1961.
2. Dramatists, American—20th century—Biography   I. Title.
PS3521.A727Z67   812'.5'2   79-12819   ISBN 0-19-502623-3

Printed in the United States of America

To the Wulfmans:
Jeanne
Robert
Clifford
David

Acknowledgments

It is a pleasure to report that while writing about George S. Kaufman I have had the close and generous co-operation of his family. My heartfelt thanks go to Anne Kaufman Schneider, his daughter, for countless hours of conversation about her father, for the loan of manuscripts and letters by both her father and her mother, and for easing my path to many members of her father's circle. I am equally grateful to Irving Schneider, Kaufman's son-in-law; Beatrice Colen, his granddaughter; Ruth Kaufman Friedlich, his sister; Allan Friedlich, his nephew; and Leonard Bakrow, his brother-in-law. I must also express my thanks to Leueen MacGrath, Kaufman's second wife, for sharing her memories of her husband with me. At the same time, I hope that no reader of this book will construe these acknowledgments as indicating that the opinions expressed in it are not my own, or that I was encouraged to pass over any details of Kaufman's life for the sake of presenting an idealized portrait rather than a naturalistic one. Nothing could be further from the truth.

Many other men and women have also contributed to my knowledge of Kaufman's life and work. Since their names appear in the notes, I have resisted the temptation to list them here. I wish, however, to make an exception of five persons, to all of whom I am especially grateful: the great actors Groucho Marx, Alfred Lunt, and Lynn Fontanne; and Marc Connelly and Morrie Ryskind, two of the playwrights with whom Kaufman most frequently collaborated.

Persons whose names do not appear in the notes and for whose aid I am grateful are Marilyn Evert, Walter Evert, John S. Paul, Laurence Shyer, Carmel Wilson, and my editor and friend, Sheldon Meyer, whose encouragement has meant a great deal to me.

I wish also to thank the staffs of the libraries of Columbia, Harvard, Princeton, and Yale (with a special bow to the library of the Yale School of Drama for last-minute information), the Wisconsin Center for Theater Research at the University of Wisconsin–Madison, the Library of Congress, the Walter Hampden Library of The Players, the Theater Collection of the Museum of the City of New York, and the New York Public Library Theater Collection at Lincoln Center. Especially to the last-named Collection am I indebted, as I have been since my undergraduate years, when its home was still at 42nd Street. To all the staff at Lincoln Center—Paul Myers, Dorothy Swerdlove, Monty Arnold, David Bartholomew, Roderick Bladel, Donald Fowle, and Maxwell Silverman—I offer this expression of gratitude.

Quotations from Kaufman's published plays are taken from the earliest printings. Those from the unpublished plays are taken from copies in the libraries listed above and the collection of Anne Kaufman Schneider. Drawing on these sources, I have been able to read virtually all the plays that Kaufman completed but did not publish. This includes many that were never produced. Two plays that I was not able to find are *Business Is Business,* written in collaboration with Dorothy Parker, and *Eldorado,* written in collaboration with Laurence Stallings. Kaufman did not keep copies of these plays among his papers, nor did he or his collaborators copyright them. At Princeton in the collections of scripts produced by George C. Tyler and Sam H. Harris, and at The Players in the collection of scripts produced by Max Gordon, are many unpublished Kaufman plays, as well as unpublished plays by other writers that Kaufman directed. At the Wisconsin Center for Theater Research I was able to read unproduced film and television scripts by Kaufman and still more unpublished plays. At Lincoln Center I found the only copy known to me and to Kaufman's family of *Strike Up the Band,* his first musical with George Gershwin. For plays known to have been copyrighted, but not included in any of these collections, I went to the Copyright Division of the Library of Congress. Those plays have since been moved to the Manuscript Division. Like most New York dramatists of his day, Kaufman took his plays as they were finished to the Rialto Typing Service for professional typing, and as he picked them up he always looked for some expression of approval from the typists. I am told that he got it with only one: *You Can't Take It with You.* A man who had no confidence that the popularity of his works would outlast his own time, he would probably be astonished to know how many researchers have read these dim and yellowing copies in recent years.

In addition to the collection of letters from her father and to and from her mother in the possession of Anne Kaufman Schneider, other collections which yielded letters of importance to my work are the papers of Kaufman and of Moss Hart in the Wisconsin Center for Theater Research, the papers of Alexander Woollcott at Harvard, the Tyler and Gordon collections at Princeton, the Bennett Cerf papers at Columbia, and the Brooks Atkinson papers at Lincoln Center. Also at Lincoln Center I was able to read typescripts of early plays by Moss Hart, including the original version of *Once in a Lifetime*. As should be clear from the context in which they are cited, still other letters, most of them by Kaufman, were lent to me by their recipients.

In Chapters 1 and 2 when no other source of information on Kaufman's family and his activities is cited, the reader may assume that my source was Ruth Kaufman Friedlich. On such matters for the remainder of the book, when no other source is cited, it was Anne Kaufman Schneider. All figures on the runs of plays are taken from the annual *Best Plays* series, originally edited by Burns Mantle. Those on production costs are taken from *Variety*.

To keep the notes within reasonable bounds, I have not annotated newspaper reviews of productions, provided the paper and date are given in the text. In quotations from newspapers and magazines, where the title of a play was originally in roman type, I have changed it to italics, for the benefit of scanners.

New York
May 1979

M.G.

Contents

George S. Kaufman

—1—

Beginnings

When he died on June 2, 1961, George S. Kaufman was in his seventy-second year. More than forty of the plays of which he was the author (all, with rare exceptions, written in collaboration with other dramatists) had reached Broadway during his long career in the theater, and more than twenty-five of them had been hits. Though this represented a prodigious amount of creative effort, it had been far from enough to consume Kaufman's energy. He directed most of the plays himself and alternated his work on them as writer and director with activities of many other kinds: directing plays by other dramatists, "doctoring" ailing productions on the road, script-writing for Hollywood, creating blackout sketches for musical revues, spinning out humorous verse and prose for newspapers and magazines, and making appearances on radio and television talk shows. In addition there were, of course, the false starts on scripts that ended in the wastebasket and the plays that, though completed and produced, had to be abandoned on the road to New York. Though the illnesses that attend old age plagued him in his last years, all in all, his life was a good one, a long-running success.

Yet the public reading his obituary had no sense that it had lost a classic American author. Kaufman himself was partly to blame for the under-valuation of his plays. Though he paid meticulous attention to the details of the production of every one of them, not only during rehearsals but throughout the run, he cared very little about any play after it closed. It is odd that the writer who pared each script down to the bone for maximum comic impact and the director who ruthlessly chastened careless actors should think so little about posterity's regard for his work. A streak of impatience made him want to get on to the next job, for a play, he believed, was a thing of the moment, and each had to be followed by something new, different, and good—and as soon as possible. Over the years, he made an effort to promote a Broadway revival of only one of his plays, *Of Thee I Sing*, and consequently it was the only one to receive a major new production during his lifetime.

Many other twentieth-century American playwrights, among them Eugene O'Neill, Thornton Wilder, Tennessee Williams, and Arthur Miller, became classical writers in their own lifetime and were happily and gratefully aware of it, even going so far as to attempt to amplify their renown with large-scale works that called attention to the breadth and depth of their learning. But Kaufman had no wish to write in the masterpiece style. That a writer should be jealous of his reputation and eager for a place in literary history was in his view altogether reasonable, but he himself was one to whom long-lasting fame did not matter. What mattered was the fair treatment of the public that had paid the price of tickets, and the accumulation of sufficient resources to provide for a comfortable life. One reflection of his indifference to literary fame was his perfect willingness to sell his works to Hollywood without a contractual provision for control over the screenplays. Not one of his works did he himself adapt for the screen. He knew that Hollywood purchased properties with no intention of preserving their authenticity, and he knew that the public knew this and would not hold him responsible for whatever happened in the transformation. If the proffered sum was satisfactory, he sold and said no more about it.

Though from the early 1920s the stock rights to his plays provided Kaufman with a substantial supplement to his income from new works, it was not until 1965, some four years after his death, that directors and producers began to perceive the enduring merit of his writing. The Broadway production of *You Can't Take It with You* presented in that year under the direction of Ellis Rabb marked the beginning of the rise of his posthumous reputation. The new companies of professional actors that were establishing themselves in Minneapolis, Los Angeles, San Francisco, Washington, Philadelphia, and other cities were inspired by the success of that production to find a place for Kaufman's plays in seasonal programs along with standard works of the international repertory. Theaters in both western and eastern Europe began to send in requests for the professional rights. Bids were made for special television adaptations, as well as for permission to turn the plays into musicals for Broadway. Major New York productions of *Dinner at Eight* and *Beggar on Horseback* were undertaken in 1967 and 1970, respectively. In the season of 1975-76, when, in honor of the Bicentennial celebration, plays from the national past were rediscovered by the dozen, Kaufman's works were repeatedly staged. The most ambitious of the revival series, that of the John F. Kennedy Center in Washington, included Kaufman and Edna Ferber's *The Royal Family*. Of all the indications of his growing reputation, none was more impressive than the fact that this production, also directed by Rabb, ran for six months on Broadway after the Washington month, whereas the other Bicentennial revivals of the Kennedy Center, including plays by O'Neill, Wilder, and Williams, soon disappeared.

What kind of man was the author of these many hits? Evasive or aggressive? Sensitive or thick-skinned? Comfortable or morose? Hesitant or cocksure? At one time or another, every man is all that these adjectives imply, depending on the stimulus of the moment. But in Kaufman the shifts of mood, from friendliness to disdain or from agonized self-doubt before hearing the verdict on his latest play to elation if it was well received, were striking and not a little awesome to those close to him. Wrote one of his most intimate theatrical associates, ". . . what a strange man he was, one of the strangest I have ever met in more than half a century in show business." "George was scary," said the wife of one of his most cherished friends. "He was only happy when working in the theater," added another acquaintance. "He was a deeply unhappy man," said yet another. He was also a hypochondriac who shied away from shaking hands—for who knew what germs those outstretched fingers might carry? "For a year after George Gershwin died of a brain tumor," said Kaufman's sister, "my brother had headaches." But, "He was a profoundly witty man." And "He had a way with the ladies."[1] Above all else that could be said about him, he had a passion for work. Even while writing one play and directing another, he developed ideas for still another and the one after that. If, while writing and rehearsing, he still did not have enough to occupy his mind, he would try to inveigle friends and acquaintances into turning out scripts that he could direct or produce later on.

This passion for work, intense as it was, did not wholly eclipse his other passions. He liked card games, especially poker and bridge. At the latter he developed a skill so keen that even professionals were impressed. His appearance, late in the afternoon, at the Regency or the Cavendish, New York's leading bridge clubs, was more or less expected whenever he was in town. He could joke about the game, as in his introduction to a book by Charles Goren, the prominent professional, in which he wrote that, though in all the bridge columns South seemed to hold the best hands, his carefully planned ruses to get that position never netted him a winner.[2] But he took it seriously, all the same, and played it to the end of his life. To a partner at the Regency who asked to be excused to visit the men's room, he replied, "Gladly. For the first time today I'll know what you have in your hand." His other great game was croquet, which in the 1930s developed into a kind of pedestrian polo for Broadway and Hollywood writers and their friends. Kaufman, Moss Hart, Alexander Woollcott, Harpo Marx, and various friends of both sexes played with such fanaticism that a single match could last an entire day. Planning days in advance for teams of equal strength was part of the fun. In 1947 it seemed to him the most natural thing in the world to suggest to his daughter that she curtail her honeymoon by a day to be present for croquet at his country home in Bucks County, Pennsylvania.

Women moved into and out of his life in a continuous procession, but none was encouraged to believe, while his first wife was alive, that she would be the next Mrs. Kaufman. Never a braggart Don Juan, he told nobody about his romances. Yet his acquaintances had ways of knowing whom he had conquered—or had been conquered by. One was through his unconscious habit of referring to the woman by her last name only, though this was not infallible, because he also addressed a few favorite actresses in that way. The other was through his way of chiming in, whenever one of the women in his life was mentioned, with some such comment as "A lovely girl. I took an interest in her."[3] Those in whom he "took an interest"—on one occasion, notoriously— were many, but none was known to have turned on him when the affair came to an end.

As for friendships, they did not come easily. It was not that people disliked him, though undoubtedly some did, but that not many were truly comfortable with him. So austere was he, so much the moralist (apart, of course, from his surrender to the promptings of sex), that most of his acquaintances felt an oppressive sense of their own shortcomings in his presence. They also feared the lash of his wit. None could match him in the art of putting a fine edge to an observation. Perhaps Groucho Marx came closest, but one major difference in the wisecracking styles of the two men was that Groucho had no intention of wounding, whereas Kaufman sometimes did. Elmer Rice, the playwright, spoke for many when he commented that Kaufman was a man who said "many devastatingly witty things, but never a kind one."[4] Yet he was often kind, in actions if not in words. A deeply ingrained abhorrence of sentimentality bridled his tongue at those moments when he might have been expected to offer a word of cheer or consolation or praise. With women he was more at ease than with men, and this put most of them at ease with him. Of the men who could be described as his friends, the foremost was

Moss Hart, who entered his life in 1930 and with whom he was in touch thereafter almost every day for the rest of his life. There were few other cronies, however; Kaufman was not the sort to call up another man and suggest that they meet for lunch. But the young wits with whom he repeatedly lunched at the Algonquin Hotel in the 1920s were certainly his friends as the term is generally understood; it was simply that for most of them his reserve was too great to permit intimacy and that if they bored him by repetitiousness or the telling of self-serving anecdotes he would reveal his displeasure with shattering brusqueness. If Kaufman called someone for lunch with mere socializing, not business, in mind, that person was almost invariably an alluring woman.

But as for food, Kaufman was in the main indifferent to what has come to be called "gourmet cooking." If any foods could tempt him, they were meat and chocolate candy. One of his minor pastimes was making fudge. Once, when he occupied a bungalow at the Garden of Allah hotel in Hollywood near that of Natalie Schafer, the actress picked up her ringing telephone late one evening and heard his voice plaintively suggesting that she come over and make fudge. Her guests also heard it and thought that this was a code term for making love.[5] It was not, however; Kaufman meant what he said, and as soon as her guests departed, Schafer made for his kitchen. At home in New York or in Bucks County, Kaufman was a thoughtful host despite his lack of a "gourmet" palate. Both his first wife and his second employed capable cooks and enjoyed party-giving, and he himself was never averse to it.

In matters other than food his tastes were equally unextravagant. He seldom smoked and did not care much for drink. He did care for good clothes, and not only his suits but his shirts and underwear and his long, white, billowing nightshirts were made for him. His lean, six-foot frame was always draped in excellently cut, conservative garb. This was in part a calculated compensation for his plain, beaky face and unruly pompadour (not that the women in his life found him unattractive), and partly a reflection of his fastidiousness. For personal possessions he cared not at all and collected nothing at any time. If he owned anything that he was proud of, it was a drawing of Mark Twain that Twain himself had signed. That drawing occupied a place of pride in his otherwise spartan bedroom, perhaps spurring him to sharpness and understatement as a writer. Yet from the beginnings of his success in 1921 Kaufman and his family lived well. Sensible, even tough in doing business, he nevertheless was no pinchpenny and not a man to deny his wife the pleasures that his ample income could provide.

Money meant comfort to Kaufman, and comfort made possible the continuation of his career. He worked, one could say, in order to be able to keep on working. He needed to be close to the theater—to feel the emanations pulsing from Broadway. In 1936 at the urging of his wife he bought a fifty-nine acre farm in Holicong, Bucks County, to provide a change of scene on weekends. But the time that he spent there, on the "farm," as the Kaufmans referred to it, was in no sense a withdrawal from the New York stage. Other New Yorkers who were also Bucks County property-owners included Oscar Hammerstein II, S. J. Perelman, Ruth and Augustus Goetz, and Moss Hart. To the farm on weekends came his theatrical and literary friends. Though not a native New Yorker, he found a spiritual home in the city on first moving there in 1913, and whenever far away from its spell he claimed to be miserable. Especially in Hollywood—"the Coast," as Broadway professionals called it—was he often fretful, despite the invitations that came his way daily and that he usually accepted. Even to the extent that he did enjoy his stays in the West, he was reluctant to admit it. As for the place of his birth, Pittsburgh, that was a city to which he returned only when one of his plays was routed there on its tryout tour. In the years of his daughter's adolescence he told her from time to time that one day he would take her to see the haunts of his youth, but that day never came.

The parents of the playwright were Joseph Kaufman and the former Henrietta Myers. They were married in Pittsburgh on January 17, 1884; the groom was twenty-seven years of age and the bride twenty-five. Joseph's family name had originally been spelled with two "n's," but his father, Simon Kaufman, on coming to the United States from Germany in 1848 had dropped the second "n" to make the name seem less German. For the same reason, he abandoned the German pronunciation of the name, "Kowfman," in favor of "Koffman." Joseph Myers, Henrietta's father, had settled in Allegheny (later incorporated into Pittsburgh, but then a separate city) about 1834, having come from Heidelberg. He was the uncle of Simon Kaufman, and the younger man had in fact gone directly to him for assistance and advice on his own arrival in the United States. Joseph and Henrietta, or Nettie as she was always called, thus were second cousins. The match was considered a good one, the consanguinity of the newlyweds not being viewed as genetically perilous, as it might have been in later times. Nor did it prove so; four healthy children were born to the couple, and though one died in early childhood, the others lived more than their three score years and ten. Two of the children preceded George into the world: Helen, who was born on October 6, 1884, and Richard, who was born in 1886 and died only two years later. George was born on November 16, 1889. The fourth child, Ruth, was born on November 16, 1895.

Like most American families of German-Jewish origin, the Kaufmans and the Myerses preferred not only to marry within their religion, but to marry within the German-Jewish circle. To such as they, who resolutely refused to consider themselves different from Christian Americans in any aspect of life other than the religious, the recent waves of Jews from Eastern Europe seemed to suffer irremediably and disastrously from an inability to assimilate to American culture. To eyes accustomed to American ways, the Russian and Polish Jews were glaringly different—too different to be taken into one's family, to say nothing of one's club (in the case of these Pittsburgh families, the Concordia Club, which Joseph Myers, Nettie's father, had helped found and whose members were Jews of German origin). Simon Kaufman raised nine sons and a daughter; Joseph Myers, three sons and a daughter (a second daughter died in infancy). All were taught to be proud of their lineage.

In addition to suitable pedigree, both families had a good footing in business. Though their most illustrious descendant, George, was to say of them that they "managed to get in on every business as it was finishing and made a total of $4 among them,"[6] that was a slur they did not deserve. Simon Kaufman had prospered as a pants manufacturer, and the Myers family had made a small fortune in the meat-packing business. The families were not in equal circumstances, however; the Kaufmans, though able to live on a handsome, tree-lined street, and to feed and clothe their numerous children, had to be content with a rented house, whereas the Myerses could afford to own a large, well-staffed house in an upper-middle-class neighborhood. The Myers family was able to maintain this house despite an altogether improbable event in which Joseph Myers suffered the loss of a major share of his wealth when, during a party one evening in Nettie's girlhood, the house was invaded by bandits well enough dressed to be mistaken for guests. Not only were the real guests robbed of jewelry and cash and rendered defenseless by chloroform, but all the family's valuables on the premises were stolen. With incredible foolhardiness, Joseph Myers had kept his major assets, negotiable government bonds, in a strong box in the cellar of the house, where the thieves had no trouble finding them. Nothing was ever traced. Nettie, then a student in an Ursuline convent school, happened to have in the pocket of her dress a ring given her by another student at the school. The pocket was slashed and the ring taken.

In both the Kaufman and the Myers families appreciation of learning and love of the arts were taken for granted. The Myers family included amateur painters and musicians, among whom was the future Nettie Kaufman. As a student with the Ursulines she won a medal for general achievement in scholarship. She could speak both French and German. Joseph, though he had only a few years of schooling, was a voracious reader. In his adulthood he always had a den well stocked with books. His favorite writer was Voltaire, and his collection of books included the complete works of that philosopher-satirist. Particularly to his taste were the English naturalists Darwin, Huxley, and Tyndall. He was also fond of the theater. Whenever he found it necessary to go to New York on business, he went to some of the new plays, and on coming home he would tell the children about them. A contemplative man, if one who had difficulty in fixing on a career, he encouraged his son's intellectual growth. It may have been that, by example, even his failures were of help to George, who, once he had found the work he liked, stayed with it doggedly.

Nettie Myers Kaufman, on the other hand, was anything but helpful. All her life she was a deeply neurotic woman, troubled with illnesses which were as much imaginary as real, but nonetheless debilitating. To her children, Nettie's complaints were endlessly distressing. Though they could understand that the complaints were in substantial part a way of getting attention, they could not easily shrug them off. When young, Nettie was able, despite her anxieties, to maintain her household with that efficiency expected of a woman of her background. But later in her long life, which came to an end in 1940, four months after the death of her husband, she required psychiatric nurses.

To Nettie may be traced the quirks with which George Kaufman was notoriously afflicted as an adult: an avoidance of physical contact with virtually everyone apart from the women with whom he had sexual relations, a fussiness over food, an imperious way with such minor figures in life as waiters and cab drivers, and imagined illnesses. Nettie was overprotective, constantly worrying lest George become ill or endanger his life in the sports that boys enjoy, such as swimming and climbing trees. By himself, her even-tempered husband could not prevent her from harassing the boy with her fears. Yet Nettie did not act so in conscious knowledge of the harm she was doing. Like all neurotic people, she was not wholly to blame for her condition. No doubt she would have chosen to be less difficult had that been possible. In part her temperament came from her mother, who all her life displayed a haughty, overbearing personality. Moreover, the death of Nettie's firstborn son, Richard, had much to do with her suffocating concern for George. Richard had been the victim of inadequate medical care. He suffered from diarrhea when less than two years old; the resultant dehydration, which the family doctor did not know how to treat, was the actual cause of his death. She was determined that George should live. Consequently, any minor ailment that George contracted was treated as a major calamity. Both George and his sister Ruth had wet nurses; Nettie apparently feared that it would endanger their lives if she herself nursed them. George's nurse, Annie Burns, did not like vegetables and imparted her distaste to him, a distaste that never left him. Sweets and meats, then as later, were the only foods he cared for.

Yet, even on this decidedly unbalanced diet, he grew strong enough to engage in sports. He played sandlot baseball with the neighboring boys and joined them in rooting for the Pittsburgh Pirates. But these and other athletic pleasures were preceded and followed by Nettie's constant nagging about his health and her frequent death scenes, which implanted in George an unshakable abhorrence of sentimental scenes, whether in life itself or on the stage. He rebuffed sentimentality at every turn, even to the extent of decrying the love songs in the musicals for which he supplied the dialogue. Moss Hart in 1943, in court proceedings involving a charge of plagiarism against himself and his collaborator, remarked for the public record, "As a matter of fact, George and myself don't portray love very well on the stage. We have been accused of this and accept it."[7] But since this inability never amounted to a seriously damaging limitation on Kaufman's range, one cannot impute to poor Nettie a malign effect on the American stage! Quite the contrary, most would say, since the very tartness of the comedies has played a major part in preserving them.

No doubt Joseph would have been happier with another sort of woman, but his temperament was so relaxed that he could endure Nettie's personality without apparent suffering. Though never uxorious, he remained monogamous until his death. His best defense against Nettie's outbursts was to excuse himself and leave the house for a while, returning when he guessed that she had calmed down. But of all the good qualities that could be claimed for him, and were claimed by his friends, he himself was a cause of insecurity within the family home. In the years of George's boyhood, he changed occupations continuously, leaving one job for another, gripped as he was by the chimeric notion of one day coming to rest in wholly satisfying, ceaselessly challenging employment.

His adventurous spirit had first revealed itself in 1878, six years before his marriage, when he went with two other young Pittsburghers to the West, for whatever work might offer itself in the mines of Leadville, Colorado. One of the three, Isaac Frank, was trained as an engineer. All three were hired by

Bill Tabor, the "Silver King," to survey the Little Pittsburgh Mine. But mining was not the sole occupation of young men in Leadville in those years.
Joseph was also pressed into service as an Indian fighter and a vigilante. For
four years he stayed in the West. Isaac Frank went on to amass a fortune
in tinplate stock.

Three decades were to pass before Joseph stayed in another job for as long
as four years. Meanwhile, three of his brothers, whose less fanciful intelligence was balanced by greater practicality, began moving up: Gustave in the
construction of bridges and the design of the Ferris wheel (named for his
partner rather than himself because of his feeling that it had no dignity),
Sidney in improving the typewriter, and Sol in tinplate and steel. Nettie's
brother Lou, operating the meat-packing business founded by his father, also
did well; occasionally he would drop in on the Kaufman household to pass
out silver dollars to his nephew and nieces. Though Joseph's children never
wanted for anything of importance, it was never certain from year to year
that the respectable, *bürgerlich* existence to which he accustomed them
would continue undiminished. At the same time, George was not overim-
pressed by his rich uncles. One of them, or perhaps all of them rolled into
one, he metamorphosed into a buffoon in *George Washington Slept Here*.

The first home of Joseph and Nettie was in Allegheny. Joseph was then
employed by Kaufman and Klee, the pants-manufacturing firm of which his
father was a founder. Shortly thereafter he secured the major executive position of superintendent of the works for the Crucible Steel Corporation. This
came to a hasty end when, inspired by the doctrine of Samuel Gompers,
whom he knew and admired, he attempted to persuade the corporation to
decrease the workers' daily stint from twelve hours to ten. A variety of jobs
followed, as did a number of changes in Joseph and Nettie's address. At the
time of George's birth in 1889 they were living in Pittsburgh at 6230 Station
Street, where they stayed until 1900. In that year Joseph founded his own
company, Vulcan Machine and Foundry, for the manufacture of tool steel.
The Vulcan plant was in the near-by town of New Castle, and the family
moved there to a house at 28 Croton Street. In 1905 the company failed, in
part because of Joseph's indifference to success: the business had been going
along too well to provide a challenge. When he attempted to revitalize it,
realizing that it was slipping away, he found that he had been negligent too
long. Back came the family to Pittsburgh, where they took half of a double
house at 6102 Walnut Street. The woman occupying the other half kept
boarders and wanted the Kaufmans' ground floor for the expansion of her
establishment. Not too well supplied with cash, they were willing to oblige,

and decided to take their meals with her. Joseph once more began to move from job to job, and four years passed before he found work that struck him as congenial. Through it all he was somehow able to keep Nettie surrounded with the trappings of a good life. There was always a maid, invariably renamed "Influenza," "Piazza," or "Veranda" by George.

Though Nettie's constant anxiety put permanent scars on her son's psyche, George had a boyhood that was not without its pleasures. It was not only that he occasionally played ball, but that other activities proved to his liking and formed his character. Both Nettie and Joseph liked card games, including pinochle, hearts, and three-handed whist, and George took to this kind of family entertainment with delight well before his teens. Reading was also an early passion, and in time it became so much of an addiction that Joseph had to urge his son out of the house and into the fresh air. As soon as he learned to read, at the Liberty School in Pittsburgh, George found delight in comic verse and prose. The family owned a copy of Carolyn Wells's popular *A Nonsense Anthology*, a thick collection of comic verse, and the Kaufman children consulted it repeatedly. They also had a fondness for Gilbert's *Bab Ballads;* among the poems in it, "My Name Is John Wellington Wells" was a particular favorite, and young George could and often did recite it. He also liked to tap out the meters of Gilbert's rhythmic poems with a pencil against his teeth. Poe was another favorite, for he too wrote in pulsing rhythms. For every birthday or other important occasion, George wrote a humorous poem. It was self-training that repaid him nicely in later years when as a beginning writer he succeeded in making a name for himself with newspaper contributions of light verse. In his teens George also developed an appetite for adventure stories of the sort published in *Argosy*, a pulp magazine of wide circulation. Speculating that he might have a talent for creating such stuff, he sent manuscript after manuscript to the magazine, only to have each one return with a rejection slip.

Of the major prose writers whom George enjoyed as a boy, the favorite was Mark Twain, and he would laugh out loud while reading Twain's novels. Not only did he read them, he bought copies of them out of his pocket money. This enthusiasm was never to leave him. Though his gift was different, since Kaufman lacked the descriptive skill that directed Twain toward the writing of fiction and books of travel, one can see a resemblance: Twain and the adult Kaufman both possessed a cast of mind that mingled a cynical view of society with sturdy personal integrity.

Young George also developed a great liking for the stage. He would go to the plays of stock and touring companies and to vaudeville shows. At fourteen he wrote his first play, a melodrama called *The Failure,* and with this early work formed the habit of writing with a collaborator. On this maiden effort his coauthor was a boy a year and a half younger than he, one Irving Pichel, also a member of one of Pittsburgh's German-Jewish families and later an actor and Hollywood director of note. In the form in which the two later entered it for copyright at the Library of Congress in 1914, it was a three-act piece with a conventional happy ending and a large cast, but in its original form it was shorter and simpler. The plot had to do with a conflict between a young artist and his father, a businessman. At the climax, the father slashed a canvas on which the son had been proudly working. There was nothing funny here—nothing, that is, to suggest the direction in which the mature Kaufman's talents would develop. The boys were very proud of their work and acted it repeatedly. The climactic scene they liked to perform in Ruth's room with a sheet from her bed substituting for the canvas. Nettie, fearful as always that some illness would befall her children, would invariably interrupt the action, ordering the boys to let the eight-year-old girl get some sleep.

At this point in his life George was revealing an idealistic bent of which *The Failure* was only one indication. He attended religious school faithfully at Temple Rodef Shalom, which his grandfather Myers had helped to found and at which his parents were congregants. At fourteen he was confirmed in the Reform Jewish faith at Rodef Shalom by the temple's English-born rabbi, Dr. J. Leonard Levy. Rabbi Levy, who enjoyed working with the young, had set up a dramatic society. At his suggestion, George participated in it. Soon he was showing such promise as an actor that Levy urged the family to encourage him for a career on the stage. With this success George became irrevocably stagestruck. That he may have been shy in personal relations had nothing to do with his feeling in front of an audience. The separation between them rendered the theatrical event impersonal.

As George passed from childhood into adolescence, he reached six feet, but did not noticeably fill out. He was a weedy youth and was destined to remain lean all his life. Joseph was concerned about his son's failure to gain weight and about his habit, which was fast becoming ingrained, of staying indoors with a book no matter how pleasant the day. Not much could be done about this habit at home, where he had a room to settle into. Therefore Joseph ordered a change of scene when his son reached fifteen. An old family friend owned a ranch in Idaho where a gang of cowboys rode out regularly every day to supervise the livestock. Joseph thought that this was a place to send George. Arrangements were made; the fifteen-year-old took a train for Idaho. Once there, however, he discovered that nobody was empowered to force him to ride, and after one tentative, experimental effort at straddling a horse he gave it up. He stayed on in Idaho for the rest of the summer, passing the time pleasantly enough in his usual fashion: reading. No change in either his physique or his temperament was discernible; on his return he was as lean as ever and still reluctant to touch the vegetables that his mother insisted on. He was also withdrawn, sensitive, and subject to moods. Adolescence was not proving easy.

The self-consciousness that every adolescent acquires as he sees his body developing toward adulthood and senses the awakening of sex took a surprising turn for George and his friends. In 1905, when he was fifteen, he and six other Jewish boys, including Irving Pichel, formed a celibates' society, the Black and White Club. This informal organization served them as later the Boy Scouts would serve generations of American teenagers: it encouraged them in the preservation of personal integrity and sexual morality. It was to their credit that they conceived of it on their own. With the courage and idealism of the very young they swore that they would abstain from sex until they married. Whether they were all able to keep this vow would remain a secret of the grave. Yet the firm opinion offered late in life by one of the seven, William Frank, was that they all kept it.[8] In later years George's first wife, Beatrice, would tell intimates that she and her husband were both virgins when they married. The boys had set down their moral intentions in black and white—hence the club's name—and, if Frank was correct, that act had a profound effect on their judgment as adults.

In 1909 Joseph Kaufman found a job that made sense to him—that is, a job that seemed to need him and that offered an outlet for his energies. The Kaufman creative ability that had already manifested itself in the careers of his brothers was about to reveal itself in Joseph's personality after long years of dormancy. The company that offered this work was the Columbia Ribbon Manufacturing Company, whose home office and plant were located in Paterson, New Jersey. Since 1840 Paterson had been the American silk-weaving and silk-dyeing center, and Columbia Ribbon was one of many companies engaged in the manufacture of silk products. Among its wares were bows to adorn women's shoes and striped bands to encircle men's straw hats. From other plants came a range of products that included coffin linings, wall hangings, and printed fabric for dresses—in short, whatever could be made of silk, for Paterson was to silk what Pittsburgh was to steel. With silk Joseph was to be more successful than he had been with steel.

Having accepted the offer to manage the Columbia Ribbon mill, Joseph

Kaufman moved with Nettie and Ruth to Paterson. Two years earlier Helen, the elder daughter, had married Frank Gordon Lieberman, and they were living in Georgia. George, now twenty, stayed behind in Pittsburgh. In Paterson, Joseph took rooms for his family in a boarding house, but they all regarded this arrangement as only temporary. After a few months, they moved to nearby Passaic and into a house that Joseph rented.

Though he was now on the threshold of manhood, George was still not educated for a career. He had had a normal kind of schooling up through his teens: grade school and secondary school first in Pittsburgh and then in New Castle, and high school in Pittsburgh from 1903 to 1907, when he was graduated. The four years at Pittsburgh Central High had been satisfying ones, for they included the opportunity to act in a school play and to write for the school publications. But in neither of these activities did he, in 1907, chart a career. Nothing, in fact, had prompted him to a vocational choice so far. Yet some choice was necessary. Irving Pichel, his friend and collaborator, was to go to Harvard, but it does not seem to have entered George's mind to seek admittance to that university.

Still, Joseph had set aside some money for his son's education. It was up to George to make a decision. He chose to enter law school. It was possible then to proceed directly to law school without giving up four years to earn a Bachelor of Arts degree. George enrolled for the study of law at Western University of Pennsylvania, the institution that in that same year, 1907, became the University of Pittsburgh. Just three years later, in New York, eighteen-year-old Elmer Reizenstein, later Elmer Rice, also proceeded to law school without a B.A. Rice, in his eventual career as a dramatist, drew often on his knowledge of the law for the plots of his plays. He kept at his studies, becoming a member of the New York bar. But George Kaufman did not keep at his. An illness diagnosed as pleurisy overtook him before the end of his first semester, and on the advice of the family physician he withdrew. Yet he had been serious enough for the little while that he had remained a student. One memory that persisted in the family was the sight of George poring over Blackstone.

With the further pursuit of formal education out of the question, George tried for a while to earn his keep as a member of a surveying team. The work out of doors was supposed to do him good after his respiratory ailment. But it was a kind of occupation for which he had had no preparation whatever, and of course he was bad at it. His constitutional antipathy to the outdoors was another hindrance. Later on he got a certain amount of fun out of saying that as a result of his ineptness on the team the new town of Mc-

Cullom, West Virginia, was located on ground three feet lower than that originally selected for it. From this highly unsuitable work he turned in 1908 to other jobs in quick succession. He studied stenography, and with that newly acquired trade he got a job on the public payroll as a clerk in the Allegheny County tax office. From it he stepped up a bit to a post as stenographer to the controller of the Pittsburgh Coal Company. On this job, he later said, he at least learned the definition of "controller": someone who begins to dictate letters at five forty-five.[9] Somewhat more seriously, it could be said that out of this sort of work and the preparation for it he learned one skill that proved useful to him as a dramatist: typing.

By 1909 it had begun to look as though George was destined to have a career much as his father's had been, with one brief spell of employment following another in meaningless succession. In Pittsburgh he simply moved to the boarding-house side of the double house in which the family had lived, and there he stayed until Joseph himself provided a job for him. This, too, was not the most congenial work for George, who at twenty was a shy, introverted chap who would have preferred to be alone with a good book than in the office of a stranger who might or might not be in the market for some of Columbia's hat bands. But Joseph in his younger days had peddled the gentleman's trousers produced by the Kaufman and Klee Company, and he had later traveled through New England selling his own Vulcan tool steel to manufacturers—and if a man so untuned by temperament to the competitive world of business could do these things, why could not his son? George did it for three years, until 1912, knowing all the while that it was not to be his life's work.

The road out of this tiresome occupation was not playwriting but the facility in writing light verse that George had fostered since early childhood. Though Gilbert's verse was his model, George's light verse never seriously rivaled it, for he lacked the nimbleness with polysyllabic rhyme that distinguishes the *Bab Ballads* and the operetta lyrics. But he had the born satirist's ability to spot, describe, and tellingly mock pretension and vain optimism, and for this ability there were outlets by the score in American newspapers.

In that era, before not only television but radio, it could be expected that any town with a thousand inhabitants would have a paper of its own. There were 2600 American dailies in 1909. Many carried a column to which an aspiring writer could send his work without waiting to be asked, and certainly without the intervention of an agent. The New York papers offered such opportunities to their readership; until as late as the early 1970s the New York *Times* frequently published unsolicited poems on the editorial page. Of all the Manhattan columns of humor that printed light verse as well as prose aperçus, the most famous were those edited and written by Franklin Pierce Adams, "Always in Good Humor" in the *Evening Mail* from 1903 to 1914, and "The Conning Tower" in the *Tribune* from 1914 through 1921 and in the *World* from 1922 to early 1931. His popularity with readers made him powerful in his dealings with editors and publishers. In the teens of the century the major beneficiary of Adams's power was George Kaufman.

Like Kaufman, Adams was a Jew. His Yankee-sounding name seemed intended to conceal his ethnic origin, but in fact it was the name of his father before him. Also, like Kaufman, he was not a New Yorker by birth. His native city was Chicago, where he was born in 1881. But he took to New York with gusto on moving there in 1903, and explored its theaters and restaurants and cultivated its artists and writers from that year until arteriosclerosis overtook him in the 1950s.* In a quiet way he was a witty man both on the printed page and in conversation, and an admirer of the wit of others. Lean, moose-nosed, and swarthy, he was utterly unprepossessing as a physical specimen, but his consideration for his friends and his contentment in sharing, not dominating, the conversation made him an attractive man. To the illustrator Neysa McMein he once made the suggestion that she ought to paint him, because he had a face like that on an old Greek coin. McMein replied that it was rather more like the face of an old Greek waiter.[10] This companionable give and take was typical of him, as was his delight in casually dropping the names of friends into his column. From not only his friends but from the public at large, he encouraged the submission of items for the column, and every year he awarded gold watches to the authors of those items that he considered the best. Many of the writers whom he favored became as famous as he, if not more so. Beginning in the fall of 1909 one whose work he printed frequently was George Kaufman. Among the others were Marc Connelly, Edna Ferber, Ring Lardner, Herbert Bayard Swope, Sinclair Lewis, Dorothy Parker, and Alexander Woollcott.

Adams's own observations in the column were terse second thoughts on municipal and national events, as well as insightful reflections on the intellectual aspirations of suburban women and the financial aspirations of businessmen. He signed them "F.P.A." and by the beginning of the 1920s these were the best-known non-presidential initials in the United States. As a humorist, Adams stood in a line of succession that included Artemus Ward,

---

* Adams died in 1960.

Mark Twain, Finley Peter Dunne, and Kin Hubbard, of whom only Mark Twain was to be remembered for specific writings. Adams was deft at creating light verse, but to achieve immortality in that sub-genre is given to few, and those few, like T. S. Eliot, are invariably better known for having created a body of serious work. Yet Adams could strike off sparks and twinkles of humor. "Mr. Bernard Shaw says that schoolteachers ought to have babies," he once wrote. "Well, he ought to know; he's had schoolteachers." Or: "More of the milk of human kindness is what Mr. [Otto] Kahn says young businessmen should have. Suggested slogan: The milk of human kindness from contented financiers." Adams also became known for his imitation of the style of Samuel Pepys. But unlike Pepys, who wrote in his diary in code and kept it to himself, F.P.A. printed reports of his daily forays into metropolitan high life for all the world to see. To give the column eye appeal he had it set up in a variety of type faces, so that an item in black letter might be followed by one in italics which in turn might be followed by one in pica or elite, and so on to the bottom of the page. There was a certain gentility about all this that in later years would prove cloying to palates with a taste for the gossip columns of Walter Winchell and other such reporters. But F.P.A.'s daily notes and gleanings produced smiles on commuter trains and at middle-class breakfast tables for two generations. Adams thought highly of Kaufman's contributions and printed them regularly, and he even became sufficiently impressed to invite Kaufman over from New Jersey for lunch. The admiration was mutual, and with the first meeting a friendship started up between them that lasted the rest of their lives. As late as 1922, when he was not only the author of a successful comedy but a fully employed newspaperman, Kaufman continued to send in items.

Following the example of Adams, Kaufman decided to bulk up his name with a middle initial when he mailed in pieces to "Always in Good Humor." Adams was not the only columnist who was known by three initials, though he was foremost among them. Another successful columnist was B.L.T.—Bert Leston Taylor, who contributed a column to the Chicago *Tribune*. Kaufman decided on the initial S, and, though it meant nothing whatever, he would later say that it stood for Simon, in honor of his paternal grandfather. Years later, in the 1970s, Edmund Wilson, never an enthusiast of Kaufman's work, wrote testily that the barrage of submissions to Adams's column signed "G.S.K." was intended to make the public curious about what the initials stood for and what sort of person owned them, as though Kaufman was letting the world know that he possessed some skill and would eventually cross over to New York and take his place in popular literature.[11] Perhaps this was so: it would have been strange if Kaufman had intended to remain forever only a contributor to Adams's column.

No sooner did Kaufman develop a modest reputation as a versifier than he began to wrestle with the notion of trying another form of expression: the theater. It had been, after all, as a playwright that he first tried to write seriously in adolescence. In 1910 he examined some of the ways in which to break into that difficult, none too encouraging medium. One was suggested to him by Adams, who for most of the next decade made what almost amounted to a subsidiary career of finding ways to help George Kaufman. At Adams's suggestion he began to think of himself as possibly an actor, and he enrolled in the Alveine School of Dramatic Art, making the trip from Passaic to New York once a week to attend class. In the early fall of the year, through another acquaintance whose name unhappily is lost, he got a letter of introduction to the popular playwright Charles Klein, who was casting a new piece called *The Gamblers*. The letter worked. He was hired for a part in the play. Then, however, bad luck set in. A letter that Klein wrote to summon him to rehearsal got lost in the mail, and of course Kaufman did not appear.[12] Had he opened in the play, he would have been in for a run of 192 performances, more than enough to categorize the play as a hit as such things were measured in 1910.

In the same year came a second theatrical opportunity, but not of the same sort. Having read in *Billboard*, the theatrical weekly, that a stock company in Troy, New York, needed a manager, Kaufman decided to apply for the job. It did not carry a salary; rather, the manager was to receive a share of the profits, provided he invested $100 in the company. Having saved some money from his Columbia Ribbon commissions, Kaufman had no trouble getting the job; nor would anyone else who could have supplied the cash. Once in Troy he was quickly disillusioned. Along with a request for his train fare home, he telegraphed the family a message they never forgot: LAST SUPPER WITH ORIGINAL CAST WOULDN'T DRAW IN THIS HOUSE. Home again, he went back to the same old work at Columbia Ribbon. No matter how dull, at least it meant a little money in his pocket.

But the idea of making his way in the theater was now fixed in Kaufman's mind. Apart from directing and designing, he had tried almost everything else that went into the making of a theatrical production: writing, acting, and backstage work. In 1911 he had a fresh look at his juvenile manuscript, *The Failure,* and thought he saw something in it worth saving. Pichel was then a freshman at Harvard. The two were still good friends and saw each other whenever Pichel managed a visit to New York, which he sometimes did along with another undergraduate, Robert Edmond Jones, who was to have an illustrious career as a stage designer. Kaufman and Pichel rewrote their play, polishing it and expanding it into three carefully constructed acts.

In its expanded form, the plot was slightly different from the sketchy piece that they had performed over and over with Ruth Kaufman as their entire audience. It was not a father-and-son relationship that the play unfolded, but one between a young man and a surrogate father, a university professor chosen by his late, real father to raise him and invest his inheritance. Pichel's knowledge of university life was put to use. The professor, an Egyptologist, they named Radagasius Jones; the young man, a painter, they named Walter Randolph. It is Professor Jones, not Walter, who is the failure: the book on which he has been working for years is still unfinished. His campus nickname is "Old Neverdone." What has caused the delay, which in turn costs him the presidency of his college, is that he has had to make extra money by tutoring undergraduates in order to pay for Walter's education. The securities left by the boy's father were worthless, but Jones has concealed that fact from the young man. When Walter charges him with having misused the inheritance, his patience snaps, and he tells Walter the truth at last. When Walter refuses to believe him, Jones throws a paperweight through a portrait of his daughter only recently completed by Walter. This canvas was to have received a $5000 prize! Though all the signals set out by the young playwrights point toward a tragic conclusion, in the end most of the problems right themselves. Walter decides to go to New York to make enough money to repay his debt to Jones, and Jones, now free of the need to support him, can get back to work on his book. He is not really a failure after all.

Too wordy to be acted, *The Failure* came to nothing, and in 1911, at twenty-two, Kaufman may have begun to think that he himself might become a failure. But in the next year something happened: Adams got him what promised to be a very good job. He was to be the writer and editor of a newspaper column all his own.

The newspaper by which Kaufman was hired was the Washington *Times,* published by Frank Munsey. The paper needed a humor column on the order of Adams's "All in Good Humor," and Munsey, reasonably enough, turned to Adams himself for advice on the best man to head it. Yet there was a problem in the recommendation. Munsey was anti-Semitic. His many newspapers, which included dailies in New York, Boston, Baltimore, and Philadelphia, in addition to the Washington *Times* and others, printed the elaborate cartoons of Rube Goldberg, but hired no writers known to be Jewish. "Just a wee bit *rishes,"* Alexander Woollcott later described Munsey in a *New Yorker* "profile" of Kaufman.[13] The world is a Yiddish term meaning "malicious," hence its application to anti-Semites.

How Munsey came to accept Adams's recommendation is one question. How he could not have known that Adams himself was a Jew is another. How Adams could have recommended a young Jew to an anti-Semite is yet a third. Munsey may not have recognized the name Kaufman as Jewish, though most persons so named are Jews, and the meaning of the word, "merchant," describes a vocation with a traditional appeal to Jews. However the failure of understanding between Adams and Munsey came about, it resulted in an offer to Kaufman and his acceptance of it. He moved to Washington in the fall of 1912 and began his column with the issue of December 9. He called it "This and That with Sometimes a Little of the Other," and for writing it he was paid $20 a week at the start, later $25. On December 6 Adams publicly offered felicitations with a note in "Always in Good Humor": "He is a young man of unusual ability and strong originality, and in wishing him a tremendous success we are but spokesmen for a large number of his friendly admirers. Vale, G.S.K.!"

The column was a stiff test of Kaufman's ingenuity. It required a daily supply of verse, as did F.P.A.'s column, and a steady flow of social and political comment. This was Washington; humor was humor, but in the capital city it demanded political coloration. Kaufman, having got through high school only, had to demonstrate a grasp of American culture and politics for which no formal training had prepared him. He did so almost at once, satirizing big business, political institutions, and class consciousness with insight and wit that at least matched Adams's. On lame-duck President Taft's decision to vacation in Panama, he wrote: "Mr. Taft will spend his Christmas with his family on the isthmus." On high finance: "A fair Exchange has no business in Wall Street." On the banalities of the press: "A committee of six has been appointed to drag the files for the record of a daylight robbery that was not 'daring.' Slight success is anticipated." On sports: "By seasoned pitcher is meant one with a lot of pepper." Two events of 1913 were commemorated at length: the Wilson inauguration and the exhibition in New York of *avant garde* painting known as the Armory Show, in which the American public was first exposed to Marcel Duchamp's cubist "Nude Descending a Staircase." G.S.K. and his reader-contributors were as puzzled and amused by this painting as was the rest of the public.

In Washington, Kaufman lived frugally. With so little money coming in and no father near by to help with rent or food, he had to be careful. But he managed. His *real* business in Washington, he later recalled, was playing stud poker at the National Press Club. "That was what hardened my character."[14] The card sense that he had developed as a boy in Pittsburgh came in handy as a means of expanding Munsey's limited largesse. It does not seem to have been a bad period in the young man's life. To his family he described it as a happy time. Each day he clipped the newly printed column from the paper and pasted it in an album.

For the very first of his daily columns he composed a poem called "Roundelirium" which ran as follows:

> Why shouldn't I kick off the lid
>   And romp a while before I die?
> A lot of other fellows did;
>   Why shouldn't I?
>
> Though but an ordinary guy,
> Why must I keep forever hid?
> The other thing is worth a try.
>
> And later on, if they should bid
>   Me seek the timber, I'll comply;
> If they should whisper, "Beat it, kid,"
>   Why SHOULDN'T I?

This proved to be prophetic. His employment came to an end after just one year. Munsey did not meet his new columnist before hiring him, but took him on solely on Adams's recommendation, without an interview. At no time during the year did Munsey give any indication that he was other than pleased with the material Kaufman was turning out for him. But one day late in November he dropped into the offices of the paper and looked over his crew. Among them was Kaufman, his lean body bent over a desk, his high-bridged nose jutting out of the long narrow face and supporting the rimless glasses, his head topped with dark, combed-back hair. Munsey saw him for the first time, and with an eye trained in such matters spotted him as an alien presence in the otherwise white Anglo-Saxon environment. To his managing editor he said, "What is that Jew doing in my city room?" Thus came to an end the agreeable days in Washington. Kaufman was notified of his dismissal, which was scheduled to follow the submission of his copy for December 1. The paper then began to fill in with the columns of Bert Leston Taylor of Chicago.

Kaufman was both hurt and angered, but not so shocked that he was unable to talk about the incident with intimates. He told the family immediately that Munsey had sent him packing for being a Jew, and he told Adams. Later, when he had a wife and daughter, he told them about it. New acquaintances heard the story over the years, including Woollcott, who wryly but delicately retold the incident in the pages of the *New Yorker*. But in the interviews that Kaufman gave and the autobiographical articles that he wrote on becoming a national figure, he played it down. On those occasions he said only that Munsey fired him for bumping into him at the door of the city room, a reason quite as senseless as the true one. Thus, for the benefit of the public he made a joke of the matter, though in fact it was no joke to him.

During Kaufman's year in Washington, Joseph, Nettie, and Ruth moved across the Hudson to Manhattan. Joseph had left Columbia Ribbon and purchased a business of his own, the New York Silk Dyeing Company. In this small business, the first he had owned since the Vulcan tool-steel disaster, he found an enterprise that his years with Columbia had prepared him to run successfully. He never left it. At his death in 1940 he was still its owner, and by the terms of his will it then went to his employees. For close to thirty years it remained a source of stability in the senior Kaufmans' home life, though what it brought in was always supplemented by gifts from their son.

George Kaufman benefited from his parents' move to Manhattan. Their new apartment was a large one on the Upper West Side at 241 West 101st Street, between Broadway and West End Avenue. One of its nine rooms was made available to him, and he gladly moved into it. He stayed for three years. Of all the cities in the world, New York was the one that could make the fullest use of his talents. By moving there he put himself in the right direction, bringing to an end his occupational nomadism. He became what he was to remain: a New York-based writer. Once again he had the help of Adams, who in less than two months after the Washington debacle got him a post as a reporter on the prestigious New York *Tribune*. Adams himself had just moved to the *Trib* from the *Evening Mail*, taking with him his column, which was renamed "The Conning Tower."

Starting out on this new job, Kaufman was given a variety of minor newsbeats, such as burglaries, the arrival and departure of transatlantic liners, and the checking in of notables at leading hotels. F.P.A. was still happy to take an occasional item from him for "The Conning Tower."

Some free-lance opportunities also came his way, providing the evidence that his reputation as a humorist was growing. For *Puck*, the comic weekly, he supplied some items on the plots of current films. The *Tiger*, Princeton's undergraduate humor magazine, asked him for a contribution to its spring

1914 number, which was portentously designated an "all star" issue. In response he dashed off ten quatrains under the title "On the Value of a College Education," concerning two sets of brothers from the same town and what happened to the member of each set who went to college and what happened to the member of each set who did not. Some of what he wrote about the first pair ran as follows:

> And so the first one went away
>   To a distinguished college,
> And later he could never say
>   Enough in its extollage.
>
> By reason and by virtue of
>   His college education,
> His place in life is far above
>   The ordinary station.
>
> And what of him who went to seek
>   A regular position?
> A dozen meagre bones a week
>   Is now his sad condition.

And of the other pair:

> When just on the eve of attaining
>   Their manhood, the older one (Bob)
> Went in for collegiate training;
>   The other one (Jim) got a job.
>
> To-day Bob, who aimed at the gall'ry
>   Of fame and undying renown,
> Is drawing a regular sal'ry
>   Reporting the news of the town.
>
> And Jim who went in for no caper,
>   But clung to his little old job,
> Is owner-in-chief of the paper
>   That's paying the sal'ry to Bob.

As for the moral:

> A moral I'd write, if I could—one
>   To fit this ridiculous rant;
> The reason I don't is a good one:
>   I can't.

Running through this is no defensive strain, no suggestion that Kaufman envied the chance that the young Tigers of Princeton were getting; the puz-

zled note of the moral rings true. Yet it was not long before Kaufman made
an effort to improve his own chances in the world by returning to the classroom.

But that was not quite yet. In the meanwhile a young man named Herbert
Seligmann came into his life to draw him into the first real adventure of his
twenty-five years, and also to collaborate with him on a play. They met
through a family connection: Seligmann's father was a friend of Kaufman's
Uncle Gus. The two elder men played cards together, and their wives were
close. The play that young Seligmann and Kaufman wrote was a cynical trifle
called *The Lunatic*. It is a one-act piece set in the reception room of the Luna
Private Sanitorium, Ltd. In it a rich young man named John Winters is a patient in the sanitarium, not because he is out of his mind, but because he
bet a friend, James Kennedy, that he could get in by pretending to be sick.
He has fallen in love with the nurse and wants to be released, but is detained
by the doctor who owns the sanitarium. Ultimately he and his friend Kennedy, who comes to visit, have to buy their way out at the cost of $40,000.
The nurse is very pleased that they can rake together the money, because she,
as it happens, is married to the doctor.

The play came to nothing, but the friendship continued. In the spring of
1914 Seligmann's fiancée left him for a young man who not only had a great
deal more money than he, but was very attractive into the bargain. Kaufman,
hoping to console his friend, agreed to accompany him on a trip to Europe.
Not only was it Kaufman's first trip out of the country; it was the first crossing of the ocean that any of the Kaufmans had made since the emigration of
his grandfather, Simon Kaufman, in 1848. Kaufman had saved enough out
of his *Tribune* salary to make it possible. The paper granted a leave, and the
faithful F.P.A. gave the two young men a fine send-off in "The Conning
Tower."

They booked to sail on the *Kroonland,* a Red Star liner, on July 3 and to
return five weeks later. In the week before their sailing, items referring to the
coming event began to appear in the column. "Sir," G.S.K. wrote to the column, "don't you think the custom of sending gifts to Europe-goers is ridiculous? While I think of it, the Kroonland and I sail for disappoints east *next
Saturday morning* at ten o'clock. Pier 61, North River, foot of 21st Street. My
stateroom will be 169." Other items followed, including one to the effect
that it would perhaps be better if presents were sent to him at home. Adams's
creation, Dulcinea, the imaginary suburban housewife who spoke nothing
but banalities, made her contribution to the excitement of the moment the
day before the sailing, when Adams printed a note from Kaufman that read,

"I told Dulcinea I'll be in England and she said to give her regards to the King."

In the clubby atmosphere that Adams fostered for the column by having a family of regular participants, much as television talk-show hosts would do forty years later, G.S.K. was no shadowy presence. Adams expected him to receive "thousands of dozens" of bon voyage gifts, and since this was a time when presents *were* sent to staterooms, perhaps some arrived for him. Thanks to the good offices of the *Tribune's* reporter of ship news, each of the young men had his own stateroom, though they had paid for only one and expected to share it. And it may have been because of the frequency with which the initials G.S.K. had appeared in F.P.A.'s column that at meals they found themselves seated at the captain's table, along with a baroness and the wife of an admiral.[15]

The two young men ignored the reports that war would soon break out in Europe. Their first stop was London, where they were soon in the midst of a new kind of internal brawl, the suffragette movement. They attended one political meeting in a hall in which doughty gents held the doors closed against a mob of women who threatened to break them down. When it was time to move to the Continent, where they had planned stops in Amsterdam and Paris, Seligmann stayed behind and Kaufman went on alone. The paper and his family heard from him frequently during these weeks, but not a word about impending danger, since he felt none at the time. In Paris he wrote to the family that he had had a disappointment at a *charcuterie:* the first letter had fallen off the sign, and he had stepped inside because he needed a haircut, only to find the place hanging with sides of beef. His trip came to an end only one week before the firing of the first shots of the First World War.[16]

Returning home, he took up his work again at the *Tribune.* But now the work began to be rather more interesting. He was sent out to get material for Sunday feature stories on the development of the Authors' League and the pleasures of Coney Island, and also on such somber matters as unemployment and the work of the Legal Aid Society. For these stories, which were illustrated and spread across the entire page, he got a byline. The familiar G.S.K. of "The Conning Tower" was at last stretched out to "George S. Kaufman."

Moving up from cub reporter to feature writer, Kaufman took more steps toward the goal that for years he had been eyeing: a place in the theater. At Columbia University, whose southern edge was just thirteen blocks from the Kaufman apartment, it was possible to take courses without matriculating for a degree. On Friday evenings Professor Hatcher Hughes gave a course in playwriting in the "Extension" division of the university. With some prompting from Adams, Kaufman enrolled in it in the fall of 1914. The course entailed not only the writing of original scripts but visits to the theater and the analysis by the class of the plays attended.

Hughes himself was a playwright, and, though neither innovative in his methods of construction nor dazzling in the range of his ideas, he was a competent craftsman who in 1924 would receive the Pulitzer Prize for *Hell-Bent fer Heaven,* a backwoods melodrama. University courses such as the one he gave at Columbia had been proliferating across America ever since George Pierce Baker had begun, ten years earlier, to encourage his Radcliffe and Harvard undergraduates to write plays. Like Baker, Hughes had a preference for the tautly constructed "well-made" play of stern morality, as exemplified by the writings of Henry Arthur Jones and Arthur Wing Pinero.

Broadway usually offered a supply of such plays, along with farces and melodramas by the dozen: ephemera with plots of the flimsy sort that would be favored by Hollywood from the 1920s through the 1940s and by the television networks after that. There were also musical comedies and Shakespearean revivals. Now and then a producer with more pluck than a sense of box office would offer one of the recent, provocative works from northern or central Europe, or perhaps a play by Shaw. But in the fall of 1914 there was nothing by Ibsen, Strindberg, Hauptmann, or any other representative of the "new" Continental drama; nor was there any work by the newest of all—the German and Austrian expressionists, inventors of prickly anti-naturalistic tragedies on social themes. Jones's *The Lie* was produced, but did not open until December 24, too late for the course. There were some American equivalents, however: Hubert Henry Davies's *Outcast* and Owen Davis's *Sinners.* One Shaw play was offered: *Pygmalion,* with Mrs. Patrick Campbell, the original Eliza, repeating her great London performance. A production of *Twelfth Night* was given with a good cast that included Phyllis Neilson-Terry as Viola, but after eight performances it disappeared. One of the season's sensations was Elmer Rice's *On Trial,* with its clever, influential use of the flashback. It is a reasonable guess that Hughes's class saw the Shaw and Rice plays, and perhaps *It Pays To Advertise,* a popular farce by Roi Cooper Megrue and Walter Hackett, but whatever Kaufman may have had to contribute to the classroom discussion of any play is lost forever. What he learned from the course, also at a guess, was the careful method of construction that is the essence of the well-made play.

In August 1915, half a year after completing the course, Kaufman entered for copyright a slight, one-act play entitled *That Infernal Machine.* It may have been the product of his studies under Hughes, since he wrote it with another Columbia student, Wymberley de Renne. It is about a shy businessman named James Walker who cannot summon the courage to propose to his stenographer, Edith Roberts. She asks his friend, Robert Butler, to bring in a dictograph and persuade Walker to propose to her on a record. This works out as planned, but Edith, ashamed of herself, deliberately breaks the record. Walker then finds that he has the requisite courage, and all ends happily. One can see in this the influence of the one-joke sketches that were inflated into three-act farces by Megrue, Hackett, George M. Cohan, James Montgomery, Winchell Smith, and other popular writers of the time. It can at least be said for Kaufman and de Renne that they kept it short.

No sooner was the Columbia term concluded than Adams found Kaufman a job that promised to be more rewarding than his *Tribune* assignments, and that doubtless was more remunerative. Ever since Adams had left the *Evening Mail,* that paper had been seeking a suitable replacement for him. When the editor turned to Adams himself for advice, Adams suggested that he hire Kaufman, the G.S.K. of countless allusions in "All in Good Humor" and "The Conning Tower," and one-time editor and writer of his own humor column in Washington. Kaufman got the job, with instructions to prepare his first column for February 5, 1915.

The first title that he chose for the column was "Be That As It May," but later on, on June 29, he renamed it "The Mail Chute," perhaps to encourage submissions from his readers. However entitled, it was the same compendium of poetry, comment on the news, and short, humorous paragraphs on the human comedy that newspaper readers expected. It was much like Adams's column both before and after his move to the *Trib,* and much like Kaufman's own "This and That." On the first day Kaufman began with a poem called "Breaking the Ice," in which he surmised that not much attention had been paid to the first writings of Homer, Virgil, Shakespeare, Byron, and Browning, and that therefore he did not expect much attention to be paid to him. It concluded,

> Yes, yes, I know—I've mentioned five
> Who are a bit above my station;
> Tomorrow, though, I shall derive
> From them a *little* consolation.

This was not a bad way of getting started, but it turned out, like his opening sally at the Washington *Times,* to be more prophetic than he expected. The column did not go well, though it did not go poorly. It lacked the snap that "The Conning Tower" had acquired through its swelling list of bright contributors, including G.S.K. himself. Nor did Kaufman know how to make an effective use of borrowings from columnists in other cities when his own invention failed, as F.P.A. did. Still, his wit often came through. Audiences at Shaw's plays, he noted, had the habit of talking through the performance, leading him to observe, "We had a good time at *You Never Can Tell* . . . but we hesitate to recommend it. Those we persuaded to go might find an entirely different audience, and not like it at all."

In May a syndicate headed by Edward Lumely and the veteran journalist S. S. McClure took over the *Evening Mail* for the purpose (less subject to public outcry than it would be a year and a half later), of providing pro-German propagandists with an American mouthpiece. Though Kaufman's column was politically neutral, it was not to the new owners' taste, and they decided to dismiss him. The last day on which the column appeared was July 16, 1915. Kaufman did not bid his readers a formal goodbye. Instead, as a face-saving gesture he headed the day's opening poem "Wanderlust" and wrote in it that he felt a great urge to travel. Toward the end of the column he returned to this theme, noting that it kept coming back to his mind. It was his way, and as good a way as any, of departing with a smile. But he did not travel far, only to Schroon Lake, in upstate New York, for a rest. F.P.A. noted in "The Conning Tower" that Kaufman had now mastered the technique of "columnicide," having been fired by two papers, and could give lessons.

But Kaufman had become too well trained and disciplined a newspaperman to be without a job for long. The *Tribune* offered to take him back, and he accepted the post, which was as a reporter in the drama department, whose chief was burly, unkempt, sometime Harvard student Heywood Broun, Kaufman's senior by less than a year. In this position, Kaufman's main work was to gather the news from the producers' offices and shape it into notes for the paper. Broun himself was the paper's principal reviewer. His job was one that Kaufman eyed with envy.

With entrée assured to the producers' offices and plenty of complimentary tickets to the plays, Kaufman was closer than ever before to the profession that really appealed to him. But being a dramatic reporter and being a Broadway dramatist were in no way the same thing, and a dramatist was what he hoped to become. Columbia had another interesting course in the "Extension" program: Clayton Hamilton's Saturday morning course in modern drama, from Victor Hugo to Arthur Wing Pinero. In the fall of 1915, not long after coming under Broun's wing, Kaufman enrolled in that course. Like Hughes, Hamilton was a playwright as well as a teacher, though he never had such a success as Hughes was to have with *Hell-Bent fer Heaven*. Only a year before Kaufman became his student he had a play on Broadway, *The Big Idea,* which he wrote in collaboration with A. E. Thomas. But it ran a mere twenty-four performances. Like Hughes, Hamilton preferred the well-made play of conventional outlook to the work of more recent, more daring dramatists—hence his course in modern drama ended not with Shaw, but with Pinero. Between the two of them, Hughes and Hamilton, it was not likely that the young Kaufman would turn himself into a path-breaking contriver of new structural methods.

Dividing his time between the paper and the campus, Kaufman kept himself busy, if not satisfied. An occasional free-lance opportunity came along to provide evidence that he was becoming known, but as the winter and spring of 1916 came and went he was marking time. He would have liked greater responsibility, and especially a promotion to the post of drama critic. It was not forthcoming, nor could he have expected it to be.

In the summer of 1915 Ruth Kaufman met a young man from Des Moines named Allan Friedlich, and early in 1916 she told Joseph and Nettie Kaufman that she was going to marry him. "Dull!" said her brother after meeting him, but Ruth was unmoved, knowing that George made this pronouncement only because he did not want to lose her companionship. It occurred to Ruth that he too would do well to marry, since he would then have to leave home and their querulous mother. With his tie to the family, his shyness, and his sweet tooth, he was a bit of an adolescent still.

Ruth's marriage took place in New York on June 6, 1916. The newlyweds went for a few weeks' visit to Rochester, where Allan Friedlich's father was then living. They were to go from Rochester to Des Moines, where Friedlich was to have the management of a clothing store owned by his family. While in Rochester they were much entertained by, and came to know well, the pillars of the city's Jewish community. Their visit coincided with Kaufman's vacation, which he had arranged to spend on a Lake Erie steamer. Ruth and Allan Friedlich thought it would be a fine diversion for him if at the end of the two-week cruise he could join them briefly in Rochester. They were eager for him to meet their friends, among whom were some unmarried young women.

— 2 —

Beatrice

When Kaufman arrived in Rochester on July 8, 1916, after his holiday on Lake Erie, he was met by the Friedlichs with the news that they were planning a party for him that evening, a Saturday. During the evening after watching Kaufman as he chatted with the guests, they held a private consultation about the next day's plan, which was to drive to Niagara Falls for lunch. They wanted to take along one of the Rochester girls as a date for Kaufman and had to decide on which before the party broke up. They settled on Beatrice Bakrow, lively and amusing, as the one, and it happened that she was free for the day.

Though the distance was less than a hundred miles, the round trip made for a full day's outing. Young George Kaufman and young Beatrice Bakrow, sitting in the back of Allan Friedlich's car, had plenty of time to study each other. What Beatrice saw was an ungainly fellow, self-conscious, ill at ease, though not bad-looking (but no collar ad), and uncomfortably long-legged for the back seat. What Kaufman saw was a woman of twenty-one who was somewhat overweight and quite tall, though very attractive (but no Follies beauty). They liked what they saw and approved of what they heard each other say, each discovering that the other was a most intelligent human being.

They also discovered that superior intelligence was not all that they had in common. On both sides Beatrice, like Kaufman, was of German-Jewish descent. Her grandfather Adler, like Simon Kaufman, had come to the United States in 1848. Settling in upstate New York, he had acquired a stock of clothing and had become an itinerant peddler. In time he set aside enough money to open a tailor shop in Rochester, and this expanded into a successful clothing factory. As Beatrice was later to write of him, "He prospered greatly during his life and at his death he was, for those times and in that city, a rich man."[1] He sired seven children, two sons and five daughters. One of the daughters, Sara, married a Kentuckian, Jules Bakrow, who came to Rochester as a traveling salesman. Jules took a place in his father-in-law's firm and became one of the firm's ablest salesmen.

Jules and Sara Bakrow had three children, of whom Beatrice, born on January 20, 1895, was the second. Her brother Julian preceded her into the world by four years; her brother Leonard came two years after her. In the Jewish community of Rochester, the Bakrows and other families of similar origin—that is to say, families whose forebears had come from Germany before the American Civil War—constituted an elite and were well aware of the fact. Growing up in this milieu, Beatrice became increasingly conscious of the snobbishness of her family and came to resent it. When she became interested in boys from families outside the Jewish "400," her parents were quick to express their disapproval. Throughout her life she carried with her the memory of the foot-taps of her father in a room upstairs when in the living room she entertained a boy whose family had come from eastern Europe. The world in which she was raised lacked none of the luxuries that the American upper-middle class took for granted, but it was confining. Her mother wanted as full a life for her as the family wealth and Beatrice's own intelligence would make possible, and Sara Bakrow's vision of that paradise included a son-in-law from within the Bakrows' own charmed circle.

Neither of Beatrice's parents was well educated; not once in her life did she see her father reading a book. But the senior Bakrows respected learning and had every intention of giving their children a good education. Because one of Sara Bakrow's brothers was head of the Board of Education in Rochester, it was decided that Beatrice should go to public high school rather than a boarding school. She did well, but later in life, when she allowed herself time to think it over, she became convinced that it was not her study habits that won high grades for her, but a good memory and her uncle's position. After graduation she went off to Wellesley, along with her most intimate friend, Dorothy Michaels, whose family was also in the clothing manufacturing business.

Beatrice's Wellesley career had a duration of just one year. No account of what happened to her there could match her own:

> We [Beatrice and Dorothy] achieved a monumental insularity at Wellesley, making, during that year, no friends, and indeed hardly attempting

to make acquaintance with the hundreds of members of our class. I fancied myself in love with a boy at Harvard and the fact that this passion was fairly one-sided in no way lessened its intensity. I was in and out of Boston, where I knew quite a lot of people, as often as possible and the fondest recollections I have of the rest of the year were of fudge cake made at the Wellesley Inn.

As for studying, I must have done some, but what I remember best is writing compositions in English for a friend of mine who received through them a much higher mark than mine. The blow fell at midyears, and for some reason which eludes me in retrospect I was completely unprepared for it. Out of five subjects I had failed three. The next semester I tried very hard to pull myself together and I succeeded in passing everything, but my return for the sophomore year was dependent on my passing examinations in all the subjects which I had failed during the first semester. I succeeded in two and failed again in botany, a course which consisted in taking a passionate interest in the development of the bean from infancy through adulthood, a subject in which I was not able to arouse the slightest enthusiasm. I was also supposed to be able to draw the bean in all its stages both above and below the ground. In retrospect I do not know why this was as impossible for me as it seemed, but it was the end.

I was sent for by the Dean and told that I had been dropped from the sophomore class of Wellesley, 1916. I telegraphed my mother and boarded the night train for Rochester with both apprehension and sadness, as it suddenly dawned upon me that my mother had set considerable store on my college career. This feeling became a conviction. Before seven the next morning I was met at the station by my brother Leonard, then seventeen, who greeted me with a simple sentence which told all. "You're going to catch it," he said.[2]

To Sara Bakrow her daughter's dismissal was a calamity of immeasurable magnitude. She told Beatrice that no decent man would ever marry her, and Beatrice believed her. To atone, Beatrice took some courses at the University of Rochester. She found, however, that she was still no student, and when the right man happened by, she put an end to her effort at formal education. That man was George Kaufman. Her friend Dorothy also left Wellesley without being graduated, but not because of academic problems. She had met a Harvard man, Robert Nathan, the writer, and at the end of her sophomore year they were married.

Before Kaufman made his foray into Rochester, there was someone else in Beatrice's life—someone more serious, that is, than the Harvard undergraduate. One of Sara's sisters lived in Cincinnati, a city with a large Jewish population. In 1914 it was decided that Beatrice should spend the Christmas holidays with her aunt. Overweight, of course, and dressed in clothes modeled precisely as to both style and size on those of a slim cousin, off Beatrice went, "fairly bursting in pale blue velvet." Yet she could not have made too unattractive a picture, for a young man of Cincinnati fell in love with her and proposed. He was a rabbi who had just completed his studies at Cincinnati's Hebrew Union College, the center for studies in Reform Judaism, and was soon to leave for a pulpit in Grand Rapids, Michigan. From him Beatrice accepted a ring composed of two twining silver serpents with eyes of rubies. Her aunt disapproved of the engagement and sent her home, where her parents received her with indignation. "You will marry him over my dead body," said Jules Bakrow, and very soon Beatrice returned the ring, grateful for the firmness on her father's part that had saved her from a way of life to which she could never have adjusted.[3]

After leaving Wellesley, Beatrice was not always happy. Her father's concern lest she make an unsuitable marriage was suffocating, and every day she dreaded the tension at the dinner table that arose over that problem. But the appearance of Kaufman let in some air. On the outing to Niagara Falls he was witty and charming, and his sternness with a negligent waiter at a restaurant to which the party went for lunch was impressive. (Later in life his attitude toward waiters would not be so gratifying.) There was lively conversation in the back seat on the drive home—livelier than Ruth and Allan Friedlich knew. The next morning when the Friedlichs came down to breakfast in Allan's father's house, they were told by the maid that Kaufman had already gone out. Beatrice had come by and whisked him off to meet her family.

Jules and Sara Bakrow and their sons were not so enthusiastic as she about this young stranger from New York, thinking him oddly diffident for their high-spirited Beatrice. But when she told them, that same day, that he had proposed and she had accepted, they revised their opinion. No matter how he appeared in public, he was obviously aggressive in affairs of the heart![4] The family was not overjoyed at the prospect of her going off with a man whose weekly salary came to only $35, but offsetting this was the fact that, apart from money, Kaufman's background was not dissimilar to their own—that and Beatrice's obvious happiness in the engagement. Besides, the Bakrows could afford to continue Beatrice's clothing allowance after the wedding, if it should prove necessary (as it did). The first persons to be told of the engagement after the family were Robert and Dorothy Nathan, who were summering in Rochester. Beatrice took Kaufman to the Nathans' house above the shore of

Lake Ontario. Spotting them below on the beach, the engaged couple rushed down to them. There all four joined hands and performed a little dance of celebration on the sand.

Back in New York Kaufman carried on at the *Tribune,* collecting the news from the Broadway offices and typing out his Sunday features. It was at about this time that he joined the Friars Club, of which Adams also was a member.* Membership in the club carried considerable prestige in the world of show business, and such luminaries of the theater as George M. Cohan, Sam H. Harris, Irving Berlin, and Victor Herbert belonged. It also was a congenial place for a poker game.

During this interim between bachelorhood and a new way of life, Kaufman received an opportunity from an unexpected quarter to make himself known as a playwright. Burns Mantle, the drama editor of the *Evening Mail,* was asked by a young man named Henry R. Stern to supply a list of talented young writers who might become the clients of a new sort of authors' agency that he hoped to found. The son of a music publisher, Joseph W. Stern, the young man had theatrical connections. It was his idea to develop new playwrights, not simply to take on as clients a stable of established writers. The fledgling dramatists would have the agency's help in the placement of their work and also (and this was new) in its development, for Mantle and Stern would offer suggestions for the improvement of the manuscripts submitted. The agency's fee for this double function would be double the usual fee, which was 10 per cent. In his list, Mantle set down Kaufman's name, having come to know him during his time on the *Evening Mail.* Soon thereafter Kaufman submitted a manuscript entitled *Going Up.* After many revisions that Kaufman carried out in accordance with their advice, the play struck them as "quite wonderful."[5] On March 10, 1917, Stern's company copyrighted what was presumably the final form of the first act. Over the summer Kaufman continued to work on the play, and by August 3 all three acts and a prologue had been copyrighted.

A farce on the criminal practice of check-raising (increasing the dollar amount indicated on a check), *Going Up* has to do with a young, would-be writer named Sam Blaine, who lives in a West Side boarding house and cannot pay his rent. When a friend of his, an amoral type named Bob ("Skin") Flint, suggests that he raise a check from the sale of a story from $8.00 to $80, he decides to do so, and therewith starts a train of actions, many quite

* The Friars Club is unable to provide the date.

outside the law, that ends happily for him and for the young woman with whom, in the course of things, he falls in love. The play is noteworthy for its use of the flashback, a borrowing, almost certainly, from Elmer Rice's *On Trial*. The events of the prologue are supposed to take place after the first act, and suspense is created by detectives who are looking into the check-raising incident that the audience soon will see take place on stage. The dialogue of the play, if not so finely honed as would be the lines of Kaufman's mature comedies, frequently sparkles. "Do you know how much you owe me?" Sam's landlady Rose Gersten asks him in the first act.

> SAM Well, I haven't exactly kept count. But I know I've been here about eighteen or twenty bread puddings, but—
> ROSE It's been six weeks, Mr. Blaine. That's $48.
> SAM Imagine $48 worth of bread pudding!

Amusing and lively though the script was, Mantle and Stern discovered that they could not find a producer for it. Eventually they gave up not only on the farce but on the agency itself, though not before one happy occurrence. John Peter Toohey, the press agent for the eminent producer George C. Tyler, read and liked the play and showed it to Tyler. The producer did not care enough for the play to mount it, but he filed Kaufman's name in his mind for future reference.[6]

The marriage of Kaufman and Beatrice Bakrow took place on March 15, 1917, a little more than eight months after the couple became engaged. During the interval Kaufman visited Rochester as often as his working schedule and his finances permitted, and on the days when he arrived Beatrice would awaken in a state of "wild excitement," as she herself put it.[7] On one such visit she asked her fiancé what his mysterious middle initial stood for. Since it did not actually stand for anything, they decided between them that it should stand for "Sniggie," and with that nickname Kaufman thereafter signed most of his letters to her, sometimes shortening it to the original S. Beatrice had long since told him that she did not like to have her name shortened to "Bea," and though some acquaintances addressed her in this way, he never did.

Thirteen years later Alexander Woollcott was to report that Kaufman left for his wedding from the Friars Club with $75 pinned to his undershirt.[8] He was accompanied by Frank Adams, whom he had asked to be his best man, and Herbert Seligmann. After the ceremony, which was performed at a country club, the couple, Adams, and Seligmann hastened back to New York on the night train, the early morning papers in their arms. Glancing at these, they discovered that a revolution had erupted in Russia, and they talked about it during the journey.[9] Since Kaufman could get no time off from his job at the *Tribune,* the couple had no honeymoon.

The lack of this traditional period of adjustment created no problems. It took little time for them to be accustomed to marriage. Both rejoiced in their new life. Though the living quarters Kaufman could afford were not as spacious as her parents' home in Rochester was, Beatrice was content in them. The couple took an apartment in the Majestic Hotel at Central Park West and 72nd Street, across the street from the old and famous Dakota apartment building and on the site where later was to stand the Majestic apartment building, a monument to the Art Deco style. The Majestic Hotel itself was a dingy Victorian, but that did not matter. Bliss was a two-room suite with a bedroom just big enough to accommodate two beds and a bureau. Kaufman and Beatrice were a very modern couple to start off their marriage with separate beds! But one senses it was not so much their desire to be modern that decreed this way of life as it was a tentativeness born of their innocence and Kaufman's natural shyness.[10]

Their living room was not much larger than the bedroom, and their book collection consisted of one work only: Bernard Shaw's dramatic criticism, *Our Theatres in the Nineties*—good reading for a young man planning a career as a playwright. The only meal prepared was breakfast, and it was always the same: oranges, soft-boiled eggs, and instant coffee made with the water used for boiling the eggs. Though Beatrice loved food, she did not care to cook and, except when necessity dictated and then in only the most perfunctory way, did not do so at any point in her twenty-eight years of marriage.

Kaufman's hours on the *Tribune,* a morning paper, required him to work in the evenings, a situation which provided an excuse for dining out. The two would take the subway to the stop nearest the paper's offices on Park Row, and Beatrice would watch placidly while Kaufman called the theatrical press agents for news, assembled his notes, and wrote his column. In her presence he dashed off hard-edged quips for his Sunday round-up of the news. Of an unsuccessful Russian play, *Nju,* he wrote that its producers had received requests to take it out of town, "and it seems only fair to add that the requests came from out of town." On another day he noted, "Those serial pictures are showing a decided improvement. *Gloria's Romance* had twenty-five installments, or thereabouts, and *Patria* has only fifteen."

After every opening Kaufman and Beatrice would wait in the office until Heywood Broun returned from the theater and wrote his review, and then all three would skip out to end the evening with a visit to a restaurant on 41st

Street. Already a good friend of Kaufman's, Broun became Beatrice's friend as well. He had every hope of marrying Lydia Lopokova, the Diaghilev ballerina whom he had first met in 1915 when she was attempting a dramatic, non-dancing role in a production offered by the Washington Square Players. They became engaged, but Lopokova broke off the engagement to marry Randolfo Baroncini, Diaghilev's chief administrative aide. The Kaufmans nursed Broun through his grief, which took the form of a great thirst for strong drink. Mercifully, he required their services for four days only; at the end of that time he became engaged to the newspaperwoman Ruth Hale and was himself again. He had known her even longer than he had known Lopokova; attracted to him and eager to marry him despite her feminist views, she had been standing by during the engagement.*[11]

Over all this happiness hung the menace of the war. The United States entered it on April 2, 1917, not three weeks after Kaufman and Beatrice were married. Broun and Ruth Hale were married on June 7 and the next day left for France, he to serve as a correspondent for the *Tribune* with the American Expeditionary Force and she to work on the staff of the Paris edition of the Chicago *Tribune*. Frank Adams accepted the offer of a captaincy in Army Intelligence. Kaufman, however, remained out of the services. It was not only his marriage that kept him out, but his eyesight, his meager weight, and his record of having suffered from a chest condition, the pleurisy that caused him to drop out of law school in 1907. He was to remain a civilian.

Late in May, not long before Broun was married and sailed overseas, the *Tribune*'s publisher, Ogden Reid, sent Broun back to the sports department of the paper. It may have seemed reasonable to Kaufman that he should be asked to step into the vacant post of critic, but such was not Reid's plan. Kaufman was allowed to review one play in June, two in August, and one more in September, but late in August the paper hired another man as critic, a Phi Beta Kappa graduate of the University of Michigan named Ralph Block, who was one year Kaufman's junior.† Of one of the plays that he reviewed, Kaufman wrote, "*Mary's Ankle* is quite passable August entertainment, but it will never, never do in September." The *Tribune*'s powers apparently felt the same way about him as reviewer, though they were happy enough to print his Sunday columns. But writing the Sunday pieces, which meant merely embroidering the week's sheaf of publicity releases, was a dead end. Though Kaufman hoped and planned for a career in the theater, he saw

---

* In 1925, after divorcing Baroncini, Lopokova married John Maynard Keynes.
† Block eventually moved on to Hollywood, where he wrote scripts and became a producer. He is credited with the discovery of Carole Lombard.

that if journalism was to provide the base on which his literary reputation was to grow, then he would have to move on to some other paper.

Luck was with him in this. The New York *Times* offered him a job as drama reporter, and he accepted it. He handed in his Sunday, September 9, copy to the *Tribune* and went to work the next day at the *Times*. Soon thereafter, when Brock Pemberton vacated the post of *Times* drama editor to become assistant to Arthur Hopkins, one of Broadway's busiest producers, Kaufman replaced him. In that post Kaufman remained until August 16, 1930, by which date his salary had reached $80 a week and he had become one of Broadway's most successful playwrights, with an income that made possible a domestic staff of three servants and a nurse for his child.[12]

Kaufman's starting salary cannot have been much of an improvement over his final pay at the *Tribune*. But the lack of meaningful financial benefit was offset by prestige, a value that newspapers and publishing houses were not likely to underrate when figuring the salaries of their employees. Though in 1917 New York was served by some dozen Manhattan-based daily papers, to say nothing of such famous dailies as the Bronx *Home News* and the Brooklyn *Eagle*, the *Times*, thanks to the vision of its publisher, Adolph S. Ochs, stood out from all the others. Ochs, who bought the paper in 1896, had made it *the* newspaper of record, the one American daily in which full accounts of all events of national consequence could be read, where major political addresses and such documents as Supreme Court decisions and international treaties would be printed and would be permanently preserved in a library edition on rag paper. The *Times* under Ochs was sparing in feature items; it lacked, for example, comic cartoon strips and, except for those reprinted on Sunday from other papers, political cartoons as well. It carried no such columns as F.P.A.'s. Other papers might provide their readers with such amusements, but Ochs's readers, presumably of the highest seriousness, were expected to get along without them. (Those readers who were not so serious could buy a second paper and enjoy *its* cartoons and columnists.) Only on Sunday, in the catch-all cultural section, which in 1917 also included war news, a fashion page, and, sometimes, educational news, did the paper free itself a little from its policy of editorial austerity. On becoming drama editor of this respected if not very lively paper, Kaufman inherited a section that by virtue of its subject had more liveliness than most: an occasional verbal contraction could even be found in the reporting of the Broadway news! As the arbiter of what news (or gossip or releases from the producers' and talent agents' offices) should be reported, Kaufman automatically acquired power.

He was not, however, the department chief. That rank was always held by the principal reviewer.

Kaufman's effect on the content, appearance, and style of the *Times'* drama reporting was gradual and cumulative. On the Sundays before his arrival the department's page gave off fewer sparkles than did that of the *Tribune,* though thanks to Pemberton's lively intelligence it was not completely lacking in appeal. (Kaufman himself reported in the *Tribune* on April 8, 1917, that Pemberton had a quip ready for the day when Theda Bara should decide to stop making films in New York and move to Hollywood: "Westward the curse of vampire takes its way.") But many of the city's other drama departments could match that of the *Times* for completeness of coverage, including those of the *World* and the *Daily News.* Kaufman could claim, however, that he expanded the Broadway coverage, getting more notes into the daily edition and, with the backing of the Sunday edition editor, Lester Markel, causing the Sunday articles and news column to spill over to a second page and sometimes a third. After Kaufman's arrival, playwrights were asked to supply Sunday articles about their upcoming works, and reviews with stars and producers such as Kaufman himself had written for the *Tribune* began to appear. So readable did his pages become that eventually his oldest friends were inclined to attribute to him the use of two phrases that frequently adorned the Sunday pages, but which were introduced by other editors. One was the column heading "What News on the Rialto?" (from *The Merchant of Venice*), and the other was the "straw-hat trail" as a designation for the summer-theater circuit. The first appeared before he came to the paper, and the second not until after he left it.

A day at the *Times* drama desk was well structured, but not excessively demanding. It began late in the morning, allowed for a lengthy lunch, and reached a climax in the early evening when everyone on the staff went out to the theater. As soon as the curtain rang down on an opening performance, a review of the play had to be written, and the writing had to be accomplished swiftly, so that the piece could make the late edition. Thursday was the day on which the all-important Sunday pages were readied, and on that day Kaufman was busier than usual. On any day the office was an agreeable place in which to work, with plenty of time for exchanges of wit and gossip. So highly regarded by the paper's management was Kaufman that it was always possible for him, once his career as a playwright commenced, to get away to sit in on the rehearsals of his plays and to attend the out-of-town openings. It was not until 1928, when he established himself as a director as well as a writer, that his absences became a problem. Before then, on evenings when he was not attending an opening and therefore had some time on his hands, he would never fail to leave the diversion of the moment—bridge, poker, a dinner party—and make his way to the paper's offices in time for the final shaping of the next day's drama page.[13]

In temperament and literary style Kaufman's associates in the *Times* drama department varied markedly. The most outstanding stylist and most probing analyst of drama among them was Stark Young, who served as critic for a brief period in 1924 and 1925, when the post was given to Brooks (then J. Brooks) Atkinson. Later, when he was a critic for the biweekly *New Republic,* which afforded him a more lenient schedule than the *Times* in which to prepare his reviews, Young came into his own as one of the most sensitive American commentators on drama and the stage. His predecessor from 1922 to 1924 was John Corbin, a somewhat stodgy writer. Corbin took over the post as a replacement for the flamboyant, logorrhaeic Alexander Woollcott, who left in 1922 for a highly paid post as critic for Frank Munsey's *Herald.* It was Atkinson's opinion that Kaufman enjoyed the paper most when Woollcott was his chief.[14]

That may have been so, since both Kaufman and Woollcott possessed a snapping, wisecracking wit, and since Woollcott and Beatrice became fast friends almost as soon as they met. Together, the playwright and the critic could bring the tempo of any gathering, whether professional or social, up to the level of *molto agitato.* After both had left the *Times,* Woollcott wrote about their association in the department, and not wholly as a joke, "I was his uneasy chief for three years from 1919 to 1922 and he was never really satisfied with me."[15] Yet they got on well together. They were very different, Woollcott being a heavy eater, a show-off with an exceptionally demanding, egocentric personality, a lover of travel, and a lover of women in only a platonic way. But if he had no interest in women sexually, Woollcott enjoyed them as companions, provided they were intelligent, and none so much as Beatrice. For this reason, and because they shared the same social circle, Kaufman remained in constant touch with him. Yet they made an extraordinarily odd couple, the lean, austere, precise G.S.K. and the unkempt, obese Woollcott, who sometimes referred to himself in baby talk as "Acky Wooky." To Harpo Marx, his great friend, Woollcott looked like nothing so much as "something that had gotten loose from Macy's Thanksgiving Day Parade."[16]

To Lester Markel Kaufman seemed, as he did to many lesser *Times* employees, "a pretty neurotic fellow," and greatly dependent on the strength of Beatrice. Markel seldom saw him in the office, but frequently ran into him at the home of Harold Ross and his wife, Jane Grant, on West 47th Street, where Woollcott also lived. It was Markel's impression that during Kaufman's years on the *Times* his only intimates were the members of the circle—in fact, a broad one—with whom he took his lunch at the Algonquin Hotel. Woollcott was his only *Times* colleague who lunched virtually every workday at the Algonquin. Markel was always puzzled by the fact that though Kaufman was not gregarious, he enjoyed an audience. He was worth listening to, but quite capable of ignoring the feelings of others for the sake of a joke.[17]

One of Kaufman's late-night jokes at the *Times*, typical of the puns he and his friends loved, circulated around Broadway for years and eventually came back to embarrass him. A fumbling performance by a young, Italian-born actor named Guido Nadzo inspired him to report to Atkinson and other colleagues in the department that "Guido Nadzo was nadzo guido." This was too good not to be repeated, and many years later, on March 22, 1938, when the actor made an appearance in Clare Kummer's *Spring Thaw,* both Atkinson of the *Times* and Richard Watts, Jr., of the *Herald Tribune* remembered it and used it in their reviews. On March 30, *Variety* reported that the actor had never heard the pun before and was "burned up" about it. Kaufman, though not really to blame for this double assault on poor Nadzo, sent him a note of apology. Whether the note assuaged the actor's sore feelings was not divulged, but never again did he act on Broadway, though during the previous thirteen years he had appeared in fourteen plays—by no means a humble record.

Another *Times* colleague and frequent if not daily luncheon companion of whom Kaufman was fond was Herman J. Mankiewicz. Mank, as most of his acquaintances called him, served as Kaufman's assistant from 1923 to 1926 and also was an occasional book reviewer for the paper and drama critic for the *New Yorker.* Though a heavy drinker even when he was in his twenties (he was born in 1897), Mankiewicz managed to make of Kaufman not only an admirer, but a collaborator and protector. The two first met in 1917, when Mankiewicz, just out of Columbia, was hired as a drama reporter by the *Tribune.* On several Sundays in that year the paper carried by-line articles by both him and Kaufman. Both writers left the *Tribune* in the fall, Mankiewicz to go to France as a serviceman. After the war, before joining Kaufman at the *Times,* Mankiewicz worked in Berlin as a correspondent for the Chicago *Tribune.* He had plenty of energy and a tough, terse style not unlike Kaufman's.

So useful was Mankiewicz to the drama department that Kaufman kept him on the staff despite his drinking, which, on occasion, was not merely embarrassing, but infuriating. The most notorious instance occurred on the night of October 22, 1925, when he was sent to review a production of Sheridan's *The School for Scandal* featuring Gladys Wallis, the wife of Samuel Insull, the Chicago utilities tycoon. As Lady Teazle, Mrs. Insull—who was much too old for the part—gave a performance that drove Mankiewicz out of the theater and into the nearest speakeasy. Attempting later to peck out some sort of review, he passed out at his typewriter, where Kaufman found him. What Mankiewicz had written was unprintable, and Kaufman, in a rage, tore it up. Mankiewicz's wife, Sara, was present at the time and managed to get him home. The next day Mankiewicz persuaded Sam Zolotow, another member of the department, to intercede for him with Frederick Birchall, the assistant managing editor of the paper, who had the power to dismiss him if he chose. Bizarrely, Mankiewicz sent a bottle of whiskey as a peace-offering to Birchall. Hearing that Birchall was willing to overlook the incident, Kaufman was mollified. Mankiewicz went back to work, but he soon accepted a lucrative contract to write screenplays and headed for California. In 1940, when writing the script of *Citizen Kane*, Mankiewicz made use of the Lady Teazle incident. In that film Jed Leland is sent to review the operatic performance of Susan Alexander, the wife of newspaper magnate Charles Foster Kane. He finds it intolerable, drinks, writes scathingly of it, but, before finishing, passes out at the typewriter, where he is found by Kane, who decides to complete the review himself and then publishes it.[18]

At the end of their first year of marriage, in the late winter of 1918, Beatrice found that she was going to have a baby. The couple had comparatively little to live on, but they could take comfort at least from the knowledge that Kaufman's job on the *Times* was secure. The routine of their life pleased them. Kaufman remained in close touch with his parents, who continued to live on the Upper West Side and who doted on Beatrice. Dorothy Nathan was still Beatrice's intimate friend, and she lived in New York and thus was able to provide companionship for Beatrice during her pregnancy. Brought together by their wives, Kaufman and Robert Nathan also became friends. Though never as close as Beatrice and Dorothy, they admired each other enough to discuss the possibility of collaborating on a play.

Meanwhile, before the two young men could sit down and work together, Kaufman had a lucky break—one that involved him in months of writing and rewriting and added little to his bank account, but one that gave him the greatest opportunity for professional advancement he had had since F.P.A. first began finding jobs for him. It was a new kind of venture, or adventure, for him, and was one whose outcome he could hardly have foreseen. The events leading up to this moment covered almost three years, during which Kaufman was quite oblivious to what was in store.

In 1915 George C. Tyler read two short stories by a writer named Larry Evans that had to do with the escapades of a "gentleman crook," an amateur thief drawn on the model of A. J. Raffles, the fictional character created by the English author E. W. Hornung. Tyler thought he saw a play in them and got in touch with Evans. Tyler had been active as a producer since 1897, at first with the firm of Liebler and Company and then, beginning in 1916, on his own. Aggressive and imaginative and possibly more the intellectual than he himself realized, over the years he had offered the public Eleonora Duse in repertory, Shaw's *Pygmalion,* the comedies of Booth Tarkington, and the sentimental pieces created by J. Hartley Manners for his wife, Laurette Taylor. Tyler had some trouble persuading Larry Evans to fashion a play out of his stories, but he persisted, despite Evans's remark that he (Evans) "couldn't even write an intermission, let alone a play."[19] Evans consented at last and brought in a young actor named Walter C. Percival to assist with the adaptation. Tyler liked their script, but he saw that it needed work and persuaded Rupert Hughes, the novelist and playwright, to make some changes, without billing. It was then the fall of 1917, and Tyler felt that, with Hughes's revisions, the play, called *Among Those Present,* was ready to be tried out. With Shelley Hull in the lead, Tyler sent it to Richmond, Norfolk, and Philadelphia. In those cities the reviews were disappointing, leaving Tyler certain that on Broadway the play would never make its way. Still, he did not want to drop it altogether, and, when trying to decide what to do next, he thought of calling in Kaufman, whom he remembered as the intelligent young author of the farce *Going Up,* the same man who, as a writer for the *Tribune* and *Times,* often came around to his office looking for news. Kaufman agreed to take over.

Tyler's determination to make something of the play was based on his awareness of the taste of the moment. "Crook" plays were popular. Some years before, in 1910, Hornung and Eugene W. Presbrey had fashioned a play called *Raffles, the Amateur Cracksman* from Hornung's stories. Liebler had produced it, and it had been a hit. More recent popular plays of the same sort were Max Marcin's *Cheating Cheaters,* Winchell Smith and John E. Hazzard's *Turn to the Right,* and Paul Armstrong's *Alias Jimmy Valentine,* which Tyler himself had offered. The central figure in the new play was Jimmy Burke, alias "the Dancer," a jewel thief with the manners of a clubman. Knowing that the Hollister necklace, a string of exquisitely matched diamonds, is to be used in an amateur theatrical production for a war-related charity, Burke accepts one of the parts: that of a gentleman jewel thief. The performance is to take place in the home of the author, Percy Glendenning, who lives in Westchester County, New York, an area then second only to Long Island in the affections of Broadway authors of comic melodramas. Though the police are onto his identity and keep an eye on him, Burke does succeed in stealing the necklace. But he also falls in love with the girl who owns it, and therefore cannot bring himself to make off with it. Since the rules followed by crook-play writers required that the crook should get away, Jimmy eludes the handcuffs and slips back to New York.

Kaufman was not the first rewrite man called in, and he was not the last, but his revisions were so much more extensive than those of the others that his name was the only one added to those of Evans and Percival. Though he may have overstated the matter, he reported, by way of Burns Mantle's column in the *Evening Mail*, that he went over the script almost fifty times.[20] With his name on it, the play was sent to Chicago, where it opened on February 10, 1918, with a new leading man, H. B. Warner, the young English-born actor who had "created" the part of Jimmy Valentine and who later would have a prominent career in Hollywood. Kaufman thought that an effective switch on the usual plotting of the "crook" play would be to let Burke turn out to be a detective, while the real crook was a figure who everyone presumed was the detective. Warner found this an unattractive arrangement, preferring the romantic coloring that the part took on at the end when Burke's decency in leaving the jewels behind was disclosed. To Ruth Friedlich, who, like her brother, came to Chicago for the opening, he volunteered the opinion that Kaufman would do better to stick to his journalism.[21] When Tyler withdrew the play for further rewriting after the eight-week Chicago engagement, Warner decided that he had had enough. He declined to sign for the next revised version, no matter who might be contracted to write it and no matter when it might be done.

Tyler had no wish to take Kaufman off the play. Instead, he simply signed on some more writers, in a gesture that prefigured the policy of Hollywood producers of the 1930s and 1940s. Broadway play-doctors William H. Post and Brandon Tynan were brought in without billing, and they went over the play with Kaufman through the spring of 1918 and into the summer. In August, Tyler took the play to Washington. Cyril Keightley, a popular leading man, played Jimmy. But he, too, disliked the new ending and withdrew. Now finding that he was devoting practically all his time to this single project, Tyler, who normally would have been engaged with plans for the season ahead and even beyond that, simply moved up a young actor named Robert

Hudson from a minor role to the lead. Though the play still did not seem to be turning into a hit, Tyler kept at it. He engaged the Knickerbocker Theater in New York and announced an opening on September 9. A one-night stand was booked for Trenton three days before, and after the curtain rang down on it Tyler finally decided that the original ending written by Evans and Percival was preferable to Kaufman's, and restored it. Tyler then came up with a new title, *Someone in the House,* under which the play at long last opened.

The saga of Kaufman's entry into the canyon of Broadway did not have the traditional happy ending. No rave notices greeted the production. After only thirty-two performances, Tyler withdrew the play. It was not so much a case of too many writers spoiling the fun as it was of tedium induced by the formula plot consisting of the ingenious ruses of the gentleman crook and the overfamiliar setting of a posh suburban estate peopled with bright young things. On the other hand, one of the young performers was truly bright, and she gathered a sheaf of appreciative notices. That was Lynn Fontanne, whose career as a major presence on the American stage was begun with her appearance as Helene Glendenning, the playwright's wife, in *Someone in the House.* The English-born actress had been brought over to America two years before, in 1916, to appear in a comedy by J. Hartley Manners called *The Wooing of Eve.** That production closed out of town, but Fontanne stayed on under contract to Tyler and appeared in more plays under his management, including a second version of *The Wooing of Eve.* Both Tyler and Laurette Taylor, Fontanne's patron, thought she might improve her looks by putting on some weight, but at the same time recognized that she had uncommon talent and versatility.

It was as a replacement for another actress, Ethel Dane, who first took the role, that Tyler cast Lynn Fontanne. Wanting to launch her with a splash, he asked Kaufman to turn the part into one sure to draw attention. This Kaufman did, paradoxically, by patterning it after F.P.A.'s Dulcinea, the well-known symbol of banality. "You know, if there's a breeze going at all, we get it here," Helene Glendenning says. "Would you believe it—we sleep under a blanket every night." And "You know, I love dressing for dinner. There's such a flavor of the old world about it. I love the old world." And even "Where there's smoke there's fire." Fontanne could speak these trite phrases in such a way as to render them charming. But she felt at the time that she and Hassard Short, who played her foot-stamping, oversensitive

---

* Fontanne had made one previous visit to New York. In 1910 she played on Broadway for three weeks in an English comedy, R. C. Carton's *Mr. Preedy and the Countess.*

husband, were *too* good, and that the cleverness they revealed in their exchanges, some of which were ad-libbed, distorted the plot by shifting attention away from Burke, the play's hero.[22] But there was no denying that she captivated the audience, and the importance of that fact was not lost on either Kaufman or Tyler.

Nor was the value of the role of Percy Glendenning lost on them. A "nance" or "pansy" role, as it would have been described at the time, it was drawn by Evans and Percival in keeping with the notion that the homosexual is inevitably effeminate. Though in Kaufman's version he was given a wife, he remained effeminate, and the laughter that Short drew from the audience was owing to the emphasis on that aspect of the part. It was not long before Kaufman developed another such comic character at Tyler's suggestion, and with him a second enchanting female speaker of banalities.

While *Someone in the House* was still running, Kaufman was quoted in Mantle's column about this first effort at play-doctoring. "Offhand," he said, "I can't recall anybody who didn't take a crack at this piece at one time or another. I have a plan to bring all the authors together some night if Madison Square Garden has an open date. I think we ought to know each other; I imagine there must be some fine fellows among us."[23] The piece was a valiant effort to sound enthusiastic, though he knew the comedy was doomed. To Tyler he suggested that the play, which opened during the influenza epidemic of 1918, might be advertised with the slogan, "Avoid crowds. See *Someone in the House*."[24] But the sale of the film rights to Metro Pictures no doubt offset his and Tyler's disappointment in not mounting a hit.

Though Kaufman got no special kudos for his fiftyfold reworking of *Someone in the House*, the production started him out. It marked the first time that his name appeared on a Broadway play, and it demonstrated that he could be counted on to do his job, no matter how tedious it was. Before long, producers would get into the habit of calling him when a comedy was, in their parlance, "in trouble." Thus began the career in the theater that paralleled his employment as a journalist until at last in 1930 he found he could content himself with the theater alone.

Outwardly all seemed well in the fall of 1918, since not only was Kaufman earning the respect of Tyler in a way that promised greater things to come, but, to glance beyond the limits of Times Square, the war at last appeared to be drawing to its close, and the Kaufmans' friends in the service would soon be donning civilian clothes and returning to their familiar rounds in New York. But in November an event occurred that sharply affected the

Kaufmans' lives and sent them spinning off in unconventional patterns of behavior.

While Kaufman was wrestling with the script of *Someone in the House,* Beatrice's pregnancy proceeded without unusual difficulty, and they began to think of names for the child, deciding finally that if it should be a boy, they would call him John. In anticipation of the addition to the family, they moved out of their cramped rooms at the Majestic and took a two-bedroom apartment on West 80th Street. It was from this new home, on November 8, that Beatrice went to the hospital, accompanied by her husband, for the delivery of her child—and to which Kaufman returned alone to contemplate the fact that the baby, a boy, had been stillborn.

What followed for the Kaufmans, as for many other couples suffering a similar disappointment, was the end, for all time, of their mutual sex life. Though a second stillbirth could not occur, since Beatrice was no longer able to conceive children, the shock of the event rendered Kaufman impotent with her. Yet he did not want her to leave him. Nor did she wish to end the marriage, though she was sad that its physical aspect had been destroyed. From that time on, though remaining close in all other ways and never experiencing a diminishment of their love for each other, they began to take sexual gratification wherever they could find it. Promiscuity forced itself upon them. But Beatrice, no matter how successful she may have been in living up to the new conditions of her marriage, and no matter how much aid she received from the psychoanalysts whom she consulted through the 1920s and 1930s, could never completely suppress her sorrow over Kaufman's physical retreat from her. Sometimes, since this at least seemed to be permitted, she would climb into his bed and put her arms around him in simple longing.[25] Many of the men in her life resembled him, if not in appearance, at least in some aspects of personality. To Alexander Woollcott, Kaufman once said, "You know, Beatrice is always picking up these sensitive, ambitious young Jews." To this Woollcott replied, "Sometimes she marries them."[26]

Thus it happened that both Kaufman and Beatrice, who had been late to put into practice their knowledge of the facts of life, swiftly lost their inhibitions. Yet each always returned to the other for real affection; what they sought from their sexual partners was carnal satisfaction and nothing beyond it. Undemonstrative though he was, Kaufman addressed her as "Dearest" in the long, news-filled letters that he wrote almost daily when his work took him away from her and in which, over the signature "Sniggie," he declared his desire to return to her. Nor when he returned did he fail to embrace her.

She, of course, welcomed these signs of love and correctly construed them as sincere. Few of the women in his life resembled her: all had more physical beauty than she, and almost invariably they were not Jewish. In their individual ways—he by searching for differences, she by searching for similarities —each revealed a fondness for the other even in infidelity. But neither of them considered their extramarital relationships to constitute a breach of fidelity in any way that mattered deeply. No threat to the marriage ever arose, however serious their affairs seemed to be. In the profundity of their mutual understanding and trust, they remained true to each other.

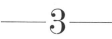

First Success

The decision of George and Beatrice Kaufman to follow their sexual in-
clinations without consulting each other struck their friends and acquaintances as unconventional, but hardly scandalous, as might have been the case
twenty years earlier. As a result of the shock effect of the First World War,
American moral attitudes were undergoing a pervasive change, and the
casual acceptance by this one couple of a mode of living that would have
profoundly troubled their parents' generation was only a small reflection of it.

There were other kinds of changes in the making as the decade came to
an end, and they also affected the sphere within which the Kaufmans moved.
The shock to complacency, the very awareness that the world, ostensibly so
well ordered before 1914, could blow up without rational cause, was evi-
denced in all directions: in the acceptance of new forms in the arts that had
begun to develop in Europe even before the war, in the questioning—slight
but unmistakable—of received attitudes toward labor and the structure of
society, and in the new frankness with which the promptings of sex were
discussed in public and between the sexes. In this last matter, which more
than anything else signaled an end to the dominance of the Victorian point
of view, the impetus was provided by the dissemination of the writings of
Sigmund Freud, whose name had been familiar to Americans since his visit
to the United States in 1909 to receive an honorary degree at Clark University. If the Eighteenth Amendment put a new stricture on freedom by pro-
hibiting the sale and possession of liquor, the Nineteenth, ratified in 1920,
vastly increased the self-respect, independence, and public visibility of half
the nation by granting the vote to women. The very *brio* of the American

refusal to put up with the ban on alcohol was in itself a sign of the times. In this much altered world, George and Beatrice Kaufman, trying to conceal their disappointment in not having a child, went on with the business of living.

Beatrice, having no maternal duties to keep her at home and enjoying the idea of independence, made a second important decision: to take a job. Before the end of 1918 she went to work as an assistant to the press agent of the Talmadge sisters, Norma and Constance, two of the silent screen's most popular actresses. For that work she did not have to go to California, since it was in New York that the star-making power of the press resided. (For that matter, Norma spent most of her career making films in the East rather than in Hollywood.) From this beginning Beatrice went on, over the next twenty years, to a series of posts related to the arts. Without such work to do, she would not only have been bored, but would have been regarded with some disdain by her women friends and Kaufman's male associates.

During the months of trying to bend *Someone in the House* into presentable shape, Kaufman had discovered that being drama editor of the *Times* was not a full-time job. He had hours to spare for his own writing, and no shortage of energy and inventive power. In the first half of 1918 he and Robert Nathan worked on *Third Man High,* a political farce. In view of the romantic quality of the novels with which Nathan would make his name in the 1930s—notably, *Winter in April, One More Spring,* and *Portrait of Jennie*—politics was an unlikely literary subject for him. However, though Kaufman seldom had much to say about politics among his friends, it was never without interest to him, as his successes of the 1930s would show. The year in Washington, including the evenings spent at the poker tables of the Press Club, had given him insight into political maneuvering, and his friendship with Heywood Broun made him familiar with the liberal and socialist positions. Kaufman developed and, privately, expressed admiration for Eugene V. Debs, the Socialist leader, and when the time came that he could afford it he would make financial contributions to liberal political causes, such as the effort to free Tom Moody, the San Francisco labor martyr.[1] But it was no such blazing issue of the day that he and Nathan examined in *Third Man High.* Their subject was the tepid, familiar one of the penchant of politicos to make self-serving compromises. In their script, the Republican powers of a Midwestern state turn out to be more honest than their Democratic rivals, and the young man who, almost by chance, is nominated for governor on the Democratic ticket decides at the close to throw his votes to the Republican candidate and accept a well-paid post as head of advertising for Metropolitan Films. But this ending only pushes home the message that *all* party politics is beneath contempt. And in the authors' view, the movies are just as bad. What calling, they ask, other than politics could be so humiliating that one would gladly give it up for a job with a film company?

Kaufman and Nathan copyrighted their play in June 1919. Perhaps Kaufman took it to George Tyler, but if so, nothing came of it. The wooden characters and predictable plot did not add up to an actable play. Meanwhile, Kaufman's path, which on most days led from the *Times* building to the producers' offices to the theaters and back to the *Times,* crossed that of another young writer, Marc Connelly. With this genial man, whose ambitions were identical with his own, Kaufman was to work closely for the next five years.

Marcus Cooke Connelly was born on December 13, 1890, fifteen miles southeast of Pittsburgh, in McKeesport, Pennsylvania. His parents were actors who had left the theater after the death of their first child from pneumonia, a melancholy event that they realized would not have happened had they not been touring but had settled into a regular home life. They found a hotel for sale in McKeesport, bought it, and did settle into such a life. Young Marc's father died in 1902, and when his mother lost the hotel in the panic of 1908, he went to work as a newspaperman in Pittsburgh to support her. In 1916 he wrote the book and lyrics of a show called *The Amber Empress,* for which the music was composed by Zoel Parenteau, another Pittsburgher. Though *The Amber Empress* lasted only two weeks, it brought Connelly to New York, where he stayed. His next chance in the theater came in 1918, when he became the ghost writer for the lyricist Henry Blossom on a musical called *Follow the Girl,* which ran three weeks. Undaunted by the two early closings, Connelly supported himself by writing verse for the original *Life,* a comic weekly, and next by hiring on as a reporter for the *Morning Telegraph.* One of his tasks on the paper was to gather items from the producers' offices for the paper's daily stage column, "Beau Broadway," edited and written by Rennold Wolf.

Kaufman and Connelly made the same rounds of offices day after day and attended the theater on most evenings. Both would drop into a theater and stand at the back of the house to watch as much as they felt like watching of the play on view. The evening on which they spoke to each other for the first time was May 5, 1919, when both were attending a Jerome Kern musical called *She's a Good Fellow,* starring the Duncan Sisters. Wrote Kaufman some three years later, when life was considerably easier for both young men, "Marc was the most distinguished person in the audience; by laughing at the

Duncan Sisters louder than anyone else he unquestionably distinguished himself."[2]

They continued to meet at theaters and to lounge side by side behind the orchestra seats, and frequently they would walk uptown together after their chores on the *Times* and *Telegraph* were over for the night. (At the time, both lived on 80th Street; Kaufman on the West Side and Connelly across the park on the East Side, in an apartment he shared with Deems Taylor.) The tall, lean, thick-haired Kaufman and the even taller, rounded, balding Connelly soon became friends. That they approved of the same plays, hailed from the same part of the country, and were alike eager for theatrical success helped to foster the friendship. In temperament they complemented each other, for Kaufman, who was tense and energetic, was able to enliven the naturally phlegmatic Connelly, and Connelly for his part could calm and cheer the sometimes dour Kaufman when the occasion demanded it. To both it seemed reasonable that they should try to write together.

They began with the libretto to a musical about two feuding Southern families, their inspiration coming from accounts of the continual fighting between the Hatfield and McCoy clans in West Virginia and Kentucky. The title was *Miss Moonshine*. When an attempt fell through to have this produced by Charles Dillingham with Irene Franklin, a popular young musical comedy performer, in the lead, the script went into their files, and each got to work on another project, but with the understanding that one day they would try again with something else.[3]

Kaufman's interim effort was another piece of rewriting for George Tyler. This time, however, Tyler did not hand him a script whose authors were on hand for consultation. Nor was it something that seemed so obviously in need of repair as the Evans and Percival script. Tyler had got hold of a romantic melodrama about a severely *un*romantic scientist. The piece was the work of the Danish playwright Hans Miller and had had some success on the Continent. It struck Tyler as right for George Arliss, one of his leading character actors. Tall, thin, dignified, and blest—or curst, depending on the eye of the beholder—with a long upper lip that was irresistible to caricaturists, the English-born Arliss had made his American debut as a member of Mrs. Patrick Campbell's company in 1901, and had not been out of work since.

Miller's play, originally called *Duval, M.D.*, but retitled *Jacques Duval* by Tyler, was unlike any stage piece that Kaufman had had to do with until then, apart from *The Failure*. Except for a brief flash in the last act that was intended to prepare the audience for a happy ending, it had no humor whatever, not even the smiling good nature that sometimes took the place of humor in melodrama. Yet Kaufman, who had yet to make his name in the practical theater, could not turn down the invitation to work on it. Tyler, for his part, was remarkably generous with his adapter, for he not only altered the name of the play but kept Miller's name off it, giving credit to Kaufman alone and thus making it all but impossible to cash in on the European success.

The plot concerns a French medical doctor, Duval, who succeeds in finding a cure for tuberculosis. He is that sort of scholar-scientist who subordinates everything to his research, including his marital obligations. Naturally, his wife, Marie, is attracted to another man, in this case the Marquis de Charvet. In the university town where the play is set, word of Marie's flirtation and Duval's experiments with tubercular patients spreads, and the medical faculty of the University, led by the officious Dr. Michaelis, is troubled. Charvet, very ill, calls on Duval in his office. Duval is aware of Charvet's feeling for Marie, but, discovering that the Marquis has tuberculosis, decides to cure him with the new medicine. (Whatever may be the full list of reasons why Charvet is ill, one, intimated by his valet, is that night after night in all weathers he stands beneath Marie's window.) But Charvet dies, leaving Duval in worse odor with the medical faculty than ever. An investigation is demanded, and Duval wants it believed that he deliberately poisoned Charvet because of Marie's romance with the Marquis, rather than jeopardize the ongoing work of refining the medicine. In the end Marie produces a suicide note sent to her by Charvet; it was an overdose of heroin, deliberately taken, that had killed him, not Duval's medicine. The result of this disclosure is general happiness, for Duval's work will no longer be threatened, and, furthermore, he and Marie are reunited.

Presumably working from a literal translation, Kaufman turned in a distressingly dull script. There had, in any case, already been an unsurpassably entertaining play written in English whose plot dealt with some of the same details: that was Shaw's *The Doctor's Dilemma*, written in 1906. Any dramatist, neophyte or not, would have been hard pressed to equal it. From Chicago, where the play opened on November 10, 1919, the reviewer for *Variety* wrote, "As for the script, George S. Kauffman [sic] did a good, clean-cut job of playwriting in the adaptation . . . but he was helpless in his efforts to introduce through the heavy tone of ether and iodoform which permeates the play one single breath of natural, fresh air."[4] Ashton Stevens, the critic of the Chicago *Herald & Examiner*, wrote that Kaufman "made a good job" of it, and other Chicago reviewers offered similarly faint praise, none of which promised a run.[5] This time Tyler decided against further rewriting.

He sent the play to three other cities on the tryout circuit, but in the last of them, Boston, he laid it to rest. It was the first of only four plays to which Kaufman signed his name that expired on the road.

With this Danish disaster safely stowed in Cain's storehouse, the resting place of the sets of defunct Broadway productions, Kaufman was free to resume his talks with Connelly on a plot that they might work up into a comedy. Whatever they were to write together, not for a moment did it occur to either to spend their time on drama with a serious message. As Connelly later put it, they were "just two young guys hoping to make their way."[6] However they might feel privately about works of weighty intellectual content, their own writing was not to be marked with the heavy stamp of "literature." Beatrice, earning a little money of her own and able to afford a cook, was developing a keen pleasure in entertaining. One person whom she found it particularly agreeable to ring up with an invitation was her husband's bachelor friend Marc. Later, with two successful collaborations behind him and Connelly, Kaufman joked in print about the atmosphere of their early discussions:

> Marc came up to our house for dinner one evening, and various and sundry plays came under discussion. A little later one night when he was having dinner at our house we agreed that writing plays was not particularly difficult. About a week after that it happened that Marc was up at our house for dinner, and we decided to write a play together. At a dinner at our house a few weeks later, when Marc chanced to be present, we made up our minds to go ahead with it. Just at present we are kept from writing another one because Marc is having a little indigestion.[7]

Nearly a year went by without any of their ideas germinating a three-act play, when suddenly, in the fall of 1920, two breaks occurred. The first was that from Tyler, whom he had met through Kaufman, Connelly received an invitation to refurbish the script of an operetta in 1886 called *Erminie*. The original libretto was by Harry Paulton, a busy Broadway writer of the late nineteenth and early twentieth centuries, and was based on Charles Selby's *Robert Macaire*, a once-popular English melodrama that had first been performed in 1835. Tyler remembered the operetta fondly from his youth and assumed that, with Francis Wilson of the original cast and DeWolf Hopper as the stars, it would find a new audience. Connelly commenced work on it, and almost at once Tyler got another bright idea. Remembering Lynn Fontanne's extraordinary charm as Helene Glendenning in *Someone in the House,* he asked Kaufman to write an entire play for the same character, who would again be played by Fontanne. Kaufman rose to the challenge, but, having fallen into the habit of working in tandem with another writer, he told Tyler that he would have to have a collaborator and that the person he wanted was Connelly. Initially Tyler was reluctant to accede to this request; if Kaufman was to have someone with him on the project, it should be, Tyler believed, a writer with more experience.[8] But when Kaufman refused to give in, Tyler at last signed Connelly.

Erminie was scheduled to open on January 3, 1921. Even as it was trying out in Boston, Connelly was polishing Act III of the new comedy for Fontanne. Kaufman puffed the revival nicely with an article entitled *"Erminie— Thirty-Five Years After"* which he wrote for the New York *Times* Sunday magazine section of January 2; but, praise the work though he did, he somehow forgot to mention his friend Connelly as the adapter. The revival ran eight weeks—not a bad run, but not good enough to recoup the money put up by Tyler and his coproducer, William Farnum.[9] More promising was the new comedy, which the authors decided to call *Dulcy*.

Writing *Dulcy* was a happy experience for Kaufman and Connelly. All that Tyler had given them by way of suggestion or instruction was that they turn Adams's Dulcinea into some sort of comic heroine, thus making it possible for Lynn Fontanne to project her vast allure without distorting the play's other values. Whatever else went into the play was left to them. Helene Glendenning had been a young matron living in Westchester County, and it struck them that the character should remain in Westchester and again be a matron, but that, unlike Helene, she should be the wife of a man with his fortune still to make, and that she should try her best to assist him to that goal. *Both* Glendennings were somewhat foolish creatures, but only Dulcy Smith, not her husband, Gordon, would be so in the new play. Yet, despite her bumbling and her meddlesomeness, to say nothing of her clichés, she should be lovable, and she should succeed in her effort to aid her jewelry-manufacturer husband to get the best terms possible in a business merger.

Such a part was a challenging one for an actress: without the requisite skill, she might let the dullness of her remarks dominate all aspects of the role. But Fontanne was a proven commodity; as Helene she had shown that she had comic skill, and to spare. She and Tyler were quite pleased with the scenario, and so, for that matter, was Adams, who was to receive 10 per cent of the authors' royalties.[10] It took Kaufman and Connelly no time at all to work up a detailed outline of the action.

Nor did it take long to develop the dialogue. Within a month they completed their script. Their method of collaboration was a somewhat unusual one, but it seemed to work. Each writer would choose from the outline those scenes that he thought were best suited to his temperament and would write a draft of them by himself, submitting them later to the other partner for consideration. When the second partner finished reading what the first had handed him, they would polish the material together. Though nothing that could be called a problem arose over this division of labor, Connelly was a bit taken aback to discover that Kaufman left all the work on the love scenes to him. Sentimental expression made Kaufman uneasy. It produced physical reactions in him, such as shivering. Fortunately, however, there was little need for sentimentality in the dialogue of *Dulcy;* only in the last-act recon-ciliation scene between the heroine and her husband did the authors see the need for tenderness. On many nights they hung around the *Times* office, waiting for Woollcott to go home and leave his typewriter to them; on others they went to Kaufman's place on West 80th Street. Wherever they worked, as they went over the scenes they hooted with laughter at their own cleverness.[11]

Before the New York opening, the play went on tour. Tyler scheduled a week of performances in Indianapolis beginning on February 13, to be followed by a stand in Chicago through the spring and early summer. His choice of Indianapolis was governed by the fact that it was the home of Booth Tarking-ton, many of whose plays he had produced, including such highly profitable comedies as *The Man from Home* and *Clarence.*[12] Tyler could rely on Tarkington's good theater sense and craftsmanship to help him out if *Dulcy* should be in trouble. But it was not in trouble. Tarkington was so impressed that he agreed to write a preface to the play when it was published later in the year—so much impressed that he declared *Dulcy* better than Goldsmith's *She Stoops to Conquer,* a comparison possibly prompted by the fact that both plays are momentarily concerned with missing jewels and elopements.

Tarkington was also impressed, and faintly amused, by the state of Kauf-man's nerves before the opening. An old theater hand, having had his first hit as a writer for the Princeton Triangle Club in his undergraduate years, Tarkington had seen some nervous playwrights before, but never like this one! He wrote to John Peter Toohey about it in June:

> Kaufman of the *Times,* by the way, was nervous in Indp'ls about the success of *Dulcy*—he seemed more open to gloomy forebodings than any playwright I ever saw and I have a guess that as the time approaches for his N.Y. opening he may become nervous again—which would be funny to see, because misery about to be luminously relieved *is* usually funny. Don't miss that first night, because it's going to be a jovial one for every-

body concerned. Of course it isn't good to tout too strong—but if ever touting *was* safe, *Dulcy*'s it.[13]

But before New York, there was the Chicago opening to be endured. Tyler had every expectation, after the week in Indianapolis, that *Dulcy* would prove to be a hit, as it did. But it was impossible to keep Kaufman calm. No reassurances could do the trick—the play would flop, and he *knew* it and continued knowing it until the reviews were in. Concerned about his friend's torment, for torment it was, no matter how funny it may have struck Tarkington the week before, Connelly remained calm, though before the evening was over even he began to feel somewhat uncomfortable in the face of Kaufman's despair. He had invited the beautiful actress Margalo Gillmore to the opening and was looking forward to both the performance and her presence in the next seat to his. Kaufman was not so calm. Having dinner alone with Connelly, he said, "W've been kidding ourselves and we might as well admit it." During the interval between the second and third acts, by which time the audience had indicated its enjoyment, Connelly and Margalo Gillmore found him in the scene dock staring at the floor. "The show stinks," he said. After an exasperated protest from Connelly, he added, "It's artificial."[14] Not until he read, late at night, the reviews in the morning papers did he understand the truth of the situation: *Dulcy* was a great success.

Tyler and his writers remained in Chicago for a few days for the inevitable tinkering and pruning. Thinking that it was possible for Kaufman to look back calmly on his evening of terror, Tyler suggested that he assume the character of Connelly and write a piece for the Chicago *Tribune* on what it was like to be confronted by a tormented collaborator on such an occasion. Percy Hammond, the reviewer for the *Tribune*, ran the article in his column on February 27. In part, it read:

> Up to last Sunday night . . . I always thought that a collaborator was a fairly useful creature. It was really the ideal way to write a play, having a collaborator. He comes around with an idea for a play and says what do you think of it, and should the first act be laid after lunch or in the garden, and you say yes, and when will the advance royalty be ready? Then, during the next few weeks, he sketches the plot in greater detail, while you go to his house for dinner occasionally and agree with him. Then, during the month that follows, he begins to put the dialogue together, while you do the really hard work, such as telling your friends about it. I never could understand all that talk about playwriting being so difficult. It's really very simple, once you get the system. But that was all prior to last Sunday night, when *Dulcy* opened in Chicago. I don't know

just what should be done with a collaborator on opening night—I'm about half for chloroform and half for strangulation. Personally, I never was calmer in my life. Around 8 o'clock, for example, when I saw people actually paying money for tickets, I calmly ran up and down the balcony stairs about six times, just to prove that I was in full possession of my faculties. It was shortly after that that I entered the theater and discovered George Kaufman, my collaborator.

My first thought was that the ushers had forgotten to take the white cover off one of the seats, but when I looked again I saw it was Kaufman. I introduced myself.

"Do you think they're enjoying the play?" he asked, giving a wonderful imitation of a phonograph record of the early nineties.

"It's hard to tell until the curtain goes up," I answered.

The lady who was with me then assisted me to my seat, although I could have walked twice the distance without any help at all. At the end of the first act I felt sure the play was a hit. I pushed a lot of dramatic critics out of my way and went out on the sidewalk hunting for Kaufman.

"My God! Wasn't it terrible?" he asked.

"What?" I inquired.

"The play," he answered.

"*This* play?" I repeated.

"If you could call it that," he said.

I went back to my seat and the second act began. Once more the audience seemed to like it. I was feeling pretty chipper again when I found my way out during the next intermission. The living corpse was waiting for me.

"They—they seem to like it," I faltered.

"There's a train at 10:30," he said, "we can catch it."

There would be other openings that would make Kaufman's pulse race and cause his face to blanch, and his self-doubt would never entirely vanish, despite the authority, so reassuring to his actors, that he would eventually develop. But the evening of February 20, 1921, at the Cort Theater in Chicago was the worst. To avoid a repetition when, after a hiatus, *Dulcy* opened at the Frazee Theater in New York on August 13, he stayed home and let Beatrice telephone him with word of the play's reception after each act. This was sensible, since the evening was warm, and an un-airconditioned theater, as all were then, was no place for a writer with hell enough raging inside him. It was also a taxing evening for Lynn Fontanne, who had been so badly troubled during a dress rehearsal over a lover's quarrel with Alfred Lunt that she feared she might be replaced in her part! On hand for the opening was not only Lunt but Noel Coward, an impecunious young Englishman who was then trying to make his way in New York and had become an intimate friend of both Lunt and Fontanne. Lunt, too, was a Tyler player; in 1919 he had displayed his genius in the title role of Tarkington's *Clarence*. He and Coward chose to stand at the back of the house, being too excited to sit. In the last few minutes before the curtain went up, they fortified themselves with soft drinks.[15] "From the moment that Lynn flounced on in the first act," Coward wrote, "wearing a smart black velvet gown and appearing to be completely in command of herself and the play, we knew that everything was going to be all right, as indeed it was, and by the time the applause had died away after the second act we discovered that not only were we no longer pinching each other black and blue, but that we were quite relaxed and actually enjoying ourselves."[16]

In *Dulcy*, it was, first of all, Lynn Fontanne as Dulcinea who provided the attraction for the audience. The actress was spared nothing in the way of clichés, and was undaunted even by such lines as "Two heads are better than one." All the reviewers praised her, having been won by the warmth and good humor that she brought to the role. Within the context of a comedy too satiric to be naturalistic, she was remarkably candid and believable. Yet, of course, the character was not new, having been developed for *Someone in the House* and, for that matter, having had a long life in "The Conning Tower." Nor was it only because of Fontanne's fleshing out of the role that the play went over; Kaufman and Connelly revealed a flair for creating a sense of community among their characters, for painlessly laying down the exposition and preparation for events to come, and for turning out jokes in quantity. They were young, but they were masters of the well-made comedy. Thus, at the outset, in dialogue between Gordon Smith (Dulcy's husband) and Bill Parker (her brother), the audience was held by the lightly comic discourse on business conditions signifying this play was in part a satire on the business world at the same time that it paved the way for more serious talk on business that was to come:

> GORDON I say, how's business?
> BILL (*As though announcing a death.*) Haven't you heard?
> GORDON (*A bit cheerily.*) Oh I don't know—I have an idea it may be picking up presently.
> BILL (*Tapping the newspaper.*) You've been reading Mr. Schwab. (*He quotes.*) "Steel Man Sees Era of Prosperity."
> GORDON Well—I think he's right at that.
> BILL Yes. (*A pause.*) Rockefeller expects to break even this year, too.

Such a deftly worked bantering tone was necessary if the audience was not to think this only a rehash of materials used in the recent past by a horde of Broadway writers. The business deal was a staple of comic plots. Among those authors who had made successful use of it centrally or peripherally were George M. Cohan in such works as *Broadway Jones* and *Get-Rich-Quick Wallingford,* and Clare Kummer in *Good Gracious Annabelle* and *A Successful Calamity.* The hyperactive advertising agency, a fairly recent concomitant of big business, had also come under the eye of Broadway dramatists, most notably in Megrue and Hackett's *It Pays to Advertise,* and *Dulcy* also had one of its operatives, a young man named Sterrett, who promises the jewelry tycoon, Forbes, that he will make the nation "Forbes-conscious." Kaufman and Connelly also borrowed from the "crook" play; one element in their plot is a scare developing over a missing string of pearls. In addition, the presence of an effeminate male showed that Kaufman had not forgotten the comic value of Hassard Short's performance in *Someone in the House.*

What gave new life to these borrowings was the flow of wit. When Gregory Kelly, as Bill Parker, spoke his line about Rockefeller, he was the first of many actors to utter a Kaufman-and-Connelly wisecrack. This sort of verbal thrust became the identifying feature of their plays and of Kaufman's comedies, later, with other dramatists. A snapping, jumping kind of line, it gives a nervous rhythm to the plays. If too much comic business is added, as sometimes happened in the last years of Kaufman's career, when as a director he warred with himself as a playwright, the effect is unsettling. But in *Dulcy,* which was produced under Howard Lindsay's direction, all went smoothly. Bill Parker, in love with Forbes's daughter and distressed to see her throw herself away on the unmasculine Vincent Leach, a movie scenarist, slides sinuously through the play to comment laconically and cynically on big business, including the film industry, and on advertising. His best moments come before, during, and after Leach's incredibly prolonged telling of the plot of his new film *Sin,* which interweaves stories of sin through the ages in a manner resembling D. W. Griffith's narrative technique in *Intolerance.* Parker, with a few words here and there and a funny turn when he awakens from a profound sleep induced by the narration, puts all films into the dust heap, where Broadwayites Kaufman and Connelly thought they belonged.

The rough treatment of Leach in other ways than as the butt of Bill Parker's jokes also pointed to the direction that Kaufman's work would take. As a representative of a kind of big business that both Kaufman and Connelly considered shoddy in its methods and products, Leach was made to suffer a veritable bombardment of authorial insults. Everything he does is foolish, including his attempted elopement with Angela Forbes, since, it is implied, he does not really care for women. When she agrees to run off with him, he speaks in the jargon of the silents: "Love cries for its own!" Business is attacked from still more directions. When another character, Schuyler Van Dyck, agrees to put up the capital to back Gordon Smith and thus makes it unnecessary for him to join up with Forbes, Van Dyck turns out to be insane. So much for the business world! It is the "bromidic" Dulcinea who somehow has the best business sense of all. Though her efforts to help her husband come close to ending in disaster, she, who really knows nothing at all about the way deals are actually made, manages to bring about a magnificent offer from Forbes. The "little woman," as contemporary jargon put it, proves to be shrewder than the males who allegedly run things.

As the reviews of the opening performance implied, Kaufman and Connelly had got hold of a winning combination of plot devices and verbal effects. Not even the stinginess of Tyler's production budget, a frequent problem for his authors and directors, kept the play from looking good and sounding fresh. There were, of course, a few complaints. Woollcott, Kaufman's chief, hinted in the *Times* that the play was not quite good enough for so luminous an actress as Fontanne, and in the *World* Broun observed that Gregory Kelly made rather too much of his comic opportunities—in other words, that he mugged. But such reservations could not stop the play. A run of 246 performances on Broadway was followed by a successful tour (which in turn was followed by the marriage of Fontanne and Lunt) and a sale to Hollywood.

— 4 —

Widening Circles

To be young and talented and living in New York in the 1920s, with money to spend and the promise of plenty more of it to come—this, the happy situation of Kaufman and Connelly after the opening of *Dulcy*, was the best life imaginable. Connelly thought it was as fantastic as a child's dream of pleasure in which the whole sky was filled with balloons and anyone could pull down as many as he wished.[1] The possibilities were limitless! Whatever the team wrote, there was sure to be a producer and an audience for it. They were home free.

Not yet the artistic capital of the world, New York was at least the artistic capital of the United States, and in the new era signaled by the Armistice its creative energy brought forth new canons of taste and judgment. Novelty was in heavy demand. Eugene O'Neill, by far the boldest playwright the nation had yet produced, was not only revolutionizing American drama, he was winning the attention of Europe. F. Scott Fitzgerald, spokesman for the young, was bringing contemporaneity to the novel of manners. Jazz was becoming respectable, and if no American composer comparable to Schoenberg or Stravinsky was on the scene, there was something to praise in the jazz-inspired Broadway music of George Gershwin and Irving Berlin. Short-sightedness (figurative, at least) prevented critics from adequately praising American painting, but the day would come when museums vied for the canvases even then being painted by Edward Hopper, Stuart Davis, Georgia O'Keeffe, and John Marin. The city itself was rising in a building boom such as had never taken place before; where isolated towers had stood, sky-scrapers erected side by side created canyons of brick and limestone. Prohibition, as the "wets" had predicted, was not working, and the particular way in which it failed, with the emergence of the speakeasy as a center of social activity, added to the hectic pace of urban life. In the course of an evening those who liked their liquor followed a trail from bar to bar in search of guaranteed-imported scotch and gin (as opposed to the synthetic stuff concocted out of who knew what substances in some Greenwich Village cellar).

The search for novelty led in some quarters to an examination of the values of popular culture. Edmund Wilson, in essays written mainly for the *New Republic,* and Gilbert Seldes in his book, *The Seven Lively Arts* (1924), commented astutely and influentially on such familiar phenomena as Charlie Chaplin's comedies, the Ziegfeld Follies, burlesque, jazz, and the comic-strip art of George Herriman—not out of preference for them over artistic inventions of higher seriousness, but because these subliterary entertainments, though not new to the 1920s, revealed a seriousness of their own as reflections of the time. Magazines in profusion were available as outlets for writers of poetry, fiction, criticism, and drama through the decade. Among the most prestigious ones at the outset were the *Dial, Smart Set,* and *Vanity Fair.* In 1924 they were joined by the *American Mercury* and in 1925 by the *New Yorker.* The editors of those magazines, far from confining their lists of contributors to established writers, reguarly published unsolicited manuscripts. Kaufman and Connelly were occasionally contributors to the periodicals of the 1920s, and members of the circle of which they were a part wrote for, edited, or published the most successful of them, *Vanity Fair* and the *New Yorker.* Of the latter it could be said that George and Beatrice Kaufman were present at its birth, if not, indeed, at its conception.

When the need to relax from the rigors of their jobs as journalists, editors, and playwrights overtook them at midday, the circle of bright young New Yorkers of the 1920s gathered at the Algonquin Hotel, at 59 West 44th Street, for a long lunch, an exchange of witticisms and gossip, and a drawing up of plans for the evening. So famous did their table become that in the press it was emblazoned with upper-case letters: the Round Table. Round it was, and situated in the center of the hotel's Rose Room, where its occupants became a focal point for the stares of all other guests in the room, including not a few tourists who came just to look at them. The craning of the necks of those unfortunate guests seated with their backs to the table was another familiar sight in the Rose Room.

George and Beatrice Kaufman were early members of the Algonquin set, though they were not the first New Yorkers active in the arts to be charmed by the hotel's amenities. Before the existence of the Round Table, the hotel, which had opened in 1902, had been a favorite among writers and actors, for to them, of all his guests, the manager, Frank Case, extended his warmest welcome. According to his daughter, Margaret Case Harriman, the two writers to whom the institution of the luncheon group owed its existence were John Peter Toohey, Tyler's press agent, and the portly, sulky, but compulsively gregarious Alexander Woollcott. Knowing of Woollcott's fondness for sweets, Toohey took him to the Algonquin one day in 1919 for a piece of angel food cake, and Woollcott was much taken by the ambiance of the place, to say nothing of the cake. Soon afterward a luncheon was held at the hotel to celebrate the return to civilian life of Woollcott and other veterans, and it was then, because the occasion was so much fun and the food so good, that the idea of lunching regularly at the hotel was formed. Originally, the group did not meet in the Rose Room, but in another room, the Pergola, and they did not sit at a round table, but a long one plus small ones flanking it. When Case seated these special guests all together, the publicity that the table generated guaranteed the Algonquin Hotel a place in American social history, though the Round Table barely outlasted the 1920s.[2]

The Round Table regulars numbered almost thirty. Since they were all working people with the somewhat unpredictable hours and duties imposed by the crafts of journalism, the theater, and fiction-writing, not every one of them could be present every day. But as frequently as possible they repaired to the hotel, and in keen anticipation, because almost from its inception the Round Table, with its constant flow of news and gossip, became essential to their well-being. Apart from the Kaufmans, Toohey, and Woollcott, those who came included Frank Adams; Heywood Broun and his wife, Ruth Hale; Connelly; Dorothy Parker; Neysa McMein; Robert Benchley; Robert E. Sherwood; Laurence Stallings; Harold Ross and his wife, Jane Grant; Brock Pemberton and his brother, Murdock; Deems Taylor; music critic William Murray; press agent David Wallace; Arthur Samuels (editor of *Life*); actresses Margalo Gillmore and Peggy Wood; young poet (and husband of Peggy Wood) John V. A. Weaver; Margaret Leech; Edna Ferber; and Herman J. Mankiewicz. In the beginning, Adams was much the best known, with Ferber not far behind. With the success of *Dulcy*, Kaufman and Connelly were suddenly in the spotlight, and they were to remain in it. Benchley, Parker, and Sherwood were at the time on the staff of *Vanity Fair*, but would soon leave, the two men resigning in disgust when Parker was dismissed for unfavorably reviewing a performance by Billie Burke and thus bringing down upon the magazine the wrath of Burke's husband, Florenz Ziegfeld. It would not be until 1927 that Sherwood made his reputation as a playwright; before that year, when *The Road to Rome* opened, he was admired for the perception he revealed in his film and drama criticism. Stallings, then a newspaperman, would achieve distinction in 1924, along with his collaborator Maxwell Anderson, for *What Price Glory?* It was the toughest and best play of the 1920s about the First World War, designed to show the mesh of comic and tragic incidents that the war constituted for the front-line soldier. Ross, also a veteran of the war—he, like Woollcott, had served on the staff of *Stars and Stripes*—was editor of the *American Legion Weekly* when the Round Table was set up, but he was already laying out in his mind a scheme for another kind of magazine that he would one day edit. His dream came true in 1925, when, with outside backing, he founded the *New Yorker*. His wife, Jane Grant, who was, along with Ruth Hale, one of the founders of the Lucy Stone League, was on the staff of the New York *Times*. Beatrice Kaufman, having left the Talmadge sisters, served for a while as playreader for the producer Al H. Woods and then moved on—and up—to become an editorial assistant in the publishing firm of Boni & Liveright, presided over by Horace Liveright. Woollcott got the Algonquin and its famous patrons exactly right when, in a piece for *Vanity Fair* in 1929, he observed that the hotel "stood at the Windy Corner where New Grubb Street crosses the Rialto."[3]

The people in the Round Table group were known by many labels over the years. Some newspaper columnists (and, ultimately, historians) referred to them as the Algonquin Wits. In her novel of 1923, *Black Oxen*, Gertrude Atherton referred to them as the Sophisticates, and introduced them compositely as background for a sensational plot about rejuvenation. To themselves they were at first the Board, when Case put them at a long table. But when he moved them to the round one, they began to speak of themselves as the Vicious Circle—accurately enough, in view of their acerbic remarks when commenting on not only outsiders but one another. Once encountering Neysa McMein in a sequined dress, Woollcott exclaimed, "Neysa, you're scrofulous with mica." On another day Woollcott, fingering a book written by himself, said to Adams, "What is so rare as a Woollcott first edition?" Adams told him, "A Woollcott second edition." Returning from a lecture tour, Woollcott told Frank Sullivan that he had spoken to ten thousand women in St. Paul. Sullivan asked, "What did you tell 'em? No?" Once when Connelly was seated at the Round Table, another regular came up, patted him on his bald spot, and said, "Your head feels just like my wife's behind." Connelly reached up a hand, patted the same place, and replied, "By God, you're right."[4]

This raillery was usually uttered in a spirit of camaraderie, though with Woollcott one could not always be sure. Though many if not most of his friends were Jews, the huffy critic was quite capable of rattling off the occasional anti-Semitic remark. On one afternoon at the Round Table he expressed his disapproval over an opinion voiced by Kaufman with "Shut up, you Christ-killer." With extraordinary tact, Kaufman stood up and announced calmly that he was leaving. Then, turning to Dorothy Parker, whose father was Jewish, he said, "And I hope that Mrs. Parker will walk out with me—half way."

In addition to the regulars, the Round Table was now and then graced by the presence of some of their most talented friends. Ina Claire, the stage comedienne who was one of the most glamorous of the irregulars, was to be remembered for remarking that she would like to take off her shoes and run through the rigid pompadour of Harold Ross. Two satirists, Frank Sullivan and Donald Ogden Stewart, sometimes turned up for lunch; the former was to give luster to the *New Yorker* as the "cliché expert" and the composer of an annual Christmas poem honoring the achievers of the year; the latter, who later became a screenwriter of note and an advocate of leftist causes, was admired in the 1920s for his humorous books on American manners. Most gifted of all the occasional guests was Ring Lardner, novelist, story writer, and sports reporter, whose ear was finely trained to catch the twists and ellipses of colloquial American speech. No one seated himself unbidden at the table; neither fame nor money nor talent nor all three in combination were sufficient to ensure a welcome. Wit and the ability to evoke it in others were two prerequisites, and a third was the common sense not to try to dominate the conversation. Though Morrie Ryskind, newspaperman and playwright as well as wit, came often to the Round Table, he was so frequently accompanied by a band of friends whom the others did not like that his own presence eventually was resented. S. Jay Kaufman, a newspaperman not related to George Kaufman, was kept away also. It was not that the regulars considered that one writer named Kaufman was enough. They found S. Jay Kaufman pretentious and condescending. Horace Liveright, though Beatrice's employer, was made to feel unwelcome for the same reason. Beatrice herself snubbed him. "Look here," Liveright told her, "those kids at what you call the Round Table are starving to death. I could *publish* them." Said she, "Do you think so?"[5]

The hotel that housed the Round Table stood in a section of the city boasting a high concentration of clubs: the Columbia and Century on West 43rd Street, the Lambs, Harvard, and New York Yacht on West 44th, and the Coffee House on West 45th. The Algonquin itself, with a substantial clientele of familiar guests, had something of a clublike atmosphere. In that sense it was the perfect hotel for the neighborhood. Strictly speaking, the Round Table, however, was never a club; no one was formally elected to it, and no vote of the regulars was necessary to keep away Liveright or S. Jay Kaufman when a cool glance could do it. But the men among the Round Table regulars, along with a number of their friends who lunched elsewhere, met so frequently and for what, in their view, was so serious a purpose that they felt justified in designating themselves a club. This overlapping body, as much talked about in the 1920s as the Round Table, was the Thanatopsis Literary and Inside Straight Club, which gathered every Saturday afternoon for a poker game that lasted through the night and into the daylight hours on Sunday.

The game began in an apartment that Ross, before his marriage to Jane Grant, shared with John T. Winterich, who had served with him in France on *Stars and Stripes*. Woollcott, Broun, Adams, and the two roommates were the original group, but Toohey, Kaufman, and Sherwood soon were asked to join them. The year was 1920, and Sinclair Lewis's *Main Street* was a new literary sensation. In it Adams found, to his amusement, that the women's study group of Gopher Prairie was called the Thanatopsis Club, the name having been adopted from William Cullen Bryant's poem, "Thanatopsis." That, he felt, should be the name of the poker club, with some elaboration. It had just the right tone and the necessary irony. No matter what they concerned themselves with privately, none of the players was given to "musing on death," as the word was defined, over the poker table.[6]

Once in a great while, Beatrice, Neysa McMein, Jane Grant, Esther Adams (F.P.A.'s wife), and other women would sit in, but the Thanatopsis sessions were a man's game, with whatever that might imply in squalid accumulations of bread crusts, cigarette butts, and leaky ice buckets, as well as language a little too strong even for the women of the Round Table. The game became famous enough to attract many male celebrities, such as Harpo Marx and, when he was in town, Charlie Chaplin. Arthur Krock of the *World*, who was later an eminent editorialist on the *Times,* sat in frequently. Ring Lardner played often, as did Raoul Fleischmann, the financier and heir to a yeast fortune who became the principal backer of the *New Yorker*. Herbert Bayard Swope, executive editor of the *World,* for whom gambling was a passion, sometimes joined the game, though the stakes were rather low for his taste. In the beginning they were $100, and as the years passed they reached $500. At that, it was possible to lose on a grand scale. Kaufman, one of the best, if not the best player in the group, acted as banker.[7] His training at the National Press Club during his year with Munsey had been useful.

The meeting place of the Thanatopsis was more often than not a second-floor room at the Algonquin that Case let the players have free. Their loyalty to their host often struck him as feeble, however. They did not always stop to think that the Algonquin was a hotel and as such made room service available to guests; they were as likely to send out to a restaurant or delicatessen for food as to order it from the hotel's own kitchen. Once, after a tub of ice cream had melted all over the carpet on a hot summer night, Case discreetly put up a sign reading "Basket Parties Welcome." For a change, or when the room was engaged, they met elsewhere: the Kaufmans', the house shared by the Rosses and Woollcott at 412 West 47th Street, or the posh Colony Restaurant. Jane Grant was fond of her husband's friends, but she did not much relish picking up after them when the sessions were held at West 47th. Glasses were frequently knocked over, and the bathroom was left filthy.[8]

The game itself was serious, the players well-schooled in the niceties of bluffing and in knowledge of the odds on drawing to their cards. Though Kaufman's card sense was keen enough to become legendary, Adams was also adept at the game, and Ross and Woollcott demonstrated a talent for it that they had developed during their idle hours during the war. Poker, much more than bridge, was the newspaperman's game; the ability to take the long risk and adopt an air of nonchalance while drawing to a pair of aces was not so different from the confidence game played daily by any crack reporter. Yet there were always moments when the players' concentration on a hand could be broken by a quip. On one evening—it must have been a less lively one than usual—Kaufman got off a pun that all the players remembered ever afterward. Glancing at a wretched hand, he threw it down with a cry of "I've been trey-deuced!" On another evening he impressed his cronies by putting a snobbish visitor in his place. When the guest informed the table that an ancestor of his had fought in the Crusades, Kaufman replied that he, too, had had an ancestor in the Crusades, Sir Roderick Kaufman, who was there "as a spy, of course."[9]

The art of putting down the suddenly uppish player was finely developed by the regulars, and they were quick to demonstrate their appreciation of the same talent in a guest. Swope seldom spoke of the fact that he was a Jew, though he did not deny it. One evening, however, he asked those present whether they knew he had "a little Jewish blood." Present at the game was Paul Robeson, who reportedly said, "And did you-all know that I'se got a tinge of the tarbrush?"[10]

On the other hand, poker sometimes proved itself a dangerous game to these players, well practiced though they were. Partly because of Broun's losses at the games, he and Ruth Hale sold their house on West 85th Street.[11] At a Sunday night game at the Swopes' house in Great Neck in 1925, Ross, who had gone deeply into debt to develop and launch the *New Yorker*, lost as much at poker as he already owed for the financing of the magazine. He returned drunk from Great Neck, to be met by Jane Grant, who had left him there much earlier in the evening. When, after putting him to bed, she discovered what had happened from notes in his pocket, she concluded that there was only one solution to this terrible new problem: suicide. When Ross awoke, she seriously suggested it to him. But Fleischmann, who had been present at the game and felt that the other players had taken advantage of Ross, bought up Ross's I.O.U.'s, thus making it possible for the magazine and Ross and Grant to keep going. According to Grant, the Thanatopsis members had an informal agreement to play only in the one weekly game that began on Saturday afternoon; Ross's disgrace had occurred at an "outlaw" session.[12]

The massive presence of journalists in the Algonquin-Thanatopsis set meant that its members were certain to receive publicity, sometimes without deserving it. Everyone seemed to be looking at them, day after day, as a result of the frequency with which their daily doings were recounted to the public. The first number of *Time* magazine, dated March 3, 1923, carried a review of Gertrude Atherton's *Black Oxen,* and alongside the review ran a piece on the real-life counterparts of the novel's "sophisticates." How could readers get to see these people in the flesh? "Go into the Algonquin some noon. Anyone can do it." Who would they find there? Parker, Adams, Broun, and Hale, of course, and "George Kaufman and Marc Connelly, too, are usually there," reported Henry Luce's scribe.

Much was written about the Algonquinites' habit of patting one another's back in print. The name of the game was log-rolling, and though the Vicious Circle denied engaging in such a practice, nobody believed them. One choice example was on view in the first number of the *New Yorker*, published on February 21, 1925. At the top of page one, in lieu of a masthead, was a list of advisory editors that included Connelly, Kaufman, Alice Duer Miller, Parker, and Woollcott, along with artists Rea Irvin and Ralph Barton. Later in the year Broun and Laurence Stallings were added. If not entirely bogus as a panel of advisers, the list was drawn up primarily to smarten the appearance of the magazine. Herman Mankiewicz, amused by this and sure that not much would be forthcoming from the panel, remarked, "The part-time help of wits is no better than the full-time help of half-wits." But even the vague phrase "part-time" was too suggestive of endeavor to describe the advisory function of the writers on the list, for Ross made his own decisions. Eventually he was embarrassed to recall this public deception, describing it as the only dishonest act of his life.[13] But it was equally dishonest on the part of those who lent their names. Though explainable as an expression of their fondness for Ross, it was also helpful to them as yet another means of keeping themselves before the public. Kaufman's name remained on the panel through the issue of July 2, 1925. He became an occasional contributor of humorous essays and poems to the *New Yorker,* but not until 1935.

Opinions on the talents of the Vicious Circle varied among outsiders. Envy arose often when the conversation of non-Circular wits turned to the Round Table. Peggy Wood's father, a newspaperman, looked at the Table, at which the press was generously represented, and pronounced it a "collection of first-rate second-raters."[14] Frank Ward O'Malley, illustrator and writer, and Frank Case's good friend, once glanced at the Round Table, which he knew to be just above the Algonquin's boiler, and asked Case, "If the boiler should explode right now and come up through the floor, do you know what the newspapers would report tomorrow?" Playing straight man, Case asked what and was told, " 'Yesterday the boiler at the Algonquin exploded'—that's all."[15] A time would come, late in the 1920s, when up-and-coming younger writers would speak disparagingly of the Algonquin crowd, being put off by the mutual admiration within the group. Toward the end of the decade, Ross took two of his best young men of the *New Yorker* staff, E. B. White and James Thurber, to the Algonquin to lunch one day, only to see them react with simple boredom. Remembering the event in the 1970s, White told Thurber's biographer, "Woollcott was just an old poop then."[16]

Eugene Wood's judgment of his daughter's friends was not far off the mark, though no doubt diplomacy would have called for politer phrasing. Some *were* second rate. One, Alice Duer Miller, was less than that; her romances, thinner than the paper on which they were printed, were destined for oblivion even before her death, though her poem *The White Cliffs of Dover* (1941) would be remembered by historians of the Second World War. The Table's only other novelist, Edna Ferber, was more talented and more serious about her craft. It was, however, in her very seriousness that she invited disparagement. Popular and financially successful, she strove to be something more: a recorder in fiction of the forces that had helped to build America. Though many admired writers among her contemporaries were regional novelists, describing primarily that section of the country best known to them, Ferber tried to be the voice of *all* regions and thereby win an important place in literary history. In this she did not succeed; Willa Cather's and Sinclair Lewis's novels of the Midwest, Ellen Glasgow's of Virginia, Faulkner's of the Deep South, and Steinbeck's of the West would always be more highly praised than her romantic delineations of the national past. In 1924, five years after the Algonquin lunches started, Ferber began a collaboration with Kaufman that would result in six plays written over a period of twenty-four years. Ironically, in view of her aspirations, it would be through the best of these, rather than her novels, that she would remain before the public after her death. She was an early dropout from the Round Table, preferring to keep long daylight hours at her desk. Many years later she made an unheralded return visit to the Algonquin at lunchtime in the hope of finding some of her friends there, only to discover that they all had deserted the Round Table permanently:

> I didn't even know that the group had sort of melted away and one day, having finished a long job of work, and wishing to celebrate, I flounced into the Algonquin dining room, sat down at an empty place at the Round Table—and found myself looking into the astonished and resentful faces of a family from Newton, Kansas, who were occupying the table on their New York stay. I mumbled an apology and left.[17]

The table's only serious composer, Deems Taylor, would not make a permanent contribution to American music, but would achieve the distinction of having two of his operas, *The King's Henchman* (1927) and *Peter Ibbetson* (1931), presented by the Metropolitan Opera. It would require a music critic of blatant intellectual snobbery to rank this music above that of Irving Berlin, an occasional guest at the table.

Of almost all the rest, it could be said that what they did they did very well. Peggy Wood was a favorite light comedienne and musical comedy performer through the 1920s and 1930s, both on Broadway and in London's West End. Had illness not overtaken him, John Weaver, her husband, might have fulfilled the promise shown by *In American,* his highly praised volume of idiomatic, vernacular poetry published in 1921. Margaret Leech, after her marriage to Ralph Pulitzer, became a historian commanding both popular and academic respect. Dorothy Parker and Robert Benchley, who were close friends, developed a following in the days of the Round Table that they were able to keep throughout their lives, despite the formidable drain of energy that their alcoholism cost them in time. Both an essayist and a film actor shamelessly exploiting his public image as an amiable drunk, Benchley at his death in 1945 left behind a massive legacy of subtle, understated comedy. Parker, the only member of the Vicious Circle, not excluding Kaufman, to become a legend in her own time, wrote increasingly less as the decades passed, but her stories and poems would remain in print in response to the public demand for them, and some of her acidulous wisecracks would be repeated appreciatively more than half a century after she had uttered them.

Press agentry and journalism were not occupations to be undertaken by anyone with a desire for eternal fame, especially the former. At least it could be said of each Round Table regular in either calling that he fulfilled his professional obligations expertly. Of some of the journalists one could say more than that. Woollcott, through his very quirkiness—his "old poopiness," perhaps—and his immense talent for publicizing himself, was not to be easily dismissed, though he had no long-term effect whatever on the shape and tone of American theater and literature. Broun, by virtue of his pungent style in commenting, not only on theater, but sports and politics; his complete commitment to radical causes; and his successful effort to organize the Newspaper Guild, would be remembered. But if among the journalists who regularly came to the Round Table one could be called great, that one was Ross. After a year of ups and downs, the *New Yorker,* the magazine he had dreamed about for some half-dozen years before at last getting it into print, steadily and surely increased its influence and its circulation until, in the 1930s, it became a national symbol of urbanity. Its stories, "profiles," reportage, criticism, and cartoons were to be collected and published in hard covers in a yearly flow of at least a dozen volumes. So firm was the base founded by Ross that the magazine not only survived his death in 1951, but grew even more impressive as a gauge of new talent and a reflection of the city's liberal élan.

The talents of the playwrights in the Circle were varied, but on the whole sound. Stallings would always be remembered for *What Price Glory?,* if his other plays were neglected, including one that he wrote with Kaufman. Sherwood, not yet a playwright when the Round Table came into being, would win two Pulitzer Prizes for drama and a third for biography. As for Kaufman and Connelly, they found that the demands made on their talents by producers and publishers were enough to keep them busy around the clock. With their energy replenished by the Algonquin's food, they kept moving.

One offer that they accepted soon after the opening of *Dulcy* came from Arthur Samuels of *Life,* the humor magazine. From December 1921 through November 1922 they provided the magazine with a monthly calendar that combined accurate historical data with whatever whimsies leapt to their minds. Readers were treated to such notations as this, for January 31: "Thirteenth Amendment adopted, 1865. One school child in Reading, Pa., is able to say what the Thirteenth Amendment is all about, 1922. Actor takes a full three minutes to write a check during the action of a play, 1971." And this, for April 20: "S. Loo Chung, of Canton Falls, China, pays election bet lost on Ming Dynasty by rolling lichi nut length of Great Wall, 1352-1412. Bell tinkles when actor pulls stage bell rope, 1922." So it went throughout the year, each month's collection of irrelevancies decorated with vignettes by John Held, Jr. Evident throughout the calendar was the new, irreverent, "debunking" attitude toward the past. Most of the Algonquin writers, not Kaufman and Connelly alone, felt the desire to turn the past upside down in this fashion, Parker in light verse, Benchley in comic essays, Sherwood in plays, and Stewart in satiric fiction. Kaufman continued to send squibs to Samuels's *Life* after completing the calendar.

In addition to the calendar, a new comedy, to be produced by Tyler, occupied Kaufman and Connelly's free hours in late 1921 and early 1922. The producer asked them to write a vehicle for Helen Hayes, who had been under his management since 1917, when she went on tour as Pollyanna in the play of the same name.[18] She had been on the professional stage since 1905, when her mother, Catherine Hayes Brown, an archetypal stage mother, let the five-year-old girl take a part in a stock-company production in Washington, where they lived. Her enjoyment of the work was never in question; nor did it seem to impair her emotional or intellectual growth to be almost continuously before the public at such an early age, when most children were content to spend the hours between meals and naps with their toys. Her greatest successes as a teenager were made in Barrie's *Dear Brutus* (1918), which Charles Frohman presented, and in Tyler's triumphant production of Tarkington's *Clarence* (1919), in which she played an adolescent suffering from a crush on the title character. Slight in appearance, but durable, intelligent, determined, such was Helen Hayes in 1921 when Kaufman and Connelly fashioned *To the Ladies* for her.

It took only one week for the team to come up with the outline of a plot that won Tyler's approval, but the actual play was not so easy to compose. On January 15, 1922, with rehearsals only one week off, the last act was still not written, and the first two acts needed improvement. The general plan was to satirize big business in as many ways as came to mind, not unlike the idea motivating the turns of action in *Dulcy*. However, the authors wanted to write *To the Ladies* not from the viewpoint of an individual at the executive level, but from that of an ordinary white-collar employee. Otto Kruger was signed to play the ambitious but ineffectual jobholder, Leonard Beebe, and

Hayes, of course, was to play his wife, Elsie. Connelly loved music—hence the background chosen for this plot: a piano-manufacturing corporation. As first conceived, the play would have been not quite the comedy of triumphant scheming that *Dulcy* was, but a triumph of emancipation. Leonard, attending a company banquet, was to become so disgusted by the flatulence and absurdity of the officers that he would decide to renounce his chance for promotion and remain a clerk. But Tyler did not approve. He wanted a last act that would show Leonard indeed making a success, and doing so through the efforts of his wife. That required such intensive rewriting that it was not until a day or two before they were to read the play to the assembled cast that Kaufman and Connelly were ready.[19]

What the team finally worked out was a three-act examination of the modern business milieu, each act with its special area of investigation. In the first act Leonard is shown as a young man with no more than average intelligence who is much impressed with magazine advertisements for get-rich-quick schemes and methods of self-improvement. In the second the scene is the company banquet, at which young employees use whatever means come to mind, ethical or otherwise, to impress their bosses. In the third the audience gets a look at newfangled "efficiency" devices that create as many problems as they solve. Underlying the entire work and controlling the action is Elsie's effort to help her husband succeed. Her climactic moment, and that of the play, takes place at the banquet, where promising new men in the company are expected to make a speech. Leonard with difficulty has memorized one from a book of speeches for all occasions, only to hear it from the lips of another young employee whose turn comes first. Elsie rises to this occasion, announcing that her husband is suffering from laryngitis but that she knows roughly what he intended to say and will say it for him. Her impromptu address wins Leonard his promotion. In the final act, which is the only one free of sentimentality, the audience sees Leonard doing his honest best to live up to the obligations of his new position, but almost fired when Kinkaid, the head of the company, learns the truth about his "laryngitis." Again Elsie saves him. She has a powerful ally in Mrs. Kinkaid, who makes all the personnel decisions for the company without her husband quite realizing it. Believing, with good reason, that Elsie is as smart as she, Mrs. Kinkaid has developed the practice of consulting her whenever an important promotion is in the offing. This is made clear at the final curtain, when the two ladies plan to meet for lunch the following Tuesday, "as usual." The authors' first choice for the final exchange of dialogue was something rather different. It went as follows:

ELSIE Dear, we have more than enough money for two now. I've been
    wanting to tell you—
LEONARD Yes, go on.
ELSIE That I think we need a Buick.[20]

This was the true, unsentimental Kaufman. But Tyler demanded a revision.

To the Ladies was less amusing than *Dulcy*. Kinkaid was not much fun
compared with C. Roger Forbes, the jewelry magnate driven wild by Dulcy's
maneuvering. Nor were the minor characters up to the mark of Vincent
Leach, the walking subtitle, and Tom Sterrett, the "advertising engineer."
Only one minor character was given a real chance: Miss Fletcher, Leonard's
wisecracking stenographer. When the play went on the road after its Broadway run, this part was taken by Jean Dixon, whose father was an old acquaintance of Tyler's and who herself soon became an intimate of Helen
Hayes and her mother. The happiest consequence of the production, apart
from the money it put into everyone's pockets, was the introduction of this
comedienne to Kaufman, who would find longer and better parts for her in
later years.

Despite its faults, *To the Ladies* was a modest hit, running for 128 performances. When it opened on February 20, 1922, Kaufman and Connelly
thought of a way to use the occasion for exploiting the reputation as cut-ups
that their frequent newspaper interviews had begun to give them. Instead of
appearing in person in response to shouts of "Author!" they borrowed a pair
of department store dummies, dressed them up, and had them wheeled on.
To Kaufman, it was not just a stunt, but a means of escaping the proceedings.
Still, he did not have anything to worry about. A sale to Hollywood followed,
as did a road tour, albeit a truncated one.

When the play went on the road, Tyler was taken aback by the failure of
most audiences to respond to the satire as written, so strong was their identification with the Beebes in the struggle to secure Leonard's promotion.
They were too involved to laugh at the banquet scene, which to them was a
finely etched reflection of their own worries.[21] It appeared that the comedy
was not satiric enough for a robust run in New York and too much so for
the road. Shouldn't, the out-of-town audience asked, the man of the house
always be in charge? To enhance Hayes's characterization as a mass of energy masked with a guise of frail femininity, Kaufman and Connelly asked
her to speak with a soft southern accent, and threw in a word or two to indicate that Mobile was the character's birthplace. This part was the forerunner
of many roles the actress was to play in which a genteel appearance and de-

portment belied her character's determination. It was a stage image that would
sustain her for over half a century.

Quite as courageous offstage as on, Hayes accepted the role without hesitation, even though it would require her to demonstrate one skill that she did
not at the time possess: the ability to play the piano. When their first draft
was ready, Kaufman and Connelly called on her and her mother in their
apartment on East 19th Street to read it to the young star. Neither the team
of writers nor the Hayes family were self-assured on this occasion. It would
have been a let-down for Kaufman and Connelly if Hayes had spurned the
play, but it also would have been a disappointment to the actress if they had
found her unsuitable in the role. At that moment she and her mother were
hard up, with a bank balance of only $150, and she was at pains to place
their few pieces of living-room furniture to the best advantage. Kaufman was
no sooner there than he remarked, "Of course you play the piano. Your piano
has an important bearing on the play." Connelly amplified this by explaining
that she would not only play but sing two spirituals (in keeping with her
character's place of birth). Without hesitation, Hayes replied that she could
play, and when Kaufman completed his reading of the script, it was decided
that she would take the part. Her next move—taken as soon as the door was
closed on the writers, as they later learned—was to investigate the possibility
of renting a piano and hiring a music teacher. With the piano installed and
the teacher to help, as well as some coaching from the black woman who
cooked for her and her mother, she was ready when the play went into rehearsal. The authors were at least satisfied with her efforts at the keyboard, if
not overwhelmed. "She isn't exactly a piano artist yet," Kaufman told an interviewer after the opening, "but she can play those two pieces."[22]

Maintaining as much of a division as he could between his two professional
selves, the playwright and the drama editor, Kaufman had to take a firm hand
with John Peter Toohey, Tyler's press agent, during the run of the play.
Toohey badgered him with items to print about Hayes that might have drawn
trade and would have kept the actress in the public's mind. Rebuffed every
time, he finally asked Kaufman what he would have to do to get the actress's
name in the *Times.* "Shoot her," Kaufman told him.[23]

Even without Toohey's items, *To the Ladies,* though no record-breaker, did
well enough at the box office to improve the Kaufmans' standard of living.
From their apartment of West 80th, which, though less cramped than their
old quarters on Central Park West, was far from stately, they moved to a
largish place at 200 West 58th Street that provided not only separate bedrooms, as required by their way of life, but a study for Kaufman. If not fash-

ionable to the degree that the Upper East Side had become, the West Fifties in the teens and twenties of the century was one of New York's "best" neighborhoods. Some of the most ornate and costly one-family houses of the city could be found on those side streets, and on West 57th, 58th, and 59th stood some of the city's best-designed apartment buildings, with units roomy enough for families employing a battery of servants.

Living on West 58th, the Kaufmans were near one of the favorite haunts of the Algonquin crowd: Neysa McMein's studio on West 57th. Never distracted from her work unless she cared to be, McMein could sketch or paint with total concentration when surrounded by her friends, undisturbed by their frisky games of charades (which they called The Game) or the piano-playing of George Gershwin or the face-making of Harpo Marx. There, in a space less cluttered by chairs and tables than Frank Case's Rose Room, were to be seen some of the brightest talents of the stage and journalism, along with a few adventurous representatives of Wall Street, such as Raoul Fleischmann and Bernard Baruch. Also likely to be present, if he was not out of the country, was the mining engineer John Baragwanath, whom McMein married in 1924. Though many of these men and women would have lunched together only a few hours earlier at the Algonquin, they were delighted to meet again. There was always something new to gossip about over a Prohibition cocktail at six in the afternoon.

But others who never had the time for an Algonquin lunch, and many who could not yet afford one, also came: among them, the Lunts, Gregory Kelly and Ruth Gordon, Jean Dixon, Helen Hayes, and journeymen writers Ben Hecht and Charles MacArthur, formerly of Chicago. It was there that, in a moment of sufficient magic to become almost hallowed in the memory of those present, Hayes and MacArthur met and fell in love. Handsome, and dashing in a way that made their friends wonder how the modest actress could appeal to him, MacArthur went up to her, held out a paper bag, and expressed regret that he could offer her only peanuts, not emeralds.

With his daily duties for the *Times* never to be ignored, Kaufman had to keep an eye on his watch while at the McMein studio—when he was not glancing among the women present for a prospective affair. But there was pressure from Tyler as well as from the *Times*; the producer always had a project to talk over with his team. More often than not Beatrice would gather up her husband and his collaborator and take them to the Kaufmans' apartment for dinner and a quick discussion of the next comedy before Kaufman had to hurry back to 43rd Street and the drama department.

5

Ferber; Four Brothers

With Kaufman's fame as a theatrical craftsman on the rise, newspaper columnists took care to inform the public on his latest doings and sayings. Foremost among them in turning him into a national figure was, of course, Frank Adams, who wrote such pseudo-Pepysian jottings as these:

> June 3, 1923: Beatrice Kaufman come to dinner, and tells me that George hath made a sentence with the word punctilious, thus: A man had two daughters, Lizzie and Tillie, and Lizzie is all right, but you have no idea how punctilious.
>
> December 1, 1923: To an inn for luncheon, and saw G. Kaufman and I asked him when Beatrice was coming home, and he said he had a letter from her that she would be back bright and early Monday morning, but he, being conservative, would wager only she would be early.
>
> July 17, 1923: So home, and Beatrice Kaufman and George there to dinner, and we had a merry time of it, and George was hard put to it to devise a sentence using the word paraphernalia, till finally there was born the conceit that a man, grown ill from devouring the waxen covering of a jar of jelly was asked, Does that, &c.
>
> July 29, 1924: To G. Kaufman's for dinner, and H. Ross says he was lying out in an orchard this afternoon and an apple hit him upon the head, and the idea came to him to discover the law of gravitation, and then people would no longer have to walk upstairs, as it would lead to the invention of the elevator. But George said he was lying in an orchard too, only it was a fig orchard, and a fig hit him on the head, and that made him think of gravitation, and then it was but a step to the invention of Fig Newton, an idea he is going to try to sell to some biscuit concern or other.[1]

These column entries by Adams suggested to readers that for the Kaufmans and their friends life was a grand romp, forever free of responsibility. It was not that, to be sure, though neither Kaufman nor Beatrice would have claimed to be weighed down with care. Since his earliest newspaper days, Kaufman had known that work, and plenty of it, was the best daily program for him. Beatrice, though never putting in so much time at her job as he, learned from him that a routine of work was essential for the enjoyment of leisure. Kaufman's post at the *Times*, little though it paid, contributed to his comfort by providing him with an excuse to leave any tedious gathering. "Back to work," he could always say, and march out. Often when he left a party and headed for the *Times*, it was with the purpose of meeting Connelly there to talk over a new script. After *To the Ladies*, when the "boys," as Tyler called them, were in full stride, the plays followed one another at the rate of two per season. Kaufman pushed from script to script, burying his unconquerable dread of the opening night under plans for the next, still unwritten play. Connelly, not cursed with such a drive, was carried along by the force of Kaufman's personality. For four years they raced with Kaufman's demons.

The office at the *Times* was also a place where Kaufman could meet the young women who were beginning to occupy many of his evening and weekend hours. Some were unattached women whom he met at parties and who were drawn to him by his good manners. Though he was much too honorable a man ever to make a sexual conquest by the promise of a role in one of his plays, a number of the women in his life were, inevitably, actresses. With them he would often go to Atlantic City: no hotel detective was likely to make trouble for him there. Though never boastful about these casual relationships, even he, reticent as he was, could not hold back from friends the memory of the chorus girl who, in the act of love-making, kept calling out, "Oh, Mr. Kaufman! Oh, Mr. Kaufman!"

Beatrice was as much the aggressor as Kaufman in extramarital affairs, and equally discreet. How many of the young men she met became her lovers remained her secret, though it was never a surprise to spot her at a party or a theater with someone new at her side. If no woman of the hipless, bosomless 1920s had a less fashionable shape than the well-rounded Beatrice, her attentiveness and warmth compensated amply for her physique. She had such appeal that all the young men who met her tended to fall in love with her, including even those who did not find women sexually alluring. To Noel Coward, her good friend for twenty-five years, the prospect of seeing her again provided one of the best reasons for visiting New York.[2]

As outgoing as Kaufman was diffident, Beatrice derived pleasure from entertaining friends at home. She often gave dinner parties at the apartment on West 58th Street. Kaufman's two professions and her own work for Horace Liveright and, later, for Coward-McCann put her in touch with a much larger collection of contributors to the arts than the few who lunched at the Algonquin, and through new and intimate friends Margaret Leech and publisher Ralph Pulitzer, she also came to know prominent politicians, national as well as local. Pulitzer's commander in chief at the *World*, Herbert Bayard Swope, a figure of massive influence in his own right, also introduced her and Kaufman to political and intellectual leaders. The houseparties that Swope and his wife, Margaret ("Maggie"), gave at their Long Island home were famed for the lavishness with which the gustatory whims of guests were attended to, as well as for poker and crap games at precipitous stakes. Beatrice could not afford to emulate Margaret Swope in keeping a kitchen in operation at all hours —few could, or cared to—but she was adept at the art of making her guests feel at home. As her confidence as a hostess grew—and it grew rapidly—she decided that it was not necessary to achieve intimacy with the celebrated before extending them an invitation. "Promise them a good dinner," Beatrice sometimes said, "and they'll come."

Contented though he often appeared to be to leave Beatrice and their friends before the end of the evening, Kaufman was not viewed by his acquaintances as a recluse and did not think of himself as such. He was a good companion at any time when the preparation of a new script did not crowd almost everything else from his mind. Despite the barriers to intimacy he sometimes erected, despite his growing, pronounced hostility to underlings and his reluctance to shake hands with anyone, he was and would remain a social being. He belonged at one time or another to each of New York's theatrical clubs—the Friars, the Players, and the Lambs—as well as the Dutch Treat Club, an association of writers, illustrators, and publishers who met once a week at a hotel for fellowship and luncheon with an honored guest and once a year staged a show written and performed by members for themselves and guests. In addition, there was the Thanatopsis in the 1920s, and, later, when bridge had become more interesting to him than poker, there were the Regency and the Cavendish, New York's preeminent bridge clubs, to which he went for recreation in the late afternoon. The staffs of these clubs were not spared the lash of his wit. Once after biting into a piece of toast at the Regency, he turned a baleful eye on his waiter and said, "I suppose you've never heard the expression 'warm as toast'?"[3]

One is inclined to guess that Kaufman joined the Dutch Treat and the theatrical clubs not on his own initiative, but at the urging of his friends. It would have been the ever-helpful Adams who suggested, in the late teens of the century, that he join the Friars. Kaufman retained membership in that club as late as 1925. In the years when he joined the Players and the Lambs, 1936 and 1944, respectively, he was at the top of his profession and doubtless a most welcome recruit. It was under the prodding of Max Gordon, then his producer, that he joined the Lambs; there the two men could get lunch or dinner in the vicinity of Broadway during the rehearsal weeks of new plays without wasting valuable time.

In 1922 it was still the Algonquin to which Kaufman turned his steps at lunchtime. After *To the Ladies* opened and no longer required his close attention, he and Connelly and others of the Round Table regulars conceived the notion of putting together a musical show that would exploit their identity as a group. They were inspired by the success of *Chauve-Souris,* a revue concocted by a band of Russian actors. After trouping the show across Europe to great acclaim, the actors had brought it to New York, where it opened on February 4 at the 49th Street Theater. The Algonquin set thought that it might be amusing to stage their own revue at the same theater on a Sunday night, when the Russians would be resting. To suggest a parody of the Russian show, they chose the title *No Sirree!* Admitting, in the opening chorus, only that the material was written mainly by Woollcott, Toohey, Benchley, Kaufman, Connelly, and Adams, they concealed the authorship of individual sketches behind the collective billing, in the program, of "the Vicious Circle of the Round Table Hotel." Among the additional contributors were Dorothy Parker, who wrote the lyrics to a song called "The Everlastin' Ingenue Blues," and Deems Taylor, who supplied some of the music for the sketches. The sole performance took place on April 20, 1922.

Kaufman's contribution to the evening's pleasures was a sketch called "Big Casino Is Little Casino," a parody of the improbably contrived melodramas of Samuel Shipman, some of which bore paradoxical titles, such as *Friendly Enemies* and *East Is West.* (The latter was probably his most memorable work; it is the tale of a girl supposedly Chinese who turns out to be Spanish and thus is acceptable as the fiancée of a young San Franciscan.) Kaufman's sketch has to do with the reversals of fortune of a district attorney and the daughter whom he banishes from his home because she refuses to approve of his views on crime and punishment. At first it appears that she is bent on ruining him financially, and then that she has sacrificed her own recently made fortune to benefit him. The high-sounding jargon spoken by Shipman's characters is echoed by the butler, Dregs, who at the opening says, "Life is a puzzle, and few are able to unravel it." By design, the plot of the play is no more easily unraveled than is the puzzle of life.

The authors who contributed to the show appeared in many of the sketches and were assisted by the women of the Round Table. Irving Berlin conducted the orchestra for all the musical numbers. Kaufman and Connelly had one of the numbers all to themselves: "Kaufman and Connelly from the West." Robert E. Sherwood was cast to sing Parker's blues song, for which he was backed by a chorus of Broadway actresses that included Helen Hayes, Tallulah Bankhead, Lenore Ulrich, and Winifred Lenihan (who, the next year, would create the role of Saint Joan in Shaw's play). Neysa McMein, Ruth Hale, Jane Grant, Alice Duer Miller, and Beatrice all had a moment on stage. Of all the evening's sketches, the best liked by far and the only one to endure was Robert Benchley's parody of a community-association officer's report to the members. It was "The Treasurer's Report," in which the humorist spun out some figures that added up only to fine comic nonsense. According to Benchley, he had promised to provide *something* for the show and was urged, less than an hour before curtain time, to offer the report, which he had only just invented. His name was left off the program, but fate compensated for the omission. Berlin hired him to repeat the bit in the next season's *Music Box Revue,* and he was asked by the Fox Film Corporation in 1927 to film it as a one-reel short. Soon after that he published it in a volume of his sketches.[4]

Inasmuch as the audience that attended *No Sirree!* did so by invitation only, the papers did not send their reviewers to it. The *Times*'s critic, Woollcott, could not in any case have passed sensible judgment on it, since he was in the cast. But his paper did carry a review the next morning. Laurette Taylor, nearly as capable with her pen as in her performances on stage, sat in for him and with uncompromising acerbity offered New York her opinion of the proceedings. She was plainly bored and saw no point in hiding the fact. "I do think," she wrote, "that the performers were 'competent,' some of them 'adequate' and others their usual selves." Her kindest words were for Kaufman and Connelly: "I do think that the two who will come out of it the best now will be the ones that would have no nonsense but came downstage and sang, 'I'm Kaufman, and that's Connelly.'" Nobody in the cast seemed to have minded her slighting of their collective effort. Their real end had been to enjoy themselves, which they did, and then to partake of the Swopes' lavish hospitality at a post-performance supper.

Despite the apparent shortcomings of the evening (as were eventually made clear by the failure of any of the contributions save Benchley's to sur-

vive), Kaufman and Connelly were pleased enough with the way it had gone
to approach George Tyler with the proposal that he mount a similar revue,
intimate in scale and satiric throughout, but fully professional, and give it a
run. He was willing, and approved of their plan to importune their friends
for some of the material and supply the rest themselves. They accepted billing
as general directors, but the stage direction was left to Howard Lindsay. On
November 7, 1922, the revue opened at the Punch and Judy Theater under
the title of *The 49ers*, which was chosen for no better reason than that the
theater was located on 49th Street. These latter-day forty-niners found no
gold.

Not much of the revue was written by Kaufman and Connelly. Kaufman's
sole contribution was "Life in the Back Pages," a sketch in which a "typical"
American middle-class family converses in the language of magazine ads.
Connelly's contribution, "Chapters from 'American Economics,'" was mer-
rier, though also slight. It consisted of two dance numbers, the autumn dance
of the hatcheck girls, who celebrated the seasonal increase in business, and
the spring dance of the small-town mayors, who celebrated the rise in retail
sales created by the seasonal shift of the public from heavy to light underwear. Better—in fact, best of all in the revue—was Ring Lardner's "The
Tridget of Greva," the first of his many nonsense-plays. It featured three fish-
ermen, each in his own boat, indulging in such conversational gambits as

> "Can you imitate birds?"
> "No. Why?"
> "I'm always afraid I'll be near somebody that can imitate birds."

And

> "Is your wife still living?"
> "I'm not sure. I haven't been home for a long while. But I heard she
> was dead."
> "What did she die of?"
> "I think she got her throat caught between my fingers."[5]

Benchley and Parker provided "Nero," a parody of fustian historical drama
that may have owed something to Max Beerbohm's *Savonarola Brown*; among
their characters were Robespierre, Queen Victoria, Grant, Lee, and Mussolini.
For contrast, Broun's non-comic sketch with sociological import, "A Robe for
the King," was included. The most ambitious of these numbers was, appropriately, the finale, a miniature musical comedy called "The Love Girl" that
played upon the conventions of the operettas created by Rudolph Friml, Sigmund Romberg, and their less famous imitators. Arthur Samuels supplied

the music, and F.P.A. the lyrics, every one of which included the word "love" in its title. The only exception to this feast of romance was an interpolation by Sherwood called "Back, Back, Back to Akron."

The kindest comment that could have been made about the material was that it was uneven. Broun himself wrote an unfavorable review of his contribution.[6] Nevertheless, *The 49ers* might have made a go of it had not Tyler, growing impatient with the relentlessly satirical tone of the show as it was shaping for production, insisted that the role of master of ceremonies be given to May Irwin, a raucous comedienne and "coon shouter," long in the tooth, whose delivery and very appearance were at odds with the purpose of the revue. Kaufman and Connelly, hoping to create a spoof of outmoded theatrical styles, found themselves burdened with a performer whose method was itself outmoded. Her presence spoiled the reception of the show, and Tyler, whose showmanship usually did not fail him, decided to replace her after the opening night. He wanted either Kaufman or Connelly to step in, remembering that both had been effective in *No Sirree!* Kaufman would not accept this challenge, and in fact could not because of his commitment to the *Times,* but Connelly, who enjoyed performing whenever he got the chance (as he often did at Neysa McMein's studio, the Ross-Grant ménage, and other gathering spots), was happy to oblige. Billed as the "Trail Blazer," he went on for May Irwin on the second night. Though he had expected to be replaced by a professional comedian, if one could be found to take over, he stayed with the revue until it ended its run—unhappily, only two weeks after the opening.[7]

For Kaufman and Connelly the two short-lived revues were but interludes in their ongoing task of supplying comic scripts to Tyler. In 1922 they wrote *Merton of the Movies,* an adaptation of the novel of the same name by Harry Leon Wilson, and wrote and rewrote the comedy that in the next year would reach Broadway as *The Deep, Tangled Wildwood,* but was called *West of Pittsburgh* on the road in 1922 and as a work in progress was spoken of by the team as *Turn to the Left, Little Old Millersville,* and *The Old Home Town. Merton* proved to be the most popular of all their collaborations, *Wildwood* the least.

Together the plays offered a comment on the cultural change that had begun to take place in small towns across America. Shaken by the war, stirred by images of an ampler life shown in the movies, caught up in the revolt against Victorian prudery, and, of course, made defiant by the Eighteenth Amendment, small-town residents, envious of the advantages of city life, suffered from acute dissatisfaction with their provincialism and were seeking paths out of it. If Sinclair Lewis was the pre-eminent delineator of this new force in American Life, he was not alone among the writers who examined it. Even Carl Van Vechten, the most dedicated chronicler of New York's Upper Bohemia, made it his subject in one work: *The Tattooed Countess,* a novel set in Iowa. And it was, quite obviously, the impulse behind the decision, usually left unanalyzed, of Fitzgerald's ex-collegians not to return to the Midwest after graduation, but to settle in the East. Harry Leon Wilson's (and Kaufman and Connelly's) Merton Gill is something of a comic, male counterpart of Lewis's Carol Kennicott in his fierce drive for a style of life that would permit him to achieve self-expression. Hollywood, not Chicago, is the beacon that draws Gill, and there he hopes to find fulfillment as an actor —in serious roles, exclusively. As for the residents of Millersville, "west of Pittsburgh," they will not be content until their town rivals New York in up-to-dateness, which means bootleg booze, the latest dances, and the newest of new phenomena, a radio station. By the time Kaufman and Connelly were finished with them in *The Deep, Tangled Wildwood,* the townspeople had begun to talk about a subway system.

In creating the comedy the team had their sights set on two goals. First, they wanted to invent a series of jokes at the expense of the nation's Millersvilles, but at the same time they wanted to spoof the kind of play made popular by Winchell Smith and various collaborators in *Turn to the Right, The Fortune Hunter,* and *Lightnin',* plays in which folksiness was commingled with a mildly melodramatic plot about financial skullduggery. It was for that reason that one of the working titles was *Turn to the Left.* The basic notion was to take a jaded New York playwright, whom Kaufman and Connelly grandly named James Parks Leland—a name with the same cadence, to be sure, as George S. Kaufman—and send him back to his home town for a refresher course in simplicity. His wish to return to the place is prompted by the failure of his most recent play. Leland is every inch the Gotham sophisticate, as revealed by the very sight of his apartment, which is elegant in decor and boasts a Japanese butler and a view of Central Park. Rushing back to it before the final curtain on the opening night of the new play, he begins to reminisce with a friend, Harvey Wallick, about Millersville, "a nice little American town, filled with simple, provincial people," one of whom is Mary Ellen, a girl who looks good in blue. He decides to go back, despite Wallick's warning that times, people, and places have changed.

The central problem for the collaborators as they put their play together was one that they themselves did not recognize. In all its versions, *Wildwood* remained a heartless piece of play-making. Had the authors felt a touch of

the nostalgia that overwhelms their protagonist, the comedy would have benefited from it. It has the jokes that audiences expected to find in every Kaufman-and-Connelly script, but virtually all of them are aimed at sitting targets:
the "boosters" of Millersville. Neither Kaufman nor Connelly, it was clear,
had the slightest wish to give up the comforts of city life, yet they apparently
could not, or would not, understand why others might want such comforts. It
was a denial of the daydreams that each had had some fifteen years earlier
in western Pennsylvania and that had brought them where they very contentedly were in 1922.

Predictably, nothing that James Parks Leland sees in Millersville corresponds to the images in his mind. The town is indeed a microcosmic Manhattan. His Aunt Sarah's house is no longer a rustic homestead, but a place of
great elegance. Instead of fishing in the Chippeho River as they used to do, the
Millersville residents have gone in for gambling, dancing, and drinking Prohibition hooch. Mary Ellen, no matter how demure in blue she may once
have been, is now a flirt; even worse, she takes in stride the extramarital bed-
dings of her friends. Almost everyone has become rich on shares in a dye
factory. The one poor person is Deacon Flood, who, in what at first seems
to be a switch on Deacon Tillinger in Winchell Smith's *Turn to the Right,* is
the intended victim, along with his niece, Phyllis Westley, of some double-
dealers. But Flood, true to his dramatic kind, is shown at the close to be just
as dishonest as the next man. He had intended to cheat not only the cheaters, but also his niece! Before the curtain goes down he is organizing a daring
little scheme to sell some acres of quicksand to an airplane manufacturing
corporation. The happy ending is reached, none too soon, when Leland proposes to and is accepted by Phyllis, who, though she has been living for some
years in Paris, is unspoiled and unassuming. She and Leland have a fine plan
to get out of Millersville and take up residence in a nicer community:

> LELAND It *will* be wonderful.
> PHYLLIS We'll be almost beside the lake.
> LELAND We'll look right over it. And in the morning, when the sun
> comes up . . . It's all gold and silver. And you can look right over
> the trees and see the other lake over on the West Side.
> PHYLLIS I've always wanted to live near Central Park.

Such was the final, Broadway version.

Looking back on the failure of the play late in life, Connelly put it down
to the willingness of himself and Kaufman to listen to the opinions of anyone at all with more theatrical experience than they had at the time. They
thought, according to his recollection, that nothing but blind luck had been

responsible for the success of both *Dulcy* and *To the Ladies!*[8] But such a notion sounds more like one held by Kaufman when set upon by opening-night
megrims than by Connelly at any time. It may be that poor advice hurt the
play, but the fact remains that when it reached Broadway on November 5,
1923, it was a more enjoyable work than it had been in the version that Tyler
opened in Atlantic City on May 23, 1922. In that version Leland and Wallick
buy control of the dye works and close it down, thus forcing Millersville
to be true to its old self. After traveling in Europe for a year, still shaking the
dust of Broadway from their heels, they come back to find that their scheme
has worked, for the town has reverted to its sleepy rusticity of yesteryear . . .
except that a plan is under way to open a radio station, an event that will
be sure to start the process of sophistication in motion again. This about-face
from sentimentality, in which Kaufman's hand was especially evident, made
sense by showing up Leland's presumption, but it was not dramatically effective because of the slackening of tension created by the year's break in the
action.

Tyler opened and closed the play, then entitled *West of Pittsburgh*, on the
road in the spring of 1922. It languished in the authors' trunk for the entire
1922-23 season, but was fished out for revising in the summer of 1923, in time
for a trial showing, as *The Deep, Tangled Wildwood*, in Indianapolis in September. In that city, a lucky one for the writers, it drew good notices, one of
which they wrote themselves:

> Just as *Dulcy* completely stopped bromidic utterance, just as *To the
> Ladies* made everyone stop going to banquets, and just as *Merton of the
> Movies* completely closed every motion picture theater in the United
> States through the suicide of every movie star of any importance, so will
> the new work of the handsome young playwrights eradicate all the things
> that make life unpleasant in small towns. Maybe it will annihilate the
> small towns. You never know how powerful written words can be.[9]

But the New York critics were not amused when the new play came to town
on November 5. Nor was the public: sixteen performances were all that the
play was accorded.

Even as they were mulling over ideas for the plot of the Millersville saga
in early 1922, the writers began to consider how to make a play out of Wilson's *Merton of the Movies*. It was Frank Adams who had called the story
to their attention. He had been enjoying it as it appeared in installments in
the *Saturday Evening Post,* and one evening at a Thanatopsis session he happened to mention it to Connelly. It took two months, from February 4 to
April 8, for the magazine to print the entire novel, but, having read one in-

stallment, the collaborators asked for and received galleys for the remaining ones from the magazine's editors as soon as they were set. The story appealed to them as much as it had to Adams. They negotiated for the stage rights, giving Wilson half the royalty. Tyler, who agreed to produce the adaptation, advised them to construct a solid plot around the title character, implying that he would prefer plot rather than character to be stressed in the play.[10]

A writer with many popular satires to his credit, Wilson was no stranger to Broadway. With Booth Tarkington he turned out more than a dozen plays, of which the best-known was a jingoistic comedy, *The Man from Home;* that play, about wealthy Americans on the prowl for European titles, was produced by Tyler in 1908. When writing fiction about the young, as in *Merton,* he employed a style somewhat like Tarkington's, interweaving the essentially sympathetic portraits of his characters with benign spoofing of their gaucheries. A touch of Horatio Alger is also detectable in his style. Especially is this true of his accounts of the rise of Bunker Bean on Wall Street and Merton Gill in Hollywood; not pluck alone, but a good supply of luck as well takes them to the top.

After reading the last galleys late in March on the train taking them to the Boston opening of the road company of *Dulcy,* Kaufman and Connelly began to consider how best to adapt the story. Their work on it carried through the summer, when, as had been their practice before, they separated, each planning to write certain sections of the play to show later to the other. July found Kaufman in Maine and Connelly in Nantucket. On September 18 the script was ready, as promised, for rehearsal, with two attractive young performers heading the cast: Glenn Hunter as Merton and Florence Nash as "Flips" Montague, the girl in Merton's life. Though the playwrights did not take altogether seriously Tyler's injunction that they put the emphasis on situations rather than characterization, the producer was happy with the script. Nor did he balk at the number of settings, which included some expensive ones for backlot scenes. He knew he had a hit, and doubtless was aware that the "boys" would have no trouble finding someone else to put it on should he decline.[11]

One can see what materials the novel had that inspired confidence in the adapters. Merton's bumbling, fumbling attempts at acting provided a natural stage spectacle. At the same time, he was, for all his vainglory, a sympathetic character—someone to root for. A clerk in Gashwiler's General Store in Simsbury, Illinois, he is seized by a monomaniacal desire to become a Hollywood star, but not merely for the sake of stardom. His ambition is "to give the public something better and finer" on the screen. This he does, eventually, but not quite according to plan. It is distinction in serious roles to which he aspires, but it is fame as a comedian which he achieves, along with a contract to star in comedies for the same Buckeye Studies whose pictures he scorned in Simsbury. His "serious" acting is mistaken for high comic art. Along the way he is befriended by "Flips," so nicknamed because she is a stunt girl who doubles for the stars. With her entrance into Merton's life, the figure in the carpet comes into focus. Merton, like Gordon Smith and Leonard Beebe, could never succeed on his own, but needs the encouragement of a devoted, self-confident woman. *Merton* fitted perfectly into the Kaufman-Connelly pattern.

Neither playwright had ever visited Hollywood when they wrote *Merton*. But that did not faze them. Wilson provided local color in such abundance that they were able to throw out most of it and still have enough left for a convincing depiction of the place. No less an authority than Harold Lloyd remarked on the authenticity of both novel and play, as well as on the picture version that soon followed. "That," he said in his memoirs, "is a story I read and a play and picture I saw with more emotions than the author. It will be a great surprise to Harry Leon Wilson, no doubt, but I was Merton—or one of many Mertons."[12]

Wilson, with an eye to serialization, had not spared the verbiage. When printed as a novel late in 1922, *Merton* ran to more than three hundred pages of rather small type. The playwrights had to cut the material drastically to produce a script of the customary playing time of roughly two and a half hours, with intermissions. Wilson's description of the kind of fatuous films then being made by all but a few directors had to be pruned away. Ruthlessly discarded, for example, was his reference to a film sequence in which a California eucalyptus towered over a Klondike cabin and another in which a grove of orange trees covered part of the acreage of a Long Island farm. Also gone was, necessarily, the excellent comic scene of Merton's attempt to train himself, back in Illinois, for cowboy roles by riding an ancient but intractable draft horse at a gallop through the alleys of Simsbury.

But at the same time that they tightened the work, the team found spots for the wisecracks that were required of them as playwrights. Merton, for example, dreaming out loud about the glamorous Beulah Baxter, his favorite star, says to a sympathetic but jaded woman casting director, "I'll bet she sacrificed to get up where she is." Replies the casting director, "*I'll* say she did." When, toward the end, it seems that Merton is to be a star, he says to the director who once used him as an extra, "I guess you'll never forget how terrible I was." Replies the director, "Oh, I don't know." In addition to these new lines of dialogue, the playwrights also introduced a new character: a figure who wanders mysteriously around the lot where Merton works without saying a word and calls on him after the "premier" of his first film to offer praise. He, it turns out, is to be head of the Motion Picture Industry and once was Secretary of Agriculture. In fact, he is a dramatic portrait of Will Hays, who was hired, only months before *Merton* was produced, by the Motion Picture Producers and Distributors Association to keep up the good name of the film business by casting out of it anyone whose unsavory private life became public knowledge. A sneaky, gumshoe type, he amused the New York audience.*

From the first tryout performance, *Merton of the Movies* was presumed to be a hit. The tryouts commenced at the Montauk Theater in Brooklyn on October 9, 1922. The reviewer sent by *Variety* was so struck by the comedy as to guess that from that time on the fan magazines, whose gushing style was parodied throughout the dialogue, would lose their readers. It was not to be, but at least he was correct in predicting a long life for the play. He further observed that Hollywood's royal couple, Douglas Fairbanks and Mary Pickford, not only were present but seemed, despite the spoofing of their means of livelihood, to be enjoying themselves. The Manhattan opening, which took place on November 13, brought "corking" notices, as *Variety* put it a few days later. This time the great Valentino was in the audience. Showing that it could take a joke, a major film studio, Famous Players-Lasky, bought the rights and released a silent version in 1924, with Glenn Hunter, the original Merton, recreating the title role.[13]

Merton was settling into its run of 398 performances at the Cort Theater when *The 49ers* closed, unlamented, at the Punch and Judy. With *The Deep, Tangled Wildwood* in abeyance, Kaufman and Connelly were free for a while. To keep in practice, they wrote a parody in three scenes of Dickens's *A Christmas Carol*, which, perhaps for want of a prod from the muse, they gave the same title. Partly made up of material that they had tried and abandoned, it detailed what happened when Bob Cratchit's family, after trying in vain to achieve financial success through the self-help schemes advertised in magazines, goes into the kindness business. Abetted by Scrooge, who thinks that Tiny Tim's "God bless us everyone" is the greatest advertising slogan ever invented, the family sets up a kindness corporation (products unspecified in the script) and is so prosperous that it can afford to buy out the Kindness Trust. Much of this was taken from Kaufman's "Life in the Back Pages," but

---

* Readers of the Samuel French acting edition of *Merton* will not find this character. He was excised for the benefit of stock companies with limited resources, human and financial.

a fillip at the close originated in the abandoned curtain line of *To the Ladies.* Paraphrasing the words written for Elsie Beebe, Mrs. Cratchit shyly announces that the family is going to have an automobile.

At this time or soon thereafter Kaufman by himself composed a sketch that was for decades to augment his income through stock rights. Coming to his parents' apartment one day when his mother was entertaining some friends for bridge, he was amused to discover that it was not really bridge that brought the ladies together, but a love of gossip.[14] Nettie and her friends were much more interested in exchanging mildly malicious bits of news than in the play of the hand. It struck Kaufman that this situation could be made even more amusing if the game were poker and the cardplayers were men who comported themselves across the table precisely like this female foursome. The result was "If Men Played Cards as Women Do," which was first offered to the public in Irving Berlin's *Music Box Revue of 1923.* The four players of the sketch are called John, Bob, George, and Marc—names that, at least to the opening-night audience, suggested Toohey, Benchley, Kaufman, and Connelly. Though they speak and act in a virile fashion (according to the stage directions), they concern themselves conversationally with clothes, housekeeping, engagements, and babies, and are not wholly certain which suit in the deck is which. Brief as it is, the sketch establishes a sense of intimacy among the four players that shows Kaufman in the process of mastering one of the essentials of his craft: the ability to create a microcosmic society whose members seem to know one another extremely well.

For no major reason, but for a number of minor ones that added up to serious irritation, the two authors never offered Tyler another script after *Merton* and *Wildwood.* The break was not caused by bitterness, though Tyler's tendency to drive them hard for revisions and his tightfistedness over scenery and costumes had been causes of strain almost from the first. There had been a particular dust-up during the production of *To the Ladies,* when Tyler demonstrated a not altogether unexpected intransigence over the setting for the Beebes' living room. The lampshades were relics of the earliest days of electricity, relics from some Tyler production of long ago, and Kaufman, having decided that they must be replaced, went to a dime store and found some new ones that served admirably. "Another Clyde Fitch!" Tyler exclaimed, referring to one of the most determined disciples of dramatic realism of the turn of the century. But it was no joke to his "boys." In writing his memoirs ten years later, Tyler could only say, "I guess I deserved to lose Kaufman and Connelly." Coming from him, that was no small admission. Even so, in 1939, when Tyler was in retirement and hard up, Kaufman organized a fund for him with contributions from himself, Connelly, the Lunts, George Arliss, Mrs. August Belmont (formerly Eleanor Robson, one of Tyler's leading actresses), Booth Tarkington, and others who had worked for the producer in the years when he was one of Broadway's dominant figures.[15]

Though eventually both Kaufman and Connelly took a turn at producing plays on Broadway, in 1922 neither writer considered that serving as their own producers might be the best alternative to continuing to work with Tyler. Their flutter, as members of the Vicious Circle, with *The 49ers* had provided no incentive to continue in the unfamiliar role. Nor was either ready to test his skill at directing a script; they were content to leave that task to Howard Lindsay or Hugh Ford, at Tyler's decision. But both writers kept an eye on each successive production as it ran on Broadway and on the road tours that followed. In the spring of 1923 when an English production of *Merton of the Movies* opened in London, Kaufman sailed for that city. Though his letters from London have not survived, it was presumably to attend the opening that he made the trip, his first abroad since the crossing with Herbert Seligmann in 1914. Neither Connelly nor Beatrice accompanied him. (Beatrice had only recently returned from a holiday abroad with Margaret Leech.)

Unhappily, *Merton* did not repeat its Broadway success in the West End. Produced by Robert Courtneidge and directed by Hugh Ford, who had staged the original Broadway production, the play offered two young Americans, Tom Douglas and Patricia Collinge, in the leading roles. Though Patricia Collinge was said to be outstanding as "Flips," Douglas was all but inaudible on the opening night as the result of an attack of nerves, and his poor performance was largely responsible for the play's early closing. Perhaps it was for this reason that Kaufman's trip was also a failure. When he returned to New York, he told Frank Adams that America was good enough for him.[16]

Kaufman and Connelly made no public announcement to the effect that they were looking for a new producer, but in the spring of 1923, when an invitation came their way to throw in their lot with another management, they accepted. Their association with Tyler had yet to run its course, for not until the fall of the year was *Wildwood* offered on Broadway. Meanwhile, however, the proposal made to them by Rufus LeMaire was tempting in an odd way. The project was a musical, and they were to supply a book for it on any subject they liked, provided it would fit under a title already chosen: *Helen of Troy, New York*. The songs were to be written by the team of Bert Kalmar (words) and Harry Ruby (music); some, in fact, had already been composed when LeMaire tendered his offer to the playwrights. Kaufman and Connelly were not overjoyed with the title, but found that they could fashion a plot on which it would not hang too uncomfortably. It was a piece of comic nonsense about the Yarrow Collar Company, its executives, and its employees.

The production got off to a bad start for a number of reasons, all of them the unpredictable, unsettling, and yet not uninteresting kinds of events that befall the unwary show-business entrepreneur. LeMaire, though soon (in the late 1920s) to embark on a Hollywood career that led to his success as an executive at Universal Pictures, was a novice at producing in 1923. Previously, he had been an agent. No sooner had he come to terms with Kaufman and Connelly, and handed them a thousand-dollar bill to split as an advance, than he found himself without enough cash on hand to meet his next payments to both pairs of collaborators. There was nothing to be done but to take in an associate producer with a knack for finding money. LeMaire turned to George Jessel. Though not yet the famous fund-raiser and after-dinner speaker that he was to become in middle age, Jessel did not fail LeMaire.[17]

First Jessel and LeMaire contrived a rather daring piece of chicanery to bilk the celebrated gambler Nick the Greek and two of his bootlegger associates out of some cash. Jessel sent LeMaire a telegram, using the false but solvent-sounding name, Eugene V. Kahn, and promising to put up $25,000. This was to be used as a come-on for the trio of prospective investors, who presumably would confuse Eugene V. Kahn with banker Otto H. Kahn. It would have worked had not Nick and his friends been short of cash at the time. Jessel put up $10,000 of his own and, after observing that LeMaire was paying extravagant salaries to the actors under contract and was then taking 10 per cent as their agent, Jessel insisted that he be made a partner. Another $10,000 was needed to back the production, and this came from Sidney Wilmer and Walter Vincent, the owners of a string of theaters in Pennsylvania and Virginia who had gotten their start in show business as the authors of vaudeville sketches nearly thirty years before. They were branching out to the extent of looking for new shows to back, and heard and admired the Kalmar-Ruby score.

Next came the problem of tryout bookings. Again the unexpected took place. A representative of a group of civic-minded businessmen from Fairmont, West Virginia, a town with a population then of about 20,000, came to call on Jessel with a proposition. Hoping to attract new business to Fairmont (which is in the north central part of the state, about sixty-five miles south of Pittsburgh), this gentleman and his group were building an up-to-date theater that was expected to provide the town with first-class dramatic productions and vaudeville acts. A veritable Millersville! It was Jessel himself whom the stranger hoped to book for the theater, but *Helen of Troy, New York,* for which he contracted. This was the theater's first attraction. It opened on June 4.

Nothing went well. Harry Ruby, a wit as well as a melodist, wrote to Groucho Marx on the proceedings: "Thanks for your cabled good wishes. I'm sorry you asked how the show . . . opened out of town, but I'll answer your question as soon as I can stop crying."[18] Indeed, the confusion and general discomfort were almost bad enough to cause tears. First of all, it seemed to Jessel that the Kaufman-Connelly dialogue was somewhat too smart for its own good, and he had been bold enough to say so. This resulted in some coolness between the Georges; though they shared a Pullman drawing room on the trip to Fairmont, conversation between them was sparse for most of the journey. Connelly rode in another car, but dropped in on the pair and found after a time that things were easier between them. Jessel had managed to break the ice by pointing through the window at a shack with a clothesline from which hung a pair of red drawers and saying, "Mr. Kaufman, let's get off the train, go into that shack, and forget." That may have warmed up the conversation between the two men, but it did not result in a softening of the book's brittle dialogue.

But the snap of the dialogue did not constitute a major problem. No one, after all, could complain about such lines as the ingenue's remark to a male collar-model, "You do all your work with the *outside* of your head." This sort of thing was the Kaufman-Connelly stock in trade, and if Fairmont should prove resistant to their style, Broadway had almost always enjoyed it. Other, unforeseen difficulties arose to plague the Fairmont opening. Though work on the theater was not quite completed, a still more serious problem stemmed from the fact that the traveling company did not include musicians, and those in Fairmont were not up to the demands of the score. One elderly comedian, Tom Lewis, who was known to be a slow learner, went up in his lines disastrously on the opening night and suddenly began reciting a vaudeville monologue that he had performed long before and that made no sense whatever in the musical. He went on for ten minutes before Ruby, Kalmar, Jessel, and LeMaire could get him back into his role. Fortunately, Kaufman and Connelly were taking a breather outside the theater at the time, and they had no inkling of the disaster taking place inside. Finally, at the exceptionally early hour of ten-thirty the show was over. The authors had fully expected their material to run long and were prepared to do some drastic cutting. The reason that it did not was that the Fairmont audience wasted no time in laughing.[19]

From its hapless run in Fairmont, *Helen of Troy, New York* went on to Newark, and it came into New York on June 19. The break-in performances had somehow done what they were supposed to do; the show got good notices on Broadway and had a run of 191 performances, or just under six months. While not record-setting, this was no disgrace. Queenie Smith, who had the second feminine part, outshone Helen Ford, the star, and soon became a star herself. To her rather than to her authors went the honors of the occasion.

Scarcely had LeMaire and Jessel rung down the curtain on the show for the last time than Kaufman and Connelly, along with their producers, were sued for plagiarism by a young woman named Elaine Sterne Carrington, who said that she too had written a play called *Helen of Troy, New York*. The New York *Times,* reporting on the suit, commented with beguiling simplicity that Carrington had given her script to her agent, Julia Chandler, and "the next thing she knew it was being produced and Kaufman and Connelly were holding themselves out as the authors."[20] She claimed that her work bore not only a titular but a substantive resemblance to the just-closed musical. But her case came to nothing. *Helen of Troy, New York* proved to have been a not infrequently used title, and the fact that it was imposed by LeMaire on Kaufman and Connelly caused a further weakening of the claim. Nor did the plots of the two works have much in common. Yet it took until January to answer the charges. This was not the best way to start 1924.

It was not a portent of additional problems, however, for that year brought the team still another hit, and this made up not only for the nuisance suit but for the quick collapse of *The Deep, Tangled Wildwood* in the previous November. All the while *Helen of Troy, New York* was in preparation, the coming showdown with the Broadway reviewers over *Wildwood* was looming, and they had had to spend much of the summer refurbishing it. But they began yet another project before the *Wildwood* opening. With the quick closing of that hapless piece, and the termination of their association with Tyler, they were free to bear down in earnest on the new work. This was for the most prestigious and aristocratic of all Broadway's producers, Winthrop Ames.

Ames, a member of the tool-manufacturing family of North Easton, Massachusetts, had had fifteen years' experience in the New York theater by 1923. Before coming to New York in 1908 he had enjoyed three successful years of stock-company management in Boston. What took him away from his native state was an invitation to serve as artistic director of the New Theater, which a group of wealthy, civic-minded New Yorkers had funded and were then building, as a lavish home for repertory, on Central Park West. The New Theater opened in the fall of 1909 with Ames in charge, but after only two years he left it to build his own theaters, the Little and the Booth. By 1920 he had a series of artistic and commercial successes to his credit. Though Tyler was not the least venturesome of producers, Ames took more risks than he with artistic drama—that is, with plays having pronounced intellectual content and settings that lent themselves to striking theatrical design. And his offerings could be counted on, as Tyler's could not, to live up to their authors' expectations in the way of such design.

In the category of the artistic lay Paul Apel's *Hans Sonnenstössers Höllenfahrt,* or, in rough English translation, "Hans Sunpuncher's Trip to Hell," a title suggesting the fall to the depths of a man with his eye on the heights. Ames saw in this work a vehicle for the satiric wit of Kaufman and Connelly. The play was a minor product of the expressionist movement that touched all the arts in Germany from about 1910 to the mid-1920s, coming to a peak during the First World War. Apel was one of the least considerable of the expressionist playwrights, a figure not destined to be remembered by the historians of the movement and no match, intellectually or artistically, for such internationally acclaimed expressionist dramatists as Georg Kaiser and Ernst Toller. The plays of the movement were characterized by a sharp break with observable reality, the break usually manifesting itself in settings (often skeletal) that exaggerated certain specific aspects of the environment at the expense of others—an office, say, with only a huge desk that in its isolation suggested the power and drive of a highly placed businessman—and characters bearing not names, but labels, such as the Cashier, the Secretary, or, even more vaguely, the Man, the Woman, the Child. It was a drama primarily of social concerns, not of conflicting personal values—a drama, as has often been remarked, of Man, not of men.

The American theater embraced expressionism only when it was waning in its birthplace. The most memorable New York productions of expressionist imports were certain offerings of the Theater Guild: Kaiser's *From Morn to Midnight* in 1922 and Toller's *Man and the Masses* in 1924. A few American plays could be pointed to as examples of the style. Among them were O'Neill's *The Emperor Jones, All God's Chillun Got Wings,* and *The Hairy Ape,* and Elmer Rice's *The Adding Machine.* Apel's comedy, which had first been performed in Germany in 1912, was held under option by several New York producers in succession, including the Guild, before it came to Ames's attention.[21] Ames gave his authors only an outline of the plot, not an entire translation from which to work.[22] He took the view that the play should be completely rewritten for an American setting and was confident that Kaufman and Connelly were capable of accomplishing this, since they had already demonstrated a flair for showing up the pretensions of the American middle class.

Working from the outline, Kaufman and Connelly constructed a story roughly similar to the original, but more entertaining—seemingly wilder in its departure from reality, but making its own good antimaterialist sense. The two Americans were not programmatic stylists like the expressionists, and they did not hesitate to incorporate naturalistic scenes into the play, along with a pantomime (actually a scenario written by Ames alone) of such art-theater prettiness that it could be described as *im*pressionistic. The result was an anthology of styles that led one commentator on the *Times* to describe the play as a parody of expressionism, an interpretation that was fair enough and that may well have pleased the two writers.[23] Ames chose Woodman Thompson as set designer and produced with his customary regard for visual values. A strong cast was assembled, with the subtle comedian Roland Young in the leading part of Neil McRae, as Apel's Hans Sonnenstösser was renamed. Deems Taylor, the adapters' friend and poker-playing companion, supplied the music, as he had the year before for Rice's *The Adding Machine*. A new title was chosen, as abstract as the German original, but less cumbersome: *Beggar on Horseback*. After road work in Wilmington and Washington, the play opened in New York on February 12, 1924, to gratifying notices. It held on for 224 performances, a rather brief run in relation to the prestige that the authors gained from the production.

McRae is a composer of serious music who orchestrates popular songs in order to keep himself fed, clothed, and housed—though not very well. Though he is the composer of a symphony and the music for a pantomime, his great impracticality—that conventional trait of artists in literature—makes it seem unlikely that he will ever rise above the genteel poverty of his cold-water flat. He is tolerably content, however, and Cynthia, a young girl who lives in an adjacent apartment, is obviously in love with him and just as obviously right for him. But, on the advice of a well-meaning friend, Dr. Albert Rice, he proposes to Gladys Cady, the daughter of a rich industrialist. She could supply the cash to pay for a composer's life of contemplation, and to spare! In a dream, however, he sees the folly of this plan and kills not only the fickle, silly girl, but her snobbish brother, her pompous father, and her bone-headed mother. At his trial—still in the dream, of course—he offers his pantomime "A Kiss in Xanadu" as evidence of his talent. But with Cady himself (revived, as are all the family) the presiding judge, Neil is sentenced to life in a Cady-owned art factory, where he is to turn out popular tunes. Waking from this dream at last, he comes to an amicable parting with Gladys, and finds Cynthia standing by.

To keep the momentum of the dream sequence going in the interval between the acts, actors dressed as newsboys handed out copies of a paper called *The Morning-Evening* (with which, the authors noted, "has been combined *The Evening-Morning*, retaining the best features of both"), the lead story being an account of the multiple murder, but with space left over for a parody of virtually every department of the standard big-city daily. The authors' chum Woollcott was not neglected; a dramatic review went, in his treacly style, "Rather like an April or May morning came this lyric thing last night to our hearts and memories. Your correspondent, for one, must admit that he cried constantly."

This and the wildly spinning dream episodes of Neil's introduction to Cady's business (the making of overhead and underground aerial widgets), the murders, and the trial prevented the action from slipping into a cloying gentility, despite the over-all niceness and proper morality of McRae and Cynthia. A threat to the levelheadedness of the play was Ames's pantomime, "A Kiss in Xanadu," which reviewers described, without irony, as lovely. In this section of the play a Prince and his Princess, bored with their marriage, sneak out of their palace separately one night, disguised, have a brief fling with each other, and return before morning to their old and tiresome life. Perhaps intended as an antidote to the sweetness of this conceit was a dream-within-the-dream in which McRae finds himself married, not to Gladys, but to Cynthia. In a tart mockery of the idea of love-in-a-cottage, the couple live by selling the eggs laid by their little red hen and the milk given by their little dun cow. The diminuendo of the close of the play further diluted the sentimentality of the whole. No kiss completes the action. The deepening of the affection of McRae and Cynthia is signaled only by Cynthia's request to be useful. "Do you want me, Neil?" she asks. His reply to the question is another question. "Do I want you?" It is the hand of the antisentimental Kaufman that is apparent here as the curtain falls, just as surely as that it was the hand of the music-loving Connelly that shaped the central conflict of the plot.

As yet another Kaufman-and-Connelly hit, *Beggar on Horseback* became a little-theater staple of the 1920s and found its way into some textbook anthologies as an example of expressionist drama. An English production, with A. E. Matthews as Neil, did well in London in the 1924-25 season. Even while the play was still running in New York, Kaufman and Connelly, perhaps jaded by the critical praise, turned out a brief parody, "Beggar off Horse-back," for the revue *Round the Town* produced by Herman J. Mankiewicz and S. Jay Kaufman. *Round the Town* opened on May 21, 1924, and ran for fourteen performances. In the parody, McRae wants to be a ticket specu-lator and become rich. He also wants to marry the rich girl, Gladys, despite the opinion of his friend, Dr. Rice, that this seems oddly undramatic. Taking Rice's advice, he goes to sleep and dreams about what marriage to the poor girl, Cynthia, would be like. It would be terrible! At a restaurant, where they have only about a tenth of a cent to spend, all they can afford is bread crumbs, or, as the waiter says, a look at a steak. Waking up, McRae finds Gladys with him. When she coyly reveals that she is pregnant, he decides to marry her.*

Famous Players-Lasky, a subsidiary of Paramount Pictures, bought the film rights to *Beggar on Horseback* and released the picture under that title in 1925 with Edward Everett Horton in the role of Neil McRae. For the New York showing at the Criterion Theater, which it controlled, Famous Players wished to try something new and original, and commissioned Kaufman and Dorothy Parker to write a one-act play to be presented live as a prologue. Kaufman and Parker were a curious combination, inasmuch as neither had ever been known to show affection for the other, and, according to reports, on this occasion, their sole collaboration, they did not do their work particu-larly well. Entitled *Business Is Business*, their play was a farce which ran for forty-five minutes and was divided into four scenes. Like *Beggar on Horse-back*, it offered the audience a disapproving, satirical view of the typical busi-nessman's obsession with the piling up of wealth. John W. Berryman, a shoe manufacturer, is adept not only at making money, but at publicizing himself, and by offering great sums to charity he cannily keeps his name and the name of his company before the public. His most dashing public-relations gambit is to offer his city a statue of himself to be set up in a park that will be named for him. Reviewing the play for the *Times* along with the film, Mordaunt Hall found it clever and "filled with scintillating ideas." But a sharper and more convincing review was written by *Variety*'s "Bisk," who considered the play too subtle for the picture audiences and noted that the Criterion's cus-tomers seemed unimpressed by it. He found that, no matter what the authors may have intended to suggest through the character of Berryman, their main objection to businessmen was that they did not read Joyce or listen to Schoen-

---

* To this revue Kaufman also contributed, on his own, the lyric to a song, "If One of Us Was You, Dear" (music by Jay Velie), and, with Mankiewicz, a skit, "Moron Films, Educational, Travel and Topical." Connelly contributed a skit, "The Girl from WJZ."

berg. One suspects that that particular set of values was the gift to the play of Parker rather than of her collaborator, who might have been willing to take a glance at the last chapter of *Ulysses* sometime, but would not willingly have listened to Schoenberg's atonalities.[24]

Maintaining their hectic pace, Kaufman and Connelly accepted another proposition in 1924, during the run of *Beggar on Horseback*. Sidney Wilmer and Walter Vincent, undaunted by the fact that *Helen of Troy, New York* had failed to recover its production costs, offered not merely to back but to produce a second Kaufman-and-Connelly musical. Off the shelf came *Miss Moonshine*, their early, unproduced script about two feuding families in Appalachia. Retitled *Be Yourself*, it went into production with Queenie Smith as feminine lead opposite Jack Donohue, a popular dancing star. Lewis Gensler and Milton Schwarzwald shared the task of composing the music and also fashioned the lyrics for most of the show's twelve songs. Lyrics for some of the tunes were written by Ira Gershwin. Though Gershwin had contributed the lyrics to some half-dozen Broadway musicals before *Be Yourself,* including three to the music of his brother, George, this was the first time that he used his own name. Previously he had billed himself as Arthur Francis, a name that combined that of the third Gershwin brother and their sister Frances. On three of the numbers Kaufman and Connelly collaborated with him, and Connelly alone worked with him on another.

The opening took place on September 3, 1924, to thin praise. After ninety-three performances Wilmer and Vincent closed the show down. It might have had a better chance had not *Rose Marie* opened only the night before. Following that triumph, almost any musical was likely to strike the reviewers as an anticlimax. But the blame ultimately must fall on the two writers, who essayed nothing new for the occasion and merely refurbished an old script with which they had tried in vain to interest managers in the past. Kaufman even more than Connelly was at fault. At last he seemed to be overreaching himself, for while *Be Yourself* was being readied for the stage, he was deeply involved in the writing and road-testing of another script, with another collaborator, Edna Ferber, and that, too, was not a hit, though it fared better than the musical. At the root of the trouble was a breach, in no way rancorous, but irreparable, between Kaufman and Connelly.

Broadway rightly knew them to be a congenial pair, but one problem in their association was beyond their ability to solve. Kaufman was a compulsive writer, continually looking beyond the project at hand to a series of others and requiring no diversion other than his favorite games. Connelly, already corpulent at thirty-three, enjoyed to the full the comforts that his success had made possible. In 1923, on a trip with his mother, he discovered Europe, and he would happily make many other ocean crossings in the years to come. He was not driven to turn out a Broadway script every six months, though when yoked to Kaufman he did so. They took refuge in the notion that it would be good for each to try to write on his own, but the reason for their artistic separation was not on that plane. Even after the break Kaufman kept on chivvying Connelly. Why did he not write more? Why did he spend so much time merely making dramatic adaptations? (One of them was *The Green Pastures,* which won the Pulitzer Prize in 1930.) In 1934, when Dickens's *Life of Our Lord* was syndicated with much publicity in American newspapers, Kaufman remarked that "Charles Dickens dead writes more than Marc Connelly alive."

Neither author considered a press announcement of the separation to be necessary. It became obvious only in the season of 1925-26, when each offered a play written entirely on his own, Kaufman's being *The Butter and Egg Man* and Connelly's *The Wisdom Tooth.* But as early as 1923 Kaufman had begun to look for another collaborator, and found one in Edna Ferber, whose work he knew well. His approach to her was by letter, for at the time he was in London and she in Chicago. Kaufman had read and admired a story of hers called "Old Man Minick" concerning an elderly, self-important widower who goes to live with his son and daughter-in-law in their smallish Chicago apartment and unconsciously deranges the harmony of their marriage. Kaufman suggested to Ferber that they turn the story into a play.[25]

At first Ferber was doubtful. It was not that she lacked respect for Kaufman's achievement or disapproved of him personally, but that she thought he had overestimated the dramatic potentiality of her story. She suggested alternatives, making it clear that she was receptive to the idea of working with him. That they would hit it off well must have struck both as likely, in view of what they had in common. Like Kaufman, Ferber was of German-Jewish stock and a native Midwesterner. She was born in 1885 in Kalamazoo. When she was still a child her family moved to Ottumwa, Iowa, and then to Appleton, Wisconsin. In 1910, after early experience as a newspaperwoman in Appleton and Milwaukee and the acceptance of a few of her stories by leading magazines of the day, she moved to Chicago and embarked on a full-time career as a writer of fiction. Success came quickly. Her first novel, *Dawn O'Hara,* was published in 1911, and soon she was attracting a following with stories about Emma McChesney, a traveling saleswoman. Thus she became a nationally known figure long before Kaufman did. While the McChesney stories in *American Magazine* were delighting readers in every state, Kaufman was still the little-known G.S.K. of Frank Adams's columns.

Ferber did not find it easy to give up the Midwest. She resisted as long as she could the importuning of her publishers to come to New York even for a visit. She found that Chicago offered a continuous procession of characters to pique her literary imagination. But New York was the center of publishing and the center of the theatrical world, though the latter fact meant little to her at the time. Her first trip to New York took place in 1912. She enjoyed it, but still felt no desire to leave Chicago for good. Not until 1924 did she take a long lease on an apartment in New York and begin to think of that city as her home. In the intervening years she frequently came back to it for extended stays, but contented herself with hotel suites or furnished apartments.

Early in her Chicago years Ferber began to receive feelers from New York producers about the dramatic rights to the McChesney stories. But, busy with other projects, she held off until 1914, when, at the behest of Charles Frohman, she agreed to dramatize them herself in collaboration with George V. Hobart, a Broadway man-of-all-work. It was Frohman's thought that Ethel Barrymore, his brightest star, was right for the role of the saleswoman. In view of Barrymore's appealing looks and aristocratic bearing, Ferber felt that this was a curious choice. She acceded to it, however, and thereupon became starstruck. For the rest of her life she was fascinated by the stage and its people, and after her move to New York she counted the most talented actors and the most popular playwrights of the day among her intimates.

Problems arose during both the writing and the production of the play. Hobart, who had a string of long-running farces, musicals, and melodramas to his credit, had achieved so many easy successes that he had begun to underestimate the public. To Ferber it seemed that much of what he was putting into the plot would strike the audience as incredible. Harboring doubts through the entire collaboration, she was distressed and saddened when in May 1915, Frohman, whom she liked and respected, went to his death aboard the *Lusitania*. Frohman's well-organized staff took over the script, which had come to be called *Our Mrs. McChesney,* and brought it to Broadway on October 19. A run of 151 performances followed—by no means a failure in 1915—though the notices were not lavish with praise. One of the most unfavorable read, "We think that *Our Mrs. McChesney* is the most inept material which has been brought to the stage this season." This was the voice of Heywood Broun in the *Tribune.* Soon he and Ferber would become fast friends.

Two more unfulfilling tries at playwriting followed this one in Ferber's career: *$1000 a Year,* a collaboration with the lawyer-author Newman A. Levy (a shipboard acquaintance of Ferber's), which was withdrawn during its tryouts, and an adaptation of her "The Eldest," which she wrote hurriedly for the Provincetown Playhouse after discovering that the theater was on the point of opening an unauthorized adaptation by someone else. Though these experiences did not lessen her fondness for the stage, she remained primarily a writer of popular fiction. Throughout her writing career she could count on healthy sales for her books and vigorous bidding for the film rights. In 1923, even as Kaufman posted his letter from London about "Old Man Minick," she was writing *So Big*, which would win the Pulitzer Prize.

Kaufman was no sooner back from London than he was immersed in the task of readying *Be Yourself* for a fall opening. That meant meetings with Ferber had to be sporadic and, from her point of view, not at all satisfactory. Looking back on their first session some fourteen years later, Ferber wrote that it took place in the Kaufmans' apartment and that Beatrice was also present. The session went well, because Ferber was already so charmed by the prospect of working with Kaufman that she would not let it go badly.[26]

What drew Ferber to Kaufman was not alone the fact that they had sprung from similar stock. It was sometimes conjectured that Ferber no sooner came to know him than she fell in love with him. Possibly she did. A spinster to the grave, she was nevertheless attracted to men, and especially to those men who, like her literary characters, had advanced to the front rank of their profession. One man upon whom she doted was Alfred Lunt, the possessor of splendid acting ability and great magnetism, to say nothing of good looks. In the presence of Lunt's wife, Lynn Fontanne, Ferber could not conceal her jealousy, which took the form of extreme rudeness. Finally, after decades of forbearance, Fontanne felt that she had had enough of Ferber's snubs and began avoiding her company, as did Lunt. At Ferber's death in 1968, the breach was still not healed. Beatrice was sometimes subjected to the same treatment and complained of it with a wry smile. "Why is Edna so rude to me?" she would ask her friends, though to such a sophisticated woman the answer was plain. When Ferber was rude, she was horrid. Tennessee Williams, writing in 1972, remembered even then an unpleasant moment from his early years in the theater when he was introduced to her. "The best I can manage," she said, "is a mild 'Yippee.' "[27]

Like most women, Ferber appreciated Kaufman's suave manners and interesting looks. But had there been nothing more to him, she would not have been much moved. She knew many men who had such qualities. She also knew many men who were his match in intelligence, among them, for example, William Allen White and Herbert Bayard Swope. But few men anywhere demonstrated such devotion to work as he, and this quality, added to the others, rendered him irresistible. As much as he, she lived the hours at the typewriter to the full, closing the door on all distractions from early morning to mid-afternoon with a firmness that was not to be contradicted. She enjoyed writing, and she enjoyed writing about writing; her memoirs are crowded with paragraphs describing her work habits. In *A Peculiar Treasure* she wrote with obvious pleasure of those hours when she was closeted with Kaufman as they labored to construct a play. Usually, the work sessions took place in her apartment, beginning at eleven in the morning. Kaufman would enter on the dot, dressed to perfection. As a brief delaying tactic—certainly no symptom of a block—he would tie and retie his shoelaces. Treating her place as his own, he would inspect any papers lying on her desk. One day he picked up a Western Union blank placed on the desk by Ferber and read a note in her hand accusing him of being "an old snooper."[28] When the press of social activities in town became too heavy, they would pack up their manuscript and take themselves off to Atlantic City, White Sulphur Springs, or, as with their first collaboration, to the near-by city of White Plains, New York.

Their problem in shaping up the dramatic version of "Old Man Minick" was providing the title character with a sound reason for moving out of his son's home at the end of the play. The original story includes a scene in which he hears his daughter-in-law tell a friend she cannot have a baby as long as he stays with them, because he occupies their only spare room and they cannot afford a larger apartment. Learning this, the Minick of the story makes up his mind to move into a near-by residence for aged gentlemen, among whose "guests" he has already made many friends. But it was no easy matter to dramatize this, since no matter where the old man stood while eavesdropping, there was something quaint, pat, and unpleasantly artificial about the scene. The play was two months on the road before Kaufman and Ferber came to a reasonable solution.

Had Kaufman's attention not been divided between this play and *Be Yourself*, work on it might have progressed with less frustration. The new comedy opened in New London on August 20 and went on to Norwich, Hartford, New Haven, and Providence before the authors straightened out the plot to their satisfaction. Between Providence and Buffalo, the last stops before Broadway, Kaufman and Ferber took out all mention of the wished-for baby, and for the scene in which Minick overheard the dialogue about it they substituted another in which the old man tried unsuccessfully to enter the conversation of his daughter-in-law and her friends and thereupon recognized that he would be better off somewhere else. To justify his decision to move out, they let him say that he had a good many years left, and that in moving to the "home" he would have the stimulating society of other elderly men like himself—men who, the audience could see, enjoyed nothing so much as a hot, largely uninformed debate on world affairs. At the close, declining the young couple's suggestion that he stay on with them and teach them pinochle, his favorite game, he says, with Kaufmanesque severity, "I got my own life, same as anybody. And I know just what I'm going to do with it. I ain't going to waste it teaching pinochle to anybody."

In addition to revising their plot on the road, the authors also changed the title. Before Buffalo, the play was called *Old Man Minick,* like the original story. But as it began to be borne in on them that to audiences this title hinted of antiquity and decrepitude, they shortened it to *Minick.* This was not especially informative, but the same could be said of the best-selling *Babbitt.* In the advertisements and programs, the play was offered as the work of Edna Ferber and George S. Kaufman. For this production, Kaufman invented the rule that when his collaborator was the initiator of the play, whether with an original story or novel or with a completed draft of a play or merely an outline or an idea, that person's name took precedence over his in the credits.

The changes worked by the collaborators to lure the public were only partially successful. The Broadway opening took place on September 24, exactly three weeks following that of *Be Yourself. Minick* fared better than that lackluster entertainment; its run of 141 performances compared favorably with the musical's ninety-three. But this was no glittering hit, even so. Ferber attributed the listlessness of the production to miscasting. The English-born O. P. Heggie, who played Minick, had trouble mastering the nasal, Midwestern accent required for the part, and in addition he looked too young for it. But Heggie was not alone to blame, for the play fell flat. Ferber's original story had a folksy sentimentality, and audiences had come to expect wisecracking antisentimentalism when Kaufman's name was on the program. None of the characters had warmth enough to make an audience care about his future; young Minick and old Minick might almost have been strangers to one another, so little mutual affection did they demonstrate. Moreover, the plot, as reviewers pointed out, was too thin to last the evening. Responding to this criticism, the authors told a *Tribune* interviewer that they were more interested in character than in plot. Perhaps so, but what they created was only a domestic comedy of modest proportions.[29]

To Woollcott goes the credit for introducing the Kaufmans to Harpo Marx, who was to become a lifelong friend. On May 19, 1924, an entertainment called *I'll Say She Is* opened on Broadway, featuring four young men named Leonard, Adolph, Julius, and Herbert Marx. Those were the names given them by their parents, but to their public, which existed in virtually every town that could boast of a vaudeville house, they were known as Chico, Harpo, Groucho, and Zeppo, nicknames bestowed on them by a fellow vaude-villian, Art Fisher.* For a year and a half they had been trouping in their show, but finally, after much prodding from Chico, they decided to bring it to New York. The theatergoers of the city were overjoyed.

Written by Will B. Johnstone, a cartoonist for the New York *Evening World,* and his brother Tom, *I'll Say She Is* was partly a musical comedy with a tenuous plot about a young woman seeking for ways to make her life thrilling and partly a revue that incorporated the prankish, farcical mugging and romping of the three elder brothers, with special attention given to Groucho's seemingly impromptu wisecracks, Harpo's silent cavorting and face-making and his virtuosity at the harp, and—always the most eagerly awaited event of the evening—the prancing of Chico's fingers over the piano keyboard. (Zeppo, the most conventionally handsome of the lot, but the dullest per-former, had to be content to serve as juvenile lead and straight man.) Though they were already well known and had long since made their New York de-but in vaudeville, the brothers were billed below the title when the show opened. Thereafter, they would be great stars.

From the Marx Brothers' point of view, *I'll Say She Is* was an inspired title, because under it anything was possible. But neither the brothers nor the title had what was necessary to send a *frisson* of anticipation up the spine of most reviewers on the day of the opening. Woollcott was not expecting any-thing earth-shaking when he decided to represent his paper, then the *Sun,* at the performance. Ordinarily he would have sent an underling to such an en-tertainment, and he might have done so on this occasion had he had the choice of another play to attend. But he went—and the next day he trumpeted his delight to the *Sun's* readers. In particular, it was Harpo who captured his eye and heart: "Surely there should be dancing in the streets when a great clown comic comes to town," he wrote, "and this man is a great clown." After the second performance Woollcott called on Harpo in his dressing room and took him off to a Thanatopsis session, where the comedian found himself in

---

* The program for *I'll Say She Is* listed them by their true names, except for Harpo, who was billed as Arthur Marx. In their earliest years of trouping, before the First World War, the act included a fifth brother, Gummo. But this Marx, the next-to-youngest, took no pleasure in performing and dropped out of the act. Ultimately he became a success-ful talent agent.

the company of Adams, Benchley, Broun, Swope, Ross, Connelly, and, of course, Kaufman. It was an evening to remember.[30]

Thus began the friendship of Woollcott and Harpo that lasted until Woollcott's death nineteen years later, a friendship so close and deeply cherished that they never forgot the day of its origin and frequently celebrated it with an exchange of sentimental letters. To Harpo, who felt that his life was much enriched once he was taken up by the Algonquin circle, it seemed only reasonable that he and his wife should name not one, but two of their four adopted children for Woollcott: William Woollcott Marx and Alexander Marx, the latter born after his namesake's death in 1943. As Groucho once remarked, Woollcott "was in love with Harpo in a nice way."[31] Never could Woollcott have doubted that his love was returned, "in a nice way."

Harpo was not married when he met the Kaufmans, and, like most young men, when he was introduced to Beatrice he was instantly drawn to her. Their friendship was loving and durable, but never overtly physical. Close as they became, they shied away from love-making, going no further in that direction than to indulge a mutual enjoyment of swimming in the nude. Harpo was too healthy of mind to arouse Beatrice, and from his point of view the relationship was exactly right as it was. There were plenty of girls to whom he could turn for brief affairs. For either to make of the other a casual lover would have been bad casting. Kaufman in his own way also loved Harpo, finding in him a warm, undemanding companion and a worthy opponent at the poker table or on the croquet court.

Zeppo did not often see the Kaufmans, but Chico and Groucho played minor roles in their social life. Though Chico was the one who usually set the brothers' business deals, at least in their pre-Hollywood years, he was, paradoxically, a compulsive gambler whose games frequently made him late for business sessions or for performances. Such a man could never gain Kaufman's respect, but at least Chico had one virtue: an ace bridge player, he was always available for games when Kaufman made visits (sometimes protracted) to Hollywood in the 1930s and 1940s. Kaufman once described him as "an odd combination of business acumen and financial idiocy, a man who will bet you that three Rolls-Royces will pass the next corner within three minutes. Or that they won't."[32] Groucho, the most intellectual of the four, commanded Kaufman's admiration and gave his own in return, often remarking that Kaufman was the wittiest man he had ever known,[33] and that Kaufman's literary style had served as an example to him in the development of his own. On at least two occasions Kaufman tried to persuade Groucho to appear in plays without his brothers; this was a sign of special esteem. But, finally, it must be said that Groucho did not care for Beatrice, who was too much her own woman for his taste, and for this reason more than for any other he remained—by choice—on the periphery of the Kaufmans' circle. Though Kaufman necessarily saw him repeatedly from 1925 to 1935, the span of years over which he wrote for the Marxes, it remained Harpo alone of the brothers who became a close friend.

In 1923, the year before they discovered Harpo, the Algonquin set discovered a new pleasure: the centuries-old game of croquet, which had originated in France and had been imported to American shores from England in the 1870s. None became a more avid player than Kaufman, unless it was Harpo after he joined the circle, though all became addicted to the game. Their favorite playing ground in the early 1920s was on the Swopes' property in Great Neck, next door to the home of the Lardners. But it was also possible to play in Central Park if one secured a permit, and when Dorothy Parker did so in the fall of 1923, it was an occasion for glee. Benchley christened the loose association of Central Park sportsmen the West Side Lacrosse Club, possibly hoping to find a name as memorable as the Thanatopsis. The name did not stick, but the addiction did not lose its hold on the players.[34]

No matter what they might choose to call themselves, the players turned croquet into a game that was a far cry from the genteel, backyard pastime it was to most others who took it up. Early on, at the suggestion of Neysa McMein (so her husband, John Baragwanath, was to write), the group decided against fixing a boundary to the playing field. With infinite pleasure they knocked the ball of an opponent into the woods and gullies and bodies of water hundreds of feet away. Teams were chosen with a thought to strategy rather than to power alone; experienced players who knew one another's strengths and weaknesses were carefully matched on opposing sides. Like chess champions, these mallet men and women gave thought to the alternate possibilities of play and their probable consequences, rather than muddling through shot by shot. But physical coordination was also important in their game. To make it as difficult as possible to score, they played with extra-narrow wickets. Nor would the ordinary, toy-shop variety of mallet do; they bought the best-quality imported ones from Abercrombie & Fitch.

Thus equipped, Kaufman and Beatrice, Harpo, Woollcott, Adams, Parker, Benchley, McMein, Baragwanath, the Swopes—in short, the entire Broadway-Park Row nexus—joyously swung at wooden balls in the city and on Long Island in the 1920s, and thereafter in Bucks County and Hollywood, and on Neshobe Island in Lake Bomoseen, Vermont, as well. At most games, bets were not placed, and by disallowing the exchange of money, the players only intensified their delight in outmaneuvering one another.

In good weather they often played through the entire day. One early evening in the mid-1920s when the players had spent the day in a prolonged game at the Swopes' home, it occurred to them for the first time to rebel against the dark. Someone (Harpo later claimed that it was he) got the idea of facing all the players' cars to the field and switching on their headlights, so that play could continue. Next door at Ring and Ellis Lardner's, where Marc Connelly and Dorothy Parker were dinner guests, everyone was puzzled by the movement of the cars, until in a few minutes they heard the first crack of wood on wood. Usually a blithesome mallet woman herself, Parker found this evidence of mania hard to take. "Jesus Christ, the heirs of the ages," she said.

Another playful activity of Kaufman's that started in the 1920s was his participation in the annual shows of the Dutch Treat Club. He joined the club in 1925 or 1926. The club yearbook for 1926 was the first to list him as a member, but in the book for 1925 his name appeared as the author of and an actor in a sketch called "The Still Alarm," presented in the show that year, and as an actor, with Donald Ogden Stewart, in a two-character sketch, "In Conference," by Ring Lardner. Adams, Connelly, Benchley, John Peter Toohey, Swope, Lardner, Sherwood, and Deems Taylor, of the Algonquin-Thanatopsis set, had preceded him into the club.

"The Still Alarm," later used in *The Little Show*, a revue of 1929, was a spoof of the *froideur* of English drawing-room comedies. In it the occupant of a hotel room and one of his friends, along with a bellboy and two firemen, respond with aplomb to the blaze that is engulfing the building. When one of the firemen takes a violin out of the case he has been carrying and begins to tune it, the hotel guest, Bob (played by Benchley in the club show), asks for an explanation. The other fireman (played by Kaufman) replies, "Well, you see, Sid doesn't get much chance to practice at home. Sometimes, at a fire, while we're waiting for a wall to fall or something, why, a fireman doesn't really have anything to do, and personally I like to see him improve himself symphonically. I hope you don't resent it. You're not anti-symphonic?"*

In subsequent years, Kaufman took part in four more of the annual shows. For the 1926 show he contributed and acted in a sketch called "Shop Talk," in which the social vocabulary of undertakers was shown to be virtually identical with their professional jargon. (The second role was taken by Henry

---

* In *The Little Show* Bob and the First Fireman were played by Clifton Webb and Fred Allen, respectively.

Clapp Smith, of the publishing firm of E. P. Dutton.) The next year he appeared in Ring Lardner's "Dinner and Bridge" as a waiter serving the workmen repairing the Queensboro Bridge. Since no waiter, however willing or prompt, was safe from his verbal thunderbolts, it can only have been Lardner's fine sense of irony that led to this bit of casting. In 1932 Kaufman and Connelly wrote and performed in a sketch called "Service"; in this a ticket broker (Kaufman) makes increasingly extravagant sales pitches to an exacting customer (Connelly). Finally they settle on a performance at the customer's home combining features of George Kelly's *The Show-Off* and Jerome Kern's *Sally,* with Ed Wynn, Alfred Lunt, the Marx Brothers, and the Warner Brothers. For the 1933 show the two old friends wrote and acted in "Or What Have You?," in which a medic (Kaufman) probes into the ailments of a patient (Connelly). In view of the ever-quickening rhythm of his processional activity, with its incessant obligations to producers, publishers, and collaborators, one can only assume that Kaufman enjoyed the opportunity to get up on a stage and draw laughter and applause from his fellow Dutch Treaters. But in 1936 he left the club, perhaps because the press of work made attendance at the lunches impossible, or perhaps because he feared that in the high-spirited, uninhibited atmosphere of the Dutch Treat he would be questioned too closely about a scandal that had recently erupted in his private life.

—6—

Anne

In 1925, perhaps before, as George and Beatrice Kaufman considered the breadth and fullness of the life that the Broadway successes had made possible for them, they were sharply aware of one central lack. Both were sensible enough to realize that the responsibility of parenthood would inevitably alter their social arrangements—would cause them to give up some of the hours they committed daily to the whirl and bustle of literary and theatrical Manhattan—but at the same time they felt that a child would complete the structure of domesticity, unusual but utterly satisfactory to them, that they had built up over the years of their marriage.

Some, though not many, of their community of friends stood as examples to them of the contentment that could be achieved through parenthood. Broun and Ruth Hale, for example, had a son, Heywood Hale Broun, who was such a delight that Frank Adams filled paragraphs of his columns with accounts of visits with the boy. (Adams himself was childless in 1925, but wished for children and would soon have them.) Dorothy Michaels Nathan, still Beatrice's closest friend, had a daughter. Not intimates precisely, but no strangers to the Kaufmans, were the Lardners, who had four engaging boys in whom were combined a love of sports and a promising appetite for literature. Among the childless were Harpo, who remained single until 1936, and Woollcott. Ferber was and would continue to be wedded only to her desk, or as mean-spirited acquaintances said, to her bank account. Connelly had not yet married, and his marriage in 1930 to the former Madeline Shurlock would be childless. Harold Ross and Jane Grant had chosen to have no children. None of these men and women appeared tortured, but it was true that they were all somewhat special cases. Unlike the Kaufmans, they felt themselves to be better off as they were.

If the Kaufmans were to have a child, it was obvious that they would have to adopt one. That would have been true even if Beatrice had been able to conceive. They decided that they would look for a baby girl and made an inquiry at the Louise Wise Adoption Services, an adjunct of the Stephen Wise Free Synagogue, on West 68th Street.

The staff of the Wise Services, then a very small agency, was aware that the Kaufmans retained their identity as Jews for social reasons only and that they never attended religious services, not even on the High Holy Days of Rosh Hashanah and Yom Kippur, when among most Jews religious observance is deemed obligatory. Mrs. Wise herself interviewed them, and in the agency's printed form under the question as to the child's prospect of receiving religious training she wrote "Hopeless." But in the Kaufmans' favor as adoptive parents was the fact that they could afford to give a child a good home and that they were an intelligent, self-possessed pair. In the early fall of 1925 the agency notified them that a baby girl, born on June 23, awaited them. They were told nothing whatever of the child's parents—not their names, their ages, their occupations, or whether they had conceived the child in wedlock or out of it.

The couple's choice of a girl was understandable in view of the memory of their past disappointment. But one suspects that more positive emotions governed the choice. Beatrice, it seems reasonably clear, liked, or thought she liked, the very idea of having a daughter beside her who would grow up to be more than a daughter, to be, in fact, a friend. One further suspects that the child was to be an extension of her personality, a little girl of such manners, taste, and learning as to be a credit to her, an adornment to her already imposing presence. It also seems likely (to heap speculation upon speculation) that Kaufman equally relished the prospect of having a daughter, for, despite his memberships in all-male clubs, he thoroughly delighted in female society.

The Kaufmans named their daughter Anne. They prepared for her arrival by increasing the size of their living quarters at 200 West 58th. Since the apartment next to theirs was vacant, they rented it to accommodate the child, perhaps overestimating the spatial requirements of a three-month-old infant. To occupy the apartment with their daughter they engaged a nurse. This nurse was replaced after a year by another who spoke German and whom Anne quickly learned to love. That from the first the child seemed happy and responsive was noted by Frank Adams, who in his Pepysian persona reported on December 12 that she was "as sweet a child of five months of age as ever I saw, and ever in merry mood and laughing, as unlike George as well might be."[1] At not quite thirty-six and thirty-one, respectively, the Kaufmans were hardly too old to undertake this new responsibility, but perhaps they were too used to the old pattern of their life together to adjust easily to the change. It was not only physical distance, but emotional distance that they put between themselves and their child. However, they were not always alike in their responses to the child's emotional and developmental needs. Oddly enough, Kaufman, renowned for shunning demands on his feelings, was the one to whom the actual presence of the child in the household was especially welcome. True, he could absent himself to his study or the *Times* building without prolonged explanation if he did not want to play with his daughter; he needed only to declare that the new script or the paper's drama section was calling for his attention. But he imparted to his daughter the sense that he loved her, and imparted it more firmly than Beatrice ever succeeded in doing. In his view, Anne *was* his child; he took offense at the occasional references to her in the press that described her as his "adopted" daughter. His nickname for her was "Poky," and though this stood for "slowpoke" and revealed an occasional mild exasperation with her for not hurrying to finish her food or prepare herself for bed, it became a term of endearment.

For Beatrice, the effort at creating an ambiance of affection was more difficult. Beatrice was no failure as a mother, but her showing was poor. One guesses that she took the responsibility more seriously than her husband and developed a sense of guilt over the absences from the child caused by the demands of her social and professional life—and perhaps by her love life as well. In effect, she had acquired a pet for herself, and its requirements in the way of care and training were a bit more than she had bargained for. If originally she thought that she wanted the child close to her as a friend, she soon came to realize that emotional intimacy could not develop between them unless they were often together, but that kind of closeness, the closeness of doing things and going places together, she seldom could manage. Beatrice was happier if the child's nurse also went along. In addition to the nurse, a cook, a butler, and a chauffeur were also on hand to help relieve the strain of motherhood; their combined presence reinforced the barrier between mother and daughter, and it grew higher as the years passed.

With a look ahead—not far, but to the end of Anne's first decade—one can see how curiously mixed was the record of the Kaufmans as parents. They were remarkably successful in the task of informing the child painlessly that they were not her actual parents. Though, like most adopted children, she amused herself with fantasies as to the identity of the two persons who had brought her into the world, at heart she was not nagged by worry over the question, and accepted without conscious concern the fact that George and Beatrice Kaufman were the only persons in her life whom she could think of as her parents. At first, she imagined the typical adoption agency to be a kind of kennel where two married adults could go to choose a child and lift it out of its cage or cubicle, but, forbidding or pathetic as this may sound, it was not disturbing to her. When, as inevitably happened, she became conscious of the fact of her father's fame and professional stature, as well as the difference between wealth and poverty, she realized how fortunate it was that she had been the child lifted out of the agency by him and Beatrice. Kaufman, worried that at some future date she might run afoul of anti-Semitism, took care to explain the existence of that evil to her in a tactful, nontraumatizing manner, though, fulfilling the prophecy of the Wise Services, he made no effort to instruct her in religion or to see that she got such instruction elsewhere. Unlike her parents, Anne was never sent to religious school, nor was she confirmed.

As they watched their daughter learn to walk and talk, the Kaufmans attended to her development as a social being, though in this it must have been Beatrice who was the more effective of the two. Virtually every adult whom Anne met in her childhood was a celebrity or on the way to becoming one, and most were celebrated for their wit. Anne, exposed to such persons as soon as she entered the family, was soon able to meet them on their own ground, and to delight them. Adams reported a moment in the spring of 1929, when the child was less than four years old, that illustrates the ease with which she conducted herself. Having stayed overnight in the Kaufmans' apartment, Adams got up to have breakfast. Anne, probably the only member of the family who had gotten out of bed, raced along to the kitchen in front of him and said to the cook, "That man is here again. Isn't that nice?"[2] Marc Connelly remembered an encounter with her in the summer of that same year at Sands Point, Long Island, where the Kaufmans had taken a house. Being driven along a country road, he saw Anne walking along with her nurse and invited them into his car. As she settled herself beside him, he looked at her arms and remarked that they were very brown from the sun. "Not *too* brown?" she asked in mock alarm.[3]

But the Kaufmans could make mistakes with their child, and usually, it would seem, out of a curious inability to perceive the depth of her feeling. At a very early age Anne once became so irritated with her mother that she flushed Beatrice's wedding ring down a toilet, thinking that no ring would mean no marriage. (Beatrice was unable to retrieve it; but as it happened, she had long since ceased to wear it.) The most serious upset occurred in the summer of 1934. The Kaufmans had long since given up the apartment on West 58th Street and were living in a house at 14 East 94th Street. Anne, then nine, had been a student at private schools in the city—the first two years at the Walden School and the third at the Lincoln School—but still had the German nurse, Friedl Schulein, to look after her when Beatrice was otherwise engaged. The child was devoted to her and was with her constantly. But one summer afternoon in 1934, not Friedl, but Beatrice herself took Anne to the movies, and on returning home, Anne raced up the stairs, as she usually did at such times, to see the nurse. This time, however, Friedl was not to be found, and Anne was told by her mother that she would not be coming back. The shock to the child was intense, all the more so because no explanation of the dismissal was ever given. In unconsolable grief, she withdrew into herself and refused to speak to Beatrice, on whom, whether rightly or wrongly, she placed the blame. From that time on, she believed that she must be wary of Beatrice, never feeling certain that she could judge her mother's temperament correctly.

Later in life Anne realized that in dismissing Friedl her parents had acted out of anxiety over the rise of Hitler. Anne had learned to speak German well, and sometimes, under the pervasive influence of the nurse, spoke English with a noticeable trace of a German accent. Such a state of affairs could only have been regarded as intolerable by the Kaufmans, in view of the situation abroad. At this time, and for the ten years previous, the household staff also included a German-speaking cook. Unlike the luckless Friedl, she was retained, and would remain with the family until the outbreak of the Second World War, when, after employing her for some twenty years, the Kaufmans thought that it would be prudent to let her go.

It need hardly be said that no decision of Beatrice's to tend to her child herself had prompted the dismissal of the nurse. Two days after that event, a French-speaking governess, a "mademoiselle" named Jeanne Velay, arrived at the house. She had been engaged some time before, and the forty-eight-hour interval was presumably intended to provide a cooling-off period for Anne. No sooner did Mlle. Velay arrive than she, the child, and the parents got into the family car and were driven to Katonah, in Westchester County, where the Kaufmans, along with Alexander Woollcott and S. N. Behrman, had rented a house.

So acute was her grief and so much at a loss was she that Anne felt as though her life was without direction or purpose. She found it impossible to speak to anyone and during the first two meals looked mutely at the food on her plate without tasting it. At first Beatrice was not the sole enemy; Mlle, Velay, the usurper, also belonged in that category. But in the silence of the third evening a plan came into Anne's head. Beatrice did not know French. What if Anne made a friend of the governess and learned it from her? Then the two could converse without Beatrice's understanding—might even converse *about* Beatrice. Later, Mlle. Velay was to tell Anne—then "Chou" to her "Fleur"—that she had never known a child to learn the language so quickly.

——7——

Hit after Hit

After collaborating with Connelly on seven productions and with Ferber on one, Kaufman surprised Broadway by composing a comedy entirely on his own, the first full evening's entertainment that he had attempted without a coauthor since the unproduced *Going Up*. On this occasion he set his plot in territory so familiar to him that he was willing to risk going it alone. His subject was the making of a Broadway production.[1]

As a drama-desk man with ten years' experience behind him, Kaufman knew every type of producer in New York and had no difficulty distinguishing between those, on the one hand, whose critical judgment was sound and whose press releases were honest and those, on the other, who lacked taste and distributed handouts about casting plans that were not much more than hyperbolic expressions of wishful thinking. As a playwright he had had experience of four managements, of which only one, the LeMaire-Jessel office, could be described as demonstrating a basic indifference to honesty, as Jessel was cheerfully to admit in his memoirs. A rumor floated about that the methods of this management had put the notion into Kaufman's head of writing the play.[2] Though there was doubtless some truth in this, he had in mind a number of Broadway veterans, some more honest and some less so than that pair. Some producers had very little literary discrimination, no solid backing, no scruples about plagiarism, and a perfect willingness to cut all budgetary corners in order to ring up the curtain on some kind of show. Drawing on his accumulated knowledge of show business and its entrepreneurs, Kaufman wrote with a sure touch. When he was finished, he gave the play, *The Butter and Egg Man,* to Crosby Gaige, a respected producer who frequently socialized with the Round Table–Thanatopsis set. After thirteen years with the long-established firm of Arch and Edgar Selwyn, Gaige had only recently set up an independent office. Kaufman's play was the second that the office mounted.

The title of the comedy was a phrase familiar to those New Yorkers who haunted the speakeasies and read the tabloids. It had been invented, or at least popularized, by Texas Guinan, the rowdy night-club operator who was fast making a name for herself as one of the city's most successful defiers of the Eighteenth Amendment and the Volstead Act. It was she who gave the period two of its favorite catch phrases, the salutation "Hello, suckers," which she used when greeting her patrons, and the command, "Let's give this little lady a great, big hand," which she shouted at them when introducing a new entertainer. She gave it yet another one evening when she introduced an open-handed but unknown spender, who insisted on setting them up for the house, as a "big butter and egg man from the West." Probably (reports vary) he was just that, a dairy farmer, and so informed Texas Guinan; but by 1925 the phrase had begun to attach itself to any out-of-towner with a bankroll and a willingness to toss it to the winds. Kaufman borrowed it to designate a very young man, Peter Jones, from Chillicothe, Ohio, who comes to New York with $20,000, representing almost all his resources, to invest in a play in the hope of making a sufficient return to buy a hotel in his home town. The choice of Chillicothe was not lacking in special meaning; it was there, in 1867, that George C. Tyler was born.

As to generalities of plot, *The Butter and Egg Man* bears a close resemblance to the first four Kaufman-Connelly hits. Like *To the Ladies, Merton of the Movies,* and *Beggar on Horseback,* it exhibits as its protagonist a polite, willing, but far from brilliant young man who is aided toward his goal in life by a young woman who is quicker than he and maternal enough to love him for his helplessness and innocence. It shares with those plays, and also with *Dulcy,* a second-act calamity that in real life might be expected to do permanent damage to the young man's career, but one he is able to surmount—with the young woman's help. The pattern, it would seem, was too good a thing to be tampered with. In Kaufman's plot for this comedy, Peter does buy into a play, *Her Lesson,* but it is a very poor one. When its shoestring producers, Joe Lehman and Jack McClure, decide to close it down in Syracuse after the first performance, Peter, having learned something about fast talk from Joe and Mac, persuades a none-too-bright assistant hotel manager, Oscar Fritchie, to buy a share. With this supply of cash he is able to pay off the original producers, keep the show on the road to improve it, and then bring it in to New York, where—utterly improbably, one must say—it turns into a hit. But trouble occurs in the third act: a lawyer turns up on the day after the opening with a claim that one of his clients had once written a magazine story which the play resembles in one hundred and forty-six details. If Peter does not turn over two-thirds of the profits, the lawyer will have the production closed. Peter, now not so slow as he once was, sells the production back to Joe and Mac, who know nothing of what they are getting into, for $100,000, and with that money he and Fritchie can buy the hotel in Chillicothe. Meanwhile, of course, Jane Weston, the attractive stenographer of Lehmac Productions, has been on hand to encourage Peter at every turn. She too will go to Chillicothe, as Mrs. Peter Jones.

What turned this play into a hit of 243 Broadway performances and a popular road attraction was the smart snap of its comic lines, most of which Kaufman distributed between Joe Lehman and his wife Fanny, a caustic, knowing kind of "dame" such as he and Connelly had introduced in *To the Ladies* as the stenographer Miss Fletcher and in *Merton* as the casting director. The role of Fanny is longer and better than those earlier parts. An ex-vaudevillian once known as Fanita the juggler, she is the one in the family with money, somehow saved from her years in the business when Joe, formerly an agent, handled her bookings.

Along with her money, Fanny has the good sense not to put it into Joe's play, having had a glance at the overweight, superannuated ingenue cast in the leading role. Fanny's habitual tone and its contribution to the play are made manifest on her first entrance as she exclaims, "I just been taking a peep at that trick troupe of yours. . . . I caught that bit where the leading lady was supposed to be sixteen or something, climbing up apple trees. The stuff to make them trees out of is reinforced concrete." In five seconds this develops into an exchange between her and Joe:

> LEHMAN . . . You wouldn't 'a' had a sou if I hadn't dug you out of that Texas honky-tonk an' steered you onto Broadway! I put you in regular vaudeville, that's what I done for you!
>
> FANNY Well, you got yours, didn't you? All the acts is on to agents like you. Twenty-per-cent Joe.
>
> LEHMAN (*With incredible scorn.*) Fanita, the world's greatest juggler! Hah! If it wasn't for me you'd be keeping four clubs in the air right now for some Gus Sun that nobody ever heard of!
>
> FANNY Don't you go four-clubbing me! I done six clubs for the wow at the finish, and done it for years!

LEHMAN Aaah! There ain't a stage between here and California ain't got
dents in it from them clubs of yours! They wouldn't let nobody sit in
the first five rows! Fanita!
FANNY Yes, Fanita! And I'm as good today as I ever was.
LEHMAN Just about!

To amuse those in the audience who were theater addicts, Kaufman
dropped into the dialogue the names of producers William A. Brady and Sam
H. Harris, as well as the titles of several recent successes. *Within the Law,*
the name of a popular melodrama by Bernard Veiller, is suggested by Peter
as a substitute title for *Her Lesson,* and *Her Lesson* itself turns out to be
a mixture of elements from many familiar plays, including *Abie's Irish Rose,
Rain, The Shanghai Gesture,* and *Within the Law* as well. The last two
plays were among those produced by Al H. Woods, who also gave Broadway
Getting Gertie's Garter, Up in Mable's Room, and *Parlor, Bedroom, and
Bath.* Tastless, roguish, but also likable, Woods was one of many colorful
producers of the day. Kaufman came to know Woods not only through his
duties as *Times* drama editor, but because Beatrice worked for him briefly as
a reader of new plays. To round out Joe Lehman's character, Kaufman gave
him Woods's practice of addressing everyone, regardless of sex and age, as
"Sweetheart." This was as habitual with him as addressing everyone as "Kid"
was with George M. Cohan. Both appelatives were, like Texas Guinan's
stock phrases, parts of the Broadway myth.

Possibly less familiar to the audience was the material that Kaufman offered in the second act: a conference called by the producers to see what, if
anything, can be done to save the play. As (one assumes) had happened with
his own plays since the first of them, *Someone in the House,* into a hotel
room walks everyone connected with the play, and some who are not, soon
after the curtain falls on the last act. Fanny, having expected disaster from
the start, and having said so, is gloating and at peace with the world. Lehman
and McClure, desperate for suggestions, invite the opinion of even the hotel
switchboard operator, a girl named Kitty who tells them portentously, "You
see, the people here are funny, sort of. If they like a show, they'll go to see it,
but if they don't like it—they won't." To this Joe replies, "That's a hot lot of
news." Fanny of course has a contribution: "Are you going to put anything
in that five-minute spot where Martin [the star] couldn't think of the next
line? . . . Because if she's going to wait like that every night I figure it'd be
a great place for a specialty. I could come on with the clubs—"

If not a great show, *The Butter and Egg Man* was a good one that attracted
not only the Broadway audience, which might be expected to recognize the

titles and proper names that Kaufman threaded through the play, but the road audience as well. Gaige opened the play for a three-day run in Stamford, Connecticut, on June 11, took it to Washington, D.C., for a week, and then closed it down for the summer. The Broadway opening took place on September 23. The reviews were generally excellent, though some reviewers wondered whether a play of such "inside" material could prosper.

Gaige gave the play a first-class production, but had some difficulty in finding a director for it. He persuaded Kaufman himself to try, for the first time, to direct, but after a few rehearsal sessions it was clear that someone would have to take over for him. According to Gaige, Kaufman "was so diffident that the work made him self-conscious."[3] He was not yet ready to exercise the strength of his personality on stage with a crowd of seasoned professionals. In his place Gaige hired James Gleason, who had played the role of James Parks Leland in *The Deep, Tangled Wildwood*. Earlier in 1925 he had achieved a resounding success with a wisecracking farce entitled *Is Zat So?*, which he wrote with Richard Taber and in which he played the leading role of a lightweight boxer's manager who becomes a Fifth Avenue butler, taking along the fighter as his assistant. This play was still running when *The Butter and Egg Man* opened. As it had happened, Kaufman himself had reviewed it for the *Times;* though his notice had not harmed the play's chances, it had been something less than a rave, offering praise for the acting but finding fault with the construction, the central situation of the plot, and the dialogue.* Denman Maley, who had played Leland's pal Harvey Wallick in *Wildwood,* was cast in a small but well-written comic role. Gleason's wife, Lucille Webster, remembered for her delineation of the casting director in *Merton,* played Fanny. The best-known actor in the cast was Gregory Kelly, who played Peter Jones. Though as Gordon Smith in *Dulcy* he had been criticized for overacting, he was praised for being restrained in his delineation of Peter.†

On the opening night, the only non-laugher in the house was, as usual, Kaufman. Charlie Chaplin, as the reviewers pointed out, was present (as Woollcott's guest) and had a very fine time, as did the many other show-business figures in the audience. But Kaufman, according to Woollcott in his column "Second Judgments on First Nights" in the *World,* for October 15, "maddened his neighbors" in the audience by getting up to pace, and, after

---

* The review was unsigned, but it is attributed to Kaufman in the Samuel French acting edition.

† On the road he repeated his success, but in 1927, while playing in Pittsburgh, Kelly suffered a heart attack. He was moved to New York to be near his wife, Ruth Gordon, who was then appearing in Maxwell Anderson's *Saturday's Children,* and on July 9 he died.

the fall of the curtain on the last act, notified the company, whose ears still rang with the sound of applause and laughter, that the play was a failure.

London also liked the play when it opened there in 1927.* It was the first of Kaufman's plays to appear in translation when, in April, 1927, it was published as *Le Gentleman de l'Ohio* in *Petite Illustration* as an item in that magazine's theater series. The introduction by Louis Thomas, the editor of the magazine, offered only a backhanded compliment, however, for Thomas intimated that he chose the play only after first considering Anne Nichols's *Abie's Irish Rose, What Price Glory?*, the plays of O'Neill, and those of Clare Kummer.

It so happened that Connelly also readied a comedy, *The Wisdom Tooth*, for the 1925-26 season. The play opened on February 5, 1926. Its content and tone, when compared to those of *The Butter and Egg Man*, enabled critics and audiences to draw some conclusions as to which member of the team had contributed what to their collaborations.

A frankly sentimental piece, *The Wisdom Tooth* invites sympathy for the plight of a young man named Charley Bemis, a senior clerk in a Manhattan business office who lacks the courage to speak back to anyone who attempts to browbeat him, and whose only virtues are thrift and good manners. He lives in a rooming house on the Upper West Side and is attracted to Sally Field, a young newspaperwoman who also lives there, but he has the devil of a time letting her know that he cares for her. In a prologue, he and other clerks in the office discuss with concern the firing of a young stenographer for no better reason than that she refused to give in to the boss's advances. Charley would like to speak up to the boss, but cannot do so. At the dentist's office, where he goes to have a troublesome wisdom tooth seen to, he is so intimidated by another patient who twits him for looking into a book of fairy tales in the waiting room that he gets up and leaves, his tooth still untreated. Later at the rooming house another lodger forces him, against his better judgment, to express admiration for Calvin Coolidge. In dreams that comprise Act II and most of Act III he sees the ghosts of his grandparents, who raised him, and hears of their dismay on finding him now so timorous, when they had thought that he would grow up to be President. He also sees himself as the courageous little boy he was, who was not afraid to say that he believed in fairies. With that he wakes up, telephones his boss to reprimand him for firing the stenographer, and is promptly fired himself. But no one need worry. He will manage nicely, for not only is he a new man, but Sally, impressed by

---

* Tom Douglas, the American actor who had made a hash of *Merton* in London, took the lead in this production and acted it without mishap.

the change in him, is standing by, and furthermore he has almost $9000 in the bank.

Quite obviously, much of this plot corresponds with those of the Kaufman-Connelly plays—for example, the sour view of big business, with its hypocritical top-level executives, and the comic treatment of the innocent male who requires the moral support of an experienced young woman. The long, central dream sequence takes the play very close to *Begger on Horseback*, in particular; one reviewer, the *Sun's* Gilbert W. Gabriel, described it as a sequel to that success. But Connelly, after all, was not the world's first playwright to repeat himself. What apparently he could not do was to repeat the tart humor of the earlier plays. *The Wisdom Tooth* is drenched with bland, smiling sunniness, but lacks the crackling wit that a Broadway audience had come to expect from a Kaufman-Connelly play. Woollcott, who admired the play (not at all surprisingly), remarked in his review that at the opening night he heard the muted crying of Neysa McMein and Rebecca West. Those worldly women were not the only persons who enjoyed it. The comedy ran for 139 performances—not a bad run, though the Little Theater where it played was truly little.

On December 8, 1925, only a little more than three months after the opening of *The Butter and Egg Man*, Kaufman's second opening of the season took place. This was just as excruciating an event for him as the first, but in the end somewhat more rewarding. The new work, called *The Cocoanuts*, was a musical with songs by Irving Berlin, and the Marx Brothers, Kaufman's new friends, as the stars. So much of a hit did the Marxes make of this vehicle that they were able to keep it on Broadway into the summer of 1926, to tour with it for two lucrative years, and, playing it in front of movie cameras, to make a most auspicious screen debut in it in 1929. This same work added something new to Kaufman's reputation; once it opened, he was considered to be a peerless expert on the brothers' talent and the sort of material to set it off to best advantage.

To place the Marx Brothers in a musical with a book by Kaufman and songs by Berlin was the idea of Sam H. Harris, a producer of spotless reputation, the polar opposite of the type represented by Joe Lehman. For fifteen years, beginning in 1904, he had been the partner of George M. Cohan, and was still very close to him; the wives of the two men were sisters. Cohan and Harris dissolved their partnership in 1919, when, at the time of the actors' strike leading to the establishment and recognition of Actors' Equity, Cohan, unlike Harris, refused as a producer to acknowledge the union or as an actor to join it. Soon after this break-up, Harris became associated with Berlin in the building and management of the Music Box Theater, where each year from 1921 to 1924 they offered the intimate and highly successful *Music Box Revues,* each with a cascade of newly written Berlin melodies.

The producing, composing, and writing talent assembled for *The Cocoa-nuts* put into the shade the crowd responsible for *I'll Say She Is.* The Marxes had made it to the big time. According to Harpo, the brothers had for a long while had their hearts set on capturing Harris as producer of whatever was to be their second show. Florenz Ziegfeld, Charles Dillingham, and the Shuberts all made offers, but not Harris. It was through Berlin, whom they all knew well, that the Marxes got word to Harris that they would like to appear under his banner. This, as Harpo recalled, resulted in an invitation from Harris to the brothers to perform some of their routines for him in his office. After seeing them, Harris said that he would be in touch. In Syracuse, where they were trouping in *I'll Say She Is,* which was still a road attraction after its Broadway run, Harris telephoned to say that he was sending up a blackout writer to meet them and rough out some sketches for a new revue. This was not at all what the brothers had hoped for, and when the writer appeared they insisted that he wrestle with them and teased him so mercilessly that he departed at once.[4]

Securing Kaufman as book writer for the Marxes was not a matter of merely placing a telephone call to him. As Harris soon learned, he was not wholly taken with the idea of writing for the Marxes, despite the fact that he liked them personally. The troublesome element was the brothers' unpredictability on stage; when it suited them to do so, they would ignore the material provided by their writers and proceed on their own, though keeping within the framework of the original. If not vain, Kaufman nevertheless did not relish the prospect of having his lines being cut or altered. Nevertheless, he accepted, perhaps with assurances from Harris that the brothers would be kept in control. He went to work once *The Butter and Egg Man* had opened, settling into a suite in Atlantic City with Berlin.

Though at first Kaufman intended to write the book entirely on his own, and in the end took sole credit for it, he decided to call in a young acquaintance to help him with it. This was no secret. Kaufman widely acknowledged that he received help on the project from Morrie Ryskind, whom he had known since the teens of the century, when both were contributors to Adams's column. While at work on the book, Kaufman happened on Ryskind on the street and simply asked him whether he would like to take part. Ryskind, who was then making a living as a journalist with comic verse as his specialty, was delighted by the invitation.[5]

For *The Cocoanuts* Kaufman invented the slimmest of plots. There was no need to worry—the brothers would flesh it out with their own special kind of fooling around. Groucho (referred to in the script as Julius, his real name) played Henry W. Schlemmer, the proprietor of a run-down hotel, the Cocoanuts, in Cocoanut Beach, Florida. The Florida land boom supplied the background for as much as there was of a plot. Harpo, his familiar curls topped by a battered hat, and wearing his coat with the trick sleeves capable of holding pieces of silverware by the dozen, played Silent Sam, a guest at the hotel. Chico, also in familiar character, played, one regrets to note, Willie the Wop, another guest. Since these three Marxes by now had established their characterizations with the public, it was only necessary to give each of them sufficient opportunity to do what was expected, which included, of course, a session at the harp for Harpo and one at the piano for Chico. It was also necessary to find something, though precisely what did not matter very much, for Zeppo. Kaufman turned him into a desk clerk at the hotel; this role was the smallest that he ever performed in the major vehicles of his brothers.

Since a musical could not exist without a romance, Kaufman thought one up between Polly Potter, the attractive daughter of a grande dame known only as Mrs. Potter, and Bob Adams, another hotel clerk, who aspires to become an architect. To Mrs. Potter, no matter what Bob wishes to be, he is just a clerk. Says she, "One who clerks is a clerk, Polly." Mrs. Potter would prefer her daughter to marry Harvey Yates, whom she takes to be of good family. But he is in fact a larcenist, and with Penelope Martin, an old flame of his, he steals Mrs. Potter's necklace. Though Bob is framed for the theft, Harpo and Chico establish the identity of the real thieves by revealing a map in Yates's hand showing where the necklace is hidden. Bob is then free to marry Polly. And somehow, to tie up loose ends, Schlemmer makes a conquest of Mrs. Potter.

To play that role, Harris was inspired to cast Margaret Dumont, a little-known actress in early middle age. It was her first appearance with the Marx Brothers. She would act in one more Broadway show and eight films with them. As a result, she would become an essential part of the team, as Zeppo, who withdrew from it in 1933, never was.

Having seen their performance in *I'll Say She Is*, Kaufman knew enough about the Marxes to realize that their antic physicality and Groucho and Chico's characteristic word play would make up most of the show. Heavy plotting would simply get in the way of what the audience would come to see. Along with the two scenes between the lecherous Groucho and the dignified Dumont, the highlights were a farcical bedroom scene in Act I showing the theft of the necklace and a scene in Act II showing a detective inquiring about the missing jewels. The former involved so much popping in and out of closets and under beds that Groucho was impelled to remark, "This is like working for Al H. Woods." The Act II scene was staged as a minstrel show. When in reply to questions from the detective Mrs. Potter said, "Yes, sir," an end man would chime in with "That's my baby." Naturally, her next answer was "No, sir," prompting the end man to come in with "Don't mean maybe." This led to much business with tambourines, and the cast broke into a Berlin number called "Minstrel Days."

But as shrewdly and firmly based on an understanding of the brothers' performing strengths as it is, the book of *The Cocoanuts* is not merely a scenario. At the opening, many reviewers assumed that Groucho ad-libbed throughout the evening, so casual was his delivery of the lines. Among the bits of dialogue that they cited were his observation that the Florida land boom was "the greatest development since Sophie Tucker," his compliment to Dumont that her eyes shone "like the pants of a blue serge suit," and his soothing reply to an irate hotel guest complaining of a leaky ceiling that he would send up some ceiling wax. Without the Marxian nasal delivery and the jiggling eyebrows, these lines have little comic sheen; but no matter how they may read, they were all written by Kaufman, possibly with Ryskind's help, and were in the script. The writers recognized Groucho's skill in delivering memorized material as though it had just sprung to his mind, and they spent long hours of the day, sometimes from ten in the morning to eleven in the evening, inventing "ad libs" for him.[6] It was Kaufman's *Times* colleague Herman Mankiewicz, wearing his second hat as *New Yorker* drama reviewer, who had the most sensible comment to make on this:

> Because we stuck around the rehearsals of the play . . . we can clear up a mystery that has been bothering a number of the newspaper critics. These honest fellows, it seems, expressed their doubts the morning after the opening whether most of the comedy in the show was by George S. Kaufman, officially the author, or by Groucho Marx, so naturally and easily were the nifties delivered by Groucho. Well, they can take our word for it that Groucho is the author. Furthermore, we are a bit annoyed at their denseness. Else how could they have failed to guess, so naturally and easily are the songs sung by Mabel Withee and Jack Barker and Janet Velie and Frances Williams, that Miss Withee, Mr. Barker, Miss Velie, and Miss Williams composed the score?[7]

The truth was that the brothers in 1925 were somewhat in awe of Kaufman, as well as of Harris. Both at that time were much better known than the Marxes; to appear in a piece written by one and produced by the other represented the single biggest stride forward of their careers, and they knew it. Though undoubtedly they interpolated new business and dialogue into the show as the Broadway run progressed, and especially in its subsequent two years on the road, they were careful in the tryout weeks and the early months of the run to stay within the script. A scene had occurred in Boston to make it clear to them that they were expected to respect the production. Kaufman, the thorough professional, was capable of exploding in the presence of anyone lacking regard for correct professional conduct, and when, at a ten-o'clock rehearsal in Boston, the Marxes appeared late, one such explosion occurred. He threatened to leave the production on the spot, but was persuaded to remain with it by Ryskind, who had no immediate prospect of other work.[8]

Another problem of the sort from which the production suffered was the temporary decline of Irving Berlin's gift as a composer. *The Cocoanuts* proved to be his only musical, for either Broadway or Hollywood, up to his last, *Mr. President*, produced in 1962, that did not yield a single hit song. The score included Charleston and tango numbers in response to current rages, some love songs, and a patter song called "Five O'Clock Tea" that Groucho especially enjoyed,[9] but nothing that would join the already lengthening list of Berlin "classics." "Florida by the Sea," celebrating the charms of the state where the action took place, unfortunately was not a patch on "An Orange Grove in California" from the *Music Box Revue of 1923*. In this matter, Kaufman was no help to Berlin, for he airily refused the fine though low-key "Always" when Berlin offered it to him. Thirty-five years later he wrote about the time when he and Berlin were sequestered in Atlantic City to write the show. In the middle of one night Berlin came into Kaufman's room, woke him up, sat on his bed, and sang a new number he had just composed. This was to be the show's big, romantic ballad, and its title, though seemingly inevitable, had never before been used for a popular tune. "The song was the little number called 'Always,'" Kaufman wrote, "and its easygoing rhythms were just up my street. I learned it quickly, and as dawn broke we leaned out the window and sang it to the Atlantic Ocean—its first performance in any hotel. It was destined to be sung millions of times after that, and invariably better."

> That task done [he continued], we then talked about it. At the time, I was woefully ignorant of music, and by dint of hard work over the years

I have managed to keep myself in the same innocent state. To this day I do not quite know the difference between Handel's "Largo" and—well, Largo's "Handel." But I have always felt that I knew a little something about lyrics, and I was presumptuous enough then to question Irving's first line, "I'll be loving you, always." "Always," I pointed out, was a long time for romance. There were almost daily stories to that effect in the newspapers—stories about middle-aged husbands who had bricked their wives up in the cellar wall and left for Toledo with the maid. I suggested, therefore, that the opening line be just a little more in accord with reality—something like "I'll be loving you Thursday."[10]

Not content to spend 1925 on only this show and *The Butter and Egg Man*, Kaufman also worked on a comedy called *The Good Fellow*, in collaboration with Herman Mankiewicz. The writing of this play took place in the summer months, before the opening of *The Butter and Egg Man* and before the onset of pressures on Kaufman to begin writing the Marxes' musical. Working with Mank was always a mixed blessing, not only to Kaufman, who had affection for him, but to all his other associates of the 1920s and after, up to his death in 1953. What was good about it was Mank's dry wit, which he often loosed at his own expense. What was bad about it was his compulsive drinking, which quickened the self-destructive impulses in his nature that were evident even when he was sober. But Kaufman was willing to take a chance. The disastrous *School for Scandal* affair had not yet taken place, but even when it did, it failed to destroy Kaufman's regard for Mank. It is possible, even probable, that Mank had contributed some lines to *The Butter and Egg Man* earlier in the year, though Kaufman's name alone was attached to it, for in the office when not writing reviews they would sometimes compose lines of dialogue together.[11] Yet another work of theirs in 1925 was a two-character sketch called "Nothing Coming In," about a shadily operated pawnshop. (A sign prominently displayed in the shop reads "Particularly High Loans on Anything from the Metropolitan Museum.") By the time *The Good Fellow* reached Broadway, Mank had left both the paper and the city to take up his new career at Paramount Pictures.

Crosby Gaige, having enjoyed good fortune with *The Butter and Egg Man*, also snapped up *The Good Fellow*. Again he asked Kaufman to direct, and again Kaufman agreed, only to withdraw before the production was ready. When the play was first unveiled, on June 21, 1926, in Long Branch, New Jersey, then a popular beach resort, his name was on the program as director. But after the next stop, Mamaroneck, New York, Kaufman handed control of rehearsals over to Howard Lindsay. It was obvious at that time that the play was weak and in need of repairs in both the writing and the direction. Kaufman set himself the task of revising the script before the re-opening at Atlantic City on September 20, but he would not trust himself to continue as director.

In Atlantic City and later in New York, where the play opened on October 5, it was clear that virtually everything about *The Good Fellow* was wrong. The leading role, that of a "joiner" who rejoices in his leadership of the Knights of Corsica in Wilkes-Barre, Pennsylvania, was taken by John E. Hazzard, an actor primarily known for his musical-comedy performances and also a playwright who, with Winchell Smith, had written *Turn to the Right*. Since Kaufman had parodied that rather simplistic melodrama in *The Deep, Tangled Wildwood,* it is not easy to understand why he was willing to cast Hazzard in *The Good Fellow.* But Hazzard was popular as a performer; moreover, he had a modest following on Long Island as the reviewer for the Great Neck *Home News.* Presumably, it was thought that he would carry the show. His performance was poor, however, and he had difficulty remembering his lines, to the distress of the other actors.[12] Though his notices were not uniformly bad, they did not augur success. Nor did the playwrights' notices. A thin piece relying for its laughs on prolonged spoofing of the rituals of fraternal lodges, it resembled *To the Ladies* insofar as that play had spoofed the rituals of business organizations. For both plays the high point was the Act II gathering in which all the time-worn, ceremonial foolishness of "belonging" could be exposed. Much of it was funny in *The Good Fellow,* just as the banquet scene had seemed funny to reviewers of *To the Ladies.* But something more was needed to make the play work, and whatever it was, Kaufman and Mankiewicz were unable to supply it. The plot concerns the series of embarrassments that become the lot of Jim Helton (Hazzard's character) as he struggles to raise the capital needed to meet the expenses of the national convention of his beloved Knights of Corsica, which, thanks to his powers of persuasion, is to be held in Wilkes-Barre. Not only does he borrow $5000 on his life insurance, but he borrows the same amount from his daughter's fiancé, much to the girl's chagrin. Even this is not enough money, however, and in the end he must admit failure and return both loans. At the same time he resigns from the lodge, to the relief of his family. Yet, with typical Kaufmanian antisentimentality, at the final curtain he begins to entertain the notion of accepting an invitation to set up a Wilkes-Barre Chapter of another lodge, the Benevolent Sons of Isaac.

Seven performances were enough to satisfy Kaufman's public. It was the briefest Broadway run accorded any play he ever wrote. A film sale somewhat offset the monetary loss. Back from Hollywood for the tryout and opening, Mank, as he later confided to his wife Sara, was disappointed with the casting, in which he had not had a voice. To at least one member of the cast, Victor Killian, the writers appeared somewhat cool toward each other before the opening. They did not become estranged, but were powerless to turn their leaden scenes into something brighter. In the opinion of Marc Connelly, who in the 1920s knew Kaufman's work habits better than anyone else, much of the blame for the failure rested with Mank, for Mank, he thought, had not been the steady, reliable coworker that Kaufman required. But this was hindsight expressed long after the event and may have reflected Connelly's own unhappy experience with Mank the following season. Fetching out of his trunk a sketch which was originally intended for Beatrice Lillie, Connelly, with the collaboration of Mank, expanded it into a three-act comedy, *The Wild Man of Borneo.* This play opened in September 1927 and ran only fifteen performances.[13]*

A small by-product of *The Good Fellow* was better than the play itself. This was a letter Kaufman sent to the *Times* in 1930, some three months after his retirement from the paper. Chiding his old employers, and himself as well, he wrote,

> In your Sunday gossip, talking about Mr. Mankiewicz, you say that he once collaborated with me on a "half-forgotten" play. The reference, of course, is to *The Good Fellow,* produced about four years ago.
>
> I feel I must protest against your use of "half-forgotten." I have been conducting inquiries and am pleased to say that I find no one who remembers it at all.
>
> I think you should be a little surer of your facts before rushing into print.[14]

An entire season passed before Kaufman had a new work ready for production. In view of his record of the years immediately preceding, this was a long period for him to be without a project. When the suggestion for a new show came along, it was for a musical—not Kaufman's favorite form of work, but something that would presumably pay. The producer who approached him at this time was Edgar Selwyn, a reputable, conscientious man of the theater who had been an actor and a playwright before moving to play production in 1912. His presentation of Bayard Veiller's *Within the Law* that year made him rich. Two years later he, his brother Arch, and Crosby Gaige founded a production company that remained in existence for twelve years,

---

* Mankiewicz wrote one more, even less successful play, *The Meal Ticket,* without a collaborator. That work opened and closed in Philadelphia in 1937 during a tryout run.

after which the three principals went their own ways. He had also been (and was to be again later) a motion picture producer. In 1916 Selwyn and one Samuel Goldfish formed the Goldwyn Pictures Corporation, the name of the corporation combining one syllable from each of their surnames. (Legend had it that they originally had combined the other syllables of their names, but were persuaded by tactful associates that the public might not care to see the offerings of the Selfish Company.) Selwyn left the Goldwyn Company in 1919. His former partner changed his name to Goldwyn.

Selwyn's proposition was that Kaufman should supply the book for a musical whose composer would be George Gershwin. Though hailed in all quarters as a major force in serious American music since the first performance of the *Rhapsody in Blue* on February 12, 1924, Gershwin was as much the devoted Broadway composer after that event (and the presentation of the *Concerto in F* in 1925) as he had been before. The lyrics would be written by Ira Gershwin, whose reputation had grown since the days of *Be Yourself*.

While George Gershwin spent the spring and early summer of 1926 in Ossining with his brother, at work on the songs, George Kaufman got his book into shape on West 58th Street. He had no writing collaborator with whom to develop the dialogue, but at least once he made the trip to Ossining to consult his musical collaborators.[15] The title agreed upon for the show, which had an antimilitarist theme, was *Strike Up the Band,* and the most imposing problem faced by any of the collaborators was the composition of the title song, a march. George Gershwin wrote four versions and discarded each of them, to the bewilderment of his brother, who found them all to be satisfactory. Finally, when the brothers met with Selwyn in Atlantic City as the show was shaping up in the next spring, the composing Gershwin played a fifth tune for the versifying Gershwin and promised that he would retain it in the score, as in fact he did.[16] With that matter out of the way, everyone's troubles appeared to be over, at least for the moment.

The idea that Kaufman hit on for the book combined his now familiar dramatic theme, the self-serving instinct of the businessman—a theme just short of becoming an obsession with him—and a new concern, the folly of war. On the face of it, the idea was a good one. As the play begins, the United States has just concluded the celebration of National Cheese Week. In dialogue between Horace J. Fletcher and Edgar Sloane, an associate, the audience hears of some of the week's events:

> SLOANE There was a very large celebration in Des Moines, Iowa.
> FLETCHER A big cheese town.

SLOANE The parade was led by a naked girl symbolizing law and order and was followed by the entire male population.

FLETCHER That shows you how popular cheese is.

As "a glorious climax to National Cheese Week" (Fletcher's phrase), the news comes that Congress has voted a 50 per cent tariff on imported cheese. Naturally enough, Switzerland protests this blow to her economy, and amid the reverberations of her complaint Fletcher offers to finance a war against the Swiss. It will be the Horace J. Fletcher Memorial War. "I'll not only pay all the expenses of the war, but give the government 25% of the profits," he promises. "What did they make out of the last one, handling it themselves? Nothing."

From this brisk beginning in Fletcher's cheeseworks, the plot moves forward at a much slower rate. Kaufman found a few too many opportunities for satiric thrusts. With prompting from the hotel owners of Switzerland, it is decided to hold the war in that country. The hotels will offer special rates to the participants, and of course the Swiss scenery in itself is an incomparable attraction. Fletcher goes along to check up on his war—after all, it is his own personal production. His daughter, Joan, and the young reporter Jim Townsend, who is in love with her, also come along, as do another young couple and a rather rapacious middle-aged spinster looking for a husband (Fletcher, if possible). Also on hand is George Spelvin, an operative in the Secret Service; that name may have struck Kaufman as eminently appropriate for a man with such a job, since by tradition it had long been used in cast-lists as a cover name for an actor taking two roles.

Jim discovers that Fletcher's cheese is made of Grade B milk. Joan does not believe this and thinks that Jim in decrying her father's cheese is exhibiting un-American behavior. To make matters worse, Jim wears a Swiss watch. Ultimately it is established that, though the cheese is made of inferior milk, Fletcher himself has always been unaware of the fact. Edgar Sloane is a Swiss agent, and all along he has been lessening the quality of Fletcher's American cheese by substituting Grade B for Grade A milk in Fletcher's factory. Moreover, he has been snipping buttons off the uniforms of American soldiers so that they will catch pneumonia in the Alps. Meanwhile, having no real fighting to do, the American soldiers have been knitting for the folks back home. Fletcher, not at all happy with the slow pace of events and the lack of publicity given his war in the papers, screams like an angry playwright who is dissatisfied with the production his brainchild is receiving:

I thought it would be a real war, like 1917! There was a war for you— lots of front-page publicity, glory for everybody! But this lousy war! Nobody ever hears about it! Do you know what the tabloids have printed about this war in the past months? Three pictures of nurses and that's all. This is the most terrible war that—take my name off this war! I don't want to have anything to do with it!

It is the soft-spoken Spelvin who discovers Sloane's treachery, apprehends him, and, carrying out a plan devised by Jim, captures the entire Swiss army. Thus he brings an end to this show-business war.

Selwyn, who admired the show, did well by it, hiring such performers as Edna May Oliver, Jimmy Savo (as Spelvin), the popular leading man Roger Pryor, and Morton Downey. Even so, *Strike Up the Band* did not click. Attending the opening at Long Branch on August 29, 1927, a *Variety* reporter thought that a commercial success was unlikely, but that at least the two Georges and Ira should achieve a *succès d'estime*. He invoked the names of Gilbert and Sullivan and declared the work to be "close to an operetta." But whether operetta or typical American musical comedy, *Strike Up the Band* proved to be no sort of success at all. From Long Branch Selwyn moved the production to Philadelphia, where it played to small houses for two weeks, the second week bringing in only $9000. That low figure resulted in a loss for the week of $22,000, which Kaufman himself in embarrassment later described (in print) as a record.[17] It was too much of a loss for Selwyn, who closed the show on the spot. He liked it, however, and made up his mind that one day, when the circumstances were favorable, he would take it up again.

This was Kaufman's second out-of-town failure, but a much more telling one than his adaptation of *Jacques Duval* had been eight years earlier under Tyler's management. Despite the presence of George Arliss in the cast of *Duval,* that production was not so prestigious as to create a stir when it collapsed. Kaufman himself had been little known at the time, apart from his journalism. But by 1927 no Broadway playwright, not even O'Neill, bore a more famous name, and few musical-comedy composers and lyricists were as much admired as the Gershwins. All three men were to blame: Kaufman's book was clotted and overwrought, its satire too galling, especially at the close, and the Gershwins' score was not comparable to their scores for the earlier *Lady Be Good!* and *Oh, Kay!* Of the many musical numbers, only two stood out, the title song and "The Man I Love," the latter having originally been composed for *Lady Be Good!* in 1924 and dropped during that show's tryout tour. Good as they were, those two numbers were not enough to carry the show, and, for that matter, neither was quite right for its purpose. "The Man I Love," though destined to become one of the Gershwins' most popular songs, was rather low-keyed for the stage, and the rousing military march "Strike Up the Band!" was possibly *too* rousing for a play intended to decry the waging of war. George Kaufman loved the march, however, and ten years later claimed that it was his favorite among the songs of all the shows with which he had been associated.[18]

By 1927 Kaufman was too much the practiced showman not to know that his book was mediocre, and too much the team player not to regret having let down his associates. Writing a few words about his experience with the show, he once offered an anecdote about an encounter with its principal backer, a gentleman from Kentucky whom he called Mr. Levy. A few years after the Philadelphia closing, Levy approached him in a theater lobby and introduced him to Mrs. Levy as George Gershwin. (Seen in a dim light through half closed eyes, the two Georges did have a certain resemblance to one another.) Why, Levy wanted to know, in view of all the successful musicals for which he had composed the scores, did *Strike Up the Band* have to be the one that failed? Wrote Kaufman, "I have always flattered myself that I made the only possible answer. I said, 'Kaufman gave me a lousy book.' "[19]

Kaufman's adjective was too strong, but, undeniably, the book needed improvement. His failure to provide it was in part due to the fact that his attention through the first half of 1927 was divided between *Strike Up the Band* and *The Royal Family*, a new work-in-progress with Edna Ferber, which was slow to develop: it occupied much of the two writers' time from November 1926 to June 1927, when they wrote "Curtain" to the third act.

Since *Minick,* Ferber had been close to both Kaufmans, though seldom failing to make it clear that George was the one she preferred. She was as much a part of their set as she cared to be and as her sense of obligation to her work permitted. Seldom finding the time for a long lunch at the Algonquin, a late afternoon gathering at Neysa McMein's, or a late-night party at the Ross-Grant-Woollcott house, she did, nevertheless, occasionally drop in on her friends at such places and times, and she was gregarious enough to enjoy entertaining them at her apartment in return. Her intimates were playwrights, actors, drama critics, and a sprinkling of publishers and editors. Her affection for the theater was among her strongest emotions, no matter the poor luck she had so far experienced with her own plays.

Though Kaufman's name preceded hers on the programs of *The Royal Family*, it was she who conceived the notion that the private life of a family of actors would be a first-rate subject for the two of them. The most distinguished American family of actors was, of course, the Barrymores. No matter what disappointment Ferber had felt over *Our Mrs. McChesney,* one of the delights of her life to that date had been the time spent in company with its star, Ethel Barrymore—that and the professionalism and goodwill of its producer, Charles Frohman. This had been an experience worth the letdown she felt over Hobart's two-dimensional writing. She was never to forget Ethel Barrymore's total surrender of herself to the demands of her profession, even when performing in a mediocre play.

The family to which Ethel Barrymore belonged had been performing in New York and on the road for three generations, and with such style that in the popular press they *had* become Broadway's royal family. Ethel and her brothers, John and Lionel, were the children of Maurice and Georgie Drew Barrymore. Georgie's mother was Mrs. John Drew, who not only had been an energetic trouper, but had been the manager of a theater in Philadelphia. Mrs. Drew's son John was also a popular actor, as was Sidney Drew, her adopted (some said illegitimate) son. Mrs. Drew, who died in 1897, was not the first of her family to take to the stage, but merely the first in the United States; her English forebears had been acting since the eighteenth century. In the 1920s Ethel and the Barrymore brothers were known to every theatergoer and to much of the rest of the population as well. Ethel, who was destined to become the spokeswoman for her generation of the family, had been a star since 1901, when she took the role of Madame Trentoni in Clyde Fitch's *Captain Jinks of the Horse Marines* under Frohman's management. Lionel experienced a great theatrical triumph in 1919 in Sem Benelli's *The Jest*, costarring with John, but he never enjoyed appearing on stage. After appearing in a disastrous *Macbeth* in 1921 he became a film actor exclusively. John's *Richard III* (1920) and *Hamlet* (1922) revealed a striking talent for classical acting. But in 1925 he moved permanently to Hollywood, where his extramarital affairs, drinking, and fist fights were as well publicized as his acting talent, which, despite all his excesses, never deserted him. Ethel, married to the socially prominent Russell Colt in 1909, enjoyed her association with the level of society that her husband represented, but she soon found that the theater and married life did not blend well for her. Three children were born of the marriage, however, and not until 1923 was it dissolved. Through all her years with Colt she kept at her job, not only in New York but on the road.

When word spread that Kaufman and Ferber were writing about a family of actors, it was an easy assumption that this famous family was their inspiration. Despite the writers' frequent disclaimers to the effect that the only member of the clan on whose personality they had drawn was John,[20] for the temperamental Tony, a Broadway actor who made the mistake of going to Hollywood, no one in the audience of the 1920s could have failed to think that the very existence of such a family had put the notion of writing the play into their heads. On the other hand, Julie Cavendish, the central character, at thirty-nine is about ten years younger than Ethel was at the time, and her daughter Gwen at nineteen is older than Ethel's daughter then was. But the matriarchal Fanny Cavendish, Julie's mother, an old trouper now impatient with the new breed of actors who think more of creature comforts than of their art, is a fine reincarnation of old Mrs. Drew, Ethel's grandmother. And perhaps a touch of Sidney Drew is present in the personality of the improvident Herbert Dean, Fanny's brother. Not to be overlooked also is the fact that the trisyllabic names Cavendish and Barrymore have the same cadence. From Ferber's own family, however, came the names Julie and Fanny, the former from her mother, Julia Ferber, and the latter from her sister, Fanny Fox.

Ferber's principal stock in trade in fiction was the sentimental depiction of the American dynastic family. *The Royal Family* is also such a depiction, but invigorated and vivified by Kaufman's wit, with the consequence that, though the similarity to Ferber's novels is evident, the play is superior to them. By the same token, the play has greater depth of characterization and considerably more humanity than any of Kaufman's earlier plays had. The combination of the two writers' skills was in balance throughout the writing, resulting in a work that is neither too sentimental nor too cynical. It has warmth, and it also has humor.

The plot consists, essentially, of the tribulations and joys of Julie Cavendish, the leading actress of Broadway and the divorced mother of an ingenue who is rising in prominence. Julie's mother, Fanny, though ill, is determined to go on a prolonged tour booked for her by Oscar Wolfe, the producer who for decades has presented all the members of the family in whatever kind of play they fancied. Julie is beset throughout the three acts by family crises: Tony, her brother, has had a fight with his Hollywood director and also is involved in a threatened breach of promise suit; he must flee to Europe. Gwen, engaged to a young stockbroker of very social family, cannot bear the interruptions in her private life caused by her obligations to the stage and is determined to quit the theater altogether. Herbert Dean, Julie's uncle, who is over-age for the parts he likes to play, wants Julie to put his querulous wife, Kitty, into the cast of her own play so that he can act in a new one without her, for Kitty, in his opinion, is too old-looking. If she were in his play, she would rob him of his chance of success. In addition, Dean always needs a loan. Fanny, determined to have a last season on the road, is a constant cause of worry to Julie because of her precarious health. Finally, Julie has a problem all her own: whether or not to marry the strong, silent Gilbert Marshall, who, having discovered platinum in South America, wants to take her away from Broadway to the pampas.

Underpinning this prolonged set of anxieties is the collaborators' belief in the importance of the theater and their admiration for those who serve it. This takes many forms and embraces tones that range from the flippant to the deeply affecting. Gwen, quarreling with her fiancé, snaps out, "I can give you the names of actors and actresses of three hundred years ago—dozens of them! Name me two Seventeenth Century stockbrokers." Julie, on the verge of hysterics as the result of the many pressures on her, rants about the hellish demands of her profession, ending with a vow never to set foot inside a theater again. But when her maid, knowing that she has a performance that very evening, reminds her that it is already eight o'clock, she grabs for her coat with a cry of "Oh, my God!"

Fanny, infirm but ever young in her love of life and of acting, which have become the same thing for her, has the most urgent speech of all:

> Every night when I'm sitting here alone I'm really down there at the theatre! Seven-thirty, and they're going in at the stage door! Good evening to the door man. Taking down their keys and looking in the mail rack. Eight o'clock! The stage hands are setting up. (*Raps with her cane.*)
>
> Half hour, Miss Cavendish! Grease paint, rouge, mascara! Fifteen minutes, Miss Cavendish! My costume! . . . More rouge! . . . Where's the rabbit's foot! . . . Overture! . . . How's the house tonight? . . . The curtain's up! . . . Props! . . . Cue! . . . Enter! . . . That's all that's kept me alive these two years. If you weren't down there for me, I wouldn't want to live. . . . I couldn't live. You . . . down there . . . for me . . . going on . . . going on . . . going on. . . .

Her collapse at the end of this cry from the heart suggests that it is the actor's duty and reward to die in the service of his profession.

The three Cavendish women are not the only defenders of the actor's art. Dean, down on his luck for the moment, and unable to get the kind of epic role he would like, is quite content to accept a booking in vaudeville in a fatuous one-act farce, with a role for his wife. Tony, having sped back from Europe in a new cloud of amatory troubles as dense as the one in which he left, has come across a German play composed in a radically novel technique. For this daring, different work he is willing to sacrifice the riches of Hollywood, if Wolfe is willing to produce it. It is a new version of the Passion Play, and Tony's role is, of course, Jesus Christ.

In a play of many juxtapositions of varied mood, no turn of the action is more striking than that saved, appropriately, for the end. Fanny, like all the others, is happy with plans—the cross-country tour booked by Wolfe—and ignorant of the fact that her doctor has warned Julie against allowing it. On stage alone in her living room while the others are in the library congratulating one another on new jobs, she settles into her favorite chair with her back to the audience, holding the glass with which a moment before she had been toasting the future of her great-grandson, her late husband's namesake. Suddenly the glass drops from her hand, and the hand drops to her side; she is dead. It is the perfect terminus to her long career, since she dies knowing only that the entire family will soon again be gracing the nation's stages. The scene is held briefly as the others come in, one by one, and find her.

Though this is a curtain guaranteed not to leave a dry eye in the house, and hence unlike anything else in the Kaufman repertory, it appears to have been Kaufman's invention, or at least the ending he preferred to whatever others the team may have considered. In a sense it is antisentimental, since it takes away something from the general joy of the moment, as do the endings of the two immediately preceding Kaufman plays, *The Good Fellow*, in which Helton, though he has renounced one lodge, is about to take up another, and *Strike Up the Band,* in which preparations begin for war against Russia even as the new peace is being celebrated. Ferber would have preferred something different: "Every member of this stage family," she later wrote, "should have gone on to the fall of the curtain, even though the audience might know that Fanny was going on the road to her death. We should have seen her starting off on her last road tour, vain, stage-struck to the end, gay and courageous."[21] Ferber fancied herself in the role of Fanny; undoubtedly she would have preferred to act the scene as thus described, rather than as it was written. (Her opportunity to play the role came in summer stock in Maplewood, New Jersey, in 1940. Kaufman and Beatrice saw her perform.[22]) But the scene was, and would remain for future audiences, much too good to be tampered with.

When Kaufman and Ferber had completed one act of the play, they sent it to Broadway's newest, youngest (born 1900), most promising, and most magnetic producer, Jed Harris. Starting in 1925, he had already offered three plays, of which two had been hits: *Love 'Em and Leave 'Em* by George Abbott and John V. A. Weaver, a comedy of the amours of young department-store workers, and *Broadway* by Philip Dunning and George Abbott, a crime melodrama set behind the scenes in a Broadway night club. At the time he was looking over the script of *The Royal Family*, he was readying the production of what would prove to be another hit: *Coquette,* by Abbott and Ann Preston Bridgers, which was to star Helen Hayes as a tempestuous Southern beauty. (Abbott served only as rewrite man on these scripts. They did not originate with him.) Crosby Gaige was a silent coproducer of *Broadway,* and it may have been at Gaige's country house at Peekskill, New York, that Kaufman and Harris met. But they could have met anywhere in the world of the New York theater of the mid-1920s, for everyone knew, loved, and showered invitations on Harris in those years. "Destiny's Tot" was the nickname bestowed on him by Noel Coward, who took a great fancy to him. (To their mutual friend S. N. Behrman, Coward once exclaimed, "I've simply passed out over Jed Harris.") Harris later wrote that Kaufman sent him *The Royal Family* after they had discussed it while taking a stroll. He liked the first act well enough to agree to produce the play when it was ready. But no sooner had he made the decision than some unexpected problems suddenly clouded what until then had been a particularly sunny creative atmosphere.[23]

Neither Kaufman nor Ferber had thought of their play as a *pièce à clef,* despite its correspondence in certain details to the lives of the Barrymores. To them it seemed quite reasonable to ask Ethel Barrymore to act the part of Julie. Both writers were unprepared for her response. Not only would she not act in *The Royal Family,* but she went so far as to consult a lawyer about securing an injunction forbidding a production of the play. Her counsel, Max Steuer, a criminal lawyer of note, advised that she had no grounds for a suit. John Barrymore might possibly sue, since Tony, the character created in his image, was something of a hell-raiser, but neither Julie nor any of the other Cavendishes went beyond the legally permissible as a Barrymore portrait.[24]

What so enraged Ethel Barrymore was not precisely the portrait of herself that she saw in Julie or that of her grandmother that she saw in Fanny or even that of her brother. Rather, her rage was created principally by the characters Herbert and Kitty Dean. That the Barrymore family could be thought to include such a pair was too much for her to endure.[25] Though she could do nothing about it in the courts, she made her indignation known to friends and, by avoiding them, to Kaufman and Ferber.

Because of Ethel Barrymore's rejection of the part and her profound disapproval of the play, which she did not choose to keep a secret, the role of Julie was difficult to cast. Ina Claire was the authors' next choice, but she turned it down, as did Laurette Taylor. It went, finally, to Ann Andrews, a competent but less interesting actress than those the authors had preferred. Over the dissenting voice of Harris, Kaufman and Ferber insisted on giving the role of Fanny to Haidee Wright, an English-born actress with a conspicuous lack of comic flair. The role of Tony was assigned to Otto Kruger, an attractive young actor who made the most of it and received higher praise from the critics than did his colleagues. Wolfe was played by Jefferson de Angelis with a slight Jewish accent. Ferber, for one, considered his performance the best of all. But Harris thought poorly of the entire cast and fired them all after a week of rehearsals. Only the threat of losing the play to Winthrop Ames caused him to reconsider. He rehired them and became reconciled to their imperfections, as did the authors.[26] The director of record was David Burton, but Harris himself was constantly present, and prodigal with suggestions to both the director and the authors. The authors also were on hand for rehearsals, but Ferber's attention was partly diverted to another production in progress: the musical version of her celebrated novel *Show Boat,* with music by Jerome Kern and book and lyrics by Oscar Hammerstein II. Produced by Florenz Ziegfeld, it was scheduled to open on Broadway on December 27, 1927, one night before the Broadway opening of *The Royal Family.*

When *The Royal Family* tried out in Newark and Atlantic City it was clear that Kaufman and Ferber had brought off a success. The New York reception amply confirmed their expectations, though the reviews made more of the parallels with the Barrymores than the authors would have liked. The run, 345 performances, was Kaufman's longest to that time. A road tour followed, and a second company was engaged to play in the West. Paramount Pictures bought the film rights. Released in 1930 as *The Royal Family of Broadway,* the film offered Ina Claire (at last) as Julie, Henrietta Crosman as Fanny, and Frederic March as Tony. (March had developed his Barrymore-aping performance while touring in the play.) London managements did not rush to buy the rights, and when the play at last opened in the West End in 1934 the title was changed to *Theatre Royal.* In this production, directed by Noel Coward, Marie Tempest appeared as Fanny, Madge Titheredge as Julie, and Laurence Olivier as Tony.

8

The Director

As the decade of the 1920s waned and his fortieth birthday loomed, Kaufman exhibited the stamina of a much younger man. If anything, his energy seemed enhanced, and he was constantly on the search for new outlets for it. A good night's sleep and a box of chocolates were virtually all that it took to maintain his strength for the overlapping tasks of putting on one play, outlining another, seeing a third through rehearsals and tryouts, and performing his daily stint at the *Times*—as well, of course, as putting in an appearance at the parties that Beatrice so much enjoyed giving. In the late 1920s he found two additional pursuits to fill out his days, both of which were of enduring interest to him.

These were the post-Tyler years, when Kaufman appeared to be shopping around for a new producer with whom to make a permanent alliance. In the four years immediately following the break with Tyler, no fewer than seven managements presented his work, not counting S. Jay Kaufman and Herman J. Mankiewicz, the producers of *Round the Town*, and Famous Players, which commissioned *Business Is Business*. With none of these many managements were Kaufman's contracts negotiated by an agent; not until the 1930s and 1940s, when, in succession, Leland Hayward and Irving P. Lazar came into his life to act for him in the sale of his plays to Hollywood, did he feel the need to hire such a representative. Nevertheless, as generally untroubled as his dealings with producers were, he took an active interest in the movement underway in the 1920s to ensure every author, novice as well as veteran, fair play at the hands of producers. Though not an instigator of the movement, Kaufman was one of its most faithful advocates.

Efforts of at least a slight effectiveness to protect the rights of dramatists had been made at the close of the nineteenth century, with the founding of the Society of American Dramatists and Composers in 1891.* Through the work of Bronson Howard, its president and a leading dramatist of the two preceding decades, the society successfully promoted legislation to stop the acts of literary piracy whereby authors had been deprived of rightful royalties from their plays. The pirates were hacks who revised and retitled plays and then produced them as their own. By putting an end to this practice, the society had made a start in the establishment of authors' rights, but much more work was yet to be accomplished. Additional, though largely fumbling attempts on the part of dramatists to preserve and extend their control over their own work were made in the teens of the century under the aegis of the Authors' League of America, which came into being in 1913. Those playwrights who joined the League tried to persuade the Managers' Protective Association to adopt a standard contract to be used for agreements between playwrights and producers. They wished to gain control over stock and revival rights, which many of their number had to concede to get a Broadway production, and they also wanted to protect the plays as written from those producers who were in the habit of cutting, padding, or in other ways altering an author's original script. Other goals were a reasonable division between author and producer of profits from film sales, power of approval of cast and director, and, for composers and lyricists, complete control of the performance of their songs outside the production. In these matters they were unsuccessful; the producers were too powerful to be threatened by the writers, who made their approach not as a tightly knit group, let alone a closed shop, but only as a loose association of individuals who shunned the idea of fining one another for violations of the standard contract, should they ever arrive at one.

The establishment of Actors' Equity in 1919, and its recognition by the producers in the same year as the result of the actors' strike, set an example for the playwrights. Those holding membership in the Authors' League set up the Dramatists' Guild within the League's framework. Though these playwrights shrank from the prospect of affiliating with the American Federation of Labor, as the actors had done, they leaked word to the producers that this might be their next step, with the result that in 1920 the Managers' Protective Association accepted the principle of a standard contract. Unfortu-

---

* In the 1880s Steele Mackaye and Clay M. Greene founded the American Dramatic Authors' Society for the same purpose, but made no headway. Their organization soon expired.

nately, however, this contract was not enforceable, because it did not include the principle of the closed shop for playwrights.

Not until 1925 did an event occur that put starch into the members of the Dramatists' Guild. This was a report that the Fox Film Corporation was entering into an agreement with the managers that would seriously lessen the proceeds to playwrights of sales of their work to Fox. The agreement also threatened to create a situation in which plays not adaptable to the screen might not be produced. Under the leadership of George Middleton and Arthur Richman, writers with a good Broadway record, the Dramatists' Guild speedily signed up new members. A committee was appointed to look into managerial abuses, and an agreement to abide by its recommendations was circulated among members for their signature. Kaufman, who was among the first members of the Guild, signed the agreement promptly. As the Guild increased in membership and prepared for a fight with the Managers' Protective Association, the leadership once more took up the idea of the standard contract, and early in 1926 a committee of twelve playwrights was named to consider what such a contract should include. Kaufman was put on the committee because it was thought that his years as drama editor of the *Times*, to say nothing of his own experiences as a playwright, had brought him into contact with producers of every stripe. Another of the committee members was Eugene O'Neill.

As a result of the committee's work, a Basic Agreement affirming the rights of the dramatists was drawn up and presented to producers for their signatures. On April 27, 1926, under the threat of losing the scripts of Guild members, who were bound to respect the agreement, most of the major producers signed. Their leader in negotiations with the dramatists was William A. Brady, who was sympathetic to the aims of the Guild. Those who refused to sign were Anne Nichols, author of *Abie's Irish Rose,* who produced her own scripts; the maverick George M. Cohan, who earlier had refused to join Equity; and the Shubert brothers. The Shuberts not only refused to sign, but went so far as to bring suit against the Guild. In the following year, however, the dominant brother, "Mr. Lee," capitulated, and the Shubert organization signed the agreement. Their suit was proving too costly to be continued. In the years to come, the Dramatists' Guild contract with producers would evolve into the strongest, most favorable on Broadway.[1]

Kaufman's service on the Guild's contract committee was but the beginning of his years of work on behalf of the Guild. He became Chairman of the Board in 1926, and in 1933 he was elected Vice President, a post he frequently held thereafter. When in 1936 the Guild established the Dramatists'

Play Service, for the publication of "acting versions"* of members' plays and the management of amateur rights to them, he became a member of the advisory committee of this new organization. As an officer of the Guild, he took his duties seriously, no matter how tiresome the meetings became on occasion. A younger playwright, George Sklar, who served on the board with him from 1934 to 1940, wrote this about Kaufman's appearance and demeanor at the Guild:

> There was nothing of the comedy writer about him; nor about Robert Sherwood. Both chaired most of the meetings, which were anxious affairs, conducted seriously even though half the Algonquinites were present. Kaufman, dour of face, his forehead creased in wrinkles of doom, his voice tenebrous with gloom, spoke as if he were in constant pain. We were involved at one point in a strike, at others in the serious matter of whether we should back or break our relations with the Screen Writers Guild. Every meeting seemed to have a serious concern. There was no fooling around. Kaufman was businesslike. No board of directors of any corporation could have been more efficient and to the point. The Guild was important to him—to all of us. And the witticisms came afterward.[2]

Kaufman's second new pursuit of the late 1920s was perhaps of greater moment to the public. In 1928 he became a stage director, and no sooner did this happen than he became one of the most sought-after Broadway directors. He would remain so for the next thirty years. The shyness that had overcome him when he tried to take his actors through rehearsals of *The Butter and Egg Man* and *The Good Fellow* fell away when Jed Harris sent him the script of an exceptionally brisk piece of writing, Ben Hecht and Charles MacArthur's *The Front Page*.

This play followed *The Royal Family* on Harris's schedule. As a wise-cracking comedy it clearly resembled Kaufman's own plays, but it was, if anything, more cynical in its view of human nature. Its cynicism was expressed in some of the harshest dialogue to be heard on Broadway since Anderson and Stallings had shocked the audience with the doughboy speech of *What Price Glory?* in 1924. With a cast of characters consisting mainly of male newspaper reporters, Hecht and MacArthur lost no opportunity to jar the ears of the audience with salvos of bawdy epithets from which only the expletives were removed. Kaufman, with a decade and a half of journal-

---

* Acting editions are printed primarily for amateur troupes; accordingly, they include more detailed descriptions of settings and of actors' movements and intonations than the hardcover editions intended primarily for libraries and collectors. Several of Kaufman's plays that did not achieve a long Broadway run may be found only in such editions.

ism behind him, knew such men and the patterns of their speech quite as well as the authors did. It was shrewd of Harris to engage him.

Yet one may wonder whether Harris would have approached Kaufman had he not had a serious falling out the year before with George Abbott, who had directed four of his productions. This estrangement, created by a dispute over royalties due Abbott from his play *Coquette,* was one of the first of several withdrawals of friendship that Harris's unpredictable temper brought about. Among others soon to be alienated were S. N. Behrman, Richard Maney, Edgar Selwyn—and George S. Kaufman. But for the moment Harris and Kaufman were on good terms.

Having been newspapermen in Chicago, Hecht and MacArthur knew the craft of journalism and took a nostalgic delight in summoning up an account of the way of life of its practitioners in that nervous, energetic city. With seven newspapers competing for the customers' pennies, a corrupt municipal government, a Prohibition-bred crime syndicate, and an insular fear of left-of-center opinion, Chicago afforded them some gaudy dramatic opportunities. A young playwright, Maurine Watkins, had made excellent use of the city's atmosphere two seasons earlier in a grainy comic melodrama about a husband-slayer named Roxie Hart whose travesty of a trial becomes a nine days' wonder. That play was entitled simply *Chicago,* as though to suggest that the city's name alone was exciting enough to summon a line of customers to the box office. One season earlier Bartlett Cormack, another ex-journalist, had had a success with *The Racket,* a melodrama centering on an attempt of Chicago racketeers to corrupt the police. Like *Chicago,* Hecht and Mac-Arthur's play concerns a murder charge. The protagonist, however, is not the defendant, but a young newspaper reporter named Hildy (for Hilde-brand) Johnson, of the Chicago *Herald & Examiner,* whose worth to his boss, Managing Editor Walter Burns, is such that Burns will stoop to any trick, however low, to keep him on his staff.

For years MacArthur had held a job on the *Herald & Examiner,* while Hecht had been a reporter for the Chicago *Daily News.* From the distance of a thousand miles, Chicago was bathed for them in a romantic glow, though they were astute enough to realize that nothing had been romantic about it in reality, especially that part of it where they set the play, the press room of the Cook County Criminal Court. But Burns, at least, was drawn from life. His prototype was the *Herald & Examiner*'s Walter C. Howey, a cutthroat editor relentlessly pressing his reporters for the big scoop and willing enough to risk a brush with the law while gathering material for a story. Burns/Howey made a worthy opponent for Hildy, the dashing journalist who represented the image that the tricks of memory had made for Hecht and Mac-Arthur of themselves in their newspaper days. Hildy wants to leave the paper and move with his fiancée to New York and a job in advertising, much to the disapproval of Burns. The central matter of the play is the effort made by the two to save from the gallows a harmless radical named Earl Williams, who has been found guilty of a bogus murder charge. With that business accomplished, Hildy departs at last for New York, wearing a watch given him by Burns on which is inscribed, "To the Best Newspaperman I Know." But Burns tells an assistant to send a telegram to the Sheriff of La Porte, Indiana, with instructions to yank Hildy off the train when it reaches that town and return him to Chicago. Says Burns, "The son of a bitch stole my watch."

Harris took the play to everyone's favorite tryout town, Atlantic City, where it opened on May 14, 1928. There it had a good press, if one discounts the inevitable cavils over this or that salty phrase. It was evident that this was a comedy that in its briskness and its emphasis on life's seamy side would have something of the appeal of Dunning and Abbott's *Broadway*. In Atlantic City for the opening were not only the actors, the producer, and the director, but a small crowd of Algonquinites invited down by Harris. Among them were Marc Connelly, Woollcott, Harpo, and Harold Ross, along with Richard Maney (Harris's press agent), and still others, including, in the words of Ben Hecht, "a small harem that was kept well out of sight."[3] They —celebrities and harem—were installed in the Marlborough-Blenheim Hotel, and since the production was not in trouble, they passed the time pleasantly enough with card games and badinage. For Harpo and Woollcott this excursion was but a prologue to a long holiday on that well-beloved playground of the 1920s, the French Riviera. They were booked to sail on Saturday, May 19, with Alice Duer Miller and Beatrice. Though Beatrice often accompanied Kaufman to tryout performances, on this occasion she stayed away.

During the tryout week Jed Harris allowed an incident to occur that, though no worse than foolish, imprinted itself on Kaufman's mind as a mark against him. Harris, finding something wrong with the production, as might any producer during an out-of-town run, called his authors and his directors to his room for a conference. There, to their discomfiture, they found him lolling in a chair in hairy nakedness. In that state he kept them for an hour while he talked about the play. To Kaufman, this was coarse and insulting, and, for that matter, neither Hecht nor MacArthur was amused. As they filed out, the conference over, Kaufman said only, "Your fly's open."[4]

Jed Harris, following the practice of the age, dismissed the company after the trial run, called for some revisions, made some changes in the cast, and reopened the production on August 6 in Long Branch for a week's run prior to the Broadway opening on August 14. *The Front Page* was pronounced a hit on Broadway. Its run of 276 performances, though not extraordinary by later standards, was profitable, and the comedy began its long history as a standard item in the American repertory. The reviewers, being newspapermen themselves, were able to confirm the authenticity of the reporters' jargon; most felt an obligation to complain about the roughness of the language, perhaps out of a sense that their profession was being maligned! Specially praised among the actors were Lee Tracy (Hildy) and Osgood Perkins (Burns). Kaufman also received praise, though, as was usual with the mention of a director in a review, no detailed analysis of his contribution was offered by the critics.

Nevertheless, a legend of Kaufman as director soon began to build, as actors in the cast told their friends something about his method. It was reported that his sense of timing was uncanny—that he knew not only where the laughs would appear, but how long each would last to the second. Recognizing that *The Front Page* had only a slim plot and no philosophical implications beyond those that might be found in a pulp-magazine suspense tale, he made the most of the characterization and the comic lines. Tempo was all important, and if to achieve the correct tempo meant cutting the dialogue—"taking out the fat," as he put it—then it was necessary to cajole the authors into agreeing to the cuts. These were the bare essentials of his technique, which, from the Hecht-MacArthur comedy to Peter Ustinov's *Romanoff and Juliet* in 1957, remained the same, whether or not he himself was the author of the play at hand.

Kaufman's directorial manner, authoritative without being overbearing, allayed the anxieties of his actors and his producers, no matter how flimsy the script might be. The confidence that he inspired with each production was no guarantee of success, but producers so warmed to him that at the start of every season he was presented with a pile of scripts to choose among, each allegedly crying for his touch. After *The Front Page* he directed forty-three productions, of which twenty-four were of his own plays. Without asking or receiving credit, he also lent a hand to many other plays in rehearsal. Sam Harris once said that whenever Kaufman passed a theater and saw a group of actors standing outside, he immediately began rehearsing them.[5] The producers whom ultimately he preferred to all others were Sam Harris (unrelated to Jed Harris) and Max Gordon, and he usually invested in their productions. One consequence of his financial participation was that he had more of a voice in the over-all preparation of each production than a director usually commands. Alone among directors, he expected to have the set constructed and available very early in rehearsals, and sometimes as soon as a week after they had begun. His orders were often costly in the execution, but seldom were they countermanded. For example, when directing Gertrude Tonkongy's *Town House* for Max Gordon in 1948, he was informed that a staircase in the setting that was to disappear below the stage would run into pipes in the theater's basement, and he demanded that the pipes be moved.[6] He argued that the design was exactly right as it was and must not be altered. Having risked his own capital, he got his way.

Until almost the very moment that the rehearsals of the play began, the actors saw little of Kaufman. From the outset of every production he projected a personality courteous but distant, precisely as he did in all other moments of his life, except where his most intimate acquaintances were concerned. He did not, for example, lunch with the actors between rehearsal periods, and it would have been unthinkable for him to confide in the company that he himself had a financial interest in the production. He usually walked around outside the theater, weather permitting, until the last minute before the company assembled, then entered quietly and said, "Places, please"—those magic words that summoned a performance.

Not as flamboyant or dynamic a director as, say, Noel Coward or Moss Hart might be, he was nevertheless impressive in rehearsals by virtue of his very dignity and calm. His manner provided the company with a sense of security: if he was unruffled, why should they be agitated? Never stooping to flattery, he was able, even so, to make a performer content with his job. One actress, Natalie Schafer, whom he directed in two productions, and who sat in on rehearsals of some others, recalled in later years, "He made you think you were better than you were."[7] This, of course, did not mean that he was content with mediocrity, but that he was able to build confidence in those performers still young enough to lack it. Often, sitting in the back of the house with his head in his hands, he created just the opposite effect, leaving the actors with the alarming sense that nothing they were doing could possibly be right. But they learned soon enough that that was not the case; he was simply listening to the tempo of the lines and asking himself whether it should be speeded up or slowed down.

During the early days of the rehearsal period, Kaufman would take himself up onto the stage and walk around among the cast, whispering a word or two in an actor's ear if an intonation or a movement seemed inappropriate. That he never subjected the cast to a tantrum made him something of a marvel on Broadway, where the director quite often went into a rage. His way of achieving the necessary improvements was either by means of the onstage whisper, when that was appropriate, or, if more than a whisper was required, to take the actor aside and outline his suggestion. Stress this word rather than that one, break the line here rather than there, cross on this line, turn your head a quarter inch more to the left, speak more slowly: he offered instructions of this sort continually, shaping each performance in accordance with the cadences of the dialogue as he or another author had written it. Getting it right, an actor might hope for the reward of a smile. The smile was almost never forthcoming, but the actor might still know, from Kaufman's very quietness, that all was well.

It was rare that an actor would question Kaufman's advice, so firm did he seem in his conviction, yet so gentle was he in offering the suggestion. Those rare occasions when he spoke brusquely to an actor were ones on which the lines of a script came under question. To an actor in George Oppenheimer's *Here Today* who complained that one of his lines did not flow, Kaufman replied, "The line flows. You don't."[8] If an actor should be so bold as to change a line, whether inadvertently or—fatal error!—intentionally, he would not soon forget his director's annoyance. But this sort of carelessness or boldness was not so likely to occur during rehearsals as after the play had settled into its run, when, as sometimes happened, a bold or ambitious actor would attempt to build up his role with a few verbal embellishments. One of the most repeated tales about Kaufman had it that at a performance during the run of *Of Thee I Sing*, when a leading actor, William Gaxton, attempted such a lark, the irate director sent him a telegram reading, "Am in back of the house. Wish you were here." But if in rehearsal a performer, or, as it might happen, a stage manager came to him with a suggestion for a new piece of business, he would listen and, if it worked, would say, "Good. Let's put it in."

When, indeed, a line did not flow for an actor, Kaufman could always spot and solve the problem. For example, the expert comedienne Jean Dixon, who appeared in four of his plays, stumbled repeatedly over a line in *June Moon*, until Kaufman recommended that she shift the emphasis from one word to another, thus removing the problem by showing her how to make better sense of the entire line.[9] Normally, however, he did not care to give line readings to his actors—that is, he did not care to demonstrate how he himself would speak the line on stage. Nor did he care to show his actors exactly how and where to move. Rather, his method was to let the actors find their own most comfortable readings and movements, but to correct them mildly when it was necessary to do so, and sometimes with a joke. When Michael Wager, the juvenile lead in *The Small Hours,* paused rather lengthily in the middle of a speech, Kaufman asked him why he had done so. Wager pointed out that in the typescript Kaufman had put ten dots to indicate the pause. "Make it *two* dots," Kaufman told him.[10]

As sensitive to the beat of dramatic language as an orchestra conductor to the rhythm of music, Kaufman was ruthless with himself and his collaborators if in rehearsal a script proved to have dead spots or scenes in which the language was so dense that it delayed stage movement, or scenes in which the laughs came so rapidly that one topped and killed another. It was no hardship to him to cut and revise his work; when necessary, as it was with every production, he got to work, tapping out the new pages on his typewriter with a speed that astonished his cast. He was just as unsparing of those other playwrights whose works he staged. He could afford to turn down scripts that he considered unalterably weak or whose substance was not to his taste, such as Sidney Howard's dramatization of Lewis's *Dodsworth.*[11] But when he did choose to direct a script, he would make it clear to the writer that it would not go into production until he was satisfied that it was worth the effort. Unlike Jed Harris, who bedeviled his writers endlessly with demands for revisions and then did not always get a good script for his and their pains, Kaufman was not a destructive taskmaster. But he knew what he wanted, and usually this was the elimination of dead moments. Of one script that he directed, Joseph Fields and Jerome Chodorov's *My Sister Eileen,* there were six complete versions before rehearsals began and, of course, some rewriting during them. Kaufman vetoed the suggestion of a tryout tour to precede the opening, but following the opening he did ask for some rewriting of the final scene, despite excellent reviews.

Kaufman's concern with timing made him a vastly different type of director from the many who practiced the introspective art devised in Russia by Constantin Stanislavsky and promulgated in the United States by the Group Theater and its offshoot, the Actors Studio. One much-repeated anecdote about him had to do with a brush that he had in rehearsal with an actor trained in the Stanislavsky method. When the actor, puzzled about a movement recommended to him by Kaufman, asked what should be his motivation for carrying it out, the terse reply was, "Your job." Perhaps the story is true, perhaps not. It was true to Kaufman's general approach to theater, in which the effect of the production was to be the exhilaration of the audience, and this was to be achieved by the sensitive pacing of comic effects. He almost never cared to direct the exquisitely poignant moment of tragic self-revelation.

He became a first-rate director of the kind of play of which he was also a first-rate author.*

Kaufman once told Jean Dixon that he had just been to see O'Neill's *Strange Interlude,* that dramatic equivalent of the three-volume novel which exacted some four hours of attention from its audience, not counting an hour's recess for dinner. Kaufman had not only seen it, but had liked it. "Yes," said Jean Dixon, "and I know who was with you: Beatrice." When Kaufman nodded and asked how she could have guessed, she replied, "Because that's the only woman you could have stood to be with for so long a time."[12]

That Kaufman might think it odd if someone guessed that his theater companion was his own wife was in itself a comment on the kind of marriage that theirs had become. Neither partner felt an obligation to consult the other about social plans; conversely, they sometimes found themselves making dates with each other so as not to have conflicting engagements for those occasions when one of them felt that he or she would particularly like the other's company. Knowing how much satisfaction Kaufman derived from his playwriting, Beatrice felt free to disappear when he was deeply involved in the preparation of a script, but at such times the exchange of letters, with the unironical salutation of "Darling," was intense. During the summer of 1928, when Kaufman was busy with the final work on *The Front Page* and was outlining a new vehicle for the Marx Brothers, and when Anne, who would turn three in June, could be safely left with her nurse, Beatrice saw no reason to dismiss as impractical Woollcott's suggestion that she, his "Lamb Girl," junket with him and Harpo and Alice Duer Miller to the Riviera. This was Beatrice's first trip abroad since she had traveled with Margaret Leech to Italy in 1922.

Woollcott, who resembled nothing so much as a medium-sized aquatic mammal of fierce, peculiarly anthrophobic temperament, was not a man to inspire love at first sight. But he had gathered to his ample bosom a circle of close friends who endured his wounding brusqueness as a burden to be borne in exchange for his loyalty and generous aid in time of psychic or financial distress. He could be counted on—and he counted, relentlessly, on others to see him through the hours when the demands of journalism were relaxed and he was thrown on his own resources. He did not know how to be contentedly alone. All his life he was driven by the spirit of his birthplace, the

---

* For these insights into Kaufman's directorial method I am much indebted to Fred Astaire, Henry Ephron, Janet Fox, Victor Killian, Irving P. Lazar, Sam Levene, Barna Ostertag, Irving Schneider, Mary Wickes, and Murial Williams.

Phalanx, situated near Red Bank, New Jersey, a community that was formed in the 1840s as an experiment in social cooperation. Though the canning business that the members of the Phalanx established as a cooperative proved unsuccessful as such and was ultimately taken over by Woollcott's maternal grandfather, the community itself continued to exist. In 1887, when Alexander was born, most of its fifty or sixty members dwelt in an eighty-five-room house—more or less one big family. Though from the ages of two to eight he was taken by his parents to live in Kansas City, Woollcott spent most of his early years in the Phalanx. Ever afterward, he sought a surrogate cooperative society. Hamilton College supplied it, of course, as residential colleges always have done; the United States Army supplied it, and so also did Harold Ross and Jane Grant in the house on West 47th Street. When Woollcott sought an apartment elsewhere, he begged Alice Duer Miller to break off a few rooms for him from her own large apartment in the Campanile, a cooperative building on 52nd Street at the East River, and she did so. In 1924, he saw for the first time Neshobe Island in Lake Bomoseen, Vermont, and decided, along with Neysa McMein, that it should be bought and turned into a club for a select membership of their cronies. Among the other original members, whose number was kept to ten, were the Kaufmans, Alice Duer Miller, and actress Ruth Gordon. The membership changed over the years, but included only such persons as commanded a respectable place in the arts and journalism.

Though in the habit of vacationing on the island, where he soon established himself as the lord and master and where croquet and cribbage were the order of the day, Woollcott was eager to travel abroad in May 1928. His contract with the *World* was due to expire that month,* and, though Herbert Bayard Swope, his editor, had dangled a new contract before him, Woollcott was determined to make a career as a free-lance writer. A holiday on the Riviera would supply a refreshing interlude, and it might give him something to write about. He planned the summer joyously, taking a lease on a villa near Cap d'Antibes. This was a place of Olympian splendor compared with the house on the island, which until the 1930s had neither electricity nor indoor plumbing.

Woollcott, though asexual and probably impotent (as the result of a severe case of mumps in young manhood), was no misogynist. Beatrice and Alice Miller were two women whom he deeply loved. Others were Ruth Gordon and Neysa McMein. For the entire summer Alice Miller and Beatrice were to be with him, and Ruth Gordon would join them later, after the run of her play. That left out only McMein, but Harpo, whom he adored, would com-

---

* Woollcott had left the *Sun* in 1925.

pensate for that lack. Though no group could have been more worldly than the four New Yorkers who set sail on the *Roma*, there was something delightfully adolescent in their plans, as though they were planning to act out the story of the Rover Boys (and Girls) on the Riviera.

Before the long holiday was over, it seemed that everyone of importance in the arts who was in the vicinity of the villa had come to call. Foremost among them was George Bernard Shaw, who, with his wife, surprised Harpo alone when this most antic of the Marx brothers was clad only in a towel. (Shaw playfully yanked the towel away.) Among others who dropped in were Somerset Maugham, Mary Garden, and Grace Moore, the last-named having known the Algonquinites since the years when she had been a leading performer in the *Music Box Revues*. Two of the celebrated persons whom they saw that summer were surrounded by a special air, an air redolent of glamor in decay. These two were Scott and Zelda Fitzgerald, who were spending the summer chiefly in Paris, where Zelda, determined to possess fame in her own right, studied furiously to become a ballerina. On one occasion when they traveled south, they too came to the villa. For the rest of her life Beatrice would remember the game they played one evening, in which a prize was to be awarded to the person who could attest to having done something so extraordinary that none of the others had done it. "I've done something that no one else here has done," said Zelda. "I've gone mad."[13]

The group passed two glorious months gambling at Monte Carlo, swimming, dining sumptuously, entertaining and being entertained. But before returning they explored the territory beyond the Riviera, while keeping the villa as their home base. The last of their excursions was to Naples, so that Beatrice could visit the aquarium and see again a marine creature, the *sensitivo,* that had caught and held her eye on her travels with Margaret Leech. In his memoirs, Harpo described the scene:

> The *sensitivo* was a fantastic kind of shellfish. It drew into its shell whenever any strange object came near it, then poked out of its shell when the object was pulled away—all in a weird, synchronized movement. Beatrice would watch it and play with it for hours. The real reason she was so fascinated, she said, was that she knew a lot of people who were *sensitivos*. She refused to name any names, however.[14]

Named or unnamed, one person of whom the conchiferous Neapolitan *sensitivo* undoubtedly reminded her was the bespectacled New York *sensitivo* with whom she shared her home and those aspects of her life that mattered most. To him she happily returned aboard the *Ile de France*, which sailed up the Hudson on August 14, just in time for the first Broadway performance of *The Front Page*.

9

With Ring Lardner

While Beatrice was reveling in the pleasures of the Riviera and *The Front Page* was resting between engagements at Atlantic City and Long Branch, Kaufman was being his usual productive self. The other, gentler Harris, Sam H., had asked him to prepare another show for the Marx Brothers, and he had accepted the offer. With an eye to an opening in October, Kaufman remained in New York City and worked on the script. Morrie Ryskind worked with him, no longer an anonymous aid but a fully credited collaborator. The title was *Animal Crackers*. Rehearsals would begin in the dog days, at the tag end of the summer, but Kaufman did not plan to direct them. Oscar Eagle, who had directed *The Cocoanuts*, was engaged to stage this new work; presumably, he was as capable as anyone of bringing order to a Marx Brothers performance. Following the pattern established by *I'll Say She Is,* this was to be a musical; Bert Kalmar and Harry Ruby, a songwriting team admired by Groucho, were commissioned to write the numbers. They met no opposition from Kaufman, since to him one songwriter was not much different from any other. As Harry Ruby once put it, ". . . playing a song for him was like playing to a dead man. There was no difference between playing it for George and playing it for the wall."[1]

Working with the Marxes was never easy, since it was all but impossible for them to stick to either a schedule or a script. But both Kaufman and Ryskind knew enough about them as individuals and as a group to construct a scenario that would show their well-established stage personae to advantage. That there would be trouble getting them to follow the script to the letter, especially on the road, was a dead certainty. But the brothers had, on the whole, respected the lines of *The Cocoanuts,* and the collaborators sweated through the summer days to create more "ad libs" for Groucho and Chico.

As before, they had a fifth important stage presence to account for, Margaret Dumont, who would move through the script with an elegant unconcern for the physical assaults of Harpo and the verbal thrusts of Groucho. She was a dignified society matron to the end. Kaufman and Ryskind imagined her character this time in her own home—a Long Island estate, of course —and made the occasion a weekend party. They gave her an appropriately grand name, Mrs. Rittenhouse, though that was more suggestive of the Main Line than the North Shore. For Groucho they invented the character of Captain Spalding, an African explorer just back from the Dark Continent, and the social catch of the season. Chico was to be Ravelli, an orchestra leader; and Harpo, the Professor, Ravelli's partner. Kaufman and Ryskind found a place for Zeppo as Spalding's secretary.

No plot for the Marx Brothers could be complex; the public that came to watch their cavortings and listen to their non sequiturs had no time for any business with a closer connection to Art in its upper-case sense than the specialty numbers of Harpo and Chico. For *Animal Crackers* the writers wanted to eliminate even those numbers, but were prevented from doing so by the brothers' stubborn determination when the show tried out in Philadelphia in October prior to the New York opening. Harpo felt that without his solo the show would lack beauty, and Chico insisted that if time was found for the harp solo, a piano solo (always the hit number of any Marx Brothers production) would have to follow.[2] The plot, like that of *The Cocoanuts,* turned on a theft. Not only does Mrs. Rittenhouse have Captain Spalding to show off to her guests, but she also has arranged a special viewing of a valuable canvas by one Beaugard. Among those present, in addition to the Marxes, are Roscoe W. Chandler, a financier who is also a noted patron of the arts; Mrs. Whitehead and Mrs. Carpenter, wicked sisters who, as hostesses themselves, are envious of the double coup of Spalding and the painting that Mrs. Rittenhouse has brought off; and, necessarily, two younger persons to provide for the romantic interest, one of whom, Wally Winston, is a gossip columnist for the *Morning Traffic.* Mrs. Whitehead and Mrs. Carpenter precipitate the action by arranging with Hives, the Rittenhouse butler, to substitute a fake painting for the original, thus confounding their hostess. In the end, the Marxes themselves are able to restore the true Beaugard and expose the substitution for the shabby trick that it is. Pretty young Arabella Rittenhouse becomes engaged to Wally Winston, much to the contentment of her mother, who shows a becoming lack of snobbery in the matter. John Parker, a young painter who also has made a copy of the Beaugard, but an excellent one, is recognized as a most promising artist and is to be launched on a career. It is the best of all possible worlds! Kalmar and Ruby were no more able to produce a hit song for this Marx Brothers show than Irving Berlin had been with *The Cocoanuts,* but in "Hooray for Captain Spalding" they at least came up with a catchy number that was to serve Groucho as a kind of theme song for years.

As before, Kaufman and Ryskind provided a flood of throwaway lines for the brothers that the audience was always ready to think were the Marxes' own invention. An exchange between Groucho and Chico in the first scene, with Margaret Dumont on hand to react with a puzzled expression, typifies the authors' style:

> MRS. RITTENHOUSE [*to Ravelli*] —You are one of the musicians? But you weren't due until tomorrow.
> RAVELLI We couldn't make it tomorrow. It was too quick.
> SPALDING You're lucky they didn't come yesterday.
> RAVELLI We were busy yesterday, but we charge you just the same.
> SPALDING This is better than exploring. What do you fellows get an hour?
> RAVELLI For playing, we get ten dollars an hour.
> SPALDING What do you get for not playing?
> RAVELLI Twelve dollars an hour.
> SPALDING That's more like it.
> RAVELLI Now for rehearsing we make you a special rate, fifteen dollars an hour.
> SPALDING What do you get for not rehearsing?
> RAVELLI You couldn't afford it. You see, if we don't rehearse we don't play, and that runs into money.

In a scene "in two" between Spalding and Chandler before the curtain, occurs this calculated "ad lib" for Groucho:

> CHANDLER Tell me, Captain Chandler—
> SPALDING Spalding; you're Chandler—you're Chandler, unless the program has been making a fool out of me.

It was Groucho's on-stage naturalness—behaving rather than acting—that caused the audience to think that he was shaping his own lines as he went along.

A disturbing element in the script is the character of Roscoe W. Chandler, whose resemblance to Otto H. Kahn was obvious in the extreme. The German-born Kahn, head of the investment-banking firm of Kuhn Loeb & Co., was one of the 1920s' most generous supporters of the arts, dipping into his capacious pocket for funds for the Metropolitan Opera, the Theater Guild, the Provincetown Players, and other institutional theaters, as well as for individual singers, playwrights, actors, and painters. He sought no self-aggrandizement through his benefactions; nor, though many of them were described as loans to the recipients rather than outright gifts, did he expect to be repaid. His generosity was too extensive to be concealed from the public, and because of it he was much admired. But in one other aspect of his personal life he had created mild annoyance in certain quarters. For what were apparently social reasons only, not conviction, he had given up the Judaism into which he had been born and had joined the Episcopal church. Kaufman and Ryskind, though no more devoted to the faith of their fathers than Kahn was, considered this deviation a fit subject for satire and made Chandler the possessor of a guilty secret: in younger days he had been Rabbi Cantor of Prague, where Ravelli had known him. Word of this reaches Wally Winston, who publishes it in the *Morning Traffic,* not realizing that Chandler owns the paper. It is an indication of the evolution of taste that the scenes involving Chandler, though no doubt amusing enough to the original audience, would in time lose their comic edge and become merely vulgar. Chandler, reading the *Traffic* as he eats his breakfast, spots the story about himself and at once becomes the stage Jew, excitable, lapsing into Yiddish, aquiver with self-pity. Though the same actor, Louis Sorin, played the role in the film version (1930), the character became less the conventional Jewish comedian, and references to his having been a rabbi were dropped. (Kaufman did not work on the screenplay; it is credited only to Ryskind, with continuity by Pierre Collins.)

As always, the brothers found their own occasions for laughter during the run of *Animal Crackers.* At their hotel in Philadelphia during the tryouts, they spent one hilarious night playing baseball in Groucho's room, abetted by Harry Ruby, whose love of the sport was legendary. Ruby pitched, and Groucho played first base.[3] On another night, at a party given for the cast by Kalmar and Ruby, the brothers relieved the tension that had built up in them during the performance by sailing plates of food out the hotel windows. When there were none left to hurl away, they eyed Ruby's piano and got it halfway through the window before common sense prevailed and they hauled it in again. Groucho and Harpo were not content to go quietly to bed, however. Harpo left the songwriters' suite, walked along the hotel corridor, banging his fist on every door that he passed, and then went down to complain to the desk clerk that some oaf was banging on the doors. Groucho, not wearing his stage moustache and therefore not recognizable, also went to see the desk clerk, complaining that a crowd in the Kalmar-Ruby suite was making so much noise that he, a tired businessman, was unable to get to sleep.[4]

Onstage, the brothers were as unpredictable as off. When the fit was on, they were quite capable of tearing Margaret Dumont's slip out from under her dress as a test of her composure. Unable to remain in Philadelphia for the entire pre-Broadway run, Kaufman left Ryskind and the songwriters to maintain order. They did their best, but night after night some piece of action not in the script would be presented to the audience. Sam Harris came to inspect the proceedings at a matinee and, provoked to irritation by what he witnessed, went backstage to complain to his stars in Groucho's dressing room. Pretending to be irritated in turn, they opened his fly, exposed his male member, and pushed him through the door before he quite knew what had happened. In New York the brothers continued to take liberties with the script, though there they ran the risk of doing so in front of Kaufman, who made it a practice to drop in on his plays. After one matinee performance at which they had departed from the script, he went backstage to protest. Groucho countered with, "Well, they laughed at Edison, didn't they?" Replied Kaufman, "Not at the Wednesday matinee, they didn't."[5]

At some point late in 1928 Kaufman collaborated with Ryskind again; the result, however, was only a sketch, "Something New," written as a spoof of the flashback, which had become an overused dramatic device. In 1929 Kaufman moved on to two new collaborators, Ring Lardner and Alexander Woollcott, each of whom he saw more of socially than he did of Ryskind. These were men whose companionship he especially enjoyed, despite the sharp contrast of their personalities with his own. They were also quite unlike each other. Lardner, tall, thin, exceptionally reserved, a heavy drinker, good-natured, easily offended by obscenities and *double-entendres,* the happily married father of four sons, was no more like Woollcott than matter is like antimatter. Nor did semiliterate ballplayers and prizefighters, the typical Lardner protagonists, have a place in Woollcott's florid, sentimental chronicles of hard-won success in the Horatio Alger vein. It is true that both in their time wrote about songwriters, but Lardner did so in such sardonic stories as "Rhythm" and "Some Like Them Cold," in which he offered piercing insight into the limitations of minor talent, whereas Woollcott's subject was Irving Berlin, whose rise from the Lower East Side he chronicled in a maudlin book. For the first half of 1929 Kaufman alternated work-sessions on projects with these writers, and without confusion. His left hand knew perfectly well what his right hand was doing.

The collaboration with Lardner was the first of the two to get under way. Kaufman had read "Some Like Them Cold," which was first published in 1921 in the *Saturday Evening Post* and was included in the volume of Lardner's tales called *How To Write Short Stories,* which Scribner's brought out in 1924. In the fall of 1928 he suggested to Lardner that they make a play out of it. The two had been friends ever since the establishment of the Thanatopsis Club, whose sessions Lardner frequently attended. Though bridge had superseded poker in Kaufman's favor by the late 1920s, he still saw Lardner on occasion, both in town and in Great Neck, where the Lardner family lived until the spring of 1928. The Swopes and Groucho Marx, as well as the Lardners, lived in Great Neck, and Kaufman went there frequently on urgent business: croquet.

One measure of the friendship between the Kaufman and Lardner families was the fact that in 1928 Lardner celebrated the vivacious personality of Beatrice in a *New Yorker* piece called "Dante and—," a far-fetched parody of Woollcott's style:

> George often says that Beatrice won his heart through his sense of humor. As they were walking up Broadway together, he spied a small eft on the curb and made as if to scrunch it.
> "Don't step on him!" cried Beatrice. "It might be Mary Pickford and her mother."
> Kaufman was then at work on the play *Dulcy,* and Beatrice collaborated with him under the name of Marc Connelly. (It has always been one of her foibles to use noms de plume. For a long while she signed herself Beatrice Fairfax in a newspaper column of advice to boys and girls; she assumed the name Beatrice Lillie when she appeared in the *Charlot Revue;* she has written many plays under the sobriquet of Owen Davis, and in 1926 she won the women's national tennis championship as Mrs. Bjurstedt, the former May Bundy.) *Dulcy* was a hit and George proposed.[6]

Having included "The Tridget of Greva" in *The 49ers* and having acted in "Dinner and Bridge" at the Dutch Treat Club's annual revue, Kaufman had already paid his respects to Lardner as a playwright. The zest for the irrational that Lardner revealed in those nonsense plays was not the quality that Kaufman sought from him on this occasion, however; he needed Lardner's ability to depict an idiosyncratic personality in the round in only a few pages. The story "Some Like Them Cold" is an exchange of letters between a young man from Chicago and a girl he picks up in that city's LaSalle Street railroad station while waiting for the train that will take him to New York. The young man, who signs his letters "Chas. F. Lewis," is fully revealed in these letters as unintelligent, uneducated, and self-centered, and thus one of the types suitable for the leading role of a Kaufman comedy.

Lewis's ambition is to become a famous composer of popular songs. Mabelle Gillespie, the girl, writes him everything she thinks he will want to hear: how funny his jokes are, and how famous she is among her friends for her sense of humor; how much she admires his industry, and how much she loves to cook, sew, and stay home nights; how impressed she is by his expectation of becoming rich, and how high is the value she sets on homemaking. At first each is desperate to make an impression on the other, but eventually hints creep into Lewis's letters that he has met another, "ice cold" girl. His last letter to Mabelle informs her that he is engaged, but at the same time that he would like to continue the correspondence. Her pathetic reply offers the transparent lie that somebody new has just entered her life who would certainly not approve of her writing to another man.

At first Lardner turned down the proposition, though not out of disrespect for Kaufman. He had just been stung, and badly, by George M. Cohan, who had produced a dramatic version of his baseball story "Hurry Kane" under the title *Elmer the Great*. Though only Lardner's name was attached to the play, it owed more to the heavy hand of Cohan than to Lardner. Impressed, as was the public at large, by Cohan's personality and versatility, Lardner had rashly signed a *carte blanche* contract that gave total control of the script to Cohan. The result was a sentimental comedy quite untrue to the original; after only forty performances it closed. It was to that grim experience that Lardner reacted when Kaufman approached him. Very soon afterward, however, he telephoned to say that he had changed his mind. What brought about the change was a spontaneous, altruistic impulse: he wanted to create a role for Florence Rice, the daughter of his good friend Grantland Rice.[7] When Kaufman agreed to this stipulation, they had made a deal. Work began early in 1929, with a view to an opening in the fall after some summer tryout performances. Sam Harris, the great friend and former partner of Cohan, was to produce, with no objections from Lardner. *June Moon,* the hit play that the collaborators delivered, worthy of their reputations though it was, bore only about a 50 per cent resemblance in substance to "Some Like Them Cold."

The collaboration proceeded without any problems other than those that might occur to any pair of writers putting together a Broadway play—that is, the need to revise and fine-tune the work until it would hold the audience. The initial requirement from Lardner's view—to make a part for Florence Rice—was quickly solved; she was to play a relatively small part, that of a jaded secretary. Of the two authors, it was Lardner whose hand was the more evident in the finished product. He wrote the first draft, submitted it to Kaufman for revision, and then went over the manuscript again to make a third draft with which they went into rehearsal.[8] Lardner often came to New York on weekends from Great Neck to discuss the revisions. When summer arrived and the Kaufmans rented a house in Manhasset, both writers came into town on weekends, leaving their families in the country while they themselves endured the heavy metropolitan weather for the sake of the play. During this summer Kaufman, who seldom drove, rammed the family car into the wall surrounding one of Manhasset's large estates, the home of Charles and Joan Payson. After this incident, he never took the wheel again.

Lardner was determined to have a hit this time, and his concentration strongly impressed Kaufman. In 1940 Kaufman reminisced about the experience of writing with him: "One of my collaborators, Ring Lardner, is dead. I think, perhaps from the standpoint of comedy, that that is the most unfortunate thing that has happened in the American theater."[9]

The script that finally opened on Broadway differed from the "final" draft edited by Lardner with which they went into production; it benefited strongly from the insights into the roles that the authors had gained from the rehearsals and the tryout performances. From the start, however, it was a conventional three-act comedy preceded by a prologue. Quite apart from the vast difference between this literary form and a story-in-letters, *June Moon* differs from "Some Like Them Cold" in its characterizations and its conclusion, which offers the pairing-off of the young man and the first girl, not the "ice cold" creature whom he later meets. In the prologue, the young man, now called Fred Stevens, meets the girl, called Edna Baker, not in the Chicago railroad station, but on a train en route to New York from Schenectady. Fred is now a lyricist, not a composer, and Edna works in New York as a dentist's receptionist.

What happens in the play is that, though Fred at first sees something of Edna in New York, he is very soon taken up by the hard and predatory Eileen Fletcher, the mistress of music-publisher Joe Hart, and must go through a period of anxiety in his emotional and professional life before he becomes engaged to Edna and has the pleasure of seeing one of his songs in print. Eileen is the sister-in-law of Paul Sears, who is on Hart's payroll as a composer, but has not had a hit in three years. The last one was called "Paprika" ("Paprika, Paprika, the spice of my life"). Were it not for Eileen's connections with Hart, Paul would be out of a job. He has written a new song, "Montana Moon," with a lyricist named Fagan—a man who is obviously extravagant, since he has put the moon and a state in the same title. But even with that lavish combination, Hart and his partner do not want the song. In need of a new lyricist, Paul teams up with Fred almost as soon as he meets him. Fred seems to be the right man for him, because he is young, energetic, and new to the scene. As a sample of his lyrical wares, he recites "Life Is a Game," which goes, in part,

> Sometimes the odds seem dead against you;
> What has to be, has to be,
> But smile just the same, for life is a game,
> And God is a fine referee.

In the course of the play Eileen, with the help of Sears and his malcontent, wise-cracking wife, Lucille, shows Fred the town, making him spend his very limited funds night after night in pursuit of local color for the lyrics he is supposed to write. He does not write about New York, however; instead, he and Sears write a love song, "June Moon," and Hart, who has found a new girl, accepts it because it will provide Fred with enough money in royalties to maintain Eileen's interest in him. At the final curtain, however, Fred is back with Edna, much to his relief.

Lardner loved popular music and had considerably more than an amateur's knowledge of song construction. He had written songs for Nora Bayes and Bert Williams in the teens of the century, and all through the 1920s he had hoped for the chance to write songs for a Broadway musical. (After *June Moon* he got his wish. Ziegfeld asked him to write some lyrics for *Smiles*.) Lardner knew enough about the popular-music profession, with its dozens of one-finger composers and semiliterate lyricists for each Berlin, Gershwin, Kern, or Porter, to create a script that for all its distorted characterization was clearly grounded in reality.[10]

Lardner wrote four parody songs for the show: two love songs and two novelties. The latter pair are offered in the script as the products of that sort of composer who insists, and possibly believes, that all the great songs were stolen from his works. In "Hello, Tokio," he writes about an American who is in love with the photograph of a Japanese princess and is trying to reach her on the telephone. The other is the lament of an unwed mother:

> I don't ask to share your life,
> Live with you as man and wife;
> All I ask is give our child a name—
> Not just a first name.

The love songs from the play were published by Harms, one of the leading houses, and were moderately successful. Of the two, "June Moon" and "Montana Moon," the former is the more lilting, and by no means a poor example of the songwriter's craft. Not entirely fair is the description of it given by the case-hardened publishing-house pianist, Maxie Schwartz: "It's a tune that's easy to remember, but if you should forget it it wouldn't make any difference." The covers of the songs allowed that they were "eavesdropped" by both Kaufman and Lardner, but in the program and printed text of the play they were attributed to Lardner alone.

A play on such a subject required wisecracks in abundance, and in *June Moon* they rattled like bursts from a repeater rifle. Maxie was given about half of them. The following is an exchange between him and Fred, who is so awestruck by the flavor and color of New York that he wants to write a song about its immigrant population:

> FRED . . . Take the Jews—do you know there's nearly two million Jews in New York City alone?
> MAXIE What do you mean alone?

In Act II, one of their exchanges goes:

> FRED Well, suppose "June Moon" is a big smash? What's the most we could make off of it?
> MAXIE It's hard to say. Take a sing like "Swanee River" and it's still going big.
> FRED Yeah, but that's because it was in a big production like *Show Boat*.
> MAXIE How's that?
> FRED And with that girl to sing it, that sits on the piano.
> MAXIE You're thinking of Ruby Keeler in *The Wild Duck*.*

More subtle—too sly in most instances to be effective out of context—were the countless quips assigned to Lucille, played by Jean Dixon. The most gifted member of the cast and, as the years would prove, the most durable, Jean Dixon was at first reluctant to take the part. When Kaufman offered it to her, she had just completed a run in a high-comedy role in George Kelly's *Behold the Bridegroom* and hoped to continue in such parts. Also, she had recently been disappointed that Kaufman would not let her play Julie in *The Royal Family*, a role she had coveted.[11] Nevertheless, she agreed to play Lucille. At first finding herself uncomfortable in the part, and getting no help from Kaufman with line readings, she recalled certain mannerisms of an inti-

---

* It is Keeler and *Wild Duck* in the version published by Scribner's. In the Samuel French acting edition Maxie says, "Sophie Tucker in *Strange Interlude*."

mate friend and used them in her characterization, thus suddenly making everything come right. For all its wryness, the part of Lucille is not altogether unsympathetic, and she was able to play it without alienating the audience. Blest with extraordinary clarity of diction, she gave each syllable its proper weight. Realizing their good fortune in having her in the cast, the collaborators introduced new lines for her in the rehearsal period. Yet, expert as he knew her to be, Kaufman never paid her a compliment—not during the run of *June Moon* or during the runs of two later plays of his in which she acted. Unable to utter such remarks, he later sought another way to show his thanks: in the 1930s he gave her a gold cigarette case with her name picked out in diamonds.

On July 30, *June Moon* opened in Atlantic City for a week's run, which was followed by a week in Asbury Park. These performances established that the script needed more work, since only Act I seemed to be in good order. Running into an acquaintance on the Boardwalk who asked him what he was doing in Atlantic City, Lardner replied, "I'm down here with an act." When the play was withdrawn after the Asbury Park engagement, the authors tinkered with the casting of minor roles, invented a new character, Miss Rixey, to be Eileen's successor in Hart's affections, and altered some of the existing dialogue. Sam Harris felt that Fred and Edna were too unsympathetic to hold the audience.[12] The collaborators had given them only one kiss, a peck in Act II that, according to the stage directions, "would easily get by the censors," and that was not enough of a show of affection. What the writers supplied, in an effort to appease their producer, was a scene in Act III in which the two characters reminisce about one of their outings together when a small boy spurned a dime offered him by Fred for finding Edna's lost watch, and when they topped off the day by visiting a flea circus. If Harris had required more sentiment than that, he would have had to find two other writers.

After a break of six weeks, during which they made these improvements and Kaufman was intermittently busy with *The Channel Road*, his collaboration with Woollcott, *June Moon* played the last week of September in Washington and the first week of October in Newark. All was then ready for the Broadway opening on October 9, these last two weeks of tryouts having brought further improvements in the script. In what was clearly an autobiographical short story, "Second-Act Curtain," published in *Collier's* on April 19, 1930, Lardner wrote about the last-minute work, renaming himself Booth; Kaufman, Chambers; and Harris, Rose; and referring to Vincent Youmans by the composer's own name. In the story, Rose tells his two playwrights after the Wednesday matinee in Newark that the second-act curtain needs fixing. Going into New York, Booth stops at a speakeasy to buy a bottle of whiskey, checks into a hotel, and begins thinking about the scene. He decides that it ought to end with a song, calls Chambers for an opinion, and gets Chambers's approval, provided the song is funny. After sleeping a while, he has a call from Rose, who does not approve of dropping the curtain on a song, because, for one thing, the play has too many songs already. But a good song comes into Booth's mind, and, fearing that it may not be original but something he has heard somewhere, he calls his friend Youmans to consult him about it. Youmans, hearing Booth whistle the tune, tells him that he had indeed heard it somewhere before: in the score of Youmans's own *Great Day*. Booth then falls asleep, to awake at seven in the morning with the empty bottle beside him and the telephone cord wrapped around his neck.

Apart from the ending, the story has the ring of truth about it. Moreover, the second-act ending as played on Broadway and published agrees with certain details of it. A music-minded window-cleaner plays "Hello, Tokio!" in Hart's offices as Maxie comes back into the otherwise empty room. Maxie, deciding that since the window-cleaner is doing *his* job, he should do the window-cleaner's, picks up the sponge and gets to work. Thus the scene has both a funny song and funny business. Though the programs show that the window-cleaner was in the play from the beginning, according to his biographer, Lardner invented this piece of business not after the Newark run, but after the summer tryouts. At that time, if this report is accurate, he took a room at a hotel, called for a piano, and gave a party, during which a window-cleaner came in and, apparently indifferent to the carryings-on in the room, proceeded to wash the windows.[13]

Though it may have been that Lardner looked for the solution to the second-act problem at the bottom of a bottle of speakeasy liquor, he kept good control of his drinking habit during the writing and rewriting of *June Moon*. This was a piece of work whose success he was counting on—not because he needed the money, but because he was more than a little stagestruck. With the Washington and Newark notices pointing toward a hit on Broadway, Lardner amused himself by writing a comic essay called "Let George Do It" for a flier advertising the play and also wrote some outrageous notes on the actors for the inevitable "Who's Who in the Cast" in the program. They are the work of a man who was having a good time. The flier reads in part,

> One difference between Mr. Kaufman and me is that he selects his collaborators at random (and a mighty pretty place, too), while I make it a rule never to work with anybody I can't call George. . . . Last year, as .

is almost too well known, I turned out *Elmer the Great* with George M. Cohan. This season I am teaming with Mr. Kaufman. And in 1930, I expect to pair off with George B. Shaw, an announcement which may surprise Bernie himself.

The following are samples of the cast notes:

> JEAN DIXON is a great favorite with the producers and authors because she won't accept a salary. "It's just fun," is the way she puts it. She makes a good living betting on the whippet races at Grant's Tomb.
> FLORENCE D. RICE is the daughter of Grantland Rice, the taxidermist. Miss Rice's parents have no idea she is on the stage and every time she leaves the house to go to the theatre, she tells them she has to run down to the draper's to buy a stamp. On matinee days she writes two letters (that's what they think). She is very proud of her wire-haired fox terrier, Peter, because on the night the play opened in Atlantic City he sent her a wire.
> JOHN BARRYMORE is one of the famous Barrymore triumvirate, consisting of "Lionel, Ethel and Jack." There was a difference of two dollars in what was offered him and what he thought he was worth, so he is not in this play, but sends regards.

The play ran through the season for a total of 273 performances. In mid-season Harris put together a road company; it played in Chicago for ten weeks and then made its way around the Midwest and California. The New York company also went on tour when its Broadway run was over. Harry Rosenthal, a professional pianist who, at Lardner's insistence, took the part of Maxie in New York, though he had never acted before, became something of a celebrity and ultimately got star billing in a company of the play that traveled the "subway circuit" in Brooklyn and the Bronx. The comedy became a stock-company staple of the early 1930s, was filmed, was broadcast on radio, and was eventually (in 1974) televised.

As much as Lardner had looked forward to the success of the play, it actually proved more than he could deal with. He had held himself under control too long, and no sooner was *June Moon* opened and drawing a line at the box office than he began a bout of drinking that lasted for three months. His health, always fragile, suffered a further weakening after this collapse. Nevertheless, his creativity did not desert him; as before, he continued to send a flood of stories and essays to national magazines, and began a new career at the *New Yorker* as radio critic. Kaufman, remaining fond of him personally and still much impressed by his talent, agreed to write another play with him. The protagonist was to be an alcoholic, though not an alcoholic writer. As he had with *June Moon*, Lardner intended to complete a first draft and send it to Kaufman for editing. But by the late spring of 1933 his health began a rapid deterioration, and he could no longer write. He had completed only the first act and a part of the second. On September 24 he died, aged forty-eight.[14]

With Woollcott on *The Channel Road,* Kaufman never had a chance of success. "Ball of Fat," by Guy de Maupassant, on which they based the play, had neither a plot nor characters of the kind for which he had a natural sympathy. Only the persuasiveness of Woollcott was responsible for the collaboration. He it was who promoted the idea that they should work together and suggested possible subjects. They arrived at "Ball of Fat" by the process of elimination, as Kaufman with a faint air of exasperation remarked:

> He [Woollcott] had, he said, six different ideas for plays. Five of them, I thought, were just terrible, and the sixth was Maupassant's "Boule de Suif." So that was the one we leaped at. No play ever dropped into its acts and scenes more rapidly, although there are a lot of people who think it might have been just as well if it had taken a little longer. Anyhow, it went quickly enough. Mr. Woollcott, it seems, had been nursing the idea for a long time, and came to the task with the whole thing pretty clearly in mind.[15]

Though they had been colleagues on the *Times* in former years and were still friends, they were an ill-matched pair—the sentimentalist and the cynic—and not much was likely to come from a meeting of their minds. Nor did it.

"Ball of Fat" is lean—a well-constructed, economical story. The setting is Normandy during the Franco-Prussian war. Some citizens of Prussian-occupied Rouen receive permission to leave their city by diligence for Dieppe, which is held by the French. The travelers represent all classes of society, down to the plump, handsome prostitute Elizabeth Rousset, the "ball of fat" of the title. During the tedious, weather-delayed journey, none of the other passengers will speak to her until it is discovered that she alone has brought food with her. Then, of course, their attitude changes. They eat her chicken and drink her wine, converse with her and learn that her reason for leaving Rouen is that she, an ardent patriot, cannot bear the sight of the Prussians. At the inn in the town of Totes, where they spend the night, the Prussian captain who is in residence refuses to let them pass on to Rouen unless Ball of Fat will grant him her favors. She refuses, shocked by the very notion. But after they have been delayed two days and the others present her with a host of reasons why she should change her mind, she allows the Prussian into her room. The next morning the company recommences the journey, but on this leg of it none of them will speak to Ball of Fat. Nor will they share their food with her, the only one who this time has forgotten—has been too rushed to remember—to bring along something to eat.

Writing years later to Burns Mantle about *The Channel Road,* Woollcott described it as being one-third de Maupassant, one-third Woollcott, and one-third Kaufman.[16] Yet this is a questionable distribution of credits, for the play would seem to have next to nothing of Kaufman about it, and rather more of Woollcott than of de Maupassant. Virtually every line is too studied and florid for the stage. If Kaufman edited Woollcott's orotund phrases with his customary, vigorous wielding of the pencil, one can only conclude that Woollcott prevailed upon him to restore the cuts. In addition to the heavy language, an unfortunate change was made in the plot. The ultimate, unsentimental humiliation of the prostitute was not allowed to occur in the play. Instead, poetic justice triumphs. Though Mlle. Rousset is snubbed by all the passengers after her sacrifice, only she and two nuns are allowed to continue to Dieppe. The deceitful Prussian detains all the others.

Kaufman and Woollcott labored over their drafts through the summer of 1929. At the outset, Woollcott asked to write alone; "and for a dollar I let him," wrote Kaufman, who at that point was polishing *June Moon* with Lardner prior to its Atlantic City opening. Early in July, though *June Moon* was set to open in Atlantic City on July 30, he and Woollcott sequestered themselves in the house in Katonah that Woollcott, the Kaufmans, and S. N. Behrman had leased as an occasional retreat. In August, when Kaufman was temporarily free from his duties with Lardner, he and Woollcott wrote the second act in Woollcott's apartment on the East River at 52nd Street and then wrote the third in the St. Regis Hotel, to which Woollcott had moved to escape the noises of the building going up in the vicinity of his apartment. When they were finished they took their manuscript to Arthur Hopkins, who more than ten years before had been so impressed with an army play by Woollcott as to hope that he would eventually write one for Broadway. Hopkins took *The Channel Road* at once and rushed toward production, but requested a new third act. By that date, in September, Kaufman was preoccupied with *June Moon,* then playing in Washington. Woollcott came to Washington, where Kaufman managed to find two days to refurbish the third act with him.[17] Satisfied, Hopkins assembled his cast and began rehearsals, directing the play himself.

Altogether, *The Channel Road* was a hurried job. It opened on October 17 (only a week and a day after *June Moon*) to respectful but tepid reviews. Most of the critics complained about the quality of the acting, apart from that of Anne Forrest as the prostitute and Siegfried Rumann as the enemy officer. Even so, the public curiosity over what the combination of Woollcott and Kaufman might turn out kept the play going for sixty performances. This was not an unimpressive number in view of the notices and in view of the general falling-off of business—show business and all other kinds—that began on October 29, when Wall Street panicked.

Before the season reached its end, two more Broadway productions had Kaufman's name on them. The first of these was a new version of that disaster of 1927, *Strike Up the Band,* which Edgar Selwyn had never entirely abandoned. It was his opinion that the book might work if its satiric bite were made somewhat less sharp. Kaufman himself was thoroughly tired of the script, however, and had no wish to become involved with it a second time. He made no objection to Selwyn's suggestion that it be turned over to Morrie Ryskind for revising, with credit going to himself as the author of the original. Selwyn, Ryskind, and the Gershwins, who wrote some new numbers and struck out some of the old ones, readied the show for a trial run in Boston. The play opened there on Christmas night in 1929 and came to Broadway on January 14, 1930. The comic team of Bobby Clark and Paul McCullough were the stars. Ryskind's alterations included a switch in the product over which the United States and Switzerland go to war. Previously it was cheese, now it was chocolate, and this sweetening of the plot rendered the show more digestible. Ryskind also made the war take place in a dream of the American manufacturer, so as to increase the element of fantasy. The producer, the song writers, and the adapter performed their respective tasks well, for, despite some critical cavils about the disjointedness of the book, *Strike Up the Band* had a run of 191 performances. Not so Bertram Bloch's *Joseph,* on the other hand, which Kaufman directed and John Golden produced. The play opened on February 12, 1930. Starring and substantially backed by George Jessel, this was a comedy about the biblical Joseph told in the debunking style of the 1920s that had been much more effectively employed in such works as Donald Ogden Stewart's *Parody Outline of History* and Eugene O'Neill's *Marco Millions.* Jessel played the title role, as Brooks Atkinson put it, "with all the racial blandishments of a ticket speculator,"[18] in other words, as a Jewish caricature. Thirteen performances and it was gone.

During this season, in which the stock-market exploded and many Broadway houses were turned over by their bankrupt owners to Hollywood and "wired for sound," Kaufman could claim that at least he had had one hit and that, no matter how badly his speculating friends had been hurt by Wall Street, his own finances were not a source of worry. To the producer Max

Gordon, who lost virtually everything, he offered the loan of $1500, leaving himself for the moment with only $1000 in the bank.[19] But royalties would come flooding in from his many copyrights, new plays would roll out of his typewriter, and pleas would never cease to be made for his directorial services, no matter how severely theatrical production would be curtailed as a result of the market debacle. In the summer of 1930, as stock prices reached new lows and unemployment figures rose in a steep trajectory, he took the step that until then he had always wished to avoid: he resigned his post at the *Times*.

——10——

Enter Moss Hart

> I have a pet theory of my own, probably invalid, that the theatre is an inevitable refuge of the unhappy child. Like most pet theories, this one also contains the fallacy of too broad a generalization. But certainly the first retreat a child makes to alleviate his unhappiness is to contrive a world of his own, and it is but a small step out of his private world into the fantasy world of the theatre.[1]

Thus wrote Moss Hart at fifty-five in his memoirs, *Act One,* looking back over a lifetime to the beginnings of his earliest fascination with the stage. For nearly three decades, since his first theatrical success, *Once in a Lifetime,* his talent and industry had been lavishly rewarded with fame and money. Since receiving the Pulitzer Prize in 1937, he had also had prestige. More recently, marriage and fatherhood had further enriched his life. But the beginning had been bleak, and contentment had been a long time in coming.

Hart was born in Manhattan on October 24, 1904, and raised in the Bronx. His mother's father, who lived with the family, was an English Jew who had come to the United States as a young man. Hart's own father was also an English Jew. Hart's mother had met him on a trip to England that she made with her sister and parents when she was eighteen. It was a journey undertaken in the face of great poverty and paid for out of the savings of twenty years. The senior Hart followed the eighteen-year-old girl to America, but did not marry her until ten years later. His father-in-law was a cigar-maker, and he entered the same trade. The household, established in a Bronx apartment, was one in which creature comforts were utterly unknown. There was never enough money; often the family ate dinner by candlelight, not out of some notion that it was fashionable, but because no one had a quarter to feed the gas meter. On such nights they would find their way to bed in the dark. Usually the family kept boarders to help with the rent.

In addition to Moss, his parents, and his grandfather, the family included a brother five years his junior and an aunt, his mother's sister, whose *folie de grandeur,* improbable in such a place, was so severe that not only did she refuse to assist in the household tasks, but she was constantly waited on by Moss's mother. Inevitably, tensions were acute. Young Moss enjoyed his grandfather despite the old man's self-centeredness and stubbornness, but he could not communicate with his father and brother, and did not care much for his mother. His aunt, whom his father loathed, was cast out of the apartment when Moss was ten for giving away some books that had been presented to Moss's father by a departing boarder. Despite her airs, the aunt had provided the only moments of relief from this claustrophobic environment that Moss had as a small child, for with money sent her monthly by her English relations she often took him to the theater. They did not go to Broadway, however. Their playgoing was limited to such fare as the Bronx provided. Still, it was theater, and very early Moss decided he would make his career in the theater—and make enough money to compensate for the deprivations of his childhood.

Leaving school after the eighth grade, young Hart went to work to help support the family. Before he was twenty-five he wrote a play that was produced on the road and collaborated on another that ran briefly in New York. He discovered that he possessed only slight talent for acting, but that he was a good director, though in that capacity he worked only with little-theater groups. His chief claim to fame, and it was hard won, was as a social director in the Jewish resorts in the Catskill Mountains, the "Borscht Circuit," as the entertainment press called it. As a social director, he was obliged to plan amusements for the guests all summer long: to direct plays, to attend to the comfort of those awkward or homely young women ignored by the male guests, to act in sketches, to invent themes for parties—in general, to keep things hopping—and to add to everyone's pleasure by being an entertaining, sociable creature at every waking hour. It was not a thankless job, since the guests enjoyed his effort on their behalf and took to him personally, but it was not what he hoped to do for the rest of his life. Moreover, the money it brought in over the summer was not so much that he could afford to be idle the rest of the year; when it was off-season in the Catskills, he directed amateur troupes. Nor could he yet afford to install the family in spacious living quarters. They had moved from the cramped apartment in the Bronx to a somewhat preferable one in Brooklyn, but the new place was hardly lavish.

The way out of Brooklyn, the way out of the Catskills and penury, ran through Hollywood. In 1929 Hart had visited Hollywood only in his imagination, which was fed by the film section of *Variety*. What he read there gave him the idea for a play. The film world was making an adjustment to sound, that innovation with which it had only flirted until the moment in 1927 when Al Jolson, in *The Jazz Singer*, said, "You ain't heard nothin' yet," and began to sing. The reception of this film made inevitable the domination of the motion-picture industry by sound, but, as *Variety* reported, the studios were not prepared for it. There was much talk of voices that were too high-pitched or too low, of virile-looking actors with effeminate voices, of foreign-born stars with guttural accents. Since many of these performers were in Hollywood under high-paying contracts, the studios were as eager as they to find the means of improving their voices. Accompanying the problem of the sound of the actors' voices was the problem of finding words for them to speak. Not a single Broadway playwright of proven talent was ignored by the studios in their search for literate dialogue. Uncomfortable at the prospect of leaving New York, some ignored the appeals—Kaufman among them—but others went out in such numbers that the studios did not always have a project for them when they arrived. This made good copy for *Variety*, and Hart, reading it, decided that it would also make a good play.

In the plot that he devised, three vaudevillians, experienced but still young, decide to give up their act and go to Hollywood, where they pass themselves off as veteran teachers of elocution. Two men and one woman make up the team, and they are a mixed lot. One of the men is dim-witted but sweet-natured, and a compulsive eater of Indian nuts; the other, a born leader, is the go-getting type; and the woman, the most intelligent of the three, is given to speaking ironically on all occasions. In Hollywood they have their initial moment of glory, their later moment of exposure as the charlatans that they are, and, since this is a comedy, their ultimate triumph. George Lewis, the nitwit, is paired off with Susan Walker, a would-be actress who is as bird-brained as he, and the other two troupers, Jerry Hyland and May Daniels, also make a pair, but only after a period of estrangement. Suffusing every scene is the sense that the powers of Hollywood had so little understanding of what they were doing that the success of any picture was purely accidental. This impression was in part created by the *Variety* reports of the new travail over sound, but the notion that the studios were run by big-spending, blow-

hard ignoramuses and egomaniacs had begun to circulate almost with the
origin of the film colony in the teens of the century and had already been the
stuff of countless satirical novels, plays, and even films. *Merton of the Movies,*
for example, had delighted the public in all three forms. Hart, as he later
revealed in his memoirs, was at first reluctant to turn his hand to comedy
when he set out to be a writer, but was urged to do so by a play publisher.
When he decided to try comedy, he knew it would have to be in the tradition
of Kaufman and Connelly. The team had already broken up by that date, but
the memory of their work remained with Hart, as it did with other aspiring
young writers and the public. He finished the Hollywood play, *Once in a
Lifetime,* in just three weeks.

Over the next ten months, Hart learned the first lesson of the theater—
that plays are not so much written as rewritten—and he learned it from a past
master at the art of rewriting. The second half of *Act One* is a generous tribute to Kaufman, with whom Sam Harris and his aide, Max Siegel, persuaded
him to collaborate on a new version of the script. As soon as he finished the
first draft, Hart read it to his little-theater troupe in Newark (one of three he
was directing at the time, the other two being in Brooklyn) and was so be-
dazzled by their enthusiastic response that he took the advice of Dore Schary,
a member of the troupe, who told him to submit it to the other theatrical Harris, Jed, who was still at his peak and was soon to add to his prestige with a
widely praised production of *Uncle Vanya.* Much to young Hart's astonishment, Jed Harris agreed to meet with him and read the script. But after keeping him waiting in a hotel lobby for two days, Jed Harris said nothing about
producing *Once in a Lifetime* when they met, though he commented on it in
depth, and did not hand back the typescript. Meanwhile, without consulting
Hart, a friend of his, Lester Sweyd, had given a copy of the play to an agent,
Frieda Fischbein, who in turn took it to Sam Harris's office. (Though Hart
ignores the issue in *Act One,* Fischbein apparently gave the play to a number
of other producers first. Both Sweyd and Fischbein believed that their efforts
on Hart's behalf were misrepresented in his book.)[2] When Sam Harris, in
California at the time, received the play, he was quick to read it, but thought
it would serve best as the framework for a musical. He was willing to produce
it as such, with the music to be composed by Irving Berlin. Hart responded
quickly and negatively. Though soon enough he would collaborate with Berlin on a show called *Face the Music* and in the years to come would write or
direct musicals with songs by Cole Porter, Rodgers and (Lorenz) Hart, Kurt
Weill, and Lerner and Loewe, he could not at this moment, in his twenty-
fifth year, endure the threat to his authorial pride of Harris's suggestion. An

extraordinarily good-natured man, Siegel revealed no indignation over this rebuff and merely passed the word on to his chief. Sam Harris, obviously impressed with the script, offered a second suggestion. He would produce the play if Hart were willing to collaborate on a revision with Kaufman, assuming that Kaufman would agree to the arrangement.

Before this partnership could be formed, Hart thought it necessary to tell Jed Harris of the turn of events, since Jed Harris had not definitely rejected the script. This gesture on Hart's part nearly cost him the production with Sam Harris. On the telephone Jed Harris remarked that Hart was probably correct to let Sam Harris have the play, since he, Jed, would be putting all his creative energy into *Uncle Vanya*. He suggested that Hart would do well to pass on to Kaufman his recommendation of the play. To Hart this seemed a good idea, for despite his faithful reading of *Variety* and his pastime of sharing theatrical gossip with other stagestruck young men over afternoon coffee, he had never heard that Kaufman and Jed Harris were not on speaking terms. An unbridgeable rift had opened between the two men. The origin of their mutual hostility, if any single incident could be said to have begun it, was the typical outburst of fury with which Harris greeted the publication in the *Times* on January 13, 1929, of parts of an unfavorable out-of-town review of his production of S. N. Behrman's *Serena Blandish*. In the 1920s the *Times* often printed road reviews of incoming plays as a service to readers who might wish to book tickets in advance, and Kaufman as drama editor made the selection. Nothing could cool off this feud once it began; it was white-hot and unending. Neither party to it could ever resist the opportunity of speaking out against the other, though there is no record of Kaufman's ever attempting to spoil a young person's chance by recommending his work to Harris. When Hart, knowing that the script was already in Kaufman's hands, brashly but rather fearfully telephoned to give him Harris's message, he heard Kaufman reply that he would not be interested in any play that interested Jed Harris. Having said this, Kaufman hung up.

The least damning construction one might put on this devious plot of Jed Harris's would be that he recognized the potentiality of the script and wished to do Kaufman out of a good thing. Hart had done nothing to give him offense—except, to be sure, having decided to work with Kaufman. It was fortunate that Kaufman had already been sent the script. He picked it up, read it, and decided it had something worth developing, despite Jed Harris's recommendation. He notified Max Siegel that he was willing to go ahead on the project with Hart.

When Hart decided, almost thirty years later, to set down these events in a book, he forgot, it would seem, that he had written about them once before. The earlier account is much briefer. It is an essay titled "Men at Work," and, with an essay by Kaufman called "Forked Lightning," it was printed as an introduction to the volume of six of their plays published in 1942. There are discrepancies between the two accounts. In 1942 Hart recalled that he and Kaufman began their daily sessions, which he called "Days of the Terror," at ten in the morning; in 1959 he moved them up an hour, to eleven. In 1942 he wrote that, after sequestering themselves in a Philadelphia hotel room to revise the script of *Once in a Lifetime* before the Broadway opening, the two of them went for a stroll at three in the morning and spent half an hour on a children's carousel; in *Act One* it was he alone who did this. In 1942 he wrote that he had conceived the "idea" (his word) of *Once in a Lifetime* while attending a performance of *June Moon;* in *Act One* he wrote that he had already begun to write the play when he saw *June Moon.* (During the Broadway run of *Once in a Lifetime* Hart told an interviewer that he had seen *June Moon* on its opening night from a balcony seat.)[3] In both accounts, errors in dates leap off the page. But the important fact, which renders irrelevant such matters as whether the two men got down to work at ten or at eleven, was that the script that Hart offered Kaufman was no shoddy, neophyte effort. For some ten months, from December 1929 to September 24, 1930, the date of the Broadway opening, they toiled over the play in Kaufman's fourth-floor study.* This uncomfortably attenuated stretch of time included two dismal weeks in late May and early June when a version of the play was tried out in Atlantic City and in Brighton Beach, Brooklyn. Never before had Kaufman worked with a man so much younger than he, and a stranger of unproven talent, at that. Shy as always with strangers, Kaufman prefaced his remarks to Hart with "Er," which to Hart's ears became a form of address. Kaufman was powerless to unbend so far as to call his young colleague "Moss," and perhaps thought "Mr. Hart" too formal for the situation. For Hart also the relationship lacked definition: straight to the end of this first collaboration he addressed his collaborator as "Mr. Kaufman," and apparently he was never invited to do otherwise. Still with some rough edges to his personality, Hart, then a heavy smoker of cigars, was insensitive to the fact that Kaufman was severely tried by the waves of smoke that filled the study. But the author's talent was evident in the original script, and its gleam shone through the smoke. Though during the many months of work they at least twice altered the structure of the play and refined its plot, many of the

---

* The Kaufmans were then occupying a house at 158 East 63rd Street.

wittiest lines retained were in Hart's original script, and most of the suggestions for revisions of the structure originated with him.[4]

In his years as a subway commuter from the Bronx to his various Manhattan jobs, Hart had formed the habit of reading the *World* and took special
pleasure in F.P.A.'s column, particularly the Pepysian effusions with which
on a Saturday Adams recounted his adventures of the week. Hart knew by
reputation, as did all of Adams's readers, the entire Algonquin set and fancied
that theatrical success would bring him entrée to that charmed circle. A taste
of what might lie ahead was provided by Beatrice Kaufman, who, some
months after the writing had begun, invited him to a "tea," as a cocktail gathering could still be termed in 1930. Hart's first meeting with her, which occurred by chance one day as he was climbing the stairs to Kaufman's study,
had no magical effect upon him, but the party to which she eventually invited him, and at which he saw for the first time in the flesh those rare creatures so glowingly described week after week in "The Conning Tower,"
replenished his meager store of energy for the completion of the script before
the late spring tryouts.

At this time Hart became deeply attached to Beatrice, and before long she
grew equally fond of him. Their mutual fondness never took physical expression, apart from friendly caresses, but, once developed, it was undying.
He admired her look of sleek sophistication and was touched by her evident
concern for his well-being and her hope for his success. For his part, he was
precisely her type: young, neurotic, handsome, and Jewish—perhaps a little
less polished, less touched with finesse, than Kaufman had been when they
met, but bearing a resemblance to him nevertheless, since both were wiry and
tall. If one may trust contemporary photographs, Hart had very good looks,
with dark wavy hair coming to a peak over a wide forehead, and with pin-
nacled eyebrows that hovered above dark eyes. The pictures also showed
some youthful pudge, but this soon vanished. It made no difference to Beatrice that at this time Hart sometimes mispronounced or misspelled words, or
that his suit sleeves stopped too far above his shirt cuffs; these were signs of a
deprivation for which she hoped he would soon be compensated.[5]

The purpose of the late spring and summer road tours offered by a producer
had always been the uncovering of flaws in the fabric of the play, which
could then be repaired in time for a fall opening. Though *Once in a Lifetime*
had gone well enough in rehearsal, its flaws gaped widely when the curtain
went up before paying customers. Some minor problems were evident in the
casting, though the company included Aline MacMahon and Hugh O'Connell, solid actors, in the most important of the three leading roles—May Dan-

iels and slow-thinking George Lewis. Lawrence Vail, the Broadway play-wright hired by Hollywood and promptly forgotten, was played by Kaufman himself, in a brave gesture for one so terrified of opening nights as he. For some reason he chose on this occasion to bill himself as "Calvin Brown," a pseudonym adopted the season before by Marc Connelly as the writer of a revue called *Say When*. He was recognized, of course, as soon as he came on stage, and his very presence was good for a laugh. He played the part well, if not brilliantly. His performance was all that redeemed the second act, the only act in which in this version Lawrence Vail took part.

To his and Hart's dismay, the first-night audience in Atlantic City on May 16 found little to laugh at after the first act, and even that act was lacking in continuity. Once the point was made that the trio were determined to crash Hollywood as voice teachers, not much of value seemed to be happening on stage. Yet the scenes were crowded with people and movement. There were caricatures almost without number: the powerful executive whose favorite adjective was "colossal," the waiter hoping to succeed as a scriptwriter, the actress (Susan Walker) of no talent whatever who was inclined to recite Kipling's "Boots" to anyone willing to listen, the grafting female gossip columnist, the nervous performers whose vocal tones might be all wrong for such a choosy instrument as the Vitaphone. There was also something familiar about George Lewis's career; in keeping with the formula established by Kaufman and Connelly ten years earlier, he was sure to become a success in spite of himself. All this added up to just too much of a stir; moreover, Kaufman's pacing of the action resulted in a thunderous performance, though at that there were some dead spots. Nor was there any depth to the relationships, or any conflict of importance. On looking over what they had created together, Kaufman told Hart during the Brighton Beach week that he had nothing more to give the play, and that Hart was free to take the script and give it as it now stood to any producer who was willing to mount it.

Hart knew that if Kaufman and Sam Harris dropped a script, no producer in New York would pick it up; Kaufman's offer was absurd, as he must have known, though he had not meant to be unkind. With the resilience and the ability to improvise that his Catskill education had given him, Hart went home to the family's drab Brooklyn apartment, slept soundly, and awoke with the intention of developing a scenario for new second and third acts that might appeal to Kaufman before he took up something else, as he assuredly would do within a few days. The Catskill resorts, to say nothing of Brooklyn and the Bronx, were places where one also developed *chutzpah,* and Hart in bearding Kaufman with his scenario revealed that he had plenty of it. But the years as social director had benefited him in still another way: in the acquisition of charm. That all-important quality, so frequently remarked upon in later years as the keystone of his personality, must have served him with Kaufman in this new effort to interest him in the play. They were still not quite friends, despite the months of work, but neither did coolness exist between them. When Hart presented himself at Kaufman's house on the Monday following the Brighton Beach closing, he was permitted to recite the scenario. Kaufman was struck with its inventiveness and got on the telephone to the Harris office with a message that the play was to go back on the road in the early fall in preparation for a Broadway opening.

Because Beatrice had sailed to Europe for the summer with her daughter,[6] the family residence was untenanted except by Kaufman. Thus, at Kaufman's suggestion, Hart moved in with him for the rewriting. With an end put to the dull subway trips to and from Brooklyn and also to the forced frivolity of the Catskills, his life was rapidly changing. He had one last weekend at the Flagler, the resort hotel where he had worked during the preceding summer, and at that time he decided he wanted no more of that world. He also had the doubtful pleasure of seeing another of his plays, *No Retreat,* performed in midsummer by a troupe on Long Island; a turgid piece about the rivalry between two actors who are father and son, it was optioned for Broadway but was never produced.[7] Otherwise, the summer was a long stretch of workdays on the top floor of the Kaufman house.

For the new version, which opened in Philadelphia on September 1, the team tightened the second act by drastically reducing the role of the aspiring scenarist and removing his female collaborator altogether, threatening May and Jerry with the closing of their elocution school, and somewhat strengthening the role of George Lewis, who had gone over well in the tryouts. For the last scene of the third act Hart invented a Hollywood restaurant, the Pigeon Coop, in which the patrons sat in what appeared to be cracked eggshells.* This was intended to give a visual lift and provide a final instance of Hollywood's vaunted opulence. Before that was shown, it was to be made clear that George Lewis, as the director of the first picture starring his ingenue friend, Susan Walker, shoots the wrong script, forgets to tell the electricians to light the crucial scenes, and, with his beloved Indian nuts, is responsible for curious popping noises on the sound track—and yet turns out a film that is pronounced a triumph by the critics and becomes a hit of "colossal" proportions.

In addition to reshaping the script, Kaufman and Hart recast several of the

---

* Hart refers to it as the Pigeon's Egg in *Act One.*

parts. Of all the substitutions, including the actors playing the roles of Jerry, Susan, and the gossip columnist Helen Hobart, that of greatest consequence was the replacement of Aline MacMahon by Jean Dixon in the part of May Daniels. It was not dissatisfaction with MacMahon's performance, which had been generally praised, that caused the writers and Harris to make this change. Hart had designed the role with Dixon in mind after witnessing her adroit delineation of the wisecracking Lucille Sears in *June Moon,* and from the outset he, Kaufman, and Harris had tried to persuade her to take it. She had been tempted by it, and pleased by their attention, but had felt that if she accepted the part, she would forever be typecast as a sardonic "dame." However, when she attended a dress rehearsal before the company left for Atlantic City, she was so taken with the role that she expressed regret that she had let it slip by.[8] Neither Kaufman nor Harris needed to hear more, for despite the merit of Aline MacMahon's performance, the addition of Jean Dixon's name to the cast would provide a degree of insurance. A good trouper, MacMahon took her release from the play without a show of bitterness and in time was rewarded with opportunities to resume the part on the West Coast and in the film version.

Among the original actors who were retained was Kaufman himself, the famous playwright who played the famous playwright, and by his appearance he gave a lift to the sagging second act. But his decision to continue in the role meant that at last he would have to resign from his post at the *Times,* since he could not take his place on stage six nights a week and fulfill his duties as the paper's drama editor. During the two weeks of the tryouts, the *Times* docked his salary for absence for the first time in the thirteen years that he had held the job.[9] In August, before the start of rehearsals, he and the paper came to a friendly parting.

In Philadelphia the collaborators found that their summer exertions had resulted in only a partial improvement of the script. Though they now held the audience through the first and second acts, they detected a sharp letdown in the third. There was no question about bringing the play into New York, but a serious one about its chance of succeeding there. In the second rewriting the personality of May had been deepened and her relationship with Jerry more sharply defined than in the early versions; this at least was to the good. She was permitted to leave the wisecracking posture occasionally, and she and Jerry were given a conflict whose resolution contributed to the tone of the play at the final curtain. Even so, audiences left the theater dissatisfied. In the end it was Sam Harris who provided a clue to the trouble. He had a showman's ear—one trained, that is to say, to catch the modulations of a script. To Hart he confided his concern over the very noisiness of the play; not once in it, he complained, did the audience have a chance to relax. Seizing on this, Hart redesigned the third act, removing the Pigeon Coop, which at a cost of $20,000 had proved to be nothing more than an expensive sight gag. To provide the desired moment of calm in the swirling action, he invented a scene between May and Lawrence Vail, who happened to be traveling back to New York on the same train, Vail boarding it in Needles, Arizona, where he has been taking a rest cure in a sanitarium for writers abused by Hollywood. Their Pullman car is the same one in which May, Jerry, and George had been seen on their way to Hollywood in Act I. In this new scene, May gets the Los Angeles papers to read the reviews of George's picture and finds, to her astonishment, that it is a hit. She then decides to return to her partners, who love her in their different ways.

Kaufman was reluctant at first to introduce these extensive revisions, for the Philadelphia run was nearing its end when Hart offered them, and the actors had already been subjected to almost daily changes in the dialogue. But, impressed by Hart's plea, he did so. He himself was responsible for one line. On the night that the train scene was first introduced, he warned Jean Dixon he was going to speak a line that was not in the script. This turned out to be Vail's jaded response to one of the rave reviews: "The whole thing couldn't be a typographical error, could it?" It brought down the house.[10] A few days later, on September 24, the play reached Broadway, as would not have happened had not Hart been determined to get it there. It was an unequivocal hit. After taking his bows as a member of the cast, Kaufman unexpectedly stilled the applause and said, "I would like the audience to know that eighty percent of this play is Moss Hart."

Unused as he was to the grind of giving eight performances a week, Kaufman eventually tired of his role. At first, however, he enjoyed himself in the part, and with good reason, since the audience always greeted his appearance with applause, and he had some of the play's best lines. A running gag (invented by Hart and present in the original version) was the frequent sight of a uniformed page bearing a sign announcing the whereabouts of the studio head: "MR. GLOGAUER IS ON NUMBER FOUR [OR FIVE OR SIX]." Vail, furious that he can never get an appointment to see this great man, finally shouts at the page, "Wait a minute. Now I'll give you a piece of news. I'm going to the Men's Room and if anybody wants me I'll be in Number Three." This speech usually rewarded him with the biggest laugh of the evening. Early in the run Kaufman wrote a piece for *Theatre Magazine* called "How I Became a Great Actor" in which he spoofed his performance:

Of course it was a herculean task. The part was a long one, and I had only until September to learn it. Many a night I sat alone in my room until the wee hours, gulping down cup after cup of strong black coffee, pounding the words into a brain already wearied by the long grind. But I kept on, and when the opening night arrived walked onto the stage of the Music Box and spoke every "if," "and," and "but." And if it had not been for a certain pardonable nervousness I would have spoken some of the other words, too.

The rest is history, of course, but in the interest of fair play there are two or three points that I would like to set straight. It has been said in some quarters that I could not have been so *terribly* good, or else people would have taken the horses out of my carriage and hauled me to my home, the way they did with Jenny Lind. As a matter of fact every effort was made to do this, and the plan was defeated only because they were unable to get the right horses.

It seems that the horses who do this work were on another job that night—I believe some star was opening down on the East Side, although it would not surprise me if certain people deliberately arranged for the horses to be elsewhere. (There is a good deal of jealousy in the theatre— I've found that out.) At the last minute there was talk of taking the gasoline out of a taxicab, but it was realized that that wouldn't be the same thing.[11]

All this was fun, but only for a while. In April 1931 he relinquished his role to Robert B. Sinclair, a young man on Sam Harris's staff, who hoped eventually to be a director. On May 4 Hart took over the role from Sinclair.

Both Robert Sinclair and Hart had played the role of Vail in California before they assumed it on Broadway. Sid Grauman, the celebrated Los Angeles showman and theater-owner who had built the Chinese Theater on Hollywood Boulevard, arranged with Sam Harris to present *Once in a Lifetime* on the West Coast. Hollywood, having long since learned to take jokes at its expense, wanted to see the play. Hart and Sinclair codirected the company, and Hart was scheduled to play Lawrence Vail, since California, if it could not get Kaufman, demanded at least to have Hart. Unfortunately, Hart fell ill before the Los Angeles opening, which took place on January 27, and had to surrender the role to Sinclair. Soon, however, he recovered and went on in the play, which even without him had been doing excellent business. Carl Laemmle of Universal Pictures was impressed enough with the comedy to buy the film rights, though this masochistic gesture was decried by some of his associates in the business.

It was Hart's name that held the audience, not his performance, which was poor (and did not improve in New York).[12] But in spite of his uninspired acting and some ironic remarks to interviewers that Beverly Hills and the studios lived up to his expectations, he was promptly taken to the bosom of the film colony. The lions of Metro-Goldwyn-Mayer, the richest of the studios, stalked him with a contract. It was only a question of time before he succumbed. He discovered, as other playwrights had done before him, that with only one hit to his credit the options available to him were pleasantly if bewilderingly numerous.

He also rejoiced to find that his sudden fame was accompanied by a large weekly inflow of cash. His arrangement with Kaufman gave him 60 per cent of the royalties from *Once in a Lifetime* to Kaufman's 40 per cent. With two companies doing business at close to capacity, a movie sale, and a sought-after talent to ensure the future, he had never to worry about money again. On the very day after the opening, even before the royalties had begun to come in, he responded to the promise of security evident between the lines of the reviews. From their shabby Brooklyn apartment he moved his mother, father, and brother to Manhattan, insisting that they leave behind them their furniture, their clothes, even their kitchen implements. The break with the old life was to be complete; there were to be no reminders of the twenty-six years of want. He found many ways to make up for past deprivations, and without hesitation he acted on them. No more subway rides, for one thing, only taxis! No more ill-fitting clothes, only the best tailoring the city had to offer, and silk shirts and silk underwear, and above all, gold: gold cufflinks, gold tie clips, even gold garter clasps, until it seemed that he had turned into a shimmering blur of precious metal. To his circle of friends, which soon included Kaufman and Beatrice and the set in which they moved, it was a pleasure to watch. Taking a kind of parental pride in his achievement in the theater, they thought it only fitting that he should try to make up for the drabness of his early youth. Amazingly, he remained unspoiled; he was prodigiously open-handed with those to whom he felt closest, sometimes leaving them wondering if, despite his steeply rising income, he could actually afford the presents which he showered on them.[13]

But the rapidity and depth of the change in his way of life proved punishing to his emotions. His adjustment was difficult. To accomplish it he turned to psychoanalysis in about 1933 and continued with it for many years. Beatrice, always sympathetic, and herself a patient in analysis at the time, was the one friend to whom he turned most freely in moments of crisis. She never failed him, but she knew, as did he, that progress could only come through the analytic sessions, not through the give and take of their conversations and letters. Perhaps of all the uses to which he put his new wealth, this expenditure was the wisest of all, since not only did it make possible the continuation of his career but, eventually, the sharing of his life in marriage.

But all that, the unhappiness and its vanquishment, lay in the future when the reviews of *Once in a Lifetime* came in. Hart suffered no diminishment of his capacity for work; like Kaufman, he seemed to thrive on it. Even before the opening, Kaufman suggested that they collaborate on a second play, though he did not have a subject in mind at the moment. Hart did have some subjects ready for exploring, but he doubted the wisdom of working with Kaufman again, or at any rate so soon, if he was to develop a distinctive talent.[14] Yet it was inevitable that they should work together again, in view of the success of their first collaboration and the compatibility of their talents. Before they did so, however, Hart, sorting over the offers and propositions that sped his way, decided first to do the book for a musical, *Face the Music,* which Irving Berlin would provide with songs and Sam Harris produce. After that, there was the attractive proposal from MGM to come out and strengthen some feeble properties in its possession.

Hollywood was in pursuit of Kaufman also. For years he had been deaf to offers that he make the trip west and work on screenplays, but some executives at Paramount who had witnessed his performance as Lawrence Vail had other plans for him. They asked whether he would care to act in a film. The studio was preparing a picture, *Tarnished Lady,* in which the leading character was to be a society woman financially embarrassed by the Wall Street plunge and desperately in need of a job. The role had been assigned to Tallulah Bankhead. Opposite Bankhead's character was her employer, the Jewish owner of a department store. Paramount dangled this part before Kaufman, but not even with the lustrous star as a lure was he tempted to bite. Nor would he have had to travel to California to make the picture, since it was to be shot in Astoria, Queens. In his place the studio hired Osgood Perkins, who gave a sauve, professional performance.[15]

11

Max

G.S.K., who knew his G.B.S., sometimes referred to his friend Max Gordon as "the comparable Max."[1]* Kaufman's wit had an acid bite when he was capricious, as he was in these instances. He admired Gordon, one of Broadway's most energetic producers, and profited from his investments in Gordon's offerings. But Gordon, no matter how heavily laid on was his brash, "show-biz" manner, possessed a nature sensitive to slights. This was a fact that Kaufman chose to ignore when the mood for irony possessed him. Yet he could be solicitous of Gordon's well-being, whether the problem overtaking the producer was financial or, more serious and more frequent, a nervous collapse. Gordon, respectful of Kaufman's theatrical skill and grateful for his concern, was also impressed by his strict moral sense as it revealed itself in their business dealings. A man who kept his promises and was proud to be known as such, he was happy to find in Kaufman someone who did the same. His word for Kaufman was "honorable."[2]

Gordon, born Mechel Salpeter in New York in 1892, produced one-act plays for the booming vaudeville circuits of the 1920s before he struck off independently as a producer of Broadway plays and musicals. During the 1920s, with his partner Al Lewis, he was associated with Sam Harris on several productions, including John Colton's *Rain* and Samson Raphaelson's *The Jazz Singer*. Though Lewis and Gordon were a highly successful team, leading all other managements in the production of one-acts, Gordon wanted to be on his own, with full control over his productions. The year in which

* Kaufman, of course, was alluding to Shaw's estimate of Max Beerbohm—"the incomparable Max."

he chose to assert his independence was 1930, when his bank account had shrunk to almost nothing in the wake of the crash and outside financing was difficult to find. Nevertheless, he succeeded in getting together the funds needed to stage an intimate revue, *Three's a Crowd*, which ran for eight well-paying months in the unpromising 1930-31 season. Max Gordon was on his way.

Though he did not become Kaufman's regular, "official" producer until after the death of Sam Harris in 1941, Gordon had come to know Kaufman well during the 1920s through Harris and was associated with him on numerous projects during the 1930s. Both Kaufman and Moss Hart invested in his productions, as they did in Harris's, and became his advisers, as they were to Harris. Kaufman often complained about Gordon's repeated telephone calls to him, which seemed to reach him at inconvenient times, and, more often than not, it seemed, when he was in the bathroom. At least once in this long association the producer requested advice too late to use it: "George," said Gordon after the failure of a play about Napoleon, "remind me never to do another play where a fellow sits down and writes a letter with a feather." Sometimes Kaufman and Hart advised his writers, as on those occasions when they directed plays for him, as well as on other occasions when they did not direct but dropped in on rehearsals and tryouts, as they constantly did when Gordon produced Clare Boothe's *The Women* in 1936.[3] In 1938 they let their names appear as associate producers with Gordon on *Sing Out the News*, a political revue. In 1931, in the hope of following *Three's a Crowd* with a new revue that would ride the wave of its popularity, Gordon for the first time turned to Kaufman, and Kaufman agreed to supply him with sketches.

The idea of approaching Kaufman originated with Howard Dietz, who had written the lyrics to Arthur Schwartz's songs for *Three's a Crowd*, as he also had for *The Little Show* and *The Second Little Show*, both produced by Tom Weatherly and Dwight Deere Wiman. All three revues were "little" shows in the sense that the casts were small and the scenery, though fresh and innovative, was not spectacular. The shows were a reaction against the ornateness of the *Follies*, the *Scandals*, and the *Vanities*, whose producers were out to dazzle the eye of the audience with all that money could buy in the way of feathers, beads, and metallic fabrics, in addition to a lavish roster of big-name talent. The common ancestor of the more intimate productions was *The Garrick Gaieties*, a revue with songs by Richard Rodgers and Lorenz Hart that the Theater Guild offered in 1925. One quality that most of these shows shared with the extravaganzas of Ziegfeld, George White, and Earl

Carroll was that the authorship of the sketches and songs was shared by a number of writers. This meant that, no matter how appealing the individual numbers were, the point of view and over-all tone were not always well-defined, as might be true of an anthology of poetry whose compiler had no principle of selectivity to guide him. When Gordon turned to Dietz for a new show, Dietz replied that he would participate only if the producer agreed that all the songs should be by Dietz and Schwartz and all the sketches by Dietz and George S. Kaufman, whose *The Still Alarm* had been one of the most applauded sketches in *The Little Show*. Dietz also wanted Fred and Adele Astaire in the cast. Gordon assented. The title ultimately chosen was *The Band Wagon*.[4]

As it happened, Gordon had nothing like the money for such expensive talents as Kaufman and the Astaires, though he took a chance and signed them up. The situation heated almost to flash point on the day when Kaufman brusquely bearded him with the rumor that the money for the revue was not on hand. This was the same George Kaufman who had come forward with the offer of a loan when Gordon's sinking stocks had nearly pulled him under in the market crash. But that had been personal, and this was business. Finally Gordon got the necessary cash from ticket brokers in exchange for his promise of choice seats for their clients when the show opened.[5]

In addition to the Astaires, the stars in the cast included the Viennese dancer Tilly Losch and two adroit comic actors, Frank Morgan and Helen Broderick. The Astaires, popular musical-comedy stars for more than a decade, were the chief drawing power, but, as it was known that Adele would leave the cast before the end of the run to marry an Englishman, Gordon and Dietz wanted to show Fred to good advantage without his sister. Therefore he was given a dramatic dance number with Tilly Losch, "The Beggar's Waltz." It was not overlooked that Losch was a talented solo dancer; for her, Dietz and Schwartz wrote what proved to be the strongest song in the show, "Dancing in the Dark." Taking a chance, Gordon asked a very young designer, Albert Johnson, to create the settings. When Johnson's plans were complete, they included two revolving stages, one placed inside the other, that could move in opposite directions. These were used to excellent effect as a merry-go-round in the number "I Love Louisa." Equipped with such stages, *The Band Wagon* was somewhat more elaborate than the earlier Schwartz-Dietz revues, though it avoided the razzledazzle of the *Follies* and its progeny. So happy were Gordon and Johnson with the revolving stages that they got copyright protection for them and inserted a note in the program to warn other producers against the unauthorized use of them.

Dietz was an adept lyricist; he was equally at home with comic and sentimental material. A laconically witty conversationalist, he had also developed
a terse writing style, the result of years of experience as head of advertising
for Metro-Goldwyn-Mayer. When he and Kaufman began their collaboration, Kaufman was still acting in *Once in a Lifetime*. It was Dietz's practice
to come to the theater after the performance, when the two would go over the
material. The final drafts were Kaufman's, but Dietz furnished many of the
ideas for the sketches, as well as lines. In keeping with the taste of the time,
the writers did not ignore the bedroom and bathroom when searching for material. In "The Pride of the Claghornes," for example, a Southern gentleman
expresses outrage that the girl whom his son intends to marry is a virgin. In
"The Great Warburton Mystery," a spoof on detective stories, it is not a finger-
print that reveals the culprit when a murder is investigated, but the imprint
of his posterior on a cushion. In "Pour le Bain," so much admired by Gordon
and the writers that they placed it immediately before the finale, a woman
(Helen Broderick) visits a supplier of plumbing equipment to buy a toilet
and finds that the errand is almost too embarrassing for words. But not all the
pieces were of that stamp. Frank Morgan, delivering a monologue in front of
the curtain, alluded to the recent problems with the police that had beset
Earl Carroll, whose *Vanities* were notoriously nude: "For a while we thought
we would have the girls undressed and call the show "The Patrol Wagon."
At another point in the evening Morgan went over a plunging financial
chart and told the audience, "In a few years from now these are going to be
known as the good old days. What is called down in the dumps today will be
known as up in the dumps by *that* time."

Before the show went into production, Dietz told Max Gordon that he
wanted his own name to precede Kaufman's in the credits. Kaufman, of
course, was not present when Dietz made this bold move, and Gordon at first
was at a loss as to how to deal with it. He suggested that Dietz toss a coin
with him to solve the problem. Happily for himself as well as for Kaufman,
Gordon won the toss, and the credit line that went into the programs was "A
Revue by George S. Kaufman and Howard Dietz." Dietz was also given credit
for the over-all supervision of the show, a task that Kaufman could not undertake because of his acting commitment. The sketches were staged by Hassard
Short, who, having long since given up acting, was much in demand as a director of musical productions. Kaufman was present as often as possible, however, for it would not have been within his character to stay away altogether.
For some members of the cast his presence during rehearsals was unnerving,
since he sat in unbroken silence, his head in his hands, giving no sign of ap-

proval whatever. Tilly Losch and the Astaires, though seasoned performers, were convinced that he did not care for their work.[6]

But as it happened, the work of everyone who contributed to *The Band Wagon* merited approval. That the revue would be a major hit was evident at the dress rehearsal; Noel Coward, whose presence in New York was occasioned by rehearsals of *The Third Little Show,* for which he provided some material, shouted "Bravo!" after every number of this competing revue.[7] The notices that followed the Philadelphia opening on May 12 were so warm that Kaufman said he would be content to bring them to New York and leave the show out of town.[8] But the New York notices were quite as good. Though the run of 260 performances fell eleven short of that of *Three's a Crowd, The Band Wagon,* with its sumptuous Dietz-Schwartz numbers, its revolving stages, and its dancing stars, became the more memorable of the two, earning a prominent place in American theatrical history. It also would hold a prominent place in the affection of Max Gordon as the show in which he first worked with Kaufman.

——12——

Political Perspectives

The season of 1930-31, the first full season of the Great Depression, witnessed a downturn in Broadway business unprecedented in the history of the American stage. Producers were hit by a double onslaught, for not only were their sources of financial backing severely reduced because of the Wall Street crash, but their audience was lured away to film theaters, where for as little as a quarter the hard-pressed entertainment-seeker could watch a feature picture, a newsreel, an animated cartoon, and possibly a second feature. For those without enough loose change for even this low-priced feast, radio, with increasingly sophisticated programming, offered entertainment that, after the initial outlay for the set itself, cost nothing at all. The Shubert organization, the giant among theater-operating concerns, went into receivership. One by one the long string of playhouses on 42nd Street, the heart of the theater district in the 1920s, went over to films. Radio also took over many legitimate houses.

Nevertheless there was still a Broadway, and new producing firms came into being to bring to the stage new visions of American life as transformed by the collapse of the economy and the threat to peace created by the rise of totalitarianism in Europe. Such new organizations as the Group Theater and the Theater Union maintained their existence only by dint of a continual struggle for financing and decent scripts, but they managed to provide some of the most provocative and best-staged works of the decade. The national government's own Federal Theater also offered many worthy social plays during its four-year lifetime. The prestigious Theater Guild, searching for high-quality works by Americans to place on its schedule, discovered that the most interesting new American plays were based on political and economic themes, and duly accepted them. Whether produced by insurgents or mainstream organizations, the most memorable new plays of the decade offered reflections on a nation experiencing incisive social change.

For Kaufman and the writers whom he knew best, the Depression was a national calamity affecting their social conscience but not seriously threatening their personal financial security. Kaufman's talent remained as marketable after the crash as it had ever been. Finding a producer had not been a problem for him since his first hit, and inasmuch as Sam H. Harris, who had always been esteemed for his show-business acumen and his honesty, was able to ride out the shock to the economy with loyal backers, Kaufman could continue with the producer whom he then preferred to all the rest. His collaborators of the 1920s were equally blest. Marc Connelly's *The Green Pastures* opened in February 1930 and ran for 640 performances in New York; on the road it reaped a second fortune, and in the sale to Hollywood, a third. Edna Ferber's fiction was in constant demand for serialization in national magazines, for publication in book form by Doubleday, and for filming. Herman J. Mankiewicz, valued as a screenwriter, shuttled between Metro-Goldwyn-Mayer and Paramount, two of the richest studios. Ring Lardner poured out a flood of short pieces for the *New Yorker* and other magazines, though his health was in cruel decline. Morrie Ryskind was less certain of his economic future than the others at the beginning of the decade, but, as the result of more collaborations with Kaufman and the offer of a good Hollywood contract, he was soon out of danger. The thirteen million Americans reported to be unemployed at the worst of the Depression did not include these writers. Both Kaufman and Ferber suffered large paper losses in the Wall Street debacle, but the shock for both was mitigated by the public acceptance of whatever writing they offered.

The development of social concern took place more rapidly and was more extensive with some members of the Kaufman circle than with others, as was to be expected. The Algonquin was no longer their meeting place, largely because they were all too busy to take time off for two-hour lunches, but the members of the Round Table set were still in touch and aware of one another's activities. Ferber became increasingly indignant over the unchecked rise of Hitler, until in 1939 she published an outspoken volume of memoirs, *A Peculiar Treasure,* as a gesture in defiance of anti-Semites, foreign and domestic, individual and organized. Two of the Algonquin set, Donald Ogden Stewart and Dorothy Parker, became thoroughly radicalized before the decade's end, the former abandoning his old acquaintances altogether in favor of a new set of Communist party members and followers. Among Kaufman's playwriting friends of many years, those whose works revealed the deepest awareness of the changes affecting American life were S. N. Behrman and Robert E. Sherwood. Among new friends to share in this awareness and bring it to the stage was Lillian Hellman. Nor was Kaufman's own writing untouched by the trouble and discontent felt across the nation. Always impressed by the dedication of Eugene V. Debs, the early Socialist leader, in 1932 Kaufman cast his vote for Norman Thomas, the Socialist presidential candidate, and acknowledged the fact in print.[1] Though he did not vote Socialist again, he remained a political liberal, supporting Roosevelt in the campaigns of 1936, 1940, 1944, and, on the municipal level, favoring Fiorello La Guardia, for whom Beatrice became a campaign worker. During the 1930s Kaufman contributed seven essays to the liberal *Nation* and one to the radical *New Masses.*

It was Morrie Ryskind who, of all his major collaborators, was the most politically minded. In the beginning a liberal of the old school that harbored distrust of big government, he became frankly conservative in 1940, when Roosevelt announced for a third term, an act in which he saw a threat to the American democracy. But, in 1930, he believed that biting satire on governmental folly was a kind of theater fare an intelligent public would accept, and in that view Kaufman concurred.

On January 15, 1930, the second night of the run of *Strike Up the Band* as revised by Ryskind, Kaufman and Ryskind stood at the back of the Times Square Theater to view the performance. This was the first Broadway musical of the 1930s, and it was going well. The reviews published earlier that day had left no doubt that the show would be a hit. Yet neither writer was particularly pleased with it, despite the merit of the performances and the excellence of the Gershwins' score. What troubled them was the dilution of the satiric quality of the original book as written by Kaufman in 1927. Though Ryskind had accomplished the feat of transforming a failure into a success, he was no more pleased with the new, soft-edged version than Kaufman was. While they were standing side by side, Edgar Selwyn, obviously delighted to have produced the show, came up and observed that the first, hard-hitting version could never have filled a Broadway house as this one was doing. His remark had the effect of a challenge. Turning to Ryskind, Kaufman said, "Let's do one just for ourselves. We'll get it produced somehow." With that, they decided to write a satiric musical on American politics in which nothing would be smoothed down or held back.[2]

Though Kaufman was preoccupied with the revisions and rehearsals of

Once in a Lifetime for almost the entire first eight months of 1930, he found the time to confer with Ryskind. For a working title they hit on *Tweedledee,* which would bear out the theme that the candidates of the two major parties were as indistinguishable as Lewis Carroll's Tweedledum and Tweedledee. As for the plot, it would center on a presidential campaign in which the major issue was the choice of a national anthem. With this somewhat arid scheme in mind, they invited the Gershwins to join in the project. The choice of songwriters was shrewd, not merely because of the brothers' mounting fame, but because George Gershwin's rhythms and Ira's lyrics could be counted on to impart a brassy modernity to the finished piece. But demands on the Gershwins' time were as heavy as those on Kaufman's. While the playwrights were weaving the plot, which they did in hours that Kaufman snatched from his ongoing sessions with Hart, the songwriters were creating the score for *Girl Crazy,* which Vinton Freedley expected to offer in the fall, and in April they signed a contract with Fox to write the songs for *Delicious,* a vehicle planned for the studio's favorite romantic team, Janet Gaynor and Charles Farrell. For this project it would be necessary for the Gershwins to go to Hollywood in November, as soon as *Girl Crazy* no longer required their attention. Nevertheless, the two teams arrived at a tentative arrangement, and Kaufman and Ryskind set to work on a scenario which would provide the brothers with cues as to where the songs might be placed. George Gershwin liked the idea of composing the competing anthems, which he thought should be sung contrapuntally as a first-act finale.[3]

As Ryskind and Kaufman sorted out more ideas for the plot, a problem with what they had so far invented suddenly made itself felt. The problem was that the plot offered no romantic interest whatever, but only the intellectual substance of the idea of the electorate foolishly falling into a state of anxiety over which of the two nearly identical parties was the better. It was Ryskind who first became aware of this lack. He insisted that they throw out the battle over the anthem and contrive another plot on a subject that would bring some romance into the script.[4] What they settled on was the most direct and sensible of solutions. The campaign would have to do with romance, and one of the presidential candidates, the protagonist, would be promoted by his party as a man in love and about to be married, and therefore the candidate for whom a right-thinking electorate should and would vote. The uninspired title *Tweedledee* was dropped in favor of *Of Thee I Sing,* one nicely suited to a musical about an issue presumed to be of national importance.

The second scene of the final script of the musical reflected Kaufman and Ryskind's debate over this issue. One can almost catch echoes of their conversation while reading it. In a smoke-filled room the national committeemen of the party (unnamed, of course), whose candidate is John P. Wintergreen, try to find a campaign issue. Hoping to hear the authentic voice of the people, they ask the chambermaid to tell them what she cares about most in life. "Money," is her prompt, Kaufmanesque response. But that, say the committeemen, is too common a concern to serve as an issue. What else does she care about? "Well, maybe love," she replies. They reject this at first as merely foolish, until suddenly it begins to seem just possibly right:

> WINTERGREEN Put women into politics and that's what you get. Love.
> GILHOOLEY Love!
> FULTON (*Slowly*). What's the matter with love?
> THROTTLEBOTTOM [the Vice Presidential candidate]. I like love!
> FULTON People *do* care more about love than anything else. Why, they steal for it, they even kill for it.
> WINTERGREEN But will they vote for it?
> FULTON You bet they will! If we could find some way to put it over— why, we could get every vote. Everybody loves a lover; the whole world loves a—(*Stops as he gets an idea; looks fixedly at Wintergreen*)
> WINTERGREEN What's the matter?
> FULTON I've got it.
> THROTTLEBOTTOM He's got it!
> FULTON You've got to fall in love!
> WINTERGREEN You're crazy!
> FULTON You've got to fall in love with a typical American girl!

With love thus becoming the fulcrum on which the plot turned, everything in the show settled into place.

In the fall, as soon as *Once in a Lifetime* was launched and Kaufman had no other professional duties than his eight performances a week as Lawrence Vail, the two playwrights composed a scenario that ran to fourteen pages. They gave a copy to the Gershwins to take to Hollywood with them. The brothers read it and liked it, but Ira was puzzled by one detail: what did the P. in John P. Wintergreen's name stand for? "Why," said Kaufman, "Peppermint, of course."[5]

The playwrights also gave a copy of their scenario to Sam Harris. The producer was in Palm Beach, his favorite retreat, when it reached him. Kaufman and Ryskind were doubtful as to whether Harris would care to undertake the production, inasmuch as the work made an attack on all three branches of government and did so on the grounds of the venality, the egomania, and (in the instance of the Vice President) the sheer stupidity of those at the top. On the other hand, they had been careful to avoid alluding to any real officeholders, past or present, with the exception of a mild reference to Coolidge. Harris wired back, "It's certainly different." Kaufman rightly interpreted this message as an agreement to produce.[6]

In California the Gershwins got to work on the score sooner than Kaufman and Ryskind knew. Ira was inspired to add "baby" to the play's title and used the entire phrase in a short, antisentimental lyric to serve as a combination campaign song and pop "ballad." His brother supplied this lyric with an upbeat melody that would work as an anthem or march, if such was needed, as well as a love song. The brothers also worked out the tune in which the ingenue Diana Devereaux proudly admits to being the illegitimate daughter of an illegitimate son of an illegitimate nephew of Napoleon. As was usual with him, George Gershwin could not refrain from playing the title song to friends who asked to hear his latest work. His pleasure and skill at the keyboard had long since become a part of his legend, and it was impossible to keep him away from the piano at any social gathering if the premises contained one. Thus it happened that reports of the brothers' progress were carried back to Kaufman and Ryskind by friends returning from visits to the West. They themselves had to wait until late winter, when the Gershwins returned, before hearing the two songs.[7]

No further progress on either the script of *Of Thee I Sing* or the songs took place until the summer of 1931. Kaufman was still acting in *Once in a Lifetime* until mid-April, though with decreasing enthusiasm as the weeks crawled by, and George Gershwin occupied himself with the orchestration of his newest concert piece, the *Second Rhapsody*. Also in the early months of 1931 Kaufman and Howard Dietz began their collaboration on *The Band Wagon*. When he dropped out of the cast of *Lifetime*, Kaufman suddenly found himself with altogether too much time on his hands. He turned to the stack of plays in need of doctoring that was always on his desk. One of the scripts was *Hot Pan*, the work of Edward J. Eustace, a young writer who used the pseudonym Michael Swift. Kaufman looked it over and decided it had possibilities.

Hot Pan had reached Kaufman through an unusual channel. Apart from the occasional sagging script that he might read through at the request of an author with whom he was on friendly terms, the plays that he considered as candidates for the Kaufman touch were brought to him by producers. But *Hot Pan* was delivered to him by a dress manufacturer. It happened that in 1928 Isidor Polisuk had seen the play at the Provincetown Playhouse, where it opened on February 15 and remained for nineteen performances. *Hot Pan*, a satiric comedy set in California during the gold rush, made a savage attack on American greed. For good measure the author threw in the six other deadly sins as well. The American way with Latins and Indians who had prior claim to desirable land, one miner's villainous pre-empting of another miner's stake, the neglect in the courtroom of due process, the venality of the church: Swift dealt with these matters and more, making the mining camp of the title a microcosmic image of the entire nation, which, in the mood of the 1920s, he saw as destroying its spiritual self in the hectic process of economic expansion. Polisuk enjoyed *Hot Pan* very much and was unhappy when it closed. Two years later he gave $100 of the profits of his dress business to Swift for permission to have the play rewritten by an experienced dramatist.[8]

When Kaufman agreed to rewrite *Hot Pan,* he said that the trouble began in the third scene of Act I, and that only about one-quarter of it was satisfactory as it stood.[9] (That was the approximate percentage of what he had considered to be satisfactory in *Once in a Lifetime,* which on first reading he had pronounced not bad.) Apparently neither he nor Polisuk entertained the notion that he should rewrite the play with Swift, the original writer. His suggestion was that Laurence Stallings be brought in as his collaborator. The two writers had never been close; nor were they often in each other's company, though Stallings had been one of the original members of the Round Table set. But the aggressive masculinity that stamped Stallings's prose made him the appropriate writer to collaborate on *Hot Pan.* He agreed to work with Kaufman, and Harris agreed to produce the script in the fall. Polisuk, believing he was onto a good thing, put up $15,000 toward the production. Kaufman also invested in it, as he was in the habit of doing with his plays.

Though busy with *The Band Wagon* until it opened on June 3, Kaufman spent many days of the late spring tugging Swift's play this way and that with Stallings, and through the summer, though resuming work with Morrie Ryskind and the Gershwins on *Of Thee I Sing,* he continued to meet with Stallings. During most of the summer Beatrice was in Europe again, once more accompanied by Anne, leaving Kaufman comfortably established in a rented house in Manhasset. The play, retitled *Eldorado,* went through three revisions. After the last, in Kaufman's opinion, it was still not right, but it was in sufficiently promising shape for him to press Harris for a fall opening. Polisuk also felt that the script was inadequate and, swallowing his disappointment, suggested to Kaufman that they cut their losses and drop it. But Kaufman persisted, reasoning that before an audience they would find solutions to the problems that still lingered. This, after all, was the purpose of tryout performances. Harris arranged for the production to open in New Haven on October 19, splitting the week with Hartford and proceeding the following week to Newark. He stinted nothing on the production, hiring—with Kaufman's say-so, of course—such able actors as Osgood Perkins, Esme O'Brien-Moore, and young Will Geer, among a cast of fifty. Settings were designed by Cleon Throckmorton. With Kaufman and Stallings sharing the direction, the large cast went into rehearsals in September.

Talent and industry notwithstanding, *Eldorado* at the New Haven opening seemed, to both playwrights and their producer, to be nothing less than a dire mistake, and the reviewers for the New Haven *Register* and the *Journal Courier* offered little in the way of encouragement. The play was formless, hinted the reviewers; despite the sharp characterization, the barbed dialogue, and the great number of satiric thrusts, it was a static performance. Nor were the next two cities on the schedule warmer in their reception. Nothing was to be done except to close down in Newark. For some three months afterward, Kaufman continued to entertain the hope of taking up the script again. In the winter, however, he decided conclusively to drop it. He then told Polisuk that he had nothing more to give the play. Late in 1932 it was reported in the papers that Morrie Ryskind and Robert E. Sherwood expected to revise the Kaufman-Stallings script for a new producing firm, but nothing more was heard of this project. In fact, nothing more was heard of *Eldorado* in any regard until January 26, 1937, when a suit instituted by Polisuk against Kaufman came to trial.

The gist of Polisuk's contention was that Kaufman had failed him twice, the first time by refusing to abandon the script in the summer of 1931 instead of rushing into production with a feeble last act, and the second time by not persevering after the Newark run. Suing to recover the $15,000 that he had put into the production, he asserted that Kaufman had not played fair because he had allowed the two hit musicals, *The Band Wagon* and *Of Thee I Sing,* to dominate his thoughts. In reply, Kaufman maintained that Polisuk's argument regarding the musicals was not to the point, because in his own opinion he had not let his work on them prevent him from giving his full power of invention to *Eldorado.* Either a writer had the lucky flash of insight that provided a solution to a play's problems, or he did not. He said that had an idea offered itself, he would have been happy to make a fourth version, because, though it was true that he had two hits on Broadway at the time, he would have been delighted to have three. As it was, he had spent a good deal of time already on *Eldorado,* and had nothing to show for it. After listening to these arguments, Judge Ferdinand Pecora decided the case in Kaufman's favor. It may have been the first case in which a backer sued a playwright for not writing a hit.

No sooner did *Eldorado* close in New Haven than Kaufman put *Of Thee I Sing* into rehearsal. From the beginning it had the mark of success on it. With George Gershwin's composition of the *Second Rhapsody* completed, he and Ira were ready to finish the score of the musical as soon as Kaufman and Ryskind handed them a typescript of the book. They did so in August 1931. It took the playwrights only seventeen days to turn their fourteen-page scenario into a two-act book. Those were not consecutive days of concentration, but were spread over five weekends at Manhasset, interrupting Kaufman and Stallings's struggle with the intractable *Eldorado*. Once they had the book to work from, the Gershwins rapidly completed the score. By early fall it was ready, and George Gershwin was delighting his friends with it at Sunday night parties in his Riverside Drive apartment. Kaufman and Ryskind, worried by this overexposure of the score, warned him that if he kept it up the audience would think the play was a revival. Kaufman was in the habit of cracking jokes about this compulsion of Gershwin to show off his latest songs, though aware that the jokes would have no effect whatever. After *Of Thee I Sing* had opened, he remarked to a reporter that with the comedian Joe Cook he was working on a new invention that might solve the problem. (Cook had already invented a shower that never got you wet.) "It's a device for keeping composers away from the piano until after the show is produced," Kaufman explained. "It will probably require the services of eight men. We thought at first about a device for keeping the piano away from the composers, but that, we decided, might be too difficult." Kaufman also said that he had an idea for a new competition to add to the next Olympic games: a race by twelve composers to reach a piano placed fifty feet away. As always, he was grudging in his comments on the songs and unhappy about losing playing time to them. If the Gershwins could reprise a song in the second act, why, he asked, would it be wrong for him and Ryskind to repeat a funny scene? Moreover, he made it clear that he did not care for the tacking on of the vehement "Baby!" to the phrase "Of Thee I Sing."[10]

In consultation with Kaufman, Harris developed a nearly flawless production. For the role of John P. Wintergreen the team chose William Gaxton, a popular musical-comedy performer, and for Alexander Throttlebottom, the mousy Vice President, Victor Moore, the corpulent, ungainly comedian whose quiet, tentative delivery never failed to please the audience. The role of Mary

Turner went to the film actress Lois Moran, the young woman whose personality F. Scott Fitzgerald drew on for the characterization of Rosemary Hoyt in *Tender Is the Night*. The reviews were to bear out the wisdom of these choices, though to many critics the popularity of Gaxton, a wooden performer, would remain a show-business mystery.

For the tryout run Harris booked the show only in Boston. It opened in that city on December 8 to excellent notices, word of which whetted the appetite of the extensive New York following of both Georges. In Boston and again in New York George Gershwin doubled the excitement of the opening night by conducting the orchestra. Among the opening-night celebrities in New York was Jimmy Walker, the city's strutting mayor, who experienced the questionable pleasure of seeing his mannerisms mimicked on stage by Gaxton as Wintergreen. Raves greeted the show, ensuring a long and profitable run even in the depths of the Depression.

A lampoon of national politics, when it reached Broadway *Of Thee I Sing* stood at too great a remove from reality to be dagger-sharp. It was not quite the piece the writers had envisioned; Kaufman's original book for *Strike Up the Band* had a keener edge. In the new show the names alone of the President and Vice President softened the effect of the whole. Moreover, at some moments the plot situations, far from being stern satire, were in danger of tumbling over into a pit of banal farcicality, and especially in those scenes involving the humbling of the nine ancient Justices of the Supreme Court. At the outset of the run Gaxton and Moore lowered the tone by departing from the original dialogue for the sake of easy laughs. Infuriated by this, Kaufman stopped it with a reprimand to the actors and a warning that the stage manager would report any further violations of the script directly to him. However, their performances were never wholly free of face-making and exaggerated intonation.[11] Yet despite these occasional lapses on the part of the playwrights and the team of comedians, and an occasional distracting Yiddishism in Ira Gershwin's lyrics, the new musical offered more wry comment than the Broadway audience was accustomed to hear on the tendency of the major parties to let trivial side issues dominate their campaigns and the habit of officeholders to seek self-aggrandizement. Through it all, George Gershwin's lively music never failed to provide support for Kaufman's rapid pacing of the action. Seldom on the musical-comedy stage had songs and dialogue been so well integrated. One result of this effective blending was that to many of the reviewers the term "musical comedy" seemed not quite grand enough, and, invoking the names of Gilbert and Sullivan, they designated it an operetta.

Even so, the enthusiast of musical comedy can only have felt as the curtain went up that he was in the right theater. Thanks to Ryskind's persistence, for Kaufman was not happy with the idea, the scene that greeted the eye at rise was a torchlight parade set to George Gershwin's music against a cityscape of skyscrapers, churches, and speakeasies. True to form, Kaufman would have preferred to take up the curtain on a scene of dramatic action, but he accepted Ryskind's assurance that with music they would take firm hold of the audience's attention.[12] The marching crowds were revealed to be supporters of presidential candidate John P. Wintergreen. Among the slogans on their banners were "Vote for Prosperity and See What You Get," "Turn the Reformers Out," and "The Full Dinner Jacket." Their marching song, "Wintergreen for President," had for its brief lyric only a repetition of the title phrase and one couplet, perfect in its inevitability: "He's the man the people choose— Loves the Irish and the Jews."

Wintergreen agrees to marry the winner of a national beauty contest, but instead, at the last minute, he decides to marry Mary Turner, a young woman on the staff of a newspaper run by Matthew Arnold Fulton. Not only is she beautiful, but, as he tells the world in one of the Gershwins' most lilting numbers, "Some Girls Can Bake a Pie," she knows how to make corn muffins. Wintergreen wins the election easily, casting the last four votes himself. Next, the jilted contest-winner, Diana Devereaux, having missed her chance to be first lady, decides not to be a lady at all and sues for breach of promise. Her suit becomes an international issue when it is discovered that she is of French descent, for the French nation views the snub to her as a snub to itself. Almost impeached in the middle of this to-do, Wintergreen is forgiven when Mary reveals that they will soon be parents. Everyone shares in their joy. Not even the villainous Miss Devereaux is neglected, for, as it is explained, when the President cannot fulfill his duties, they are taken over by the Vice President. She can have Throttlebottom, arch bumbler of the Administration.

Animating this fluff were passages of rapid-fire dialogue reminiscent of those that the team had written for the Marx Brothers. One, from the beginning of the second act, is shared by two new Cabinet officers, Louis Lippman and Francis X. Gilhooley, and their President:

> LIPPMAN . . . Listen, Jack. I don't know anything about agriculture. I told you I wanted the Treasury.
> WINTERGREEN What's the matter with agriculture?
> LIPPMAN Agriculture's all right—it's those farmers. Wheat, wheat! All they know is raise wheat! And then they raise hell with me because nobody wants it.

WINTERGREEN Why do you let them raise so much?

LIPPMAN How can I stop 'em? I did all I could. I invited the seven-year locusts, but they didn't come. Even the locusts don't want their lousy wheat. And they're always complaining about being in one place all the time—they want to travel.

GILHOOLEY You call that trouble. How'd you like to have a lot of sailors on your neck?

WINTERGREEN What do *they* want—*two* wives in every port?

GILHOOLEY Yeah. And any port in a storm. And no storms. And they won't stand for those bells any more. They want to know what time it is the same as anybody else. . . .

During the year's run of the play, a series of three events generated by its success kept it in the news. The first was a complaint, issued by the France-America Society, that the references to France in the play were so lacking in dignity as to be an offense against propriety. The second newsworthy event was in the main more agreeable, though it too involved the show in a controversy.

On May 2, 1932, Kaufman, Ryskind, and Ira Gershwin were notified that they had won the Pulitzer Prize for drama. The decision came as a surprise, both to the authors and to the public, because never before in the fifteen-year history of the prize had it been awarded to a musical comedy. Emphasizing the fact that the Pulitzer Prize was given for *literary* excellence, the judges ignored George Gershwin in their citation, honoring only the three whose contributions had been verbal. The prestige of the prize, which far outweighed its economic benefit ($1000 divided among the three writers), seemed to some commentators to be threatened by the judges' choice. Brooks Atkinson and Heywood Broun, for example, took exception to the decision on the ground that the judges had violated their trust, which was to honor the best *play* of the year. Editorial columns as well as entertainment columns were given over to the debate. Happily, most of the opinions offered on the issue favored the choice, though the competition included O'Neill's *Mourning Becomes Electra*, which most critics preferred to his *Strange Interlude*, the Pulitzer Prize winner of 1928. Sagely, the winning authors made no comment in self-defense, but simply pocketed their money. Since $1000 could not be divided evenly by three, on the joint decision of Kaufman and Ryskind the leftover penny went to Ira Gershwin, because he was the eldest.[13]

The third publicity-generating event took place in December 1932, when the young radical poet Walter Lowenfels went to court to claim a share in the profits of *Of Thee I Sing* on the ground that it had been plagiarized from his unproduced play *U.S.A. with Music*, which he published in 1932. Lowenfels cast his net wide, bringing suit against not only both teams of writers, but also against Sam Harris and Irving Berlin as owners of the Music Box Theater, where the show was playing; Alfred A. Knopf, the publisher of the text; George Jean Nathan, who had written a foreword to the book; and the Gershwins' music-publishing company. He demanded an accounting of the profits so far amassed by the work; now that a second company had been mounted and was running in Chicago, he estimated the figure to be between $750,000 and $1,000,000. He offered parallel passages between *Of Thee I Sing* and his own play, which was a burlesque in episodic form of recent public events as viewed from the political left. The defendants, aware that Lowenfels had very little money, agreed to waive their privilege of requiring him to post a bond to cover the costs of the trial. Had they not done so, the case would have been thrown out on a technicality. Their reasoning was that it would be far wiser to have the case decided on its merits; they themselves were in no doubt as to the outcome, having never seen Lowenfels's book. Judge John M. Woolsey agreed with them that the claim was groundless. "Obviously," he noted, "the plaintiff cannot claim a copyright on words in the dictionary, such as the names of the seasons in the principal lyrics, or in the usual English idioms, or on ideas; therefore the alleged parallelism of phrase does not infringe on anything that was copyrightable in the plaintiff's play, and the plaintiff's contention to this effect may be entirely disregarded." Nor did he find a convincing similarity in the choice or depiction of events.[14]

The publication of the text and lyrics of *Of Thee I Sing* also generated some publicity, for Knopf announced, correctly, that this was the first American musical play to be put into print. It was a highly successful book, going into seven printings between April and October of 1932.

With so much evidence of critical and popular esteem heaped in front of him, it might have seemed that Kaufman would at last cease to be troubled by his old, nagging doubt about his talent. Yet it still lurked, astonishing his friends and relations with its intermittent surfacing. Only when he was at work on a new script and its actual production was he completely sure of himself. Once the curtain went up on the new play, the self-torment recommenced. In July 1932, two months after the announcement of the Pulitzer award, Kaufman's sister Ruth Friedlich and her husband came to New York from Des Moines for a holiday, bringing along their three children. Kaufman got the youngsters fourth-row seats for *Of Thee I Sing*. They were thrilled by the show, but puzzled afterward by their Uncle George, who not only wanted to know whether they had liked it, but seemed positively worried lest they might not have.[15]

Well before the occurrence of any of these incidents that followed the opening of *Of Thee I Sing*, Kaufman began to busy himself with new productions. As usual, the would-be collaborators were clamoring at his door. Harris also was after him, not only for new manuscripts, but to direct plays by other writers. His relationship with Harris, always a serene one, put them on the basis of equality, for Kaufman not only provided Harris with his best (if not unfailing) insurance against disaster, but also was an investor in Harris's productions. As 1932 began, no indications of an improvement in the national economy were evident on any front, but, thanks in particular to *Of Thee I Sing*, the Harris office felt no financial pinch, albeit no film company jumped at the play, which had an asking price of $150,000 and was in any case not typical movie fare.[16] Harris's first offering of 1932 was another political musical, *Face the Music,* with a book by Moss Hart and music and lyrics by Irving Berlin. Kaufman agreed to direct this production with Hassard Short.

In writing the book, Hart showed that he was his own man, for *Face the Music,* though satirizing certain aspects of American politics, owed nothing to *Of Thee I Sing.* Hart based it on the recent hearings on corruption in the government of New York City which had been held by Judge Samuel Seabury. Eyebrows had been raised and impolite laughter had been prompted by these hearings, for the politicians and policemen charged with having dipped into the public treasury asserted that the swelling in their bank accounts had resulted not from theft, but thrift. They had saved their money, and as one of them said, had put it away in little tin boxes. Mayor Walker, who had countenanced and benefited from this massive corruption, would resign in the fall, but he was still in office when the musical opened on February 17, 1932. There is no record of his having attended the opening performance.[17]

The starting point of the plot was the frank astonishment of the middle class at the unaccustomed poverty into which the Depression had swept it. An out-of-luck producer of poor repute, Hal Reisman, wants to put on a show, but can get no backing until he meets Mrs. Martin Van Buren Meshbesher, the wife of a policeman whose tin boxes are full to bursting. The Meshbeshers and other policemen and their wives back the show in order to make use of their new wealth before the investigators uncover it. In the complications that follow, the producer and his backers are brought into court, but all comes right in the end.

Face the Music had a string of good tunes to offer the audience. Berlin's songs proved more melodic than George Gershwin's for *Of Thee I Sing,* and his lyrics on the whole were more articulate than Ira's. Especially beloved by the public was the Depression-inspired "Let's Have Another Cup of Coffee," which predicted, against heavy odds, the imminent return of prosperity and metaphorical rainbows. The extent to which Kaufman added to the book is not known, though it would have been an instance of rare restraint on his part if he had not made some suggestions, and uncharacteristic of Hart if he had spurned them. School-of-Kaufman wisecracking was as evident here as it had been in the original script of *Once in a Lifetime*. One good example of it is a reflection of the precipitous deflation of the era, in a scene that takes place in front of vaudeville's famous home, the Palace. A signboard announces a bill of ten acts, including Ethel Barrymore, Al Jolson, Maria Jeritza, the Marx Brothers, Maude Adams, Eddie Cantor, Albert Einstein (!), Lou Holtz, Rex the Wonder Horse, and Aimee Semple MacPherson, with free sandwiches at intermission, at prices of ten, fifteen, and twenty-five cents. "They've got an awful nerve," says Reisman, "charging a dime for that show in these times. Why, at the Roxy you can get four feature pictures and a room and a bath for a nickel." The public supported the musical, and had not Mary Boland, who played Mrs. Meshbesher, withdrawn to meet a Hollywood commitment, the run presumably would have stretched through the summer. Her departure closed the production after 165 performances. The company was reassembled for a tour in the fall, however, and a return Broadway engagement of thirty-two performances followed.

Before *Face the Music* opened, Kaufman had already begun to block out a new play with Edna Ferber. The most importunate of the collaborators, Ferber was happiness itself when immured with Kaufman, a typewriter, and a work in progress. She had pursued him with a number of ideas after *The Royal Family,* but none had yet jelled into a three-act plot. One that struck her as particularly promising centered in the events preceding a Park Avenue dinner party. Neither writer was more responsible than the other for this idea; it arose, in one of the many sessions at which they pursued new playmaking notions. They invented an appropriate title for it: *Dinner at Eight.* It was to consist of episodes that showed the hostess framing plans for the evening and her guests keeping busy in diverse, stageworthy ways on the day of the party. Kaufman was much less attracted to this outline than Ferber was; in his opinion it would be difficult, perhaps impossible, to forge the links between the guests that would give unity to the work. To her sorrow, Ferber found that her favorite producer, Winthrop Ames, took the same view when she discussed the idea with him. But she persisted, being certain that she and Kaufman could make something of the idea.[18]

The pair of writers met to begin a serious discussion of the plot soon after the opening of *Of Thee I Sing,* and dramatic devices that would mesh to create a sturdy structure sped to their minds. Kaufman mentioned a recent success, Vicki Baum's *Grand Hotel,* that was similar in structure to their scheme, and worried that reviewers might charge them with unoriginality. He himself had been sent a copy of the Baum script in 1930 with a request that he consider directing it.[19] But Ferber swept this fear away as inconsequential; after all, she maintained, they had discussed their scheme over a period of three years.[20]

Exchanging ideas on the project through the winter and early spring of 1932, Ferber and Kaufman concluded that the play should comment satirically on the pleasures and rituals of the rich and socially prominent. The dinner party would provide the means whereby they could examine not only the higher reaches of society but also the servant class. Much more material came to them than they could make effective use of. Some of the discarded episodes included one in the office of the dinner's caterer; one in the shop of a dressmaker; and one outside the hostess's house, where the guests' chauffeurs would be seen discussing their employers. "So many of these ideas suggested themselves," Kaufman told an interviewer, "that we were obliged to hew terribly close to the line. Otherwise there would have been no end to the play."[21] But even without these excursions into fields rather distant from the central events of the play, the authors still found the means to express their distaste for pomp and their disapproval of the rich and spoiled. They spent ten days of the spring in Atlantic City shaping up the first act and completed the remainder of the play during the summer in Manhasset.

Dinner at Eight was in its final form and ready for casting by the middle of August. While resting, as it were, before the plunge into these activities, Kaufman undertook the staging of *Here Today,* a comedy by George Oppenheimer that Sam Harris had scheduled as his first offering of the season. One of the founders of the Viking Press, Oppenheimer at the time was gradually moving away from publishing toward a full-time career as a writer. In 1931 he, with another young playwright, Ruth Goodman, had outlined the comedy. Before their work was finished, Ruth Goodman married Augustus Goetz and went abroad on her honeymoon, leaving Oppenheimer to revise and complete the script on his own. Though Ruth Goetz would eventually become well known, along with her husband, for contributions to Broadway and Hollywood, she did not share in the credit for *Here Today,* having agreed to remove her name from it and reduce her percentage of the royalty from one-half to one-quarter, inasmuch as most of the play that finally went into rehearsal was the work of Oppenheimer—along with substantial but uncredited contributions by Kaufman. When Harris received the play, which came to him not from Oppenheimer but from Kaufman, he declared himself willing to produce it.[22]

Kaufman himself had been given the script by Beatrice, not by the authors. Meeting Oppenheimer in the late 1920s, she promptly took to him and befriended his new publishing house by sending young writers of promise to him and his partner, Harold Guinzberg. Oppenheimer adored the slightly older woman and took every opportunity to be with her. At the parties that the Kaufmans gave on Sunday evenings, he became a regular guest. At this time of his life Oppenheimer, who never married, was always becoming engaged and disengaged. With more affection than malice, Beatrice said that one would be wise to invest in the Cunard Line, because wealthy parents were always sending their daughters abroad to get over a romance with him. She encouraged his writing, and when she heard that he had written a play, she asked to see it. After reading it, she made up her mind that only her husband was to direct it. Tucking himself into bed one night, Kaufman rubbed against an object that turned out to be Oppenheimer's script, placed in the bedclothes by Beatrice. As she had hoped, he read straight through it. When he was finished, he too thought that he should stage it.[23]

By the time *Here Today* was set before the audience, it owed so much to Kaufman that Oppenheimer asked whether he would like to be billed as coauthor and to accept a share of the royalties.[24] Kaufman, who could better afford than Oppenheimer to be generous, declined the offer, assuming, as he had done before and would do again, that such editorial suggestions as he made were a part of the director's task. When the play was published subsequent to the opening, Oppenheimer dedicated it to him and thus made public acknowledgment of his debt. It would be impossible to identify the senior George's lines, however, since even at its conception the play was influenced by Kaufman's wisecracking style. The central character, Mary Hilliard, was patterned after the most quoted wit of the century, Dorothy Parker, and the character's two friends, Stanley Dale and Philip Graves, were drawn from the personalities of two of Parker's closest friends, Robert Benchley and Donald Ogden Stewart. But the resemblance began and ended with the wisecracks, for the play was a lightweight entertainment at best, more farcical than any of Kaufman's plays.

In *Here Today* two debonair New Yorkers, Mary Hilliard and Stanley Dale, try to rescue their friend Graves from a romantic entanglement with a demure Boston girl, Claire Windrew. Mary is the ex-wife of Graves; in the end, having succeeded in freeing him from Claire, she is happily reunited with him. This modest plot is enlivened with Parkeresque jibes at Boston, high society, and the foibles of the elderly; also brought into it is Parker's well-known trick of speaking sweetly to a parting guest and reviling him the moment he was out the door. So obvious was the identity of the three characters that Benchley, reviewing the play for the *New Yorker,* was moved to say, "Incidentally, it has been rumored that a couple of characters in the play are based on real celebrities, and I guess there must be something in it, because if Stanley Dale wasn't meant to be Theodore Dreiser, then I must have been seeing things!"[25]

Rehearsals of *Here Today* began early in August with Oppenheimer and (briefly) Ruth Goodman Goetz on hand. Ruth Gordon was featured in the leading role of Mary Hilliard. Oppenheimer, who had never seen Kaufman in his professional milieu before, was struck by his air of authority and his animation. It seemed to him that Kaufman was far more content there in the theater than he ever appeared to be at social gatherings.[26] If any part of his mind was caught up in plans for the more demanding *Dinner at Eight,* the *Here Today* company never suspected it. In Atlantic City, where the play tried out, business was good, apart from one matinee that coincided with a total eclipse of the sun, which proved more attractive than the play. Later in New York, however, where the comedy opened on September 6, audiences were sparse, for the reviews left little doubt that this was thin, early-season stuff. After thirty-nine performances Harris took it off. Yet the play found an audience eventually; with the restoration of some of the sentimental passages excised by Kaufman and a slight revision that did away with a beach setting, it was taken up by the managers of stock and summer theaters. In such less demanding environments, it added to Oppenheimer's income every year of his life.

While *Here Today* was in rehearsal in August, a crisis arose in the life of Max Gordon, to Kaufman's concern. Suffering from steep losses in the stock market and in danger of losing what little money he had left, Gordon was also struggling to pull together another Schwartz-Dietz revue, *Flying Colors.* The show had an abundance of good songs, and Tamara Geva, Clifton Webb, Charles Butterworth, and Patsy Kelly to perform them, but lacked the dash of *The Band Wagon.* Gordon, beset by brokers making margin calls and hurt by treachery on the part of Jerome Kern, who would not allow him to produce his new show despite their recent shared success with *The Cat and the*

Fiddle, also had to contend with a stubborn set designer, Norman Bel Geddes; an inexperienced choreographer, Agnes de Mille; and sketches that would not jell. At a rehearsal he found himself sobbing uncontrollably. Disconsolate, weeping, shouting, unable to sleep, he nevertheless tried to bring order to the production as the company made plans to travel to Philadelphia for the dress rehearsal and the first tryout performance at the Forrest Theater. At the rehearsal, however, Gordon fell into even deeper despair; only the agility of his general manager prevented him from leaping from the top railing of the circular staircase of the theater.

Sam Harris and Kaufman, who had invested in the revue, and other friends and associates rallied to Gordon's aid, arranging for him to enter a rest home for what was clearly a severe nervous breakdown, and doing what they could to save the production. After the Philadelphia opening, which took place on August 23, Kaufman hurried to the rescue. Getting away from the *Here Today* rehearsals as often as he could, he traveled to Philadelphia to see what could be done. Sharpening the dialogue of Dietz's sketches and adding one of his own—"Service," which he and Marc Connelly had written for the Dutch Treat Club—he improved the production considerably. When *Flying Colors* opened in New York on September 15, it gathered a sheaf of good notices, though most stressed its resemblance to the four Schwartz-Dietz revues that had preceded it, especially *The Band Wagon.* Holding on for only 188 performances, the production was too expensive to recover its production cost, but it was not the disgrace that Gordon feared it would be. He regained his health, and Kaufman, having for the second time come to his aid at a critical moment, turned without further interruption to the task of readying *Dinner at Eight.*[27]

The Depression, which gave no sign of coming to an end, provided the means of bringing into focus the attitude that Kaufman and Ferber had toward their characters. In the best of times a self-involved society woman might seem foolish when drawing up the guest list for an elaborate dinner party honoring titled foreigners whom she scarcely knew. Even more foolish would such a woman seem, then, when planning a costly menu in 1932, as the breadlines lengthened. The production was of necessity an expensive one, requiring glamorous evening clothes for the actresses and eye-filling settings on a revolving stage, but the plot was as ruthless in its exposure of social myopia as any of the plays offered in the decade by the Group Theater or the Theater Union on a stringent budget.

Apart from Macbeth's banquet, no more disastrous dinner party in drama was ever conceived. On the day of Millicent Jordan's dinner honoring Lord and Lady Ferncliffe, her husband Oliver loses control of the shipping business that the family has run for generations, and, a crueler blow, he is discovered to have a fatal heart disease. The Jordan butler and chauffeur wound each other in a knife fight and destroy the lobster dish that was to be the dinner's *pièce de résistance*. Paula Jordan, Millicent and Oliver's only child, decides to break off her engagement to a promising young businessman out of infatuation with an aging, alcoholic actor, Larry Renault. Renault, expected at the dinner, commits suicide on the threat of eviction from his hotel, and the guests of honor at the last minute decide to go to Florida, first sending a perfunctory telegram explaining that Lord Ferncliffe is "ill."

Nor is that all. It is one of the dinner guests—Dan Packard, a robber baron from the West—who has seized control of Jordan's company. Another of the guests, the retired actress Carlotta Vance, an old, trusted, but whimsical friend of Jordan's, has made this possible by selling her Jordan stock to a dummy concern that Packard has set up for the purpose. Packard's vapid wife, Kitty, a former hatcheck girl, is in love with Wayne Talbot, Jordan's physician, who is the only one who knows how sick Jordan is, and who is also a guest—along with his wife. Immediately before leaving home for the party, Kitty Packard is forced to surrender a valuable bracelet to her blackmailing maid, who knows about Kitty's affair with Talbot. Whether aware of it or not, with the exception of Carlotta, every person present at the dinner has been somehow hurt by the day's events, including Packard, who accepted the dinner invitation only because he wanted to meet Ferncliffe. Even Hattie and Ed Loomis, Millicent's middle-class sister and brother-in-law who are substituting for the Ferncliffes, are unhappy, simply because this is not at all their sort of evening. Dora, Millicent's maid, learns quite by chance that the butler, whom she had married that very day, already has a wife in Switzerland; thus her hope of happiness to come is also destroyed. Perhaps most cruelly punished of all is Paula Jordan. Though she has not been invited to the party, she, like the guests, is unaware that Renault is dead. When she leaves the house to meet her fiancé, it is with the intention of breaking off their engagement and telling him of her affair with the actor.

Though none of Kaufman's plays could be devoid of humor, *Dinner at Eight* has fewer comic moments than most. Many of the most amusing lines go to the thoroughly spoiled but good-natured Carlotta Vance, a character widely recognized as being drawn partly in the image of Maxine Elliott, the actress who was rumored to have been the mistress of J. P. Morgan. Reminiscing (Act I, scene 2) about her youth and lost loves, she says, "Look at Lily Langtry! Not half my looks, but she got her Edward. I picked the wrong period. Too young for Edward and too old for Wales. I fell between princes."

Putting the production together was made difficult only by the decision over what performer would play Carlotta. When the choice settled on Constance Collier, the English actress, it was discovered that she was engaged to appear in a London revival of Noel Coward's *Hay Fever*. Her producer, Charles Cochran, released her to Sam Harris at the last moment, but by the time her ship docked in New York harbor rehearsals had already begun. Because Jo Mielziner's settings were very heavy, Harris and Kaufman decided to forgo a tryout tour and instead offered a series of invitational previews. As was becoming his custom, Kaufman selected a Saturday night, October 22, for the official opening, since this would give the reviewers an additional twenty-four hours in which to frame their notices. (The Sunday papers went to press too early to include reviews of Saturday evening openings.) The first night was especially suspenseful to Ferber, because her niece, Janet Fox, was making her acting debut as Tina, Kitty Packard's maid. The audience, Ferber felt, sat on its hands.[28] When the reviews trickled in, late on Sunday night, their tone, on balance, was respectful enough to make the play a hit. In the first months of the run, which lasted for 232 performances, the weekly take at the box office set a record for the theater. Some of the reviewers were troubled by the ruthless cynicism, especially as it affected the ironic final scene; to others the opulence of the production seemed excessive. High praise went to Conway Tearle as Larry Renault, and to the scene of Renault's suicide. Ann Andrews, who played Millicent Jordan, and Constance Collier were also admired. As to comparisons with *Grand Hotel*, Kaufman had predicted correctly: though no reviewers went so far as to suggest that he and Ferber had stolen the structure and ironic conclusion from Vicki Baum, some of them, reasonably enough, pointed to the similarities between the two works.

A film sale to Metro-Goldwyn-Mayer followed, and Herman J. Mankiewicz made the screen adaptation, in collaboration with Frances Marion. Though the screenwriters did not lighten the seriousness of Jordan's illness, they softened other Kaufman-Ferber severities. Packard, goaded by Kitty, decides against wresting control of the shipping company from Jordan, and Paula, notified in the nick of time by Carlotta that Renault is dead, takes up again with her fiancé, who knows nothing about the affair. With these concessions to what it perceived to be the taste of the film-going public, the studio shot the picture. The cast included Wallace Beery and Jean Harlow as the Packards, Lionel Barrymore and Billie Burke as the Jordans, John Barrymore as Renault, and Marie Dressler as Carlotta Vance. They were directed by George Cukor. The result was an exceptionally well-made film—the best ever made from the Kaufman repertory, with a fine balance of comic and serious tonalities sustained to the end. The reviews were full of praise, both for the film as a film and for the talents that had created the original play, but because the same studio had only recently released an all-star version of *Grand Hotel*, they included a second round of invidious comparisons.

— 13 —

London Revisited;
Miscalculations in New York

With *Dinner at Eight* doing big business at the Music Box, Charles Cochran exercised his right to a favor from Sam Harris in return for surrendering the services of Constance Collier: he requested permission to produce the play in London. He also wanted Kaufman to duplicate the New York staging, and Kaufman agreed to do so. Plans were completed quickly. Passage was booked for him on the *Europa*, a German liner due to sail on November 18. Traveling with him was Robert Sinclair, who was to fill in as assistant director. Ferber also wished to be in on the fun, but decided to cross on a ship leaving New York two weeks later.

Before the *Europa* sailed, Kaufman was briefly involved in a futile rescue operation on behalf of friends. The Gershwins' new musical, *Pardon My English*, due to begin its tryout tour in Philadelphia on December 2, was rumored to be in shaky condition. Aarons and Freedley, the producers, asked Kaufman to look in on rehearsals with a view to strengthening the ramshackle book. It was at once rumored that he was on the point of assuming the direction himself, though this was not true. After witnessing one or two rehearsal sessions, Kaufman, the play doctor, threw up his hands at the helplessness of the case. Morrie Ryskind, who had written the book with Herbert Fields, was so distressed by the changes introduced by the producers that he asked to have his name taken off the show. Jack Buchanan, the popular musical-comedy star who was one of the principal leads, bought his way out of his contract while the show was on the road. (The other star was Jack Pearl, a dialect comedian with a radio following.) Later, Kaufman wrote to Beatrice from England, "Sorry to hear about the Gershwin show, but of course it was inevitable. They may patch it together for a few months, but it will never be more than that." He was generous in his estimate; after a much-delayed opening (the curtain rang up on January 20) the show ran a meager forty-six performances.[1]

As this series of misfortunes was overtaking his friends, Kaufman faced the challenge of staging a play in unfamiliar conditions for the benefit of an audience whose tastes he knew very little about. This was his third trip abroad, but the first in almost ten years. Unhappy if away for long from Broadway and his home, he was not pleased to realize that he would not be with Beatrice and Anne during the coming Christmas season, which, to the Kaufmans and their friends, was always a busy time of parties and the exchange of presents. Never before had he been away at this period of the year. Moreover, this would have been a somewhat special holiday season, because the family had recently taken a lease on a large house at 14 East 94th Street, which Beatrice had had the fun of decorating.

But there were compelling reasons for his making the trip, of which the greatest was that the play could not be placed confidently in the hands of an English director, so intensely American was it in its references and social viewpoint. Kaufman's other reason for voyaging to London was that he wanted to look at two West End plays in order to decide whether they were right for Broadway, under Harris's banner. These were *Wild Violets,* a Robert Stolz operetta adapted and staged by Hassard Short, and Somerset Maugham's *For Services Rendered,* an antiwar tragedy.

Not stinting on creature comforts, Kaufman took a suite at Claridge's. According to an issue of *Variety* that he saw not long after his arrival, he could well afford this opulent hotel. On November 29, in a page one story, the show-business trade sheet alleged that he was making more money per week than any other playwright or any producer on Broadway. With the royalties and profits coming in from *Of Thee I Sing* and *Dinner at Eight,* he was said to be drawing some $7000 a week, possibly more. Since at that particular moment the musical had suffered a sudden drop in weekly business, he found this rather ironic, though in writing about the report to Beatrice he did not contradict the magazine's estimate of his income. To both Kaufmans the story was somewhat embarrassing, coming as it did in the midst of the harsh economic downturn. In a second letter concerning it, he wrote, "It doesn't matter—people forget these things very quickly."[2]

It was to be expected that invitations should pour into his mailbox at Claridge's. He was asked to weekend houseparties, Christmas parties, dinners, and luncheons. To the extent that he could free himself from his appointed task, he accepted them. Through various gregarious American friends, Woollcott especially, he had already made the acquaintance of many nontheatrical Londoners, among them Lady Sibyl Colefax, Rebecca West, and the American expatriates Paul and Lilly Bonner. Some of the theater people whom he saw while there were Raymond Massey and his wife, Adrienne Allen; Herbert Marshall and his wife, Edna Best; Noel Coward; Romney Brent; and Adele Astaire. Woollcott himself bustled into town en route to New York from Russia, where he had spent the preceding month. Kaufman, remembering how Woollcott, as a daily reviewer, used to tell his readers that certain exciting plays sent him dancing in the streets, suggested that if he did that sort of thing in London he should mind the left-handed traffic.

Many of Kaufman's activities duplicated those he enjoyed at home. For bridge, an increasing addiction, he went to Crockford's. That club was happy to have him as a member, and he played there often during his stay, but he thought it not to be compared with the Cavendish, then his favorite bridge club in New York. His letters to Beatrice also hinted of other pleasures. "My life is full of ladies—in the titled sense, I mean," he wrote. "It is pretty hard to meet just an ordinary woman." Yet he did meet them, as the days tumbled by. Beatrice of course was not lonely in New York. At the moment she was much involved with George Backer, the publisher and financier.

Kaufman did not care for *Wild Violets,* but he thought well enough of *For Services Rendered* to recommend it to Harris. He also admired *Children in Uniform,* a tragedy set at a German boarding school for girls, written by Christa Winsloe. He deeply regretted that he had missed the opportunity to stage the play in New York, though it bore no resemblance in tone or content to the plays he had directed. It was due to open on Broadway during his stay abroad. Sorry that he could not be there for the first night, he urged Beatrice to attend it.[3] Also playing in London, but in an outlying theater, was *To the Ladies.* The notices for it were so enthusiastic that he collected them and sent them to Connelly.

Ferber was no sooner on the scene than Kaufman approached her with the suggestion that they try another play together. She refused, however, making it utterly clear that she had no intention of collaborating with him again. They did not quarrel over this and did not allow it to mar their personal relationship, but the incident added to Kaufman's already mounting perplexity about the next season. What turned Ferber against the arrangement that she had always found so congenial was, at a guess, a simple instance of piqued vanity. With *Dinner at Eight,* as with their earlier plays, she did not receive due credit in the press for her share in the collaboration.

Additionally, Kaufman as both director and virtual co-producer with Harris, had obviously possessed the weightier power of determining the look and tone of *Dinner at Eight*, and would have it on any future collaborations between them. Eventually Ferber got over her irritation and wrote three more plays with Kaufman, all of which bore her stamp as conclusively as the first three. For the time being, though annoyed, she entered into the task of readying the London production, conferring with Kaufman, Sinclair, and Cochran about casting, and trying to stay warm in the winter chill. One day, with time on their hands, she and Kaufman made a thorough exploration of the Palace Theater, which Cochran had booked for the play. They rambled through its Andean balconies to their highest peaks. The steep climb upward left both with the impression that the nuances of the play would be lost on much of the audience. "How any playgoer is persuaded to occupy those seats, Heaven alone knows," Kaufman wrote later in the New York *Times*. "The sheer physical hazard is enormous—London galleries are pitched at a terrific angle, and I'm sure the whole gallery audience has to be roped together. If one ever goes, they all go."[4]

Ferber could not manage to keep warm in the vast theater. Suddenly done in by the unaccustomed damp, she fell ill with influenza, and, though all Harley Street seemed to troop through her rooms at Claridge's with medicines for bronchial complaints, she did not recover in time for the opening night. Kaufman was anxious about her health, but not so moved as to forgo the pleasure of reporting to Beatrice that a London paper had printed a reference to "Miss Ferber and her author-husband Marc Connelly" and that the Paris *Herald* "carried an item saying that Miss Ferber was in London and staying at Christie's, which, as you know, is famous for its antiques. Miss Ferber was a little pained."

Kaufman's direction of *Dinner at Eight* was like nothing the English actors had ever experienced. He had some difficulty with Irene Vanbrugh, who played Millicent and was a slow study. There was also trouble with Lyn Harding, who, as Dan Packard, was unhappy with having to appear *en deshabille,* his suspenders hanging down and the collar of his dress shirt unbuttoned, while quarreling with Kitty, until Kaufman took him aside in his usual way and quietly explained that the scene required such un-English carelessness. But once these very minor problems were disposed of, Kaufman achieved a crackling pace with the production; the actors, not used to such a rapid tempo, were quite startled to discover that they were expected to maintain it even in that normally sacred moment when tea was being poured. With Vanbrugh, Harding, and Basil Sydney leading a cast of other able

actors, the production was an unqualified success. The play was also a revelation to the audience. The first-nighters were more than usually fashionable,
with full-dress suits conspicuous in the boxes. Wrote one American newspaperman who witnessed the scene, "It was remarked to me during the performance by one who is a frequent theatregoer here that not in years had so
'electric' an atmosphere marked a London audience. People were not only
entertained by the play; they were fascinated by the demonstration of what
a master craftsman can accomplish. Nothing like it has ever been seen in
these parts." Kaufman's reaction was, as usual, mild—with the play well
launched, he boarded the *Europa* two days later and sailed for home.[5]

Landing in New York on January 12, 1933, Kaufman scarcely took time
to reacquaint himself with the city before getting down to the all-important
decision of what to write for the fall. He had already chosen Morrie Ryskind
and Woollcott as his collaborators for the season, but was uncertain as to
what the substance of their works should be, though with these two very
different men as co-creators the results were certain to be two sharply contrasting plays. It did not occur to him that he might cease fretting over this
matter and enjoy a leisurely spring on the returns from the two companies of
Of Thee I Sing, the New York and London productions of *Dinner at Eight*,
which soon would be joined by a West Coast company and a Paris production (*Lundi à Huit Heures*), to say nothing of an imminent London production of *Once in a Lifetime*. But it was not so much a question of maintaining the family treasury at its current level, though that issue was not to
be ignored. Beatrice *was* inclined to worry about the inroads made on it by
their household expenses, Anne's education, her own wanderlust, the taste
of both herself and Kaufman for costly clothing, and Kaufman's contributions to his parents. But as much as for any other reason, Kaufman made
plans because he could not bear to be idle.

As to which project should come first, that he had long since decided.
With the success of *Of Thee I Sing*, Kaufman and Ryskind jointly concluded
that they should take advantage of their prestige as a team by offering something new as soon as was practical. But neither had come up with a workable
suggestion before Kaufman left for London, and as they sat in the living
room on East 94th Street a week after Kaufman's return, they still had
nothing to work on. In the end it was Beatrice who made up their minds for
them. She suggested that they write a sequel to their musical that would take
up the lives of the Wintergreens at the end of four years in the White
House.[6] They seized on this, ignoring the fact that it was a rare sequel, dramatic or fictional, that lived up to the quality of the original. The Gershwins

expressed their willingness to compose the songs, and Gaxton, Moran, and Moore agreed to recreate their characters.

Over the winter and spring of 1933, the writers discussed ideas for the book and kept in touch with the Gershwins, interrupting themselves long enough to dash off a piece for the *Nation* on recent political and economic developments. Entitled "Socratic Dialogue," it was a barroom debate between themselves. "Waiter! Two beers," calls out Ryskind. "Make mine the same!" says Kaufman. But in spite of the comic tone, it was a serious lampoon, chiefly of the Reconstruction Finance Corporation, the agency set up in the last months of the Hoover administration to salvage failing banks, insurance companies, railroads, and other large corporations. As liberals who admitted in this article that in the previous fall they had voted for Norman Thomas, they were skeptical of this use of public funds:

> MR. K. But what about the Reconstruction Finance Corporation? Aren't they supposed to help out?
>
> MR. R. Oh, sure. They keep right on lending money—good jails and bad. No matter what happens.
>
> MR. K. Let me get this straight. The Reconstruction Finance Corporation just keeps on lending money?
>
> MR. R. That's right. On condition that there's no security.
>
> MR. K. Well, whose money is it? Whose money are they lending?
>
> MR. R. It's very simple. You see, they take the money that the depositors put into the good banks—
>
> MR. K. And lend it to the bad banks.
>
> MR. R. Now you've got it![7]

Brief though it was, this piece indicated that the cure-resistant national ills of 1933 had firmly engaged their minds, and that if they chose to write about them for Broadway, the result would not necessarily be a romp.

As usual, Kaufman was shuttling back and forth between collaborators, trying to give equal time to Woollcott while conferring with Morrie Ryskind on what would obviously be the more complex project of the two. Other matters intervened to distract him, temporarily, from both works. In February he went to Washington with the producer William A. Brady and the playwright Austin Strong to protest a bill then before the House of Representatives and already passed by the Senate that would restrict the employment of alien actors to only those few of previously established reputation of the highest order. That Congress might consider this protectionist measure at all was understandable in view of the effect of the Depression on the acting profession, which even in the best of times offers no guarantee of employment. But it was the opinion of Kaufman and other writers and producers that such a bill, if passed, might mean that performers of rare talent would be delayed in the progress of their development, or possibly would never get the opportunity to advance in their profession. He cited the case of Lynn Fontanne, who had made little progress in her native England, but once brought to this country under the aegis of Laurette Taylor had soon become one of the most sought-after actresses on Broadway.[8] His eloquence helped to defeat the bill.

The second major distraction of the spring was the arrival in May, on a visit from Hollywood, of Mary Astor, the beautiful screen actress, to whom a mutual woman friend had made the suggestion that she would not be disappointed if she telephoned Kaufman and introduced herself. She made the call, and with it began an affair that lasted for more than three years.

Toward the end of May, Kaufman and Ryskind chose a title, *Let 'Em Eat Cake,* and they began to put dialogue down on paper. From Atlantic City, still the best place for uninterrupted work, they signaled their progress to the New York press in the unusual form of a list of their favorite critics, with annotations. First on the list was Madam Rajah, "of the Atlantic City board-walk, who predicted, at a special 75¢ reading (regular reading 50¢) that *Let 'Em Eat Cake* would be a bigger hit than *Of Thee I Sing.* (We are now writing in a part for her)." Second was Sam Harris, "whose confidence in the sequel is so great that he has refused to advance a nickel on it." Another critic deserving of mention was their chambermaid, who threw out the first draft of their script. When it was recovered, they decided that she had been right to throw it out, and threw it out themselves. Among other noteworthy critics were their wives and the Gershwins, and, finally, the unknown person who was sure to sue them for plagiarism. "Whoever it is," they pleaded, "we would like to know his name immediately, because if the show is a flop, we intend to sue him."[9] Later in the summer, Kaufman came back, with Woollcott, to Atlantic City, where the two writers prepared a draft of the play that was to follow *Let 'Em Eat Cake* on Harris's schedule.

By mid-August the musical was ready for rehearsal, and Harris booked a Boston opening on September 15, with bookings in other cities to follow. The show stayed on the road five weeks, coming into New York on October 21. At no point along the way were the portents especially encouraging, though the reviews at least indicated that each team was bent on something new. For Kaufman and Ryskind, it was a shift from the rather mild, benign satire of the earlier show to a less compromising and more bitter analysis of current politics, abroad and at home. For the songwriters, it was an effort at even more sophisticated music than before. George Gershwin yielded to an impulse to make counterpoint the basis of the score, and for every number he developed two contrasting melodies. When the show reached New York, the reviewers were disposed to like it, inasmuch as they still felt grateful for the pleasures of *Of Thee I Sing*. But they could not summon the enthusiastic praise that would ensure a long run. Other members of the opening night audience were moved to only mild applause.[10] Ninety performances were all that the work received.

In later years, looking back on the failure of *Let 'Em Eat Cake*, Morrie Ryskind put the blame on the mood of the age, observing that by 1933 audiences had begun to see international politics as no laughing matter, in view of the ascendancy of the Nazis in Germany, and were numbed by the continuing grind of the Depression at home. The actors also felt that the climate had so worsened as to make the satiric thrusts of the show hard to take.[11] Perhaps the Kaufman-Ryskind team had been unwise to test the public's sympathy for their charlatans again, especially with so unsympathetic a book as the one they offered. Though they had not lost their talent for creating comic lines, the over-all mood of the work was unpleasant. Too frequently the stage was full of men with guns.

From the opening number, Kaufman and Ryskind seemed to be foundering. It was a repetition of the opening of *Of Thee I Sing*, except that the audience hears of a new Presidential candidate, John P. Tweedledee. The idea was clear enough, but off-putting, for the name dehumanized the events. On election day Tweedledee is the victor, to the astonishment of Wintergreen and his cronies, who cannot accept the notion of being thrown out of work. To regain power and an income, Wintergreen leads a revolution, deposes Tweedledee, and sets himself up as an American dictator. His symbolic garb is the blue shirt, as opposed to the brown shirt of Hitler and the black shirt of Mussolini, the prototype being a shirt that Mary herself had made as a present for Wintergreen while he still was President. The high point of the action is a baseball game held to decide whether the former allies of the United States will repay their war debts. It is played between one team representing the League of Nations and another made up of the nine Supreme Court Justices, representing Wintergreen's party. When Throttlebottom, the umpire, makes a decision unfavorable to the American team, the revolutionary army threatens him with beheading; the scene is more grisly than humorous, if humorous at all. In the end Wintergreen restores democracy and, stepping down, hands over the destiny of the nation to Throttlebottom. Tweedledee will not take the job, because he has had a better offer from Cuba.

On this occasion the Gershwins' songs, though coming at frequent intervals in the action, offered relatively minor support. It could be argued that the numbers were integrated altogether too well into the fabric of the book. For "Union Square," a number performed by a chorus of malcontent radicals, Ira provided good comic lyrics in which the throng sang of its disapproval of everything from the House of Morgan to the Roxy organ, their motto being "Down with Everything That's Up." The score yielded up only one number that had a life of its own after the show closed: the contrapuntal love song "Mine," sung by Wintergreen and Mary against a chorus of salesgirls and customers in the shop where Mary sells her blue shirts. But the true culprit was the other George, along with his partner. Their failure of invention, noticeable on every page of the printed text, is most obvious in the second act when Mary tries to save her beleaguered husband by announcing in song, precisely as in *Of Thee I Sing*, that she is pregnant. Wintergreen, urging her on, says, "Try it. It worked once."

A tour followed the Broadway closing, but did not succeed in recouping the production cost. If anything of value, apart from "Mine," came out of the production, it was the consolidation of the popularity of Gaxton and Moore as a team. Immediately after the tour they made some highly success-ful appearances together in vaudeville and were soon signed for the new Cole Porter musical, *Anything Goes*. They were later paired in two more productions, the final one being Kaufman's *Hollywood Pinafore* in 1945.

On November 25, only five weeks after the opening of *Let 'Em Eat Cake*, Harris and Kaufman suffered another disappointment when *The Dark Tower*, the new Kaufman-Woollcott play, opened to mixed, unpromising reviews. The way toward their second effort at collaboration had been made cautiously by both men. Kaufman all along was especially concerned lest Woollcott think he bore him a grudge over the dreary *Channel Road*, but was reluctant to hold a postmortem on that play. In a letter to Woollcott, undated (characteristically), he wrote,

> I don't think the fact that we haven't discussed *The Channel Road* means a thing, so far as our communicativeness is concerned. I think we both felt that we knew what was the matter with it, and that it didn't need much discussion. It seems to me that has nothing to do with writing other plays, and I also think we are a good combination—especially after that taught us several things.

The substance of the play, an on-stage murder never solved by the police, showed that in the main it was the product of Woollcott's imagination. Murder cases, especially those unsolved, had long held a fascination for him.

He enjoyed armchair attempts at unraveling their mysteries and conducting analyses of the criminal mind. In *The Dark Tower*, however, it is not the murderer, Damon Wells, who is the real villain, but his victim, the sinister Stanley Vance, who is married to Wells's sister Jessica, a distinguished actress. So powerful is Vance's hold on her emotions that in his presence Jessica is perpetually in a waking trance, though when away from him she is aware that he is not only unloving, but pathologically self-involved. Vance is also an ex-convict. The trick of the plot is that Damon Wells, a fine actor, kills Vance in a disguise so heavy that the audience cannot penetrate it. When the deed is done, he simply resumes his own identity and eludes the police. But at the close, in a scene intended to be great fun for the audience, he has occasion to redisguise himself and then on stage divests himself of the borrowed accoutrements, gradually revealing himself as the decent young man he is supposed to be.

But this was not fun enough to redeem the play, which contains some of the dullest pages in the entire Kaufman repertory. The talents of the two writers blended as unhappily as in *The Channel Road*. Given the grave difference in their temperaments and preferences in literary tonality, this was inevitable, though Kaufman in his eagerness to have a play to offer had blinded himself to the fact when searching for a collaborator. He sensed trouble before the official first night, however. The play opened "cold"—that is, without a preliminary tour. Prior to the opening some previews were held, and the audience for them was invited. For the official first night, Kaufman was determined to have a sympathetic crowd on hand. The rather perfunctory applause that had greeted *Let 'Em Eat Cake* in October was still an irritating memory to both him and Sam Harris. Their intention was to bring together an audience less blasé and cynical on this occasion, with the expectation that the critics would be impressed by the general response. To that end Kaufman pared down the press list by a third and returned the checks of many habitual first-nighters who had written in for tickets, making his own decisions as to who would and who would not sit in the orchestra. Woollcott was happy with this stratagem. To an interviewer he said,

> A premiere night should be a pleasant occasion but it has become an unbearable one. You certainly don't want your friends and relatives at a premiere. George Kaufman isn't silly about that. He's a terrible audience and doesn't want people in the theater like himself. He hasn't laughed or applauded in fifteen years.[12]

Not all the friends of both writers were excluded from the first-night audience, of course, though one who was invited soon ceased to be a friend to

Woollcott. Intimates for more than ten years, Ferber and Woollcott had recently suffered a severe falling-out, the exact cause of which remains unknown. The breach was not thought to be beyond repair until, as it happened, Ferber trod heavily, if inadvertently, on Woollcott's vanity by arriving late at the *Dark Tower* opening. Furious, Woollcott vowed to see her no more.[13] Ferber was not distressed by the termination of the friendship, since friendship with Woollcott was never easy. In any event, she was spared the seemingly interminable expository scene at the rise of the curtain.

The Dark Tower held on for only fifty-seven performances, three fewer than *The Channel Road* had played. It is faintly possible that, if Kaufman had been less occupied with other projects during the months that he and Woollcott conferred on the script, something more would have come of it. But with Woollcott's zest for the fustian phrase and the bravura gesture, Kaufman was fortunate to secure even so brief a run, and yet more fortunate to make a sale of the script to Hollywood. Bennett Cerf and Donald Klopfer, the heads of Random House, then a new publishing firm, chose the play to be one of the first dramatic texts that they would publish, and that too was a fortunate event, inasmuch as it was the beginning of a professional relationship between Cerf and Kaufman that resulted in the firm's issuing most of Kaufman's subsequent plays in attractive volumes designed to meet his precise specifications. But *The Dark Tower* itself would never seem other than an aberration. The brightest spot in the entire work is a droll and suspenseful passage toward the close when a police detective comes to call on the Wells household and leaves satisfied that the case will never be solved, but not before securing a promise from Jessica that she will read his nineteen-year-old daughter's manuscript play and will send him two tickets for her next opening night. Woollcott had the grace to admit that that scene was entirely Kaufman's.[14]

For a few weeks during his work on *The Dark Tower* Kaufman was distracted not only by consultation with Morrie Ryskind and the Gershwins over *Let 'Em Eat Cake,* but also by an assignment from one of Hollywood's most honored, if also most difficult, producers. It was Samuel Goldwyn, who besought him to tailor a comedy to the talents of Eddie Cantor. Other Hollywood offers had come his way before, but this was one with an important difference. The earlier attempts to interest him in screenwriting had carried the stipulation that he fulfill the assignment in an office at the studio, so that he would be on the spot and available for story conferences if his producer required revisions. These were the usual terms set by the typical studio, no matter the renown of the writer in question. But the atypical Goldwyn wanted not only Kaufman but another major Broadway writer, Robert E. Sherwood, for the Cantor film, and he was shrewd enough to guess that he would capture them only if he allowed them to work on their home ground. Cantor, at the moment his most valuable contract player, had to have the best if he was to top the three hits he had already given the producer. A contract was devised with escape clauses that permitted Kaufman and Sherwood to withdraw after writing the original story synopsis if they cared to, or to stay on and write the first draft of the screenplay and then withdraw if they did not wish to prepare the final script. In mid-March they signed this contract, neither realizing how demanding their new employer could be.[15]

For every film starring the comedian, certain requirements existed. It was mandatory that Cantor have the opportunity to sing, dance, put on blackface, deliver a rapid line of patter, save some creature in distress, and have a romance. But it was always necessary to change the background. For the new picture Goldwyn had first thought of casting him as Androcles, the prisoner in the tale of ancient Rome who survives an encounter with a lion in the arena because the beast recognizes him as the man who once removed a painful thorn from his foot. The version of this story best known to the public was Shaw's *Androcles and the Lion*, in which the prisoner is a Christian and a Greek, rather than the Roman slave Androclus of the fable. But Shaw for years had flatly refused either to write for Goldwyn or to allow Goldwyn to film his plays. In February 1933 the Goldwyn office informed the press that Edwin Justus Mayer and Ernest Pascal were preparing a screenplay on Androcles for Cantor with a modern slant. For whatever reason—possibly the fear of encroaching on Shaw's copyright—Goldwyn soon dropped the project.[16] Nevertheless, he could not dismiss the idea of dressing Cantor in a toga. It was this that made Sherwood the logical collaborator for Kaufman on the project. A writer of intellectual comedies in the Shavian manner, he had demonstrated his knowledge of antiquity in *The Road to Rome* (1927), a shrewd and amusing piece of speculation on Hannibal's reason for not invading the city of Rome. Friends since the early years of the Round Table, he and Kaufman could be counted on to work harmoniously. Thrown together, so to speak, by Goldwyn, they spent Inauguration Day, March 4, 1933, at the Kaufmans' house, where they listened to the new President's address to the nation and exchanged ideas about the film.[17]

Once the contract was signed, Cantor came east to discuss the script with the writers, and stayed on through May. It was decided that he would play the custodian of a small historical museum in an American town called West Rome. The character would be curious about life in ancient Rome and in a dream would be transported to that city, only to find that political corruption such as he knew to be rampant in his home town also existed there. Coming out of the dream, he would express the hope of cleaning up West Rome. Goldwyn approved the story and told the writers to go ahead with their screenplay. They did so, but when they submitted it to him, they found that his demands for revisions would require more time than they were willing to give the project. Kaufman, after all, had obligations to Ryskind, the Gershwins, and Woollcott. Sherwood had a home in England where he and his wife liked to spend the summers, and in the summer of 1933 they were expecting Beatrice and Anne to be among their guests. Exercising their option, the writers withdrew altogether from the production.

Not wishing to leave Goldwyn without first finding a successor to complete the script, Kaufman and Sherwood recommended George Oppenheimer, who had recently added to his credentials as a comedy writer by creating scripts for Groucho and Chico Marx's radio show, *Flywheel, Shyster, and Flywheel*. Goldwyn was not enthusiastic about this suggestion, but with still other recommendations from Groucho, Cantor, and Arthur Hornblow, Goldwyn's principal aide, Oppenheimer got the job. Goldwyn also assigned William Anthony McGuire, Arthur Sheekman, and Nat Perrin—comedy writers, all—to the project. When the film, entitled *Roman Scandals,* was released at the end of the year as a Christmas treat, the original story was credited to Kaufman and Sherwood, and the adaptation to Oppenheimer and McGuire. This was Kaufman's first credit as the author of an original screenplay. The picture drew a good audience, but its success was no more due to the invention of the six writers than to the pace of the energetic Cantor and glimpses of the Goldwyn Girls clad only in their long, golden hair.

Goldwyn lived up to his reputation for stubbornness when it came to paying Kaufman and Sherwood for their weeks of work. He insisted that they had completed only step one of the contract, the story outline, and had not done enough on the second step, the preparation of a first draft, to be paid for it. He refused to hand over the full $50,000 to which they believed they were entitled, holding back half of it. The writers sued in 1934, but not until 1937 was a settlement reached.[18]

At the end of the 1933, Kaufman was also involved in the production of another film, though this was not for national distribution. His parents were to celebrate their fiftieth wedding anniversary on January 17, 1934, and he was determined to give them a party worthy of the occasion. He wrote a brief film script for them and himself in which they reviewed their lives and Nettie announced that she intended to become a critic so as to further her son's success. The picture was made in Fort Lee, New Jersey, and was the highlight of the anniversary party which was held at the Savoy Plaza Hotel. The guests were a mixture of Joseph and Nettie's friends, George and Beatrice's friends, and *mishpocha* (Yiddish for "family," and virtually the only Yiddish word in the Kaufman vocabulary). Ever the doting family man, Kaufman put aside his mask of aloofness when in the company of his parents, the Friedlichs, the Liebermans, and the Bakrows, and at this party all his close relations and some of Beatrice's were present. A gala evening, it gave the host as well as the guests of honor immense satisfaction.

This production in behalf of his parents was, in its way, more of a success than the two that Kaufman had undertaken with Sam Harris during the fall. It was now midwinter—too late to work up yet another play for the current season, but the right time to begin making plans for the season ahead. Several possibilities were open. Though Ferber still kept herself out of the running, there was no shortage of available collaborators. By the winter's end, Kaufman made plans to work with two old associates, Ryskind and Hart, and one newcomer, Katharine Dayton, a Washington correspondent for the North American Newspaper Alliance and occasional contributor of sketches to the *Saturday Evening Post*.

Kaufman met Katharine Dayton in February or March of 1934 through Ethel Taylor, a play agent. For years Taylor, a friend of Dayton's, had urged Dayton to put her knowledge of Washington to use in the theater. Dayton finally agreed to do so, provided the great George S. Kaufman would consent to be her coauthor. Though Kaufman was always on the prowl for new material, to approach him with a dramatic idea was never an action to be undertaken casually. One had to have nerve to face the possibility of not simple rejection, but rejection in the form of an acid rebuff. Ethel Taylor, to her credit, got through to him without trouble and set up a luncheon meeting for him and Dayton at the Algonquin. The meeting was a success; Dayton impressed Kaufman with her intelligence and her willingness to work. The fact that Washington was her beat as a newspaperwoman had an appeal in itself, since at the moment politics and the New Deal were very much on his mind, as the musicals and the *Nation* pieces had revealed. Yet when the two talked over possible situations for a comedy, they concluded that they would not write one heavily burdened with references to the current state of national affairs, but instead a satire on the trivia with which Washington social and political life was cluttered. On the next day Kaufman reported for work at Katharine Dayton's apartment, where in five hours' time they outlined a plot. Like all the collaborators before her, Dayton looked on in mild astonishment as Kaufman paced the floor throughout the work session.[19]

Though Kaufman made it clear that he approved of her as a collaborator, Katharine Dayton soon learned that she could not hold her own against the competition of Hart and Ryskind. No sooner was the play outlined than Kaufman informed her, none too gently, that he was about to go to work with Hart and that he would return to her in May, two months later.[20] That, for the moment, was that. Whatever can be said against this slapdash method of composition—that eventually it left each of the collaborators unhappy, that it sometimes resulted in an inferior product—it was the only method that Kaufman's temperament permitted. Only by pursuing a restless course from collaboration to collaboration could he use up enough energy so that he could maintain a semblance of calm. At that, stories had begun to proliferate about his tendency to scowl and mutter to himself while walking along the street on the way to an appointment. To see one project through in orderly fashion from start to finish was not for him. Hart and Ryskind knew this to be so, of course, but it came as something of a shock to Dayton to discover that she could not count on their finishing the play at once. She was anything but pleased to be dropped temporarily from the Kaufman agenda. But she was willing to wait; this was an opportunity too valuable to be thrown away in anger.

The prospect of collaborating with Hart again was immensely appealing to Kaufman. He would have been very pleased to re-establish their professional relationship on any sign from Hart that he too wished it. He did not press for a commitment from Hart, but bided his time in hope that Hart would turn to him. At last it happened. Hart appeared, early in 1934, fresh from the Coast with a plan for a new play taking shape in his head. This plan was a radical departure from the traditional kind of dramaturgy that they customarily engaged in: the play was to be written and staged back-to-fore, starting at the climactic moment of the protagonist's life and proceeding backward to the bare beginning of his career. Kaufman was immediately interested.

In the three and a half years since the opening of *Once in a Lifetime,* Hart had revealed himself to be almost as prolific and untiring as Kaufman. With the success of *Face the Music* and a second, even more highly praised show with songs by Berlin, the revue *As Thousands Cheer,* Hart had come into his own. Those hits, and the offer he had accepted from Metro-Goldwyn-Mayer to put a gloss on some doubtful scenarios scheduled for screening, had strengthened his self-confidence and had added so substantially to his personal fortune that he was free to write when and what he chose. The Hart who had once confided to Jean Dixon that he was afraid to write again with Kaufman lest he lose his individuality had become a man who viewed his own talent as being on a par with Kaufman's. Their collaboration on *Face the Music* as writer and director had clearly been satisfactory to both and had cemented the personal regard for one another that had begun to develop early in their acquaintance. It was Beatrice to whom Hart was the more closely drawn as a human being in the early years of his friendship with the Kaufmans, because of her unfailing, unguarded sympathy for him as he struggled to overcome his emotional instability. She could well understand his descents from ebullience to melancholia, since she was still undergoing analysis. (She was a patient of the well-known Dr. Gregory Zilboorg.) Apart from the series of analysts whom he consulted during the 1930s, it was only with Beatrice or Joseph Hyman, his most intimate male friend, that he could drop the social mask. No doubt the analytical sessions played as much a part in the strengthening of his ego as did his theatrical successes. Thanks to them and the two hit shows with Berlin, he felt that he could seek out Kaufman again as a collaborator without subjugating his own talent to that of the older writer.

At the end of the run of the California production of *Once in a Lifetime*, Hart conceived the notion of writing a play that would trace the life of an American family through the first three decades of the twentieth century, with scenes showing the family's reaction to or participation in historical events. The crash of 1929 was to end the play, and accordingly Hart chose as his working title *Wind Up an Era*. Staying on in California for a while after the close of *Lifetime*, he did some research for the new play at the Huntington Library in San Marino. He returned to New York by ship through the Panama Canal, writing all during the voyage and completing an act and a half by the time the ship docked in New York. Immediately after his arrival he learned that Noel Coward had beaten him to the draw with *Cavalcade*. That panoramic play, which opened in London on October 15, 1931, chronicled the experience of an English family over the same period of time and with similar attention to current history. Hart was crushed, but, still entertaining the notion of dramatizing a family history, he thought about choosing the Rockefellers as his subject. He then pared this down to a play about a successful individual career and suddenly was struck with the novel idea of presenting the scenes in reverse chronological order.[21]

In the winter of 1934, Kaufman and Hart boned up on American cultural history since the teens of the century and met three times a week to discuss the plot of their play. Among the titles considered and discarded were *All Our Yesterdays* and *Career*, until they finally hit on *Merrily We Roll Along*, a phrase weighted with ironic implications inasmuch as the play did not roll along, but backward, and was far from merry. Before they could begin the actual writing, Hart was recalled to Hollywood. Kaufman, to the astonishment of the theatrical world, agreed to follow him there on March 15. In Palm Springs they resumed their sessions as soon as Kaufman settled in. In five weeks' time they were close enough to the end for plans to be made for a September opening. Kaufman came home in April, happy in the knowledge that they had only a bit more to do. Moreover, they had developed an idea for another play.[22]

Returning to New York, Kaufman and Hart added to the last act of their play, gave a final polish to the whole, and set about the task of making ready for a fall production before moving on to other tasks for the summer. They were not free of responsibility to Harris and the play, however. Once a week they met with the producer and his staff to discuss casting and hold auditions; this continued until very close to Labor Day, September 3, 1934, when rehearsals began. But both writers had other work to do, and they managed to fit it in. Hart and Berlin were mulling over ideas for a Harris revue, *More Cheers*, intended as a sequel to *As Thousands Cheer* but ultimately abandoned. In addition, Hart was preparing the libretto for *The Great Waltz*, an adaptation of a Viennese operetta that Max Gordon had scheduled for early fall. Kaufman, apart from a four-day stint of work in early August revising Sam and Bella Spewack's *Spring Song* for Max Gordon, gave the rest of the summer over to sessions with Morrie Ryskind for the writing of yet another political satire, a non-musical comedy to be called *Bring On the Girls*. Meeting in town and in the Kaufmans' rented house in Katonah, New York, they expected to go into rehearsals immediately after the opening of *Merrily We Roll Along*.

The production of this second Kaufman-and-Hart collaboration was unusually heavy. They had not stinted themselves with *Once in a Lifetime*, which called for five different settings, but with *Merrily We Roll Along* they asked for an even more elaborate production. The play had nine scenes, each with a special setting. It called for ninety-one actors, one hundred and fifty costumes, and two assistant stage managers to support John Kennedy, the Harris office staff-member who almost always stage-managed Kaufman's plays. The cost of this lavish laying-on of actors, materials, and staff ran to an unusually large sum for a non-musical production in 1934. The heaviest "straight" play ever to be presented in Harris's Music Box Theater, it could not be toured easily. The writers and Harris decided to hold a series of five invitational previews before the September 24 opening in lieu of an out-of-town tour, as they had with *Dinner at Eight* for the same reason. Jo Mielziner, who designed the settings, was on his way to the position of Broadway's leading designer, an eminence he reached in the 1940s, but at this time he had not discovered the trick of planning an outsized production without sacrificing mobility.

It was as a physical production and as a kind of literary stunt that *Merrily We Roll Along* made its strongest impressions, not as profound drama. It became clear that the writers had not experienced a brainstorm of invention in their weeks in the desert. Their plot centered in the moral and artistic decline of a playwright, Richard Niles, who might have been a great writer had he been willing to settle for years of poverty while learning his art. Instead, he was one of those who scurried to Broadway and the remunerative work of pasting up popular but flimsy comedies. The audience was first shown him on his fortieth birthday as he waited, with friends, for the reviews of his latest comedy. From that point, the authors took him back through the stages of his life that had brought him this far. He was revealed to have abandoned the wife who had stood by him in time of struggle, the two friends whose faith in his talent had given him moral support, and the producer who had given him his first success. The predictability of the play was lessened only by the reverse method of construction; once one thought about the scenes in their normal sequence, there was nothing much to cheer about. On virtually every producer's schedule in this Depression year was such an antimaterialist play.

Yet the play contains some good, if shallow, passages. The opening scene is a marvel of show-business cleverness, though written in so high a key that all the rest is anticlimactic. In this scene the curtain rises on the protagonist, Richard Niles (originally played by Kenneth McKenna) as he and his wife entertain friends while awaiting the reviews of his latest comedy amid the splendors of a country house on Long Island. Physically, this was the sort of scene that delighted Harris, who believed that the best way to catch an audience was to give it the sight of attractive people in handsome clothes. Present to make ironic comments is the wise-cracking, alcoholic writer Julia Glenn (played by Mary Philips), one of the oldest of Niles's friends and something of a thorn in the flesh of his wife, the actress Althea Royce (played by Jessie Royce Landis). As this scene progresses and Julia Glenn's drunkenness so loosens her tongue that she insults most of the guests, tension mounts rapidly. It is relieved only by means of a shocking, Grand Guignol incident: Althea, noting her husband's fondness for the ingenue Ivy Carroll (played by Murial Williams), and burning with resentment that she, despite her age, was not cast in Ivy's part in the new play, hurls iodine in the girl's eyes, thus not only blinding Ivy but bringing ruin on herself. To cap this startling scene would be impossible, as the authors knew; but they were unaware, apparently, that even to sustain the interest that it generated would be difficult.[23]

The only other gripping scene is an explosive incident near the close of the second act, usually the high point of a Kaufman script. Here the excitement is created by Mrs. Riley, the mother of Althea Royce, *née* Annie Riley. At a party to celebrate the opening of her daughter's new play, which is also Richard Niles's first Broadway production, this exuberant woman, once a burlesque star, steals the scene with a noisy attack on the pretensions of writers of comedies of manners such as Niles and of modern star actresses such as her daughter. The writers hired an aging English comedienne, Cecelia Loftus, for the role and gave her a weekly salary of just under four hundred dollars, a large figure for the time, especially in view of the brevity of the part.[24]

It was noted by the press that two of the characters had living counterparts: Julia Glenn, whose heavy drinking, caustic wit, and penchant for making bedmates of quite young men were traits appropriated from Dorothy Parker; and Sam Frankl, a composer of great skill and popularity and a superbly clever pianist—in short, George Gershwin. Queried about this, Kaufman admitted that there were "traces" of Parker in Julia Glenn, but added that "we would not dream of insulting her."[25] There were, however, more than traces of her in the portrait. Kaufman and Hart were far more severe with Parker than George Oppenheimer had been in *Here Today*. In that comedy the unsparing acerbity shown by Parker when dealing with her inferiors was softened by the glimpses of the impish charm of which she was capable in her best moods. But Julia, as the curtain rose on her in the first scene of *Merrily We Roll Along*, was shown to be a woman near the point of total disintegration of personality. The inclusion of so obvious a caricature, like that of the kinder, amusing one of Gershwin, was a gesture calculated to increase word-of-mouth publicity; the authors, liking Gershwin but not caring for Parker, let the chips fall where they might. Altogether, it was a difficult year for Parker. Only a month earlier, she had made an equally unattractive appearance in Charles Brackett's *Entirely Surrounded*, a novel set on Woollcott's island.

Though reviews of *Merrily We Roll Along* were, on balance, more respectful than laudatory, the play ran for 155 performances—on paper a quite decent run, if not one of sufficient length to recover the production outlay. A sale of the film rights to Metro-Goldwyn-Mayer took place, but the studio merely added the script to its stockpile of properties and forgot about it; no film version was produced. A tour was planned to follow the New York closing, despite the unwieldiness of the sets. However, after two weeks in Philadelphia, the first stop, Harris decided to send the play no farther, and he made a mental note not to employ Mielziner again. Kaufman himself was not deceived by the play. He had the wisdom and the level-headedness to enjoy the criticism of it uttered by his friend Herman Mankiewicz: "Here's this wealthy playwright," said Mank, "who has repeated successes and earned enormous sums of money, has mistresses as well as a family, an expensive town house, a luxurious beach house, and a yacht. The problem is: How did the son of a bitch get into this jam?"[26]

A much worse fate awaited *Bring On the Girls*, Kaufman's second play of the 1934-35 season. The sixth work on which he and Morrie Ryskind were associated, it was the first non-musical play that the team offered the public, and that public was unprepared for the change in the Kaufman-Ryskind format. The very title caused trouble. Who would not be fooled into thinking that such a title promised music and a shapely chorus line? Yet, as they told the press, Kaufman and Ryskind never had any intention of making this play a musical and were baffled by the public's confusion.[27] They offered one song, "Down on the Old-Time Farm" (lyrics by Ryskind, music by Arthur Schwartz), but only as a parody of badly dated vaudeville numbers.

A farcical spoof on the policies of the New Deal and the men who administered them, *Bring On the Girls* was neither funny enough nor profound enough to compensate for its lack of the expected songs and dances. Kaufman and Ryskind had dipped lightly into this same well for their article, "Socratic Dialogue." When the play opened in Washington, D.C., on October 22, it was apparent that they had become more heavy-handed. As in the article, the principal target of their attack was the Reconstruction Finance Corporation. In the doling out of public funds to assist private enterprise, the writers saw a dangerous deviation from what, as liberals, they took to be the proper business of government: the improvement of the way of life of the individual. In the play they combined the function of the RFC with that of the Agricultural Adjustment Administration, which was empowered to subsidize farmers for restricting their crops in order to avoid a glutted, deflationary market.

Allowing one dull joke to follow another, Kaufman and Ryskind created a plot in which two cronies, Jim Pearson and Charlie Meredith, who have just been released from the penitentiary, where they served a five-year term for bank fraud, scheme to bilk the RFC for funds with which to run, in succession, a railroad, a farm, and a bank. The railroad runs from Black Creek, Ohio, to East Black Creek, a distance of two miles. The farm is maintained on the terrace of a rooftop apartment in Manhattan, and most of its produce comes from the neighborhood grocery store. The bank, which the audience hears little about, is dragged in at the last minute for a gag with which to bring down the final curtain. The two one-time bankers, apparently not chastened by their five years behind bars, will soon be up to their old tricks again. None of this trifling with public monies would be possible had not the ex-cons had the complicity of two good-looking but out-of-work chorus girls. Writing to the RFC to come to the aid of the railroad, which in fact they do not own but expect to buy cheaply, the two men stick into the envelope some photographs of the girls, whom they identify as the railroad's treasurer and secretary. The pictures bring aid in a hurry. Three days after the letter is sent, two RFC officials appear at the apartment, both eager to meet all the staff. These two bureaucrats are typical brain trusters, or at least they were so in the eyes of the authors. Before accepting their Washington posts, one had been a professor of anthropology at Columbia and the other a professor of Hebrew at Harvard.

The authors and Sam Harris made a major coup in the casting of this work. Jack Benny, who had recently come into his own as a radio comedian after years in vaudeville and some half-dozen indifferent pictures, agreed to take the role of Jim Pearson, the shrewder of the two bankers, though with rehearsing and performing his radio show as well as acting in the play he faced some fatiguing months. But, according to the reviews, though Benny was acceptable in his role, he was not outstanding. A first-rate comedian when delivering patter and acting out brief sketches, he had not had the training that might have enabled him to sustain a characterization in a three-act play. Porter Hall, as his sidekick, drew better notices than he.

At the opening in Washington, D.C., a representative of Metro-Goldwyn-Mayer dropped by after the second act to inquire about the film rights, but by the end of the third act he had disappeared. Still more revisions were needed, but Kaufman fell ill with a stomach complaint and returned to New York, leaving Ryskind to continue alone.[28] When the Washington run ended, Harris withdrew the play to give him some time to make his alterations of the script, though only the addition of a musical score would have fleshed the work out satisfactorily, and it was too late for that. Harris reopened the play in New Haven on November 22 and then took it to Boston and Hartford, but in those three cities it met with no more gratifying response than it had in Washington. A New York run was out of the question; on December 15 Harris closed down the production. Jack Benny, disappointed but not angry despite having been let down by so renowned a writing and producing team, told friends that he would like to try another play sometime, but only if Kaufman wrote it for him.[29]

In between the Broadway opening of *Merrily We Roll Along* and the try-out of *Bring On the Girls* in Washington an event took place which both Kaufman and Beatrice looked forward to with a certain edginess, and which was of more than casual interest to the theatrical press. Beatrice decided to come forward with a play of her own, a sentimental comedy called *Divided by Three*. Like her husband, she practiced her craft in collaboration with an-other writer. The coauthor was Margaret Leech Pulitzer, Beatrice's friend of many years. Because both women were well known in literary and social circles, their joint undertaking commanded the attention of not only the theatrical press, but the slick, "smart," monthly magazines. In one of them, *Town and Country*, it was suggested that Beatrice had everything to lose in the way of reputation for wit and sense if the play should fail and nothing to gain if it should prove to be a hit.[30]

Divided by Three was presented by Guthrie McClintic, who also directed the production. A sought-after director in his own right, he also served in every season as the director of the productions of Katharine Cornell, his wife. McClintic's hand as producer or director could not guarantee success, of course, but his association with any play guaranteed a respectable press. In this instance, anticipation was heightened because the New York opening followed only by ten days that of *Merrily We Roll Along*. The cast assem-bled by McClintic was led by Judith Anderson as Lila Parrish, an attractive woman in early middle age who is hard-pressed to cope with the demands made on her emotions by her husband, her son, and her lover. In the cast were James Stewart as the son, Teddy, and Hedda Hopper as the heroine's worldly, expatriate sister. McClintic opened the play in New Haven on Sep-tember 27, allowing a trial run of only four performances before the Broad-way premiere. Despite the imminent opening of his own play, Kaufman man-aged to get to New Haven for this big moment in Beatrice's career. Among Beatrice's opening-night telegrams was one from him which read,

CHEER UP DARLING YOU KNOW ITS A GOOD TRY BESIDES WHATS THE
WORST THAT CAN HAPPEN LOVE GEORGE.

Both Kaufmans believed that the plot was altogether too scandalous for the eyes and ears of nine-year-old Anne, and they left her at home with her governess.

Though Beatrice turned to Kaufman for advice from time to time while working on the script, *Divided by Three* bears no trace of his hand. Kaufman liked most of it, but not quite all. On the opening night in New York Hedda Hopper overheard him say to McClintic that the third act did not go well with the first two. When McClintic asked why he had never voiced that opinion before, he replied, "I'm only the author's husband, not the author."[31]

Though many reviewers echoed Kaufman's criticism, the play drew a sheaf of encouraging notices, if not those of a sort likely to draw a throng to the box office. The scene most highly praised was the climactic confrontation between mother and son during which the young man is profoundly shocked to learn of his mother's affair. The sentimentality of the ending, in which Lila determines to continue her loveless marriage out of pity for her husband, who has come close to financial ruin, raised suggestions in the reviews that the work was primarily a "woman's matinee play"—that is, one with an invalid emotional appeal. Such comments held the play to a run of only thirty-one performances. Among the reviews that Beatrice was pleased to keep was Joseph Wood Krutch's for the *Nation,* in which a favorable paragraph on *Divided by Three* was sandwiched between a long, complaining review of *Merrily We Roll Along* and two dismissive sentences on Samuel and Bella Spewack's *Spring Song,* which Kaufman had touched up.[32]

───14───

Hollywood

Ever discreet in his romantic arrangements, Kaufman did not allow even his most trusted associates to wrench hints from him as to the identity of the women in his life. Cool, unapproachable when it suited him to be, he could quell an inquiry or a wisecrack with one glare over the rims of his glasses. Thus, for all his sophistication, he reacted in panic on finding his name on the front pages of the nation's newspapers in August 1936, in headlines alleging him to have been the lover of Mary Astor, a Hollywood actress of exceptional beauty and more intelligence than the revelations suggested. Kaufman's panic was brief, but keen enough while it lasted. He had indeed been her lover, and she had been unwise enough to describe their relationship in a diary—a diary her former husband confiscated and used against her in a suit for the custody of their daughter.

Born Lucile Langhanke in May 1906—and thus some seventeen years younger than Kaufman—Mary Astor began her career in pictures in 1920, having been pushed into it by her father, a single-minded, Berlin-born autocrat. D. W. Griffith once described this curious gentleman as "a walking cash register."[1] Both Otto Langhanke and his wife, Helen, were determined that their only child should become a screen actress; they had heard—as who had not?—of the generous salaries that the studios paid their stars and warmed to the prospect of living lavishly if their daughter should succeed in films. Within a few years their fantasy became a reality. Under the new name given her by the publicity department of Famous Players-Lasky, the young woman soon developed a reputation as a good, reliable actress.

For the first three years Mary Astor worked in New York. In 1923, she was asked for the first time to make a picture in Hollywood. Though she returned to New York from time to time in the mid-1920s to make films, by the end of the decade Hollywood was her home. Her classic features, thick, russet hair, and poignant look about the eyes enabled her quickly to attract a following. After a period of difficulty and uncertainty, she made the transition to sound films, for the recording equipment revealed that she possessed a low-pitched, lilting voice that nicely matched her romantic eyes. Yet for all her popularity she was not a star; attractive as she was, she lacked that vitality and distinctiveness of personality that sets the star player apart from other actors. Nor, on the other hand, did she possess the ability to submerge herself so deeply in her roles as to become a first-rate character actress; one always knew that one was watching a great beauty named Mary Astor. Of all this she herself was fully aware, and though she was unhappy with the insipid ingenue roles usually assigned her, she was content to remain a featured player, no more. She resisted offers of stardom when they came her way, having convinced herself that she would have a longer career if she kept her name below the title.

As she disclosed in her memoirs, which were published in 1959, Mary Astor was also aware of her own sensuality and felt no need to suppress it. Her first affair was with John Barrymore, with whom she fell in love at seventeen, when Barrymore was forty. Other romances swiftly followed the break-up of this one, but none was so promising as that with Kenneth Hawks, a young assistant producer at Fox whose brother was the director Howard Hawks. In 1928, after he had secured a new, long-term contract with the studio, Kenneth Hawks married Mary Astor. The marriage was not an unqualified success, because Hawks, though in love with his wife, did not satisfy her sexually. During their marriage she had an affair with a Fox executive that led to pregnancy and an abortion. Mary Astor's guilt over that affair was compounded when, in 1930, Hawks, having become a director, was killed in a plane crash while supervising aerial camera work on a film. Recovering from her grief, in 1931 she married Dr. Franklyn Thorpe, a Hollywood gynecologist. In the following year the couple had a daughter, whom they called Marylyn.

This second marriage was not beset by the same problems as the first, but it too was not a success. In the spring of 1933 Mary Astor decided to leave her daughter in the care of Thorpe and a nurse and treat herself to a holiday in New York. Marian Spitzer, a story editor at Paramount, gave her the telephone number of an attractive man, George S. Kaufman, with whom she might see the town.

Kaufman's suavity and politeness with women and Mary Astor's susceptibility to men of intelligence and accomplishment made their affair inevitable. It mattered not at all to her that her new acquaintance lacked the conventional handsomeness of Hawks or Thorpe, to say nothing of the extraordinary masculine beauty of John Barrymore. He knew New York, and could and did show it to her. He was courtly, but in no way condescending. Some plays, including his own *Of Thee I Sing* and *Dinner at Eight,* a film, an evening at "21," a carriage-ride around Central Park, a look-in at a cocktail party, and, at every turn, bright conversation: Mary Astor accepted these offerings very happily—and just as happily accepted the suggestion that they drop in at a conveniently empty apartment on East 73rd Street. Into her diary went a sentence or two on each event.

To Kaufman these May evenings meant no more than other evenings that he had spent with other beautiful women. To Mary Astor, however, they were nothing short of rapturous. She fell in love with Kaufman and confided that fact to her diary, as well as to her friends at home when she returned. She looked for signs of similar feeling in Kaufman, but found none. His occasional notes to her never included a declaration of love. Nor did she know when she might have another opportunity to see him. Kaufman's plans for the summer included the writing of his second play with Woollcott, and work on *Let 'Em Eat Cake* with Morrie Ryskind and the Gershwins. What chance had a Hollywood actress against such a schedule? But the affair had not run its course.

It was resumed in the spring of 1934, in California. Mary Astor doubtless knew that it was not her charm that drew him there, but work with Hart on the new play. "Kaufman Off to Coast," noted the New York *Times* on February 13, for this was news in view of his past refusals to visit the West for any reason. The paper also reported that he and Hart planned to write in Palm Springs and that they expected to complete their script in six to eight weeks. Also noted was the fact that several parties were being planned for him; he was to receive the celebrity treatment.

Kaufman settled in at El Mirador, an elegant Palm Springs hotel whose chevron-striped tower was a landmark in the desert. Lonesome for Beatrice and Anne, he telephoned New York frequently and wrote even more often. Though only two of his letters to Beatrice on this trip have survived, they indicate that he sent many more. One of the two—undated, of course, but probably written in the second week of March—reveals that his habits of work and play in California were precisely the same as they were in New York:

> Well, it goes on. Raining every day in Los Angeles, they say, but not a drop here. And, not to annoy you unduly, how far away your blizzards seem. . . . The hotel crowded with people mainly dull. All kinds of

Hollywooders can't get in, and that's good for our side. However, Zeppo and Marian [Marx] will be here over the weekend. So far we have been nowhere, seen nothing. . . . Got stuck today and wrote not a line, but will resume at full tilt tomorrow. We shall finish early in April, we hope. . . . Have an idea for the show after this, and it's a pip. Like nothing ever seen on land or sea. All of which makes me feel good. Mossie burned his hand on a package of matches, but that's about over. Clara Bow and I are bridge buddies. . . .

And there you are. I hope you're finding lots to do, darling, and am sure that you are. It helps a lot to hear your voice once in a while—and it made me very lonesome for you the last time. Thanks for being nice to my parents—you're a good girl, really.

I'll come home tanned, if I don't lose it on the way. Buy yourself something nice for our anniversary, and be sure to call me up that night. I can't send anything from here except Hershey's chocolate, which I don't think you want.

Give Poky a kiss and a hug—gosh, I miss her.

S.

Kaufman and Hart concentrated on the new script, and, as they had planned, in about six weeks they put "Curtain" to the last act of the play that was to be presented as *Merrily We Roll Along*. During this period Kaufman sometimes left the desert, however, and often it was with the purpose of meeting Mary Astor. Also, for one week, the actress stayed in Palm Springs, as the guest of Richard and Dorothy Rodgers.[2]

In all other respects, Mary Astor's life continued as before: a fretful marriage, one picture following almost on the last take of the preceding one, and importunings from her parents for ever more cash. The Langhankes went so far as to sue their daughter for money. No amount of cajolery on her part could get from Kaufman a declaration of romantic love. As much of it as he had to give went to Beatrice. Finally, making a direct appeal to him, Mary Astor had to take no for an answer. "Well, I'll tell you," he said (according to the diary), "I am not going to say I love you because I don't. I was through with love long ago."[3] If, as he may well have done, he attempted to explain to her the nature of his tie to Beatrice, Mary Astor was too blinded by emotion to see the meaning of his words. In the late summer of 1934, being free of picture commitments for a few weeks, she went again to New York, and the affair resumed once more.

She arrived to find Kaufman involved in the rehearsals of *Merrily We Roll Along*, which was scheduled to open on September 29. The play neither engaged all his time nor did it require all his energy; the evenings were free for her. Their entertainments were much as they had been in the previous year:

dinners at the Colony and at "21"—"our 21" to Mary Astor—a drive through the park, and visits to theaters. The evenings also ended as before—not, however, in an apartment on East 73rd Street, but in the Essex House, a hotel on Central Park South.[4] Of their mutual friends, at least one, Jean Dixon, advised Mary Astor to curb her feelings, since, as any but the most infatuated person might have known, Kaufman would never leave Beatrice. Mary Astor thought otherwise, however, and she told Jean Dixon that she was sure Kaufman would marry her. Jean Dixon also advised that she not attend the rehearsals of *Merrily We Roll Along,* since, as Dixon knew from experience, Mary Astor was certain to find other women attracted to Kaufman in the house.[5] Yet go she did, and came away with the desire one day to play the role of Althea Royce. Unhappily for her, she could not linger in New York for the opening. But she went home convinced—rightly—that if she could not marry Kaufman, she would be able at least to find occasions to be with him.[6] These occurred during Kaufman's second stay in California, which began in January 1935.

Kaufman's first dealings with a Hollywood mogul, Samuel Goldwyn, had left him with a distaste for film writing. He and Sherwood had initiated their suit against Goldwyn soon after Kaufman's return to New York in April 1934.[7] Under such circumstances, it was no easy matter for any studio executive to persuade Kaufman to agree to write another film script. But Irving Thalberg of Metro-Goldwyn-Mayer was not a man to give up easily when he had his mind set on a project.

Metro-Goldwyn-Mayer was both the biggest and richest of all the studios in the 1930s and the only one showing a profit and paying dividends to its stockholders throughout the Depression. One of the slogans that Howard Dietz invented for the studio was "More Stars than There Are in the Heavens," and if this was a shade hyperbolic, at least MGM could claim to have put under contract more film stars than any of its competitors. Under Thalberg's guidance, the studio took care to see that it also had under contract some of the ablest and best known writers of the age. Among those who worked on scripts for MGM during the 1930s were S. N. Behrman (a specialist on Garbo pictures), Anita Loos, Dorothy Parker, Donald Ogden Stewart, F. Scott Fitzgerald, and William Faulkner. Though a time would come, long after Thalberg's death, that revisionist screen critics would look back with indifference on his career, the admiration in which he was held by such persons as Fitzgerald, Loos, and Groucho Marx would stand as a reminder that he was one of the very few in his profession in whom organizational genius and creative flair were combined. It was remarked that he could draw from anyone at the studio the most that that person had to give. Constantly on the search for talent, he raided the rosters of other studios incessantly, borrowing for at least a picture or two those performers whom he could not put under contract, so that it was a rare star of the 1920s or 1930s who failed to make a film for MGM. (It is worth noting, however, that when Mary Astor asked him for work after the advent of sound her appeal was ignored. Eventually, in 1932, she had a featured role in MGM's *Red Dust*.)[8]

In 1933, after the Marx Brothers had completed five films under a contract to Paramount that was not renewed, Thalberg invited them to work at MGM. There would, however, be only three Marx Brothers making the move, for Zeppo, bored with his thankless role of straight man, had given up acting and become an agent. Thalberg had some specific notions as to the shape the brothers' pictures should take in the future. He believed that the pace should be slowed down a little by a reduction in the number of gags, thus making it possible for the audience to catch its breath. He also thought that the plots should be less improbable than in the past and that the brothers should have opportunities to engage the sympathy of the audience. Thalberg had in mind not that they should be turned into lovable orphans of the storm, but that they should be placed in a position to come to the aid of the young lovers in the subplot. This had been their function in both *The Cocoanuts* and *Animal Crackers*. The Marxes were not immediately inclined to accept Thalberg's offer, but at last did so on the advice of Samuel Goldwyn. Goldwyn had also made them an offer, but so great was his admiration for Thalberg that he believed that the Marxes would be unwise to forgo a chance to work under his supervision.[9]

By the fall of 1934 Thalberg had on hand an original story invented for the brothers by James Kevin McGuiness, a contract writer at MGM. A scanty outline, it suggested a background in grand opera. The action was to commence in Italy and then to proceed to the United States; the cast was to include not only the brothers, but a romantic young couple as well, with a vengeful rival for the hand of the girl. Groucho was to play an opera impressario, Chico a vocal coach, and Harpo, unfathomably and incredibly, a tenor.[10] To work over this scenario, Thalberg brought in Bert Kalmar and Harry Ruby, the brothers' old friends who had written the songs for *Animal Crackers* and the screenplays and songs for *Horsefeathers* and *Duck Soup*. These writers filled in dialogue, expanded the action to include the ultimate triumph of the pair of young lovers on the opera stage in New York, named Groucho's shady character Otis Driftwood, and invented the character of Mrs.

Beatrice.

Beatrice and G.S.K
in Atlantic City.

G.S.K. and his
daughter, Anne.

The house at Barley Sheaf Farm.

Woollcott and Beatrice
on Neshobe Island.

Max Gordon at the Farm.

Sam H. Harris at the Farm.

G.S.K., Lynn Fontanne, and Marc Connelly looking at the reviews of *Dulcy* (1921). *Culver Pictures.*

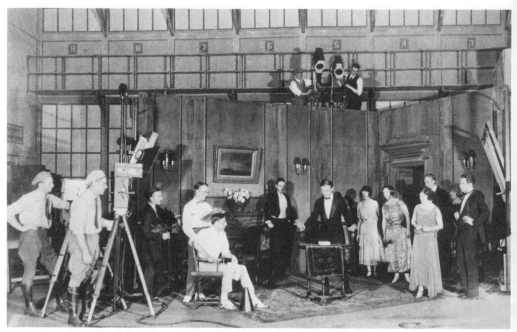

Standing at table, Glenn Hunter as Merton. *Merton of the Movies* (1922), by G.S.K. and Marc Connelly.

Roland Young as Neil McRae,
Kay Johnson as Cynthia Mason.
Beggar on Horseback (1924), by
G.S.K. and Marc Connelly.

Gregory Kelly as Peter Jones,
Robert Middlemass as Joe Lehman,
and Sylvia Field as Jane Weston.
The Butter and Egg Man
(1925), by G.S.K.

In the role of Anthony Cavendish,
Otto Kruger, bearing a distinct
resemblance to John Barrymore,
emotes with Haidee Wright as
his mother, Fanny Cavendish.
The Royal Family (1927),
by G.S.K. and Edna Ferber.

Edna Ferber and G.S.K.

Harpo, Chico, Zeppo, and Groucho. *Animal Crackers* (1928), by G.S.K. and Morrie Ryskind.

A scene from the television production of 1974, with Kevin McCarthy, Jack Cassidy, Beatrice Colen (G.S.K.'s granddaughter) as a clerk in Goebel's music-publishing house, and Stephen Sondheim as Maxie, the house arranger-pianist. *June Moon* (1929), by Ring Lardner and G.S.K. *Courtesy of Exxon Corporation*.

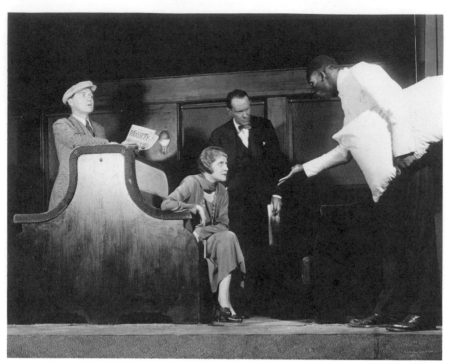

Three vaudevillians en route to Hollywood: Hugh O'Connell, Jean Dixon, and Grant Mills, with Oscar Polk as the Pullman porter. *Once in a Lifetime* (1930), by Moss Hart and G.S.K.

Ira and George Gershwin above; G.S.K. and Morrie Ryskind below. *Culver Pictures.*

In black on the left, Victor Moore as Vice President Throttlebottom, Grace Brinkley as Diana Devereaux, and William Gaxton as President John P. Wintergreen; in bed, Lois Moran as the First Lady. *Of Thee I Sing* (1931), by G.S.K. and Morrie Ryskind.

Janet Fox as Tina, Judith Wood as Kitty Packard, and Paul Harvey as Dan Packard. *Dinner at Eight* (1932), by G.S.K. and Edna Ferber.

Richard Kendrick as ex-proletarian playwright Keith Burgess and Margaret Sullavan as budding actress Terry Randall. *Stage Door* (1936), by Edna Ferber and G.S.K.

Moss Hart and G.S.K.

The Kirbys make an unexpected entrance. Fourth from left, Henry Travers as
Grandpa Vanderhof; at easel, Josephine Hull as Penny Sycamore. *You Can't
Take It with You* (1936), by Moss Hart and G.S.K.

F.D.R., as impersonated by
George M. Cohan, tries to comfort
the young couple Phil Barker
and Peggy Jones, played by
Austin Marshall and Joy Hodges.
I'd Rather Be Right (1937),
by G.S.K. and Moss Hart.

Mary Wickes as Miss Preen the nurse
and Monty Woolley as her impatient
patient, Sheridan Whiteside;
behind Woolley, Theodore Newton
as Bert Jefferson.
The Man Who Came to Dinner
(1939), by Moss Hart and G.S.K.

Janet Beecher as Catherine Apley, Percy Waram and Margaret Dale as Roger and Amelia Newcombe, and Leo G. Carroll as George Apley. *The Late George Apley* (1944), by John P. Marquand and G.S.K.

Stubby Kaye
as Nicely-Nicely Johnston,
Johnny Silver as Benny Southstreet,
and Sam Levene as Nathan Detroit.
Guys and Dolls (1950),
by Jo Swerling and Abe Burrows,
directed by G.S.K. *Culver Pictures.*

Leueen MacGrath and G.S.K.

Claypool, the well-heeled opera patroness, for Margaret Dumont. But the script did not satisfy Groucho. Despite his friendship with Kalmar and Ruby, he wanted some other writers to have a go at McGuiness's story. Thalberg suggested that two of the studio's young writers, George Seaton and Robert Pirosh, work on it, and he gave them a copy of the Kalmar-Ruby script to read. Groucho was cordial with them and at first seemed content to have them writing for him and his brothers, but ultimately made it known that there were only two writers whom he trusted to give him what he wanted. They, of course, were Kaufman and Ryskind.[11]

Getting Kaufman to California a second time was not a simple matter of dangling a lucrative contract under his nose. It took tact and persuasion. Thalberg made an offer that reached Kaufman shortly after the out-of-town closing of *Bring on the Girls,* when he was not in the best of humors. In Beatrice, however, Thalberg had a strong ally. Thinking it would be good for Kaufman to get away, she kept after him and at the same time encouraged Morrie Ryskind to put pressure on him. For his part, Ryskind did not require much encouragement from Beatrice or anyone else. Having fewer options than Kaufman, he was eager to accept Thalberg's offer. After the two writers talked it over several times, Kaufman explained his reluctance: he had promised never to write for Hollywood again. When Ryskind asked him *whom* he had promised, he replied, "Myself." Ryskind thereupon suggested that that was one promise he could easily break, and Kaufman agreed. Meanwhile, as a result of Kaufman's holding out, Thalberg's offer increased substantially, mounting at last to $100,000 for the script. But regardless of the money involved, Kaufman was not thrilled by the prospect of writing for Hollywood or, for that matter, writing once again for the Marxes, no matter how much he liked them personally. In a note to George C. Tyler dated January 16, 1935, a few days before his departure, he wrote, "I'm going to Hollywood, God damn it, this Saturday, but only for a few weeks."[12]

Once Kaufman arrived in Hollywood, settled into the Beverly Wilshire Hotel, and began to survey the scene, he underwent a slow, grudging adjustment to the ways of the movie colony. He was pleased—anyway, not displeased—to have party invitations extended to him, but accepted none that he could not get out of if he wished. The disagreeable part of his Hollywood life was that he could not determine his own work schedule. Like all other writers under contract to the studio, he and Ryskind were expected to put in a daily appearance. They had an office in the MGM writers' building; Kaufman and others called it, without affection, the "iron lung." According to a much-repeated story that originated with Kaufman, passersby could sometimes hear voices within screaming, "Let me out of here! I'm just as sane as anybody else!"[13] Kaufman was a somewhat special inhabitant of this particular zoo, to be sure, since he had come to the studio to write one picture only and expected to remain in Hollywood no longer than his task required.

Despite the unfamiliar sensation of writing to order, something he had not brought himself to do since the Tyler days, and despite the downright oddity of being three thousand miles away from real life, Kaufman had a good time. Hollywood was full of his old acquaintances. Bridge with Chico Marx provided a pleasant way to spend the evening, or a Sunday afternoon. Herman Mankiewicz, who, like the Marxes, had moved from Paramount to MGM, was delighted to see him. George Oppenheimer was also at MGM. S. N. Behrman was in and out, thinking of plots suitable for the special style of Greta Garbo. On one Sunday evening Kaufman attended a farewell party for Behrman, who was supposedly leaving the next day for New York. At the last minute, Behrman was asked by the studio to do some rewriting, and Kaufman encountered him on the lot. "Ah," said Kaufman, "forgotten but not gone."[14]

During this visit, as during the last, Kaufman extended his circle of Hollywood friends. One new acquaintance was the screenwriter Charles Lederer, the nephew of Marion Davies and an intimate friend of George Oppenheimer. Kaufman enjoyed Lederer's company, but did not let this get in the way of his making a joke at the expense of Lederer's mother, Reine Davies. Pursuing her duties as a columnist for the Los Angeles *Examiner,* this elder Miss Davies asked Kaufman to fill her in on the guest list for a party given for playwright Norman Krasna at the Trocadero, Hollywood's favorite night club of the moment. He gave her a list that included not only such authentic film figures as Sylvia Sidney, Richard Barthelmess, the Groucho Marxes, and Zeppo Marx, but Karl Marx, William Cullen Bryant, Edith Cavell, and Ethan Frome. The columnist printed the list in full; for all she (and her editor) knew, they were contract players.[15]

The most interesting of Kaufman's new acquaintances, both as a private individual and as a representative of Hollywood, was Irving Thalberg himself. Kaufman discovered, a little to his surprise, that he liked and admired this brilliant young man. According to Thalberg's biographer, Kaufman once said of him, "That man has never written a word, and yet he can tell me exactly what to do with a story."[16] Groucho, who believed that Thalberg was the most capable man in pictures and that Kaufman was the best possible writer for himself and his brothers, was delighted that they hit it off. According to his report, Kaufman said to him of Thalberg, "He's another Sam Harris. I didn't think you had people like him out here!"[17] The comparison with Harris implied that Kaufman found Thalberg not only astute and industrious, but aboveboard. One story had it, however, that it took a while for them to become comfortable with one another. "Come on, George, call me Irving," said Thalberg. "I'll call you Irving," Kaufman replied, "if you call me Mr. Kaufman."[18] With Thalberg as a buffer for him, only rarely did he encounter MGM's reactionary, power-hungry boss of bosses, Louis B. Mayer. He won a good many hearts and minds by remarking, "I'd rather have t.b. than L.B." Not once did he mention Mayer in his letters to Beatrice from Hollywood.

From Thalberg and his wife, actress Norma Shearer, came a spate of invitations for dinner and bridge. These evenings were much to Kaufman's liking: not only could he count on good bridge, he could also count on thrashing over matters pertaining to the picture. At the studio Thalberg was—famously, even notoriously—difficult to see. Curst with the habit of making more appointments than he could possibly keep, he allowed the anteroom of his office to fill to overflowing with some of the most expensive writers and actors in the country, and often ended the day having seen none of them. Kaufman sometimes warmed this "million dollar bench," but he did not let Thalberg's neglect of him create a coolness between them.

All this while Mary Astor was very much a part of Kaufman's life. Though managing to maintain a heavy schedule under a new contract with Columbia Pictures, the actress suffered from severe emotional stress. There was no apparent likelihood of her ever marrying Kaufman despite her hopes, and she knew it, but she saw no point in continuing her marriage to Franklyn Thorpe. What she did not know was that Kaufman had recently begun an affair in New York with a Russian ballerina. Thorpe was well aware of his wife's involvement with Kaufman, as she confided to her diary:

> I called for George [one evening in February] at the Beverly Wilshire at seven. He was very pleasant but a little jittery and strained, I noticed. In the car on the way to the Trocadero I said: "Feeling lowish?"
> "M—yeah—I'll tell you all about it."
> We went downstairs to the bar, sat down at a table and ordered drinks.
> "Shall I wait for you to have a drink or shall I plunge right in?"
> I was pretty mystified and worried and said: "Plunge in, I'm dying of curiosity."
> "I've had a visit from your husband."
> I practically went through the floor.[19]

As Kaufman described the meeting to her, it had been amicable enough. Thorpe's intention was to notify Kaufman that he would not allow a divorce to take place without a fight, and that Kaufman would be brought into it. Very soon thereafter Thorpe reached an agreement with Mary Astor that she could have a divorce without mention in court of Kaufman provided that Thorpe would have custody of their child six months of the year. In her diary Mary Astor wrote that she intended "later on" to sue for complete custody. The divorce duly took place without contest; good as his word, Thorpe made no mention to the press or the court of his wife's extramarital involvement.

The affair continued in full force, but after six weeks of work Kaufman and Ryskind completed the script and handed it over to Thalberg, and Kaufman, without reluctance, packed his bags and returned to New York. He had a piece of unfinished business awaiting him there: the script of *First Lady*. Remaining behind, Ryskind read the Marx Brothers' film script, now called *A Night at the Opera*, to Thalberg. Ryskind won Thalberg's approval, though during the reading the producer did not crack a smile, but only remarked at the end that it was one of the funniest scripts he had ever heard.[20] At that, Thalberg had reservations, and, true to the tradition that he had helped to establish, he was not content to give it back to Kaufman and Ryskind to revise. He returned it to the team of Kalmar and Ruby and at the same time put the team of Seaton and Pirosh back to work on it. At first neither team knew that the other was rewriting the script. Finally an *eighth* writer, gagman Al Boasberg, was also assigned to *A Night at the Opera*. After Boasberg completed his job, which consisted mainly of adding pieces of business for the brothers, Thalberg and Groucho between them conceived the notion of trying out the major scenes on the road.

The tour opened in Salt Lake City on April 13, with Ryskind, Boasberg, Seaton, and Pirosh in attendance. Apart from the brothers themselves, of the actors who had major roles in the film, only Allan Jones made the tour. From Salt Lake City the show went on to Seattle, Portland, and San Francisco, with additions and deletions of dialogue en route. One of the most important expansions of the original material occurred in a scene that was to become a highlight of the film: the scene in Groucho's tiny stateroom, which becomes increasingly crowded. Not only the brothers and the stowaway juvenile (Jones) make themselves at home in it, but incursions are made by a waiter, two engineers, a manicurist, and a girl looking for a telephone, all of whom spill into the corridor when Mrs. Claypool (Margaret Dumont) opens the door in search of Groucho.

In May, when the tour had run its successful course, the brothers and their crew of writers returned to MGM to make the film. They began with a script credited solely to Kaufman and Ryskind, but with credit also going to McGuiness as author of the story on which it was based. As written (and published three decades later), the script included all the scenes that audiences would long remember: the stateroom scene; the backstage scene in which Chico (as Jones's agent) and Groucho (as Dumont's impresario) tear up, article by article, the contract for Jones's services; the gala last night aboard the ship en route to New York (in which Harpo and Chico find an opportunity for their musical specialties); the hotel scene in which stowaways Chico, Harpo, and Jones are pursued by the plainclothes cop, Henderson; and the performance of *Il Trovatore* that ends with the establishment of the juveniles as new operatic stars. The plot itself scarcely bears retelling. It is, simply put, the story of how Otis P. Driftwood, acting in behalf of the very rich, socially ambitious Mrs. Claypool, persuades her to make a sizable contribution to the New York Opera Company. She will back the production of *Trovatore* in which the great tenor, Lasspari, and the young soprano, Rosa Castaldi, will make their American debut. The young tenor, Baroni (who is in love with Rosa), Lasspari's mute dresser, Tomasso, and Baroni's inept manager, Fiorello, sail with them as stowaways. On the night of the performance, the brothers, all of whom are in one sort of trouble or another, create such havoc in the theater while trying to avoid the police that the performance becomes an utter wreck. However, they come out on top, as always, and the young lovers are united. A comparison of the shooting script with the cutting continuity[21] reveals no structural changes, but the addition of numerous sight gags and comic lines.

To make the brothers the helpful types that Thalberg thought they should be on screen, Kaufman and Ryskind let each of the three make some sort of gesture toward bringing together the young lovers, who were played by Allan Jones and Kitty Carlisle. This is somewhat forced at the moment when Groucho, dropping his cynicism, comes upon the weeping soprano aboard ship and attempts to comfort her. She claims that the cause of her distress is homesickness, but Groucho knows better. "That's funny," he says. "I happen to have with me the greatest prescription for homesickness you ever saw. [He takes a paper from his pocket.] A fellow gave it to me just before the boat sailed. There's the prescription and, uh, take it, uh, every two hours." It is a note from her beloved Baroni. Harpo is made a character rather more tender than is usual for him when, near the beginning of the picture, he is beaten savagely by Lasspari, his employer, for donning the singer's costumes. His harp solo, in which he plays "Alone," by Arthur Freed and Nacio Fred Brown, is possibly the most beautiful of all those that he filmed.

As in their stage musicals for the brothers, the collaborators supplied gags in such profusion that they seem to streak through the dialogue like tracer bullets. Most, of course, are for Groucho. Being handed a dinner check by a waiter, he tosses it to his woman companion, saying, "Nine dollars and forty cents. This is an outrage! If I were you I wouldn't pay for it." As he and Margaret Dumont board the ship, she asks him if he has everything, and he replies, "I've never had any complaints yet." Groucho, in accordance with his authors' instructions in the script, frequently violates the cardinal rule of film-making against speaking into the camera; on each of these occasions he reveals his gift for seeming to invent his lines on the spot, when in fact he is reeling off phrases set down for him by his writers.

When the production went before the cameras in May, Thalberg chose Sam Wood as director. The selection was governed, according to Groucho, by the fact that Wood was so inept at his profession that he would not have the nerve to complain if Thalberg required a massive number of retakes, as he usually did.[22] But Kaufman, having completed the script of *First Lady* with Katharine Dayton, returned to Hollywood to oversee the production at Thalberg's request. He himself directed some of the scenes among the brothers.[23] The production gave him his first opportunity to meet Kitty Carlisle, who a decade later would enter his innermost circle of acquaintances as the wife of Moss Hart. In 1935, though she had already made some successful screen appearances, she was awed by Kaufman's theatrical reputation, and eyed him silently as he sat to one side on the set. One day when she had been called in for some scenes with Harpo, she saw that Kaufman was not sitting alone this time, but was accompanied by a woman of great beauty. That woman, of course, was Mary Astor. When the shooting was finished, Kaufman introduced the actresses to each other.[24]

The summer of 1935 saw Beatrice making her first and, as it happened, her only visit to California. She scheduled only ten days there, after which she was to proceed to Honolulu. Anne accompanied her on the trip, which began immediately after the summer closing of the Todhunter School, where the child had just completed the fourth grade.

The unprovoked, precipitate dismissal of Anne's German nurse, Friedl Schulein, in the previous summer still troubled Anne and affected her relations with Beatrice. Kaufman was well aware of the problem, but from his point of view it was Beatrice's problem, not his. Anne had come to love her governess, Jeanne Velay, and consequently was no longer cheerless over the departure of Friedl Schulein. Nevertheless, she had not quite forgiven her mother. A restraint of feeling, an armed truce of the emotions, existed between them. Jeanne Velay—"Fleur"—was to be Anne's companion for the entire summer. She left New York for Los Angeles by train while mother and daughter started out by air. Inadvertently, Anne contributed further to the distance between herself and Beatrice by becoming violently sick on the plane. When they reached Kansas City, Beatrice, though not pleased to do so, took herself and her child off the plane and booked a drawing room on the train for the remainder of the journey to Los Angeles. It was a bad beginning to what was supposed to have been a summer of relaxation.

Having gone back to the Beverly Wilshire when he returned to duty at MGM in May, Kaufman booked Beatrice into the hotel. After settling into her suite, Beatrice was both amused and annoyed to have delivered to her some of her husband's clothes that had just been cleaned. The hotel staff made the mistake of thinking that husband and wife would share rooms.[25]

From her base at the hotel, Beatrice explored this opulent world of Hollywood that seemed so delighted with the acquisition, however temporary, of her famous husband. One excursion took her as far away as the Hearst estate at San Simeon. The castle, an ornate tribute to the Spanish Colonial architectural style, sufficiently impressed Beatrice that she stuck some postcard views of it into her scrapbook. In Hollywood she was taken around by Herman Mankiewicz, Harpo, and other friends, who were as keen as Kaufman to see that she enjoyed herself.

Up to this time Beatrice had seen relatively little of the Hollywood powers. Now that she was meeting them in numbers and on their own territory, she found herself responding in ways that were not to her credit, as she herself realized. With few exceptions, the top-ranking executives were Jews born in Eastern Europe, and Beatrice could not avoid making invidious comparisons between them and Jews of German extraction, such as her own or Kaufman's family, or, for that matter, Thalberg.[26] Nevertheless, she had a good time among them. For their part, the Hollywood crowd took to her enthusiastically. One executive who took a particular liking to her was Samuel Goldwyn, despite his ongoing legal battle with Kaufman. One year later Goldwyn asked her to become his Eastern representative. Though Kaufman worried that the hard-driving Goldwyn would exhaust her with demands on her time, she took the job, and from the fall of 1936 to the fall of 1937 she hunted out young directing and writing talent to send to the West.[27]

When the ten days were up, Beatrice, Anne, and Fleur sailed to Honolulu, where they arrived toward the end of June. Beatrice had reserved rooms at the Halekulani Hotel on Waikiki, but, never one to stint where comfort was concerned, for the month of July she took a house on the beach. Dorothy Pratt (who had been Dorothy Nathan) came to stay, and for two days one of Hollywood's most celebrated actresses, Shirley Temple, came to visit. Her parents, seeking privacy for the child star but wanting her to have the chance to play like any normal little girl, asked if they could bring her over to Mrs. Kaufman's strip of beach, and Beatrice was happy to have her.

Despite this and other attractions of the island, the Kaufmans' daughter was not having much of a time. She could not relax in her mother's presence, even among the languid breezes of Waikiki. The fault in part rested with Beatrice, who, liking the idea of motherhood more than the fact, remained unpredictable in her manner toward the child, at times becoming strict, at other times affecting permissiveness. But at the end of July, in keeping with her plan, Beatrice sailed back to the mainland with Dorothy Pratt, leaving Anne and Fleur to spend another two weeks at the Halekulani. As the *Lurline* went out to sea, Anne felt a swift lifting of the spirit, and, it was evident, so did Fleur. The Frenchwoman bought herself a Coca-Cola and, in full knowledge of the fact that Beatrice would have expressed stern disapproval had she known, offered one to Anne. It was the treat of the summer.

From Honolulu, Fleur and Anne went back to Los Angeles, where Kaufman had again booked them into the Beverly Wilshire for ten days. Still busy with the Marx Brothers' picture, he nevertheless found time to entertain his daughter. For her part, she was delighted to be with him. He took her to the set of a Tarzan picture, where she could ogle Johnny Weissmuller as he swung from tree to tree. Kaufman also let her perform for a few seconds in a scene with Harpo, but the regulations of the Screen Actors Guild forbade the appearance on screen by a non-member, and the bit ended on the cutting-room floor. On the days when his obligations to MGM could not be scanted, Kaufman took her to the house of a friend who had a little girl, albeit one some six years younger, with whom she could play. It was thus that Anne spent several afternoons of her Hollywood visit at the home of Mary Astor.

At the end of August, Kaufman sent Anne and Fleur back to New York by way of Rochester, where they stopped briefly with Beatrice's family. He himself stayed on in Hollywood until the picture was finished in mid-September. With that out of the way (though already Thalberg was talking to him about the next Marx Brothers picture), Kaufman returned to Broadway. His plans were carefully drawn for the season. The first order of business was the staging of *First Lady*. The comedy opened on November 26 to reviews of the sort that guaranteed a run through the season. The second major item on the list of events was the staging of *Tomorrow's a Holiday*, a comedy adapted by Romney Brent from the German of Leo Perutz and Hans Adler. The beginning of his work on this immediately followed the launching of *First Lady*. The play opened on December 30 and closed after one week. Next he agreed to lend a hand to Robert Sinclair, his protégé, who was directing James M. Cain's *The Postman Always Rings Twice*, a production offered by Jack Curtis that opened on February 25, 1936, for a run of nine weeks.[28] Next came the writing of *Stage Door* with Edna Ferber, a task that occupied him through the spring months.

Beatrice also kept busy. In the late spring of 1935 she had been approached by Carmel Snow, the editor of Hearst's *Harper's Bazaar*, to join the magazine as fiction editor. The title was inaccurate, because she was expected to find essays as well as fiction. No announcement of the appointment was made until September, but in the meantime she had begun to search out items for the magazine. It was not only her ebullience and the shrewdness of literary judgment that she had developed while with Horace Liveright and, subsequently, with Coward-McCann that made her valuable, but the fact that she knew a great many talented writers in the United States and abroad from whom she might wheedle a few publishable pages. She stayed with the magazine for about a year and a half; the last issue to include her name on the masthead was that of December 1936.

One of the first writers whom Beatrice approached was Noel Coward. Even before leaving for California in June she wrote him asking for an article, only to find his refusal, dated July 10, awaiting her on her return. In the fall she approached him again, this time asking him to contribute to a piece on the kind of women preferred by eminent men. Again he refused, though he called her "Darling Lamb Girl." "On second thoughts not darling Lamb Girl but wicked Lamb Girl for worrying the be-Jesus out of me with beastly symposiums about whether I like women this way or that when you know perfectly well that I love only Lamb Girl to play backgammon with me."[29]

Though she could not bag this lion, Beatrice nevertheless fulfilled the expectations that Carmel Snow had of her. The two women became good friends. If the editor and her second-in-command, Frances McFadden, had a complaint to make about her, it was that she seemed to favor Jewish writers. Since she also favored them in her personal life, this was inevitable; however, she did not object when some of her choices for inclusion in the magazine were voted down. Always animated, she was a good colleague, though sometimes a rather startling one, as on the occasion when she sought the advice of

Frances McFadden on what she took to be a delicate social issue. Kaufman's nephew Frank Lieberman was to be married at the Kaufmans' house, and Beatrice asked whether in Frances McFadden's opinion it would be appropriate to invite the officiating rabbi to stay for the supper that was to follow the ceremony. McFadden confessed that she did not have the answer, but inquired about the outcome of the matter the day after the wedding. Roaring with laughter, Beatrice said that she had asked the rabbi to stay, and that not only had he eaten heartily but told her that years before he had been a chorus boy in one of Kaufman's musicals.[30]

On May 28, 1936, Kaufman was back at the Beverly Wilshire. Thalberg had persuaded him to spend two weeks at MGM doctoring scripts under consideration for filming. Kaufman's first letter to Beatrice of this stay reveals that he had already spent some time in New York going over a script with members of the MGM story department. Probably this was the new vehicle for the Marx Brothers, which eventually would be released as *A Day at the Races*. The writers of record on that script were Robert Pirosh, George Seaton, and, at Kaufman's suggestion, George Oppenheimer. Al Boasberg supplied gags, but without screen credit.

The filming of this new picture for the Marxes was scheduled to begin late in the summer, following a road tour of the central scenes. Kaufman notified Thalberg that he would like to direct the picture when it was ready to go before the cameras, but could not draw a commitment from the producer.[31] Thalberg was insistent, however, that he read and pronounce upon the script before the tour. He went through it in the presence of Seaton and Pirosh and, like Thalberg when Ryskind read the script of *A Night at the Opera*, he was poker-faced throughout. Putting it down at last, he pronounced it a perfect vehicle for the Marx Brothers.[32] But Thalberg had still other assignments for him, and before he knew it the two weeks had stretched to three.

The chief piece of business on Kaufman's mind at the time was the writing of another comedy with Hart. Had not Hart, who was also putting in time at MGM, been delayed with a film assignment, Kaufman would have had less interest in Thalberg's importunings. But eventually the two collaborators were free of their studio commitments and settled into a routine of daily stints on their play at the house in Beverly Hills that Hart had rented from Frances Marion, the screenwriter. Still a patient in psychoanalysis, and far from the end of it, Hart saw his doctor late every afternoon, after he and Kaufman were finished for the day. Nothing, nothing at all, was to interfere with this work-in-progress, not even the analytical sessions.[33]

The lives of both Kaufman and Beatrice marched at a rapid tempo that summer of 1936. Though apart, they were in constant touch by telephone and letter. Kaufman's gossipy messages were invariably bracketed between a salutary "Dearest" and a declaration of love at the close. He held back, as always, specific accounts of his romantic involvements, but offered clues of a sort. Noting how quickly in his letters Luise Rainer became merely Rainer, Beatrice must have realized that he had been attracted to this actress, the latest sensation at MGM. That spring she had received an Oscar for her portrayal of Anna Held in *The Great Ziegfeld,* and even now, as the Chinese peasant wife in *The Good Earth,* a Thalberg production, she was enacting the role that would win her a second one. It was another playwright, Clifford Odets, with whom this actress would fall in love and marry. As it happened, Kaufman and Ferber had added to the cast of characters of *Stage Door* a travesty figure of Odets. Hart, reading the manuscript of *Stage Door* on Kaufman's first night in town, liked everything about the play except this character, who did not seem quite real to him.[34]

Having spent his first evening in Hollywood with Hart, Kaufman dined with Mary Astor the next evening. Again they went to the Trocadero.[35] In that ordering of events she could not have been so unastute as to miss the value that he set on their affair in relation to his profession. Both were content to let the affair continue for a time, though the end was in sight.

At the conclusion of his first letter of the summer to Beatrice he declared, "I love you darling, and at this writing I doubt if I'll have a very good time of it here." Yet for most of the summer he did have a good time. Others with him at parties noted that he was far from miserable.[36] In addition to the pleasures of socializing with old friends, he derived great satisfaction from the progress that he and Hart were making. The new comedy went so well that within a month they were arranging its tryout tour and Broadway opening. Of nearly equal importance to him was the casting of *Stage Door.* Canvassing the scene for the right actress to play the leading role of Terry Randall, he chose Margaret Sullavan, "despite," he wrote to Beatrice, "her slight madness."

The Hollywood figure most often in his thoughts throughout his stay was Thalberg. Looking forward to 1937, the producer had in mind a film version of *First Lady,* starring Norma Shearer. This, not *A Day at the Races,* was the first picture that he wanted Kaufman to direct. For the year following that, Thalberg had arranged with Mayer and other officers of Loew's, Inc., the parent company of MGM, to set up his own producing unit within the corporation, and it was his idea that Kaufman should be a part of it to the extent of directing one picture a year. Though unwilling to work in Hollywood as often as that, Kaufman reported to Beatrice, "I didn't commit myself, but it's nice to know that I could direct a picture once in a while and make a hunk of money. I don't think it should be once a year—that's too often. . . . Anyhow, that's probably where our old age security will come from, and it's worth the trips once in a while. It has given me anew that feeling of prosperity, even though we are far from rolling in coin at the present."

Sometimes, in order to be with Thalberg, Kaufman broke dates with other acquaintances; for so punctilious a man, this was a gesture indicating exceptional regard. In addition to going to the producer's beach house for bridge, Kaufman also spent some days on Thalberg's newly acquired yacht. After the first time aboard, he wrote to Beatrice, "The yacht was fun in the main, although a bit silly. Irving loves it—it makes him emperor of a small kingdom over the weekend, as well as during the week."

As usual, Beatrice had travel plans. Early in July she and Carmel Snow sailed for London, from which they went on to North Africa. Their destination was the Tunisian port of Hammamet, where George Hoyningen-Huene, the innovative fashion photographer of *Harper's Bazaar,* had built a house overlooking the Mediterranean. Before setting out on this junket, Beatrice had the feeling that she might not be able to keep her job—not because she was not discharging her duties efficiently, but because William Randolph Hearst, whose corporation owned the magazine, might decide to hold her personal support of liberal politicians against her. Inevitably, her endorsement of liberal candidates for office made the papers. She had heard a report (false, as it turned out) that Hearst would be sailing on her ship. Kaufman was amused by this, and he wrote, "That should be fun—crossing with him. See if you can drop something in his soup."

The time passed pleasantly, at least at first. By the end of July, Kaufman and Hart had completed the second act of their play, which they decided to call *You Can't Take It with You.* But then Mary Astor's suit for the custody of her daughter came to trial. That development put an end to the pleasantness.

The actress had initiated her suit in accordance with a plan that she had devised when she divorced Thorpe. He had demanded six-months' custody of their daughter, and in order to secure an uncontested divorce she had acceded to his wish, fully intending to sue for complete custody at a later date. It was all but certain that Kaufman's name would be drawn into the proceedings, for Thorpe had confiscated her intimate diary and could be expected to try to introduce it as evidence that she was morally unfit to raise a child. Having wind of this, Kaufman notified Beatrice by cable to Paris, where she was stopping briefly on her way back from Hammamet, that she could expect some unpleasant news to circulate about him.[37]

When the case came up in late July in the court of Judge Goodwin J. Knight, Mary Astor was at work in one of the choicest parts ever to come her way: the sympathetic Edith Cortright in *Dodsworth*, a film based on Sidney Howard's dramatic adaptation of Sinclair Lewis's novel. Samuel Goldwyn was the producer. At the outset, the court sessions were held at night, so that the actress could spend the daytime hours on the set.

Though Mary Astor's lawyer was able to prevent the opposition from introducing the diary as evidence because it had been mutilated by Thorpe, he was powerless to keep Thorpe from showing it to reporters, and powerless to keep the reporters from publishing excerpts from it. Much that got into print in the tabloid press described the "thrilling ecstasy" of the actress's encounters with the playwright. The whole truth as to how many of the published "excerpts" were genuine and how many had been forged—and if forged, by whom—never came to light. The first mention of the document in the papers occurred on July 31, when it was reported that the diary was expected to reveal that its author had had an affair with a man named George. Bits of it, as printed on that day by the New York *Daily News*, the paper with the greatest circulation in the United States and the one from which other tabloids took their style, had the ring of truth. They described not an infatuation on the actress's part, but an emotional response to a charming man who was also an adroit lover. They also demonstrated Mary Astor's hope that she could protect him from scandal when she sued Thorpe for divorce. They were identical with others, printed two weeks later by the Los Angeles *Examiner*, which eventually, in her memoirs, the actress declared to be genuine. On the following day the papers revealed that in court Thorpe had identified "George" as an eminent theatrical figure and that, following this disclosure, his lawyer had cleared up the matter: the eminent theatrical figure was George S. Kaufman.

Bowing to the exigencies of film production, Judge Knight recessed the trial for one week so that Mary Astor could complete her role in the film. The strain of acting through the daylight hours and testifying in the evening was beginning to show. The alternative to the court recess, the postponement of the film, would have caused a massive layoff of actors and technicians. On the same day that Judge Knight called the recess, Joseph Anderson, Thorpe's lawyer, had Kaufman subpoenaed to appear as a witness.

With the identification of Mary Astor's lover as Kaufman, the press had something to publish that amounted to more than a routine Hollywood marital squabble. True, Mary Astor, by virtue of her professional competence and her beauty, was newsworthy, but Kaufman's fame amounted to vastly more. The mention of his name was followed by blasts of sensational reporting. On August 4 the New York *Daily News* titillated readers with "Diary of Astor Love Bares Kaufman Tryst—'Ecstasy.'" The next day the paper declared, "Mary Blushes Over Diary." Inside, on page four, appeared a summary of certain lines of the diary as (somehow) uncovered by the reporter:

> Almost three pages of closely scribbled notes in her diary were devoted to one night when Kaufman revealed himself to her as superman, in the thrilling friendship he offered her.

Papers and news magazines across the nation offered such choice bits as "He fits me perfectly . . . many exquisite moments . . . twenty—count them, diary, twenty. . . . I don't see how he does it . . . he is perfect."[38] Readers were informed that the diary was written in purple ink, was written in lavender ink, was scented with lavender. It was also reported that the actress had included in her daily jottings a "box score" of the prowess of various men in her life.

Justifiably perturbed by this invasion of her privacy, which might adversely affect both the trial and her future in films, Mary Astor maintained that she had kept no such score and that indeed all the lurid quotations had been forged, though she admitted that she had known George S. Kaufman intimately, asserting (as was true) that Thorpe had condoned the relationship. In later years, puzzling over the description of the diary entries as written in purple ink, she concluded that the reporters had received that impression from the combination of bronze ink that she had actually used and the blue lines of the book.[39] Be that as it may, it is possible that one of the metaphorically purple passages was present in the diary, but to a different effect from that suggested by the reporters. At Kaufman's request, the diary was examined privately by Moss Hart, the only friend whom Kaufman trusted enough to dispatch on such an intimate errand. Hart maintained—privately—that the actress had indeed written the phrase "twenty—count them, diary, twenty," but that it referred not to sexual performances, but to Kaufman's string of Broadway hits.[40]

The reason Kaufman did not examine the diary himself was that he was in hiding. His first refuge was Hart's rented house in Beverly Hills. Then, assuming that he would be run to earth in his collaborator's home, he escaped to Thalberg's yacht, where he spent an agitated weekend. On Monday, August 10, when the trial resumed, Kaufman failed to appear in court.

Judge Knight sent a sheriff on his trail, but by that time it was too late. Coming back to dry land from Thalberg's "weekend empire," the harried, rueful, middle-aged Lothario was whisked by studio employees to San Bernardino, east of Los Angeles, where he boarded the Santa Fe Chief for the East and freedom. "I'll put him away for a while to cool off if he ever comes back into the jurisdiction of this court," Judge Knight declared. "He could write quite a play about life in jail."[41]

That was the climax of the story. The denouement took another two weeks to play out. Judge Knight, reluctantly recognizing that Kaufman was beyond his reach, brought the trial to an end on August 13, allowing Mary Astor custody of her daughter for nine months of the year and denying a motion by Thorpe's lawyer to reopen the case. The diary was impounded, never to see the light of day again.[42] Despite the sensitivity of the Hollywood powers to any suggestion of immorality on the part of their employees, Mary Astor's career proceeded much as before. That she played a warm, generous-hearted woman in *Dodsworth,* and played well, was of help to her in maintaining the admiration of the public. Additionally, it was taken to be to her credit that she had risked her reputation in order to recover her daughter. For a time, *any* Astor picture was in demand, so sensational had been the disclosures in the press. But her *Dodsworth* performance was above exploitation; it received a respectful hearing on its merits.

In January 1937 the actress married Manuel del Campo, a handsome Mexican six years her junior. At last she had conquered her feeling for Kaufman. Until her retirement in 1965, she kept as busy as she cared to, but continued to resist stardom. Her portrayal of a concert pianist in *The Great Lie* (1941), a Bette Davis picture, secured her an Academy Award for best featured performance by an actress. As the murderess Brigid O'Shaughnessy in *The Maltese Falcon* (1941), opposite Humphrey Bogart, she gave what is possibly the most memorable of all her performances. Through the remainder of her career, however, most of her roles were colorless, and less demanding than the scope of her talent deserved. In middle age she demonstrated a second talent, as novelist and memoirist. But never did she succeed in dissociating herself from Kaufman in the mind of the public.

Not so with Kaufman, of course. It was not long before he regained his self-possession and, back in New York, turned his wit loose on the scandal for the benefit of the press. Leaving his Santa Fe drawing room in Chicago, he boarded the New York Central. In Harmon, New York, he was met by his sister Ruth, who drove him to Manhattan. The day of his return was August 12. After two nights at the apartment of Hart's parents, he came back to the house on East 94th. The next day he met the press. "Kaufman Turns Up In N.Y., Isn't Angry At Mary," proclaimed the News. "There is only one thing I resent about the case," he said. "Some newspaper referred to me as a middle-aged playwright. The reason I resent it so much is because it's true, but the thought is frightening. I have also one wonderful piece of news for the American public. I have never kept a diary. Everything I write is to be acted on the stage." Now, he added, it was time to forget the entire dreary business: "I feel I have been in the public eye long enough, and think the public ought to be glad to get me out of its eye."[43]

To the surprise of none of their associates, Beatrice took in stride the revelations of her husband's infidelity. Before sailing from London on the last leg of her journey home, she was besieged by reporters. She said, "George is a good husband. I love him very much, and he is in love with me. . . . Please do not ask me to discuss Miss Astor. She is a film actress and kept a diary. Very stupid, that."[44] On August 27 she arrived in New York on the Ile de France. Aboard the ship she avoided questions. "The story is completely dead," she told reporters. "Why can't you leave it that way? I have nothing to say. I don't even know whether I shall meet him [Kaufman] on the pier. We ought to be allowed to go back to obscurity." Reporters in the corridor heard her conferring with Irving Berlin, who had sailed on the same ship. "You're doing all right," Berlin said to her. "Just don't say anything."[45] She said nothing more.

Accompanied by his lawyer, Howard Reinheimer, Kaufman was there to meet her. With nothing to say except a terse "Come on," he took her arm and led her away. But lest this unloving reunion give rise to gossip, Beatrice offered a statement to the press the next day: "Mr. Kaufman and I are pursuing the usual routine of our lives. We have no intention of changing its order. Naturally, we both regret that an incident which must have occurred in the lives of many adults was made the focus of public interest. We honestly wish to be permitted again the peace and privacy of ordinary individuals."[46] So much for rumors of divorce. Beatrice had expressed greater irritation over her husband's affair with the ballerina, who had had the bad taste to telephone him frequently at home. The Astor scandal may have tested their marriage, but it did not threaten it. Coming back from the sunswept glamour of the Mediterranean and the Pacific, they were grateful to begin again on 94th Street.

On September 14 Thalberg died. In frail health all his life, he had caught a cold on Labor Day, September 7, and it quickly deepened into pneumonia.

Kaufman would return to MGM the next year and for some years after that, but to nobody else at the studio would he warm as he had warmed to Thalberg.

On September 25 Kaufman and Beatrice signed a contract to buy Barley Sheaf Farm, the fifty-seven acre estate of Juliana Force, the socialite-sculptor, in Holicong, Pennsylvania. Columnists and photographers lost no time in reporting on weekend houseparties at the Kaufmans' Bucks County farm. Who now could doubt that these two were themselves again?

—15—

Birth of a Classic

First Lady played 246 performances. The picture rights were sold, though not to Metro-Goldwyn-Mayer, despite Irving Thalberg's hope of filming it with Norma Shearer in the lead. Warner Brothers snapped it up as a vehicle for Kay Francis, who was widely known as the screen's best-dressed actress. It was a dressy play.

In the three years immediately preceding *First Lady*, Kaufman's only great hits had been the films *Roman Scandals* and *A Night at the Opera*. If his failures did not create the impression with the public and the press that his talent was in decline, they did demonstrate that his judgment was not flawless. Besieged by would-be collaborators, he had often overestimated the potentiality of the projects urged on him. The compulsion to work, which increased as he pressed into middle age, had kept him from closely questioning the plot concepts at hand. A sprinter, he moved from project to project too rapidly to allow himself adequate time for reflection. But with *First Lady*, he guessed correctly that the dramatic idea was marketable. Washington social trivia, it turned out, could provide the basis of a popular play, at least if the play were acted by good-looking players wearing attractive clothes in opulent settings. This play, which did not have a shred of intellectual content, easily satisfied that part of the Depression audience that demanded light but colorful fare to relieve the blackness of the times. Such theatergoers took pleasure in witnessing well-phrased squabbles over party politics, though the parties were unidentified and no political issues of consequence were aired.

The frivolous, airy content of *First Lady* did not reflect Kaufman's concern over the tenor of American politics. The collaborations with Morrie Ryskind, though dealing only lightly with such serious subjects as spoils-grabbing and incompetence in high office, told more than this new comedy did about the responsible citizen that Kaufman actually was when he allowed himself to think beyond the next play—the man who, when staying at the expensive Beverly Wilshire Hotel, had the habit of going down to breakfast with the *New Republic* under his arm. As he sat at his typewriter, he could not deny that part of his nature that thrived on making jokes no matter what serious subjects were on his mind. But some of the jokes could be serious, too. It was Kaufman the sardonically humorous companion of Swope, Pulitzer, and Sherwood, not Kaufman the glib collaborator of Katharine Dayton who, early in 1935, wrote a piece for the *New Yorker* entitled "All We Need Is Horse Sense," in which he commented on the presidency:

> In the year 1948 the depression was still with us, and it was decided that something really should be done about it. By that time several million persons had written letters to the *Herald Tribune,* complaining about the administration. Most of the writers said that the new ideas of government were proving to be of no avail, and that all we needed in a President was plain horse sense. So great was the insistence upon horse sense that the next step was almost inevitable. It was decided to get a horse.[1]

In his narrative on the term of President Hot Baby, Kaufman expressed his impatience with not only the critics of the New Deal—those who sought a President with horse sense—but also with the very Administration he was defending, which troubled him with its occasional shifts in policy. President Hot Baby, unlike most officeholders as Kaufman viewed them, would always give a straight answer. He pawed the air once for "No" and twice for "Yes." Though coated with humor, this little squib offered a keenly felt comment on the political scene of 1935, when the Depression, after five grinding years, had begun to seem the permanent condition of American life. But all such opinions and attitudes were screened out of *First Lady,* though the play was set in Washington itself and purported to depict behind-the-scenes skirmishes of the sort that led to major-party nominations for the presidency.

The collaborators constructed their plot around a feud between two handsome women in early middle age, each of whom would like nothing so much as to see her husband inaugurated President. Early on, the audience is told that the feud began when Irene Hibbard, the villainess of the piece, stole the cook of Lucy Chase Wayne, the quick-tongued, brainy protagonist. The granddaughter of a President and now a prominent Washington hostess, Lucy was intended to resemble Alice Roosevelt Longworth, Theodore Roosevelt's outspoken daughter and a friend of Katharine Dayton. Lucy is agonized by the sight of Irene behaving kittenishly with the young western Senator, Gordon Keane. She surmises that Irene expects Keane to be the next President and that to be first lady she will divorce her dull husband, Justice Carter Hibbard of the Supreme Court, and marry Keane, a bachelor. Since Lucy hopes that her own husband, a Cabinet officer, will be President, she takes it upon herself to initiate a boom for Hibbard, being confident that Irene will stick to him on those terms, but not expecting the boom to carry Hibbard all the way to the White House. Happily for Lucy, in the breathless third act it is discovered that because of a legal technicality the Hibbards are not married after all—happily, because the taint of scandal on his union immediately puts Hibbard out of the running and opens the path for Stephen Wayne. At the last minute this too pat, too coy plot gets some shaking up and a tonic dash of vinegar when Keane, who unwittingly was the primal cause of Lucy's intrigue, announces that he can never be President. Though now a citizen of the United States, he had the bad luck to be born elsewhere —in British Columbia—and thus is disqualified by the Constitution.

Though one reviewer complained of the "cutting edge" of the voices of some of the character actresses,[2] this may have been a deliberate directorial touch invoked to effect a contrast with the silvery tones of the leading character, Lucy Chase Wayne. For that all-important part, a star was required— one of the several luminous, middle-aged actresses who in the 1930s commanded the loyalty of almost the entire theatergoing public. Among such stars—Lynn Fontanne, Helen Hayes, Katharine Cornell, Jane Cowl, and Ina Claire—it was Claire who might have served the play best. She was offered the role, but could not accept it because she was committed to another production. Of the others, Kaufman and Harris considered only dark-haired, elegant Jane Cowl, and she was happy to take the part. Her magnetism was perhaps a shade less strong than Claire's, but she possessed in large measure the essential quality for fulfilling the demands of the part: a talent for projecting quick and deep perception. She was a choice of whom the critics approved no less than the public; by comparison, the others in the cast were given short shrift in the reviews. But this was inevitable, for the play was of that sort intended primarily for the women in the audience, and in the tradition of such works it allowed its graceful star to sweep all before her. This was not the usual Kaufman style of play-making, regardless of the collaborator, and it would never become one in which he was comfortable.

With this play launched, Kaufman found himself with less to do than usual over the winter months. One inescapable duty was to attend the dreaded story conferences about the next picture for the Marx Brothers; happily, these were held in New York. The polishing that he contributed to Romney Brent's *Tomorrow's a Holiday* and his assistance to Robert Sinclair on the direction of *The Postman Always Rings Twice* occupied him only briefly, in December 1935 and February 1936, respectively. The remainder of the season was free for writing. He and Hart were eager to work together again, but did not plan to do so until the summer, when both would be in Hollywood. Meanwhile, he had just time enough to write a play with Ferber.

Though Ferber had told him in 1931 that she would never collaborate with him again, she had long since realized the absurdity of that stance in view of her fondness for the man himself and the money that streamed in from their plays. She smothered her resentment over the tendency of the press to assume that theirs was not an association of equals. They had been "looking around" desultorily for a plot over the past year, conferring about several notions that came to mind but discarding each of them. Finally, on New Year's Eve 1935, a reasonable idea offered itself, and, work-hungry as always, they settled to it with a passion. Over dinner at East 94th Street, Beatrice announced that she intended to see in the new year at a party of friends and urged them to come with her. But Kaufman hastily declined, insisting that he and Ferber were going to spend the evening designing a new play. That was news to Ferber, but she was game. "Are we?" she asked—or later told a reporter from the *Times* that she had asked. "I hadn't thought of it, but it sounds like a grand idea. The world at play and we artists grimly at work, oblivious to time and all its irrelevant connotations, conscious only of the supreme necessity of—of—"

"Of finding something to write about," said Kaufman.

Later in the evening, after Beatrice left and they were well into the construction of their plot, they were puzzled to hear a noise in the streets. It was midnight; 1936 had arrived.[3]

The plot that Kaufman and Ferber were concocting as the bells rang out was set in a club-like residence for young women ambitious for a career on the stage. Between *The Royal Family* and *Dinner at Eight*, the old friends had discussed the practicality of writing a play for a cast to be composed solely of ingenues. In 1936 this notion was modified to include some males. Ferber's respect for the acting profession was the prime motivating force behind their decision to write this play, as it had been behind *The Royal Family*. With Kaufman she outlined a script in which the central character was a young woman confident of her talent and ever true to her goal of Broadway stardom, though faced with tempting offers from Hollywood of easy money and exalted billing. This was to be, then, a romance of the theater, a sentimental product of Ferber's imagination, but highlighted by the cynical Kaufman touch. It would also have a robust comedy part for Janet Fox, whom Kaufman had described, after her debut in *Dinner at Eight*, as "pretty good for a niece."[4]

The prototype of the Footlights Club, as the collaborators named the residence of the would-be actresses in their play, was an establishment, on West 53rd Street between Fifth and Sixth Avenues, called the Rehearsal Club. Founded in 1913 as a non-profit enterprise, and well enough subsidized by its directors to keep the cost of bed and board within the narrow means of the residents, for over twenty years the club had been filled to capacity with aspiring actresses of every degree of talent. In no sense luxurious, but clean, comfortable, safe, and relaxed, the club was rather like the college dormitories some of the residents had only recently left. During the writing of the play, Ferber made a point of visiting it. Concealing her identity, she called the woman in charge, Mrs. M. T. Chapman, and asked to inspect the premises on behalf of a niece who, she said, would soon be coming down from Boston to make the rounds of the producers' offices. She was shown the place from top to bottom. When the tour was completed, she had the grace to praise it. (She added, quite untruthfully, that she would make a reservation for her niece as soon as she knew when the young woman was planning to come to New York; neither of her real nieces intended to move into the Rehearsal Club.) Later, obviously hoping to avoid legal difficulties, she maintained that she and her partner Kaufman had made no attempt to describe in detail the actual club, but had used only its "general atmospheric feeling." The staff and the residents were not amused by the publicity that the play gave the club. Sightseers began to gather before its doors, and some of the boldest made an effort to get inside. Such gawkers were themselves a curious sight on the Rehearsal Club's block, which in 1936 was primarily a quiet neighborhood of brownstone houses.[5]

Toward the end of January, the two writers and Beatrice went down to Palm Beach at the invitation of Sam Harris, who continued to spend as much of the winter in that resort as his producing schedule would allow. Whether bicycling in the sun or huddling in a room in Harris's house that they had made into an office, Kaufman and Ferber worked with their own peculiar intensity. When they were ready to weave the dialogue around the bare bones of their scenario, Ferber suggested that Charleston, South Carolina, might offer a nourishing environment for their sessions. She managed to move Kaufman off the train when it arrived at that sedate city, but after two days he said that he had had quite enough of its quiet charm and insisted that they return to New York—where, he might have added, they belonged. Setting up shop in Ferber's new apartment, a penthouse overlooking Park Avenue, they resumed the routine that had gotten them through the writing of *The Royal Family* and *Dinner at Eight*: four full hours of work on the script from eleven in the morning until three in the afternoon, when Kaufman would go to his bridge club.[6] By the last week in May they were ready to place the script in Harris's hands. Kaufman then took the train for Hollywood, where Irving Thalberg eagerly awaited his presence at Metro-Goldwyn-Mayer.

From one point of view, *Stage Door*, as the new play was called, may be seen as a sequel-in-reverse to *The Royal Family*. The young hopefuls who make up most of the cast are not to be mistaken for the Barrymore-like eminences of the earlier play, but they have the dedication that great art requires—just such dedication as motivated Fanny and Julie Cavendish. This is particularly true of Terry Randall, the central character of the play. Radiant with talent, goodwill, and charm, she is bound for stardom. The role itself is a star role that provides scenes of pathos and prolonged introspection, and a moment of glory at the final curtain. With fine contempt the actress rebuffs the offer of a standard, seven-year Hollywood contract: "That isn't acting," she says, "that's piecework. You're not a human being, you're a thing in a vacuum. Noise shut out, human response shut out. But in the theater, when you hear that lovely sound out there, then you know you're right. It's as though they'd turned on an electric current that hit you *here*. And that's how you learn to act."

This attitude is understandable to most of the young women in the club, but rather baffling to Terry's pretty roommate, Jean Maitland, who accepts with pleasure the sort of contract that Terry spurns, and in the third act returns in triumph for a visit to the club, bringing in her wake a covey of studio publicity men and photographers, along with a very large portrait of herself to be hung in the club's living room. Good-natured and loyal, Jean is not portrayed harshly for her defection to Hollywood, but it is clear enough, all the same, that the authors intend her to provide a sharp contrast with the faithful Terry. Another devoted young woman is the remote, penniless Kaye Hamilton, who comes to the club in flight from her rich but insane husband, is fired from her first job during rehearsals and, unable to take this slap, poisons herself.

The most topical element in the play is the presence of Keith Burgess, the young proletarian playwright who for a brief moment stirs Terry's emotions.

In the first scene of the play he tells her, "Romance is for babies! I write about *today!* I want to tear the heart out of the rotten carcass they call life, and hold it up bleeding for all the world to see!" His dress, as he first appears, is the standard garb of playwrights with such a mission: a turtleneck sweater and an unpressed suit. Gruff and unkempt, but supremely sure of himself and his future in the theater, he is the authors' version of Clifford Odets, the rage of Broadway when *Stage Door* was conceived. Odets was the author of the Group Theater's *Waiting for Lefty* and *Awake and Sing!* In 1931, Ferber had befriended the Group Theater with a gift of $500. After Odets achieved fame with his two hits in the spring of 1935, she asked an acquaintance to bring him to a party, so that she could take a good look at him. Perhaps she did not like what she saw, for in *Stage Door* he is portrayed as all hypocrisy and humbug.[7]

Burgess's play is picked up for production by one of the most eminent producers on Broadway, but only on condition that the lead be played by a well-known star, not Terry, who was originally Burgess's choice. With much backing and filling, Burgess apprises Terry of the situation. She, of course, bows out gracefully. When next he appears on stage, he is a changed man. Arriving at the Footlights Club to take Terry to an opening, he is in full dress, including that most class-conscious piece of haberdashery, the top hat. He has sold out to the very forces he once inveighed against, for he (like the real Odets in 1936) is on the point of departing for Hollywood. "I'll write their garbage in the daytime," he says, "but at night I'll write my own plays." That is not the way it works out. In a year he is back to see Terry, but after glancing at his elegant clothes she realizes that he has "gone Hollywood" and casts him out of her life.

Burgess's departure is not the final allusion to proletarian drama in *Stage Door*. Suddenly, marvelously, the other man in Terry's life, the aide to a Hollywood executive, decides to separate himself from the corrupting influence of the studios and to produce a play, with Terry as the lead. Her role is to be that of a union maid who urges the reluctant workers to strike. "It means hungry," the girl's big speech goes, "and maybe cold, and scared every minute somebody'll come home with a busted head. But which would you'd ruther do? Die quick fighting, or starve to death slow? That's why I'm telling you—strike! Strike! Strike!" The collaborators had been listening to Odets's dramatic language, and listening closely.

The search for seventeen distinctive young actresses to portray the residents of the club began before Kaufman left for Hollywood in May. With his permission, Ferber cast Janet Fox as Bernice Niemeyer, a girl whose self-confidence and self-delusion are so enormous that she thinks she can play anything. With Ferber's permission, Kaufman acted on the hunch he had had in California and asked Margaret Sullavan to play Terry Randall. He had been aware of her strange hold on audiences since the spring of 1933, when she entered the cast of *Dinner at Eight* as a replacement for Marguerite Churchill in the role of Paula Jordan. Her appearance in that play earned her a favorable contract at Universal, a studio ordinarily less inclined than the others to develop stars. Sullavan's magnetism was as telling on screen as in the theater, but her attitude toward the craft of film-making was not unlike Terry Randall's in *Stage Door*. She found it unfulfilling and was indifferent to her status as star. Thus the part was an excellent one for her.

The casting of one of the minor parts was to have important consequences for Kaufman in later years. Janet Fox, happening into a Broadway drugstore one day shortly before rehearsals began, noticed an unusually tall, dark-haired young woman at the counter and, aware that Kaufman and her aunt had not yet been able to cast the role of Little Mary, which called for just such a person, asked her whether she was an actress. The young woman, Mary Wickes, was not only an actress, but at the moment was appearing in a production of Kaufman's archenemy, Jed Harris. Since this play, Philip Barry's *Spring Dance,* was expected to close soon, Mary Wickes went to read for *Stage Door* and was immediately offered the role. Jed Harris, his feud with Kaufman notwithstanding, permitted her to leave his play, though it had another week to run.[8] Thus began one of the pleasantest friendships and professional relationships of Kaufman's life. He was to cast Mary Wickes repeatedly in his plays thereafter, and in his last years, when, more often than not, she was in Hollywood while he was in New York, he savored her cheerful letters.

When Kaufman first read the *Stage Door* script to his cast, he was still in hiding from reporters who hoped for more copy on the Mary Astor case. After his successful, conciliatory meeting with the press on August 15, he turned his back firmly on the scandal and readied himself for rehearsals. The out-of-town performances began in Philadelphia on September 28. *Variety's* reviewer predicted another Kaufman hit and praised his direction of the predominantly female cast. It was, observed the reviewer, "less forced" than the staging of *First Lady*.[9] The writers were not so pleased, however, and made extensive revisions on the road. After a brief run in New Haven, they closed down the production for a week of still more rewriting before opening in New York on October 22. The Broadway notices were lukewarm, with complaints centering in the sentimentality of the authors' approach to their material. But Sullavan's performance was so highly praised, and so great was her popularity as a screen star, that a long run seemed a certainty.

Ignored in many of the notices, except for perfunctory mention, was Ferber, as she had been on the three earlier occasions when she had collaborated with Kaufman. Hoping to avoid another flare-up of petulance in her such as had occurred after the opening of *Dinner at Eight,* he composed a letter to the *Times* in homage to her as a writing partner, and sent it directly to Brooks Atkinson with a request that the critic see to its being printed. In part the letter read,

> Miss Edna Ferber and I have written four plays together. For some fantastic reason, and despite the simple assurance of the programs, there has been a tendency on the part of reviewers to assume that Miss Ferber is some sort of cook's assistant in the preparation of these little dishes, and that I dash them off single-handed, while Miss Ferber sharpens the pencils. Also, they seem to have the idea that Miss Ferber is then sent to the Orient or some place while I attend to the casting.
>
> * * *
>
> My collaborations with Miss Ferber have been collaborations in every sense of the word, from beginning to end.[10]

With a steady call for tickets at the box office and a company happy in its expectation of rounding out the season on Broadway, largely on the strength of Margaret Sullavan's performance, the actress suddenly exploded a bombshell. She announced that she was pregnant and would have to leave the cast, on the advice of her physician. Her marriage to agent Leland Hayward had taken place on November 15; her last appearance occurred at the 169th performance. Realizing that it would be futile to attempt to continue the New York run with another actress, Harris and the writers decided to close the play. It was their hope that Sullavan would take it on the road in the fall. When this hope was not realized because of the actress's refusal to make a prolonged tour, they gave the role to Joan Bennett, in the expectation that she would duplicate Sullavan's attractiveness to an audience of filmgoers. Kaufman was disappointed by the defection of Sullavan, but not so annoyed as to become estranged from her. On visits to Hollywood after the couple settled there, he often accepted the Haywards' hospitality. Moreover, in the late 1930s and early 1940s he let Hayward arrange sales of his plays to the studios. Ferber also became a client of Hayward's, but she was furious over Sullavan's hasty departure from the play. The actress, in her view, had no right to become pregnant at such a time. *Stage Door,* Ferber told her fans, "was a success, and in the midst of the success Miss Margaret Sullavan left it, throwing about forty people out of work, and over that we draw a veil, dear reader, as the novelists used discreetly to say."[11]

Consolation for the brevity of the Broadway run came to the authors in the form of a sale of the script to RKO-Radio Pictures as a vehicle for Katharine Hepburn and Ginger Rogers. Hepburn was to play Terry Randall and Rogers the much expanded role of Jean Maitland. The picture drew reviews more favorable than those accorded to the play, and with good reason. The screenplay, written by Morrie Ryskind and Anthony Veiller, differs in many respects from the original. In it, Terry is something of an outsider, a girl of wealthy family who has the necessary drive but a still unformed talent. Kaye Hamilton commits suicide, as in the original, but after she loses her part to Terry. It is the revelation of the suicide that deepens Terry's character and gives her the emotion to draw upon for the enrichment of her art. Both Hepburn and Rogers were well received, but Hepburn's nasal rendering of the words "calla lilies" was mimicked for more than a decade by radio and night-club comediennes. Though Kaufman was rumored to have dismissed the film with the comment that it should have been retitled "Screen Door," in fact he preferred it to the play.[12]

It was on Kaufman's first visit to Hollywood, in 1934, that he and Hart developed the first notion of *You Can't Take It with You*—the "pip," the play "like nothing ever seen on land or sea." Of all Kaufman's successes, it would prove to be not only the longest-running in its original production, but the one most frequently revived. Neither writer had the time to spare for an attack on this new dramatic idea in 1934 or the next year. It had to wait until the summer of 1936 for development. Kaufman was not so much to blame for the delay as Hart was. In January 1935 that young lover of the good life sailed on a five-and-a-half month cruise around the world on the *Franconia* with the Cole Porters and some of their lively friends, including Monty Woolley. Out of this luxurious voyage came, as hoped, *Jubilee,* the musical, which Max Gordon and Sam Harris produced. Until it opened, on October 12, 1935, Hart was not free to take on other work. By that time, Kaufman was committed to the rehearsals of *First Lady,* and soon was collaborating with Ferber on *Stage Door.* But he and Hart were determined to write a third play together. When they first explored possibilities for it, in 1936, they did not take up the "pip" of an idea, but instead considered making a dramatic adaptation of Dalton Trumbo's still unpublished *Washington Jitters,* which Hart had read in galleys early in the year at the suggestion of Trumbo's agent.[13]

Always warmly welcomed at MGM as one who could come up swiftly with the hoped-for suggestion on how to tighten up a sagging plot, Hart was even more in favor in the summer of 1936, as a result of his having won an Academy nomination for the screenplay of *Broadway Melody of 1936*. His obligations to the studio were slight, and he was left with plenty of time for writing with Kaufman and for meeting his psychoanalyst. However disturbed Hart was, the analytic sessions were supportive enough to enable him to work confidently and efficiently with Kaufman throughout the summer. Less sensitive than Beatrice to the manifestations of anxiety, Kaufman wrote to her on Memorial Day, "Moss . . . is well again—that's all I can say. I asked him in detail, and didn't get a lot—he says he is back where he was two years ago. Others who have been around him say they never see any signs of unhappiness. He looks marvelous, and to me that's that."

On the night of his arrival in Los Angeles, Kaufman dined with Hart and read him the script of *Stage Door*. Then the two went on to discuss their immediate problem: what sort of play to write. No sooner did they open the subject than the notion of dramatizing Trumbo's *Washington Jitters* lost its allure. They would not, as Kaufman informed Beatrice in one of his first letters of the season, be writing "the political thing." Trumbo, who was also at MGM, would be disappointed, but that could not be helped.

Still, they had not met to do nothing but revamp scenarios for Metro-Goldwyn-Mayer. With the fixed intention of creating a comedy for fall production, they were not to be put off merely because the promise of one tentative scheme had faded. Within a day or two they settled on something else, the idea that they had talked over in 1934. It had been Hart who at that time proposed the idea, which was a plot about an unconventional but loving and deeply contented family. As they went back over it, they decided that the emphasis should not be placed on plot, but on character and the bizarre situations that might develop among individuals who, though wishing no harm to others, lived only to please themselves. Once they decided to work on this scheme, it took the writers only three days to fix the characters in their minds. Each member of the household was given his share of special interests— snake-collecting for one of them, playing the xylophone for another—and when all were assembled, they were fitted into three episodic acts held together by the thinnest of story lines. In other hands, this was the stuff of which sentimental comedies were made: trifles that were described in the pages of the Samuel French and Dramatists' Play Service catalogues as "heartwarming" and suitable for high school production. But as developed by Kaufman and Hart, no part of the play, not even the obligatory love story, would be allowed to impede the flow of comic incident.[14]

With the characters fixed, it took less than a month for the collaborators to rough out a draft of the entire piece. They allowed themselves only about five hours a day to work, from eleven-thirty to four-thirty, with a respite for lunch. So sure were they of the material and their ability to prod it into shape over the summer that before settling down to the final draft they wired Sam Harris to begin casting. Specifically, Harris was to put under contract four expert character actors: Josephine Hull, George Tobias, Frank Conlan, and Oscar Polk. At this time they themselves engaged a film actor, Henry Travers, to play the head of the household. Harris got in touch with the actors on the same day. Much to his astonishment he received a second telegram before nightfall in which the writers instructed him to plot a road tour beginning on November 9. That date was later moved to November 26, because of circumstances over which only Judge Goodwin J. Knight could be said to have control.[15]

On June 26, Kaufman let Beatrice know how well he and Hart were proceeding. "I doubt if I can convey the quality of the Hart play in writing," he admitted.

> You know it's a slightly mad family, and has to do with the daughter of the house, the only sane one. She falls in love with the son of a conventional family, and the play proper concerns her attempts to reconcile the irreconcilable elements. The tony family comes to dinner—arriving on the wrong night—and finds everything at its most cuckoo. It turns out that the young man himself has a streak of madness in him, and at the finish he converts the girl [to his unconventional views] and they both settle down happily with [her] family. But it has a point, as you can see—that the way to live and be happy is just to go ahead and live, and not pay attention to the world. I think the play will have a nice love story and a certain tenderness, in addition to its madness. Does it sound too naïve—I don't think it will emerge as such. Of course we have some swell mad things for the family—the father manufactures fireworks in the cellar, the grandfather retired from the world in 1898 and doesn't admit that anything has happened since then, etc. Please let me know how you react.[16]

In one respect the writers departed from this outline: in the finished play the young couple do not indicate that they plan to live with the girl's family. Otherwise, the plot had already jelled firmly.

Though the title *You Can't Take It with You* would become so well known as to seem inevitable, Kaufman and Hart did not come to it at once. In turn they considered and rejected *Foxy Grandpa, Money in the Bank, They Loved Each Other,* and *The King Is Naked,* and then hit on *Grandpa's Other Snake,* which struck them as possessing a sure sign of success. Beatrice was the first to hear of this choice, in a letter from Kaufman, and she vetoed it, explaining that few varieties of life were more repellent to the average person than the snake, whether venomous or not. In the end, and with some doubt as to its attractiveness, they chose *You Can't Take It with You.* When they proposed it to Sam Harris, the producer expressed enthusiasm and encouraged them to settle for it; ultimately they grew used to it.[17]

The effect created by *You Can't Take It with You* is that of a kind of benevolent mayhem; something wild and noisy is always going on, but never to anyone's harm. Since both writers had spent their childhood within somewhat unusual families, they were not strangers to the kind of world that they described. Unlike *Once in a Lifetime,* which offered a view of a milieu that neither knew at the time of writing, this comedy, for all its characters' detachment from the humdrum life of the average human being, does not slide into fantasy. One of its strengths is that it does not burlesque the characters' manner of living, but instead invests it with immense appeal. The cast includes six family members, two black household servants, a permanent lodger, seven assorted minor but substantial roles, and three unamed F.B.I. operatives. All contribute to the continuously bustling activity, but none, no matter how eccentric, is zany. One family member, Alice Sycamore, the elder daughter, differs from her relations by having a job and going out every day into the world. Thus she provides the play with an anchor to "real" life, the life the audience experiences. But the others are not ignorant of that life; they simply prefer not to submit to its constraints, and, thanks to the modest but sufficient income of Grandpa Vanderhof, they need not. To the audience of 1936, the family's insouciant existence provided as gratifying an escape from the surrounding dreariness as the flights into opulence provided by the films of Thalberg and Mayer.

While her sister Alice labors at her secretarial job, Essie Carmichael is content to make candy for sale in the neighborhood and for home consumption and to practice ballet to the xylophone accompaniment provided by her husband, Ed. That even-tempered young man is also an amateur printer who sets such mottoes as "God Is the State; the State Is God" that he comes upon in the writings of Trotsky. He prints them, and, because he is proud of his skill, tucks them into the candy boxes. The mother of the two young women is Penny Sycamore, Grandpa Martin Vanderhof's daughter; her chief interest in life is the writing of plays and has been ever since the day, some eight years earlier, when a typewriter was delivered to the house by mistake. (Before that she was a painter, and she still has the palette, beret, and smock to prove it.) At the outset of the comedy, she is at work on two plays, *Poison Gas*, a war play, and *Sex Takes a Holiday*, a melodrama set in a monastery. Her husband, Paul Sycamore, passes the time by making fireworks in the basement, with the assistance of Mr. De Pinna, who called to deliver the ice one day six years before and never left. Presiding over this amiable lot is Grandpa Vanderhof, who quit his well-paying job thirty-five years ago out of boredom with the routine of money-making, and has never had a moment of regret. His hobby is collecting snakes; more in keeping with his high-spirited, generous disposition is his custom of attending the annual commencement exercises at Columbia, an agreeable gesture to youth. Perhaps in the make-up of his personality is a touch of Joseph Kaufman, George's beloved father.

More than in any other Kaufman play, the characters of *You Can't Take It with You* project the sense that together they constitute a veritable social unit, a community whose members know one another's habits and moods extremely well and respond to them in accordance with their knowledge. No one's actions, however outré, come as a surprise to anyone else; the popping of loud firecrackers startles no one except an intruder from the Internal Revenue Service; the snake tank, no menace, is only a familiar part of the living room furniture. Essie can pirouette to the timekeeping of her Russian dance instructor, Ed can make music, Penny, having taken up her brushes again, can paint a betogaed Mr. De Pinna, and Grandpa can throw darts, all at the same time in a scene of wonderfully integrated movement that becomes a kind of ballet when properly directed. The two preceding Kaufman-and-Hart comedies had large casts also, but a less effective meshing of personalities.

A double frame of actions holds the characters together. The first to get under way involves the family in confrontations with both the F.B.I. and the I.R.S. Grandpa it appears, never pays his income tax, and at long last the I.R.S. has discovered this interesting fact. With the operative who comes to call, Grandpa has this interview:

> GRANDPA Well, what do I get for my money? If I go into Macy's and buy something, there it *is*—I see it. What's the Government give me?
> HENDERSON Why, the Government gives you everything. It protects you.
> GRANDPA What from?
> HENDERSON Well—invasion. Foreigners that might come over and take everything you've got.
> GRANDPA Oh, I don't think they're going to do that.

> HENDERSON If you didn't pay an income tax, they would. How do you
> think the Government keeps up that Army and Navy? All those bat-
> tleships . . .
> GRANDPA Last time we used battleships was in the Spanish-American
> War, and what did we get out of it? Cuba—and we gave that back. I
> wouldn't mind paying if it were something sensible.
> HENDERSON (*Beginning to get annoyed.*) Well, what about Congress,
> and the Supreme Court, and the President? We've got to pay *them*,
> don't we?
> GRANDPA (*Ever so calmly.*) Not with my money—no sir.

It is Ed's printed slogans that bring the F.B.I. down upon the Vanderhof-
Sycamore household; having gotten wind of them, including exhortations to
dynamite the Capitol, the White House, and the Supreme Court—all inno-
cently run through his press simply as exercises in the art of printing—the
G-men enter the house to make an arrest. Investigating the cellar, one agent
interrupts Mr. De Pinna in the act of making firecrackers and drags him upstairs before he can reach for his pipe. The gunpowder for the firecrackers is
more than enough to convince the agents that Ed is indeed an anarchist, but,
ignited by the burning pipe, all this evidence goes up in smoke and loud ex-
plosions, a fitting second-act climax.

The other strand of action concerns Alice and her boss's son, Tony Kirby.
That boy will get girl is never seriously in question. Romance always has a
place in a Kaufman comedy, but never a romance that can be described as
heartwarming. True, Tony goes so far as to tell Alice that he loves her, and
she to reply in kind, but the following is more typical of their lovemaking:

> TONY (*Happily*) I wouldn't trade one minute of this evening for—all
> the rice in China.
> ALICE Really?
> TONY Cross my heart.
> ALICE (*A little sigh of contentment. Then shyly.*) Is there much rice in
> China?
> TONY Terrific. Didn't you read *The Good Earth*?

It is Tony who inadvertently brings on the coolness between himself and
Alice. When she invites him and his stuffy parents to her home for dinner,
he pretends confusion over the date and brings them one evening before they
are supposed to come. His wish is that they see this extraordinary family as
they really are, not as they might be when special company is coming. The
result, of course, is disaster: a drunken actress makes a pass at Mr. Kirby, and
Essie's dance teacher trips him to the floor; a word-association game proposed

by Penny causes infinite embarrassment when Mrs. Kirby associates "bathroom" with "Mr. Kirby" and "sex" with "Wall Street." Finally, the F.B.I. arrives, and everyone present is sped away to court. But in the end, Alice is persuaded by Tony that the differences between their families should not matter to them. The senior Kirby is also brought around; Grandpa convinces him that there is something to be said for a way of life that rules out money-making for its own sake. To tie up the last of the loose ends, word comes that the government intends to leave Grandpa in peace, and with good reason. Eight years ago, on the death of the milkman, Mr. De Pinna's predecessor as lodger, the family buried him as Martin Vanderhof, not knowing his real name. Now the I.R.S. believes that the deceased gentleman was the *real* Martin Vanderhof, and Grandpa may even get a refund.

The final draft of all this agreeable business was nearly complete just at the time that *Stage Door* went into rehearsal. A day or two before the end of August, copies went out to the players already under contract. As soon as Beatrice came back from Europe and the Kaufmans' domestic situation righted itself (a matter of perhaps one day after her return), she sat down with the script, at Hart's insistence. Though she did have a few complaints to make, on the whole she was delighted with what she read, and so informed Hart by letter to Hollywood. Hart wired back to this goddess-mother:

> YOU'RE THE MOST BRILLIANT WOMAN I'VE EVER KNOWN. YOUR CRITICISM IS SO SHREWD, SO PENETRATING, AND SO COMPLETELY RIGHT THAT I WISH I WERE BACK TO PLUNGE IN AND FIX THE PLAY IMMEDIATELY.

But such fixing as was required, and there was not much, had to wait until rehearsals and the tryout performances.

Some casting remained to be done. Of the parts still to be assigned, the most difficult was the role of Ed Carmichael, for which it was necessary to find a competent actor who was also a xylophonist. Happily, this was solved when a young actor named George Heller spotted the agent William Liebling on the street and asked whether he knew of any good parts in the offing. Liebling, to whom the Harris office had sent a list of its needs, said that Heller could have a fine part, if only he could play the xylophone. This, it turned out, was Heller's hobby, and he got the job.[18]

Originally, as recorded in their telegram to Harris in June, Kaufman and Hart had expected to open the play in Philadelphia on November 9. But they conceived that plan in the expectation that they would have a full summer of daily work sessions in which to improve their original draft, and that there would be no special problems with *Stage Door*. But Kaufman's precipitate flight from California and the time required for revising the Ferber collaboration set back the rehearsals of *You Can't Take It with You* to the last week in October. A half-week run was booked for Princeton beginning on November 26, to be followed by two weeks in Philadelphia. In Princeton a difficulty arose: Louise Platt, who was playing Alice, struck both writers and Harris as wrong for the part. Though she went on to open the Philadelphia engagement, it was clear that a replacement would have to be found. Fortunately for Kaufman and Hart, though possibly not for Ferber, an entire company of ingenues from which to choose a new Alice was performing nightly at the Music Box in *Stage Door*. Margot Stevenson seemed of particular promise. She was given a copy of the script and a ticket to Philadelphia. For the next two years she went on as Alice.

The enthusiasm of the Philadelphia audiences and reviewers made it clear that only a little tinkering was necessary. The F.B.I. men were made somewhat less menacing on their surprise entry into the Vanderhof living room, and with that slight alteration the play was in proper shape for Broadway. At the writers' request, Harris booked it into the Booth Theater, one of the most intimate of the Broadway houses. Opening on December 14, *You Can't Take It with You* garnered highly enthusiastic notices, though many of the reviewers were puzzled by the relative lack of satire in the piece. Receiving much praise was Kaufman's direction, which called for exceptional adroitness in handling on-stage traffic. Audiences began to build before the holiday season, and soon it was necessary to book tickets months in advance, a state of affairs far less common in the Depression years than it would be in the second half of the century.

It was soon apparent that this comedy, unlike the two Kaufman-and-Hart comedies that had preceded it, would appeal to virtually every region of the country, and, quite possibly, to all age groups and economic classes. Though never in doubt about the play's chances for success, the authors had written better than they thought. With word spreading out from New York about the delights of the play, audiences all over the country wanted a look. Under the direction of William McFadden, the stage manager of the New York company, a company was soon readied for Chicago, where it opened on February 7, 1937. An Eastern touring company, a West Coast company, and a Southern company also were organized and were directed by McFadden, with casting left to John Kennedy and Myra Streger, Kaufman's aide. McFadden was kept busy for more than two years by the need to check on these various companies and to tighten the performances. He also directed the London production, which, under the auspices of John C. Wilson and Sam Harris, opened on December 22, 1937. But that production was not a success, for the play struck many in the audience as just not making sense.[19]

The disdain of the London audiences notwithstanding, *You Can't Take It with You* proved itself to be the two writers' most valuable property. Having invested in the original production, as was their custom, they received not only royalties from all the companies, but a share of the profits as well. The gross revenue of the Broadway company alone by the end of the run of 837 performances was estimated by *Variety* to have mounted to $1,250,000.[20] So lucrative a production was bound to stir envy, leading to a plagiarism suit, as had almost begun to seem inevitable when a play of Kaufman's proved profitable. A writer named Virginia Gordon sued both writers and Harris in 1937, complaining that the play resembled a work called *Rash Moments*, which she and another writer had composed in 1934 and submitted to Kaufman and Hart, among other playwrights and producers. As was usual with such suits against Kaufman, nothing came of this. On November 13 it was dismissed.[21]

Another major source of revenue for Kaufman and Hart was the sale of the play to Hollywood. Aware of the dimensions of their success, Kaufman made up his mind that the sale figure would be $200,000 and that the first studio to offer that amount could have the rights. The winning bid came from a rather surprising quarter: Columbia Pictures, whose hard-headed boss, Harry Cohn, bought the rights as a plum for his ace director, Frank Capra. Cohn was aware that he was paying a record sum for a Broadway play. But no sooner had he made his costly purchase, only just beating out Louis B. Mayer, than he become involved in one of his periodic disputes with Capra. Looking around for a replacement, Cohn approached Kaufman himself, who was then back in Hollywood at MGM.[22] Fortunately, since Cohn and Capra soon became reconciled, Kaufman was only mildly interested, though he was more concerned as to how the film would turn out than he had been with any of his other properties that were sold to Hollywood. At its opening (on September 1, 1938, at the Radio City Music Hall), the film won notices as laudatory as those the play had drawn. It was, however, a distorted version of the original, for Capra and his screenwriter, Robert Riskin, placed an inordinately heavy emphasis on the role of the senior Kirby, who was shown as a Wall Street wolf of exceptional rapacity until his "conversion" by the Vanderhof-Sycamore family. In the cast were some of the most popular film actors of the decade: Lionel Barrymore as Grandpa, Jean Arthur as Alice, and Edward Arnold and James Stewart as the elder and younger Kirbys. In the naturalness and sensitivity of his performance, Edward Arnold outshone all the others.

Before the date of the opening of the film, Harris moved the play to the Imperial, a house more than twice as capacious as the Booth, cutting prices to match those of the Music Hall. Thus the play continued to draw good audiences, despite the popularity of the picture. Never before had a play run against the picture made from it.

In the spring of 1937, it was assumed by theater enthusiasts and professionals that *You Can't Take It with You* would be a strong contender for the Drama Critics' Circle Award and the Pulitzer Prize. But in March the critics gave their prize to Maxwell Anderson's *High Tor,* a blend of comedy, fantasy, prose, and verse, with an antimaterialist theme not unlike that of *You Can't Take It with You,* though with a much different sort of plot. The Kaufman-and-Hart play drew some votes in the early ballots, but none at all on the final one. Thus it was something of a surprise when on May 4 the word was passed down from Columbia University that Kaufman and Hart were the winners of the Pulitzer Prize in drama for 1937. As in 1932, when he was honored for *Of Thee I Sing,* Kaufman took the prize in stride. Back in Hollywood at the time, he commented to Beatrice by letter that he had a great lot of congratulatory notes to reply to, but said nothing about what the prize meant to him. What mattered—when did it not?—was the next play, which at that particular moment was *I'd Rather Be Right,* another collaboration with Hart.

The year 1936 was witness, just before its close, to the premiere of yet another play with the Kaufman touch, though one that did not bear the Kaufman name. This was Clare Boothe's *The Women,* a brittle comedy of manners with a cast that included not a single male. A journalist for many years before turning playwright, witty and acerbic on the printed page and in private conversation, Boothe was a frequenter of the homes of the powerful figures of whom she wrote in the columns of *Vanity Fair* and was also, when she cared to be, a dazzling figure in the upper reaches of New York society. Wealthy in her own right and respected for her professional competence, she added to both her fame and influence on her marriage, in 1935, to Henry R. Luce, the publisher of *Time, Fortune,* and, as of the fall of 1936, *Life.* Her first play, *Abide with Me,* was produced to little applause in 1935. Bernard Baruch had urged it on Max Gordon, but Gordon turned it down. At the same time, he sent word to the author that he would like to see her next play, should she care to try another.[23] Only one year later she dispatched *The Women* to him, by way of Baruch, as before, and Gordon was quick to accept it. Rehearsals began in November 1936, and at the first session the author made a brief but striking appearance in a sable coat.[24] On December 26 the New York opening took place.

The play, an unsparing analysis of the lives of rich, socially prominent women, most of them married, offered such a stream of wisecracks and so many thrusts at the vainglorious and greedy that despite its female perspective it bore a close resemblance to Kaufman's comedies. Gordon had been bound to like it. In addition to being a witty piece of writing, it was a stylish, dressy play and as such appealed to him, for he, like his mentor Sam Harris, saw the value of bringing on a cast of attractive women in good-looking evening gowns, though this time there would be no gentlemen to accompany them. On the other hand, the absence of males was enough of a novelty in Broadway drama to add to the publicity for the production. The plot itself was slight—little more than the tale of how the pleasant but fundamentally dull Mary Haines loses her husband Stephen to the scheming shopgirl Crystal Allen, and how, in a third-act crescendo, having learned to be tough, she gets him back again, as much to his relief as to hers. Thin as it was, this was plot enough to provide not only a close look at Park Avenue matrons, but a look at the women who make life tolerable for them, from powder-room attendants to saleswomen, cooks, maids, manicurists, and nurses at lying-in hospitals, with a running commentary on the men who pay for this luxurious life. Kaufman and Hart, Gordon's unofficial advisers, not only approved, but invested in the production, as did Harris. Gordon chose Robert Sinclair, Kaufman's favorite young director, to stage the play; the similarity of the writing to Kaufman's, at least in its acidity, justified the selection. Sinclair saw to it that the play got the same sort of pacing that Kaufman himself might have provided.

Because *The Women* was a Max Gordon production, because the Kaufmans were known to be acquaintances of the Luces, and because Kaufman, along with Hart, was seen at rehearsals and, not least, because in its tone the comedy had an affinity to Kaufman's work, the rumor spread well in advance of the opening that Kaufman had had a hand in the writing. Margalo Gillmore, who played Mary Haines, saw him and Hart so often at the Philadelphia tryout performances that she believed both men were editing the script—"writing a new last act every night in Philadelphia."[25] Neither Kaufman nor Max Gordon bothered to deny that Kaufman attended rehearsals and the tryouts, but neither would ever say that he had done some of the writing. When questioned, Kaufman would admit only that he had advised the author to retain a scene in the Haineses' kitchen that she had wanted to drop.

He told all inquirers that if he were the author of so successful a play, he would not conceal the fact. Gordon, for his part, would only allow that if Kaufman had doctored the play, he had never said so to him.[26]

Whatever the truth of the matter, it was obvious that Clare Boothe wrote her play under the strong influence of the Kaufman style. True, the tone is more shrill than in his plays, but often in the dialogue one seems to be hearing not the pupil's voice, but that of the master. Any fan of Kaufman's might wonder how much is Boothe's and how much is his in, for example, a passage spoken toward the close by one nameless woman to another as they cross the stage:

> —So there we were on Sattiday night and it's Atlantic City. And he says: "I gotta go home tomorrow, baby." And I says: (*Pulls up her stockings*) "Why dja got to?" And he says, "My wife always expects me home on Easter Sunday." So I says: "What's she expect ya to do? Lay an egg?"

—16—

The Farm

The stilling of the rumor that their marriage had been shaken by the Mary Astor affair was only one of the benefits that the Kaufmans received from their purchase of Barley Sheaf Farm, and the least important to them, at that, since neither gave much thought to what was said about the marriage. At last they had a permanent, regular retreat whenever the heat or the pace of New York became too much for them. Though for almost two decades the pattern of their lives had suited them exactly and, to their less fortunate friends, had seemed a model to aspire to, they proceeded, amazingly, to improve upon it.

Since the early 1920s, the Kaufmans, like most well-to-do New Yorkers who were not obliged to follow a nine-to-five routine, had had the habit of absenting themselves from town for most of the summer. If Beatrice was not traveling abroad, the rule was to rent a spacious place on Long Island or in Westchester County and to remove the entire household to it in early June. Though Kaufman might duck in and out for rehearsals or work sessions with one of the collaborators, they would keep the place through Labor Day. During the pre-farm years, when Beatrice departed for rambles on the Mediterranean shore, Kaufman was content to stay at home in New York and busy himself with the new play (or plays) and with weekends at the country houses of friends or the Ritz in Atlantic City. On occasion he would join Harpo and others of the Algonquin set at Woollcott's island retreat, of which he was part owner; on some of these visits Beatrice also went along, though more often than not she went to the island without her husband. No matter where they traveled, never before the summer of 1936 had the Kaufmans put so much distance, physical or emotional, between themselves, and in truth they had not cared for the long separation. Though they would sometimes be apart in later summers, they now had a home of their own in which to rest and relax. Dorothy Pratt had a house in Bucks County, and her presence gave the area an additional attraction for Beatrice; it was while on a visit to the Pratts that Beatrice first spotted the Force property.

As a country place, Barley Sheaf Farm met all the requirements of Beatrice for comfort save one: it offered weather no more comfortable than that of New York. Bucks County is as hot and humid in summer as the city is. Frequent rainfall cools the air a little in the late afternoon, but the climate is hardly that of Vermont or the North Shore of Long Island. One does not have to sleep under a blanket. Still it is preferable to the city, since in the country informal dress is always appropriate, and country houses, unlike New York townhouses, offer cross-ventilation to catch whatever breeze is going. (Domestic air-conditioning was virtually unheard of in the 1930s, in either town or country.) Born and bred inland, Kaufman and Beatrice felt more at home in the country than in seaside resorts, no matter how unwelcoming the country climate might be. One way to beat the heat, of course, was to plunge into a swimming pool; happily for the Kaufmans and their friends, the property included one. A quick dip made the steaminess of midsummer bearable.

The land and its buildings constituted a working farm, complete with barn, corn crib, woodshed, storage buildings for tools and heavy equipment, and greenhouse, along with the main house and a caretaker's cottage. The barn housed four horse stalls; attached to it was a studio in which Juliana Force had modeled sculptures. The main house, which had been constructed of local fieldstone in the eighteenth century to the height of two stories, had later been enlarged by the addition of a mansarded third story along with a wing of two full stories and a finished attic ventilated by dormer windows. A long, tree-lined drive provided the approach to this structure from the highway; situated deep within the property, the house was well protected from the sound of traffic. On the second floor were master bedrooms for Kaufman and Beatrice, each with its private bath, a dressing room for Beatrice and a study for Kaufman, and two servants' rooms and bath. On the third floor were Anne's bedroom and bath and two guest rooms with a bath. At a little distance from the swimming pool, and visible from the upper floors of the main house, was a duck pond. One guest of the Kaufmans, Clinton Wilder (a Princeton undergraduate at the time), would always remember the afternoon when, soaking in the bathtub, he heard a reedy tune outside and, rising for a look through the window, saw Harpo Marx, clad in the briefest of bathing suits, dancing a quickstep and piping the ducks across the lawn.[1]

The house was in relatively good order when the Kaufmans took it over, but, naturally enough, it did not quite please Beatrice as it was. Like any new householder, she wanted the place to reflect her own tastes. One room that required extensive remodeling was the kitchen; Beatrice herself never cooked a meal in it, to be sure, but she wanted a kitchen equipped for entertaining on a grand scale. Though the depths of Kaufman's indifference to interior decoration were beyond measure, Beatrice had an eye for color and a liking for decorative objects and pictures that would blend well in a room. Feeling comfortable with the mid-1930s taste for cheerfully eclectic, part Victorian, part "early American" rooms, she drove around the countryside to explore the antique shops of Doylestown, New Hope, Flemington, and other near-by towns in search of American primitive portraits, nineteenth-century prints, needlework samplers, spatter ware, Staffordshire figures, woodcarvings, and plain but attractive wooden cabinets and tables. She bought so much that she created a market for such items in the region and in the end found that she herself had been responsible for the increased prices that she was asked to pay. But the result was worth it, for all the rooms took on a welcoming look. Despite the scores of bowls, plates, pictures, and various other objects which Beatrice distributed in them, they never gave the viewer a sense of self-conscious clutter. Kaufman's room alone of all those in the house was almost antarctic in its bareness, but none of the others was over-decorated.

The installation of the new kitchen and the sprucing up of the rest of the house and the grounds were not completed until June 1937. Like all such refurbishings, they took longer than expected and were fraught with irritations; three years later, Kaufman would find a way to capitalize on this disagreeable experience by basing his and Hart's *George Washington Slept Here* on it and the similar travail that Hart underwent. When the last wall had been repainted and the last picture hung, Kaufman, ironically, was nowhere near. Ensconced in a bungalow at the gaudy old Garden of Allah Hotel on Sunset Boulevard in Hollywood, he received word of Beatrice's success with the redecoration from Beatrice herself and the few visitors from the East who had had a look. One such person was Arthur Kober, who had a house of his own in Bucks County and enthusiastically reported to Kaufman on the new look of Barley Sheaf Farm.[2] Before the summer ended, Kaufman finished his stint at MGM and his work with Hart on a new script, and he hastened east to take up residence in his new home.

Having repeatedly accepted the hospitality of such friends with country houses as the Swopes and the Pulitzers for years, the Kaufmans began to repay it as soon as both were on hand to receive guests. They developed a routine. If Beatrice was in New York, she and Kaufman would drive down to the farm together on Friday afternoon, along with Anne, in anticipation of the arrival of guests in time for dinner. If Beatrice was already in the country, Kaufman and his daughter would take the train to Trenton, where they would be met by a servant. An enthusiastic hostess, Beatrice enjoyed filling her guest rooms over the weekend, no matter the season. Her cherished principle that an honest display of hospitality (and a reputation for providing good dinners) would draw anyone, no matter how celebrated, held as true in the country as in town. Usually she took pictures of her guests and pasted them into scrapbooks, so that later she could remind herself of the visits of Thornton Wilder, Robert B. Sherwood, the Lunts, and other theatrical and literary friends. House parties at Barley Sheaf Farm were so star-studded that the editors of newspapers and magazines hastened to offer accounts of them to their readers. *Life,* the glossiest of all the picture weeklies, printed, in the issue of September 6, 1937, a spread on one weekend's doings at the farm. The guests then were Hart, Harpo and Susan Marx, the Howard Dietzes, and Lillian Hellman—with Max Gordon showing up on Sunday to get in on the fun and the publicity.

Though never so gregarious as Beatrice, Kaufman more often than not enjoyed the weekends at the farm. His right to the privacy of his study was recognized by Beatrice, whether or not guests were present; if he wished to retreat to it, as he often did, to smooth a rough draft of dialogue, she made no objection. But it sometimes happened that Kaufman was not in the mood for company, though company was present. These moments of glowering withdrawal, though rare, created acute tension within the household. On one winter weekend when he made it unequivocally clear that he preferred to be alone, Beatrice, Anne, and their guests spent an uneasy evening, after an uneasy day, huddled near the living room fire while winds whistled outside and Kaufman paced in his study overhead. Suddenly the pacing ceased, and they heard him approaching the stairs. All at once he was in their midst at the fireplace. He flung the firescreen down on the hearth and began to jump on it. Then he said, "First time on any screen."[3]

Not all the Kaufmans' guests came only for the fun of it, however. As soon as they bought the farm Kaufman realized that it would be a splendid place in which to sequester himself with his collaborator of the moment, and also that he could bring down to it the playwrights whose work he intended to direct or produce. In the seventeen years that he owned the farm, he invited to it for those purposes John Steinbeck, Ruth and Augustus Goetz, Arthur Sheekman, Herman Mankiewicz, Gypsy Rose Lee, John P. Marquand, and many others. After a late breakfast the working guests would march upstairs and settle down in the study for the usual Kaufmanian day of inventing, cutting, splicing, and refining dialogue until their taskmaster was satisfied that the day's work was at last worthy of the reward of a rubber of bridge, a game of croquet, or—though rarely for himself—a cocktail. One long, non-working weekend in the spring of 1938 when guests were present, he conceived the notion of making a comic photographic record of the birth of a play to parody the educational film *The Birth of a Baby*. A spread of stills from that film had been shown in *Life* on April 11, 1938. On April 29 the New York *Post* published the thirteen-picture story. In this series, Kaufman and Hart are the parents; Robert E. Sherwood is the doctor who listens with professional sympathy as they confide that they are pregnant with a dramatic idea. With his stethoscope to Hart's head, Dr. Sherwood listens to the beat of the idea. He then instructs the parents that they must be careful for the next six months. At last, after much travail, the eight-pound manuscript is delivered by Dr. Sherwood. Beatrice, comforted by Ruth Gordon and Alexander Woollcott, awaits the news. "It's a comedy," says Dr. Sherwood. The proud fathers decide to name it *You Can't Take It with You.*

The remaining years of the 1930s witnessed the deepening of the relationship between Kaufman and Hart. Their friendship, steadily encouraged by Beatrice, was based in part on their mutual love for her, in part on their proven harmony as a team, and in part on Hart's need for the steadying influence in his life of an older and wiser man. Though always in touch with him, Kaufman was not Hart's most intimate friend. That place in Hart's life was held by Joseph Hyman, the theater-loving businessman who had befriended him long ago when a thieving resort-owner in the Catskills had disappeared at the end of the summer without paying Hart what was due him for his months of work. Hyman's loan, $200, allowed the Hart family to move at last to a decent apartment and bought Hart some time to sit on the Brooklyn beach with a pad of yellow paper and get on with what he meant to make his life's work: playwriting. Not until 1946 would Hyman become Hart's producer, but in the meanwhile he helped with the management of Hart's business affairs and was in his way as supportive to Hart in his periods of bleak depression as Beatrice was in hers: a warm, understanding, and continually available friend. Kaufman was not that. Quirky, cranky, doubting, often against massive evidence, that each new play would bring down the house on opening night, Kaufman nevertheless had no fundamental understanding of the torment that Hart underwent through these years of popular success. To Hart's friends it appeared that the young man looked upon Kaufman as a father; he was fond of his own father, to be sure, but Kaufman was the father he would have preferred, had the choice been his. For his part, Kaufman was grateful to Hart for what he brought to their collaborations. Hart was tireless, ebullient, and brimful of ideas, and possessed a gift for spontaneous invention. He became "Mossie" to Kaufman. That diminutive, the only one Kaufman bestowed on any acquaintance, was a sign of affection, but it did not signify that Kaufman found in Hart a surrogate son or that he cared to bare his emotions to Hart. If intimacy implied the pouring out of one's most private thoughts, loves, hates, fears, aspirations, to another individual, then Kaufman was nobody's intimate! As for Hart, during his bachelorhood he was more inclined to discuss such matters with Joseph Hyman or Beatrice than with Kaufman, the father figure, but, presumably, like anyone else under psychoanalysis, he brought everything out only with his analyst, who guided the process of self-discovery.

With his bank account mounting from the royalties of *Once in a Lifetime* and *You Can't Take It with You,* his musicals, and his screenwriting for MGM, Hart indulged in extraordinary shopping sprees along Fifth Avenue, supplying himself with one gold object after another and buying still more—many more—for his friends. Kaufman, never a spendthrift, was astonished by Hart's forays into the most expensive shops in town. He told one friend who was looking at jewelry in the window of a run-of-the-mill store to ignore it, because Hart could get him the same things at Cartier's at three times the price. Encountering Hart one day on a shopping expedition in Palm Springs, he shouted, "Hiyo Platinum!"[4] But if this constant exercising of his purchasing power made Hart happy—or, at any rate, less unhappy—and heightened his creativity, Kaufman was not one to object. Hart's most elaborate gesture of all was his purchase in 1937 of a farm in New Hope, Pennsylvania, a few minutes' drive from the Kaufmans' retreat. It was all but inevitable that he should have made such a purchase; if Kaufman, idol, friend, fantasy father, had a house there, it was also where Hart's country house should be, if he was to have one at all. Kaufman, of course, was very much pleased by this; it made life easier to have his collaborator—and friend —near by. Once Hart had moved in, and had surrounded himself with an instant forest of his own planting at an extravagant cost, weekends for the two playwrights and their guests assumed a pattern: Friday evenings were spent at the Kaufmans' and Saturday evenings at Hart's, with much movement back and forth during the daylight hours for bridge and croquet.

When, in the spring of 1937, Kaufman went to Hollywood for the fourth successive year, he could do so only after Dr. Franklyn Thorpe had asked that the bench warrant issued by Judge Knight for his arrest be withdrawn. This took place on March 31. What prompted Kaufman to make the trip was the prospect of writing another play with Hart, who had gone out earlier at the request of MGM that he work on a screenplay for Greta Garbo. On arriving, Hart had discovered that he was not up to the demands of such work because of the bleak depression and the sense of futility that still hung over him. Begging off, he returned some three weeks' salary to the studio, resumed his analytical sessions, and awaited the arrival of Kaufman, whose presence would guarantee sympathetic, gloom-dispelling companionship and a familiar, gratifyingly arduous working arrangement. As usual, Kaufman had yet another project on his mind, though not one whose demands would interfere with his collaboration with Hart.[5]

That project was the dramatization by John Steinbeck of his best-selling novel *Of Mice and Men*, which Kaufman expected to stage in the early fall for production by Sam Harris. It was through the urging of Beatrice that the play came into being. Annie Laurie Williams, the agent, had shown the galley proofs of the novel to Beatrice late in 1936, in the hope that Beatrice would recommend it to Samuel Goldwyn for filming. Beatrice read through the galleys with mounting excitement. A gripping tragedy of the life of itinerant ranch-hands in California, it had, despite its brevity, more depth than most of the novels of the 1930s on manual laborers, and less propagandizing for the radical left. Noting that Steinbeck had constructed the novel in three parts to make the fictional equivalent of a three-act play, Beatrice suggested to Kaufman that he take up the possibility with Steinbeck of their turning it into a real play. Kaufman thought that Steinbeck should do the job alone, in view of the fact that he knew the kinds of characters in the book at first hand, and Kaufman knew nothing about them at all. But he felt confident about directing the play. He also suggested to Beatrice that she arrange to option the stage rights. Though by this time the novel had already appeared and received much praise from reviewers, Steinbeck had not yet disposed of any subsidiary rights. It was the possibility of having his work staged by Kaufman that induced him to conclude the deal with Beatrice.

Though he and Kaufman did not have an opportunity to meet until long after the contracts were signed, Steinbeck proved amenable to Kaufman's suggestions, as well as grateful for them. In March Kaufman wrote to suggest that Steinbeck keep "the marvelous tenderness of the book," but, if he felt right about it, that he add some touches of humor.[6] It was not that Kaufman intended to turn the work into a comedy, but that he believed humor would serve to heighten the ultimate tragedy of the play. He also suggested that Steinbeck invent more appearances for Curley's wife, the unnamed young woman who inadvertently precipitates the tragedy of the migrant workers Lennie and George and is herself a tragic victim.

Not at this time or at any later point when they were working on the play did Kaufman and Steinbeck experience a clash of egos. They did have trouble, however, in getting together. In April, Steinbeck left his home in California for New York by Panama Canal steamer on the first leg of a trip to Europe, just as Kaufman was leaving to join Hart in Hollywood.[7] Steinbeck began the adaptation soon after receiving Kaufman's suggestions and continued to work on it while en route to Europe. In his absence, on May 21, a non-professional radical troupe, the San Francisco Theater Union, mounted a version of the play without authorization. Busy with Hart at the time, Kaufman ignored this incursion of his and Beatrice's rights. In midsummer Steinbeck's first draft of the play reached Kaufman at the Garden of Allah, but Kaufman, to his dismay, could not quite make sense of it, even when comparing it with the novel scene by scene. Nevertheless, he felt confident that on Steinbeck's return the two of them could pull the thing into shape for a late October opening. With the help of Steinbeck's agent, Kaufman arranged for Steinbeck and his wife to come to Barley Sheaf Farm in August, as soon as their ship docked in New York harbor.[8] The farm, quite clearly, was fast proving to be a sound investment. All worked out according to plan: when the two authors met in Kaufman's new study they put the finishing touches on the play in short order.

But when it came to huddling in town with Kaufman, Sam Harris, and Donald Oenslager (who was to design the settings), Steinbeck suddenly grew impatient. These sorts of discussions were too remote from the rather casual dealings that he was used to with his publisher and agent, and Sam Harris's office in the Music Box was too distant from the Pacific for comfort.

After one meeting, he simply said that he felt the play was in good hands, and that therefore he was returning to California. That was the beginning and end of his personal involvement in the production.[9]

In the meanwhile, Kaufman had the pleasure of working once more with Hart. It had not been easy for them to come to a decision on the substance of the new play, but they knew that as soon as *You Can't Take It with You* had been safely started on its run they would stir up some sort of show for the next season. To follow it up with a comparable success would not be easy, however. No matter what they created, comparisons of it with the hit comedy were sure to appear in the papers. They skirted this problem partially by deciding to write a musical revue, which would mark a new departure for them as a team. As early as February they had come to this decision and were hastily communicating with various persons with whom they hoped to collaborate on the production. The title was to be *Curtain Going Up,* the songs were to be by the Gershwins, and the stars, it was hoped, would be two expert comedians, Clifton Webb and Ina Claire. Their idea was to write a musical about the making of a musical, from the conception of the plot through the composition of the score, the hiring of performers, and on through to the opening night. With remarkable sureness of purpose and confidence in their entrepreneurial skill, they decided that they would play themselves in the show, and they expected the Gershwins to do the same. There would even be a part for Sam Harris. As a first step in the development of this extraordinary scheme, they took an option on Webb's services for $3500. But piece by piece the plan fell apart. Sam Harris refused to set foot on stage, no matter how promising the material turned out to be. As for the Gershwins, they had contracted with Samuel Goldwyn to provide the songs for *The Goldwyn Follies,* his film extravaganza, and could not find the time to compose the stage score, to say nothing of appearing nightly. Since Warner Brothers had saturated the nation with film musicals on precisely this theme, it was perhaps just as well that the plan came to nothing. But had it proceeded further in the planning, it would have had to have been abandoned, for in July George Gershwin died. His death at age thirty-nine was as shocking as it was unexpected.[10]

With this scheme coming to naught, the two playwrights were without a joint project for the fall. But only briefly, for as soon as Kaufman reached Hollywood, for which he departed from New York on April 1, another scheme came to mind. This was to be a musical starring Marlene Dietrich, who was then suffering a temporary decline in her box-office allure and therefore was possibly ready and willing to risk a Broadway appearance.

Hart, drawing from his personal experience on the psychoanalytic couch, suggested to Kaufman that they write a book centering in the process of free association, the method whereby the patient in analysis reveals, through uninhibited expression of whatever comes to his mind, ultimately to himself and his doctor the root cause of his neurosis. At this stage in his life Kaufman had no first-hand knowledge of the process, but he had heard enough from both Hart and Beatrice to grasp the principle behind it and to appreciate its value. He consented to Hart's notion, and before the end of the month the pair had written the first act of their book and had exacted a promise from the nation's second most famous team of songwriters, Richard Rodgers and Lorenz Hart, to supply the score. But this scheme, too, they abandoned; novel and promising though it seemed to be, it just did not jell. Hart, however, did not discard the idea completely; some three years later he returned to it and made it the basis of a lavish, costly musical, *Lady in the Dark.*[11]

Finally, a suitable subject drifted into their heads: a satirical musical comedy about the President of the United States—not, like *Of Thee I Sing* and *Let 'Em Eat Cake*, about a fictional President, but about the man who was then occupying the White House, Franklin D. Roosevelt. Though a bold stroke, it was not without precedent: in 1925 the Theater Guild's *Garrick Gaieties,* for which Rodgers and Hart had written the score, included a sketch in which the principal character was Calvin Coolidge. Moss Hart himself, for *As Thousands Cheer,* had created a sketch about a living ex-President, Herbert Hoover, who was shown with his wife as they packed their belongings to make way for the Roosevelts. Still, to proffer an entire musical comedy about Roosevelt, and to turn him into a song-and-dance man only a trifle more elevated than John P. Wintergreen, was sure to create something of a sensation. Rodgers and Hart welcomed the opportunity to create the score, and Harris, perhaps relieved that he would not have to make a stage appearance, was willing to serve as producer.

Toward the end of May, when the libretto was nearing completion, Kaufman and Hart began to give thought to casting. Their first choice of an actor to play F.D.R. was Charles Winninger, who had created the role of Captain Andy in Ziegfeld's production of *Show Boat* in 1927 and in 1936 had repeated it in the highly successful film version. But Winninger was too content with his West Coast career in movies and on radio to consider returning east for a Broadway run. Suddenly, as the two writers were outlining a Fourth of July speech for F.D.R. to deliver at a mock-up fireside in Central Park, the thought struck them that of all song-and-dance men on Broadway, the one best equipped to enact their character was George M. Cohan, the

"Yankee Doodle Dandy" who claimed—falsely, by one day—that he had been born on the Fourth. Notoriously stubborn, arrogant, prideful, and egocentric, he was nevertheless a striking performer. If anyone could bring him in line it was Harris, perhaps his closest friend and confidant, as well as his former partner. After receiving a telephone call from the writers urging him to offer Cohan the role, Harris cabled the actor, who was then traveling in Europe. (But not in Germany: "I'm not so dumb an Irishman to go to Germany with a name like Cohan," he told the press on his return.[12]) Kaufman and Hart had been extremely guarded about the substance of the book all along; Beatrice had been urged not to breathe a word of it, and she had followed instructions. Harris had been similarly advised, and not only kept the secret from the press but, curiously, even from Cohan himself. His cable merely invited the star to perform in a Kaufman-and-Hart musical under his banner. Though Cohan accepted promptly, on the strength of his friendship with the producer, neither Harris nor the playwrights felt completely confident that he would in fact play the role, and with some anxiety they awaited his return in July. For one thing, they feared that Cohan, who fancied himself a major popular songwriter and who had, indeed, contributed many numbers to the standard repertory, might at the last minute balk at singing the songs of other writers; for another, they were worried that the role might strike the old flag-waver as unpatriotic. Though Cohan exhibited star temperament in plenty before the play settled down to its run, he docilely signed the contract, after reading the script on his return. In the meanwhile, however, Harris, though unwell, paid a visit to his playwrights in Hollywood, where they and their songwriters congratulated themselves on their catch and worried over how it would all work out.

Those who expressed the greatest worry were Rodgers and Hart. In 1932 it had been their lot to write the first songs that Cohan, since his arrival at stardom, had ever sung professionally that were not of his own composition. This was at Paramount, for the film *The Phantom President*, in which Cohan costarred with Claudette Colbert. The experience had been all but intolerable for the songwriters, for Cohan was clearly unhappy at having to sing their songs, and in fact generally unhappy at not having complete control over the production in all its aspects, which he was accustomed to having on Broadway. They were of two minds over the prospect of working with him again, knowing as they did that they could expect nothing but barely concealed contempt from him for their work. A time would come when Richard Rodgers would have as much power as any writer or producer in Broadway history, but that time was not yet; for him and his partner, it was an either-or proposition: accept Cohan as star or give up the opportunity to compose the score. Finally Moss Hart (not related to Lorenz Hart), who had known the songwriters since 1932, and who had a gift for diplomacy, persuaded them to accede to the arrangement.[13]

With this problem solved, and the book completed, Kaufman came back to New York and Bucks County at the end of June, while Hart stayed behind with the songwriters, until, as Kaufman expressed it in a letter to Beatrice, they could be safely left. In about three weeks they finished the score. Dorothy Rodgers, the composer's wife, thought up the title, an abridgment of the often-quoted saying of Henry Clay, "I would rather be right than President." This was an improvement on the title originally conceived by Kaufman and Hart, *Hold on to Your Hats, Boys,* which, Kaufman had explained in another letter to Beatrice, was the punch line of a dirty joke. A two-week booking in Boston was contemplated for the tryout performances.

The concentration of Rodgers and the two Harts on their show was suddenly made impossible by the news that George Gershwin had fallen dangerously ill. His death came soon, on July 11. The brain tumor that destroyed his life had not been quickly diagnosed, for Gershwin—like Hart, a patient in analysis—was somewhat slow to come to the view that the root of the discomfort he experienced might be physical rather than emotional. Though reports differ, according to his biographer, Charles Schwartz, the Los Angeles psychoanalyst, Dr. Ernest Simmel, whom he was consulting, insisted that Gershwin have a complete physical going-over after he complained in early June of repeated headaches and dizzy spells. This analyst, as it happened, was also Moss Hart's; both became his patients on the recommendation of Dr. Gregory Zilboorg of New York, who was Beatrice's analyst. Of his New York acquaintances, those who most frequently saw Gershwin at the last were Moss Hart and S. N. Behrman. To Behrman, it seemed that Hart was a poor counselor for the ill composer because of his conviction that Gershwin's illness was psychological, whereas Behrman thought otherwise. Hart, who remained in deep melancholy all summer long, took Gershwin's passing to heart. Communicating the sad news to Rodgers by telephone, he could not keep from crying. The death was also a blow to Rodgers and Lorenz Hart. The great Broadway composers of the day, however much they may have vied with one another for lucrative assignments, were in fact all close friends whose social lives were intertwined. In New York, Kaufman, too, was much moved, but at the same time began to worry, on no medical evidence whatever, that he might be afflicted with a brain tumor.[14]

Rodgers and his partner completed the songs for *I'd Rather Be Right* well before the summer's end, and Kaufman and Harris made plans to begin rehearsals in September and to open the two-week tryout run in Boston on October 11. This Boston date meant that Kaufman would have three plays running simultaneously in that city—*You Can't Take It with You* and *Stage Door* (with Joan Bennett) in addition to the new one. He believed this to be a record, and was proud of it.[15] So far as the scheduling was concerned, the only problem to arise was that the show required one more week on the road than had been planned for it, and this meant that Kaufman had only three weeks after the Broadway opening on November 2 to ready *Of Mice and Men* for its scheduled opening on November 23. There were, however, other problems with *I'd Rather Be Right*—problems of precisely the sort anticipated by Rodgers.

Cohan was first invited to hear the songs early in September at the home of Jules Glaenzer. Glaenzer, a Cartier executive who was a friend of Rodgers, had been a friend of Gershwin also, and enjoyed the society of show business celebrities. Moss Hart sang the songs for the actor in a way that Rodgers was later to describe as "charming," while Rodgers and his regular rehearsal pianist played the accompaniment. Throughout this presentation, Cohan remained impassive, giving not so much as a hint of reaction to the words and music. When the last bar had been played, he rose, said, "Don't take any wooden nickels," and left. Obviously, some difficult weeks lay ahead.[16]

Part of what troubled Cohan, in addition to his continuing resentment over having to sing someone else's words, to someone else's tunes, was that he sensed a lack of vitality in the score. Though he did not impart this belief to the authors and production staff on first hearing the songs, ultimately he made it clear that he had found some weak moments in the show and wanted them improved by the addition of upbeat numbers. At the outset the score had three love songs, the title song among them. As a result of Cohan's stubborn sense of what was suitable to the production, the original title song was dropped and a new, jaunty, political patter song with the same title was added. The pretty but dull "Everybody Loves You" was also dropped. The one love song that remained, "Have You Met Miss Jones?" was one of the songwriters' most charming inventions, and in the course of time worked its way into the standard repertory. But since it was "ballads," not patter songs, from which Broadway writers derived most of their ASCAP royalties, this left Rodgers and Hart with only one money-maker. Nor were Rodgers and Hart pleased that their weekly royalty from the show was less than that of the playwrights.[17]

Though Cohan gave Kaufman no difficulty during rehearsals, he kept his distance from the songwriters. To others on the production team he referred to them, with obvious distaste, as "Gilbert and Sullivan." On the Boston opening night, his festering grievance exploded, when in an extraordinary breach of professionalism he substituted some words of his own for a passage of Lorenz Hart's in the patter song "Off the Record." The songwriters had already been suffering from Kaufman's constitutional inability to treat the music of musical comedy with as much seriousness as he treated the comedy; he had raised an objection to one of Hart's lyrics and had even offered to rewrite it himself, if Hart could not supply the sort of lyric he wanted. The company had survived that unpleasant quarter of an hour, and it survived the crisis of the opening night as well, but not without some severely abraded sensibilities. The lyric interpolated by Cohan put the President in a particularly bad light; the four writers had known all along that Cohan, a conservative, cared less for F.D.R. than they did, but they were unprepared for this behavior. To make matters worse, Cohan remarked, while on the stage, that he would probably get his two weeks' notice for his action.[18]

At the back of the house, Lorenz Hart turned white with rage, as did Kaufman. After the performance, both Harris and Kaufman reproached Cohan and exacted from him a promise that he would never again commit such an act. On the following morning it was Cohan's turn to be annoyed; the New York *Herald Tribune,* which had sent up a reporter to cover the opening, carried a front-page article about the incident. Cohan, not sufficiently impressed by the fact that the first public performance of a musical comedy about an incumbent President was news whether the star misbehaved or not, accused Rodgers of informing the paper of the incident. Further diplomatic gestures were required; Kaufman, Harris, and Moss Hart calmed down the star. No further unpleasantness occurred, and relations among all concerned were eased somewhat when Kaufman gave a party at the Ritz to celebrate the presence of his three plays in Boston, and Cohan, not to be outdone, gave a lavish party the following night. Before the company left town for its hastily booked week in Baltimore, Sam Harris also gave a party. No matter how uneasy the writers and their star were during the engagement, the rest of the company, with three parties to attend, had a good time of it.[19]

Well before the Boston opening, word had spread of the boldness of the Kaufman-and-Hart libretto in putting F.D.R. on the stage. It was no cause for amazement that the press was interested. As a writer for *Life* noted in a picture story published before the New York opening, in no other nation was the depiction of the head of state on stage, and a critical depiction at that, possible.[20] The deepening division in Europe and the threat of war rising from it had served to remind Americans of the virtues of their form of government; thus this show was news. At this point in his presidency the real Roosevelt was at or very near his low in popularity as a result of an ill-advised effort he had made in late winter to "pack" the Supreme Court with additional Justices, who were to serve as assistants to those members who were over seventy years old. In five years in office he had not had an opportunity to make an appointment to the Court; many of the New Deal acts that he considered central to his hope of bringing an end to the Depression had been declared unconstitutional by the "nine old men," as he called them. But the court-packing plan, shaped into a judicial reform bill, was doomed to fail, and it died in Congress on June 14 (at about the time that Kaufman and Hart were completing their script) when the Senate Judiciary Committee reported unfavorably on it. In the meanwhile, the President had achieved some of the hoped-for results even without the complicity of Congress: some pieces of "progressive" legislation were upheld by the Court, including, on April 10, the crucial Wagner Labor Relations Act, establishing the National Labor Relations Board; and in May the eighty-year-old conservative Justice Willis J. Van Devanter retired, making possible a Roosevelt appointment at last. Roosevelt took what consolation he could from these events, resigned himself to the failure of the court-packing bill, and began to rebuild his crumbling popularity. This division between the President and the Court, though not the only issue of the Kaufman-and-Hart script, became a major item in its design.

The plot itself of *I'd Rather Be Right* amounts to very little. Early in the evening on the Fourth of July a young couple, Phil and Peggy, come to hear a concert in Central Park. It is their hope to marry soon, but their financial circumstances are such that they cannot see their way clear to going ahead with their plans. Phil's boss had promised him a promotion and a post in a new office that the company expected to open. But, with the Depression continuing and uncertainty developing over Roosevelt's fiscal policy, Phil has been told that this will not come to pass. It all boils down to the fact that Phil will not have a better job, and consequently the couple will not have enough money to marry on, until the President balances the budget. As they sit on a rock in the park to hear the music, who should come in but the President himself! Naturally, they approach him, and, kind man that he is, he promises to look into the problem of the budget. In fact he has it with him; it is the little book in which he writes down the twenty-five cents that he spends on ice cream for the couple and himself. (The preceding item is $150,000,000 for two battleships.) "You wouldn't think a little bit of a book like this could put the whole country on the bum, would you?" he says. In the scenes that follow, the Cabinet, the Supreme Court, and several members of the Federal Theater Project of the Works Progress Administration come on, all to be engulfed in satire. When it is all over the budget remains unbalanced, to be sure, but the President advises the country to take heart anyway, and persuades Phil and Peggy to take a chance and marry no matter what. It then turns out that they have been asleep all this while and that the President has been only a figure in their dream.

The pungency that the two playwrights always exhibited when working together is not lacking in this script. Most of the members of the Cabinet are given their comeuppance for indifference toward the individual taxpayer, but perhaps none so deftly as Postmaster General James Farley, the dispenser of patronage. In the first act, after all the members have entered in response to the President's summons, Farley approaches him with a letter from someone deserving of recognition.

> FARLEY Now this fellow . . . is Chairman of the Fourth Assembly district in Seattle. He wants to be Collector of the Port of New York. How about it?
> ROOSEVELT But we've *got* a Collector of the Port of New York.
> FARLEY Not in Seattle.

It is, however, the Supreme Court that bears the brunt of the satire. The "nine old men" pop up from behind bushes in the park as soon as the President suggests a law. "Ah, no! No, you don't! Oh, no!" they tell him before all the words are out of his mouth. "It's unconstitutional." They become a trifle more amenable when nine young girls appear on the scene, but never really relent. Finally F.D.R. asks them to go home to their wives: "See if they're still constitutional."

It might have been expected that, in addition to these sitting ducks, the Cabinet and the Supreme Court, the authors would choose the Federal Theater Project as yet another target for their barbs. Since 1935, under the Works Progress Administration, out-of-work professional artists across the country had been given a chance to pursue their profession under government auspices. Headed by Hallie Flanagan, formerly the director of Vassar's Experimental Theater, the Federal Theater created in most sections of the nation, but especially in New York, vital, frequently innovative companies that offered surprisingly good theater at extremely low prices, in competition, it need hardly be said, with the commercial theater in which Kaufman, Hart, and Harris made their living. Some of the freshest jokes of *I'd Rather Be Right* have to do with the Federal Theater; in offering them, the authors were, as *Variety* might have put it, "kidding on the level." In the first act, at what might otherwise be a lull, a seedy-looking man and "a dozen or more beautiful girls" enter, and the following dialogue is spoken:

> DIRECTOR Pardon me, are you people doing anything?
> ROOSEVELT Huh? Why—no.
> DIRECTOR Well, do you mind if we give a show here?
> ROOSEVELT A show?
> DIRECTOR We're the Federal Theater, Unit. No. 864.
> ROOSEVELT Oh! Well . . . We *are* kind of busy. . . .
> DIRECTOR Can't help that. Whenever we see three people together, we're supposed to give a show. We're the Federal Theater.
> ROOSEVELT Well, if it's the law . . . Say, you've got quite an organization, haven't you?
> DIRECTOR Oh, this is only one unit. It's pretty hard to go any place these days without tripping over the Federal Theater. Went into my own bathroom the other day, and there they were!
> ROOSEVELT What were they doing—taking a bath?
> DIRECTOR No, my wife was in the tub and they were giving a performance of *She Stoops To Conquer.*

Before Kaufman and Hart allow them to exit, the girls go into a song and dance called "Spring in Vienna," which, the director says, they have produced at a cost of $675,000. This was hardly a fair figure, though it was true that before Congress brought the Federal Theater to an end in 1939 it had spent more than $46,000,000.[21] The President is impressed enough by the cost of this one number to refer to himself as "Franklin D. Ziegfeld." Later, in the second act, he asks his personal secretary to bring him the Wagner Act, and in response to the secretary's call for it, onto the stage bound two German acrobats, Hans and Fritz Wagner. They, too, are a unit of the Federal Theater.

But when Kaufman and Hart wished to borrow an idea from the Project, they did not hesitate to do so. In the first act, before any mention of Federal Theater occurs, we find that Maxwell, Phil's boss, has given up his wholesale furniture business and is now selling balloons. Why? Because Roosevelt has made it impossible for him to make money. How? By taxation. Handing the balloons to F.D.R., he begins to explain why, after making $200,000 the preceding year, he has nothing left. Mentioning one tax after another, until he has named thirty of them, he pops a balloon for each, the last being the inheritance tax that will take what little he has left after he dies. This was the sort of technique employed by the Federal Theater's Living Newspaper Unit, which presented documentary plays to educate the public on urgent social issues of the day. With stunning stage effects created by the inventive use of lights, slides, and novel teaching methods, the Living Newspaper was the most consistently imaginative of the Federal Theater units. The Kaufman-and-Hart instruction in taxation was akin to that in Arthur Arent's highly esteemed *Power,* in which a Man Who Knows and two assistants pile yellow, blue, and orange boxes on top of one another to create a towering pyramid, by way of illustrating the means whereby holding companies in the energy business top one another until an industrial empire is created.

Expectations ran high for *I'd Rather Be Right* before the New York opening on November 2. The fact that Cohan was coming back in a musical generated enough excitement by itself to ensure a strong advance sale. According to *Variety,* nearly a quarter of a million dollars came into the box office before the opening. Cohan had not put on his dancing shoes since 1927, when he appeared in *The Merry Malones,* a work with book, words, and music by himself. The advance was a help to the Harris office, for the show had proved to be unusually costly. Donald Oenslager originally created a setting whose measurements were impractical for the Alvin Theater, where the show was booked, because it had been designed for a smaller theater. This setting had to be scrapped and another built, bringing the cost of the production to $150,000. Fortunately, the plot called for only one scene, an expanse of Central Park toward its southern edge.[22]

Two minor pieces of misfortune occurred to mar the pleasure of the opening night for the cast and management. According to *Variety,* Cohan had to play the performance with a rubber cast on one leg, as the result of his having tripped over a cable backstage, and Beatrice wore a new fur coat to celebrate the occasion, only to have it stolen from her seat during the intermission. The next day's reviews were highly appreciative of Cohan's performance and the writers' affectionate characterization of F.D.R., though some of the reviewers noted that, apart from the novelty of bringing a living President to the stage, *I'd Rather Be Right* was a rather conventional musical, and one without distinguished songs. But Cohan carried the day. A run of 290 performances took the play into the summer of 1938, and a tour ensued. This success, coming so soon after *You Can't Take It with You,* had the effect of fusing the names of Kaufman and Hart. Hart was thenceforth *the* collaborator, the other writer with whom playgoers automatically associated Kaufman. At least once Kaufman publicly expressed his deep contentment with their writing relationship. This occurred during the Baltimore week of *I'd Rather Be Right,* when he baldly announced to a newspaper interviewer that Hart was his favorite collaborator. It was undoubtedly true. Later, in answer to a question put by S. N. Behrman as to how the relationship had begun, Kaufman replied, "I very quickly knew, when I met Moss, on which side my bread was buttered."[23]

The unforeseen need to play a week of performances in Baltimore after the Boston run meant that Kaufman had no time to lose; he had to put *Of Mice and Men* into rehearsal if it was to open on November 23 as scheduled. Taking advantage of every available hour, he began working with the cast on November 3, the day after *I'd Rather Be Right* opened. It was all one to him, of course, since he could think of nothing better to do with his time than to put it to practical use in the theater. To the theatrical reporters, however, it seemed rather unusual that the successful playwright could not be allowed a few days in which to savor his latest triumph, and they remarked about it.

But the tight schedule was no joke, for the tone of the play was darker by far than that of any of the plays Kaufman had previously directed, whether written by himself or other playwrights. It involved tense and violent passages, including a scene in which one character's hand is brutally crushed in the superhuman grip of another; an especially harrowing scene, to which the way had to be carefully prepared, in which the only woman in the cast is accidentally murdered; and a final scene in which a man kills his only intimate in order to spare him from falling into the hands of a lynch mob. And for this, Kaufman had only three weeks.

Steinbeck's play, despite Kaufman's request that some humorous touches be added, is a somber work. At the same time, it is a skillful analysis of the mind-set of one large element of the unskilled working force: the migrant farmworkers who in the 1930s moved about the countryside taking such planting and harvesting jobs as were available. Such men were homeless; permanent transients, despite whatever dreams they had of settling down, they lived life on the road year after year. Steinbeck reveals this as part of the Depression scene through the lives of two men, George Milton and Lennie Small—the former lean, wiry, and intelligent; the latter huge (belying his name), possessed of physical strength beyond his understanding, and having only a child's intelligence. They have traveled together for years, taking work where they find it. Their great scheme, which the title suggests will come to naught, is to have a small ranch of their own, where they can work as much as they like and no more. What decrees its failure is the coupling of Lennie's unformed mind with his incredible strength. His passion is to pat soft things. A piece of velvet would do if he had one; but since he does not, he strokes live things that come his way, and, though never meaning to, he kills each of them. Steinbeck makes these creatures ever larger as the play proceeds. The first is a field mouse; the second, a newborn puppy; the third, the daughter-in-law, known only as Curley's wife, of the boss of the ranch where he and George are, for the time being, employed. At the close, George, having got hold of a gun, can save his friend only by destroying him, and in the way that, earlier in the play, one of the other men on the ranch kills an ancient, invalid dog—with a bullet through the base of the skull.

The cast included Wallace Ford as George, Broderick Crawford as Lennie, and Claire Luce (not to be confused with the author of *The Women*) as Curley's wife. Kaufman's hand was sure in directing the script, despite its difference in tone from his own writing. The production was suspenseful, and chilling in the scenes of violence, yet ultimately poignant. It became the hit that Beatrice had predicted. The run did not match that of *I'd Rather Be Right,* but at 207 performances it took the play through the season. A road tour followed, and a sale was made to Hollywood. Since the Kaufmans owned 50 per cent of the production, the play was a profitable undertaking for them, as well as for Steinbeck and Harris. In April 1938, even though competing with Wilder's *Our Town,* it was voted best play of the season by the Drama Critics' Circle. Steinbeck had no desire to come east for the opening. Nor did he attend the play at any later date in its Broadway run. To Kaufman he expressed the gratitude that he and his wife felt in a letter that followed closely on their receipt of the opening-night reviews:

> As the reviews come in it becomes more and more apparent that you have done a great job. I knew you would of course but there is a curious gap between the thing in your hand and the thing set down, and you've jumped that gap. It's a strange kind of humbling luck we have. Carol and I have talked of it a number of times. That we—obscure people out of a place no one ever heard of—should have our first play directed and produced by the greatest director of our time—will not bear too close inspection for fear we may catch the gods of fortune at work and catching them, anger them so they hate us. Already I have made propitiation—

thrown my dear ring in the sea and I hope no big fish brings it back to me.

To say thank you is ridiculous for you can't thank a man for good work any more than you can thank him for being himself. But one can be very glad he is himself and that is what we are—very glad you are George Kaufman.[24]

The capture of the Drama Critics' Award offered no greater temptation to Steinbeck to travel to New York than had the opening. He stayed at home, but sent a telegram of thanks with a thoughtful reference to Kaufman and the cast as being more deserving of the critics' praise than he. To his agent, Elizabeth Olds, he wrote in consternation over the hullaballoo raised by newspaper columnists about his not witnessing the production. "I'd like to have seen the play," he confided, "but I wouldn't go six thousand miles to see the opening of the second coming of Christ."[25]

Kaufman was not pleased with Steinbeck for his apparent indifference to the production, though he did not let Steinbeck know of his displeasure. But the production brought him, in addition to the critics' praise and a good return on his investment, consolation of a kind in a prolonged, intense relationship with the actress Claire Luce. An indication of its warmth may be gleaned from the fact that in turning over Kaufman's sixty-eight letters to her to the Morgan Library, the actress stipulated that they could not be made accessible to the public for fifty years.

Still the restless search for new projects continued. Some might have had fruitful results, but Kaufman simply let them slip by; others he rejected out of hand. Among the latter was Ferber's suggestion that they make a play out of her *Nobody's in Town*, a loose-jointed novella portraying New York in the height of summer, when the humid city is deserted by all those residents who can afford to get away. Kaufman shrugged this off with a mock-anguished cry of "Hot pavements!" and a shuffle of his feet. In the summer of 1937 Norma Shearer tried to persuade him and Hart to write a film script for her, the subject, of course, to be left entirely to them. The actress also expressed the hope that Kaufman would direct her in the film version of *The Women*, the rights to which MGM hoped to persuade Max Gordon to sell. The writers declined the invitation to write the script, and Kaufman, after briefly considering the tentative proposal that he direct *The Women*, decided against it. Though he had hoped in 1936 to direct *A Day at the Races*, he now believed that he was not ready to direct any picture. Another film idea, and a more appealing one to the two writers, was that they should write a musical based on Hart's early life, leading up to the opening of

Once in a Lifetime and his precipitate removal, the day after the opening, of his family from darkest Brooklyn to sparkling Manhattan. But this, too, they decided against, and it remained for Hart to tell the story in print twenty years later. They had other, if not better, ideas. Early in 1938 Hart returned to Hollywood, again to work at MGM. Kaufman followed him in February. As in the preceding four years, they expected to get a play down on paper in good time for an early fall production.[26]

Initially they thought of writing a kind of epic of the American stage from its beginnings to their own time. This was another of Hart's "cavalcade" schemes. In his plan, not only the legitimate theater would be featured, but all other forms of stage entertainment. Hart conceived this scenario after reading through bound volumes of *Theatre Magazine* the slick monthly periodical of the stage that began publication in 1900 and continued until 1931. Growing enthusiastic over the photographs of past productions, he thought that Broadway's outwardly ageless acting couple, the Lunts, might take on the roles of a couple very like themselves who, never changing, pursued a joint career over the centuries. Approached by Hart and Kaufman, they showed a tentative interest in the scheme. It was the writers whose enthusiasm waned. Doing proper research into American theatrical history, they discovered that too few plays of the eighteenth and nineteenth centuries had merit enough to draw on for their panorama of the past. All this was behind them when Kaufman went out to Los Angeles in February. By that date they had decided on another one-set play about family life.[27]

On this occasion Kaufman had no employment awaiting him in Hollywood; he was there solely to confer with Hart. As soon as Hart himself was finished, at the end of the month, the two boarded a steamer heading back for New York by way of the Panama Canal. With them on the voyage were the young screenwriters George Seaton and Robert Pirosh. The trip was made memorable by the report, on March 11, that Hitler's troops had invaded Austria. Clustered around a radio and having a nightcap, the four men listened to the grim news.[28]

As the steamer made its way south and east to the Canal, it dawned on Kaufman and Hart that their family play, which by now included a number of eccentrics, was, if not a carbon copy of *You Can't Take It with You*, too close to it in conception to bear scrutiny. Once through the Canal, they abandoned it and re-examined the earlier idea of a theatrical cavalcade. It began to strike them as not so unattractive after all, though in need of modification. As they neared New York, however, Kaufman began to turn his mind to his plays then running, *I'd Rather Be Right* and *Of Mice and Men.*

The ship docked in the late morning of a matinee day, and Kaufman, gathering up Seaton and Pirosh, hurried from the dock to the Music Box, where *Of Mice and Men* was still drawing good houses. Standing at the back of the house, Seaton and Pirosh looked on as he paced in agitation while listening to one of the actors invent new lines.[29]

As their discussions continued during the spring, the writers concluded that they should limit their review of the stage to Broadway since the turn of the century, with a simple framing story that would embrace a series of numbers from outstanding musicals and passages of dialogue from well-known popular plays. They also planned to sketch the recent history of the Broadway area, with an unblinking look at its decline from the peak of glamour, when the theaters were new and their architecture a source of civic pride, to the tawdriness into which the area slumped after the crash of 1929, when, one after another, the 42nd street playhouses were given over to movies. At the same time, the writers expected to convey an optimistic message: that the theater, through chronically suffering from financial shock and the competition of less expensive entertainment, never dies. They chose as their title *The Fabulous Invalid*. By June they were ready to make plans for the fall production, with the aid of Sam Harris's office. In its new guise, this affectionate glance at the stage was no longer a suitable vehicle for the Lunts; the leading roles had become less important than the historical and sociological material. Though it would not include performers of such fame, the cast was nevertheless to be very large; over seventy actors were required, and many of them would be expected to double or triple in small roles. It was left to John Kennedy and Myra Streger to find the actors and work out the complicated business of the multiple roles. Confident that he and Hart had another winning production in the making, Kaufman read the play to Harris and his staff in June. His ebullience was as convincing then as it had been with *You Can't Take It with You* and *I'd Rather Be Right*.[30]

With the production left in the competent hands of the Harris office for the time being, Kaufman and Hart immersed themselves in another project that was scheduled to precede *The Fabulous Invalid* to Broadway. Max Gordon, after *The Women*, had produced four failures in a row and was searching for a hit. He thought that he spotted the formula for one in the unpredictably successful social revue, *Pins and Needles*, which had been offered off Broadway in November 1937 under the sponsorship of the International Ladies' Garment Workers Union. This show, with sketches by five socially conscious writers, tuneful numbers by Harold Rome (whose clever lyrics simultaneously saluted and spoofed the labor movement), and a cast composed of ILGWU members, not only became one of the hits of the season, but, with changes of material to reflect the march of political events, was destined to run to June 1940. Gordon may not have been so prescient as to foresee the length of the revue's run, but his judgment told him that its success was well deserved, for the material was of a quality seldom encountered in off-Broadway productions. Gordon was particularly drawn to a number called "Sunday in the Park," in which workers celebrated their one day off from work by taking an outing in Central Park.[31] It struck him that if the show's writers could be induced to turn out some new material, he would have another hit. He arranged with Charles Friedman, the director and principal contributor of sketches to the original revue, and Rome to create the new show. Like *Pins and Needles,* it was to be a topical, left-of-center series of comic blackouts and musical numbers. Kaufman and Hart, who could always be counted on to participate in Gordon's productions, now went a step beyond merely doctoring, looking in on rehearsals, and silently contributing to the backing. For *Sing Out the News,* as the show was called, they allowed themselves to be billed as associate producers.

The three men—Gordon, Kaufman, and Hart—were all enthusiastic about this project, and Gordon especially so. He very much enjoyed the society of officeholders, and he used to entertain Kaufman and Hart with tales of various occasions on which he met and talked with politicos. He was proud of the fact that he had come to know President Roosevelt well enough to be a frequent overnight guest at the White House when his productions were playing in Washington. In *Sing Out the News* he saw an opportunity to return the President's favors by supporting New Deal politics. All three warmed to the thought of participating in the wave of political theater then in fashion. This show was to be somewhat to the left of the mild, fence-straddling *I'd Rather Be Right.*

During the summer of 1938, the producers shaped plans for an early fall opening of the revue. As the summer deepened, the international political atmosphere grew heavier as Hitler, having annexed Austria, looked toward Czechoslovakia. Rumors flew of a coming demand from the dictator that the western part of Czechoslovakia be ceded to him. Kaufman and his partners shared the anxiety of all American Jews over the clear-cut threat posed to European Jewry by the Nazis, and they were aware as well of the threat to American democracy that Hitler's expansionist ambitions had created. In its modest way, the production of *Sing Out the News* became an effort to defend the American liberal tradition. As the summer passed and Kaufman and Hart mulled over both the revue and *The Fabulous Invalid,* and the task of staging them that lay ahead, they began to give thought to still another dramatic plot in which they might speak out against the Nazis and in support of the American way of life. Beatrice, profoundly moved to both pity and anger over the reports from abroad, urged them on in this project and began to search for her own way to affirm her anti-Nazi views.

At this time Kaufman began to contribute funds to relief agencies which sought to enable German Jews to emigrate. In particular, he was moved to help any of his German namesakes who wished to flee. Germany, he soon learned, was peopled with numerous Kaufmanns who were grateful for his aid. Not they alone, but countless other German Jews benefited from his generosity. Saying little about his gifts even to friends, he insisted that he wished to be as helpful as he could, but that he preferred not to see any of his beneficiaries who might make their way to the United States.

At Barley Sheaf Farm and Hart's near-by Fair View Farm, Max Gordon, Charles Friedman, and Harold Rome were frequent guests during the summer. To Rome the rounds of conferences about *Sing Out the News* were both a revelation and a disappointment. The young composer, holder of two degrees from Yale (B.A. and M.F.A. in architecture), felt that Kaufman and Hart lacked firm political convictions. Their hearts were in the right place, but they were in the distressing habit of firing off jokes at virtually everything, left, right, and center, even joining the general satiric attacks on the WPA as the haven of loafers. Rome was also astonished by the tenseness of both men; the relative merits of various sleeping pills seemed to creep frequently into their conversation. Rome was more closely drawn to Hart, only three years older than he, than to Kaufman, who struck him as withdrawn and aloof.

As the days went by, Kaufman and Hart grew ever less content with the sketches drawn up by Friedman. It was not the left-leaning subjects that bothered them, but the quality of the writing itself. Though loath to take credit, they began to revise Friedman's work heavily and to make some original contributions of their own to the program of sketches.[32] By the end of July the show was ready to go into rehearsal, with plans drawn up for a late August tryout run in Philadelphia, prior to the New York opening on September 24.

The topics of the sketches reflected the same skeptical attitude toward current politics that *Pins and Needles* had. One sketch, entitled "Private Enterprise," showed a gathering of the rich in Palm Beach fulminating against F.D.R., who could be seen fishing on his yacht offshore. Another, "I Married a Republican," offered Hiram Sherman, the young comedian, as an angel who comes down to the Republican National Convention in answer to the delegates' prayer and is at once drafted as the party's presidential candidate. After much importuning he accepts, but at the very moment of doing so his wings fly off. A third sketch, "Gone with the Revolution," depicted a conference at MGM over the script of the studio's extravaganza *Marie Antoinette;* in it writers and executives ponder the problem of telling the queen's story without mentioning the French Revolution. More biting was "A Liberal Education," in which a small boy in the park is caught between a marching band of "reds" and a marching band of the bourgeoisie, who are about to get into a fight. The boy, son of a liberal father, tries to stop them with his father's advice against being dogmatic. Thereupon both sides fall upon him and beat him until a policeman enters and arrests him for inciting a riot. Another sketch, "International Mountain Climbers," which came immediately before the close, showed the dictators of Europe and Benes of Czechoslovakia, Daladier of France, and Chamberlain of England dressed for climbing and roped together as they ascend a peak. Sherman, as Chamberlain, was pulled to right and left and finally suffered the loss of his lederhosen. This was the 1938 counterpart of the "Four Little Angels of Peace" sketch of *Pins and Needles,* which featured Hitler, Mussolini, an unnamed Japanese, and Anthony Eden protesting that international peace was their preeminent desire.

Appended to and interspersed with these and other sketches were Rome's songs. One stood out from all the rest: it was a rousing number called "Franklin D. Roosevelt Jones," in which a black family cheered the birth of a son who was named for the President. With a cast that included, in addition to Sherman and many others, Philip Loeb and Will Geer, and expensive settings by Jo Mielziner, this revue was obviously intended not to be merely a second *Pins and Needles* but, as Harold Rome viewed it, an *uptown* version of the original.

It might have been expected that Kaufman, with his new billing of associate producer, would exert strong pressure on Rome and Friedman to polish and repolish as the show went into rehearsal. Yet he did not. True to form, he revealed to Rome, as he had to Berlin, Gershwin, and Rodgers earlier, his profound indifference to the production's score. When at Barley Sheaf Farm or on the rehearsal stage Rome sang his new numbers, Kaufman listened patiently and sometimes murmured "Good," but it was evident to Rome that Kaufman did not know how to comment meaningfully on the music and that the way music functioned in the theater was simply a mystery to him. Polite and deferential to Friedman, Kaufman made suggestions about the direction, but let Friedman hold the reins. After the revue opened in Philadelphia on August 29, to good but not greatly enthusiastic notices, it was reported that Kaufman intended to take over the direction himself in order to protect his investment. But those reports were false. Though he offered more suggestions, he wished not to be distracted from work on *The Fabulous Invalid*.[33]

When *Sing Out the News* opened in New York on September 24, it received notices similar to those that had greeted it in Philadelphia: on the whole quite good, but not good enough to encourage a run on the box office. As was to be expected, the reviewers made comparisons with *Pins and Needles*. The tenor of the reviews, in the commercial press as well as in the *Daily Worker* and the *New Masses*, was that the new show had an attractive gloss, but less bite than its predecessor. The result was a disappointing run—only 105 performances. The producing trio, who were also the sole backers, lost the entire cost of the production. For Gordon the reception of the show was an especially harsh blow, because the opening followed by only five nights the even less promising opening of another of his offerings, E. B. Ginty's *Missouri Legend*, which he had produced in association with Guthrie McClintic.

As for *The Fabulous Invalid*, that curiously conceived work was in rehearsal when *Sing Out the News* opened on Broadway. In its final form, it bore a distinct resemblance to the "living newspapers" of the Federal Theater, but it lacked the fine moral indignation as well as the vitality of those productions. Taking ideas where they found them, Kaufman and Hart were not ignorant of the successes of the Federal Theater, no matter how much they had enjoyed satirizing it in *I'd Rather Be Right*. Earlier in the year when they had planned to offer a modest one-set play, they had, it would seem, been mindful of the Federal Theater's remarkable stroke in opening twenty-one productions of Sinclair Lewis and John C. Moffitt's *It Can't Happen Here* in seventeen cities on one night (October 27, 1936). They had not planned anything quite so grand as that, but they seriously consulted Sam Harris on the possibility of opening two productions of the one-set play in tryout cities simultaneously, one to be directed by Kaufman and the other by Hart, with casts of equal caliber. After the tour, one company was to come to Broadway and the other to open in Chicago for an indefinite run.[34] They abandoned that idea when they abandoned the play itself. The example of the living newspapers was more promising. In their panorama of the New York stage from 1900 to their own day, the Alexandria Theater was the site of the action, much as a crowded New York tenement was in

Arthur Arent's *One-Third of a Nation,* the living newspaper on housing that the Federal Theater had opened to loud praise in the preceding January. The writers' use of an acting couple as guides through the years also resembled the practice of living-newspaper authors in putting into the action a "little man" whose questions provided the occasion for educating the audience on the social topic of the play. The numerous bits of action, both dramatic and musical, from past successes were somewhat like the historical illustrations provided in the living newspapers.

The Kaufman-and-Hart couple are the ghosts of the actors Laurence Brooks and Paula Kingsley, who die on an opening night after their performance, she of a heart attack and he by suicide in grief over her death. They haunt the Alexandria and other playhouses ever afterward, commenting on the ups and downs of the "fabulous invalid," but always threatened with having to give up this earthly paradise for heaven if the theater dies. This is an intolerable thought to them, since they have been told that in heaven no theater exists! Stephen Courtleigh, the rather wooden actor given the role of Brooks, had scored his first sucess earlier in the year in a Federal Theater production, E. P. Conkle's *Prologue to Glory.*

Toward the end of the play, the poor ghosts are very nearly forced to make their ascent, as, between movies and strip shows, the "legit" is virtually squeezed out of business. Happily, however, they are saved when the Alexandria is taken over by a band of young idealists and their ebullient leader. These zealots, as described in the text, resemble those in the socially conscious Mercury Theater, whose leader was twenty-three-year-old Orson Welles. Kaufman had been following the Mercury since the fall of 1937 when, to critical acclaim, it opened its first production, a pared-down version of *Julius Caesar,* directed by Welles in such a way as to suggest parallels between the old Rome of Caesar and the new Rome of Mussolini. When that production opened, Brooks Atkinson began his review in the *Times* with, "Move over and make way for the Mercury Theater!" Backstage at the Alvin, where *I'd Rather Be Right* was playing, Kaufman had waved a copy of the paper and complained, "But where I was sitting, I *couldn't* move over."[35]

The Fabulous Invalid proved to be too cumbersome to travel. Out-of-town tryout performances were out of the question because of the heaviness of the Alexandria set, the complicated musical and lighting plans necessitated by the prolonged nostalgic interludes, and the sheer number of actors, singers and dancers—seventy-three of them—required by the script. A series of previews preceded the opening, which took place on October 8. The organizational work of Myra Streger and John Kennedy had prepared the way for smooth rehearsals; Kaufman knew well in advance of his first meeting with the large cast which of the actors would be doubling or tripling in the many small roles called for by the script. In addition to Courtleigh, among the better-known actors in the cast were Doris Dalton, who played Paula Brooks, and the veteran vaudeville performer Jack Norworth, who played the ghost of the theater doorman who introduced the couple into the mysteries of spectral existence. One member of the cast was eventually to acquire fame of a sort as an extremely busy bit player in Hollywood. This was Iris Adrian, who, as the stripper Daisy LaHiff, electrified the audience with an energetic series of bumps and grinds. Later, in her Hollywood career, she was proud to declare that it was her director, George S. Kaufman, who had taught her how to do them.[36]

The notices received by *The Fabulous Invalid* were disappointing, to say the least. The opening performance went off smoothly, but the play itself proved to be awkward and ill-conceived. Even where the theater was concerned, Hart and Kaufman drew back from a frank, unashamed expression of sentimental regard. The death of the stars was too abruptly presented to seem anything other than what it was, an excuse to start up the review of stage history. Its suddenness jarred the audience instead of stirring it. Too many comic moments undercut the serious ones, as with the appearance of the ghost of Shakespeare, who assured the twentieth-century artists that the theater was a chancy business in his day, too. The selections from past successes also presented problems. Many of the reviewers were agreed that they were performed by actors, singers, and dancers who, though competent, were no match for the originals, at least as the originals were recalled by playgoers with long memories. No novice actress imitating Ethel Barrymore in a scene from Clyde Fitch's *Captain Jinks of the Horse Marines* could compete with the memory of the great star as she had appeared in youth. Nor could any young song-and-dance man, no matter how agile, ever catch completely the dash and verve of George M. Cohan offering "Give My Regards to Broadway." With Oscar Levant wielding the baton, the pit orchestra no doubt matched, if it did not outclass, most such bands of the past, but the mimics on stage were, after all, just mimics. As for the twenty-six "straight" plays which Hart and Kaufman had settled on after reading through one hundred and sixty-five scripts, though they included O'Neill's *Anna Christie* and Anderson and Stallings's *What Price Glory?*, too many were long-forgotten melodramas.[37] After eight weeks (sixty-five performances) Harris ended the run. But the season of 1938-39 had not seen the last of Kaufman and Hart.

The season was also to hear from Beatrice. In December, she was informed of the presence in New York of a talented band of Viennese refugees who were making ends meet with various ill-paying jobs and were eager to show the American audience what they could do, and had done, in the theater. Though they were not figures of international reputation, they had developed a following at home. They had performed in satirical cabaret sketches, and up to the moment of the *Anschluss* they had tossed their theatrical barbs not only at the Austrian government, but also at Hitler. With the annexation of Austria by Germany, they found it only prudent to flee the country. Beatrice asked them to come to 94th Street for an audition, and on hearing them she made up her mind to raise the money to put them on Broadway in a revue. With an eye to providing a light, warm-weather entertainment, she worked at this project over the winter months.

Both Kaufman and Hart served as consultants to Beatrice in her planning of the revue, but they were preoccupied, as always, with plans of their own. Even as the closing notice was posted for *The Fabulous Invalid*, Kaufman was making plans to start the rehearsals of their new play. This work, *The American Way*, was also a kind of pageant. Both writers, however, took the subject to be more serious than that of their sham-history of the theater. It was to be a confirmation of American democratic principles and an expression of the age-old national conviction that by dint of hard work any American, no matter how humble his origin, could rise in life. At the urging of Beatrice, they expanded on this theme.

─17─

End of an Era

Though Kaufman was in his fiftieth year as *The American Way* went into production, he was livelier than ever, his sights set further ahead than they had been even in the last years of the 1920s. Nor did his work consume all his energy; he appeared to take greater interest in his social life with Beatrice than he had in the past. Not only did it include the usual cocktail gatherings and dinners, but modish costume parties as well. Kaufman enjoyed these evenings. They brought out the ham in him; he became, on such occasions, a particularly impressive Abraham Lincoln, with false beard, stovepipe hat, and his habitual erect posture giving a striking verisimilitude to the characterization. But his real joy was still to be found mainly in work, and that included the cooperation of Hart. In his reliance on Hart's willingness to put out a play with him per season lay a risk, the risk of disappointment and rejection as Hart, growing up emotionally, felt ever surer of his ability to maintain a career without the identification with Kaufman. As they readied the new script, however, neither man foresaw the future clearly.

As planned, *The American Way* was to be presented on a grand scale: in execution, it went beyond the merely grand; it moved toward the grandiose. Still unwilling to abandon the cavalcade idea despite the failure of *The Fabulous Invalid*, Hart hoped to offer a sweeping panorama of American life in the twentieth century, and Kaufman was happy to go along. Noel Coward had become an acquaintance of Hart's, if not an intimate, and Hart, whether consciously or not, aspired to be Coward's American counterpart; indeed, the time was not far off when Hart would refer to Coward as "the English Moss Hart."[1] Meanwhile, the new play was as emotional a work as *Cavalcade,* and it was intended to be as spectacular. *Cavalcade* had played in the vast Drury Lane Theater in London; *The American Way,* Hart hoped, would play in the vast Center Theater in Rockefeller Center.

The Center, which seated over 3800, was something of a white elephant because of its very size. Though it had never been used before for a non-musical production, it could be made to serve well enough for a "straight" play of the dimensions envisioned by Kaufman and Hart, provided certain modifications were made of the stage opening. But so costly would this production be—$225,000, according to *Variety*[2]—that it would call for the combined resources of two producers, Sam Harris and Max Gordon. The figure was an extraordinarily large one for 1939. It was the largest expenditure required for any production, musical or otherwise, during the 1938-39 season. The producers and writers held the majority interest, as was their custom. The New York World's Fair, which was scheduled to open its gates on April 30, 1939, was expected to draw throngs of visitors to the city; both the producers and the writers believed that their extravaganza would find a steady audience among them.

Behind the substance of the play, if not its form, was the alarm of the writers over Hitler's territorial expansion in central Europe, which posed a threat to themselves as Jews and to democratic government in the United States and wherever else it existed. The effectiveness of exported German propaganda was evident in the attention, not all of it on the part of yahoos, given such American demagogues as Gerald L. K. Smith, Charles E. Coughlin and his Christian Front, William Dudley Pelley and his Silver Shirts, and Fritz Kuhn and his German-American Bund. As much as Kaufman, Hart was sensitive to anti-Semitic comment and a steady supporter of Jewish causes. To Kaufman the dismissal from the Washington *Times* remained a sore memory, and he and Beatrice were concerned that Anne might be subjected to anti-Semitic hostility on the part of schoolmates. Edna Ferber, a confirmed Jewish chauvinist, made a trip to Palestine in 1934, and though not so moved as to turn Zionist, was much impressed. For several years thereafter, she approached Kaufman with the proposition that they write a play about the history of the Jews.[3]

It was not, of course, only the Jewish members of Kaufman's circle who were worried over this newly exacerbated danger from the Right. Woollcott, though himself capable of voicing anti-Semitic remarks, was deeply concerned for the Kaufmans, Harpo, and the Berlins, among other friends.[4] Sherwood, who became increasingly political-minded as the 1930s lurched along, and the Luces were also alarmed over the rise of the American fascists.

Clare Boothe's successful *Kiss the Boys Good-bye*, produced in September 1938, was intended to be a parable on that painful subject. The following year she offered *Margin for Error*, a comic melodrama in which the German consul in an American city was shot, stabbed, and poisoned, as though to suggest that just one attempt on such a creature's life was not enough.[5] Through these and other figures from the worlds of journalism and politics, among them Ralph Pulitzer, Herbert Bayard Swope, W. Averell Harriman, and James V. Forrestal, the Kaufmans were in touch with public affairs. To be sure, houseparties at the Swopes', say, or the Harrimans', where they spent Thanksgiving in 1938, after the Munich Conference, were not intended to be political briefing sessions, but they did offer an opportunity for someone like Kaufman, who spent his days at work in a quite different world, to hear intelligent comment on the latest, usually dire turn of international events. Occasionally he was amused as well as instructed at such parties. At a high-level gathering at the Harrimans', when Sherwood suggested that the scene could be made the basis of an entertaining play, Kaufman replied, "Yes; the title would be *The Upper Depths*."[6]

Despite the strength of their feeling about the new demagoguery, Kaufman and Hart refrained from making Martin Gunther, the protagonist of *The American Way*, a Jew. His religion is not discussed, but he is clearly intended to be a Christian, even though he is killed by Bundist thugs. This characterization at least spared the writers from hearing that they had written out of self-interest instead of in the hope of serving a higher cause. The play traces the economic and social rise of Gunther, an immigrant from Germany who comes to the United States out of respect for the American ideal of democracy. Settling in the small town of Mapleton, Ohio, he is determined that his children shall be raised in a free country, not one dominated by such a regime as the Kaiser's. So skillful is he as a cabinetmaker, and so refreshing in his candor, that the town's leading banker, Samuel Brockton, offers to lend him the money to erect a factory. The factory prospers, and Gunther and his wife become increasingly American in speech and manner, though it is hard indeed for Irma Gunther to accept her son's decision to enlist in the Army in the First World War and thus be thrown into a fight against her relations on the German side. But the death of that son in the war only hastens the process of assimilation, for they view it as an experience shared by countless other Americans. After a run on Brockton's bank, Gunther finds himself no longer rich, but still happy to be living in a freedom-loving country. Yet all Americans do not rejoice in their freedom, as witness those who advocate the importation of the principles of the "new" Germany.

On the very night of his fiftieth wedding anniversary, Gunther is beaten to death by American Nazis as he tries to persuade his grandson, who is unemployed, not to join their organization. In this at least he is victorious, for the young man is horrified by the murder. At the close, Gunther is given the sort of funeral befitting a civic leader, complete with the singing of "The Star-Spangled Banner" by a huge throng of Mapleton citizens. During the run of the play, the curtain fell nightly on an audience groping for handkerchiefs.

Almost unrelievedly sentimental in plot and characterization, the play exhibited only those aspects of American life that were comfortably middle class. Gunther's success, though based on his stubborn honesty, is achieved with breath-taking speed. His children and their friends are so clean-cut and polite as to be ciphers. Nor does he seem particularly hard-pressed after the bank's failure, despite what is said about the magnitude of his loss. For that matter, the WPA workers who figure briefly in the play are shown to be exclusively middle class in origin. Finally, it must be said, even Gunther's death is played down, for his killers, though unmistakably Bundists, are not identified by such a label. Nor is Hitler mentioned by name. Happily, however, the overly sweet atmosphere is normalized a little by plain-speaking Winifred Baxter, a suffragette who concedes nothing to society's dictum that a woman's place is in the home. Like a welcome and unexpected breeze on a sweltering day, she comes and goes through the play's many scenes, coolly offering her comic lines to a grateful audience. A divorcée, when addressed by her married name, Mrs. Alexander, she replies, ". . . call me Miss Baxter. I like it better, and so does Mr. Alexander, wherever he is."

But if the plot was both frail and overheated, the production made up for its lacks by spectacle. The Center was, in its day, a technological marvel, equipped with all the latest in lighting boards and movable stages. One scene flowed into another without interruption of the action or the necessity of playing "in one" (down front before a drop) while the settings were changed. The music, composed and conducted by Oscar Levant, was piped down from six levels above the stage; cues to Levant to strike up the band were indicated by means of flashing lights. To bring the action as close to the audience as possible, the orchestra pit was covered over and the stage was extended outward above it. Donald Oenslager designed scenes of Ellis Island, the cozy, nostalgic Mapleton town square, a picnic ground, a country club interior, and of course, the Gunthers' home, which underwent changes as its owners' fortunes varied. To fill up the stage, some two hundred extras were employed, along with some sixty actors who had speaking parts.

There was much to look at in *The American Way;* turn-of-the-century America, so fascinating to audiences of the 1930s, was especially well carried out by Oenslager in the town square setting, with its Civil War mementoes and its hotel, courthouse, post office, bank, shops, and lighting fixtures. This place became the heart of the play, as it was the heart of Mapleton. It was the audience's introduction to Mapleton when, in the second scene, Martin Gunther showed it to his newly arrived wife, and the play returned to it in the tear-wrenching scenes of the soldiers' homecoming after the Armistice and in the funeral scene that concludes the play. Though Kaufman was the director of the dramatic action, Hassard Short, who had developed a reputation for staging spectacle, served as technical director of the production, since this task, which involved the cuing of the crowds and the coordination of the scene changes, was of a sort that Kaufman had never attempted on so great a scale.

The casting of the extras and minor characters was left to Myra Streger and John Kennedy, as with *The Fabulous Invalid*. Those small roles especially well filled were Karl, the Gunthers' son, who was played by David Wayne, and Anna, the family maid, who was played by Janet Fox. Wayne was discovered by John Kennedy and Myra Streger at an audition for a prize offered by John Golden to beginners. In the roles of Martin and Irma Gunther were Fredric March and his wife, Florence Eldridge. The couple had left Hollywood temporarily in the previous season to act on Broadway in *Yr. Obedient Servant*, a comedy of manners about Sir Richard Steele by Horace Jackson. After one week it closed, but they were determined to return, so that, like the Lunts, they could appear together, and March could have a role of greater weight than those he was usually offered in Hollywood, where, because of his good looks, he was too often cast in unchallenging romantic parts. Kaufman had known the couple since 1928, when March went on the road as Tony Cavendish in *The Royal Family*. He had frequently been the couple's dinner guest in Hollywood. The part of Winifred Baxter was, of course, a "Jean Dixon" part, but that actress unfortunately turned it down, for both it and the proffered salary were too small.[7] But even with this serious lack, the supporting cast measured up to the standard set by the Marches; Ruth Weston was praised as Winifred, as was McKay Morris as the banker, Brockton, her suitor in the later scenes of the play.

Yet despite the cast and the spectacle, the play drew reviews that were more respectful of the authors' patriotic intentions than of their dramatic achievement. Since the production was much too heavy to travel, some pre-

views were held for the purpose of testing the play before the formal opening on January 21, 1939. Kaufman and Hart tinkered with the production
up to the opening, and as a result of some hints in the reviews they continued to tinker for several days afterwards. Because Burns Mantle, an old
Kaufman fan and friend, took exception to the sight of Gunther's coffin, it
was shown as little as possible after the opening night, and was draped in an
American flag. And because the murder of Gunther was judged too tamely
presented by some of the reviewers, it was made more violent, and his as-
sailants were unequivocally shown to be American imitators of Hitler's
street-fighters. With these improvements, the play did excellent business
during the late winter. Unhappily, however, the opening of the World's Fair
did not bring the expected demand for tickets, and on June 10, when it had
run 164 performances, the producers closed it down for a month. After re-
opening, it played only eighty performances. Max Gordon, who had set up
a film-producing arrangement with RKO Pictures, expected to film the play.
But no picture was ever made of *The American Way*. In the final accounting, the play did not make a profit. The Pulitzer Prize went to the season's
other patriotic play, Sherwood's *Abe Lincoln in Illinois;* ironically, it was
this play, a Playwrights' Company production, that Gordon produced for
RKO. This was his only film in a long career in show business, and, unhappily, it, too, was a box-office failure.

Minor kudos went to Kaufman and Hart in the form of an award for pa-
triotism from the United States Flag Association, but this struck Kaufman as
more of a nuisance than an honor. To receive the award, he had to make a
speech from the stage of the Center Theater after the performance on Washington's Birthday. Hart was then in Palm Springs at work on a film script,
and that was also annoying to Kaufman. To Beatrice, who was visiting Hart
in the desert, he wrote, "And Moss won't even be here. I shall make a
speech saying that I had to fight Moss tooth and nail all the way through the
thing, because he kept wanting to come out for Communism."[8] Kudos went
to Beatrice, too, at about this time, and in a more lasting way. The published
text of *The American Way* carried the dedication, "This play is for Beatrice." No other play by Kaufman had borne a dedication.

As for Beatrice's own show, *From Vienna*, plans called for an opening on
June 20, ten days after the temporary closing of *The American Way*. Bea-
trice did her work well. To produce the play she formed the Refugee Artists
Group with a board that included, among others, her husband, Gordon,
Harris, Charles Friedman, and Howard Reinheimer (Kaufman's lawyer),
with herself as chairman. Her backers read like an abbreviated *Who's Who*

in the Theater; among them were Irving Berlin, Eddie Cantor, Ferber, Moss Hart, Rodgers and Hart, the Marches, Harpo and Zeppo Marx, and Robert Sherwood. Charles Friedman and Hassard Short assisted with the staging, Irene Sharaff with the costumes, and Donald Oenslager with the scenery. To top it all off, Sam Harris lent the Music Box, rent-free, and Kaufman and Hart bustled about at rehearsals, dispensing suggestions. Organized as a non-profit venture, the revue paid modest salaries to the performers and little or nothing to the roster of American designers and technicians whom Beatrice charmed into helping out. It was planned that if any money was made by the production, it would be used to assist theater workers abroad who wished to emigrate. Some pleasant notices were written for the revue, and, as intended, it ran smoothly through the summer for seventy-nine performances.

Another diversion of the season was Kaufman's emergence as a radio celebrity. In the spring of 1938 CBS aired the first broadcast of a panel show called *Information Please,* with Clifton Fadiman as head panelist and John Kieran, a sportswriter for the *Times,* and Franklin P. Adams as regular performers. Two outsiders were invited to participate every week, and Kaufman soon became a cherished guest. So valuable a participant was he that on occasions when Fadiman could not appear, he was asked to head the panel. Another frequent guest, and, eventually, a regular member of the panel, was Oscar Levant. Comfortable with this crowd of "experts," and enjoying the reunion of sorts with F.P.A., from whom he had drawn apart since the break-up of the Algonquin set, Kaufman liked to appear on the program. In the main he answered questions on show business and left those on other topics to the regulars. Once (at least) he was stumped by a simple question: "What was distinctive about *The Deep, Tangled Wildwood?*" The expected answer was that it failed.

Before the season was over, he and Hart completed still another script. Now accustomed to the procedure of writing a play in the spring for staging in the fall, soon after the opening of *The American Way* they had begun to think of what to do next. In March, after Hart's return from California, they made some progress on a new comedy and also looked ahead to the writing of a musical with Cole Porter, for—tentatively—W. C. Fields. Under the influence of *Our Town,* they thought of staging the musical without scenery. Suddenly, however, they set aside the comedy-in-progress and jettisoned the idea for the musical. This precipitate dropping of one set of plans in favor of another was nothing new; since *Once in a Lifetime* the plots of all their plays save *The Fabulous Invalid* had resulted from the hasty decision not to proceed with a project at hand. At this time, however, their plans were altered at the command of a third person, Alexander Woollcott, who insisted that they keep a promise made more than a year before—that they write a play in which he could act.

Their promise, rather rashly given, had been prompted by a visit that Woollcott made to Bucks County at the start of 1938. For only the second time, Woollcott was engaged to act in a leading role in a professional production. The play was S. N. Behrman's political comedy, *Wine of Choice*. Behrman had also written the first play in which Woollcott attempted Broadway: *Brief Moment*, produced in 1931. He had been something of a trial in that production, but Behrman, who liked him personally, took a chance and cast him a second time. The character in *Brief Moment* was Binkie Niebuhr, a Jewish *Feinschmecker* (epicure) and merry meddler in the lives of others, a figure loosely patterned by Behrman after his friend Rudolph Kommer, the financial adviser to Max Reinhardt. The off-stage Woollcott was not unlike the character, except that he had managed, by means of his lecture tours, radio appearances, and writings, to make himself rich, whereas Binkie lived by his wits and off the largesse of friends. The play ultimately was a failure, but in January 1938, when Hart and Kaufman had gotten the bright idea of memorializing Woollcott's quirky personality in comedy, it was going through a pre-Broadway run in Philadelphia.

The Kaufmans asked Woollcott to come over to Barley Sheaf Farm after his performance on Saturday night, January 1. He accepted, but did not spend the entire weekend with them. On Sunday he went from their house to Hart's to spend the night. Though Hart welcomed him warmly, the occasion proved altogether disagreeable, because, to Woollcott's extreme distress, Max Gordon was also present, and Woollcott, ever the prima donna, did not wish to share Hart's attention with him. Moreover, Woollcott did not care for him personally. Refusing to eat with Gordon, whose table manners rendered uncomfortable even less squeamish persons than he, Woollcott returned to the Kaufmans' for dinner.

After dinner, however, apprised that Gordon had gone back to New York, he returned to Hart's to spend the night, but insisted that Hart's own bedroom be turned over to him. He was demanding in still other ways: he insisted that a chocolate milkshake and a chocolate cake be prepared for him, all the while complaining loudly that Hart's servants were dishonest. The next day, before departing, he wrote in his astonished host's guest book, "I wish to say that on my first visit to Moss Hart's house I had one of the most unpleasant evenings I can ever recall having spent." Hart then drove him to Philadelphia in time for the Monday evening performance and, though no glutton for punishment, not only stayed to see it but had drinks with Woollcott afterward. As it happened, Hart enjoyed Woollcott's performance on stage, no matter how distasteful he had found his friend's histrionics in Bucks County. Together, over brandy, Woollcott and he arrived at the opinion that the Kaufman-and-Hart team should write a play in which Woollcott could assume the leading role.[9]

Hart, despite his appreciation of the performance which he had just seen, was aware that Woollcott's talent for acting was nothing special. On the radio and the lecture circuit, Woollcott in his own person could capture an audience, but that was not the same thing as impersonating a dramatic character. Nevertheless, on the following day Hart spoke with Kaufman about his conversation with Woollcott and suggested that writing a play for him might be a lark. But first they had to think of a plot. Hart, reflecting on Woollcott's mercurial disposition, his constant demands, and his childlike craving for attention, told Kaufman about the weekend with him and his outrageous behavior. What would it have been like, he wondered, if Woollcott had broken his leg and had had to stay? With that, the two friends looked at each other and laughed. "Well," said one or the other or both at once, "there is that play for Woollcott."[10]

Nevertheless, they did not start to write the play until more than a year had passed. In the interim, there was work to be done on *The Fabulous Invalid* and *Sing Out the News*. During the summer of 1938, while busy with these, they added *The American Way* to their schedule. To placate Woollcott and demonstrate their good faith, in the fall they journeyed to Neshobe Island, where they offered an explanation and an apology—and played croquet. But the plan for a comedy had come up, as had the plan for a musical. While Hart was away, Woollcott invited Kaufman to tea in New York to talk once more about the project. He suggested that he and Kaufman should write the play, if Hart was no longer interested, and do so on the island during the summer. But Kaufman loyally insisted that he and Hart would get around to it before long.[11]

Ferber, who no longer could bear Woollcott, meanwhile had a suggestion to offer, as Kaufman wrote to Beatrice:

> Ferber left for Phoenix yesterday. . . . I asked her why she was going, and she said she just had to. It seemed typically Ferber—always forcing herself to do something she doesn't particularly want to do, eternally hardening that character of hers until finally they can use it to build bridges with. . . . I found myself telling her about my visit to Wooll-

cott, and that led to mention of a possible play for Woollcott, and there she had a wonderful idea. Put *her* in it, she said, and they would tour the country together. She said there never would be such a tour, and I believe it. She wants a big spitting scene with Woollcott on stage, and she said not to worry about off stage. And she said she felt certain that in the little towns there would be more fuss raised about her than there would about him, which would make everything even better. My reason staggered at the possibility of such a combination.[12]

Though Woollcott was still able to take the delay in stride in February, he felt put upon by the postponements one month later. Soon after Hart's return from the West, the two had dinner together. During it Woollcott lost his temper, though, for once, not without reason. He pointed out to Hart that he had refused lecture offers and radio dates for the 1939-40 season on the strength of the two playwrights' promise. Now, he cried, it was time for them to come through. It was a typical Woollcott explosion, complete with imaginative name-calling, but Hart conceded that the bundle of petulance seated across the table from him had a point.[13]

The next day, Kaufman and Hart put their heads together to invent a vehicle suitable for Woollcott. The central situation was the one they had originally conceived at Barley Sheaf Farm. Not only was it a shrewd comic invention, but it had the advantage of requiring Woollcott to sit in a wheel chair for almost the entire length of the play, instead of whimsically heaving his great bulk across the stage. He had been sedentary, for the most part, in the Behrman plays as well, in the fashion of a corpulent Wagnerian diva around whom moved the others in the cast. Apart from this, the character was in every way to resemble Woollcott as the public knew him. As Hart later put it, ". . . in talking about Woollcott, we decided to use only public aspects of his character. That is, to be guided in the plot by his lecture tours, his broadcasts, his charm, his acidulousness, his interest in murders, and all of this had to be worked into the plot of the play. Those things were the core of the play, and the plot was something that had to be worked around them."[14]

It was not the first work conceived for the purpose of giving the public a close-up view of Woollcott. Charles Brackett had done so in his novel *Entirely Surrounded*, published in 1934 and set, as the title implied, on Neshobe Island. But Brackett had aimed for verisimilitude, not caricature, and furthermore he had permitted no mitigating softness to tone down the aspects of his character's personality. His Thaddeus Hulbert is Woollcott at his worst: unrelievedly meddlesome, imperious, spoiled, emotionally immature, and revealing deplorable self-indulgence by lapsing into baby talk, a trick of Woollcott's that not even his staunchest friends could bear. Though Kaufman and Hart designed a character to whom the same adjectives could apply, they toned down the portrait with an admixture of humor and good nature. Theirs was to be a Woollcott as the public knew him, explosive, of course, but not insufferable.

The portrait appealed to Woollcott. At the Gotham Hotel on Fifth Avenue, where he then lived whenever he could bring himself to leave Lake Bomoseen, he listened with pleasure as Kaufman and Hart read him the first act and told them that he would give them his decision on playing the role when a draft of the entire script was ready. Then, however, he decided against it. His reason, a sensible one, was that it would not be in good taste for him to exploit his own personality so blatantly. The writers were not displeased with this decision, because the role had become too substantial to be well realized by an actor who was, after all, only an amateur, his possession of an Equity card notwithstanding. At this point, the play was entitled *Prince Charming*. It was subsequently copyrighted as *Such Interesting People*, but finally reached the stage as *The Man Who Came to Dinner*, at the suggestion of Myra Streger.

Woollcott did play himself—or Sheridan Whiteside, as the character was named—eventually, but never on Broadway. In the spring of 1940, when a West Coast troupe was organized after the thunderously successful New York opening and the establishment of a Chicago company and an Eastern road company, he settled into the role quite happily and played it in California. By that time the play was so famous and Woollcott had been so much publicized as the original of Whiteside that he could not fail in it. The authors' first choice was Robert Morley, the portly English actor who had recently made a success in both New York and London in Leslie and Sewell Stokes's *Oscar Wilde*. But Morley disliked the third act and declined to take the part—only to agree to play it in London the following year.

After the part was spurned by their second choice, Adolph Menjou, the authors offered it to an actor not so well known: Monty Woolley, a bearded man, stocky of build, but, unlike Woollcott, not obese. An occasional Broadway performer and former teacher of acting at Yale, he had been the dialogue director of *Jubilee*, Hart and Cole Porter's musical. Woolley proved precisely right for the assignment. In fact, it was the making of him.

With Sam Harris again the producer and Myra Streger and John Kennedy to assist with the casting, the writers assembled an excellent company. Apart from Whiteside, none of the roles was a starring one, and, for that matter, Woolley was not billed above the title. Mary Wickes, having delighted Kaufman in *Stage Door*, played the gawky, put-upon nurse, Miss Preen. Edith Atwater, then the leading lady in Hart's personal life, was given the role of Whiteside's secretary, Maggie Cutler. David Burns, a rising comedian, played Banjo, an amiable caricature of Harpo. Cast in the important roles of Lorraine Sheldon and Beverly Carton, respectively, were Carol Goodner and John Hoysradt. It was a thoroughly dependable company.

The plot of the comedy, like that of *You Can't Take It with You*, was anything but complex; it only seemed so as a houseful of characters whirled around in it. Since Woollcott was much in demand on the women's club lecture-circuit, the writers decided that it should be at the home of a prominent small-town clubwoman that Whiteside have his accident and be immured for recuperation. After a dinner that follows his lecture, he slips on ice at the doorstep and fractures a hip. From this follow endless new developments for a period of two weeks, in the home of his unprepared hosts, after which, mobile again, he leaves the house by the same door and once more slips on the ice. That was the framework to set off a portrait of Woollcott as a master deliverer of the sarcastic phrase, a sybarite, a sentimentalist, an enthusiast of the films of Walt Disney, but also a dispenser of kindness to those whom he thought required or merited his protection, and a person with a vast capacity for sustained hard work.

But attention could not, after all, be focused on the Woollcott persona alone for the entire performance. Diversions were necessary, in the form not only of eccentric characters, but of dramatic conflict. As with *You Can't Take It with You*, the writers decided on a small-scale love plot. Though aware that this was not the kind of writing at which they excelled, they saw that it would provide a welcome contrast with the rages of Whiteside, as well as giving them a device with which to illustrate both his selfishness *and* his generosity. It could never be Whiteside himself who was to have a romance; that was something that Woollcott did not do. (Once, six years before, he crashed a luncheon party given by George Oppenheimer for Rebecca West, knelt at the English writer's feet, put his arms around her, and then rose and said, "That is my sex life for 1933.")[15] But the secretary could fall in love with a local journalist, Bert Jefferson, and Whiteside could do his best to break them up, lest she be lost to him forever. That was at most a sliver of a plot, but, like Alice Sycamore's mildly troubled affair, it was enough to keep things going for three acts. Moreover, as with Alice and Tony Kirby, it gave the writers the opportunity to create normative characters who functioned as centers of repose in the midst of frenzied action. The best side of Woollcott's nature was allowed to come through at the close, when Whiteside, having created a comic version of hell on earth for two hours and a half, gives in and offers his blessings to the loving couple.

With the questionable exception of Boothe's *The Women,* no other hit play of the late 1930s reflects so frankly the attitudes of persons not deeply touched by the Depression. Some differences between the two plays may be noted, however. Boothe wrote of an economic class so protected by inherited wealth that not even the shocks delivered by the Wall Street crash could leave it without sufficient resources to maintain a luxurious life, whereas Kaufman and Hart chose to write about public figures whose popularity and talent ensured them a robust earning power. Boothe allowed such minor characters as domestic servants, shopgirls, and nurses to point up the extravagance of the major characters with such acerbity that no playgoer could think her indifferent to the plight of the needy. Kaufman and Hart had manifested their awareness of the national situation in their comedy of the Vanderhof clan in the same year. But in the new play they chose to ignore almost completely the problems that existed just beyond the icy doorstep of the Stanley residence. Their sole reference to such matters exists in a subsidiary plot involving the Stanley children, whom Whiteside likes and who admire him, despite the agitated feelings that exist between him and their parents. June Stanley, the daughter of the house, is in love with a labor organizer, and, knowing that her father, a manufacturer, would never approve of the match, she asks Whiteside for advice. He advises merely that she run off with the young man, and she does. Nor is her father's effort to prevent the marriage successful, because Whiteside, identifying Stanley's sister as an axe-murderess who a quarter of a century earlier had killed their parents, blackmails him into dropping it.

What is most striking about *The Man Who Came to Dinner,* apart from what it offers in the way of wisecracks and sight gags, is the aura of success that radiates from every scene. It is, in part, a play about success: about how to make the most of talent and how to enjoy the rewards that it brings. Into the Stanleys' living room in Mesalia, "a small town in Ohio," are dropped the names of some of the most accomplished and lionized persons of their time. The list of the famous who are mentioned runs to some forty authentic celebrities of the 1930s, including H. G. Wells, Walt Disney, Ginger Rogers, Lady Astor, Hattie Carnegie, the Khedive of Egypt, Hedy Lamarr, and so on and on, until it becomes a sort of game to guess who will be mentioned next. In addition to Harpo, one natural scientist of note and two theatrical luminaries make actual stage appearances in the play, though not under their own names. Dr. Gustav Eckstein, a writer and naturalist at the

University of Cincinnati, and a social pet of Woollcott's, appeared as Professor Metz, who arrives at the Stanleys' immaculate house to give Whiteside a cheering present: Roach City, in which ten thousand cockroaches in a glass-topped box live out their lives as a parable for human onlookers. The stage stars were Gertrude Lawrence and Noel Coward. Lawrence is travestied as Lorraine Sheldon, a playwright's paradigm of seductiveness and egocentricity who comes to the aid of Whiteside in his effort at breaking up Maggie Cutler's romance. Coward is presented as Beverly Carlton, just as egocentric as Lorraine, and happy to score a hit at her (in what is the least believable episode of the play) by gulling her into planning a hasty trip to London and her rich but dull fiancé. (The scheme fails, it may be noted.) Carlton no sooner arrives than he sits at the piano to croon a new song of his own composition, "What Am I To Do?" To oblige Kaufman and Hart, Cole Porter wrote the song; tuneful and fey, it was a successful parody of Coward's style and one that Coward himself enjoyed. In payment for it, Porter received a specially designed cigarette case from the playwrights. Banjo, the stage image of Woollcott's adored Harpo, is asked about the health of his brothers Wacko and Sloppo, lest anyone fail to spot him as a Marx. Since the real-life Harpo carried on much as his film persona did, the writers had him no sooner enter the Stanley household than start a pursuit of Whiteside's virginal nurse. "I love you madly—madly!" he exclaims. "Do you hear what I said—madly! Kiss me! Again! Don't be afraid of my passion. Kiss me! I can feel the hot blood pounding through your varicose veins."

The Man Who Came to Dinner, whatever else it may have been—an evening's escape from the tensions of the time, a parade of "in" jokes and allusions, a compliment to a cherished friend—was first of all and still remains a very funny piece of writing that represents the combined sense of humor of Kaufman and Hart honed more keenly than ever before. The verbal wit gets into the play through the acerbic disposition of several of the characters—Whiteside, chiefly, but also Maggie and Carlton. Banjo is a mad spouter of verbal disjunctures that are funny in themselves. One is reminded on hearing them how much the early Kaufman contributed to the Marx Brothers' public personalities. With Whiteside/Woollcott, he and Hart deepened and amplified the acid self that was always there. Though Kaufman once described him as "an entrancing companion,"[16] his lines in the play are as jarring as they are funny. His first remark on stage is, "I may vomit." If Miss Preen fails to respond instantly as he calls to her in the next room, he shouts, "What have you got in there, a sailor?"

But jokes were not the authors' only comic means. The second act ends with the usual humorous Kaufmanian bustle, as Stanley expresses his rage over Whiteside's meddling, and Lorraine, fuming over the trick just played on her by Maggie and Carlton, turns hungrily to Jefferson. Then, to cap all this, six choir boys enter. They have been brought in for Whiteside's annual Christmas broadcast, and Whiteside, courtesy of his sponsor, Cream of Mush, commences his retelling of the Bethlehem story. The contrast is supremely unsettling, but no sooner does Whiteside begin his narration than Miss Preen dashes on stage screaming, "A penguin bit me." In the last act occurs the timely removal of Lorraine from Mesalia, so that the romance between Maggie and Jefferson may continue. As first written, she was to be wrapped up in a blanket and abducted by Banjo and the surrealist painter Miguel Santos. This was kept in for the opening in Hartford, but Santos was not funny enough, and had to be written out. In Boston the playwrights tried something else, and it worked. One of Whiteside's Christmas presents is a huge mummy case sent by the Khedive of Egypt. Lorraine, daydreaming about its original occupant, steps into it and out again, and both Whiteside and Banjo, watching her, get the same brilliant idea. They talk her into posing in it again, then slam it shut. She will be flown far out of the way—to Nova Scotia.

As was his custom whenever possible, Kaufman rehearsed the company in the settings. To a visitor who was writing a report of the rehearsals for *Theatre Arts*, it was clear after only a few days' work that the play was a potential hit. Like others before him, the visitor was amazed at the speed with which the team could mend a weak moment in the play and Kaufman's shrewdness in supplying action to fill in a dead spot.[17] At the Hartford opening, which took place on September 23, 1939 the writers knew that the play would go over, but saw that some improvements were necessary. Santos, as noted, had to go; the ability of the writers to revise scenes overnight that had originally included him and to invent the new means of dispatching Lorraine seemed little short of miraculous. One minor problem existed, and continued for a while, but was corrected with a sympathetic word. Woolley, bon vivant that he was, enjoyed a cocktail with his dinner, even before the evening performance, and sometimes this mild imbibition showed in his acting. Kaufman and Hart, since they themselves seldom drank, were at first puzzled as to why he seemed slow on certain evenings. When at last they grasped the truth of the situation, they were too shy to speak to the actor about it. In the end, Edith Atwater did it for them.[18]

In Boston, where it played after Hartford, the comedy soon established itself as an audience-pleaser. This came as a welcome relief to the actors, who had feared that the jokes and references to celebrities would appeal to insiders only.[19] But some additional work was needed during the Boston run. By the time the play arrived in New York on October 16, it was a brilliant, smooth-functioning piece of dramatic craftsmanship. The Broadway production enjoyed a run of 739 performances. But that was only the beginning. The play was destined to become the second most valuable of the writers' properties, as individuals or as a team, after *You Can't Take It with You*. Not only did it become a major touring attraction, but drew enthusiastic crowds in the film version released by Warner Brothers in 1942. Monty Woolley and Mary Wickes repeated their stage roles in the film, and the roles of Maggie Cutler and Banjo were taken by Bette Davis and Jimmy Durante.

Though this last theatrical season of the decade brought Kaufman one of his most lucrative hits and another round of awestruck notices in the press, it proved not to be the most joyous of times. Personal success had to be measured against the outbreak of war in Europe and the certainty that the United States would eventually be drawn into the fighting, since the Allies appeared unable to conquer Hitler on their own. To the Kaufmans, who, with the members of their circle, still felt the shock of the Munich Pact, it seemed the duty of Americans to give unstinted aid to the Allies. In a minor way, the war made itself felt in the writing of *The Man Who Came to Dinner*: a reference to Gertrude Stein telephoning Whiteside from Paris had to be changed to one to Walt Disney calling from Hollywood. If the play made no mention of the war that had engulfed Europe, the omission did not signify that Kaufman and Hart were indifferent to it, but that they chose to leave their original script virtually intact as a light-hearted comedy, rather than turn it into another kind of play, one that would reflect a darker mood.

A month after the opening of this popular work, Kaufman turned fifty. He passed that milestone with no discernible decline in stamina, but he was too much of a worrier not to view it as an important date. Making it somewhat easier for him was the sight on newsstands all over town of his picture on the cover of *Time*, whose editors chose to honor him thus on his birthday. Inside there was an entertaining, if superficial, account of his career.

The aging of those close to him was also a matter for concern. In March 1939 Sam Harris married, and very happily, for the second time, but the producer was then sixty-seven and inclined to spend much of his time in Palm Beach. He now cared to produce only the Kaufman-and-Hart plays, and how much longer he would wish to expend his energy on even these was beyond guessing. The declining health of Joseph and Nettie Kaufman was a persistent worry. In 1939 Joseph turned eighty-three and Nettie eighty. Joseph had long since handed over his silk-dyeing plant in Queens to his employees, and, with Kaufman's financial aid, the couple were living comfortably in New York. The Kaufmans entertained them frequently with dinners and plays, and sent them on trips when they had an urge to travel. But at last they had reached the point in their lives when they needed close and constant looking after. Nettie's mental instability was more and more evident, and Joseph had begun to experience some episodes of mind-wandering. Early in 1940 he had to be placed in a mental hospital, to his son's distress. That event marked the final ebbing of Joseph's strength. He died on June 14, 1940. Nettie's health worsened with his passing, and later in the year, on November 1, she too died.

Beatrice and Anne remained sources of comfort. Anne, an adolescent, was beginning to develop as a person very much like her father: she was amusing, intelligent, and something of a leader. She was elected the president of her class at the Dalton School in New York, an achievement in which Kaufman took pride. As for Beatrice, though his relationship with her remained the companionable one in which neither questioned the other's affairs, periodically he found it necessary to assure and reassure her of his undying love. As one decade ended and the next began, Claire Luce, the actress, figured importantly in his life, but did not render all other women unattractive. Briefly, and for the only time in their lives, he and Hart found themselves in a friendly rivalry for the attention of another young actress. Kaufman lost out to Hart in this contest. The actress herself lost out eventually, however, for Hart was not yet ready to make a commitment to marriage.

Signs of Kaufman's growing reputation for skilled showmanship were suddenly in evidence all around him. In November 1939, just as *Time* was honoring him on his birthday, Bennett Cerf of Random House conceived of another, more permanent, way of memorializing his achievement. Cerf, whose firm published more contemporary Broadway plays than all others combined, offered to issue a set of his collected works. When Kaufman replied that not all his plays were good enough to merit reprinting, Cerf countered with a proposal to issue one volume of sixteen of them. Eventually, this scheme was dropped, possibly because of the difficulty of securing the necessary permissions from the various collaborators, all of whom would have had to take second billing to Kaufman in such an undertaking. Two years later, however, Cerf issued a volume of six of his collaborations with Hart.[20]

Through Kaufman's appearances on *Information Please* he was beginning to create a public image for himself as a man who could always be counted on to say something dry and funny, without the "cooked" sound of the professional comedians such as Benny and Bob Hope, who did not write their own material. Inquiries began to be made about his willingness to appear on other radio programs as well as to make a lecture tour, like his crony Woollcott. The W. Colston Leigh Agency, one of the leading lecture-booking agencies, asked Cerf, an indefatigable lecturer himself, to sound Kaufman out on the tour. Though nothing came of the project, Kaufman admitted to some interest.[21] Suddenly he was putting a tentative foot into new territory and enjoying his reception.

One invitation to lecture that he accepted, though not without a qualm, came from a university drama department. According to the notes that he prepared for this event, but which offer no clue as to the identity of the university, he gave the lecture on March 4, 1940, and it was the first such speech of his lifetime. He spoke diffidently about his career as both a writer and a director. The art of direction got short shrift: "I think it's a highly overrated goings-on. If you have any ear, any instinct for the theater, you can be a director. And if you get good scripts, you'll be a good director." On playwriting, he had much more to say. Asserting that at that particular moment the playwright, not the star actor or the director, was the most important figure in the theater, he discussed his own dramatic technique. It was based, he said, on the conviction that the essential element in dramaturgy was careful construction—the "well-made play," though he did not use the term—with care taken to keep the minor characters in their places. This, presumably, was advice for which the students were grateful, but it was offset by the unrelenting, pitiless self-doubt that remained a part of his character. He felt obliged to point out that two currently running hits that rambled, Saroyan's *The Time of Your Life* and Lindsay and Crouse's *Life with Father*, had pleased him very much. (*Life with Father* he described as "the most entertaining comedy ever produced in America.") He pointed out also that his fame was not based entirely on his own efforts, but had been erected with the aid of his gifted collaborators—"although Mr. W[ollcott] I caught in an off moment. Two off moments."

Referring to the many hits of the past that he and Hart had read while writing *The Fabulous Invalid,* he reminded the audience that the successes of one age could baffle and bore the theatergoers of another. His own plays, he thus implied, might lose their freshness eventually. Nor, he suggested, was he likely to prove an influential writer, one who would achieve fame

for having bettered the theater. He and Morrie Ryskind had expected at
least to revolutionize the musical stage with the plot provided for *Of Thee I
Sing*, but "we succeeded so completely in revolutionizing the musical comedy stage that this year's musical comedy hits are *Too Many Girls*, which is
concerned with who is going to win the big football game, and *Dubarry Was
a Lady*, which is about Bert Lahr and Ethel Merman."

The late winter and spring of 1940 brought other developments of many
sorts, not all so pleasing as the attention of students. There were now three
companies of *The Man Who Came to Dinner*: the Broadway cast was settled in at the Music Box for what was clearly going to be a long run; a second company, headed by Clifton Webb, was regaling audiences in Chicago;
and a third, West Coast company, with Woollcott happily and shamelessly
playing Whiteside, had opened in Santa Barbara on February 9. Woollcott
hoped that he would be given the lead in the Chicago company,[22] but settled
for the Western tour because he knew that the company would eventually
tour the East. Kaufman, who directed both replicas of the original produc
tion, rehearsed the Western company in Los Angeles in January. Hart came
out for the fun, as did Alice Duer Miller, Woollcott's great friend. They all
stayed at the Garden of Allah, each in a separate bungalow. Residing in
other bungalows at this hotel, then the favorite of transient Eastern writers,
were Dorothy Parker and Robert Benchley, so that for a while the atmosphere was a bit like that of the Algonquin in its days of glory, except that
the Garden of Allah had palms and greenery and a pool. Hart no sooner hit
town than he remarked to the press that he cared for neither the intellectual
climate of Los Angeles nor the looks of its women. Some young women of
the area declared that they would boycott the play.[23] That hardly mattered,
however, since nearly all the tickets for the Los Angeles run had been sold
in advance. That Woollcott's performance proved to be no better than that of
any other willing amateur had no effect on box-office receipts. It was not the
prospect of witnessing virtuoso performing that drew customers to this company, but the chance of seeing the celebrated show-off disport himself merrily
on stage, and of hearing him drop one famous name after another from
the long list provided by the script, just as he did on radio. On the evening
of February 15, when the show was still playing in Los Angeles, his voice
failed him and Kaufman went on in his place, making his first stage appearance in ten years. He, too, delighted the audience.

In May during the San Francisco engagement, Woollcott's romp with the
play came to a rattling stop. Responding to the elegant cookery of Northern

California with his usual abandonment, he overate copiously and suffered a heart attack. Thereupon the production closed down. For Kaufman or anyone else to fill Woollcott's role on a regular basis was out of the question, for more than one reason: not only was he its star attraction, but, as Kaufman and Hart knew, it was important to his convalescence to believe that he might one day resume his part. Eventually he was able to do so, but that was not until January 1941, when the company reassembled in Philadelphia to make the projected Eastern tour.

Woollcott's illness gave Kaufman an anxious month, and Beatrice, to whom Woollcott was a principal confidant, went through a period of acute concern. It was a heavy addition to the great weight of worry that the worsening health of Joseph and Nettie, the senior Kaufmans, had already placed upon them. Though burdened with these cares, Kaufman believed, nevertheless, that he must develop new projects for the fall. Sure as the turning of the seasons, the coming fall would have its Kaufman-and-Hart comedy. But that, he felt, would not be quite enough to occupy him. To take up the slack in his schedule, he secured the production rights to a romantic comedy by Irwin Shaw called *Retreat to Pleasure*. Shaw, who had come to public attention with his short, moving antiwar play *Bury the Dead* in 1936, was new to this kind of dramatic writing and quite happy to take instruction from Kaufman in the techniques of improving its comic edge, and moving the characters on and off stage convincingly. As two highly productive theatrical journeymen, Shaw and Kaufman got on well together. Eventually, however, Kaufman turned the play over to Harold Clurman of the Group Theater, because he himself could find no suitable actor for the leading role.[24]

In the spring Kaufman began to take a busy part in the committee work generated by the European war. This constituted a sort of sideline for him until V-J Day, as it did for Hart and most of their associates. He had already shown himself to be much concerned about the problems of those unfortunates in flight from the Nazis, and at this point he undertook work on behalf of the British. In January the fund-raising American Theater Wing of British War Relief had been established under the leadership of Rachel Crothers, then the most prominent American playwright of her sex. With Crothers as president, Gertrude Lawrence as first vice president, and Helen Hayes as second vice president, the Theater Wing acquired the image of a women's volunteer organization. The leadership made effective use of available males, however, in the fund-raising entertainments it set up, and it also established a men's committee, on which sat both Kaufman and Hart. Beatrice became a member of the honorary women's committee, to lend her name to the letterhead. In March 1940 Kaufman and Hart participated in one of the Theater Wing's benefit performances, along with Gertrude Lawrence and other stars. That was Kaufman's first such contribution to the relief effort.

The appearance of the two playwrights on this bill occurred as they were looking for a new plot. The idea that they had first had was not, they decided, especially good: an episodic comedy taking place in a barber shop, where incidents from the lives of the various customers would be acted out.[25] They dropped that idea as soon as they began looking at it in earnest, because it would require too large a cast to be financially practical. But the idea that they next developed, and stayed with, did not summon their best efforts. The production of this comedy, *George Washington Slept Here*, which they got around to in the early fall, was troubled from the outset. One cause, possibly, of the tentative state of the manuscript from first to last was that Hart's mind was not wholly given over to it. All the while that he and Kaufman were talking their way through the making of the plot, he was also shaping, honing, and editing another plot, one entirely of his own invention.

First announced as *I Am Listening*, Hart's play in-progress reached the stage in January 1941 as *Lady in the Dark*. In final form, it was one of the most opulent musicals ever presented on Broadway, a triumph of the art of its scene designer Harry Horner, a showcase for two greatly gifted performers, the popular Gertrude Lawrence and the little-known Danny Kaye, and a treasury of sumptuous melodies by Kurt Weill and brisk lyrics by Ira Gershwin. As a play, Hart's script was only a slim thread on which these riches of performance and "production values" could be strung, but as originally conceived it was to be a full-bodied three-act play, embellished by only one song. Hart had two ends in mind when he began to write. One was to create a play about psychoanalysis so as to offer a sign of his esteem for the process that at last was beginning to make his inner life tolerable. He had a new analyst, Dr. Lawrence S. Kubie, whose ministrations were more helpful than those of the others he had tried. What better way, then, to register his gratitude than to write a play about a patient who, like himself, had benefited from sessions with an intelligent prober of the secret recesses of the mind?[26] Hart did not intend, however, to write an autobiographical play. He decided to write about a woman. During the Boston tryout of *The Man Who Came to Dinner*, he encountered Katharine Cornell, who was in the same city on tour with S. N. Behrman's *No Time for Comedy*. Then and there he pounced upon the idea for his play, with Cornell in the leading part.

Thinking it over as *The Man Who Came to Dinner* made its way to Broadway, and afterward, as the Chicago and California companies were in preparation, he invented a plot about a businesswoman, Liza Elliott, the editor of a fashion magazine, who would suddenly lose her customary drive and turn to psychoanalysis to discover the cause. A musical theme repeatedly jingling in her mind was central to the plot and would be sung by Cornell in the course of the action. When approached, the actress was happy with Hart's conception and agreed to act in the play.[27] Soon, however, Hart's deep-seated love of luxuriant spectacle asserted itself. What was intended to be a non-musical work became, in the jargon used to publicize it, a "play with music." But in reality it was a grand musical comedy with a few long scenes confined to the spoken word. For all her grandeur and her following, Katharine Cornell was no longer an appropriate choice for the heroine's role. The only established performer who could meet its demands was Gertrude Lawrence, who had long since proved herself a song-and-dance woman and who, with a series of roles conceived for her by Noel Coward and others in the 1930s, had demonstrated that she was a capable dramatic actress as well.

During the 1939-40 season Gertrude Lawrence was the star of Samson Raphaelson's *Skylark,* a romantic comedy. Kaufman was rumored to have described this conjunction of script and star as "a bad play saved by a bad performance." Perhaps so. The play was saved, in any event. Lawrence played in it on Broadway for 256 performances, and after the closing she took it on the road. It was a personal triumph for the actress, and one that quickly followed after her success in the more demanding heroine's role in Rachel Crothers's *Susan and God.* She was not at all certain that she wished to resume her identity as a musical performer. Only by great patience was Hart able to prevent himself from exploding at the delaying tactics of the actress and her lawyer-agent, Fanny Holtzman. Negotiations ran through the late winter and spring to the summer before she gave in and signed the contract, a contract that Hart, exasperated, reported gave her his farm and "the Music Box Theatre, Sam Harris's house in Palm Beach, half of Metro-Goldwyn-Mayer, a couple of race horses, and five thousand dollars a week."[28] To Noel Coward, who was visiting New York on a wartime mission for the British government, Hart had the look of a man on the point of going to pieces. Coward's intervention with Lawrence was instrumental in causing the actress to recognize the role as the first-rate vehicle that it was, a part that would allow her to dazzle the public with all her talents at once.[29] When the play went into rehearsal in late fall, with Hart directing the dramatic scenes and Hassard Short in charge of the musical interludes, *George Washington Slept Here* had been running a month and a half.

Hart kept Kaufman informed about the progress of his solo effort from virtually the moment of its conception. There was nothing unusual in his decision to initiate a project on his own; he had done so before with musical comedies. He had also written for the screen without Kaufman. The only unusual aspect of this new venture as it affected their relationship lay in the fact that from Hart's viewpoint it was a serious dramatic work, not merely another musical, and as such it was the first work for the stage that he had written alone since the establishment of "Kaufman-and-Hart" as a household phrase. His decision to write the play alone made no difference in their personal relationship, however. Throughout the year, apart from periods when Hart sequestered himself with his script, the professional and private lives of the two writers were intertwined. They were, as always, in touch on the telephone every day. At intervals during the spring they reviewed their ideas for their next collaboration, and in June, with Hart's plans for his musical still in abeyance because of Lawrence's indecisiveness, they settled down in earnest at Hart's Bucks County house to put the play on paper.

Behind their plan to write at Hart's Fair View Farm rather than at Kaufman's place was the fact that Barley Sheaf was then the scene of another collaborative endeavor. Beatrice was working there on a new play in company with a writer named Charles Martin. This young man, slim, dark, and good-looking, like the many other young men in her life, had been introduced to her by an agent. Beatrice had told the agent that she had an idea for a comedy and that she, like her husband when the muse descended, wanted a partner to share the labor. Martin was then employed by an advertising agency as a dramatist for night-time radio. Through the summer while the team of Kaufman and Hart plotted what was to become *George Washington Slept Here,* the team of Kaufman and Martin worked at a play that they entitled *The White-Haired Boy,* a farce about a popular and controversial writer whose youthful energy and giant ego made him resemble Clifford Odets and William Saroyan. When not occupied with his own work, Kaufman read Beatrice's manuscript and gave advice on the construction of the plot. Both Beatrice and Martin gratefully accepted his suggestions. When the play was finished, Beatrice sent it to Herman Shumlin, the producer of, among other works, the plays of Lillian Hellman, a good friend of both Kaufmans. Shumlin accepted the manuscript, but did not schedule it for immediate production. Impatient to have the work mounted, Beatrice showed it to George Abbott, who was delighted with it. Shumlin relinquished it in Abbott's favor, and a fall production was planned, with Abbott directing and Keenan Wynn taking the role of the writer. The tryout tour was booked to commence in Boston on October 28.[30]

The dramatic idea that offered itself to Kaufman and Hart in June once they set aside the barbershop play was partly autobiographical. Sitting in Hart's study and looking out at his well-landscaped lawn, they were suddenly reminded of the struggles that both had had to endure when renovating and planting their properties only three years before. Beatrice had directed the improvements of Barley Sheaf by herself; Kaufman, relieved of the burden of coping with carpenters, plumbers, glaziers, and the rest of the artisans hired to refurbish the place, had only had to pay the bills. But Hart, a bachelor, had seen to the work of Fair View Farm himself, with the advice of Joseph Hyman, his business manager, on how much he should spend. That advice was not heeded to the letter. Hart not only improved the house, but at extravagant cost in money and patience reforested the property and put in a winding road to the house from the highway. Capping all this was the difficulty he had experienced in finding a water supply. Welldiggers had worked their way over almost the entire breadth of Hart's land before locating a spring. Here, it seemed to both writers, was material for a play, and perhaps material rich enough to recover the outlay for the work.

As with their seven earlier collaborations, the writing of the new comedy proceeded swiftly once the two made up their minds about the subject and its treatment. In one important respect the overwhelming success of *The Man Who Came to Dinner* influenced their approach to the new subject. In large part because of their ownership of Bucks County properties, the region was widely publicized. It had become known, with good reason, as the haunt of celebrities. But they had just written a play about celebrities, and popular though it was, they could not return to their audience with another comedy whose characters were the rich and famous of the day in transparent disguise. The new play had to center on the preoccupations of ordinary people. They chose a middle-aged couple from Manhattan as their new Bucks County farm owners and put them—persons without a great deal of money to spend—through the anxieties that they, or at any rate Hart, had suffered during the unending delay of having a run-down house restored. Since by itself this was not quite enough to serve as the basis for a three-act comedy, they added some personal conflicts. The wife, Annabelle Fuller, is not at all pleased with the fact that her husband, Newton, has purchased the property. It had been his idea, and his alone, to get away from noisy Manhattan to quiet, rural Pennsylvania. That he has imperiled their financial security to buy the farm comes as a shock to her when at last he must break this piece of news. Their daughter, Madge, though she has a young man, develops a dangerous crush on a dashing married actor who is in the company of a summer theater in the area. Yet another problem is the ferocity of the neighbor, one Mr. Prescott, whose land abuts on theirs and who owns the road leading from the highway to their house. But the greatest problems remain those of repairing the house when the local labor force is sparse and tapping a source of water without digging to China. Money runs out very soon, of course, and the Fullers' fearful, reluctant appeal for aid to Newton's Uncle Stanley is of no avail. This self-important old rogue, who for decades has promised to leave them a fortune when he dies, is in fact a fraud. Left penniless in 1929, he has been exploiting his numerous nephews' hopes of a legacy ever since. Yet another blow to the Fullers is the explosion of the legend that George Washington had spent a night in the farmhouse. It had not been George Washington, but Benedict Arnold.

The play proceeds with intermittent merriment, but without a display of true wit. The characterization is slight and the twists of plot improbable, excessive, and dull. It was as though the old firm had gone bankrupt of ideas. In desperation, they extended the action by adding new problems having to do with the title to the land, the pregnancy of an unmarried servant, and the heartpangs of the daughter, none of which amounts to much. To bring the play to a close was, one guesses, especially difficult for the team. It had to come out that the Fullers could afford to keep their place and that they would worst their cranky neighbor's claims that he owned the road to the house and the land on which, finally, they had struck water. What to do? A historic map supplied by a pleasant woman who heads the County Historical Society supplies the evidence that the Fullers own both the road and the site of the well. As to getting the necessary cash to prevent the bank's foreclosure, Uncle Stanley by bluff gets them out of this difficulty by maintaining his pose of tycoon at an encounter with Prescott and threatening to bring in his lawyers if Prescott, bank-director as well as neighbor, causes trouble. Thus, all the problems vanish. But they do not vanish before the Fullers, believing that they have lost the house to the bank, decide to return it to its original condition. After belting a few whiskeys, they, their dour caretaker, and the amorous actor's wife have at the windows, the walls, the banisters, and even the roof with hammers, saws, seltzer water, and pails of garbage. The place is thus made a shambles once more, and after that a hurricane strikes. In this mayhem the famous Kaufmanian antisentimentalism is once more in evidence, but with a new, uncomic bluntness, though doubtless some members of the audience laughed at it. As a way to end the play, this vandalism struck a note that was, and remains, sour, if not repellent.

Kaufman began rehearsals in late August with a view to opening the try-out tour in Hartford on September 20. He had a new stage on which to assemble his cast for the reading: the Lyceum Theater, which, in July, he, Hart, Sam Harris, Max Gordon, and Marcus Heiman (a long-time associate of Gordon's) had bought. This theater had been built by Daniel Frohman in 1903. Gordon installed his office on one of its upper floors. It was planned that the play would open at the Lyceum in October, and that it would be the home of future productions of the various owners. When asked why, after all these years he felt the need to have a theater of his own, Kaufman liked to say that it was not his own theater that he wanted so much as his own lavatory in midtown.

The cast assembled for *George Washington Slept Here* included three well-known stage actors who, in the years immediately preceding this production, had been working exclusively in Hollywood. For Uncle Stanley, Kaufman engaged the veteran character actor Berton Churchill. Ernest Truex played Newton. For the role of Annabelle, Kaufman had the good fortune to lure Jean Dixon back to the stage. Though in its comic acidity the part resembled those she had taken in *June Moon* and *Once in a Lifetime*, it was not written with her in mind. Having been scorched by her firm refusal to appear in *The American Way*, the writers did not think of approaching her with it. Helen Broderick, the comedienne who had appeared to excellent advantage in *The Band Wagon*, was their choice, but, like Jean Dixon, she had made a name for herself as a wisecracking screen actress and had no wish to return to Broadway. Faced with this rebuff, they turned—this time with a reasonable salary proposal—to Jean Dixon, who surprised them, and perhaps herself, by agreeing to take the role without so much as a glance at the script. "For all I knew," she later told the press, "it might very well have been a bit part of a Sicilian streetwalker."[31]

It was a feeling of guilt for having disappointed Kaufman over *The American Way* that led the actress to accept this new role. As rehearsals started, she began to regret her decision. Friction developed between her and Truex, who demanded center stage and resented the moments in the action when she was called upon to imitate him. To make matters worse, she had a painful quarrel with Kaufman about one of her lines: "I'm so sick of sucking up to Uncle Stanley." When she complained that she found the line offensive, he asked since when she had become so genteel. Greatly troubled by his tone, she said, "I always have been, only you never had the grace to recognize it." With that she threw down her copy of the script, announced that she was through with the play, and walked out of the rehearsal. It was then

Kaufman's turn to be troubled; never before in their nearly twenty years of friendship had she revealed such temperament. His response, quite out of character, was to telephone her in the evening, not only to ask that she return to the cast, but to inquire how she would like him to alter the line. She suggested "buttering up" as an improvement. Kaufman consented to this, and Jean Dixon agreed to take up her role again. Later the entire line was excised from the script. The actress also found distasteful a reference to the impossible adolescent Raymond, Annabelle's nephew, as Huckleberry Hauptmann, an allusion to Bruno Hauptmann, the kidnapper of the Lindbergh baby, and Kaufman obligingly altered this to Huckleberry Capone. Thus was peace restored.[32]

But it was peace without the benison of ease. At the out-of-town opening, which took place in Hartford on September 21, the play was revealed to be in need of incisive revision. *Variety's* reviewer called it a "quickie," and complained that the script appeared to be "sleeping through the major part of two acts."[33] In New Haven, where the production next stopped, Jean Dixon appealed to Kaufman to let her out of the cast. She was still unable to achieve rapport with Truex on stage and shuddered at the prospect of spending a season on Broadway with him. A comedian himself, he resented the fact that she had the best lines, and he could not resist the temptation of coming in too soon on them—in actors' parlance, "stepping" on them—and spoiling her laughs. But Kaufman was adamant on holding her to her contract, and she said no more about it and got on with her part.[34]

Yet the situation was no better in Boston. Jean Dixon was not alone in being annoyed with Truex, who continued to kill the other actors' laughs. He also added a piece of stage business for himself that promised to cause trouble and, soon enough, did so. Perhaps to make up for his small stature, he would leap on a table in the third-act mayhem scene to squirt a syphon of soda over the wreckage of the living room. Kaufman permitted it, but warned Truex that he could easily fall off the table and injure himself. One evening it came to pass as Kaufman had foreseen: Truex fell and hurt his knee so badly that it was necessary to cancel a performance. The first few rows of the audience were treated to a stage whisper from one of the actors: "That's one line he won't step on again."[35]

The remainder of the Boston run passed without bringing a further trial of the company's nerves. Returning to New York, they braced themselves for the opening on October 11. On October 10, when the cast met at the Lyceum for the dress rehearsal, Berton Churchill was missing. When a telephone call to the actor's hotel room got no answer, Kaufman dispatched the stage manager, Henry Ephron, to roust Churchill. Within minutes, Ephron came back to the theater to report that Churchill was dead. The opening was postponed, and the Harris office notified the press that a search was in progress to find another actor of comparable reputation to fill the role of Uncle Stanley. Fortunately, Dudley Digges, a character actor who had long been a favorite with New York audiences, was available. Within a week he was ready to go on in the part.[36] Harris, in an unexpected show of niggardliness, took the position that Churchill's death was that sort of disaster categorized by the law as "an act of God," and attempted to withhold the company's salaries for the week that the play was closed. Equity would have none of this; nor would the American Arbitration Association.[37]

The reviews that followed the opening on October 18, while not ruinously unfavorable, were hardly laudatory. Broun, writing in the *World-Telegram*, said of the play, "It cannot hold a candle to *The Man Who Came to Dinner*. It is not to be mentioned in the same breath with *You Can't Take It with You*." Atkinson told *Times* readers in his second notice of the play that "the Bucks County homes of Mr. Kaufman and Mr. Hart have yielded one of their least amusing plays. *The Fabulous Invalid* of two seasons ago at least represented some thinking and involved a notable stage production. But *George Washington Slept Here* represents nothing in particular except the annual necessity of writing a play." Kaufman and Hart, as these and other reviewers suggested, were paying the price of being Kaufman and Hart: they had established standards for themselves which they could not always meet. In the *Sun* Richard Lockridge said it most pointedly: "*George Washington Slept Here* would be a mighty funny little play to be written by a couple of playwrights named Joe, and everybody could predict that they were going places." The Harris office tried to use Lockridge's review by taking out advertisements that quoted it and gave the authors' names as Joe Kaufman and Joe Hart. John Peter Toohey, then the press agent for the firm, got a few items about the play into Broadway gossip columns—for example, that Uncle Stanley was modeled after one of Kaufman's own rich uncles and that the ineffable child Raymond, though named for the manager of Hart's farm, was actually a portrait of Hart at age fourteen. When, late in October, it became legal, at last, for the New York theaters to offer Sunday performances, Harris scheduled them for the play in the hope of improving the box-office take. With aid coming thus from one quarter and another, *George Washington Slept Here* enjoyed a run of 173 performances. Close to the end, on March 6, 1941, a piece in the Bucks County *Times* unwittingly gave a clue as to why it got no more. By performance 150, according to this essay, the number of items destroyed in the third-act havoc ran to 1200 window panes, 550 light bulbs, 1500 banister spindles, 1200 plates, and 76 pairs of curtains, in addition to which the contents of 150 seltzer bottles had been sprayed over the wreckage.[38]

But all was not lost. Stock rights were made available as soon as the production closed, and the managers of summer theaters scrambled to secure them in the belief that the country-house owners among their patrons would relish the sight of the Fullers suffering through renovations as they themselves had. On the Eastern "straw hat trail" in 1941, it was the most popular new play, with ten productions scheduled.[39] To offset further the loss on the run, a sale of film rights was successfully negotiated with Warner Brothers. The studio wanted the comedy for Jack Benny, and, recognizing that Annabelle had the best lines, produced a revised version in which it is the wife who pines for a country place and the husband who cares only for town.

Looking back a quarter of a century later, Henry Ephron thought that the play might have had more of a chance on Broadway if Churchill had not died. Digges was good, but, in Ephron's opinion, the energy of the production was somehow vitiated when he took over. It also seemed to him that Kaufman, recognizing that Jean Dixon was the outstanding member of his company, paid too little attention to the others' performances. The actress, looking back over the same number of years, thought that Kaufman and Hart might have made a better thing of the comedy if their minds had been squarely on it as it made its way to the Lyceum. Though neither writer was indifferent to it, of course, each had his mind on another project. To Hart the impending production of *Lady in the Dark* was virtually all-important, and Kaufman had agreed to direct a new comedy, *My Sister Eileen,* by Joseph Fields and Jerome Chodorov, for Max Gordon. It was Hart who took the play to Gordon and gave him the notion of inviting Kaufman to direct it. The young authors believed that he did it to give his friend something to do while *Lady in the Dark* was in preparation. Kaufman read their many drafts of the comedy and recommended changes and more changes even as the production of *George Washington* was getting under way. But all the while he too had an eye on *Lady in the Dark;* he hoped for Hart's success, but recognized, without having to be told, the fact that if the play was the hit for which Hart yearned, the old partnership would probably come to an end.[40]

In the meanwhile, Beatrice's comedy, *The White-Haired Boy,* had had its brief moment and was no more. Under Abbott's direction, it opened in Boston on October 28, with Kaufman sitting hopefully beside his wife. She

had not wanted to go into rehearsals until *George Washington Slept Here*
had its Boston opening, which she, of course, attended. Shaky as that comedy
was, it at least had touches here and there of the hands of master craftsmen.
That Beatrice and Martin were no more than apprentices by comparison
was all too evident at the tryout performances. The intended laugh lines
were dull, the action was frantic, and the playwright protagonist was, in the
words of *Variety*, "all too grimly fatuous."[41] Though it was scheduled to come
into New York on November 6, Abbott decided to withdraw it after the Boston
week. After this, her second effort at playmaking, Beatrice, disappointed but
realistic, realized that if she was to be a writer at all, her best course lay in
the pursuit of a career in journalism. In 1934 she had pasted into her scrapbook all the telegrams she received before the New Haven opening of *Divided by Three*, and the reviews as well. In 1940 she still had the scrapbook,
but after the debacle of *The White-Haired Boy*, she decided against saving
any such mementoes of that play's fleeting life.

Matching her disappointment was the annoyance that Kaufman was put
to by still more plagiarism suits. Both *Stage Door* and *The American Way*
were suddenly alleged by various unknowns to have been purloined from
their manuscript plays. Like all the others, these suits were decided in Kaufman's favor, but his patience was tried. To Woollcott he wrote,

> Ferber and I went down about a month ago and spent two days in court
> being sued on *Stage Door*. And now it turns out we stole *The American
> Way* too. The questions on *Stage Door* were keen and to the point:
>   "Now having planned the play, did you and Miss Ferber thereupon
> sit down, indite, write, and compose said play?"
>   "No, you dumb son of a bitch, we went to the ball game that day and
> came home and there it was, finished."[42]

For Hart, good fortune lay in store. The worry that had hung over him
through the tryout tour and first Broadway weeks of *George Washington
Slept Here* lifted on November 16, when, in Grand Rapids, Michigan, Gertrude Lawrence gave her last performances on tour with *Skylark* and became free to commence rehearsals of *Lady in the Dark*. John Golden, the
producer of the Raphaelson play, had insisted that he had a call on the star's
services for a tour throughout the season, but, with an appeal to Equity, she
was released from it at last. Contemplating an exceedingly elaborate production that required four revolving stages and hundreds of costumes at a
financial layout of $130,000—a staggering figure then—and lengthy musical
numbers alternating with the dramatic scenes, Harris and Hart extracted
from Equity the privilege of holding five weeks of rehearsals instead of the

customary four. Since so unwieldy a show could not be trouped from city to city on a tryout tour, they scheduled three weeks of performances to be given in Boston, beginning on December 30.

Meanwhile, Kaufman was busy with rehearsals of Chodorov and Fields's *My Sister Eileen,* which was scheduled to open in New York on December 26, with no out-of-town tour. The play was based on a group of *New Yorker* sketches by Ruth McKenny about the adventures in Greenwich Village of herself and her sister, two young women who had come to the city from Ohio in search of careers in journalism and the theater. It had taken the playwrights several weeks of hard work to put their script into a form that satisfied Kaufman, but so happy were they to have a Gordon production under Kaufman's direction that they raised no objections to his demands. Knowing of his sweet tooth, they plied him with candy whenever he met with them; it was not good candy, but he accepted the thought for the gift. Both were impressed, as others had been, not only by the intensity with which he approached the task of directing the play, but by his skill in drawing from the actors performances of just the proper shade. For the central role of Ruth McKenny, the authors wanted Shirley Booth, and, all for amity, Kaufman agreed. The actress, who was not yet the star that she would become in the 1950s, came to read for the role. Though she looked, to Chodorov, like "a busted bale of hay," she had the humor and the grace that the role required.[43]

With its barrages of wisecracks and bustling activity, *My Sister Eileen* bore a resemblance to the Kaufman-and-Hart comedies. But Fields and Chodorov included one scene of a sort not to be found in any work of the more famous pair: a sentimental passage of dialogue in the third act in which it is revealed that the two sisters are in love with the same man. Marveling at his expertise in leading the actors through their lines, the authors were unprepared for his response to this scene when the company arrived at it. He could not face it. Putting down his copy of the script, he turned to Chodorov and Fields and said, "All right. You two wrote it. Now you can direct it."[44]

Not much talk circulated on Broadway about *My Sister Eileen* before the opening. Nor was the advance sale large. An incoming production with good out-of-town reviews could be counted on to create its own publicity, but since this comedy was to open "cold," no such reviews had been in circulation. On Sunday, December 22, an event distressful to all concerned with the production occurred, and Gordon gave serious thought to putting off the opening until the cast had recovered from it. Driving home from Los Angeles after a weekend hunting trip in Mexico, the real Eileen McKenny and her husband, Nathanael West, the novelist and screenwriter, were involved in an automobile smashup. West, a notoriously bad driver, failed to obey a stop sign before turning onto a highway. Both died without regaining consciousness. The cast found it painful to go on with the play, and Chodorov and Fields, who had known West in Hollywood, had to steel themselves to complete some last-minute revamping of the script. It was Kaufman who urged the company to pull itself together and open on schedule, with the suggestion that the unfailing excitement of an opening night would sustain their performance. He was right. The two preview performances were disappointing, but on the official first night, with new lines to bolster the third act, the company rose to the occasion. So well received was the comedy that it stayed on Broadway for 865 performances, to become the ninth-longest-running play on Broadway at the time of its closing.[45]

With this production behind him (though the authors tinkered with the final scene even after the opening), Kaufman lost no time in getting to Boston for Hart's last days before the premier performance of *Lady in the Dark*. Like many, if not most musicals in preparation, this one was overlong. Hart, immensely eager to gain a new reputation as a writer—an independent writer—of serious plays, besought Kaufman to advise him on how to pare it down to practical length without disturbing the quality of the performance. As they labored over this task, cutting a passage of dialogue here, a song there, and striving for an effect of seamlessness, Kaufman found it necessary to eliminate one of the scenes of a character named Alison Du Bois, a fashion writer on the staff of Liza Elliott's magazine. An attractive madcap with a limitless enthusiasm for anything describable as "chic," the character bore a resemblance to *Harper's Bazaar*'s Diana Vreeland, a living legend in the field of fashion reporting. Hart had had Natalie Schafer in mind when he created the part, and she had been cast in it. Kaufman sensed that the shortening of her role was no small disappointment to her. As she sat in the orchestra of the Colonial Theater, and fought to hold back her tears, she saw Kaufman's lanky frame sidling along the row of seats. They had not met before that occasion. He sat beside her and explained, or tried to explain, that her role would be stronger for the pruning, since all the good things in it remained, and only the weak, unhelpful lines were gone. To this show-business wisdom she made no direct reply; instead, remembering the treats that had been given her in childhood to compensate for disappointments, she turned to him and said, "Please get me an ice cream soda." Kaufman happily ran up the aisle and out of the theater to comply with her request. He did not know, but might have been even happier if he had, that in doing so he took the first steps toward forming one of the longest-lasting, most successful of his romantic relationships.[46]

As for *Lady in the Dark,* it opened to sustained applause in Boston, with Kaufman and Beatrice in the audience. No question remained that in New York it would become one of the biggest draws of the season. The performances of Gertrude Lawrence and Danny Kaye, the presence in the cast of Victor Mature ("a beautiful hunk of man" as the Kaye character described him), the melodic score by Weill, and the witty lyrics of Ira Gershwin—his first since his brother's death—and the unstinted spilling of *grande luxe* across four revolving stages made for an evening of such glamour as would seldom be seen again. It was enthusiastically welcomed by an audience in need of escape, an audience sensing that the Depression was drawing to a close but made tense by the Nazi conquests abroad. The demand for tickets set a record for sold-out houses.

To Hart the success of the play supplied the hoped-for confirmation of the strength of his talent. True, he had drawn on the skills of a composer and a lyricist of distinction and thus had not created the work wholly on his own, but at least he could claim that the concept of the play was his. He did not announce that he would never write with Kaufman again; on the contrary, over the next three years he did write with Kaufman on several occasions. But he would not again feel an obligation, either personal or financial, to collaborate with the senior playwright every spring. To tell this to Kaufman was painful to Hart, but it had to be done, and Hart did it.[47] To the columnist Robert Rice, who, as the son of the prolific playwright Elmer Rice, knew something about compulsive playwriting, Hart offered a comment for publication:

> One reason for writing *Lady in the Dark* was my increasing disinterest for plays with plots; for what is known as "the well-made play." I'm speaking not only as an author, but as a fairly regular member of the theater audience. I've become much more interested in characters than in stories.
> Another reason is that over the last few years I've literally sabotaged every serious idea I've had for a play. And so my psychoanalyst made me resolve that the next idea I had, whether it was good or lousy, I'd carry through. This was my next idea, and it was about the toughest one I've ever had to realize.
> And now, as the result of *Lady*'s success, and my own trend along a path of playwriting that isn't George Kaufman's métier, I can afford not

to feel obligated to write a play every year, or to continue to work with George just for the sake of collaborating with him.

But don't misunderstand me. George Kaufman is the swellest person I know, and I haven't broken with him one single bit. *Lady in the Dark* just isn't his kind of play. If I get another idea that is, sure I'll go back to work with him. If not, then I won't. Right now I have no ideas at all. I'm going to take a rest.[48]

——18——

Wartime

When the curtain rang up on 1941, Kaufman, as author, was represented on Broadway by *The Man Who Came to Dinner* and *George Washington Slept Here* and in Chicago by the former; as director, by both these plays and *My Sister Eileen;* and, as investor, by all of them and *Lady in the Dark,* which was warming a huge nightly throng in Boston while preparing for the scheduled New York opening on January 23. With weekly royalties and investment returns from these productions mounting comfortably into five figures, with additional income from the rental of the Lyceum, where *George Washington* was playing, and with returns coming to Beatrice from her investments in all the productions, the economic future of the Kaufman family was solid. Soon there would be a Chicago company of *My Sister Eileen* to bring in even more, to say nothing of the royalties from amateur productions that Samuel French and the Dramatists' Play Service sent in monthly. Even the chronically worried son of the improvident Joseph Kaufman could now forget himself long enough to draw an untroubled breath once in a while. But a day was not full enough that included nothing more than a late-afternoon session of bridge at the Regency Club, an evening's socializing, and an inspection tour of his plays to see whether the companies were speaking the dialogue as written. Kaufman needed something more to do.

In this year of tension and uncertainty, all that could be safely predicted for the future was that somehow, at some point, the United States would be drawn into the fighting. The number of theatrical charities and benefit performances related to the war proliferated, and in them Kaufman found an outlet for his energy. His first such activity of the year not only helped the

Allied war effort, but inadvertently served a second, infinitely lesser cause: it allowed Ethel Barrymore to revenge herself on Kaufman, after some thirteen years, for his alleged depiction of her clan in *The Royal Family*. With Gilbert Miller in charge, the American Theater Wing planned a gala "Carnival for Britain" to take place at the Radio City Music Hall at midnight on February 21. Kaufman and Vinton Freedley were to organize the evening's bill. Between them, they had no difficulty in getting up a good program, since most professional performers were glad to serve the interest of England. But (and it was to become a part of Broadway lore) they suffered one major disappointment. All three of the theater's illustrious Ethels—Barrymore, Merman, and Waters—were then starring on Broadway, and to Kaufman it seemed only reasonable that they should be on the bill together. Merman and Waters were happy to oblige, but Barrymore declined to have anything to do with Kaufman. She parried his request with a line spoken by Julie Cavendish in *The Royal Family* when asked to take part in a benefit: on the evening of the twenty-first, she expected to have bronchitis. Merman and Waters did well enough without her. On separate sides of the stage they emerged from hansom cabs. Assisted by Howard Lindsay, Joe Cook, and Bill Robinson, each sang two numbers with which she was associated. No singer, though a good amateur pianist, Ethel Barrymore would have suffered from the competition.[1]

A few days later, on February 24, it was announced that Kaufman and Robert E. Sherwood, among others, had been named to the Army and Navy Committee on Welfare and Recreation, whose purpose it was to develop entertainment for service men. On May 8, at Seagirt, New Jersey, this committee put on its first show, under the direction of Leonard Sillman. Eventually the committee's work was taken over by the United Service Organization (the familiar USO), but without further assistance from Kaufman, Sherwood, and Sillman, who were informed by the Wall Streeters in charge that in their opinion the organization's funding could be managed better by the financial community than by theater workers.[2]

In March the itch to get something under way for fall presentation became too distracting for Kaufman to ignore. He had no chance of luring Hart back to his study—so much was clear—and he did not care to write again with either Connelly or Ryskind (neither of whom at this point may have cared to write with him). That left, of the major collaborators of the past, only Ferber. He had vetoed one proposal that she put forward: that they write a play set in Saratoga Springs in the "Gilded Age" of the nineteenth century. That idea she was busy turning into a novel, which eventually she published as *Saratoga Trunk,* but in the meanwhile she was willing to interrupt herself long enough to write a play with him, if they could agree on a serious enough subject. The play that they had often discussed—tepidly on Kaufman's part, one suspects—about the history of the Jews did not rise again, but the idea that replaced it had the same generating force behind it: the desire to take a stand against Hitlerian tyranny. The new plan was that they should write about the distinguished European refugees who were beginning to appear in New York in numbers great enough to make their presence felt in the city's creative and professional life. It might have been predicted that when Ferber and Kaufman took up this subject, the profession whose refugee members they would write about was their own, the theater.

The better to concentrate on their play, Kaufman and Ferber decided to isolate themselves for ten days in early March at the Greenbrier Hotel in White Sulphur Springs, West Virginia. There they expected at least to outline the plot. But this one play, assuming that they would be able to create it, would not serve as a complete Kaufman season. Before leaving New York, he found another play to put on his fall schedule. That was *Premiere,* a satiric murder mystery by Arthur Sheekman and Margaret Shane. Kaufman had known Sheekman, a writer for the Marx Brothers and an intimate of Groucho's, for many years. He had been one of the team who replaced Kaufman and Sherwood on *Roman Scandals* when the two playwrights refused to rewrite their script. Shane was a newspaperwoman and novelist. Sheekman had earlier sent a copy of the script to Kaufman and notified him that it was to be performed at Columbia University on March 3 by a student cast. Kaufman attended the first performance, along with Max Gordon. They were not the only Broadway operators present; Lee Shubert was also in attendance. The authors had elected to conceal their identity under a single pseudonym, Grant Woodford, presumably to avoid embarrassment and loss of prestige (always a danger to a Hollywood writer) if the play should prove to be a disaster.[3]

Nobody was disappointed, however. Kaufman was so pleased that he made an offer for the professional rights on the spot. He expected to produce the comedy himself. Though one of the authors had already arrived at an informal agreement with Lee Shubert for the rights, the prospect of a production supervised by Kaufman was too bright with promise to be overlooked. Sheekman and Shane quickly came to terms with Kaufman. Shubert was cut in for a 17.5 per cent share. And, Kaufman explained, Shubert would turn out to be very lucky to have only that much if the play failed.[4]

Satisfied that he had got hold of something good, but recognizing that the script needed improvement, Kaufman set the authors to work on alterations with a view to a fall production. Their first change was in the title, which became *Mr. Big,* which had been one of their working titles.

That business out of the way, Kaufman left with Ferber for White Sulphur Springs. Some months later, he wrote about their stay at the resort for the *Times.* To his readers he made it clear that the refugee idea had never shone brightly in his imagination, and that such dim luster as it possessed began to fade even as he and his collaborator set foot on West Virginia soil: "A splendid cold rain greeted us as we came down the steps; the car had pulled off into a siding, and there wasn't a porter in sight. It was precisely at that moment that the refugee idea began to slip. As days passed, it was destined to get worse and worse, but I should say that the instant of our descent of those car steps was when it first started to go."[5] Yet they remained at the Greenbrier for the scheduled ten days in the hope that somehow they could spin a plot at whose center would be an émigré playwright of international fame and on whose periphery would be a woman of an old New York family who would lend the playwright a house on Gramercy Square in which to live until he and his family were established. As a model for the playwright they had in mind Ferenc Molnár, who had recently come to New York from Budapest.

The continuing wetness of the weather and the lack of diversions had a dampening effect on their spirits. Whenever the rain stopped, Ferber went out for an invigorating walk, as she frequently did in New York or Connecticut, to which she had recently moved. But for Kaufman, who cared nothing for physical exercise, the atmosphere of the Greenbrier was continuously oppressive. Finally, the pair of friends abandoned their original idea; it dawned on them that they knew too little about the psychology of refugees to describe it convincingly in dramatic action. Yet something was salvageable from the dreary sojourn. What had been peripheral to their plot suddenly took the center, and the central issue of the plight of the refugees shifted ground in turn: they decided to write about an old New York family that finds itself making a home for its expatriate relations at the outbreak of the war in Europe. This new notion came too late to be developed in White Sulphur Springs, but they carried it away in their heads. Later in the spring, when the mild weather came, they went off to Atlantic City to examine it further.

Meanwhile, disquieting news arrived from Florida. Sam Harris, wintering in Palm Springs as usual, complained of intestinal pain and on March 4 underwent an exploratory operation. Though reported by the press as appendicitis, it was cancer from which he suffered. To Woollcott, Kaufman sent a brief but poignant note: "Sam Harris is desperately ill and we are all heartbroken."[6] Harris, then sixty-nine, was not strong enough to recover quickly from the surgery. He remained in his winter home until he was sufficiently out of danger to be moved to his New York apartment in the Ritz Towers. When possible, he visited his office, but only rarely did he have the stamina for such activity. With the unlamented closing of *George Washington Slept Here* on March 19, he was represented on Broadway by only *Lady in the Dark*. In spite of the gravity of his illness, he confidently made some plans for the fall. Kaufman and Ferber notified him of their intention of having a script ready by September, and this work, still unwritten, he entered on his schedule. The playwrights let the scheduling stand, content to let Harris imagine he would be strong enough to produce their play, but knowing that almost certainly they would have to find another producer.

Though that cloud hung over them, the summer was a more than usually full one for the Kaufmans. To one event of the season that heaped honor on him, he paid, or affected to pay, scant attention. It was the festival of his plays held at the Pasadena Playhouse under the direction of Gilmor Brown. The Playhouse, founded in 1918 and renowned nationally as both an acting school and a subscription theater, in 1935 had begun the practice of offering a special summer season of works by a single author or a series of plays related by subject. Shakespeare's plays were given in the first two summers, and subsequent seasons were devoted to the plays of Shaw, Maxwell Anderson, and James M. Barrie, and a series of plays on the Southwest. Kaufman's season opened on June 23, 1941, with *Beggar on Horseback;* the plays that followed were *George Washington Slept Here, Dinner at Eight, Minick, Once in a Lifetime, You Can't Take It with You, The Royal Family,* and *The Man Who Came to Dinner*. The season, which gave the Playhouse a box-office bonanza, marked Kaufman's elevation to a new level of public regard. Though a reporter for the New York *Times* commented that the honoring of Kaufman was "a wartime variation"—that is, a decision on the part of the Playhouse director to give an anxious public a chance to laugh—the fact was that the choice of Kaufman reflected the growing admiration for him as a solid, reliable contributor to the contemporary stage. Yet he stayed in the East while the Festival took place, never once appearing at it. Shyly and slyly, but revealing clearly that he could not be budged, he declared that he did not know what a drama festival was. He sat it out in Pennsylvania and Connecticut, at work on his *new* play.[7]

For Beatrice, the summer had a glow not quite like any other. A new young man entered her life, and if it was possible for anyone to be in love with two persons at once, then Beatrice was in love with both her husband and this young man. In the spring she had been asked to be an occasional contributor to *PM,* the new tabloid-size, progressive daily newspaper published by Ralph Ingersoll, and now and then she made appearances at the paper's offices, as much to see friends there as to look for assignments. On the staff was William Walton, handsome, intellectual, and, at thirty-three, some fourteen years younger than she. No sooner did they meet than they were drawn to each other. The difference in their ages did not seem to matter to either of them; nor did the fact that Walton was married and a father. Though she did not ask Walton to Barley Sheaf Farm that summer, she delighted in presenting him to her friends in town. Kaufman was aware of the relationship, but was no more troubled by it than he had been by her affairs in the past.[8]

Beatrice offered Walton free admission to her secret life, such as it was, commenting openly to him on her prolonged psychoanalysis, teasing him about the fact that he was not Jewish, speaking with true affection of her husband, and constantly bringing into their conversation the great but platonic passion of her life, Moss Hart. She also confided that though she was still in her forties, she sensed that physically she was running down. Little signs had begun to appear of a circulatory problem—an irregular rhythm of the heart—and some ominous bumps had developed along the line of her jaw. They were diagnosed as skin cancers. It was perhaps because of these signs of mortality that Beatrice gave so much of herself to Walton, as though realizing that this was to be the last great romantic relationship of her life, which, in fact, it proved to be.[9]

At the time this affair was beginning, the tension created for the Kaufmans and their friends by Harris's illness came to its end. Harris died at his apartment on July 7. For Kaufman, it was an occasion not only for grief but uncertainty about the future. Their relationship had always been singularly amicable. No producer of the day had had a firmer hold on the affection of his fellow professionals, or had surpassed Harris in probity. Kaufman as well as the others who had worked with him were depressed at the prospect of continuing in the theater without him. Kaufman was left in a quandary over arrangements for the production of his play with Ferber. Preparations for the mounting of *Mr. Big* were going forward under the old team of Streger, Toohey, and Oenslager, and this would be a George S. Kaufman production. The thought of adding to this labor the preparation of the Ferber collaboration, a heavy, demanding work, did not appeal to him. Buttonholing Max Gordon, Kaufman suggested that he take over the play.

Gordon was, of course, the logical successor to Harris as Kaufman's producer, inasmuch as he and Harris had participated in each other's enterprises for the past decade. Like Harris, he was dependable and honest, a man who never equivocated. Those qualities, however, were not enough to make Kaufman always easy with him. Some quirks and crudenesses of the man—his table manners, his habit of telephoning when the message was not important—deprived him of dignity and, thus, in Kaufman's view, rendered the prospect of working only with him something less than a pleasure. Nevertheless, he was the inevitable choice. Kaufman's terms were steep, and his language indicated to Gordon where he (Gordon) stood in Kaufman's esteem. Between them, Kaufman and Ferber intended to keep 80 per cent of the play; Gordon could have the remainder. "It will mean a great deal of prestige to you," Kaufman said, "doing a play by Edna and me—even if it isn't a hit."[10] Though nettled by this, Gordon held his tongue, knowing that if he did not take this play on these terms he would not get any others from Kaufman.

But the play was still unwritten. In July the two writers settled in at Ferber's new country house, Treasure Hill, in Easton, Connecticut. By virtue of its moderate climate and the relative scarcity of show-business neighbors, this was a work-rendezvous superior to Barley Sheaf Farm, where the dankness would warp the typing paper and distracting invitations sped along the telephone wires at all times. But weighing heavily against the advantages of Ferber's house was the touchiness of her personality. Age had done nothing at all to mellow her. Beatrice, never happy in her presence, later passed on to Woollcott a little of what Kaufman told her about his stay at Treasure Hill. Every morning Ferber stormed into the work room, "breathing fire," and said, "I've been thinking about that scene we did last night. Now, maybe you don't care about honest writing, but I do." One hour after they finished their draft, Kaufman was at the railroad station waiting for his train out of Connecticut and wearing his summer work costume, a pair of shorts.[11] In the first week in August, following an interval in which Ferber began the final draft of her novel, *Saratoga Trunk*, she came down to Barley Sheaf Farm, and the pair dug in for the final honing of their play.[12]

The summer was also a busy one for Anne. Turning sixteen in June, she was developing into a young lady of attainments. Witty (to the delight of her father), and beginning to reveal an intellectual curiosity, she had no difficulty in forming a circle of friends. Her parents had denied her nothing of importance during her childhood, but at the same time had taken care not to overindulge her. She entered into and departed from adolescence without giving indications of being spoiled. She tended to accept what was allowed her without outward complaint, though underneath she could feel a growing determination to establish herself as an independent person, to get out in the world on her own, as soon as possible. Her parents decided to send her to Holmquist, a girls' boarding school in Bucks County, from which she could come to them at the farm on weekends. She was to begin at Holmquist in the fall. In the meanwhile, she came to know some engaging, energetic undergraduate males who were determined to enjoy the little period of freedom left to them before, as was inevitable, Selective Service reached out to claim them.

Enrolled at near-by Princeton was Patrick Watson, the stepson of Sam Harris. At Princeton, Watson was a member of the undergraduate dramatic organization, Theatre Intime. Among his good friends in the Intime was Clinton Wilder, who had entered the university from the Lawrenceville School in 1939 and had begun to read for parts in the Intime's productions. During the break between terms in 1941 he had accompanied Watson to the Harrises' house in Palm Beach, where Harris was soon to fall ill. After the producer's death in July, Harris's widow—called "China" because of a faintly Oriental look about her eyes—spent the remainder of the summer in the Bucks County home of the Oscar Hammersteins. Watson and Wilder, suffering through sweaty summer classes in an effort to fill some gaps in their credits toward graduation, spent their weekends there. China Harris, who warned the boys to beware of the Kaufmans' sharp-tongued daughter, took them one weekend to Barley Sheaf Farm. They returned to the farm often after this initial, experimental visit, for Anne proved to be very good company. But it was, of course, also a pleasure for them to see something of Kaufman and Hart, and to have glimpses of Harpo, who, with his wife Susan, was staying with the Kaufmans, and Danny Kaye, who, on summer furlough from his role in *Lady in the Dark,* came with his wife, Sylvia Fine, to visit Hart. To Wilder especially, who unlike Watson had not previously known such exalted members of the theatrical profession, these weekends were stimulating occasions.[13]

To the undergraduates one of the treats of the summer of 1941 was the presentation at the Bucks County Playhouse of *The Man Who Came to Dinner* with Kaufman as Sheridan Whiteside, Hart as Beverly Carlton, and Harpo as himself. When it became known that the Broadway production would close on July 12, making the play available to stock companies, Theron Bamberger, the proprietor of the Playhouse, was struck with the idea of offering the play to his customers with the authors and their antic friend as the stars. It was scheduled to open on July 29, the earliest possible date, with Edith Atwater resuming the role of Maggie Cutler and Janet Fox filling in as Miss Preen. So overwhelming was the demand for tickets that, with the agreement of the actors, Bamberger scheduled extra matinees. Even so, the Playhouse could not satisfy all the requests for tickets.

The play had the one week of rehearsals usual for summer stock, but not with Kaufman as director. He was content to leave rehearsals in the hands of William McFadden, the Playhouse's staff director. For three days prior to the rehearsal period, he went to Atlantic City with Anne to get up in his role. On the beach she fed him his cues; though the author of the script, he found it none too easy to master the part. Reports of the performance varied, but with such a cast it hardly mattered whether any member of it was convincing in his role; New Hope was jammed with cars for the entire week. To Edith Atwater's mind, Harpo gave the best account of himself. Doubtless for many in the audience, it was a surprise to hear him speak on stage; though barely able to read, he managed to learn his lines. On the opening night Beatrice sat in the first row, as though by her presence to urge her husband to do his best. It astonished some members of the audience who recognized her that this woman, usually a model of self-control, should appear nervous throughout the performance.[14]

Beatrice took herself and her daughter off to Nantucket after the play completed its run. Ferber, not wanting to miss her niece's performance as Miss Preen, had arrived at Barley Sheaf Farm in time for the last night and was scheduled to remain for a week of work sessions with Kaufman. But Beatrice had no intention of playing hostess to her for so long a visit.

When her week was up, Ferber returned to Connecticut to work on the final draft of her novel. At that time, the play was pronounced officially ready for production. Publicized briefly as *Three Acts,* it was soon retitled *The Land Is Bright.* Kaufman himself lost no time in beginning rehearsals of the cast of *Mr. Big,* which was scheduled to begin its tryout tour on September 6 in Hartford.

Between them, he and Myra Streger had assembled a company of skilled, if not stellar, actors that included Hume Cronyn, Florenz Ames, Oscar Polk (a Kaufman "regular"), and two recruits from Hollywood, Betty Furness and Fay Wray, the latter a star in films, but rather an unknown quantity in the theater. This first Kaufman-mounted play was no shoestring production venture. But it failed, and dismally. Its gloomy destiny was evident in Hartford, where the audience found little fun in the authors' gibes at political office-seekers and seemed only fitfully interested in the discovery of the murderer. Kaufman kept it out another three weeks and strove to improve the pacing and the jokes, but to no avail. On September 30, a Tuesday, the play opened on Broadway, and on Saturday it closed. The undertaking was a painful reminder of the comment once made by Kaufman that satire is what closes on Saturday night. Brooks Atkinson remarked in the *Times* that whenever Kaufman decided to produce another play, his career as producer could only take a turn for the better.[15] Lee Shubert was in luck after all.

Rehearsals for the unfortunate *Mr. Big* had progressed only two weeks when Kaufman began rehearsing *The Land Is Bright*, dividing his days between the two productions. Max Gordon, whose love of politics and politicians was only slightly less intense than his love of the theater and its artists, elected to try out the play in Washington, where he could hobnob with friends in office and pay social calls at the White House. The play was political in the large sense of advocating, none too subtly, that the United States enter the European war. The title itself offered homage to Winston Churchill; it came from a poem by Arthur Hugh Clough that Churchill quoted in a speech of April 1941. Kaufman and Ferber printed the stanza from which the title was taken as an epigraph in the program for the play and, later, the published text. For the trial run, the patronage of official Washington was assured; newspapers reported that in the opening night audience were, among other capital city luminaries, Mrs. Roosevelt, Vice President Henry Wallace, and Senator Alben Barkley. Business was brisk.

In New York, where it opened at the Music Box on October 28, the reviews were mixed. There was more of Ferber than Kaufman in the play; her sentimental fondness for dynastic families and her tendency to relish the ways of the rich weighed heavily against the few bright lines that she and Kaufman allowed themselves. More damaging, possibly, was the fact that after the first act (so well constructed that it might have existed on its own as a one-act piece), the second and third acts sloped downward into anticlimax. The action covered a forty-five-year span. The characters, consisting of a staggeringly rich family with a fortune originating in Western railroads, were shown in the difficult, drawn-out process of achieving social distinction and a civilized, magnanimous outlook on their fellow men. First met in its Fifth Avenue mansion (the scene of all three acts), the Kincaid family is still an unpolished, Western clan whose head is avid for power to match his wealth. At the end of Act I, he is shot and killed by a former partner outraged by his high-handedness. In the second and third acts, the family gradually takes on some graces to match its airs. At the close, painfully aware that their massive riches were the product of their chief forebear's systematic plundering of the federal government in the expansionist years of the last century, they are prepared now to do their patriotic duty: the current head of the family's companies intends to volunteer for a job in Washington, and his elder son has enlisted in the Army Air Corps. In their various ways, all the Kincaids have come along nicely and are ready at last to contribute something of themselves to the country that has made them rich. A talky play, it proclaimed its patriotic message over and over. Singled out for flattering praise was Diana Barrymore, who appeared in the second act as a neurotic, thrill-seeking flapper and in the last, some fifteen or sixteen years older, as a mature matron living contentedly in the West as the wife of a cattle-breeder. If anything lifted the last two acts above the mundane, it was her artful performance. This was, however, not enough to save the play, which Max Gordon reluctantly closed after 79 performances.

The Land Is Bright was not the only well-meaning play of late 1941 to fall short of its producer's expectations. Maxwell Anderson's *Candle in the Wind,* Norman Krasna's *The Man with Blond Hair,* and Fritz Rotter and Allen Vincent's *Letters to Lucerne,* each a play about the Nazi menace, lost at the box office despite some merit in the writing, as did other, less interesting plays on the same theme. More anti-Nazi plays opened in the new year to little applause. With the mounting expectation that the United States would soon join the Allies, it seemed only reasonable to producers to offer works on aspects of the war. None took, however—with the striking exception of *Let's Face It,* a musical with songs by Cole Porter that starred Danny Kaye in the role of a young man caught in the peacetime draft. What Max Gordon lost on Kaufman and Ferber's anti-Nazi piece he more than made up on a comedy remote from the issues of the war: Fields and Chodorov's *Junior Miss,* directed by Hart. Kaufman and Hart, who were among the backers, also profited from the success of the play, which opened on November 18. Broadway, three thousand miles away from the war that was reducing London to rubble, was still aglow nightly, and the throngs who were drawn to it had no taste for reminders of the European horrors. Suited to their mood were easy-going works such as *Junior Miss,* the still-running *My Sister Eileen, Lady in the Dark,* and Noel Coward's *Blithe Spirit,* which opened on November 5. (Max Gordon was a participant in *Blithe Spirit* as well as in the other three plays; Coward presented him with a 15 per cent share in it.[16]) Soon all this changed, and the glitter of Broadway was dimmed down in a "brown out" as the great advertising signs were switched off in an energy-saving gesture. But that was not to happen until after December 7.

On that day the Kaufmans were apart. Beatrice was in Bucks County, and with her was William Walton. All that fall Beatrice had delighted in his company in town. She derived pleasure from being seen with him and from the prestige that she acquired in his eyes from her association with theatrical celebrities. She wrote about this to Anne at Holmquist in November, though without revealing the true nature of her relationship with Walton:

> I went to the opening of *Let's Face It* with Bill Walton of *PM* and later I took him to a party at the St. Regis that George Cukor gave. One of those all-star casts and he had never seen one before. Elsa Maxwell, Elsie de Wolfe, Joan Crawford, Marlene Dietrich, Swopes, Paleys, Selznicks, etc. etc. The part that undid him the most was my general position in this group—I guess he had never stopped to think that maybe I got around a little. It was quite amusing, but only briefly because really they're boring silly people and the groupie on *PM*, all working for something they believe in, makes much more sense.

But not until the first weekend in December did Beatrice invite him to the farm. It was a weekend crowded with the usual Bucks County socializing. Moss Hart had been lent a television set—then a rarity—with help from Max Gordon, who had a contract with the National Broadcasting Company to develop properties for the new medium. Somehow, they were able to get a picture on it. At Hart's for the weekend was his brother Bernard, a young man renowned for his wit and, like Moss, the warmth of his personality. Anne came for lunch on Sunday and understood at once the real meaning of Walton's presence in the house. But after lunch, Walton had to return to New York and his job at *PM*. When the news of the attack on Pearl Harbor broke, a little before three in the afternoon, Beatrice was alone with Anne. They listened to it together, and then Beatrice called her husband, to talk it over with him.[17]

On December 7 Kaufman was in that part of the American mainland where the reaction to the event in Honolulu was the most intense—California, which, of all the states, had the largest number of residents of Japanese extraction. Those unfortunates were soon rounded up and immured in special camps without official inquiry into the constitutionality of the procedure. After the initial shock, business in Hollywood, like business everywhere in the United States, resumed as usual. Though he had expected that America would go to war eventually, Kaufman at first was no less shocked than everyone else. He had arrived in Los Angeles on Thursday, December 4, with much business to accomplish. Leland Hayward, Ferber's agent, who had just concluded an exceptionally shrewd deal with Warner Brothers for *Saratoga*

Trunk, whereby the studio had control of the film rights for only seven years instead of in perpetuity, was attempting to sell the same studio the rights to *The Land Is Bright.* Kaufman was much in favor at Warners in 1941, for the studio had bought and filmed *The Man Who Came to Dinner* and expected to make good money from it when it was released the next year. Now the studio was preparing to film *George Washington Slept Here.* Hayward also hoped to make a deal for Kaufman at this studio as producer-writer-director, rather like the scheme that Thalberg, not long before his death, had broached to Kaufman at MGM. The plan would allow Kaufman to make films for the studio at his own convenience. Possibly his willingness to contemplate such a commitment to Hollywood was in part attributable to Hayward's famous persuasiveness, but possibly also to his own dread of finding himself with time on his hands, now that he could no longer count on the annual springtime plotting with Hart. At Warner's Capra was directing the film version of Joseph Kesselring's *Arsenic and Old Lace,* a smash hit of the previous season; Kaufman was expected to visit the set two days after his arrival in Hollywood. He was also expected to pay a call on Harry Cohn at Columbia. Hayward had done his work well.[18]

There was still other business on Kaufman's mind—plenty of it. From the Garden of Allah, where the staff had reserved his favorite bungalow for him, he wrote to Beatrice soon after settling in. "I will enjoy it here," he told her, "but I know I'll be glad to get back." Among those he reported having seen as the days sped along were the Marxes, Chodorov and Fields, and the aging playwright Zoë Akins, whom he hoped to talk into turning out a script that he could direct one day. Of the Marxes, it was Groucho who dominated his reports to Beatrice. In the back of Kaufman's mind was the thought of talking Groucho into coming back to New York for an appearance in some kind of show: either a revue or a musical comedy—possibly something about Sherlock Holmes.[19] The Marx Brothers' act had broken up for the time being with the completion earlier in the year of their final MGM film, *The Big Store,* and thus Groucho was free to work as a "single." No plans were formulated between the playwright and the comedian on this visit, however, for Groucho was having marital troubles—indeed, his first marriage would soon end—and Kaufman was fearful of being drawn into a discussion with Groucho about the situation.[20]

It was probably at this time that Kaufman made an arrangement to collaborate with Herman Mankiewicz again after an interval of fifteen years. They met often for talk and for bridge. "I know," Kaufman was reported to have said to Mankiewicz, "that you only learned to play bridge today, but what *time* today?" The ever-perverse Mank that year had jarred his Holly-wood cronies by betraying the intimacy he had long enjoyed with Marion Davies and William Randolph Hearst; their relationship became the center-piece of his screenplay for Orson Welles's *Citizen Kane.* This put into jeopardy his friendship with Charles Lederer, Marion Davies's nephew. But Kaufman, no respecter of Hearst's feelings, had only admiration for the film and was amused to find in it a version of Mankiewicz's drunken evening at the *Times* in 1925. The least competitive of wits, Kaufman delighted in Mankiewicz's verbal brilliance, which the years of much too much drinking had done nothing to dull. Possibly it was with a thought to the contract that Hayward was trying to secure for him at Warner's that he planned to work on a screenplay with Mankiewicz. He also briefly considered turning James Hil-ton's new novel, *The Hopkins Manuscript,* into a film.[21]

Impatient to get home to Beatrice now that war was declared, Kaufman left Hollywood before concluding the deal with Warner's. But his visit to Capra's set convinced him that film directing was not beyond his range. "I must say," he confided to Beatrice, "it didn't look hard, and there were a couple of things I thought I could do better, but don't tell anybody."[22] The hoped-for sale of *The Land Is Bright* did not come off, but the contract nego-tiations were eventually concluded successfully. In March, Warner's an-nounced that they had secured Kaufman's services to direct, write, and pro-duce three pictures and that work would commence on the first of them in the coming winter.[23]

Before returning to New York, Kaufman began to ponder the question of what role he would play in the war effort. Hollywood friends, particularly the younger actors, were already making plans to enlist. Lederer and George Oppenheimer were impatient to get into the war. Of all his collaborators, the most eager to see action was Ferber. While still at the Garden of Allah, Kaufman received a telegram from her announcing that she was to sail to the Pacific on December 13 as a correspondent for the Army Air Corps. It was not to be, however, for the mandatory physical examination that she un-derwent revealed a cardiac irregularity that rendered her a poor risk for the high-altitude flying that the job entailed. Disappointed, she later asked vari-ous friends for advice on what to do instead. When she called Kaufman—so the story went—he told her that she could be a tank. What he himself might do best, as the fifty-two-year-old head of a household, was to write skits for the shows produced for the military and munitions workers, and sometimes to perform in them, as well as to urge others to turn out material for the same purpose. That was no different from the volunteer service he had rendered for the past two years, but the fact that the nation was now at war gave the work a new urgency. Soon he turned out two sketches with Hart and some others with George Oppenheimer.[24]

In the early spring, after winning an Academy Award, along with Welles, for the screenplay of *Citizen Kane*, Herman Mankiewicz came to New York with his wife, Sara, and settled in at the Carlyle Hotel for talks with Kaufman about their projected screenplay. Though for years Beatrice had doted on Mankiewicz, she was disturbed by the state of his physical health, which had declined so badly that he continually made unpleasant sounds. She still found him brilliant, but decided that she would rather hear about his conversational brilliance from others, rather than have him in her home where he would be brilliant and belch or worse simultaneously.[25]

From New York, Kaufman and Mankiewicz took themselves to Barley Sheaf Farm, where they concocted a film script called *Sleeper Jump*, the theatrical profession's term for overnight train travel between the performances of a road show. The script is an eccentric piece of work for Kaufman, but in all respects (other than its downbeat ending) is typical of Hollywood screenwriting of the 1930s and 1940s. Like countless comedies of the time, it has a bustling, well-populated plot, abundant sight gags, and quantities of suggestive lines and situations, though none going beyond the bounds set by the Hays Office. The work is an account of a transcontinental tour made by a troupe that has just ended a long Broadway run. Composed of actors of all sorts—an old actor who forgets his lines, an intellectual young actress who immerses herself in *War and Peace,* two young actors who have designs on the women in the company, a temperamental leading lady—the company experiences all weathers and endures with equanimity all sorts of accommodations and audiences. In short, it is a typical tour. But the play within the film, the supposedly successful piece enacted by the company on tour, is of a sort for which Kaufman himself would have had little patience in the real theater. It is a "costume" piece set in the Civil War on the Confederate side, with perhaps a glance at *Gone With the Wind.*

The plot of the film script has two strands of action. The minor one—baffling as a Kaufman-endorsed, if not Kaufman-invented, design—is about a young actress who is an ex-convict and, though unjustly charged, fears that her past will be exposed. The major one is about a hard-drinking, self-destructive actor, the former husband of the leading lady, who is cast in the touring company when the male lead walks out on the play to accept a Hollywood contract. This character, named Harvey Evans, scores a success with the reviewers and revives his ex-wife's affection for him, but in the end finds his new success too heady and seeks the solace of scotch. The minor plot, ending happily in a truncated chase and a comic brawl, is regrettably banal. The other is more intriguing, for in the end the portait of Evans has a familiar look. It is none other than Mankiewicz himself, in partial disguise.

Sleeper Jump was finally copyrighted in July, but was never filmed. According to Mankiewicz's biographer, Kaufman set it aside on the advice of David O. Selznick, who found it slight.[26] Whether Warner Brothers had an opportunity to look it over is unknown. Nor did Kaufman ever provide the studio with a suitable script. Eventually his agreement with Warner's was terminated by mutual consent, without his having made a single film under it.

Equally futile was Kaufman's effort to bring Groucho back to Broadway. This was a double disappointment, because for a brief moment it seemed just barely possible that his collaborator on a script for the comedian would be Moss Hart. They thought that Groucho would be fun to watch as Sherlock Holmes, but finally agreed with him that an entire evening of him in the role would lose its luster by the end of the second act. He had already, in the summer of 1941, vetoed a suggestion from the management of the Bucks County Playhouse that he do the part there. When Kaufman tried to lure him into a revue instead, he turned down that proposal also, and with a battery of excuses ranging from a distaste for putting on his false moustache again to reluctance to part with a "dame" he had just met in Culver City.[27]

Kaufman did not give up easily. As he cast about for something else that might appeal to Groucho, he saw a volume entitled *Franklin Street,* the memoirs of Philip Goodman, which was published posthumously on February 25, 1942. Goodman, a onetime advertising man and theatrical producer who had died in 1940, had been an acquaintance of his for many years. Ruth Goodman Goetz, the producer's daughter (and George Oppenheimer's collaborator on *Here Today*), was also an acquaintance of Kaufman's and, with her husband Augustus Goetz, a Bucks County neighbor. The last two chapters of *Franklin Street* were her work, prepared from her father's notes. Kaufman found the book much to his liking, for it offered a series of gently amusing anecdotes about late-nineteenth-century life in a German-Jewish family not unlike his own. He was especially pleased with the chapter on a ham actor named A. Lincoln Ladd who ran an acting school that Philip Goodman attended as a boy. This, he thought, would make a fine comic role for Groucho.

Kaufman's idea was that the adaptation of the material should be made by Arthur Sheekman, Groucho's friend. That Sheekman had presented him with *Mr. Big*, one of the worst failures of his career, did not faze him. Ruth Goetz, on the other hand, expressed doubt when he approached her with a request that she let Sheekman go to work on her father's book. Kaufman countered by suggesting that she collaborate on the play with Sheekman. Soon it was agreed that Sheekman, Ruth Goetz, and her husband would write the play together. Since Kaufman could be expected to modify their drafts somewhat, and since Groucho was certain to make some suggestions of his own, assuming he agreed to appear in the play, Ruth Goetz could expect to have four collaborators on the adaptation, though two would receive no credit. As it turned out, Groucho liked *Franklin Street*, which he read at Kaufman's suggestion, and consented to act in the adaptation. Max Gordon agreed to produce it.[28]

Though the Goetzes had an apartment in New York and Sheekman was living there temporarily, it was decided that the writing of the script should take place at Barley Sheaf Farm. The Goetzes were to occupy one of the Kaufmans' guest rooms instead of coming daily from their own place in Bucks County. Thus Kaufman was able to keep an eye on his writers at all times, rather like a movie magnate who expected his scenarists to do all their writing on the lot. They began very late in the spring and continued into June. Though on the surface it was a pleasant enough time for all concerned, what with good food, late afternoon swimming and croquet, and Kaufman's quips to laugh at during meals and in the evenings, it was nevertheless an unsettling experience for the Goetzes, if not for Sheekman. From their standpoint, it looked as though Kaufman's sense of dramatic values had gone off, and badly. They were by no means pleased with the work that they were handing him day after day. He, however, was reasonably content with it. Though he revised each day's work every evening, and made shrewd changes in it, the script still did not strike them as viable. Before they knew it, before a second draft was ready, he and Max Gordon were casting the roles, were booking a New York theater, were plotting the road tour. They were aghast. A heavy piece of machinery had been switched on, and they were powerless to turn it off.[29]

All this while the war was an inescapable source of worry. Most of Beatrice's young men were in the services, or were soon to enter them. An exception was Hart, who at thirty-six was too old for the draft at this point in the war; like Kaufman, he busied himself with civilian volunteer committees. But William Walton, also over age in 1942, was eager to go overseas as a writer and in late spring became a correspondent in Europe for *Time* magazine. At home, the progress of the Allies was the leading topic of conversation. The German-born cook employed by the Kaufmans for two decades was dismissed, though Beatrice knew that she would not be easy to replace. Through Max Gordon they periodically received a budget of news from official Washington. Beatrice herself was not without friends in office; her briskly efficient committee work in behalf of La Guardia and Roosevelt had put her in touch with numerous elected and appointed officeholders. Looking for ways to be useful, she volunteered to roll bandages for the Red Cross like many another American woman, though this was utterly, almost absurdly, uncharacteristic work for her, as she well knew.[30]

For a few months, the Kaufmans' preoccupation with the war created tension between them and their daughter. At Holmquist Anne had come to admire a Quaker teacher of history, a pacifist, and under the influence of this woman she took issue with the militant attitudes of her parents. This was her first serious intellectual dispute with her father; in the first months of 1942 it dampened her weekends at the farm and increased her wish to achieve a way of life independent of her parents. The contention, severe while it lasted, wore itself out when the young men whom Anne knew and liked began to enter the services. In the summer of 1942 she was sufficiently reconciled to her parents' view as to spend a few weeks working in the office set up in the Lyceum Theater for the Lunchtime Follies, an agency established by the American Theater Wing to provide tabloid shows for civilian munitions workers during their noon breaks.

Kaufman and Hart resumed their writing association on behalf of that same organization in 1942. The Lunchtime Follies organizational committee was headed by Hart and George Heller, the Executive Secretary of the American Federation of Radio Artists (and the actor who had played the xylophone in *You Can't Take It with You*). The first Follies, a miniature revue titled *Fun To Be Free,* presented at the Todd Shipyard in Brooklyn on June 22, offered two sketches by the old team: "The Man Who Went to Moscow," a spoof of Hitler's effort to conquer Russia; and "Washington, D.C.," about the seeming impossibility of doing business in the wartime capital. This revue, the first of many such programs offered by the Theater Wing to the end of the war, was a hit with the workers, who chewed their sandwiches and took swigs from their Coke bottles as volunteer actors performed for their benefit. Over the next three years, for this and other agencies, Kaufman and Hart collaborated on three additional sketches, "The Paperhanger," "Dream On, Soldier." and "The Ladies," and Kaufman alone wrote a sketch in 1945 called "Freedom of the Air" for performance at army camps.

Kaufman also made broadcasts for the War Production Board and later headed the war bond drive of the National Community Theater.

Having made his casting and booking arrangements with Max Gordon for *Franklin Street,* Kaufman proceeded in the summer to encourage his writers to complete a second draft of the play, with the expectation of going into rehearsals as soon as it was ready. Then he, Beatrice, and Hart went to visit Woollcott on the island. Having finished his Eastern tour with the play in May, and having received a substantial sum from Warner Brothers as part of Kaufman and Hart's bargain with the studio when the rights were sold, Woollcott was in an even more expansive mood than usual. But Kaufman would not stay long. When he returned and read the new draft, he pronounced himself pleased with it. The Goetzes, however, were no more satisfied with it than they had been with the first; Ruth Goetz's word for it was "ghastly." It seemed to both her and her husband that if this play was good, they had completely lost their judgment. Their sense of its flimsiness was soon confirmed, and in a distressing way. Groucho, having received and read a copy, replied that he would not, after all, act in it. Kaufman was astounded and affronted by this news. To Sheekman it was also a jolt; after the shambles of the *Mr. Big* production, he was hoping for a hit and counting on the team of Kaufman and Groucho to provide it. Determined to have Groucho in the play, Kaufman called him and persuaded him to change his mind. With vast relief, the three writers and their director looked forward to the mid-August start of rehearsals. Five days before the cast was to assemble, however, Kaufman received a telegram from Groucho. The comedian lengthily and conclusively bowed out of the play.[31]

It was obvious to the writing team that Kaufman was disturbed, and deeply so, by Groucho's retreat. In an effort to save face, he told them that Groucho would not have been good in the part anyway. Sheekman also felt betrayed by Groucho. Yet neither of them suspected that the judgment implied in Groucho's refusal to act in the comedy was sound, that the play was truly an inept piece of dramatic writing, and that the character of A. Lincoln Ladd as it emerged in the script was not likely to amuse Groucho's fans or any other body of theatergoers. Kaufman sought out Sam Jaffe, known to movie audiences for his portrayal of the High Lama in *Lost Horizon.* To the Goetzes, he seemed utterly humorless, a man with the look of a sad rabbi, and they despaired of success. Max Gordon was also not happy with this piece of casting, but was too insecure in his new relationship with Kaufman to protest. After a few days of rehearsals, however, Ruth Goetz did protest, firmly. Jaffe was let out of the part, and in his place Kaufman brought in Reynolds Evans, a trusted character actor who had played many parts for the Harris-Kaufman-Gordon nexus, and would take roles in many later Kaufman plays. But the character of A. Lincoln Ladd as developed by the trio of writers under Kaufman's governing hand was a hodgepodge of personality traits, not the amusingly preposterous rogue of Philip Goodman's memory, and the many gags introduced by Kaufman did nothing to animate the inert script. Evans did not have the comic gift to redeem the inane role. The writers were not alone in their sense that Kaufman was simply incapable of making an accurate judgment of the material. To Anne it also seemed as though he had lost something of his skill and that he himself, watching this production crumble before his eyes only a year after the shock of *Mr. Big,* was aware of it.[32]

On September 17, two days before the play was set to open in Wilmington, Groucho wrote to Sheekman, "Max Gordon wrote me that your play looks very funny in rehearsal but then so does Max Gordon."[33] If Gordon was telling Groucho what he really thought, he was in a minority, for few others found *Franklin Street* amusing. As soon as it opened on the road, he and Kaufman knew, finally, what they had wrought. From Wilmington, they took the play to Washington for a week's run, and then withdrew it on September 26 with the customary but in this case transparently untruthful announcement that the script would be revised for eventual restaging. No one concerned with the play had any intention of trying to resuscitate it, ever. As for Gordon and Kaufman, they had got hold of a more promising script. Joseph Fields, having lost his writing partner Jerome Chodorov to the army, had written a fast-paced school-of-Kaufman comedy of his own. Called *The Doughgirls,* it revolved around the doings of several young women living in a hotel suite in wartime Washington. It was reported that Fields got the idea for writing a play on the crowded condition of the city when, earlier in the year, he went there and had to go all the way to Baltimore to get a hotel room.[34]

The play resembles Kaufman's writing in the rat-tat-tat rapidity of its jokes, its potshots at pomposity, and the ending in which all that has been on the point of going wrong suddenly is saved. On the other hand, the comedy has quite a different stamp from any of the Kaufman plays: many of its lines are downright bawdy, and the entire plot deals with sex. Three of the women in the play are attached to men who are on duty in Washington, but none is married to her mate. Each has hopes of marrying, and the difficulties that interfere with these aspirations make up the substance of the farce. Some amusing non-suggestive business and lines are given to a young Russian woman, a sharp-shooting sergeant whose rifle is her constant companion. It was perhaps Fields's wish not to annoy a wartime ally that resulted in this character's speech lacking the innuendoes given to the others; to do homage to his missing collaborator, Fields called the character Natalia Chodorov.

The play, with Kaufman as director, went into rehearsal in November for an opening in Bridgeport on December 5. As with *My Sister Eileen,* he kept pressure on Fields until he got the script into a form that he thought he could show the out-of-town audience. But with two hits just behind him, Fields was not so tractable as he had been. Kaufman nevertheless was insistent, and did a substantial amount of rewriting, not only during rehearsals, but in the tryout tour, which took the play to Boston and Washington before the New York opening on December 30. This proved to be the only Gordon-produced play directed by Kaufman about which Kaufman freely admitted that he was responsible for a large share of the lines.[35]

In Bridgeport it was clear that with work the play would turn into a hit. To strengthen the last act, he and Fields brought in a comic admiral to match the comic general already present, added more gags, and replaced an inadequate actress playing a small role with Natalie Schafer, the comedienne who was then playing a major role in Kaufman's private life. Though the play became better for these changes, it was not originally a happy production from the managerial point of view. (The four young featured actresses—Virginia Field, Arleen Whelan, Doris Nolan, and Arlene Francis—got on extremely well.) Kaufman, usually not tight-fisted where his associates were concerned, never picked up a single check when he and Fields took meals together on the road.[36] Despite the fact that some audiences took offense at the liberal sprinkling of sexual allusions, to say nothing of the notion of three unmarried couples sharing, off and on, a hotel suite, Fields was obdurate in his refusal to remove any of them. One exchange especially troubled Gordon. A slightly older woman in the cast, the mother of six, remarks that she can have babies at the drop of a hat and would be having one now if her husband had not gone to Australia. "Yes," a young woman replies, "and he took the hat with him." Gordon was anxious to have this passage excised from the script. Fields at last, and reluctantly, agreed to cut it, but after the opening night in New York he insisted on putting it in again, and under the regulations of the standard Dramatists' Guild contract, Gordon was powerless to intervene.[37]

What made Fields decide to restore this trifling bit of bawdry were the excellent reviews that the play drew on Broadway. Though *The Doughgirls* was recognized as fluff, it was fluff of high quality. It was so crowded with robustly comic lines, each building on those that preceded it, that audiences were indifferent to its thinness. It served the need for comic relief. The Broadway run continued for 671 performances, and a second company was created for the road, with a third put together shortly thereafter for the West.

With his participation as director of all three companies, as well as investor in the play and part-owner of the Lyceum, which housed the New York company, Kaufman had struck yet another lode. But for the time being his creative skill had dried up. If he had an idea for a play to fill out the season, or even the trace of an idea, nothing came of it. The season of 1942-43 was the first since that of *Dulcy* in which he did not offer a new play of his own writing. During the remainder of the season he did not direct another production.

But during this same span of months, he and his family were occupied with other matters. Roosevelt's suggestion about holding down personal income to a maximum of $25,000 put a bit of a scare into them. As early as the spring of 1942, when the President first mentioned this scheme to the public, Beatrice began to ask herself what could be done to pare the household expenses of a family not noticeably given to thrift. Her first gesture, rather a slight one, was to have four telephones removed from the 94th Street house, including the private lines of both herself and Kaufman.[38] Generously assisting his sisters with funds for the education of their children, contributing to the maintenance of refugees, helping out aged actors and actresses with gifts of money, Kaufman might have found it more than slightly difficult to get by on the President's suggested maximum income had the ill-advised plan been sent to Congress and approved. Even without the imposition of this limit, Kaufman recognized the need to hold down expenses somewhat. In the summer of 1942, he and Beatrice decided, with that end in view, to give up the town house in which they had lived for the preceding ten years and take an apartment at 410 Park Avenue.

With characteristic verve, Beatrice pitched into the task of readying the new place. Writing to Woollcott from the old address, she broke off her letter thus: "Here is my moving man to give me an estimate; he is tall, blond, virile, and handsome, so I am sure you will excuse me."[39] She received no help whatever from her husband, who was content to let her have her way with the apartment, just as she had had, with pleasing results, at the farm. Kaufman, unable to bear the thought of living amid a swirl of carpenters and paperhangers, took himself to the St. Regis Hotel for two weeks until all was in readiness. Then no sooner was he installed in his new study than a serious problem arose. The building was divided into two wings, and Kaufman discovered that its owner, who also lived in the building, rented apartments to Jews in only one of the two—the one in which he did not live. In a rage over this, Kaufman wanted to move out at once. But with tact and tenderness, Beatrice, who was herself capable of fury in the face of anti-Semitism, persuaded him to change his mind. Understandably, she did not care to repeat the moving and decorating process.

When that crisis had passed, Beatrice began to entertain her friends at dinner parties, and happily listened to their praise of her taste in decoration. "Everyone is mad about the apartment," she wrote to Anne on October 7; "they like it much better than our house and it is really lovely. . . . There are a few odds and ends needed, but I shall get them slowly and carefully." And again, a few months later: "Our dinner last night was the usual Kaufman triumph, with the guests staying so late that your dear papa was sending me looks of great agony around two in the morning. The Selznicks, Paleys, Moss and Miss Atwater . . . and—Orson." But as always, both Beatrice and Kaufman continued to go their own ways when it suited them. One morning when she was home from school, Anne awoke to find a note from her mother under her door. In mock anguish Beatrice notified her that they had probably lost the head of the household forever. He had sat next to Greta Garbo at a dinner party the night before, and was threatening to elope with her.

But this was not a time of unadulterated amusement for Beatrice—far from it. Though Walton returned intermittently from his duties abroad, his absence left a void in one important aspect of her life. Missing him, she warmed again to an old flame, George Backer, but could not sustain the affair for long. Woollcott's health was a grave source of concern for her. At the peak of the autumn color in 1942, she went up to the island with Backer and Neysa McMein for what would be her last visit to Woollcott in the home that he preferred to any other.[40] Always in danger of incurring another heart attack, and then recuperating from a recent operation for gallstones, Woollcott wished to see as many of his intimates as he could get to the island during the fall. Her own physical health was also troublesome. The bumps along her jaw grew larger, and her doctor recommended surgery. When this was done, Beatrice, to conceal the scars, took to wearing a veil tightly drawn under her chin and over her head. Not a vain woman, but a fastidious one, she was distressed by her disfigurement.

It may have been the decline of Woollcott's health that decided Beatrice late in 1942 to write a book of reminiscences about the people of the Algonquin Round Table and other important figures in her life. Among those others were her family in Rochester. At least every six months Beatrice journeyed to see her mother and her other relations and such old friends as still lived in the city. In January 1943 she went again, sadly aware that her mother, who had suddenly grown very frail, would not live much longer. While she was there, Kaufman, on his way home after attending the opening of the second company of *The Doughgirls* in Chicago, stopped off. It was their plan to go back to New York on the train together. On the morning when he was expected, like the girl she had been when he visited her during the months of their engagement, she awoke in her mother's house in a state of "wild excitement" and for hours went to the window in the hope of seeing his taxi drive up. At last he arrived, and, as she wrote,

> I finally saw him get out of a taxi and I hurried to the door. There he was—tall and dark—looking much as usual and I stood there silently for a moment. He put his arms around me and said: "It seems to me I came here once before to take you away from all this." This was more than I could bear and I burst into tears and rushed into my room to hide them.[41]

——19——

Sorrow

The Kaufmans' emotional interdependency abated not at all as they grew older. There was no event in his professional life that Kaufman failed to discuss with Beatrice, and no piece of work whose success would have meant anything to him without her good opinion to confirm that of the public. But they remained to the end two very different people: he cool, standoffish, impatient; and she generous, humorous, unhurried. Whereas only the family could count on him for signs of affection, cherishing as many of them as he gave, many other persons, both men and women, turned to her for warmth and signs of understanding. In the last years of her life, she was more outgoing, more the concerned friend, than ever.

She never finished the memoir that she began in 1942. What stopped her was the decision to work on a book of another sort, a tribute to one of the most intimate of her friends, Alexander Woollcott. On January 23, 1943, Woollcott suffered a cerebral hemorrhage while making a radio broadcast in New York. Rushed to the hospital, he died only a few hours later. Joseph Hennessey, his secretary, and Beatrice were named the executors of his estate, and they decided to pay homage to him by editing a collection of his letters for publication. It was this endeavor which took precedence over the projected book of reminiscences.

Some three months after Woollcott's death came the expected bad news from Rochester: Beatrice's mother, Sara Bakrow, died on April 14. After her return from the funeral, Beatrice wrote to Anne, "I miss my mother very much. I was thinking the other day that I had been quite a good daughter, but that it had been easy for me as I felt nothing but love for her. She had a truly lovely nature; nothing like my ugly temper."

Through the winter Woollcott remained much on the minds of his sur-
vivors. Beatrice pitched at once into the job of gathering and editing the
letters. She and Kaufman had at this time to decide what to do about
Neshobe Island, of which they were still part-owners. Eventually, all the
owners agreed to sell the property, for without its presiding despot, it would
no longer be as attractive a rest-and-recuperation area for the Broadway and
Hollywood people who had visited it over so many years. In February,
Woollcott and his island were the subject of examination and cross examination in civil court, during the hearing of yet another plagiarism suit brought
against Kaufman and Hart. A writer named Vincent O'Connor claimed that
The Man Who Came to Dinner was stolen from his *Sticks and Stones,* a
play with the *New Yorker* offices as its scene, and involving characters based on
Woollcott and Harold Ross. That play had been sent to Kaufman in 1936
in the hope that he would revise and produce it. He had not so much as
glanced at it, however, but had had Myra Streger read and report on it. The
suit was dismissed, like all others involving Kaufman. When it was first
threatened, Woollcott was still alive. At that time Kaufman wrote to him in
disgust, "It seems we stole the character of Woollcott from a play called
Sticks and Stones. It will probably turn out that you got it from there, too."[1]

As the winter months pressed to their end, Beatrice began to worry not
only about her mother's fragile health, but about her daughter's future. Anne
was in her final year at Holmquist; she faced the necessity of deciding what
to do in the year ahead. It was her assumption and that of her parents that
she would go to college. The problem was to decide on the appropriate institution. Beatrice, recalling her own futile experience at Wellesley, hoped
that Anne had the determination to persist through four undergraduate
years, and was insistent that she apply to those colleges that would inspire
her to do her best. Both parents hoped that Anne would select a place where
the spirit of liberalism prevailed. There was talk of Bennington, of Swarth-
more, of the University of Wisconsin. Finally, Anne set aside the thought of
all of these and chose the University of Chicago. The initial reaction of her
parents was dismay. To them it symbolized indurated conservatism, a place
where their daughter would encounter "nothing but Tory politics," in Kaufman's phrase.[2] It was a rich institution founded by Rockefeller money—that
was the cause of their disapproval. Ferber, who had lived in Chicago at the
outset of her career, had done much to persuade them to this view. That
under Robert Maynard Hutchins the University of Chicago was one of the
most progressive, innovative universities in the country, that Thornton
Wilder, whom they knew well and admired, had taught there quite happily

for six years, that it had deliberately backed away from its position as a "Big Ten" football power, had in fact dropped intercollegiate athletics—all this meant next to nothing to them. Yet another cause of their disapproval, or at least Kaufman's, was the weather of the city. Having been there in all seasons with his plays, Kaufman had wilted in the city's heat and been stung by its freezing cold. All these arguments he listed in a long letter sent to Anne at Holmquist that represented his last-ditch appeal to her to change her mind. And there was one thing more: every day she "would bump into the Chicago *Tribune*," that arch-conservative newspaper! But Anne persisted, certain that she would enjoy the sprawling, coeducational university, which contrasted sharply with claustrophobic, spinsterly Holmquist. She was accepted by Chicago. No sooner did that news reach Kaufman than he capitulated, in a loving letter:

> Well, Poky, I hear you got in at Chicago. I thought of sending you, by way of congratulation, a copy of my letter to you telling you why you shouldn't go there, but maybe you remember it. At least I have now discovered how to get you to do *anything*—just write a good strong letter the other way.
>
> But I'm delighted, darling. Your college career will be what you yourself make it. I know you will find friends wherever you go, and I have a hunch you're going to work. But, particularly, I'm pleased because that's what you wanted. Maybe some day you can explain the Chicago Elevated system to me.

She did not enter the university, however. In the summer she fell in love, and that made her change her mind about higher education. Over the preceding year she had been seeing a young man named John Booth, a classmate of Clinton Wilder's at Lawrenceville who was then taking courses at Columbia. In 1942 Booth was inducted into the army, and he was stationed at Fort Dix, New Jersey. So frequently did he manage to get away to see Anne that both his family and hers soon saw that this was a serious romance. Booth was cautioned by his mother that he might be developing expectations in Anne of a proposal. Beatrice made a rather ribald joke about the affair. When Anne requested that she send some toiletries to her at school, including baby powder, Beatrice replied, "The powder has me somewhat confused and I hope you are not tending carefully a young Booth under your bed." After her graduation, Anne, with Beatrice's help, got a summer job at *PM*. She continued to see Booth. In August she accepted his proposal of marriage and put the thought of going to college out of her mind. Because of the youth of the couple—Anne was eighteen and her fiancé four years older—the families were troubled by the prospect of the marriage. Yet neither the Kaufmans nor Booth's mother made a serious effort to persuade them to wait. The war was not a time in which any young couple could be persuaded to do that. On August 19 the engagement was announced. On September 1 the couple were married in a Jewish ceremony held at the Hampshire House, a New York hotel. After a brief honeymoon, Booth returned to his duties at Fort Dix and Anne settled into a hotel in near-by Trenton, to be as close as she could to him.

In the months preceding the ceremony, Kaufman was intermittently busy with new projects. Immediately following Anne's graduation, he took the train for Hollywood in the expectation that he would lay plans to direct a film at Warner Brothers. Though nothing came of this hope, he returned to the East with the seed of an idea for a musical planted in his mind. Over the bridge table one evening, Charles Lederer burst suddenly into a parody of some lines from Gilbert and Sullivan's *H.M.S. Pinafore*:

> He nodded his head and never said no,
> And now he's the head of the studio.

Making rhymes about friends and acquaintances to fit familiar tunes was a pastime in which Lederer frequently indulged. Kaufman had laughed at them before, but on this occasion he responded with the serious request that Lederer sell him the rights to the rhyme. Lederer was taken aback. He declined to sell the rhyme for cash, but said that he would be pleased if Kaufman bought a present for his wife. Kaufman consented to this and asked Lederer to sign an agreement to transfer the rights. He said that thanks to the inspiration of Lederer's lyric he would create an adaptation of *H.M.S. Pinafore* set in Hollywood. Two years would pass before he got the show to Broadway. In the meanwhile he purchased a set of records of the operetta made by the D'Oyly Carte Company and began to listen to them. He played them so frequently that he put Beatrice and Anne out of patience with him and his two unwitting collaborators.

For Beatrice the midyear months of 1943 were a time of uneasiness. She gave up her job at *PM*, having had little to do there of interest. Possibly the departure of Walton played a part in her decision to leave, but of greater importance was her wish to get on with the editing of the Woollcott letters. She also continued her war work; in addition to her bandage-rolling, she put in some time with the Writers' War Board on the development of a magazine. She also tried, futilely, a bit comically, and at absurd expense, to market eggs laid by hens at Barley Sheaf Farm. Very briefly she was tempted by a proposal that she take an administrative job in Washington for the duration of the war. But this she passed up for the sufficient reason that her husband could not manage his life without her. Her physical health began increasingly to concern her, and her visits to doctors made inroads on her time. The new problem was high blood pressure. During May and June she keenly missed the presence of Moss Hart, who was off on a tour of Army Air Corps installations in preparation for the writing of a play about that branch of the service. Together she and Hart spent the eve of his departure on this mission, first at a restaurant, then at his apartment, and finally in a round of night clubs. The two months that passed without the almost daily solace of conversation with him were difficult for her. This deeply felt deprivation, coupled with the contention over Anne's choice of a university, may have been the cause of her notifying her husband that she would not act the gracious hostess when during the second half of July he met with a fledgling dramatist whose play he intended to direct. But so may have the identity of the dramatist: Gypsy Rose Lee. Whether the cause was a vague restlessness or uncharacteristic snobbishness, she left it to Anne to run the household at the farm when the strip-tease artist arrived with her manuscript.[3]

Intelligent and outgoing, and viewing her career with humorous detachment, Gypsy Rose Lee was a favorite with the press and something of a cult figure at the beginning of the 1940s. Much publicity had been generated over her intellectual aspirations, and Rodgers and Hart, in the sly song "Zip" (in *Pal Joey*), had put words in her mouth to the effect that she enjoyed every writer from Schopenhauer to Walter Lippmann. She achieved a certain literary cachet by publishing two detective novels, in 1941 and 1942, and in the summer of 1943 added to her credentials by publishing an autobiographical piece in the *New Yorker*. Under the aegis of Michael Todd she enjoyed a long run in *Star and Garter,* a revue which opened on June 24, 1942, and was still running a year later. When she handed Todd the manuscript of a partially autobiographical play, *Seven-Year Cycle,* the producer expressed interest in offering it, provided Kaufman would direct it. This uninformative title was soon changed to *The Ghost in the Woodpile,* which refers to the ghost writer in the plot who tries to blackmail the burlesque-queen heroine, and finally to *The Naked Genius,* because Todd thought that the adjective "naked" would be good for business.

It is impossible to suppose that Kaufman took up the play for any other reason than that he had no other immediate prospect of work. The comedy is as slight as a puffball. It tells how stripper Honeybee Carroll, a creature possessed, like her creator, with a wish to make a name for herself as a woman of letters, finally gives up all her pretensions and marries her press agent, in a ceremony raucously stage-managed as a charity benefit by her avaricious termagant of a mother. It was no production to add to a record whose latest entries included *Mr. Big* and *Franklin Street*. Yet Kaufman accepted the assignment, and Gypsy Rose Lee came to Barley Sheaf Farm. As Kaufman plied her with questions, he made an honest effort to tighten her script. Yet when the play went into rehearsal in mid-August, it was painfully clear to onlookers and the actors that neither he nor she had confidence in it. Cast as Honeybee was Joan Blondell, an actress too soft of spirit—too nice, as one reviewer put it—for the role, but a box-office draw.[4] Philip Ober, who had been cast as the press agent, walked out during rehearsals. Throughout the rehearsal period Kaufman had the appearance of a man thoroughly revolted by what he was hearing and seeing. It was not that the play was unusually vulgar; in fact it contained no more suggestive dialogue than *The Doughgirls* did. The problem lay in the naïveté of construction and flatness of characterization. The author herself was unable to endure the rehearsals to their finish. Before they were over, she too disappeared, though she dutifully went to the opening performance in Boston on September 13.[5]

In Boston the play drew very poor newspaper notices, but was not a failure at the box office. What drew the customers was less the prospect of viewing a Kaufman-directed comedy, to be sure, than the expectation of getting an insider's view of the world of burlesque. It was a humorless show, though not by the director's intention. The New York newspapers and those in Boston passed along gossip to the effect that Kaufman was doing his best to make the play funnier. The play closed down while Kaufman and Lee tinkered, and then it went on to play Baltimore and Pittsburgh, still to harsh reviews and good business. For a brief period on the road, Lee took offense over the license that Kaufman exercised in making wholesale revisions, but at last in Pittsburgh the two made it up, each conceding to the other that the only thing to do with *The Naked Genius* was to close it. They pleaded with Todd to let the play expire on the road, since to bring it in was to court disgrace. Todd, however, would consent to no such defeatist action. Informing the press that both the playwright and the director had renounced the play, he dug in his heels and opened it on October 26. Behind his stand was a contract with Twentieth Century-Fox, the purchaser of the film rights, which guaranteed him a sizable share of the gross of the film provided the play ran at least three weeks. After four and a half weeks, and while the play was still running at a profit, Todd withdrew it, much to the relief of Kaufman, Lee, and Blondell. If all concerned in the production were embarrassed a bit, at least they had the grace not to pretend otherwise.[6] Todd was the only real winner. Out of the play he gained not only a substantial sum of money, but, in time, a wife. In 1946, he and Joan Blondell were married.

Just as this dramatic folly was going into rehearsal, Kaufman was offered another thin comedy to direct: Ruth Gordon's *Over Twenty-One*. In the interval since she had appeared in *Here Today* under Kaufman's direction, the actress had had a series of Broadway successes in roles of remarkable variety, ranging from a Southern prostitute in John Wexley's *They Shall Not Die* to Nora in *A Doll's House*, but in spite of, or perhaps because of, her intelligence and the distinctive style of her performances, she had not developed the drawing power of such other star actresses of her generation as Cornell, Hayes, Claire, and Fontanne. It was as though with every play she had to make a new beginning. In *Over Twenty-One*, she created a starring vehicle for herself based in part on her experience as an army wife. Late in 1942, at the age of forty-five, she had married twenty-nine-year-old Garson Kanin, then an army lieutenant. After the run of the play in which she was then appearing, Katharine Cornell's all-star production of *The Three Sisters*, she moved to Washington to be with Kanin, who was assigned to the Office of Strategic Services. The leading role, that of a novelist and screenwriter named Paula Wharton, she intended not as a self-portrait, but as an image of a legendary wit such as Dorothy Parker. Thus it ultimately developed that, appearing under Kaufman's direction for the second time in her life, she would again portray a Parkeresque woman.

The plot Ruth Gordon developed deals with the difficulty that Paula Wharton's husband experiences while attempting to pass through Officers' Candidate School at the age of thirty-nine, and his wife's determination to see him through it. To a degree, the husband's problems are those that were faced by Ruth Gordon's intimate friend Thornton Wilder, who went into the Army Air Corps with a commission, but once in had—or claimed to have —a struggle to learn information that the younger men around him easily absorbed. This character was also given touches of the personality of Ralph Ingersoll of *PM*. To round out the *pièce à clef*, Ruth Gordon included an iron-willed newspaper publisher resembling Herbert Bayard Swope and an omnipotent film producer not unlike David O. Selznick.

Completing her manuscript in July 1943, with some assistance from her husband, Ruth Gordon first tried to interest Howard Lindsay and Russel Crouse in producing it. After getting their firm refusal, she sent it to Max Gordon, who took it at once. Though in the hospital recovering from a pros-

tate operation, he was strong enough to bark out a hearty acceptance into the
telephone and announced that he would try to get Kaufman to direct. But
Kaufman's initial response was cool. Already burdened with the flimsy Gypsy
Rose Lee piece, he had no stomach for bolstering another paper-thin work
whose only merit lay in the amusement value of the leading character's lines.
Kaufman hesitated, and Max Gordon grew testy enough to declare that he
would produce the play with or without Kaufman as director or backer.
Finally, when Hart sided with Max Gordon on the play's potential, Kaufman reluctantly consented. Before going into rehearsal with *The Naked
Genius,* he journeyed to Washington to confer with Ruth Gordon and
Kanin, and, making it clear, obliquely but effectively, that he found the
script faulty, he began the process of prodding the author's sensibility until
she turned her work into a presentable school-of-Kaufman comedy. It remained a minor work with a trivial conflict centering on the question of
whether the aging cadet should remain in the service or resume his important civilian job of editing a major liberal newspaper, but raised some
healthy laughter at the expense of such self-important characters as the
publisher, the producer, and the OCS commandant.[7]

   Though she had known Kaufman well for years, Ruth Gordon was taken
aback by his unwillingness to laud the cast on its ability, to say nothing of
herself as author. To her question of whether he ever passed a compliment,
he replied, "No. You're supposed to be good. I'll tell you when you're not."
After that she was unprepared for his considerate conduct when writing a
sensitively phrased telegram to be sent to a young actress who had to be
replaced. Then she saw how he signed it: "Best wishes, Max Gordon."[8]

   At its first performance in New Haven on December 16 the play did not
generate much excitement in the audience. With more revisions of sorts suggested by Kaufman, it built in popularity, however. The engagements in
Boston and Washington were encouraging, and the opening in New York
on January 3, 1944, fulfilled the author's hopes and far exceeded the director's expectations. The failure of an off-stage musician to pick up his cue at
the end of the first act was a maddening moment to the overwrought Kaufman, but both Ruth Gordon and Max Gordon took it in stride. As in the past
with other productions directed by Kaufman, the reviewers assumed that his
contribution amounted to an uncredited collaboration with the author of record.
Though this was intended as praise, Kaufman ignored it. Not caring for the
play, he preferred to think of *Over Twenty-One* as entirely Ruth Gordon's.
"Our little charade," he wrote to Hart after the opening, "is an unbelievable
smash, considering that it ain't much of a play."[9]

He was strangely silent as a dramatist in his own right at this time. Apart from the benefit sketches written with Hart and Oppenheimer, he had contributed no new play since *The Land Is Bright.* That this exceptionally prolific writer should suddenly find himself with nothing to say was pointed up by Hart's great success with *Winged Victory,* his Army Air Corps play, which opened in New York on November 20, 1943. Sentimental and gaudy, it was destined for oblivion with the coming of peace, but served its wartime purpose very well. Scripts streamed into Kaufman's Park Avenue apartment with covering letters from agents who thought that with Kaufman's help they might be turned into hits. But nothing interested him for the moment. The reason was that he still lacked a compatible collaborator; it boiled down to his missing the cooperation of Hart. Approached by Billy Rose early in 1944 to sign on as writer, director, and editor of material for a revue that Rose expected to mount in the fall, Kaufman automatically turned to Hart, who was in Hollywood at the time: "Incidentally, Billy Rose has quite an exciting idea for an unusual show—revue, I suppose it is. . . . I may function as a kind of director-writer in a half-assed way, and if you have three days we might do a sketch and a half when you return. You could have it acted by six stars, anyhow."[10] As it turned out, when Rose's revue *Seven Lively Arts* opened in December, it had three sketches by Hart, one by Kaufman, and none by the two as a team, and was directed not by Kaufman, but by Hassard Short and Philip Loeb.

It took Max Gordon, finally, to lead Kaufman back to the typewriter as a playwright in earnest, with the unlikely suggestion that he and John P. Marquand make a play out of Marquand's novel *The Late George Apley,* winner of the Pulitzer Prize in 1938.

Two of Gordon's most prestigious productions in earlier years had been based on novels: Sidney Howard's dramatization of Sinclair Lewis's *Dodsworth* and Owen and Donald Davis's of Edith Wharton's *Ethan Frome.* But those plays had been handed to him, not brought into being at his suggestion. Reading Marquand's novel some five years after its publication, he thought that with Kaufman's assistance Marquand might turn it into a play. Designed as a mild satire about a provincial Boston brahmin more disappointed by life than he knows, and presented as a parody of official biography, it had at first glance not much in common with Kaufman's output. True, Kaufman had written about stuffy businessmen, but none so highly placed in society as Apley, and none developed with such an undercurrent of sympathy as Marquand felt for him. Yet, picking up the book at Gordon's request, Kaufman expressed his willingness to take on the project even before he finished reading it. In February 1944 Gordon set up a lunch meeting with Kaufman, Marquand, and Harold Freedman of the dramatic department of Brandt & Brandt, the literary agency that represented Marquand. They soon arrived at terms. The two writers were to meet in the summer at Barley Sheaf Farm to construct their play with a view to a fall production, which Kaufman would direct.[11] Much later, Marquand, sounding very much like the parody style that he had developed for the novel, wrote,

> Mr. Kaufman and I are perfect complements to each other. He knows nothing about Boston and I know nothing about playwriting. I may say, I think, that it is our joint intention to hold up to ridicule whatever folly or vice there may be in Boston's complacency, self-satisfaction and the mortmain of puritan morality, tempering it with the human and humanistic qualities that are necessarily part of people of gentle birth, education and cultivated manners.[12]

Before beginning his sessions with Marquand, Kaufman had very little on his schedule, apart from his obligation to solicit some material for the Billy Rose revue. He expected to deliver his Hollywood version of *Pinafore* to Max Gordon in about a year, but they had set no definite date. In the spring, with nothing much else in view, he agreed to stage Terence Rattigan's *While the Sun Shines* for Gordon in the early fall. Meanwhile, some problems arose within the family. In the winter the Signal Corps reassigned Anne's husband to a post in New York, and the young couple were able to set themselves up in a small apartment in Manhattan. But in April the inevitable occurred: Booth was sent overseas to Europe. To Anne this was an unbearably harsh blow. On the day of Booth's sailing she was close to hysteria. Matters were not helped when her parents insisted that she accompany them that evening to a party given by Sinclair Lewis. They believed, mistakenly, that the gaiety of the occasion would drive away her sadness. In time, however, she did dry her tears and resume the normal pattern of her days. She moved into her parents' apartment, and, having decided against resuming her education, took a job at the publishing firm of Simon & Schuster as a receptionist.

In the early months of 1944 Beatrice completed her editing of the Woollcott letters, which the Viking Press was to publish in July. Though at this time she was as active as ever in volunteer projects and maintained a crowded social calendar, her debilitated physical state worried her greatly. Even so, and despite the knowledge that she suffered from a circulatory problem, she made no effort to lose weight or to control her smoking. It was unusual to spot her anywhere without a cigarette in her hand. Her facial disfigurement troubled her much more than the heart irregularity. She underwent surgery again, for a skin graft. For weeks, swathed in bandages, she stayed in uncomfortable seclusion. But when the bandages were removed, the signs of the graft were disappointingly evident. She had expected that it would at last be possible for her to give up the veils that she had worn since the first operation, but a glance in the mirror dashed this hope. Fortunately for those around her, her zest for life remained what it had always been. Worried though she was, she lost none of her pleasure in party-giving and party-going. Nor did she give so much thought to her own problems as to fail to be stirred by the progress of the Allies across France.

When, in June, John P. Marquand began the series of visits to Barley Sheaf Farm, Beatrice, though knowing that her facial operation was not far off, made her usual effort to be the proper hostess. Her task was made difficult for her by the fact that Marquand's wife, who accompanied him, took a political stance far to her right. To John Booth she wrote on July 10,

> I am going to the country as soon as my doctor will allow me to, and settle down quietly for a couple of weeks. George is busy working on the Marquand play, which seems to be going very nicely. I had a rather trying few days with Mrs. Marquand as a house guest, because as you may or may not know she was an active America Firster who introduced Lindbergh at the last America First meeting in Carnegie Hall. I chose every opportunity to discuss politics with her, not without some success, and I have decided to take another try one day soon to make the conversion complete. Perhaps this is too optimistic of me.

It was indeed too optimistic. On the next visit of the Marquands, which took place over a weekend, Beatrice was told by a servant that Adelaide Marquand had received a long-distance telephone call but was still asleep. Snooping a bit, Beatrice asked who had called and was informed that it was Mrs. Charles Lindbergh, telephoning from the Lindberghs' house close by in New Jersey. Beatrice was infuriated by this news. Because of Lindbergh's association with the America First committee, his pre-war acceptance of a decoration from the Nazis, and the praise of them implied in his speeches before Pearl Harbor, his name was anathema to Beatrice, as it was to many others. She delivered word of the telephone message to Adelaide Marquand personally as soon as her guest awoke. When Mrs. Marquand said that she wanted to return the call, Beatrice forbade her to do so from Barley Sheaf Farm, and uttered this firm interdiction in front of both husbands. For Beatrice, this was exceptional conduct; that she was so indifferent to her husband's interests as to insult his collaborator's wife was a measure of the heat of her feeling. Yet since she knew that the Marquands were in no doubt as to the politics of both Kaufmans, she was convinced that Adelaide Marquand's behavior in giving her number to the Lindberghs was a breach of manners as reckless as her own. Mrs. Marquand burst into tears and asked her husband to take her to the railroad station. He did so, but returned from the station to continue work. Neither husband had a desire to terminate the association. Marquand, moreover, had been drifting emotionally from his wife; this was not the first time in their marriage that she had been guilty of questionable conduct. To Kaufman, nevertheless, such a display of emotion as Beatrice had made was acutely embarrassing. People did not do such things! Yet he expressed no irritation over it; he wished merely to continue writing.

Early in August this curiously composed team was ready to go into production with the play. It had to wait its turn, however, until Kaufman was finished with the rehearsals of *While the Sun Shines* and the Washington trial run of that play and its opening on Broadway, which took place on September 17. This piece of English whimsy, based on mistaken identity and set in an apartment in the vast Mayfair building known as Albany, was a long-running hit in the West End when Gordon optioned it. Though transatlantic broadcasts had rendered its references to the wartime London scene familiar, and one of the characters was an American army officer, it was too slight of plot to hold the American audience. Kaufman did what he could to revise the dialogue for Broadway, but he soon knew that he could not save it. From Washington, on September 12, he wrote to Anne:

> At 10:30 while I was quietly enjoying breakfast and the papers, there was a banging on the door. I yelled "Come in!" twice and then got out of bed in bare feet and opened the door. It was a cigar with Max Gordon around it. He followed me into the bedroom, threw my clothes off the only chair and sat down. Then he decided to telephone. My breakfast table was between the beds, so to reach the phone he had to throw himself along the other bed, on top of the rest of my clothes and my other glasses. He put in three calls and finally departed after 40 minutes. I started to nap again, but he had left word with the operator that he was in my room, so three calls came for him and woke me up. That's all, except that the show is not very good.

In New York *While the Sun Shines* had a run of thirty-nine performances or (at least this much could be boasted) twenty-five more than Broadway had allowed Rattigan's *Flare Path* two years earlier; that play also had been a hit on home grounds. The New York audience was receptive to good plays about Americans on the battlefield or the home front, but cared scarcely at all for British war plays. The audience also revealed a yearning for dramatic glimpses of a less troubled past, as was evident in the lengthy runs of such nostalgic works as *Life with Father* and *Oklahoma! The Late George Apley* was another nostalgic play, and if it did not prove so durable as those long-running hits, its fifty-one weeks on Broadway, followed by a profitable tour, did credit to the Kaufman-Marquand team and their producer. When it opened on November 23, 1944, three years had slipped by since the opening of *The Land Is Bright,* the last play officially credited to Kaufman.

The comedy that Kaufman and Marquand achieved bears only a partial resemblance to Marquand's novel. Whereas the novel embraces the entire life of its subject, the play covers only eight days in the year 1912, with a glance at the life of Apley's son thirty years later by way of an epilogue. In the novel Marquand offered his readers a double vision of Apley's life; the official biographer, a Harvard classmate of Apley's and as much an old Bostonian as he, attempts to draw a thoughtful portrait of a man who led a life thoroughly in accordance with the best standards of his social class, while at the same time the biographer unwittingly reveals that in fact Apley's life consisted of opportunities for happiness passed by in the name of duty. Bound by tradition and convention, Apley derives little contentment from his wealth and position. Even his important collection of Chinese bronzes, gathered for the ultimate benefit of Boston's art museum, gives him no satisfaction whatever. The wooded island that he purchases as a retreat for himself and his men friends is ultimately dominated by his headstrong wife and sister. Never can he forget the beautiful Irish girl with whom he fell in love while at Harvard, but, whom, of course, it would have been unthinkable of him to marry. At some points rather strained in its humor and less subtle than Marquand supposed, the novel is nevertheless an absorbing tour de force. The play is much more comic. It sounds a Broadway show-wise note in the Boston of Apley's middle age.

The authors took some liberties with historical fact, as Kaufman pointed out in a Sunday piece for the New York *Times*. Among their deliberate falsifications was a mention of Felix Frankfurter as a Harvard faculty member at the time of the play, whereas he did not begin to teach there for another two years. They also referred in the dialogue to the Copley Plaza Hotel, though in fact it had not yet been built.[13] More consequential than these anachronisms is the fact that the characters are more broadly drawn than are their counterparts in the novel. This is especially noticeable in the domineering sister Amelia, who is more outspoken with her relatives than she realizes. A character not in the novel at all, a young Harvard lecturer enamored of Apley's daughter Eleanor, drew laughs by telling the Emerson-revering Apley that he intends to lecture on "The Dead Hand of Emerson on American Creative Thought." The substance of the plot is not to be found in the novel at all, though it is true to the novel in spirit. In the play both the Apley son and daughter are in love, and with persons who, though acceptable enough to the rest of the world, count for little in Boston. Not only is Eleanor's young lecturer no respecter of Emerson, he is a Yale man. The girl in young John Apley's life is originally from the Midwest and still lives no nearer to Boston than Worcester. The climax of the play comes when Apley, striving to unbend and ready to put his blessing on his son's engagement, finds his overtures spurned by the girl's father, a prosperous manufacturer, who believes as firmly as Apley himself that the young people, so different in background, can never be happy together. In the novel the son marries a divorcée from Long Island. With Kaufman, Marquand had him marry the dull distant cousin for whom his parents intended him all along. This detail the audience learns in the epilogue, which takes place after Apley's death.

The play was a hit on its road tour, though too long and a trifle slow at the end. Taking the good advice of Robert E. Sherwood, who saw it in Washington, the authors cut the epilogue in half, took out a dull character, and invented a livelier one.[14] The New York reviewers were delighted with the play, though some who had read the novel complained mildly of the alteration of the original material. Some also were bothered by the occasional lack of subtlety in the humor, as with the characterization of the lecturer. Yet none withheld praise of Kaufman's direction, which relied less on extraneous bits of business than had his direction of such skimpy works as *The Doughgirls* and *Over Twenty-One*. The sensitive performance of Leo G. Carroll in the title part and those of the accomplished character actors Janet Beecher, Margaret Dale, and Percy Waram were also praised. Only one major piece of comic invention not fully indicated in the dialogue decorated the production. This was the entrance, at the beginning of Act I, Scene 2, of the family into the living room after stuffing themselves with a gargantuan New England Thanksgiving dinner. Each character was given a solo walk from the dining room and a special way of concealing the discomfort of an overdistended stomach. It was a directorial triumph.

As suitable a nutshell description as might be made of what the authors captured in their comedy was given by Beatrice in a letter to her son-in-law two weeks after she attended the opening performance in Wilmington on

October 19: "It is a fine piece of writing," she declared, "with its own message against the dead tradition of the past."[15]

The letter reflected Beatrice's preoccupation with the presidential contest of 1944. Through the early fall months she was agitated by the thought that, despite all the signs to the contrary, Roosevelt might fail in his campaign for a fourth term. Thomas E. Dewey, the challenger, she saw as a reactionary know-nothing who expected to reverse the progressive movement generated by the incumbent administration. Astonishing herself with a new-found ability, she made speeches in Roosevelt's behalf in New York and near-by cities. After the election she breathed more easily, but did not curtail her war-related activities or her social life. Kaufman, for the moment, was busy, chiefly with his adaptation of *H.M.S. Pinafore*. When *The Seven Lively Arts* opened on December 7, his sketch "Local Boy Makes Good," with Bert Lahr appearing as a stage hand who interrupts a managerial discussion about a show in progress, was among the more engaging items on the bill. Since Kaufman's involvement with the production was slight, he for once was able to sit quietly in an orchestra seat at the opening. After this brief diversion, he turned back to *Hollywood Pinafore*. It, over the winter, was his principal show-business concern. In whichever of the family residences he found himself, the record player spun Sullivan's melodies through the rooms.

The progress of the war was, to be sure, a concern of greater weight than *Hollywood Pinafore*. Kaufman and Beatrice shared Anne's great worry over the safety of John Booth, for the German forces had temporarily pushed back the American lines in the so-called Battle of the Bulge, and Booth was in that sector of the war. Christmas and New Year's Eve still provided an excuse for conviviality among the Kaufman circle, and this year the Kaufmans made a special effort, in the hope of cheering Anne. Kaufman also tried to cheer John Booth with a Christmas letter:

> I am sitting by a closed window with the radiator turned on and a hell of a cold wind seeping right through the glass, as nearly as I can tell. Anyhow, it is coming from somewhere. We started to have a white Christmas two days ago, thanks to that nonsense by Irving Berlin, who rides around in a car and so he can wish a White Christmas on the rest of us. By Monday it will be a dirty brown Christmas, and I dare him to write a song about that. Don't you like to hear civilians squawk? I imagine you do, because you can get madder that way.
>
> Doorbells are ringing and Christmas presents are arriving, and I have just been handed that list of fourteen employees of the apartment house, all of whom must be given hunks of money. Of course I have never seen more than four people working in the goddam apartment house in my

life, and I am convinced that the superintendent has added the names of
fictitious workers, the way one pads election rosters. And even the four
who do exist will quit on December 27th, as soon as they have my
money, and then I'll have the whole thing to do over again.

Our little family, and part of yours, will be out on the farm over the
holiday, and I may even have the pool filled, because I love to plunge
into a pool in winter time. It hardens my muscles. But if I can't do that I
shall lie by the fire, which is a little less vigorous but also quite difficult
because every once in a while I have to move away a little bit if the fire
gets too hot. (*Now* are you mad?)

We have been thinking about you considerably since the German
drive started, and wondering just where you are, and how close to it. For
Christ's sake, DUCK!

On top of this anxiety for Booth came another, though it was Beatrice who
felt it most intensely. Moss Hart volunteered to lead a company of actors on
a tour of South Pacific military bases in the spring. The play was *The Man
Who Came to Dinner*, with Hart as Whiteside. Beatrice and Hart had never
learned to face a prolonged separation from each other calmly, and this was
no exception. On the eve of Hart's departure, the Kaufmans gave a party for
him at their apartment to which they invited his show-business intimates.
Both Hart and Kaufman prepared entertainments for the guests. Hart's
contribution was a doggerel farewell ode in the style of Frank Sullivan's
annual Christmas poem for the *New Yorker,* with care taken to draw in the
names of the guests. He made no mention of Kaufman in the poem, presumably because he knew how much Kaufman disliked any remarks that he
could construe as personal or sentimental. But Beatrice was included, of
course; the honored place in Hart's poem, the last lines, were for Lamb Girl,
"the analysts' pin-up girl, Freud's favorite child." Even before parting, they
had begun to miss each other.

Kaufman's entertainment was a two-character sketch titled "Moss Hart at
the Analyst's." Kaufman himself acted the part of Hart, and Martin Gabel
played Dr. Kubie, with whom Hart was still in treatment. The jokes thrust
deeply into Hart's personality, beginning with expected ones about the
process of analysis:

> KUBIE. Tell me, Moss—have you forgotten that this is an anniversary?
> Moss. Anniversary?
> KUBIE. You're beginning your 25th year of analysis today.
> Moss. You don't mean it? Twenty-five years! (*He sits up.*) Well, well!
>   (*Shakes hands with the Doctor.*) Say, you're pretty good-looking—I
>   never saw your face before.
> KUBIE. I like yours too. I've always seen it upside down.

Moss. Well, back to work. (*Lies down again.*) What year is this?
Kubie. This is 1945.
Moss. 1945, huh? I haven't slept since 1941.
Kubie. On my records it mentions a nap you had in 1943.
Moss. It does? . . . Oh, yes, while Max Gordon was talking.

Other jokes had to do with Hart's well-known extravagance, and still others about his butler, Charles, whom none of his friends could stand and who was going along on the tour. Kubie goes over some detailed notes about Hart's expenses: "Suit of clothes for Charles, three thousand dollars. . . . necktie for Charles, two hundred dollars. . . . gold navel for Charles, nine hundred dollars." Closest to the bone were the lines on Joseph Hyman, to whom Hart had never ceased to feel grateful for the loan on which he lived while writing *Once in a Lifetime:*

Kubie. Now, I have another name down here. Joe Hyman . . . who is that again?
Moss. Oh, Joe Hyman is a wonderful man, wonderful! He did a great thing for me once, and I'd do anything in the world for him. I produced *Dear Ruth* for Joe Hyman—I wrote *Lady in the Dark* for Joe Hyman—I wrote everything for Joe Hyman. He gets half of everything I make.
Kubie. He must be a very great friend.
Moss. He is. He did something for me when I was much younger, and I'll never forget it. I was broke, and I'd written a letter to a friend of mine, and I wanted to mail it, and I had no stamp. And Joe Hyman came along and *gave* me a stamp, just like that.
Kubie. That was three cents.
Moss. No, three-cent postage hadn't come in yet—it was two cents. But it wasn't the money—It was what he said when he gave it to me. Naturally, being his stamp I thought he'd want to stick it on the letter, but that wasn't the way Joe did things. He just gave me the stamp— I'll never forget the expression on his face—and he said, "Here, Moss. Take this stamp and stick it."[16]

From Seattle, where the troupe paused before heading for the combat zone, and later, from the zone itself, Hart wrote frequently and at length to Beatrice and occasionally to Kaufman. The letters to Beatrice were celebrations of their relationship as well as detailed descriptions of events of the tour. In a telephone call to both Kaufmans from Seattle before sailing, Hart sensed that Beatrice was not feeling well and tried to cheer her with the suggestion that in a day or two she would be right again. It was a vain hope on his part, for she continued to feel, in her word, "rocky." The return of William Walton from Europe for a brief stay lifted her spirits, however, and gave her the opportunity to regale him with Hart's reports of his adventures in the South Pacific. Some were alarming to her, but others were comic. Hart had a spell of illness during the tour that required him to spend a few days in a naval hospital; an earache bothered him badly, and he caught a fungus disease. Among the amusing anecdotes was one concerning his attempt to buy an athletic supporter at an island post exchange. Told by the woman clerk that the exchange was out of medium-size supporters, he could not bring himself to ask for a small one, took instead a large one which he knew was much too big for his slim waist, then threw it away as soon as he stepped outside. Beatrice got great fun out of this tale, as Hart obviously intended that she should.[17]

But laughter was no cure for Beatrice's gradually worsening state. Her physician warned Kaufman that she might not have long to live. The doctor suggested that she get away for a change of scene. Since Woollcott's island, her favorite recreational spot in the past, was no longer available to her, she opted for Atlantic City. No young man accompanied her on this visit. Her traveling companion was Dorothy Paley, the wife of William Paley of the Columbia Broadcasting System.[18]

Kaufman proceeded slowly with *Hollywood Pinafore* and brushed aside all requests from producers that he refurbish or direct new scripts, including the Kurt Weill–Ira Gershwin musical, *The Firebrand of Florence*, which Max Gordon offered on March 22. Over the winter months he began the casting of his show, with the intention of choosing expert actors who could sing competently rather than virtuoso singers who might move awkwardly on stage. An exception to this rule was Annamary Dickey, a soprano on the roster of the Metropolitan Opera, who took the role of Brenda Blossom (Josephine in the original). Of the other leading feminine roles, Louhedda Hopsons, "Miss Butterup," the gossip columnist, went to Shirley Booth, and Miss Hebe, aide to Joseph Porter, head of Pinafore Pictures, went to Mary Wickes. The roles of Porter and the agent Dick Live-Eye were cast almost casually. Approached one day by William Gaxton with the suggestion that he revive *Of Thee I Sing* for Gaxton and Victor Moore, Kaufman replied that such an idea was out of the question because of the war; Gaxton had apparently forgotten that not only did the show lampoon the presidency, but also France. But it struck him that Moore was right for the head of the studio, and Gaxton for the crafty agent. Thus in four major roles Kaufman placed actors whose talents he knew and trusted. Rehearsals began early in April, and the out-of-town trial run began on May 7 in Baltimore.[19]

Opening in New York on May 31, the production got lukewarm notices. The general view was that not even Kaufman could do a *Twice in a Lifetime*. Kaufman himself felt that he had gone wrong in one aspect of the writing—by sticking too close to Gilbert's libretto.[20] His hindsight was correct, for the story that he chose to tell did not fit with precision or comfort into the plot invented by Gilbert. The very name of the studio, Pinafore Pictures, had a made-up sound that troubled some of the reviewers. And though Porter, the studio head, is a bumbling fool (Moore's invariable stage persona), he is a man of immense power, nevertheless, and, as with Glogauer in *Once in a Lifetime*, his movements around the Pinafore lot are announced regularly in the studio's reception room—the echo of the earlier play rings entirely too often. As in both *Lifetime* and *Stage Door*, Kaufman decries screen acting as having nothing to do with craft. This comes through the words of Dick Live-Eye, who warns Brenda Blossom against going on the stage, because, if she does, not only may she be paid as little as one thousand dollars a week, but she will have to *act*. "And should you give a bad performance upon the stage, the critics will actually *say so* in print!" (Needless to say, these prove to be persuasive arguments.) Finally, paralleling Gilbert's book, it is all right for Brenda to marry the poor writer Ralph Rackstraw rather than Porter, the man chosen for her by her father, the director Mike Corcoran, because long ago in one of her columns Louhedda Hopsons confused the studio head with the writer, and they ended up with each other's job. With her revelation made, they change places: Ralph Rackstraw is now head of Pinafore and Porter is a lowly seventy-five-dollar-a-week writer who must put on the writer's regulation garb, a set of convict's stripes. Much of this is couched in Gilbert-style dialogue, with its occasional reliance upon archaisms, such as "Hast ever thought?" and "Dost say?" One comes away from the script with a certain weariness, as did the audience in the theater.

Through the rehearsals and the uncertain tryout weeks, the missing ingredient was Moss Hart. For the first time in the fifteen years of their association, Hart was absent while a Kaufman production was taking shape. Allowed only forty-five pounds of personal luggage for his island-hopping tour, Hart did not keep his letters from the Kaufmans; nor did Kaufman keep those he received from Hart. But Hart's letters to Beatrice reveal his concern for the success of the show, his wish to be there to help, and his irritation over the news, reported by Kaufman, that *Memphis Bound*, another musical based on *H.M.S. Pinafore*, was scheduled to open only one week before Kaufman's. The letters also reveal his regret that he had not been with them at the time of Roosevelt's death on April 12 and the surrender of Germany on May 7. Perhaps Kaufman told him about the agitated telephone call he had had from Max Gordon after Truman's inauguration. "For Christ's sake, George," said the comparable Max, "they're putting on the understudy!"

With Hart away and no help coming from the ghosts of Gilbert and Sullivan, Kaufman had been hard pressed to analyze and correct the play's many problems on the road, and he had not succeeded. Moreover, he had been and still was preoccupied with worry over Beatrice's failing health. In July, in the middle of a heat wave and in the absence of any sign that the play would find an audience, he and Gordon closed it down. It was at best cold comfort to them that *Hollywood Pinafore* ran for fifty-three performances, whereas *Memphis Bound* played only thirty-six. Not long after the closing, Charles Lederer visited New York and made a date to meet Kaufman at the Regency Club. Delaying his arrival at the club to make sure that Lederer got there first, Kaufman sneaked up behind him and put a piece of Scotch tape across Lederer's lips.[21]

After the closing, Kaufman found himself for the first time in twenty-five years with no special work on hand. Hart came back, Beatrice went on a visit to her relatives in Rochester—those were the events of the summer. Kaufman passed a few days in writing a piece for the *Saturday Review of Literature* and another for the *New Yorker*. Both appeared in the week of August 11. In the former, he made fun of himself and his opening-night anxieties and then added some remarks intended to lessen the sanctity that the passing of time had lent the Algonquin Round Table. He asserted that none of the Round Table set had had an effect on the literature of the day. He cited as a typical moment in Round Table history the occasion when Frank Case printed up a special menu with inflated prices as a joke on John Peter Toohey, who complained incessantly about the cost of Algonquin meals. "And that, boys and girls," Kaufman wrote by way of conclusion, "was the Algonquin Round Table. Just that and nothing more."[22] For the *New Yorker* he wrote, at greater length, a response to the recently released film *Rhapsody in Blue*, a fantasy account of the life of George Gershwin. If a film company would pay good money for the rights to Gershwin's life and then turn it into gaudy tomfoolery, he wondered why they should not buy the rights to *his* life and then make something equally splashy of it. He offered a few moments from his early years, such as his going to the grocery store with a penny to buy candy, and suggested how they could be made into riveting musical scenes. The penny-candy incident could be stretched out with appearances by John Philip Sousa, Teddy Roosevelt, and Nora Bayes, to be followed by Lena Horne and Bill Robinson, who would come on to do some Stephen Foster numbers.

No new idea for a play offered itself to Kaufman during the summer, and none of those he was invited to direct was strong enough to rouse his interest. No script, however good, could have held its own in contrast with the drama being played out rapidly in the Pacific and ending at last with the Japanese surrender on August 14. The Kaufmans celebrated that event at Barley Sheaf Farm. Anne was with them; her husband was still in Europe, but he was scheduled to come home in the winter.

Finally Max Gordon bought a script. The thunderous reception of Mary Chase's *Harvey* at its opening on November 1, 1944, turned all Chase scripts, new or old, into valuable properties. Gordon bought one of the old ones, *The Next Half Hour*, about an Irish-American mother who thinks she has second sight, and appealed to Kaufman to direct it as a vehicle for Fay Bainter. Coy, melodramatic, fey, and without the redeeming humor of *Harvey*, it was not such a work as Kaufman ever before had chosen to direct.

Rehearsals of this vapid piece began late in September. Though at that time Beatrice's health was obviously poor, nothing was to be gained by Kaufman's staying constantly at her side. On October 6 she planned to see Phyllis Cerf. But when Mrs. Cerf came to the apartment at midday, Beatrice was in bed, obviously unwell, and repeating, "I'm so sick, I'm so sick." Her doctor was summoned, but nothing could be done. In the middle of a rehearsal session, Kaufman was interrupted with word that Beatrice had suffered a cerebral hemorrhage and was dead. *Variety* reported that he "was deeply stunned." Anne, in Boston at the time, received a telephone call from Hart, who told her only that her mother was gravely ill. From something in his voice she knew the truth at once and hurried home. At the funeral service on October 8, which was conducted by a Rochester rabbi, Hart with breaking voice spoke the eulogy. In accordance with Beatrice's wishes, the coffin was closed. At the service were virtually all the show business giants, as might have been expected. Also present were her friends from the worlds of publishing, public service, and politics; among them were two former mayors of New York, Walker and La Guardia, and Bernard Baruch. As she had requested, Beatrice's body was cremated.[23]

Immediately after the funeral service, friends gathered at the Park Avenue apartment so that Kaufman would not be alone. When he entered the living room to greet them, some recalled that in the past Beatrice had always entered gatherings with him to assist him with the chore of greeting his acquaintances. Now he was trying to manage on his own, and the effort showed.[24]

He devoted several days to writing to those who had attended the funeral or sent notes. There were a few old acquaintances from whom he expected to hear but did not, and those he never forgave. Among them, unaccountably, was Noel Coward, part of whose every visit to New York had been spent in Beatrice's company. One acquaintance overseas heard, much to his astonishment, from Kaufman before he had an opportunity to send a note. This was William Walton, to whom Kaufman wrote out of profound sympathy, knowing as he did how much Beatrice had meant to this young man.

At last the notes were all written, the obsequies complete. There was only one thing to do: to recall the cast of *The Next Half Hour* and get on with rehearsals, and Kaufman did so. After a prolonged tryout tour, the play opened on Monday, October 29, and closed at the end of the week. He was left idle and depressed.

20

Leueen

Kaufman did not recover quickly from the shock of Beatrice's death. Not only did he frequently burst into tears at unexpected moments, but at night was disturbed by dreams of such unpleasantness, or such poignancy, that he wept and cried out in his sleep. Not for months did he have the courage and will to resume a social life. In the past when he went "stepping," as Beatrice used to put it, it had often been at her bidding. Without her, he preferred to stay at home. Hart, Max and Milly Gordon, the Goetzes, the Swopes, and Lillian Hellman, good friends all, were solicitous and ultimately helpful in pulling him back to normality. Dorothy Pratt, Beatrice's intimate friend, was another who showed her concern. To Anne, Kaufman commented about this old acquaintance: "As I think I've told you, I get a strange satisfaction from talking with her. There were times when I used to find her a little trying, but a closeness to your mother has made a new bond between us."[1]

Work was the only anodyne, the only release from tension. The short-lived *Next Half Hour* was of little help, but, fortunately, there were other prospects. Max Gordon drew Kaufman out of himself with a report of *Born Yesterday* a new comedy by Garson Kanin that he expected to produce, and while talk of this project was in the air, Kaufman began playing with the idea of a new musical to be based on a short story by Nunnally Johnson. Kaufman could not expect to direct Kanin's play, for the author before entering the service had established himself as a film director and had every intention of staging the comedy himself. But Kaufman and Hart, as always with Gordon's productions, invested in it and stood by to help Kanin out with suggestions, if any were needed. Confident that it would be a hit, Kaufman also advised Anne to invest in it.

Born Yesterday delighted its backers as a droll, frequently bawdy variation on the Pygmalion myth, an almost invariably appealing theme. The Galatea of the piece is Billie Dawn, an empty-headed ex-chorus girl who comes to intellectual life under the tutelage of a young reporter for the *New Republic*. With her wits about her at last, she is shocked by the antisocial heartless-ness of the man who for years has kept her, a boorish junk-dealer of great wealth who hopes to sweep up metal from the ruins of the war and sell it for scrap, and who bribes a United States Senator to make this possible without government interference. The young woman and the reporter pre-vent this from happening and, naturally, fall in love.

Kanin eventually acknowledged that Kaufman offered jokes and some suggestions for strengthening the play during the tryout tour.[2] It could also be claimed that the play owed something to Kaufman's general style—that its rapid pace, volleys of wisecracks, and over-all satiric tone stamped it as a school-of-Kaufman comedy. And it could be said that the quickly achieved education of the heroine and the onrush of social consciousness that she feels carry reminders of similar steps to enlightenment in the plays of Clifford Odets—most notably, *Awake and Sing!* and *Rocket to the Moon*. But Kanin's jokes are more glib than those of Odets, and the liberal-populist ideology is stronger stuff, and more cogently expressed, than the political views aired by Kaufman. This was Kanin's play, and a good, enduring one, despite its lame exposition and its sentimentality. With these flaws rendered negligible by strong characterization, social expression on the side of the angels, and abundant laughs, it was certain of success when it went into rehearsal late in November 1945.

On the road to New York, however, the comedy suffered a serious setback that might have doomed it to a swift closing had Max Gordon been less alert. The role of Billie Dawn had been given to the film actress Jean Arthur, long a stranger to the stage, but an old Hollywood friend of Kanin's and the possessor of an unforgettable, silvery voice and a marksman's sense of tim-ing. At the opening in New Haven on December 20, Kaufman was en-tranced by her performance. *Variety*'s New Haven reviewer wrote, "She steps back into footlight stride with complete ease."[3] Kanin, despite his ad-miration for the star, was less impressed, though at least satisfied. But soon the company's hopes for a long run were threatened, for Jean Arthur began to show fright at facing the audience. Claiming voice problems, she missed performances. Though Kanin hoped that she could be brought around,

Gordon was angered by what he took to be malingering on the actress's part. He began to consider finding a replacement for her. Within a few days Jean Arthur underwent a nervous collapse and was ordered to a hospital by her physician.

Kanin and the agent Belle Chodorov (a sister of Jerome) recommended Judy Holliday, a very young comedienne who had never played so demanding a role. Hearing her read, Kanin, Gordon, Kaufman, and Hart were strongly impressed; they recognized in her the wit, timing, and warmth that would precisely fill the contours of the role. Though Kaufman always maintained that no other actress ever played the part so well as Jean Arthur, Judy Holliday was greeted exultantly by the press and public. On Broadway, the play enjoyed a run of 1642 performances. Holliday repeated her success in the film version and for her performance received an Academy Award. One of her last screen roles before her death in 1965, at age forty-two, was in the film version of a late Kaufman play, *The Solid Gold Cadillac,* with Paul Douglas playing opposite her, as he had in *Born Yesterday.*

As early as December 24, 1945, while *Born Yesterday* was just beginning to have its out-of-town troubles, the press reported that Kaufman and Nunnally Johnson were conferring about a musical. The *Daily News* had it that their plan was to write about a woman in politics, such as Clare Boothe Luce, then a Congresswoman from Connecticut.[4] If so, they dropped this scheme quickly in favor of a show based on Johnson's *Saturday Evening Post* story of 1933 entitled *Holy Matrimony,* which Kaufman had read on its publication and had always assumed would make an entertaining musical. They could not use the original title, unfortunately, because Johnson, one of Hollywood's most frequently employed scriptwriters, had since used it as the title of a film based on Arnold Bennett's *Buried Alive.* It centers on a young man and woman who are engaged to be married. Each of them has been married and divorced before, as have, repeatedly, their parents and the ex-wives and ex-husbands of their parents. Moreover, immediately before the ceremony the bride makes a bit of a play for the best man, who has also been married before, and divorced. On and on go the chains of marriage and divorce, to create a seeming infinitude of misalliances. Kaufman and Johnson made plans to write their new version of this saga in Hollywood in the spring. Whatever the merits of the plan, and however it might turn out, Kaufman was getting back into action, and the newspaper entertainment editors took note.

These late fall and winter months had also brought a share of anxiety to Anne, quite apart from her sadness over the death of Beatrice. She had drifted out of love with John Booth. Like many wartime brides, she had married too hastily to analyze her attitude toward the commitment she was about to make. Booth was not scheduled to return for discharge until early in 1946. In the last months before his return, she hinted in letters that she felt the marriage was coming to an end. Beatrice, in her last letters to Booth, also hinted that Anne expected to end the marriage. As for Kaufman, having grown used to Anne's presence and her assistance in running his household affairs, and hoping for no more disturbances of the tenor of his life, he did nothing to alter her viewpoint. Rather, he strengthened her in the decision she had already made.

When Booth returned in January, Anne met him at the pier and calmly told him that she intended to get a divorce. Expecting as much and reconciled to the idea, Booth offered no argument. The couple went out to dinner a few times in the next weeks, but these were not romantic meetings. They were the reunions of two old friends. Running into Kaufman on one such evening out with Anne, Booth saw such a glower on his father-in-law's face as to make him understand perfectly Kaufman's feeling about the marriage.[5] Early in February, Anne went by train to Las Vegas, where she filed an uncontested suit for divorce.

With the prospect of a sustained piece of work before him, Kaufman began to seem himself again. The talent to amuse ceased to be hidden; in fact, he enjoyed exercising it, as his letters to Anne reveal. "You may have heard the ceremony on the radio this afternoon—it was just three o'clock," he wrote.

> Mayor O'Dwyer spoke, and a band played—all very simple. It seems that I had just finished *Brideshead Revisisted,* and everyone felt that some celebration was in order. I believe they are planning a small parade tomorrow, but that will be all. The stores will remain open—I wanted everything simple.[6]

He began going out again—cautiously at first, but soon to the extent that he could say he was leading a "butterfly life." Before leaving for Hollywood at the end of February, he went so far as to plan a dinner party, though with misgivings as to his ability to bring it off successfully. "I am awaiting my dinner guests," he wrote to Anne in Las Vegas. "I don't know what I'll do with them all evening, but somebody had better sparkle with wit, because I don't know if I shall." He was also much interested in a new development in Moss Hart's life: Hart's romantic involvement with actress Kitty Carlisle. Again to Anne he wrote, "This afternoon I am having Barberry drinks with Mossie, and it seems that romance is really in the air between him and

Kitty. A week from Monday he goes to Miami to spend some time with her, and it would not surprise me if it were marriage this time. I expect to hear more this afternoon, by the simple expedient of asking him."

The woman Kaufman was seeing most frequently at this time was Natalie Schafer. She had played an important role in his life ever since the bleak day in Boston when he consoled her with ice cream after trimming her lines in *Lady in the Dark*. Since 1934 she had been married to Louis Calhern, but because that actor's drinking problem had begun to slide beyond control, it became apparent to her that continuing the marriage was senseless. In February she and Calhern signed separation papers, and she planned to follow Anne to Las Vegas for a divorce. She and Kaufman booked themselves on the same train to the West, and Kaufman planned to stop off in Las Vegas for a few days' visit with Anne. Inevitably, his and Natalie Schafer's friends sorted this out to mean that the two were planning to be married. But no such understanding existed between them, though theirs was still a romantic relationship. As Natalie Schafer knew, Kaufman had no intention of marrying at that time.

The month that followed was not one of the worst in Kaufman's life. Arriving in Las Vegas early in March, he and Schafer settled into rooms at Anne's hotel. Kaufman stayed for a few days, but Schafer, thoroughly bored by the atmosphere of the place, and perhaps feeling left out of the happy reunion of father and daughter, moved on to Mexico, where she could secure a quick divorce. She promised to fly to California afterward. From Las Vegas, Kaufman went to Hollywood as planned and settled into a bungalow at the Garden of Allah. Work on the musical was delayed because Nunnally Johnson went to Georgia to see his mother, who was ill, but old friends saw to it that Kaufman was kept busy in the interval. There were bridge and croquet, and dinner parties; the Gershwins and the Marxes entertained him. One evening at dinner at the home of Lee and Ira Gershwin, where the food was reputed to be Beverly Hills's best, Kaufman declared, while waiting for dessert, that all the sumptuous meal needed for a perfect finish was baked alaska, only to see a servant bringing that glamorous dish through the dining-room door. At the Garden of Allah, life was ever lively, with a stream of visitors entering and exiting and chatter circulating from poolside. Coming in late one night, Kaufman found a note on his desk from Harpo: "Why the Hael don't you stay home didn't think I could right did you."[7] An atmosphere of old times, of the pre-war good life, settled over the place. Natalie Schafer arrived from Mexico and also took a bungalow at the Garden of Allah.[8]

Anne was granted her divorce on March 14, and with the court's permission she resumed her maiden name. She too came to Hollywood for a visit, her first since 1935. Thinking it not quite the thing to expose her to the bohemianism of the Garden of Allah, Kaufman settled her and himself into a bungalow at the Beverly Hills Hotel. There he was immediately rewarded for his moralism by being robbed of all the clothes in his closet.

Johnson returned from Georgia, and the outlining of the musical proceeded as planned. The collaborators were unable to complete the work at this time, however, because of Johnson's obligations to his studio. But it was decided that Ira Gershwin would write the lyrics for the show's songs and that Arthur Schwartz, then a producer at Columbia, would provide the music. Some casting was also arranged. Kaufman was particularly eager to sign Mary Wickes to play one of the major roles, and that business was happily concluded. With Wickes, Gershwin, and Schwartz, known quantities as private persons and as craftsmen, to be on the team, he had an anchorhold against drifts of doubt and depression.

As a working companion, Johnson was an exceptionally good match for Kaufman, and in this lull in Kaufman's life must have seemed a good catch, too, though their joint product was a failure. Like their mutual friend Herman Mankiewicz, he was a wit whose best quips circulated from one coast to the other. Speaking to the end of his days with a Southern drawl, he liked to create the impression that he had risen to his eminent position from an origin of dire poverty in the deepest backwoods. After turning the play *Tobacco Road* into a film, he was asked for his opinion of its ragged, sharecropping characters and replied (not quite honestly), "Back where I'm from, we think of those folks as the country club set." Like other successful Hollywood writers, including Mankiewicz, he hoped one day to parallel his screen achievement with success on the stage. In the previous season he had sought it with a play called *The World's Full of Girls*, which Jed Harris produced, but this ran only nine performances. Thus he was pleased with Kaufman's suggestion that they collaborate. In the summer the team resumed work, this time in Bucks County, and finished early in August.[9]

For Kaufman it was a typical hot summer of hard work, but heightened and relieved by a major happening: the wedding of Moss Hart and Kitty Carlisle. Kaufman's prophecy that this time, after years of casual relationships, Hart would make the commitment to marriage came true on August 1. The ceremony was performed by a justice of the peace. The couple were unattended at it, but afterward at a dinner party Kaufman and other friends offered their blessings.

The title that Kaufman and Johnson chose for the musical was *Park Avenue,* a misnomer, as some critics pointed out, since the entire action took place on an estate on Long Island. In the authors' view, the title served to distinguish the characters, who were members of highest New York society, and could be presumed to have homes not only on Long Island's North Shore, but in town on Park Avenue. They designed a small-scaled, urbane show that they hoped would appeal to those theatergoers who were bored with the bland and folksy musicals of Richard Rodgers and Oscar Hammerstein II. The overwhelming popularity of the Rodgers-Hammerstein productions was beyond Kaufman's comprehension. With their smiling good nature that engulfed the stage from curtain rise to finale and their lack of ironic wit, the shows were too saccharine for his taste. Both *Oklahoma!* and *Carousel* were then running on Broadway, the latter since 1943, and their film *State Fair* had been a money-spinning success in 1945. There was no question that Kaufman envied Rodgers and Hammerstein their popularity, which he could never be convinced was justified. In 1949, when they added *South Pacific* to their string of hits and valuable copyrights, he remarked to friends, "*South Pacific* only grossed fifty-two hundred dollars tonight. Of course, since it's Sunday there was no performance, but passersby threw fifty-two hundred into the lobby anyway."[10] Nothing could ever persuade him that the famous team's kind of musical was a genuine contribution to culture. "I don't think Oscar Hammerstein knows a goddam thing about the theater," he wrote to Moss Hart still later, "except maybe those sweet birdies in the trees—for my money he's definitely, and exclusively, a birds in the trees man. I could do with a bit more birdies in me—but I'm just as definitely a son-of-a-bitch in the trees fellow."[11]

When the script was ready and the casting complete, Gershwin and Schwartz came East with their portfolio of songs. Leonora Corbett, with whom Kaufman had had a brief affair, was given the leading part of the bride's mother. Determined to show that she was a star, she demanded the right of refusal on the songs written for her. Kaufman, Max Gordon, and the songwriters called on her at her apartment in the Waldorf Towers to let her hear the numbers and were relieved to find that she approved of them. A good-looking man was there at the time, but the actress did not introduce him to them. They had all disliked their mission and were glad to leave. As they made their goodbyes at the elevator, Max Gordon asked about the gentleman caller. "He's in cotton," said Leonora Corbett. "And," said Kaufman, "dem dat plants it is soon forgotten."

During rehearsals, a wave of disappointment swept over the company.

Corbett's performance did not inspire confidence, and Jed Prouty, a middle-aged character actor from Hollywood, was painfully miscast in another major role. Max Gordon was astonished to find Kaufman so obviously faltering in his casting sense and so hesitant to make substitutions as the rehearsals went on. Prouty played the role at the opening in New Haven on September 19, but was replaced by Ralph Riggs, who in turn was replaced by J. Pat O'Malley before the role was finally given to, and kept by, David Wayne.

Casting was not the only problem. Schwartz with Howard Dietz and Gershwin with his brother or with Kurt Weill had written songs much superior to the score that as a team they provided for *Park Avenue*. None of the songs was to have much of a future, though at least one, "Don't Be a Woman if You Can," a comic lament sung by a trio of unliberated wives, displayed a hint of each writer's flair. The book, to be sure, was the production's greatest weakness. There was, first of all, too much of it; Kaufman, with his usual indifference to musical numbers, wrote so much dialogue that the numbers appeared as digressions. In addition, the book's cynicism grew increasingly forbidding as the evening wore along. Taking off from Johnson's story, the collaborators made this the first marriage for the young couple, but created in the bride-to-be a young woman completely accustomed to the idea of marriage as a temporary measure, whereas her fiancé, a Southerner, is aghast to discover how often both her parents and all their friends have been married and divorced. The series of revelations is prolonged almost to the final curtain, and virtually without relief, since most of the songs pertain to the twin institutions of marriage and divorce. In the original form of the script, one of the much-married middle-aged gents was shown to have become engaged to a lissome young girl only to find that she was his daughter, the product of a long-since dissolved and forgotten marriage. This was so repellent to Max Gordon and, so far as he could judge, to the audience that he insisted on a change. Kaufman stubbornly resisted Gordon's request until after the opening, when he too at last detected signs of revulsion in the audience. The best alteration that he and Johnson could come up with was to have the poor chap break off the engagement on discovering, not that the girl was his daughter, but that she was all of eighteen and thus too old for him. That was not the authorial correction that the ailing show required, and in any case it came too late.[12]

Because of cast changes and the necessity of rewriting songs as well as dialogue, Gordon kept the production on the road until November 4. That the New York reviews were unfavorable was no more than he had expected. Seventy-two performances were all that *Park Avenue* could sustain. Kaufman's assumption that the audience would welcome such a cynical view of modern life revealed less about the age itself than about his current mood. Still unreconciled to Beatrice's death, still living a butterfly life, flitting not from flower to flower, but from weed to weed, as Natalie Schafer put it,[13] he had suffered a blunting of his judgment. In this play he shunned not only sentimentality, but ordinary warmth.

The damp reception of *Park Avenue* was a setback to Kaufman. When it closed, he was left without a dramatic idea with which to follow it; nor did he find anything to pique his interest in the scripts that he was invited to direct. He began to confront promising writers with the suggestion that they turn out a play for him to stage. One of them was Goodman Ace, the gifted radio writer. For years Ace and his wife Jane had entranced listeners with the serial *Easy Aces,* the writing of which revealed a sharp, thoroughly debunked wit akin to Kaufman's. With the help of Groucho Marx, Kaufman set up a luncheon meeting with Ace in the hope of persuading him to write a play based on the serial. "If you write a play, I'll produce it," Kaufman said. Ace countered with the suggestion that Kaufman write a play for *him* to produce. When they finished their meal, Kaufman told Ace that he was off to play bridge and that he wanted to think while playing that Ace was beginning to write the first act. Ace was offended by Kaufman's peremptoriness, and there the matter ended, none too cordially.[14]

Though this was an arid period for Kaufman, it was a fertile one for the American stage as a whole. Tennessee Williams and Arthur Miller, who would eventually be looked on as major contributors to world drama, were finding a ready audience for their plays. But their plays were not Kaufman's kind; he could not have directed them, to say nothing of writing works resembling them. Especially was he put off by the plays of Williams, whose preoccupation in the theater with neurotic behavior Kaufman never saw the sense of. However, Kaufman did understand his own problem, the inability to come out from under the shadow cast on him by Beatrice's death. For a brief period he tried psychoanalysis, but got no help. He could not get over the loss. On the first anniversary of her death, October 6, 1946, in accordance with Jewish tradition he began the annual practice of lighting a candle to mark the day.

In the early spring of 1947, Kaufman's peace of mind was threatened by a new turn of events at home. For the preceding three years Anne had been living in the apartment at 410 Park Avenue, but now she was in love again and intended to marry. The young man was Bruce Colen, a recent Harvard graduate only a few months older than she. He had a minor editorial post at

Simon & Schuster, where she had formerly worked. An older woman friend employed at the same firm mentioned him to Anne and pointed out that he, too, lived at 410 Park Avenue. His apartment, which he shared with his mother, was two floors above the Kaufmans'. He wore a hearing aid, having been slightly deaf since birth, but this did not mar his looks. After their first meeting, which (fittingly) took place on Valentine's Day, Anne and Colen began to see each other steadily. In April Colen proposed and was accepted.

Neither Anne nor Colen found it easy to notify Kaufman of the engagement. One day Anne dragged her fiancé into Kaufman's study and ducked out, leaving the young man to face up to the dragon in his lair. To Colen it always seemed that Kaufman found it difficult to speak to him because of his deafness. On this occasion, Kaufman was stretched out on a couch, and Colen was bade to sit in a chair near his feet. He moved to be closer to Kaufman and stated his business. Kaufman sprang up to absorb the news of the engagement and then offered the opinion that the pair were too young to marry. Nevertheless, he did not interfere with their plans. On May 8 the wedding took place at Barley Sheaf Farm with Kaufman's reluctant approval.[15]

Though Kaufman was not a scheming tyrant-father bent on making a slave of his child, he was reluctant to let go altogether. Before the wedding, he reminded Anne that plans had been made for a weekend croquet game at the farm, and made it clear that he was sorry she would not be there to play it with him. He called her at Atlantic City, where the couple were spending their honeymoon, to remind her again of the game. He did not command her to return, but implied that he wished she would do so. She and Colen packed up their bags and headed for Bucks County.

If Anne's romance and marriage posed a dispiriting threat to Kaufman's domestic comfort, relief of a sort came along providentially in the form of an invitation to work once again in Hollywood. Nunnally Johnson, disappointed over the failure of *Park Avenue,* but seeing no reason to hold it against his collaborator, offered him a picture to direct at Universal. After some ten years of discontinuous employment at the studios as scriptwriter and script doctor, this was the first firm offer Kaufman had ever had to direct a specific film. The script, entitled *The Senator Was Indiscreet,* was the work of Charles MacArthur, with uncredited contributions by Nunnally Johnson, and was based on a *Collier's* story by Edwin Lanham. The plot had to do with a white-haired dullard of a United States Senator, Melvin

Ashton by name, who foolishly and, it turns out, vainly aspires to the presidency. Were it not that for more than thirty years he has recorded in a diary all the misdeeds of top-level members of his party, no one would pay any attention to him. But because of the diary, he poses a threat of some magnitude to the party's future. He blackmails his way to the presidential candidacy. Eventually, of course, this human bombshell is defused by an investigative reporter, and the Republic is saved.

On paper this sounded like a jolly satiric tale. "We don't exactly aim to be subtle," Johnson drawled in a reporter's ear.[16] With the adroit comedian William Powell cast as Ashton, it promised a good profit for Universal. The first scenes to be filmed were some location shots in New York, and when they were completed, Kaufman left for Hollywood from Grand Central Station with the Colens and many friends, including the Harts and the Kanins, to see him off, all expecting him to return with a hit.

As had never failed to happen when Kaufman went West, every possible step was taken to ensure his comfort. Once more he stayed at the Garden of Allah, and the usual after-work entertainments of bridge, croquet, and dinner parties were arranged. But the process of film-making failed to spark his curiosity. He did the work conscientiously, but without the enjoyment that was always obvious to onlookers when he was directing a play. There were many reasons for his indifference. The overriding one, simply stated, was that he was not his own man, and he knew it, no matter how gracefully Johnson and others at the studio deferred to him, for the final look of the picture would not be within his province to determine. In addition, he was utterly bored by the "piecework" aspect of filming, as he and Ferber had described it in *Stage Door*—the making of the picture by fits and starts because of retakes and interruptions for the setting up of each new sequence. When Johnson once asked him how he liked directing, he answered, "It's all right if you can stay awake." He seldom seemed to lack self-confidence, however. When he did, it was over the camera set-ups. To arrange these, Johnson brought in Gene Fowler, Jr., as his production assistant. Fowler was not the picture's cameraman, but was a young man well trained in film-making who could tell Kaufman how to get the effects he wanted.[17] A potential problem that fortunately never troubled the production was the fact that Kaufman, unlike Johnson, was not on friendly terms with MacArthur. For too many years he had been exposed to MacArthur's drinking.[18] But after delivering the script, MacArthur had nothing to do with the making of the movie. Relieving the tedium of the directorial assignment, a romantic attachment developed between Kaufman and one of the attractive, young actresses in the cast. For a fifty-seven-year-old, the attention that Kaufman received from her was indeed consoling.

In the end, *The Senator Was Indiscreet* was a disappointment, despite a few happy moments of dialogue and action. Unlike such directors as Rouben Mamoulian, Elia Kazan, and Orson Welles, Kaufman did not make the transition from stage to screen technique successfully. The film was static and stagey in the shooting, and not improved in the editing. It also turned out to be an underpopulated picture, with backgrounds relatively empty that ought to have been crowded with extras. Powell, always excellent in worldly roles, was not at his best as the silvery-haired, none-too-bright politician. The picture was released late in December 1947. It thus got to the screen in time to be eligible for the Academy Awards in the spring, but received not one. Its potential at the box office, slim at best, was further reduced by the deepening cold-war mentality of the public. In October the House Un-American Activities Committee initiated a series of hearings on the alleged communist past of Hollywood workers, touching off an explosion whose echoes would be heard for thirty years and more in the future. To make a film that satirized the highest reaches of the federal government was to risk a financial disaster, or worse—public condemnation and consequent loss of income for the participants—if one were not a celebrated capitalist prankster like Johnson, MacArthur, or Kaufman. Reviews were mixed, but most were unfavorable.

Only in one scene does the Kaufman touch show itself. This is a moment when one of the party henchmen brings to a smoke-filled hotel room a shapely blonde named Ingrid. She speaks not a word, but before the scene ends she sits beside, and titillates with her presence, every man in the room. Since this scene was not in MacArthur's script, it may have been Kaufman's gift to the film (if it was not Johnson's). Its source, one suspects, was an episode at the Swopes' Great Neck home in the 1920s, which Kaufman may have witnessed or heard about from Ring Lardner, who was there with his brother Rex when it occurred. On this evening, according to Ring Lardner, Jr., "a newly imported Swedish actress and her fiancé were among the guests. The young woman drew attention by moving from one male lap to another, causing Rex to observe, 'She's not a Swede, she's a Laplander,' and Ring to add, 'And she manages to keep one lap ahead of her fiancé.' "[19]

Returning from Hollywood early in August, Kaufman scouted around for new projects. Dramatic rights to a comic piece of his, "School for Waiters," that the *New Yorker* published on August 2, were optioned by Arthur Schwartz for the lavish revue *Inside U.S.A.* that he and Howard Dietz were planning for the spring. The presentation of this satiric comment on the bad manners and inefficiency of waiters, as turned into a sketch by Arnold Auerbach, was all that Kaufman had to look forward to in the theater. However, he had a prospect of another sort to think about, for Anne was pregnant. The baby was due in February. That the expected child might prove a source of joy to him was a possibility on which he had no comment, though he was not uninterested in the progress of Anne's condition. There was, after all, the chance that the baby would be a girl and in that case could be named Beatrice. As the months passed, he became ever more convinced that the child *would* be a girl, and from Anne he drew a promise that if so she *would* be named Beatrice.[20]

His vague discontent, his inability to peer into the murky future and see his course in it, was obliquely reflected in a conversation that he had with Alfred Lunt at about this time. In January 1947, while acting in Terence Rattigan's *O Mistress Mine*, Lunt fell ill, so seriously that he was warned by his doctor that he might not recover. After surgery, however, he quickly regained his strength and resumed his role in the play, which had shut down during his illness. Seeing him at a party some time after his recovery, Kaufman went up to him and asked how it had felt to be under the threat of death. Lunt answered that he had had such warnings before and had grown used to them. Kaufman took this in solemnly and said little in reply. It struck Lunt that Kaufman, whom he knew to be afraid of illness and death, had been disappointed with the answer. It was as though Kaufman were tacitly admitting that he would have been badly frightened under the circumstances and had hoped to hear from Lunt an admission of equally great fear.[21]

In a letter to Mary Wickes of November 2, 1947, written in response to a query about his plans and whether they included a role for her, Kaufman's tone was subdued enough to suggest a continuing malaise:

> It comes down to this, the theatre is in rather a bad way these days, and if you could get some of your Hollywood friends, like liberal old Jack Warner, to build some beautiful new theatres, including, of course, the Mary Wickes, and write some wonderful new plays . . . well . . .
>
> There seem to be hits, but people like Shaw and Euripides and Sammy Cahn have got them, and that does me no good. In a well regulated world there would be a wonderful comedy for you, and these many years

I have dreamed of helping to write it, and nothing would make me happier—well, *almost* nothing—and yet it doesn't happen. But for God's sake don't tie up with one of those long contracts out there—I'm sure you won't.

I sleep until eleven daily and wake up a day older, every time.

But soon the clouds opened up a little, for he and Ferber decided to collaborate once more. At the time, Ferber was between novels. She had hit a low in 1945 with *Great Son*, a saga of the Northwest, and was not yet ready to write the Texas epic that she had long contemplated and that would emerge from her typewriter in 1952 as the financial gusher entitled *Giant*. But Ferber, though unoccupied with her fiction, did not need Kaufman's collaborative assistance as much as he needed hers. No matter how uncomfortable had been their shared endeavors with *The Land Is Bright*, he wanted to get back to work with her. She, however, was more interested in finding a suitable apartment for herself in New York, for she had made up her mind to sell her beloved but burdensome Connecticut home. Kaufman and all her other faithful friends were bade to search out suitable quarters for her, a task made none too easy by her exacting requirements and the postwar scarcity of attractive apartments in Manhattan. To the press Kaufman happily announced on November 20, "We'll write [a play], if someone will just find her an apartment in New York."[22] It was not for another three years that she found a place in town and sold the house, but she was willing nevertheless to begin the play in the winter of 1948.

Another project loomed for the season of 1948-49, thanks to Anne. During her pregnancy, an opportunity to make a start as a theatrical producer came her way, and she grasped at it. Never before had she cared to be involved in the theater. The project that attracted her was initially developed by her friend Clinton Wilder. As one of many Army Air Corps enlisted men on the managerial staff of *Winged Victory*, Wilder had spent much of his time in the service with that production. On his release from the Army, he chose not to return to Princeton, but to take up a career as a producer. With Bernard Hart, he took an option on the dramatic rights to John Cheever's *New Yorker* stories about some ill-assorted couples who together rent and live in a New York town house. Herman Mankiewicz was their first choice as an adaptor, but after reading one act of his adaptation, they concluded that he was not the writer for the job. Unable to find any other writer suited to the task, they dropped their option, whereupon Anne and Arnold Saint Subber, a production assistant in Max Gordon's office, optioned the rights. At first they approached Fred Coe to make the adaptation, but then turned to Gertrude Tonkonogy, whose *Three-Cornered Moon,* a comedy set in Brooklyn, had been one of the pleasures of the 1933-34 season. An admirer of Kaufman, she sent him a script of hers to look over almost every season. She was willing to dramatize Cheever's stories, and set to work. To direct the venture, Anne thought of approaching Broadway's most respected director of comedy, her own father.

Kaufman expressed his willingness to take on the play. Before 1947 came to its close, Gertrude Tonkonogy was bent to her task, with Kaufman, good editor that he was, coaching and prodding to get the play that he wanted from her without letting the unsettling notion form in her head that it was as much his work as hers. But as the script took shape, he was seized with doubt about working with, and actually for, Anne. The argument he offered was that Max Gordon had a smooth-running office capable of mounting the play with efficiency and style. With this proven mechanism available, they should not waste time on setting up a new office. Anne saw through this line, which if applied generally would condemn every new enterprise before it started, but she decided not to protest it. In addition to all other considerations, which included the fact that her father would simply withdraw if pressed by her, was the fact that she had been advised by her obstetrician to have her baby delivered by caesarean section soon, almost a month before it was due. Max Gordon offered a generous deal to her and Saint Subber.

With Max Gordon, Kaufman worked out a fall schedule. *Town House* would come first, to be followed immediately by his and Ferber's *Bravo!* It was the old George S. Kaufman swinging into action, planning to open one play on a Saturday evening and begin rehearsals of another the following Monday. He expected to have Tonkonogy's finished script in hand by late spring, to complete the writing of *Bravo!* with Ferber in early August, and to go into rehearsals with *Town House* at that moment. All this came to pass. So too did his prediction that Anne would have a daughter. The child was born on January 10, 1948, and, true to her promise, Anne named her Beatrice. Soon, however, Kaufman asked her to find a nickname for the child, because he could not bear the poignant memories of the original Beatrice that the name evoked. Taking a cue from Bruce Colen's mother, who called the child "Petsy," the couple nicknamed her Betsy, the name by which family and friends would always address her. By a happy coincidence, only four days later occurred the birth of Moss and Kitty Hart's first child, a son.

Beyond offering congratulations and making presents to them, Kaufman showed no particular feeling for either of these infants though they were his granddaughter and the firstborn of the one male for whom he had lasting affection. Had it been otherwise, had he gushed and cooed, all four parents would have been shocked to see it. One glance at Betsy on a Bucks County weekend was enough to satisfy his curiosity for the week ahead. Moreover, not until after more than a year of acquaintance was he ready to warm to the child's father. Then, quite surprisingly, an event occurred at the farm that left the young man with the thought that just possibly Kaufman could tolerate him. One evening when the family and their guests, the Harts, were summoned to dinner, Kaufman, thinking that perhaps Colen might not have been able to hear, reached over and touched his arm. This was so over-whelmingly uncharacteristic that Moss Hart was moved to say, "It's obvious that he likes you."[23]

More than Anne's child, and Hart's, the two plays to be readied for production occupied his thoughts. Yet he was incapable of getting an accurate perspective on either of them. He began casting *Town House* in his mind long before he had a workable script from Gertrude Tonkonogy. As early as January 7 he wrote to Mary Wickes in California that he expected to have a role for her soon, and only a week later he wrote to her again about the play. The role was a large one, and she was glad to accept it on reading the script in May. Opposite her he cast Hiram Sherman, whose work he had followed with enjoyment since *Sing Out the News*. Other roles were taken by such favorites of his as Margaret Dale and Vera Fuller Mellish. Rehearsals began in August, and the out-of-town opening was set for September 4 in Boston.

During rehearsals, he and Gertrude Tonkonogy worked steadily to strengthen the script, but they were not of the same mind as to how it should be altered. Cheever's stories, though not lacking in comic moments, were by no means farcical, for Cheever was concerned to look closely and seriously at the problems faced by six people—three couples—in their effort to live together in fairly close quarters without impinging on one another's rights and rousing one another to anger. Kaufman's instinct was to rewrite every scene for laughs and to add comic business in rehearsal. Gertrude Tonkonogy was not pleased with this constant pointing up of humor, but was too much the admirer of Kaufman's own playwriting to make a vigorous protest. The physical production was, foreseeably, complicated by the fact that it was necessary to show two floors of the house at once. It was an expensive production for that reason, and the costs were raised further by the necessity of cutting a hole in the stage floor to accommodate a staircase supposedly leading to the basement of the house. So high was this set that the customers occupying the first few rows had to crane their necks uncomfortably to see the action on the second floor. Kaufman shrugged this problem off with a muttered word to the effect that for years persons he scarcely knew had pestered him for front-row seats, and now he was prepared to let them have them. Red bicycle reflectors were installed on a lip near the edge of the upper level of the set to warn the actors not to step off into nothingness.[24]

In Boston it was obvious that the play was in trouble, and that the trouble was due to the heavy-handed humor. Both Hart and Ferber came up to see the play and begged Kaufman to take some of it out. Though he ordered more rewriting, he did not noticeably alter the comic tone; nor did he pro-long the road tour beyond the scheduled two and a half weeks. Before the Broadway opening on September 23 he scheduled an invitational matinee for actors and other theater workers. This went so well that the cast members allowed themselves to think that they had signed up for a hit, despite the voices within predicting disaster. They were mistaken in their optimism. All things conspired to draw a celebrity audience to the opening performance: it was a Max Gordon presentation, it was the first play directed by Kaufman in two years, and it was the first major production of the season. The actresses in the cast were agog over the rumor that Clark Gable was out front. But this audience was patently unmoved by the proceedings. It offered little applause at the first- and second-act curtains, and showed not much more approval at the close. Kaufman was annoyed by this show of indifference toward his work, and let it be known. When the curtain came down on the first call, the actors heard him shout, "That's it. No more." The curtain did not rise on the actors again. Mary Wickes and Hiram Sherman were done out of their solo bows. After twelve performances Kaufman and Gordon withdrew the play.[25]

Though *Bravo!* held on for forty-four performances, exactly four weeks longer than the run of *Town House*, its failure was an even worse experience for Kaufman's colleagues and friends, because his name was on it as one of its authors. If any system of weights and balances could be devised for the ranking of literary works on an absolute scale, it would surely place this feeble comedy below Gertrude Tonkonogy's. It is a play about next to nothing, perhaps the emptiest that Kaufman ever wrote. Having the compulsion to write, but no new ideas, he and Ferber exhumed the corpse of the project that they had buried in White Sulphur Springs in 1941, the comedy about a family of refugees from Central Europe who settle in a New York brownstone. They had had a clear-headed sense of its unsuitability to their talents then. That they found merit in it six years later was a manifestation of their fear of idleness.

The protagonist of the play is a Middle-European playwright, Zoltan Lazko, whose career bears a resemblance to that of Ferenc Molnár, who was then living in New York. With him in a West Side town house are his mistress of many years, Rosa Rucker, and other émigrés who in prewar Budapest and Vienna had lived in a charmed atmosphere of praise and celebration, but in postwar New York can barely make a living. One is no less than a prince; another, a judge. The meager little plot has to do with Lazko's foolish, unsuccessful effort as a writer to turn from romantic themes to the rude American scene, along with his and Rosa's decision to become American citizens. Also thrown in is some confusion over the immigration papers of Lisa Kemper, a young actress-protégée of theirs from the old country. All comes right in the end for the entire household, thanks in large part to the assistance of Bernard Baruch, an elderly *deux ex machina,* whom Lazko encounters (off stage) on a bench in the park. Baruch's promise to intercede on Lisa's behalf saves her, saves the play in which she is about to open, and encourages Lazko to have another try at writing about his new country. "Yes, sir!" he says at the final curtain. "This time I write a masterpiece. A *real* American play. But *Wunderbar!* . . . How do they say on the radio? Zoltan Lazko writes again!"

It was a frustrating experience for Kaufman's friends to witness his futile endeavor to make something of the play. Max Gordon disliked the script from the first, but went ahead with the production out of loyalty buttressed by the hope that Kaufman would again one day hand him a surefire comedy. In New Haven, where it opened on October 21, he and the Harts glumly watched the play unfold. They knew it had no chance. With Ferber joining them, they begged Kaufman to let it go then and there, but were powerless against his silent doggedness. On at least one important matter he agreed with them: the performance of the émigrée actress Rose Stradner as Rosa Rucker. It was a dead weight on an already leaden piece of writing. In Boston, where the production next played, Max Gordon went backstage to dismiss her, since Kaufman, characteristically, would not and could not do it. Even Max, the hardened veteran of Broadway battles, was taken aback when the actress replied with an obscenity. Nevertheless, she was replaced, with the newspapers carrying the flattering message that she was too young in appearance for the role. Lili Darvas, Ferenc Molnár's real-life wife, was cast in the part. She outshone Oscar Homolka in the role of Lazko and won the best notices when the play reached New York on November 9.[26]

Bravo! was originally scheduled to come to Broadway on November 15, but was brought in early at Kaufman's insistence so that it would not open in the same week with Hart's new comedy, *Light Up the Sky*, which was set to open on November 18. Kaufman's purpose was to deny the press the opportunity to compare the two comedies. Hart's play, which began as a rather serious work about the struggle of a playwright and his producer to turn a poor play into a good one, also had trouble on the road, mirroring its content. In Boston (where the play was set, in a suite at the Ritz), Hart played down the seriousness, played up the laughs, and ended with a serviceable if lightweight Broadway comedy that ran through the season. The critics on the whole were kind to the play, and in writing their reviews were sensitive enough to avoid references to *Bravo!*, as Kaufman had hoped. When the dust had settled and the scenery of that unfortunate production was on the way to the warehouse, Max Gordon offered to give Anne one of the sumptuous, Castillo-designed gowns that had embellished the last act. She was delighted and remarked on the beauty of the dress. "It should be beautiful," Gordon replied, "It's the only dress ever made that cost $80,000."

Though the dismal box-office returns of *Town House* and *Bravo!* suggested that Kaufman's theatrical instinct was letting him down, at least he retained his famed verbal quickness. This gave him uncommon value in the eyes of television executives, for in the rapidly expanding new medium it developed that one of the most popular kinds of program was the panel show, which brought the faces and voices of the famous into the viewer's living room. As early as 1946 the men who ran the networks began to make inquiries of Kaufman, who was famous indeed and a proven commodity after his years with *Information Please*. Nothing came of the inquiries at first, but in the fall of 1948 he signed to appear on another radio talk show called *This Is Broadway*, which was conceived by Irving Mansfield, a Columbia Broadcasting System executive. Clifton Fadiman, the moderator on *Information Please*, took the same post on the new show. The third "regular" was Abe Burrows, a young comedy writer who was well established on the West Coast in radio. As with *Information Please*, a guest panelist would join these three on each broadcast. Members of the various show-business professions would appear before them, each asking advice about a special problem. Since the tone of the show was comic, the problems were never serious; the panelists had no qualms about offering direct answers.

As Kaufman interpreted his assignment, it was to show up the bogusness of the problems in a few sharp words. Audiences were quick to express their appreciation of the panel's skill. The show became such a hit that in 1949 CBS decided to put it on television, with a new name: *This Is Show Business.* Thus at the age of sixty Kaufman became a television star.

Before achieving this new distinction, Kaufman altered the quality of his life in another, more pervasive and meaningful way. In May 1949 he married for the second time.

Between the Broadway openings of *Town House* and *Bravo!* in the fall of 1948, theatergoers were treated to a new, serious, and skillfully constructed play imported from England: *Edward, My Son,* by Robert Morley and Noel Langley. It opened on September 30 after a year's run in London. The stars of the production were Morley himself and Peggy Ashcroft. Morley played the self-made businessman Lord Holt, whose every other thought is devoted to the well-being of his only child, the title character who never appears on stage. Peggy Ashcroft played Holt's unhappy, alcoholic wife. The play received gratifying notices in the New York papers and became the first hit of the season; it remained on Broadway for 260 performances. Morley and Ashcroft were familiar to the American audience, as was Ian Hunter, who played Holt's disillusioned confidant, the obstetrician who brings Edward into the world.

But new to the American stage was Leueen MacGrath, the thirty-four-year-old blonde actress who played Eileen Perry, Holt's mistress, and whose only appearances were confined to the second act. Some members of the audience may have recalled catching a glimpse of her in the screen version of Shaw's *Pygmalion.* Like Morley and Ashcroft, she had been in the West End cast of *Edward, My Son,* and she had also been in the film version (with Spencer Tracy as Holt) that had been made in England, but was not yet released. Though this small, low-voiced woman, who never failed to bring out the protective instinct in any man, was the direct opposite of the generously proportioned, outspoken, determinedly independent Beatrice, she was destined to be Kaufman's second wife.

Leueen MacGrath (pronounced "Lou-een M'Grah") was born in London on July 3, 1914, to Walter Michael Anthony MacGrath and Jean Martin MacGrath. Both parents were Irish; MacGrath, a mining engineer, served in France during the First World War and received both the Distinguished Service Order and the Croix de Guerre. Jean MacGrath wrote plays as a pastime; none of them was ever produced, however. Educated in Switzerland, Belgium, and England, Leueen in early childhood announced to her parents that she expected to have a career on the stage. It was witnessing a performance of *Peter Pan* that moved her to make this declaration. Saying goodbye to her boarding schools and convent schools in her teens, she made good on her promise to herself and entered the Royal Academy of Dramatic Art. Her first appearance on the stage took place on April 17, 1933, in a forgotten play called *Beggars in Hell.* Thereafter she was never long between roles, though not all were to her liking. In January 1937 she replaced Jessica Tandy in Terence Rattigan's hit comedy *French without Tears;* having signed a run-of-the play contract, she remained, not very happily, in the cast until the play closed in 1939, and consequently had to refuse an alluring invitation from the Old Vic. Though thoroughly professional in meeting the demands of her engagements and never failing to win good notices, Leueen MacGrath as a young woman developed neither aggressiveness about her career nor a surpassing love of acting. But the parts kept coming, and she took them. Her role in *Edward, My Son* was not large, but the character was intelligent and sensitive, and she conveyed these qualities with striking appeal. The director, Peter Ashmore, added to the memorableness of her fleeting presence by ringing down the second-act curtain on a stage blacked out except for a spotlight lingering on her small, pale, uptilted face.

Leueen had been married twice, first to Christopher Burn, then to Desmond Davis. Both marriages had ended in divorce. Free of romantic ties, good-natured, and gregarious, she enjoyed New York during the run of her play. To one coming from ravaged England, where food rationing remained in force, the city's opulence was overwhelming. It was through Garson Kanin and Ruth Gordon that she met Kaufman. Invited to 410 Park Avenue one evening, they brought her along. She had a book with her that evening, and, conveniently, she forgot to take it home with her. Seeing it the next day, and finding her name in it, Kaufman telephoned to arrange a meeting.

Kaufman very soon found that what he felt for this young woman was quite different from the emotions that had been stirred in him by any of the women he had known before. Normally capable of becoming white with rage when forced to cope with a woman who caused a delay by forgetting her gloves or keys, or who assumed the role of dependent female, he found that he enjoyed Leueen's reliant manner, her air of preoccupation, even her lack of punctuality. Not one other woman in his life had been at all like her in these ways. It was therefore startling to his friends and also to his relations to note how deeply in love he fell within a month of their meeting. This time he *was* in love, not merely seeking a sexual convenience. Neither he nor Leueen saw any reason to cloak the relationship in secrecy. To Ward Morehouse of the New York *Sun*, Leueen remarked, "I admire George Kaufman as a human being, more than anybody I know. It's rare to find anyone of such staggering honesty."[27] Yet with the memory of two failed marriages haunting her, she was reluctant to say yes to Kaufman when he proposed. In April, along with Morley, she left the cast of the play (Ashcroft had already left it). With Kaufman she planned a trip to the Caribbean as a sort of test of their readiness for marriage. They went by train to Miami and planned to sail from there. But because Leueen, typically, forgot to bring her re-entry card along, they remained in Hollywood, Florida, instead. This brief experiment in living together was a success; marriage seemed a quite reasonable possibility. On May 26 at Barley Sheaf Farm they were married by a Doylestown justice of the peace, whose other calling was the selling of automobiles.

Kaufman's love for Leueen was so intense that inevitably it precipitated a series of new problems in his life. He was in his sixtieth year, his bride in her thirty-fifth. His health was still sound, and he lacked the habits of smoking, drinking, and overeating that might have harmed it. But he fretted over the possibility that his sexual powers would suffer a decline and that his appearance also would deteriorate. There was, in addition, the burden of his memories of Beatrice. For Leueen to become mistress of the two homes that Beatrice had presided over created problems for her and Kaufman alike. Before the wedding took place, Kaufman had been approached to direct *Pretty Penny*, a revue written by Jerome Chodorov and Harold Rome, which a new producer, Leonard Field, expected to try out in summer theaters and bring to Broadway in the fall. Kaufman accepted, but did not foresee that his marriage would give rise to worries that would get in his way when he undertook work on the show.

Bookings for *Pretty Penny* were made at the Bucks County Playhouse and at theaters in Westport, Connecticut, and Atlantic City. In the cast were David Burns, Carl Reiner, and the young comedienne Lenore Lonergan, who, years before, had been praised for her performance as the best friend of the heroine of *Junior Miss*. The dances were designed by Michael Kidd, who also danced in the show; among the other dancers were two who would one day become leading Broadway choreographers, Onna White and Peter Gennaro. For the most part, the songs and sketches reflected the left-of-center political stance of the two writers. Though the sketches were only fair, Rome contributed at least two amusing songs, one about the ongoing Congressional investigation of alleged subversives, and another mocking the notion that the best things in life are free, with the agreeable title, "I'd Rather Be a Rich Man with a Million Dollars Than a Poor Man with a Pocketful of Dreams."

Despite the best efforts of the talented persons engaged, the show looked to be in trouble from the outset. It did not go over well with audiences in Bucks County; nor were Rome, Chodorov, and Kaufman deceived about its merits. But in their wish to put in new numbers and hold more rehearsals, they were frustrated by Equity's rules, which forbade any tinkering with summer productions other than changing lines in existing material. There was little that could be done to improve and save the show, though the writers and Kaufman conferred repeatedly on it. It happened that Moss Hart at the time was also staging a troubled production, the musical *Miss Liberty*, with a book by Robert E. Sherwood and songs by Irving Berlin. When *Pretty Penny* opened in Bucks County, this production was playing in Philadelphia. Hart was having a difficult time persuading Sherwood to buckle down to the obviously necessary chore of revising the book, but, aware of the magnitude of Kaufman's problems, both personal and professional, he offered to sit in on the *Pretty Penny* conferences. Much to the writer's astonishment, Kaufman refused to allow this. It was as though he had to prove to himself that he could carry off this job successfully while relying as little as possible on the judgment of anyone else. To Jerome Chodorov, it marked the turning point for Kaufman, the moment when his professional powers went into decline.[28]

The situation was soon to be made much worse. Though Kaufman admired the talent of David Burns, who had been the first actor to play the role of Banjo in *The Man Who Came to Dinner*, he did not have the patience at this time to cope with Burns's occasional quirks of temperament. He found a number of faults with the actor's performance, and, in keeping with the usual practice of the theater, delivered notes to Burns, as to others in the cast. In Westport, Burns blew up in Kaufman's face over them and delivered himself of a stream of obscenities. In thirty years in the theater, nothing like this had happened to Kaufman before. He filed the charge with the Equity Council on July 13 that Burns had conducted himself in a manner unbecoming an Equity member. The union did little about the charge. Burns was reprimanded for using "abusive language," but many members of the Council expressed the opinion that he had done so under such extreme provocation that he deserved to be exonerated. Even before hearing this unflattering minority report, Kaufman resigned as director. His departure spelled the demise of the production. Field, finding the situation

hopeless, closed down *Pretty Penny* after the Atlantic City engagement.
Everyone had lost.[29]

Too preoccupied with the effort to make a success of his marriage to brood
over this dust-up, Kaufman spent the rest of the summer of 1949 quietly
at Barley Sheaf Farm with Leueen. Because Bruce Colen was then working
in Philadelphia for *Holiday,* the new travel magazine, Anne and he were
also living at the farm. At first the two women did not hit it off, though both
tried valiantly not to seem reserved with each other in front of Kaufman.
Since Anne had a family life of her own and was not financially dependent
on her father, it was not envy or jealousy that prevented her from warming
to Leueen. What troubled her was the injustice, as she viewed it, of her father's willingness to put up with certain weaknesses in Leueen that he had
never tolerated in her or anyone else: unpunctuality, procrastination, a lack
of serious attention to the details of daily living. Soon, however, as Anne
began to feel grateful to Leueen for making her father happy, the two became fast friends. They found it amusing to make a kind of game of their
relationship, being only eleven years apart in age. Leueen was Anne's "step-
mummy," and Anne to Leueen was "my little girl." Occasionally, Anne
would bristle: she often felt that her father looked upon her as a kind of
superior servant who at a call from him could be expected to drive him and
Leueen to the farm and run errands for them, but she was capable of refusing to obey when she felt like it. In October she was troubled to find that
her father still observed the tradition of lighting a candle on the anniversary
of Beatrice's death. It was clear to her that Leueen took from this a suggestion that she could never compete wholly with the image of Beatrice in his
mind. Anne therefore told her father to stop it, and he did.

The fall brought Kaufman two new projects. The first to get under way
was a play offered to him and Max Gordon by William Walden, a sometime
staff writer for the *New Yorker.* Entitled *Metropole,* it presented an undis-
guised portrait of Harold Ross. At the center of the plot was a publisher's
effort to develop a magazine to rival his. Kaufman and Gordon cast Lee
Tracy as Hill, the editor, and brought in, among others, such favorites of
theirs as Reynolds Evans, Edith Atwater, and Arlene Francis. A fine actor
too seldom seen on Broadway, Tracy had played the leading role of Hildy
Johnson in *The Front Page* under Kaufman's direction more than twenty
years earlier. It was perhaps the memory of that production that spurred
Kaufman to stage *Metropole* at a frantic pace, as though it too were a dia-
mond-hard farce with laughs calculated to come at about the rate of one a
minute. Unfortunately, it was no marvel of mirth; in fact, it was slight of

plot and dull in characterization. The result was that to audiences it seemed nothing more than a sort of noise-making machine.

Metropole went into rehearsal in the middle of October and opened its out-of-town tour in Wilmington on November 10. It was evident from the first showing that the play was too feeble for Broadway, but Kaufman refused to give up. With his aid, Walden kept at the script through a week in Baltimore and two in Philadelphia, though local reviewers offered no encouragement. In Philadelphia, Gordon told Kaufman that it was futile to bring in the play, that to do so would merely prolong the agony. Kaufman, however, stubbornly spurned this suggestion. He realized how very poor it was, but felt that since this was Walden's first play, it would be harmful to his career if it closed ignominiously on the road. True, it was sure to close very quickly in New York, but at least Walden would have a Broadway production to his credit. Gordon protested that this would increase the loss to the backers, of whom there were many, and add to the difficulty of raising money for future productions. But Kaufman, unexpectedly compassionate, countered that he himself would make good the cost of the Broadway opening.[30]

Several *New Yorker* staff members were in the opening night audience when *Metropole* came to Broadway on December 6, but Ross was not among them. His indifference was so vast that he had declined even to glance at the script. Had he done so he would not have been pleased; indeed, this was a production that pleased no one. The play itself was dismissed as slight and unfunny, and Kaufman's slam-bang direction was held to be equally to blame for the unpleasantness of the evening. Atkinson put it in the *Times* that the comedy was "played on the level of a prolonged roar that is at first deafening and eventually stupefying." Only Tracy received unqualified praise. The upshot was that Kaufman was content to close down the play after the second performance. At a cost to himself of about $5000, he had given Walden his chance. It had been his intention to keep from the fledgling playwright the circumstances under which the comedy had come into town, but the story eventually got out. On February 22, 1950, nearly three months after the opening, *Variety* told the world about it. As with his efforts to provide for his German relations during the Hitler years, Kaufman was glad to offer help where it was needed, but uncomfortable in the extreme when his kindness was disclosed.[31]

Kaufman's second, and final, production of the season was also a failure, though the play itself was a far more promising piece of writing. Maurice Valency, a professor of English and comparative literature at Columbia, had had a success the season before with his adaptation of Jean Giraudoux's *The Madwoman of Chaillot,* in which the author offered a quite radical solution to the world's political and ecological ills: one needed only to trap underground all the avaricious men who despoiled the earth, and the troubles would end. This play ran for over a year on Broadway and was still running when Valency gave his agent, Audrey Wood, an adaptation of another Giraudoux comedy, *Intermezzo,* retitled *The Enchanted* to avoid confusion with the Ingrid Bergman film of 1939. In spite of the success of *Madwoman,* Wood had some trouble finding a sympathetic producer. Finally, two young, untried men, David Lowe and Richard Davidson, optioned the play and sent it to Leueen MacGrath, who they thought would be good in the central part of Isabel, a young schoolteacher in a provincial town in France.

The part and the play appealed to Leueen. A blend of romance and fantasy, like most of Giraudoux's writing, *The Enchanted* had good comic possibilities, but was also serious in its insistent message, rather like that of Wilder's *Our Town,* that the real marvel of life is that it is a fabric of simple pleasures. The comic quality entered through Giraudoux's treatment of the spinster Mangebois sisters, a pompous inspector of schools, and Isabel's naïve ten-year-old pupils. Fey and fragile, the play offered a risk to the producers. Lowe and Davidson planned to spare no expense in providing an impeccable production. Robert Edmond Jones was commissioned to design the setting, and the music composed by Francis Poulenc for the original French production was to be used. Isabel, one of Giraudoux's typical *jeunes filles en fleur,* was some twelve to fifteen years younger than Leueen's age at the time, but it was a part well within her range; nor did she look too old for it. She quickly accepted it.

Kaufman reacted to her decision like a young husband with a pretty bride to impress. He told Leueen that he would like to direct her in the play. That he was contending with the problems of *Metropole* did not seem to put this new proposition out of reach. He would do one, then do the other, on a tight schedule such as he had always drawn up for himself. Leueen did not seriously question his wish, though she was of course aware that the play was not of a sort that he had dealt with before. Not since *Beggar on Horseback* had he had to do with any work so whimsical, and that he had not directed. Moreover, unlike Leueen, he knew no French and had no familiarity with French culture. Yet none of this would matter if he could get to the heart of the play. He proposed himself to Lowe and Davidson, and they reported this to Valency, though with a guarded enthusiasm.[32]

Rather to their surprise, Valency was pleased with the suggestion. To their expression of fear that Kaufman's technique was too broad for Giraudoux's kind of comedy, he replied that the play would benefit from a broad approach. He liked the idea of Kaufman's name on the program, because (presumably) it would help the play's commercial chance. Moreover, since it was his intention to adapt more plays and write some of his own, he hoped to learn something from Kaufman, the acknowledged Broadway master. It did not occur to Valency that after more than twenty years of directing the plays of writers who, like Valency himself, were glad to have him take charge, he might resent the occasional authorial suggestion. But at the outset all went smoothly. It seemed to Valency that the choice of director was a very sound one.

Rehearsals were scheduled to begin as soon as *Metropole* opened. Before this, Kaufman and Valency met almost a dozen times to talk over the play, mostly at 410 Park Avenue. Kaufman struck Valency as having great respect for the material. Not a know-it-all, not wishing to pitch in and revise the script, he simply asked questions about it. He seemed to be experiencing some difficulty in understanding it, and made every effort to correct the deficiency. At the same time, it struck Valency—and this impression deepened as the work went on—that Kaufman was defensive about the extent of his learning and was not at ease with him. This was something more than Kaufman's well-known aloofness. Leueen, hoping to make the men more comfortable with each other, invited Valency and his wife frequently to dinner at the apartment, but these evenings were never successful. More and more, Valency came to think of Kaufman as inhibited, frustrated, and melancholic. Essentially, this was nothing unusual; Kaufman had always struck new acquaintances in this way. But at this moment in his life, the diffidence and impatience were deepening. Alfred Lunt and Lynn Fontanne, coming to dinner in this same period, found Kaufman bored beyond measure by the conversation at table and hardly able to conceal his relief when the party began to break up. Valency got an especially sharp impression of Kaufman's malaise one afternoon when the two were walking up Park Avenue. On that day, so Kaufman said, the *New Yorker* would arrive, on the next day *Time*, and on the day after that *Newsweek*. The arrival of the magazines on their scheduled days seemed to be as much as he had to look forward to.[33]

Rehearsals went well at first. Kaufman saw the humor of the play and had no trouble getting the actors to see it. They formed a strong cast; surrounding Leueen were the capable character actresses Una O'Connor and Frances Williams as the Mangebois sisters, Russell Collins as the sympathetic district doctor, and John Baragrey and Wesley Addy as the two rivals for Isabel's hand. They all had such a good time in the first weeks that a hit was clearly indicated. Soon, however, and quite unexpectedly, the life went out of the proceedings. There was no more fun in it, and Kaufman, as Valency viewed him, began to seem bored and unhappy with the actors. After the third week, the production seemed as certainly headed for failure as earlier it had seemed headed for success. It became heavy, almost inert, except for moments which by contrast were too light and brisk. Valency could not persuade Kaufman to reconsider his direction. When he approached Kaufman with a suggestion, Kaufman would give only a curt answer and then walk away. Finally Kaufman made it clear that if Valency insisted on offering suggestions, he should offer them as written notes. Having had the pleasantest possible collaboration with Alfred de Liagre, Jr., his director and producer on *The Madwoman of Chaillot,* Valency was perplexed and hurt by this behavior. Nevertheless, he did pass notes to Kaufman, only to see them ignored or rejected.

At the dress rehearsal in New Haven on December 28, 1949, what had been deftly and airily comic in manuscript was turned into a stolidly unfunny performance. At the close of it Valency went out into the alley by the Shubert Theater and, for the first time in his life that he could remember, threw up. He tried, unsuccessfully, to persuade Lowe and Davidson to close down the production for six weeks until it could be redirected by someone else. On January 18 it opened at the Lyceum to polite but unenthusiastic reviews. By no means all of the notices were unfavorable to Kaufman, but the over-all impression of the critics was that he had failed to capture the quiet charm of the play. As Louis Shaeffer put it in the Brooklyn *Eagle,* "He has pointed up the humorous potentialities of the script, giving quite a few lines the snap of a wisecrack, when the humor should have flowed more delicately."[34] Comments such as this one spelled failure—Kaufman's eighth (not counting *The Senator Was Indiscreet*) in a losing streak that had begun with *Hollywood Pinafore* in 1945. *The Enchanted* did not close as quickly as *Metropole,* but after forty-five performances off it went. During the brief run Kaufman and the other owners of the Lyceum sold the theater to Harry E. Gould. It had not housed a hit since *Born Yesterday.*

With no attractive prospects for the coming season, Kaufman turned to Leueen one day in the spring of 1950 and startled her by asking whether she would like to collaborate with him on a play. She agreed, but had no notion of what they might write the play about. In May they sailed for Europe with the plan of at least outlining some sort of plot. They also intended to look over the plays running in the West End, with a view to choosing one in which Leueen could appear on Broadway under Kaufman's direction.[35] In addition, they expected to visit Paris and the South of France—to have, in short, a real holiday. It was Kaufman's first trip to Europe since 1932, and Leueen's first return to her homeland since her arrival in the United States in 1948.

The trip was a success for both the Kaufmans. Leueen had the pleasure of seeing old friends again, and in the company of her new husband, whose position in theatrical circles was markedly superior to her own. With them they took several dozen eggs to give to the English friends whom they expected to see, only to find that the rationing of this once scarce commodity had ended three days before their arrival.[36] Kaufman took pleasure in being seen in Leueen's company, though the rush of friends in her direction whenever they went to the theater was a trial for him.

As always happened when Kaufman traveled, invitations streamed in—to dinners, after theater parties, and country-house weekends. On a visit to the Oliviers, he wrote in the guest book, "To Vivien Leigh and Laurence Olivier—Forivier!" For the first time since the death of Beatrice, he saw Noel Coward, and somehow was able to endure a conversation with him. To Anne he wrote, "If you see any songwriters, tell 'em I went down to Ascap for the racing, pearl derby and all." The couple also went to Cornwall for a weekend, and to Stratford, where for the first time Kaufman saw *Measure for Measure*. The production, by the twenty-five-year-old Peter Brook, so impressed him that in order to praise Brook publicly he dashed off an unsolicited article for the New York *Times* on the English theatrical season with special attention to this production and *Ring 'Round the Moon,* an adaptation by Christopher Fry of an Anouilh play, also directed by Brook. Some American friends and acquaintances were in London during their stay. Among them, briefly, were Max Gordon, who hoped to find a play worth importing. Nunnally Johnson was there and invited the Kaufmans to a dinner for Irene Dunne, who, in Kaufman's words, "it seems, has not had dinner for quite a while." If any worry lay on his mind, it was that the Harts' second child would be born without his hearing of it. Word reached him in June of the arrival of the baby, a girl. From London the couple pressed on to Paris for more theatergoing and a chat with Orson Welles.[37]

Their socializing and evenings at the theater did not destroy the Kaufmans' intention of putting together a play of their own. On the ship coming over they had noted with interest a married couple whose relationship seemed to be imperiled by the fact that the husband had outgrown his wife intellectually. It struck them that there was a play waiting to be plucked out of this situation. From Paris they went to Aigue Belle in the south of France and began to write. By August 1, the date of their arrival in New York, they had a draft of the script in readiness to show Max Gordon.

Writing the play and searching for an English play for Leueen to do on Broadway (the latter an unsuccessful effort) were not the only projects on Kaufman's mind during the summer. While still in London he received a flying visit from the American producer Cy Feuer, who with his partner Ernest Martin hoped to talk Kaufman into directing their forthcoming musical, *Guys and Dolls,* which had been in the planning stage for the preceding year. This was to be based on Damon Runyon's stories about Broadway's minor hoodlums, horseplayers, crapshooters, and night-club chorus girls, with songs by Frank Loesser. Beginning in the summer of 1949 a flurry of announcements appeared in the papers about the still-unwritten show, culminating in word that the book would be the work of Abe Burrows and Jo Swerling, a screenwriter. It was also revealed that Jo Mielziner would design the settings and direct the book and that Michael Kidd would be the choreographer. Though Feuer and Martin had hoped to open early in 1950, delays arose over the book. The notion of allowing Mielziner to direct, which originated with the designer himself, was dropped, and Kaufman became the producers' choice. Abe Burrows, his costar on television, was behind this choice and telephoned him in London from New York on July 4 to urge him to accept. Kaufman did accept the offer, and in a series of transatlantic calls laid plans to have Burrows and his wife come to Barley Sheaf Farm in August for planning and writing sessions.

This was to be yet another piece of writing to which Kaufman made substantial but uncredited contributions. Burrows did not fail to acknowledge his aid, however. "He sat with me," Burrows wrote before the opening, "worked with me, bawled me out, complimented me, taught me." To the playwright Harry Kurnitz he confided that Kaufman was "a tower of strength on the book."[38] But however much Kaufman may have contributed in the way of specific lines, the initial conception was provided by Burrows and Swerling. The principal material came from a Runyon story called "The Idyll of Sarah Brown," concerning a romance between a gambler and a dedicated young woman from the Save a Soul Mission. It was rounded out with snippets of other Runyon stories and their picturesque characters, of whom the two most prominent were another gambler, Nathan Detroit, and his fiancée of seventeen years, Miss Adelaide.

Rehearsals began on September 6, 1950. Cast in the role of Sky Masterson, the amorous gambler, was Robert Alda, who had attempted the impersonation of George Gershwin in the film *Rhapsody in Blue*. Sarah Brown, the "mission doll," was played by the young singer-actress Isabel Bigley, a comparative unknown though she had had the leading feminine role in the London production of *Oklahoma!* The second couple were played by Sam Levene and Vivian Blaine. The veteran vaudevillian Pat Rooney, Sr., was given the role of Sarah's grandfather, and a quintet of burlesque comedians and expert character actors, Stubby Kaye, Johnny Silver, Douglas Deane, Tom Pedi, and B. S. Pully, played the not very dangerous lowlifers. Kaufman shaped their performances with a sureness of hand that he had not shown since *The Late George Apley*. Having spent a large part of his life on and near Broadway, he recognized that the Runyon figures were caricatures of the real denizens of that grubby area, and he treated them as such, but allowed a moderating touch of real feeling to come through. He also seemed respectful of the songs, which were the most sophisticated compositions in both words and music that had been provided for any of his shows since he had worked with the Gershwins. Kidd's dances, which included a much praised "Crap Game Ballet," blended so well with the scenes of dialogue as to create a seamless whole.

The show opened in Philadelphia on October 14 and was instantly the talk of both that city and New York, where a run on the box office occurred. The management, wishing to take no chances on what was obviously a property of immense value, extended the Philadelphia engagement beyond the run originally scheduled. The show came to Broadway on November 24 and received unanimously laudatory notices. Kaufman's part in it suggested that he had regained the balance that had been so obviously lacking in his recent work. Wrote John Chapman in the *Daily News,* in a notice that expressed the opinion of all the reviewers, "Under the masterful direction of George S. Kaufman, [the production] is swift, crisp, and precise, with not a lagging instant."[39] Kaufman himself was aware that he had done his proper job. For the first and only time in his long career, he sat through the entire first-night performance of his own show, and down front in the orchestra. So confident was he that with Leueen he invited a few friends to the apartment for a drink—not afterward, as would have been traditional, but before the performance.

His work on this production brought Kaufman the Antoinette Perry award (the "Tony") for best direction. Burrows, Swerling, Loesser, Kidd, Alda, Bigley, and the producers also received Tonys. For three years, *Guys and Dolls* remained on Broadway, while other companies toured across the United States and played in London. For Kaufman, who was not blind to the fact his reputation had been in precipitous decline, the show constituted a personal triumph. Nor, happily, was it his last success.

——21——

New Collaborators;
Causes for Alarm

With the sheaf of rave reviews of *Guys and Dolls* under his arm, Kaufman strode into the fifties at a youthful clip. He had plenty of work to look forward to. There was talk of a Broadway revival of *Of Thee I Sing*, there was a firm plan to mount a West Coast production of *Guys and Dolls*, there was the new script that he had written with Leueen, and there were some dimly perceived but inviting schemes for scripts drifting through his head—scripts that he might write not only with Leueen, but as vehicles for her. It was all possible. Chronic worrier though he was, he was in fine health at that moment.

Behind Kaufman's suggestion to Leueen in 1950 that they write a play together was something more than the old, familiar passion for work. That was the strength of his feeling for her. By writing a play with her, he might not only reconfirm the bond between them and have an excuse to spend more hours of the day with her, but he might also build up the regard in which the public held her. This wish to create an aura around her, to add to her public image, had been behind his decision to direct her in *The Enchanted*. It became increasingly powerful within him. He wanted to write with her, to direct her, to find parts for her, and to create them. She was and had always been a very good, dependable actress in supporting roles, but Kaufman was not content to let her remain on that level. He intended to make her a star.

The play that the couple wrote abroad in 1950 was not planned as a vehicle for Leueen, however. The central role was not suitable for her. When she and Kaufman handed Max Gordon their script as they disembarked from the *Ile de France* on August 1, they were not at all certain that he would admire it. It was sure to be a costly production. Kaufman was perfectly aware of the risk of producing it. So was Gordon, though he agreed to take it on. Later, in a promotional piece for the *Times,* Kaufman joked about this, but did so half-seriously:

> From the beginning I had the idea that we would name the play "Mrs. Roberts," on the theory that some obliging typesetter might accidentally drop a letter and thus bring a nice rush of business to the box-office. Miss MacGrath, on the other hand, voted for "The Ingrown Toenail." As a result we combined the two names and called it "The Small Hours, or, Over Max Gordon's Dead Body."
>
> This brings me to Max Gordon. Mr. Gordon is the producer of the play. When we first decided to write it we told Mr. Gordon immediately and he asked a most sentient question. "Is it in one set?" he said. We said "no," but that it was in twenty-six sets, which was the next best thing. Mr. Gordon said, "The next best thing to what? The bankruptcy court?" Well, of course, this was absurd, because we were not going to use our own money.[1]

The Small Hours was a title arrived at after much deliberation. Originally the play was called *Story of a Woman,* but this was soon changed to *Man and Wife,* which in turn was changed to *The Still Small Hours.* During this while, the press releases described the play as the work of Leueen Mac-Grath and George S. Kaufman, in that order, since it had been Leueen who suggsted the central idea of the plot. Finally, however, the title was short-ened to *The Small Hours,* and at Leueen's request the authors' names were reversed. The opening was set for February 15.

With its twenty-six sets, the play was too heavy to take on a preliminary tour. It had to open cold, after some invitational previews. At this time, Leueen was rehearsing in a new work imported from England, *The High Ground,* by Charles H. Hastings, in which she played the leading role of a woman wrongly accused of murder. Her opening was scheduled for February 20.

The critics who commented on *The Small Hours* admired everything about the production but the play itself. As always, Max Gordon spared no expense. Donald Oenslager's smoothly rolling sets and the twenty-eight well-drilled cast members came in for praise. The play, however, was so thin that the sets, rather than fleshing it out, smothered it. The saga of the dull, middle-aged wife of a lively, sophisticated book publisher, it was designed to appeal to an audience eager for glimpses of New York high life. The woman, Laura Mitchell, undergoes the painful experience of fighting down her para-lyzing sense of intellectual inferiority and comes out the victor at the third-act curtain. But her story is not moving, and is all too familiar; she is one more plucky little brown wren who puts all the snowy egrets to shame. Moreover, the sheer number of characters, like the scenery, overwhelms the play; the writers did not give themselves a chance to delve into any of them. As for the dialogue, it is too arch, too clever-sounding, too crammed with references to such preoccupations of the day as publishing-house mergers, the cultural impact of television, and the widening use of marijuana to seem wholly serious. In fact, the script is a set of allusions to fads.

The son of the family, Peter Mitchell, is the pot smoker. He takes to this vice as a way of smothering his sexual anxiety. For a scene between the young man and his mother, the collaborators wrote what was surely one of the most baffling lines ever handed an actor: "I'm a latent homosexual, that's what's wrong with me." Reports of this line circulated before the play was cast, and many young actors thought it would only raise an embarrassing laugh. But Michael Wager, who took the part, had no trouble with the line and was praised for his performance. On opening night among the good-luck messages that Wager found in his dressing room were two memorable telegrams from friends: LATENTS ARE LOUSY LOVERS, and BETTER LATENT THAN NEVER.[2]

After twenty performances *The Small Hours* was allowed to disappear. The loss came to $120,000. As for *The High Ground,* it too was a failure, though praise was offered for Leueen's performance and that of Margaret Webster as the nun who establishes the alleged murderess's innocence. It was withdrawn after twenty-three performances. It may have amused Kaufman to reflect on the fact that he would soon be taking revenge in print on one nettlesome critic, Joseph Wood Krutch. Kaufman's piece entitled "My Book and I," on his inability to get through Krutch's biography of Samuel Johnson, was scheduled to appear in the *New Yorker* on May 26.

With *Guys and Dolls* continuing to draw lines at the box office, Kaufman soon shrugged off the failure of *The Small Hours* and set his face toward the next task, which was to direct the second company of the musical. In May he and Leueen boarded a train for Los Angeles, where Feuer and Martin had assembled the cast for rehearsals. The opening was set for June 4 in San Francisco. Since this was Leueen's first trip west, Kaufman intended to make it a gala one for her. Many invitations were sent to the couple, and Kaufman looked forward to showing off Leueen to Hollywood. Shy, and unfamiliar with the territory, she did not know what to expect. But she enjoyed herself, though she was no more overwhelmed by the grandeur of the place than her husband had been on his first visit. She brought back some amusing memories. One evening at a night club they sat at a table near George Jessel and one of the young girls he fancied. All of a sudden Jessel asked the waiter for a telephone, dialed and, then, lest anyone within earshot should be in doubt, delivered the line, "Hello, mother, this is George Jessel." On another evening at a party Leueen wore a new dress that she had bought especially for the trip. Greer Garson, an old acquaintance, made an admiring remark about it, and when Leueen allowed that the dress was new, Miss Garson replied, "Well, mine's not old."[3]

Between rehearsal sessions and social engagements, Kaufman pondered the future. Over the years, various producers had offered to mount a full-scale revival of *Of Thee I Sing*, only to be turned down by him. Not long before, however, Kaufman himself had decided that the play ought to be revived, and when interest in the project was shown by Herman Levin and Oliver Smith, producers of *Gentlemen Prefer Blondes*, Kaufman seized the opportunity. In California, he discussed the possibility of a revival with Morrie Ryskind, who gave his consent. It was announced in the press that *Of Thee I Sing*, with suitable revisions to account for the passage of twenty years, would be offered by Levin and Smith in the 1951-52 season.[4]

Kaufman also found the time to talk over plans with Leueen for a second collaboration. On the train coming out, she suggested as a project for them a play on reincarnation. She held no belief that human beings lived more than once, but found the notion that they might both teasing and consoling. She began talking with Kaufman around the subject in search of a plot. One came to mind about a professional woman, a sculptor, who faintly remembers her existence in past civilizations and finds herself repeating in her present life the patterns of her old one. Engaged to a stuffy though handsome man, she is actually in love with a more debonair sort who balks at being led to the altar. This second male, as stubborn as those she loved in prehistory and Roman antiquity, is an art critic who fails to admire her sculpture. After the second company of *Guys and Dolls* opened in San Francisco, Kaufman and Leueen headed back to Barley Sheaf Farm and plunged into work. On June 29 they sailed to England for a three-week holiday and took the script with them. By the date of their return, they had a complete first draft. Though earlier in the year Kaufman had talked with Abe Burrows about spending part of the summer with him on a play to star Fred Allen, that project was dropped altogether in favor of this new comedy, which the couple decided to call *Fancy Meeting You Again*. At some point during the writing, they agreed that the leading role would be right for Leueen.[5]

At the end of the summer they polished the play in expectation of a midwinter production. They were also looking forward to moving out of 410 Park Avenue and into a new apartment where the ghost of Beatrice would not hover, a place exclusively their own. Before the lease on 410 expired in September, Leueen chose a penthouse apartment for them at 1035 Park Avenue.

That pressing matter taken care of, the couple did what Kaufman and his collaborators had done with their every new script since 1941: they took it to Max Gordon. But this time the unexpected, the unbelievable, the almost fantastic took place: Max Gordon declined to produce the play. His action had nothing to do with the announcement that Levin and Smith were to produce the revival of *Of Thee I Sing*, for he had never had more than faint confidence in that project. It was purely that his well-honed showman's instinct told him to stay away from *Fancy Meeting You Again*. A pallid, multi-scened work that substituted visual surprises for wit and intellectual substance, it struck him as a play sure to cost big money and just as sure never to repay it. It took courage for Gordon to snub the play, since he knew that his action would offend Kaufman, upon whom he relied not only for scripts but for financial backing and advice. But he had no other choice. Though their relationship did not come to an end over this incident, Kaufman was nettled and showed it. Such a thing had never happened to him before; moreover, half the play was Leueen's, and all of it was designed to show off her talent as an actress.

Gordon's rejection was only a temporary setback, to be sure. There had never been a dearth of producing firms eager to mount a Kaufman play. The news spread quickly that a Kaufman comedy was available, and the new firm established by Chandler Cowles and Ben Segal asked for it. Kaufman agreed to let them have it, and because Levin and Smith had begun to have second thoughts about *Of Thee I Sing*, he turned that over to them as well. Plans were drawn up: it was decided that the new comedy would go into rehearsal on October 25.

Suddenly came a second unexpected blow, worse than Max Gordon's rebuff because it was a chilling portent of events to come. Kaufman suffered a stroke—not one so severe as to leave him permanently incapacitated, but serious, and to a degree irreparably damaging. The left side of his body was partially paralyzed, and for a time the sight was lost completely from his left eye. In a month he was well enough to leave the hospital, but a slight hesitancy was apparent in his walk, and he had difficulty with the movement of his left hand. His eye was still bad, though some sight returned to it. Henceforth it would be evident that he had no depth perception. The illness was first reported as a virus, but at least one of the papers, the *Journal-American*, learned a part of the truth and reported the impairment of his vision.[6]

As soon as he was released from the hospital, Kaufman turned back to *Fancy Meeting You Again*. His hypochondria and fear of death notwithstanding, he had to get this play on, to show the public not only that he was still a potent force in the theater, but to provide Leueen with this new starring opportunity. Rehearsals began on November 8. The cast included young Walter Matthau as the elusive lover and the expert character actresses Margaret Hamilton and Ruth McDevitt in important roles. The clever, expensive settings were the work of Albert Johnson. The tryout tour began in New Haven on November 28. It was apparent at once that the play needed much more work. *Variety*'s reviewer, though offering praise for Leueen's performance, described the script as "a combination of sparkle and vacuum."[7] From New Haven the production went to Boston for three weeks and then, since it was still not ready, to Philadelphia. In both cities the reviews were mixed. Some, it could be said, were full of praise for both the play and Leueen's performance; others were not. Weary, but putting a good face on it, Cowles and Segal opened the play on Broadway on January 14. It had been on the road for seven weeks.

Whatever merit the production had, it was not provided by the writing team of Kaufman and MacGrath. It was the gift of Walter Matthau. To the critics it was obvious that this comic young man was going to be a star. As for the play, it struck the reviewers as wan, unamusing, and lacking in point. Atkinson, still the most influential of them all, noted, "From the point of view of the audiences who are currently incarnated on Broadway, it is not up to the standard of anything on which Mr. Kaufman has collaborated before; it is not very good, even by less exacting standards." Of Leueen's performance, he observed that "it is to be feared that her acting is not much more resourceful than the writing."[8]

After one week, eight performances, Cowles and Segal closed the play to a financial loss of $55,000. Leueen was far more distressed by the debacle than Kaufman was—or than Kaufman appeared to be. "I wish I hadn't landed George into two such sorry messes," she later said. "He did pretty well without me before."[9] Nevertheless, Kaufman had no intention of giving up their literary partnership.

The cost of the revival of *Of Thee I Sing* was much higher. It ran to $240,000, an amount that Cowles and Segal did not find easy to raise. Auditions of the material were held, not only in New York but in four other cities as well.[10] The New York opening was set for May 5, 1952, with one preliminary week in New Haven and two in Philadelphia. The script needed updating, but Kaufman decided against making a wholesale revision. Though France was no longer strong enough to pose a military threat to the United States, to substitute the U.S.S.R. would bring an unwanted seriousness to the show and would affect Ira Gershwin's lyrics. It was also agreed that though in the Truman administration the vice presidency had become a more prominent position than ever before, to elevate the character of Throttlebottom was out of the question. But of course it was necessary to remove references to the Depression, for these were boom years. The writing team also decided that the show needed one more love song; from *Let 'Em Eat Cake* they appropriated "Mine." Seeking a well-known, "name" actor to portray Wintergreen, they decided on Jack Carson of Hollywood. They had hoped that Victor Moore would again play Throttlebottom, but when it became evident that he was no longer up to the physical demands of the part, they gave it to the eccentric dancer Paul Hartman. The young singing actress Betty Oakes was cast as Mary Turner, and Lenore Lonergan, who was married to Chandler Cowles, was signed to play Diana Devereaux.

Though this production promised much, it fared rather poorly. Despite the changes made in the book and lyrics, it struck the reviewers and its audience as somewhat of a fossil. This was the best musical of 1931, not a product of the postwar age. The songs were still some of the cleverest, most tuneful ever written for Broadway, and the book had its moments of laughter, but the show did not provide a view, even a caricaturized view, of American life in 1952. Though Kaufman went into rehearsals having recovered sufficiently from his illness to put the cast through its paces vigorously, he was powerless to improve Carson's voice or impart a magnetic glow to Betty Oakes. Nor could he do much to amend the book without skewing other aspects of the show. As he had done with *The Cocoanuts* in 1925, he sought outside aid. Then it had been Ryskind to whom he turned; on this occasion it was Abe Burrows, who, without taking billing, made suggestions for the book after looking over performances in New Haven and Philadelphia. Nevertheless, the book was wooden when the play opened on Broadway. The New York notices were not good enough to draw profitable houses for very long. On July 4, after seventy-two performances, the producers closed the show. Had it not been for the willingness of the cast to take cuts, and of Billy Rose, who owned the Ziegfeld Theater where it played, to reduce the rental figure, it would not have run so long.[11]

On September 17, Anne was divorced from Bruce Colen. Their marriage had long since ceased to have meaning for either of them; this step was inevitable. Always of independent spirit, Anne now enjoyed making a home for herself and her daughter and took much pleasure in a circle of friends that included many persons of the theater, including actors and producers and some of the younger writers who were also friends of her father's, such as Ruth and Augustus Goetz. She was especially close to Bernard Hart. This relationship between the daughter of one famous playwright and brother of another remained platonic, but was warm and intimate and continued to be so until Bernard Hart's death in 1964. As she had always done, Anne found time to spend with her father and Leueen, and still chauffeured them or ran errands for them, though not without occasional moments of annoyance when she felt that one or the other was taking advantage of her. As well as depending on her for such aid, in this late period of his life her father began increasingly to confide in her.

Despite his low opinion of *Fancy Meeting You Again*, Max Gordon was confident that Kaufman would turn out more hits, if he could find a collaborator with whose talents his own would mesh. Gordon's associate Marcus Heiman suggested Howard Teichmann, who taught history at Barnard College but had also had a career in show business. In Orson Welles's heyday as director of the Mercury Theater in the 1930s, Teichmann, then in his early twenties, had written scripts for the company's weekly radio series. Born in 1916, he was one year younger than Welles. Though he had not had a play on Broadway, Teichmann had at least succeeded in having options taken on his work over the years. On Heiman's advice, in the summer of 1952 Max Gordon read Teichmann's *Howe and Hummel*, an adaptation of a novel by Richard H. Rovere. Gordon did not think that the script was strong enough to produce, but it left him with the impression that Teichmann had a promising talent that Kaufman could make flourish.[12]

Teichmann and Kaufman first met on September 30, 1952, at 1035 Park Avenue. Gordon introduced them. Neither had an idea for a play, but in desultory conversation they evolved a plot having to do with minor functionaries at the United Nations. The action was to be set at a hotel near Beekman Place and the lead was designed to be taken by a glamorous female star. Before they completed a draft, word of the play had circulated, and Tallulah Bankhead, Marlene Dietrich, and Judy Holliday all expressed interest. When the draft was nearly complete, they showed it to Max Gordon, who promptly rejected it. In his opinion, it was not funny enough; moreover, he thought it showed the United Nations in a bad light. Teichmann was informed of this, not by Gordon himself, but by Kaufman. It was a severe blow to the younger writer, and one made all the worse by falling on his birthday, January 22. He believed that Kaufman accepted Gordon's verdict without demur because of an all-powerful fear of failure instilled in him by his recent quick closings. If Max Gordon thought the play was poor, it was poor—such for the time being was Kaufman's frame of mind, as Teichmann interpreted it.[13] Yet, as Teichmann found out soon afterward, Gordon's judgment at the moment was not at its sharpest. His inability to capture the musical rights to *My Sister Eileen* had sent him headlong into black depression. Under the banner of Robert Fryer and retitled *Wonderful Town*, the musical was then trying out on the road prior to a Broadway opening scheduled for late February, and gave every indication of becoming a hit. Gordon had wanted this hit for himself and believed it to be his due for producing the original play.

But Teichmann soon returned to Kaufman with a workable idea. He recalled that a few days earlier Kaufman had repeated the phrase "poor General Motors" that a bridge player at the Regency Club had uttered on hearing of a slight depression in the corporation's stock. The phrase was lodged in Kaufman's mind as the germ of an idea for a satire—yet another—on big business. Desperate for a notion that he could present to Kaufman, Teichmann coupled this phrase with the story of a rich acquaintance of his who, having been snubbed by the officers of a corporation in which he owned stock, bought up the controlling interest in it and fired the lot of them. Kaufman was quick to accept this, though with the suggestion that the protagonist be made a woman and that they write with Josephine Hull in mind. They met daily during the late winter and the spring. By summer they were able to lay plans for a fall production to star the aging comedienne, under Max Gordon's aegis.[14]

During the weeks when Kaufman was putting the finishing touches on the United Nations script, at the end of 1952 and the beginning of 1953, his attention was divided between this task and unwanted publicity that he was then receiving in the press. It was not a scandal to rival the Astor case, but it was a nuisance nonetheless. Since 1949 he had performed his weekly stint on the television program *This Is Show Business*, to the delight of viewers everywhere. But all of a sudden, on December 21, his wit turned against him and pitched him into public controversy.

There was little doubt that Kaufman was the star of the program. His wisecracks of the week were savored and quoted at dinner tables and office water-coolers across the nation. Columnists printed them frequently, to the delight of those unfortunates who did not own television sets. "Old Tangle-thatch," as John Crosby of the *Herald Tribune* called him, never let the audience down. A non-singing member of the cast of Rodgers and Hammerstein's *The King and I* came on the program with the "problem" of wanting to be allowed to sing in the show. Said Kaufman, "Why don't you some night just break out and sing? Who can stop you? You're stronger than Gertrude Lawrence. Just do it. For good measure, sing an Irving Berlin tune and get me a closeup of Mr. Rodgers's face at the time." To a team of dancers who had worked together for eight years and complained that they were bored with each other, he had some pointed advice: "I think you have a simple case of success poisoning. You've been working together eight years and you've been eating eight years and you're kind of forgetting what it's like to be out looking for a job. You're forgetting those days when you were munching on the real estate section of the Sunday paper. Quit for a while, be out of jobs and look into Lindy's window—and you'll be very glad to meet each other again." To a member of another Rodgers and Hammerstein cast, Martha Wright of *South Pacific,* he had some well-chosen words on how to find happiness: "Well, we all know money doesn't give happiness—as Senator Nixon can testify—so just give your money away. Give it to me."[15]

This quickness of mind brought Kaufman more recognition than he had ever had before, despite the many hits and the two Pulitzer Prizes. His photogenic face was known everywhere. Vain about his appearance, keeping a weekly appointment with hair-care expert Frances Fox and wearing the blue shirts that were recommended for the television camera, he cut a dashing figure on the show. It sometimes seemed that he was too popular, because on leaving the CBS studio after every broadcast he had to defend himself against a crowd of autograph seekers whom he could not bear to have cluster around him and possibly touch him and certainly breathe on him. With the umbrella that he carried in lieu of a cane after the illness of 1951, he fended them off. Many were children, but that was no excuse. "I was a child once for several months," he muttered on the show. "These autograph hunters should be at home learning their lessons, resting up in bed, eating their oatmeal, whatever they do at night—bothering their parents instead of bothering complete strangers. I would like to knock their heads together until they ring like a Chinese gong." This ill humor only pleased the public and increased the demand for his signature on a piece of paper, though no fan was ever given it. CBS and the show's sponsor, the American Tobacco Company, were agreed that he was a "property" of great value until, on December 21, he said, "Let's make this one program on which no one sings 'Silent Night.' "

Immediately, telephone calls began to come in to the CBS switchboard from infuriated viewers who construed the remark as antireligious and, more specifically, anti-Christian, since it had been made by a Jew. In the next few days "several hundred" letters (by the network's vague count) came from viewers threatening to boycott the sponsor's products unless Kaufman were dismissed. It was not the first time that Kaufman's remarks had drawn fire. Once a woman who had a dog act came on the program to complain that when she performed in Florida hotels, those same hotels would not allow her to keep the dogs in her room. As a subterfuge, she had taken to wearing the dogs around her neck as a fur piece. Her problem was whether she should continue to play such inhumane hotels. Kaufman said he was astonished to hear that the hotels would take *her*. This brought a flood of letters from dog lovers. But the dog lovers, unlike the persons who wrote about his "Silent Night" remark, did not threaten a boycott. The program was not aired on what would have been its next date, December 28, because its time had been pre-empted by a Jack Benny special. On the following day, CBS announced that Kaufman would not appear on *This Is Show Business* again.

Responses to this announcement crackled for the next two weeks. At least as many letters arrived at CBS in support of Kaufman as those insisting that he be fired. Newspapers editorialized in his favor, on the ground that if a relatively small number of irate persons—"several hundred" out of an estimated eighteen million viewers—could bring about a performer's dismissal, no one on the air would venture a controversial opinion. Thus obliquely the incident was addressed in terms of the McCarthyist syndrome that for the preceding two years had affected programming and employment on radio and television. Kaufman's fellow performers also came to his defense. When approached by CBS to take his place, both John Charles Daly and Garry Moore, prominent television personalities, flatly declined. So also did Fred Allen. Said Allen, "This thing is ridiculous. There are only two good wits on television, Groucho Marx and George S. Kaufman. With Kaufman gone, TV is half-witted."

Kaufman at first expected to ride out the storm in silence, regardless of what awaited him at the end. He went to Boston to join Leueen, who was there in the tryout tour of a new play, Peter Ustinov's *The Love of Four Colonels*. When reporters, tracking him down at the Ritz, telephoned for a statement, it was Leueen who replied. Far from intending to make a slur against religion, she said, her husband had meant only to express an objection to the use of the carol in connection with the commercialization of Christmas. Kaufman then repeated this explanation in a press release. As a result, support came promptly from the National Council of the Churches of Christ in the form of a commendation for Kaufman's "religious sensitiveness." Thus was the situation saved for him—more or less. The program was slated to lose the sponsorship of the American Tobacco Company in three weeks, after which it was to be aired on a sustaining basis. While the company still sponsored the program, Steve Allen took his place. On January 24 Kaufman returned and made this comment on the network's decision to welcome him back now that the program had no regular sponsor: "It constitutes some kind of vindication, I suppose."[16] Until the show went off the air in the fall, he appeared on it as often as his schedule permitted.

The public-relations brouhaha had not been difficult to deal with, thanks to Leueen's clever parry and his own common sense. But when Nature's destructive force made an attack upon him soon afterward, Kaufman was powerless to deflect it. This was a more dangerous skirmish. The still-youthful stride that had been his when the decade began was already lost. Now a new problem arose, and its effect was to become increasingly worrisome to him in the years ahead. In January 1953, just as it was beginning to seem to him and Teichmann that they had got hold of a subject worth their time, Kaufman fell ill. Teichmann arrived at the apartment one afternoon at one o'clock, as he did six days a week, and heard Leueen sobbing somewhere out of sight. Kaufman stepped out of his study in his bathrobe and explained that his physician, Dr. Edward Greenspan, had ordered him to Mt. Sinai Hospital for a prostectomy.[17] To those who saw him before he underwent surgery, he appeared calm, but all who knew him well were aware that he was badly frightened. His old enemy—fear of illness, of decline, of death—was on the scene.

Tests of Endurance

Though a biopsy established that no malignancy was present, Kaufman was not soon released from the hospital. Three operations were required before the surgeons were finished with their work. Kaufman spent the entire month of February in his hospital room, with Leueen or Anne in attendance during most of his waking hours. Physically his recovery proceeded rapidly, but he could not shake off the anxiety about the future that the illness had created. Though his physician had assured him that he would come through with no loss of stamina, sexual or otherwise, Kaufman could not believe it. The mere suggestion that nothing further would go wrong suffused him with the poison of doubt, and the quarter of a century between his age and Leueen's took on a sharper meaning.

Yet he continued to write, for, as always, work provided at least a temporary relaxation of anxiety. As soon as he was back in the apartment he summoned Teichmann, and the two writers went back to their comedy, which they entitled *The Solid Gold Cadillac*. By May, when a draft of the script was put into Max Gordon's hands, it was, in the authors' words, "a fairy story—the story of Cinderella and the four ugly corporation directors." Since their Cinderella, Laura Partridge, was to be played by Josephine Hull, she was no nubile beauty, but a little, elderly widow. In the years since she had played the role of Penny Sycamore in *You Can't Take It with You*, Hull had achieved fame for her performances in two additional long-running plays, Joseph Kesselring's *Arsenic and Old Lace* and Mary Chase's *Harvey*. Repeating her role of the protagonist's sister in the film version of the latter, she had won an Academy Award in the supporting-actress category. Now, thanks to Kaufman and Teichmann, another success lay in store for her.

Laura Partridge is a former actress who owns ten shares in the General Products Corporation. She disrupts a stockholders' meeting with gentle but persistent questions about the high salaries paid to the company's officers and board members. To shut her up, those gentlemen put her in charge of "shareholder relations," a job she fulfills all too well from their point of view. So warm are the letters she writes to other holders of only a few shares that they come to think of her as a friend. Since the former head of the corporation, Edward L. McKeever, is now holding down a cabinet post in Washington (as was General Motors' Charles E. Wilson at the time), the board members merrily run the company without him, and as merrily milk its profits. Informed of this state of affairs by Mrs. Partridge, McKeever comes back, but, having sold his holdings before entering government service, he has no power. Mrs. Partridge has power, however, and much more than she knows. One "little" shareholder after another gains such confidence in her that when proxies are solicited for the next annual meeting, so many are turned over to her that she gains control of the company. "Aren't they the darlingest people?" she says. She fires the crooked bigwigs and appoints McKeever president and herself vice president, secretary, and treasurer. A solid gold Cadillac is purchased to drive her to the annual meeting, and the Cadillac has a gold-clad chauffeur.

No one could deny that this was a slim plot and that it resounded with echoes of a score of plots concocted by Kaufman in the past. Here again was the "woman behind the man," the exposed nefariousness of the controllers of big business, and the over-all air of improbability. To make sure that the audience accepted the improbable chain of events, the authors planned a running narration by means of a disembodied voice that before every scene would clue the audience as to what was about to happen, always with reference to Laura Partridge as a Cinderella in the world of corporation politics. For this narration they recorded what at the time was one of the best-known voices in the nation, the dry, raspy, nasal voice of Fred Allen. Casting his mind back twenty years to the gatherings at Neysa McMein's studio, Kaufman thought of something else that would help the play: Marc Connelly's party trick of reciting "Spartacus to the Gladiators," a favorite piece with schools of elocution. Connelly had delivered it as he had been taught it as a boy, with a gesture appropriate for every phrase. At Kaufman's request, Connelly taught it to Loring Smith, the actor who played McKeever. McKeever is an actor *manqué*, and therefore just the man to take the aging actress Laura Partridge seriously. As for Mrs. Partridge, though mixed up in unlikely proceedings, she was intended to be no zany, but a direct, sensible creature, capable of uttering the occasional "hell" or "damn" without a trace of coyness. It was the conception of this role as a character who is comic by virtue of her forthrightness in a world of deceit that was the play's strength.

Though Kaufman was pleased enough with the play to have it produced, he told Teichmann that he felt it best to leave his name off it, since of recent years he had been associated only with failures. He no longer trusted the reviewers to make honest judgments about any play bearing his name. Teichmann was shocked by this declaration. The day after making it, Kaufman offered a compromise. If the play succeeded in Washington, where they intended to try it out last, then he would be willing to admit to coauthorship. But since Teichmann would not hear of this arrangement, he was forced to give in, though insisting that Teichmann's name precede his in the credits. Generously, he offered Teichmann 75 per cent of the royalties of the original production and 60 per cent thereafter.[1]

Despite his belief that he could not now get a fair hearing in the theater, a belief that reflected a serious loss of self-confidence, Kaufman was tempted by a new proposal. Feuer and Martin had followed up *Guys and Dolls* with *Can Can*, which boasted a score by Cole Porter. Next they planned a musical version of *Ninotchka*, the celebrated Garbo picture of 1939, which had been based on a stage play. For this production they went again to Porter for the songs and asked Kaufman to provide both the book and the direction. They expected to offer the show in the 1954-55 season. Kaufman accepted the offer and told the producers that Leueen would be his collaborator on the book.

But first was to come the production of *The Solid Gold Cadillac*. Max Gordon was pleased with the comedy. It required only three settings, plus the recordings of Fred Allen's voice and some filmed material to simulate television newscasts. The cost would not be negligible, but neither would it be sky high. Plans were formed to begin the preliminary tour in October. With the groundwork for the production laid, Kaufman and Leueen sailed on June 5 for a two-month visit to Europe.

One of Kaufman's reasons for making the trip was to look in on the recently opened London production of *Guys and Dolls*. But more important was the plan that he, with Leueen's prompting, had developed of leasing a house in London. It was not their intention to give up their life in New York altogether; since Kaufman's work as both writer and director tied him to New York, they expected to spend most of the theatrical season there, but to come to London for at least the summer and as much other time as could be managed. They expected eventually to sell Barley Sheaf Farm, the last, most potent reminder of Kaufman's life with Beatrice. He and Leueen arrived in London on June 10. They found the city still crowded with visitors who had come for the Coronation of Queen Elizabeth II on June 2.

As he had done before when on trips, Kaufman wrote newsy letters to Anne and awaited her answers with impatience. "I don't know if I have a daughter or not," he complained after not hearing from her for a week. She was not so mindless of her duties as all that, but was busy at home. She had begun to spend much of her time with Irving Schneider, who was the assistant producer to Irene Mayer Selznick. In his youth Schneider had been in Sam Harris's office and later became Moss Hart's secretary. Max Siegel, the Harris aide who had recommended that the producer put Kaufman to work with Hart on *Once in a Lifetime,* was Schneider's half brother. Kaufman seemed to sense that this relationship was more than casual. Writing on July 8 about plans for the next summer, when he expected Anne to accompany him to England, he cautioned, "DON'T MARRY ANYONE AHEAD OF THAT! And certainly don't marry anyone that asks you—it's like Groucho resigning from his club on the ground that he didn't want to belong to any club that would have him as a member. Well, not quite like that."

Though on this visit the Kaufmans spent almost as much time as before at plays and at social gatherings, Kaufman was somewhat slowed down by a new medical problem, lumbago. It was, in any event, the search for a house that was their principal occupation. On June 22 Kaufman was able to report to Anne that they had found one, subject to the approval of his New York lawyer, Howard Reinheimer. The house was at 17 Blomfield Road, "in a slightly déclassé neighborhood, which will become class-A when we buy." When Reinheimer gave his blessing, and after consultations with English lawyers, they took a long lease on the house. "The other day," he wrote on July 29, "I saw a solicitor named Furber, with offices at 11 Old Jewry, but I'm telling Edna it's just a coincidence."

The house needed improvements, and plenty of them, but they could not take possession immediately because the lease of the current occupant ran through the summer. With a view to establishing himself in some capacity in the London theater the following year, Kaufman held discussions with the producer Hugh Beaumont of H. M. Tennent. In the meanwhile Leueen was offered a part in a film, *Three Cases of Murder,* which was scheduled to begin shooting on July 23, and would have to stay in England longer than they had planned. Since Kaufman's work on *The Solid Gold Cadillac* required that he return to New York early in August, he had to sail alone.

Kaufman arrived in New York on August 11 and proceeded the next day to Barley Sheaf Farm to begin the push on the third and final draft of *Cadillac*. Howard and Evelyn Teichmann came to stay, and the writers began to polish the script to the finish that they hoped would dazzle viewers at the opening in Hartford on October 1. When rehearsals were in progress, Max Gordon told a reporter, "This one is it. There'll be no excuse. Josephine Hull and the whole cast are fine."[2] Still fretting over his inability to capture the musical rights to *My Sister Eileen*, Gordon was hoping to wrest a late laurel from this production.

Kaufman's anxiety about his reputation was made all the more poignant to Teichmann when Kaufman insisted that they take with them on the road another script that they had begun to write as soon as they were finished with the final draft of *Cadillac*. Teichmann knew that they had enough to do to make *Cadillac* run smoothly. The notices that the production received on the road bore out his judgment.

In Hartford, the reviewers for the daily papers and *Variety*, while making allowances for the fact that the play was being tested for Broadway and was not yet a finished product, found it wan and dull, and all too improbable at the final curtain. One serious problem that plagued the comedy at this point was the result of an error in the casting rather than in the writing. Laura Partridge was to win not merely control of the company, but the hand of Edward McKeever in marriage. But Loring Smith, who kept himself in trim with frequent games of golf, appeared to be some two decades younger than Josephine Hull. As a result, his proposal of marriage offended the audience and crippled the play. A covey of playwrights that included Hart (who had read the play earlier), Abe Burrows, and Thornton Wilder gathered after the opening performance in Hartford to discuss the play. Kaufman curtly sent them away with the announcement that he and Teichmann would do their own cutting and patching.[3]

Unfortunately, the engagement of the unlikely pair was not written out of the script before the Washington opening on October 5. For that and other reasons, the next day's notices were among the sternest condemnations of Kaufman's career. The rise of the curtain was also unnecessarily and foolishly delayed. For the playwrights and their producer, the performance was preceded by an elaborate dinner in their hotel. Supreme Court Justice William Douglas, an acquaintance of Gordon's, was present, as were Millie Gordon and Evelyn Teichmann. Music from Gordon's shows could be heard in the background, thanks to a gift from Gordon to the orchestra leader. Quite uncharacteristically, when it neared eight-thirty, curtain time, Kaufman asked Gordon to telephone the stage manager to hold the curtain, and

Gordon did so. By the time this band of revelers reached the National Theater at 8:55, the audience was stamping its feet in irritation and the actors were unnerved. During the performance, the electronic equipment projecting the recorded voice of Fred Allen began to deliver messages from a doctors' message service, and a large electric light bulb exploded back stage. Kaufman could see what was lying in wait in the morning papers and fled the city on a midnight train—with the explanation that on the following evening he was to appear on *This Is Show Business* and must ready himself for it. In pursuit, and in the hope that Kaufman would not simply give up, Teichmann also returned to New York that night. Wrote the critic of the Washington *Times-Herald*, "*The Solid Gold Cadillac,* a new play by Howard Teichmann and George S. Kaufman, presented by Max Gordon, arrived last night at the National Theater. The only remedy I can suggest is for the police department to step in with its crane and tow the wreck away, thus relieving the authors, the producer, the actors and any future audiences of further embarrassment." The critic of the Washington *Daily News* said all that needed to be said by entitling his review "Out of Gas."[4]

Adding to Kaufman's tension while the play was passing through this birth trauma was the fact that Barley Sheaf Farm was to be sold at auction on October 17, 1953. Now that he and Leueen had committed themselves to a life divided between New York and London, no pressing reason remained for holding on to the house and lands in Bucks County. The sale was only ten days off when, on the afternoon following the Washington opening, Teichmann met Kaufman at the Plaza Hotel in New York to talk over the events of the evening and what might be done to save the play. Despite the severity of the Washington notices, Max Gordon was determined to bring it in. But first a good deal of rewriting was necessary. When Kaufman informed Teichmann of Gordon's decision, Teichmann got to work at once. He spent the afternoon and evening excising the incongruous little love story and tightening what remained. The result, after further revisions in Washington and Philadelphia, was a well-running vehicle; if a thin comedy, it at least provided plenty of laughs.

The sale of the Holicong property on the seventeenth brought in some $140,-000.[5] On October 31 the antiques and primitive paintings Beatrice had collected during her ten years in the house were auctioned in more than four hundred lots. They had been left on the premises for the sale, which took the entire day.

The day of this second auction was the last that *The Solid Gold Cadillac* played in Philadelphia. On Thursday, November 5, the two writers braced themselves for the New York opening, not knowing quite what to expect, but apprehensive because of a serious lapse of memory that Josephine Hull suffered at a preview on the preceding evening. Teichmann went to call on Kaufman in the afternoon. Ill at ease, he looked at his collaborator and muttered "Nice day." Glancing up, Kaufman replied, "It was a nice day when they burned Joan of Arc."[6]

In the event, the collaborators' fears proved groundless. No mishaps occurred during the performance, and the reviews, though noting the cartoon-like, episodic construction, were full of praise for the perfectly timed performance of Josephine Hull. Though warier than usual all evening long, Kaufman invited the Teichmanns and a few friends to the apartment for a drink afterward. The next afternoon, pleased beyond measure with this triumph, he hired a limousine and with Anne and Leueen rode through a heavy snowstorm to gaze at the extended queue of customers waiting to buy tickets at the Belasco Theater box office. They sat in the heated car across from the theater for three-quarters of an hour while Kaufman drew comfort from the ever-lengthening line moving slowly in the snow. That evening the three went to see a one-man performance of the pianist-comedian Victor Borge. Spotting Kaufman in the audience, Borge announced his presence and asked him to stand up. Still glowing with pride over the reception of his new play, Kaufman stood and gratefully accepted a round of applause.

Soon after the opening, Kaufman confessed to Teichmann that he wanted to devote the rest of his life to writing a hit for Leueen. His mental energy, so far as others could tell, was directed solely toward the development of her career. Over the preceding year, the couple had found time to write a television play, *The Hat*, about the trouble that follows when two women who meet for lunch discover that they are wearing identical hats. It was never produced, but as a joint effort it confirmed the bond between them. In the meanwhile, Leueen had received good notices for her role as Private Donovan, the Good Fairy, in *The Love of Four Colonels*. But it was not a starring role, and consequently in Kaufman's view it was not important enough for her. He and Teichmann dropped the comedy that had accompanied them on their travels with *The Solid Gold Cadillac* (and had been overlooked in the tumult of that experience), and began talking about a vehicle for Leueen.[7]

Kaufman told Teichmann that he wanted this to be a serious play—a "drama," in Broadway jargon, not a comedy. He startled Teichmann by saying that he had just the title: *No Exit*. When Teichmann pointed out that this was the English-language title of an internationally famous play by

Jean-Paul Sartre, Kaufman airily replied that that made no difference. Over the winter months, they worked on the play. Teichmann for his part found it difficult to offer a display of enthusiasm for the material they were churning out: it was melodramatic and in his opinion unsuitable for Leueen. In April when they had written approximately three-quarters of the first draft, Kaufman and Leueen left for Europe, where they expected to proceed with the renovation of the house in Blomfield Road. The letters about the play that passed between Teichmann and Kaufman across the Atlantic took on an increasingly disagreeable tone as the summer sped along. Teichmann was also indignant over the fact that Kaufman would not return to New York to direct Ruth McDevitt in *The Solid Gold Cadillac* when that actress took over the role of Laura Partridge from Josephine Hull, who had fallen ill.

During the same period of time that Kaufman worked with Teichmann on the play for Leueen, he and Leueen developed their script for the new Feuer and Martin musical, to be called *Silk Stockings*. It was in the producers' hands before they sailed in April. On this trip, the couple went first to the Savoy in London, so that Leueen could supervise the extensive alterations and the painting of the house. She became ill, however, with a mysterious complaint that at first was alarmingly, and erroneously, diagnosed as meningitis. For the three weeks of her convalescence, they rented the vacation home in Portofino of Rex Harrison and Lilli Palmer, with whom Leueen had appeared in *Four Colonels*. Always unwilling to fly, Kaufman angered Leueen by refusing to accompany her on her flight to Portofino, despite the fact that she was ill. He went by boat and train. Cy Feuer sought them out there for a conference on their script. "They do go to trouble, those boys," Kaufman wrote to Anne.[8] He thought of buying out Teichmann's share in *"No Exit"* and inviting Edward Chodorov to work with him on it. Ultimately, the two took what all along Teichmann had believed to be the only sensible course: they simply dropped the play.[9]

If nothing came of the projected "drama," at least something positive was achieved in London: the house in Blomfield road became habitable by the middle of July. Ready along with it was the couple's engraved writing paper sporting the address and the telephone number. Kaufman's first letter on it was to Anne, with a report that they had been to Glyndebourne for the opera. "On the way there, incidentally," he wrote, "we passed through Uckfield, right in the heart of the pig Latin country."[10] On September 3 he and Leueen sailed for New York, where they were due to begin rehearsals of *Silk Stockings* in a month's time.

Cast as Ninotchka was the German actress Hildegarde Knef, her last name altered to Neff for the benefit of Americans. To follow the luminous Garbo would have been a heavy challenge for any actress; for Knef it was made even more difficult because she had not much of a voice. She could project it and carry a tune with it, but the sound she made was no better than a croak. By way of compensation, she had good looks and a stylish air. Cast opposite her as the American eager to convert her to capitalism was Don Ameche, no longer in demand as a film star, but nevertheless a reliable leading man blest with a resonant baritone voice. In the secondary female role of a Hollywood star who, like Esther Williams, swam to film fame was Yvonne Adair. In sum, this was a good cast, and the choice of Helen Tamiris as choreographer also promised well. But no sooner had the first reading taken place, on October 10, than delays and other troubles began. Feuer and Martin were quick to insist on revisions of the script. Rehearsals were expected to commence on October 11, but were delayed until October 21 to give Kaufman and Leueen time to provide the revisions.[11]

The out-of-town opening in Philadelphia on November 22 promised success, but ran far too late in the evening. At this time no members of the production team minded the additional work necessary to pare down the show and knead it into shape, since such work was expected on a tryout tour. But the heavy pressure applied by Feuer and Martin soon began to tell in jangled nerves and abraded dispositions. One misfortune was altogether unexpected: on the day following the opening, Yvonne Adair discovered that she was pregnant. After some trials and errors, the producers gave her part to Gretchen Wyler, who filled it effectively. Meanwhile, they dismissed Helen Tamiris and hired Eugene Loring in her place. They were hard on Cole Porter, demanding that he replace several of the songs. He thought that they underrated his best numbers and privately vowed never to work with them again.[12]

Yet another unforeseen calamity occurred when, a few days after the Philadelphia opening, it was discovered that Hildegarde Knef had the measles. The entire company agreed to keep this illness of the star a secret, so that she could continue to perform without a temporary closing of the show.[13] It became necessary to book additional weeks on the road. The original plan had called for a New York opening on December 30, but instead the production remained in Philadelphia over New Year's Day and opened in Boston on January 4. From that city it went on to Detroit. Not until February 24 did it reach Broadway.

But by that date Kaufman and Leueen had long since left the production. Shortly before Christmas, in Philadelphia, Kaufman had told Ernest Martin that he would do nothing more to the book. He had altered it so much already that it bore little resemblance to his original conception of a suavely romantic play with songs. The show was now standard Broadway fare, and he would put in no more jokes. On hearing this statement Martin dismissed him. Not in the more than thirty-five years of his career had that happened to Kaufman before. It was a blow to his pride, and, perhaps worse, it was a blow to his health. Since he and Teichmann had by this time patched up their quarrel of the summer months, Leueen asked Teichmann if he would intercede with the producers. Teichmann replied that he would do that only if Kaufman himself requested it. But Kaufman, as they both knew, was not a man to ask someone else to fight his battle for him.[14]

Returning to New York with Leueen, he was sent straightaway to the hospital by Dr. Greenspan for, as the papers put it, "rest and medical attention."[15] He had suffered a slight stroke. Lucinda Ballard, the costume designer of the show, called on him there. To her amazement, she saw that he was crying. He repeated to her something that Martin had said to him which amazed her even more: according to Martin, when the company received word that Kaufman would no longer rehearse them, they broke into cheers. Lucinda Ballard knew that this had not happened. Later, after his recovery, she heard Kaufman describe the incident again, at a party given by George Backer, and again she saw tears in his eyes.[16]

With Kaufman banished from the production, the producers brought Abe Burrows to Boston to doctor the book. He administered doses of even more gags. When Kaufman was released from the hospital, he and Leueen went to Boston to look at the results. When they saw how drastic were the interpolations and excisions made by Burrows, they asked that his name be added to theirs as an author of the book, so that they alone would not be held to account for it. Thereafter in the credits the book was cited as the work of all three. Knef asked to be released from her contract on the ground that the character of Ninotchka was a much different part from the one she had agreed to play. She was not let out, however.[17]

When at last the production reached Broadway, the travail of the preceding four months was not evident to the audience. It was a slick show. But Kaufman was not among those present. He and Leueen spent the night of the opening in Atlantic City, along with the Teichmanns, who drove them down. Still suffering from the rebuff of his dismissal, Kaufman for the first time that anyone could remember got drunk at dinner. Later in the evening, however, his spirits rose somewhat when Bernard Hart telephoned the two couples to read them the reviews, which were good enough to promise a long and profitable run. With a contract guaranteeing him and Leueen five per cent of the gross, he stood to make a great deal of money from the production.[18] Yet he was never able to shrug off the incident altogether. Ernest Martin, he said, was "Jed Harris rolled into one."

Though Kaufman did not look much altered as a result of his embroilment with Feuer and Martin, he was less agile thereafter, and gravely concerned about his health. It was impossible, however, for him to give up the search for the elusive dramatic idea that would guarantee another hit. With Teichmann he began a new comedy, called *In the Money*, about a man of no importance who inherits $850,000 from an unexpected source and then finds that all the relations who once held him in contempt cannot leave him alone—at least, not until the money is gone. He planned still more collaborations with other writers, including S. N. Behrman and Alan Campbell, the husband of Dorothy Parker. It was a sort of curse from which there was no relief, this incessant itch to write. Max Gordon abetted it, for he too was constantly in search of one more hit to swell his reputation, though he reserved the right to turn down whatever Kaufman offered. Leueen also had a project; she accepted the role of Cassandra in the production of Jean Giraudoux's *La Guerre de Troie n'aura pas lieu*, translated by Christopher Fry and retitled *Tiger at the Gates*. Michael Redgrave was to play Hector. This was set to open in London on June 2, 1955, under the direction of Harold Clurman, and was tentatively scheduled to be brought to New York in the fall.

Leueen left for rehearsals in London on March 4; since this time she was traveling alone, she flew. The tryout tour of the play began in early April in Manchester, and was to proceed to Glasgow before coming to London on June 2. Kaufman kept a promise of the year before to Anne that she would accompany him to England this year. On May 5 they sailed on the *Queen Elizabeth*, Kaufman's favorite ship. Aboard with them were other theatrical notables, including Hermione Gingold and Clifton Webb. When Anne suggested that it might be fun to invite Gingold to dinner one evening, Kaufman agreed, but, revealing the doubt that he had begun to have about his reputation, said that she might not know who he was. This, of course, was nonsense; Gingold, as amusing off stage as on, was a superb companion for him and Anne. When the ship put in briefly at Cherbourg before docking at Southampton, Kaufman took the two women into a perfume shop and told them to stock up.

In the chill of a Scottish spring, he and Anne attended the Glasgow opening of *Tiger at the Gates*. Leueen was on stage at the rise of the curtain, and at the sight of her Kaufman began to shed tears. "Isn't she beautiful?" he said to Anne.

For the months of June and July he stayed with Leueen in the house on Blomfield Road. With a woman friend of Leueen's, Anne went to Cairo, then back to New York alone. As the summer passed, Kaufman became increasingly depressed about his health, and in particular about the diminishment of sexual potency. To Moss Hart he wrote, "I passed a house that had to be renumbered. It said, '118, formerly 12.' That's me." In his many letters to Anne he made no effort to conceal his anxiety. In midsummer he wrote,

> Yesterday I stayed in bed all day, except for an hour in the garden with Peter and Natasha [Brook], and worked myself into a fine state of nerves. God, but I am expert at that. I hope I can work all right when I get home—maybe I'll have a few sessions with a psycho, though I hate it. It is not *all* emotional—there is of course a physical basis. There is a new osteopath (a woman) that I am going to over here—quite wonderful in her way, but which may not be quite the way I need. Enough of this subject—I promise not to dwell on it when I get home. But even jotting down this paragraph to you is a relief. If you answer this letter for any reason, don't bring this up—I keep as much of it from Leueen as I can, and it's very good for me to do so.[19]

Though the Giraudoux play was financially disappointing, it was so well received that a New York booking was made for the fall. Kaufman sailed back on August 11 to confer with Teichmann and Max Gordon about *In the Money*, while Leueen stayed on until *Tiger at the Gates* closed on September 3. It was only a faint hope that he held for his and Teichmann's comedy, and that soon evaporated. Getting no encouragement from Gordon, the two writers realized that it was best put aside. The preservation of his health was more important to Kaufman, and still more important was Leueen's opening night on October 3. As in London, the play drew excellent notices, but not large houses. On April 7, 1956, it was withdrawn.

One other event of the theatrical season loomed large for Kaufman and his circle. Through the fall much talk circulated about the musical version by Alan Jay Lerner and Frederick Loewe of Shaw's *Pygmalion* then being readied for a late-winter opening under the title *My Fair Lady*. Hart was the director of the show, which went into rehearsal in January 1956. So extraordinarily promising was this work that the producer, Herman Levin, was able to get the entire backing from the Columbia Broadcasting System. Reports coming back to New York during the month-long road tour generated still more excitement. Kaufman felt it intensely because of Hart's involvement. In place of the customary opening-night telegram he wrote a personal letter—a letter in which he candidly expressed his feelings:

> A letter, Mossie, instead of a telegram.
>
> I find myself feeling very emotional about *My Fair Lady,* and that, I need hardly add, is due to your participation. Of course I'm looking forward to your opening with great excitement, and thanks greatly, first, for the wonderful seats. I'm sure it will be one hell of a night.
>
> You've apparently done a wonderful job, and I'm sure you will get gigantic credit.
>
> Anyhow, this is just a letter from a full heart, so far as you are concerned.[20]

It was, as all the world soon knew, "one hell of a night." Few productions had ever received reviews of such extravagant praise as those showered on *My Fair Lady.* But the evening did not end well for Kaufman. At supper at the Plaza after the performance, he fainted and had to be taken home. Though he soon recovered, the incident was yet another indication of the deteriorating state of his health.

With S. N. Behrman he worked off and on during the season to put together a play about the Mizner brothers, Addison and Wilson, adventurers whose lives had recently been profiled for the *New Yorker* by Alva Johnson. But after making a very sketchy draft of two acts, they abandoned the project. In March Leueen flew back to London to oversee still more work on the house. A wall between two ground-floor rooms was torn down to make one large room, and the carpeting put in in 1954, whose color no longer pleased Leueen, was taken up and new carpeting was laid. To make up for her absence, Kaufman's friends and Anne kept him entertained. The Harts and the Goetzes were those whose company he most frequently sought. He also began to work in earnest with Alan Campbell on the book for a musical called *The Lipstick War.* In the past, he had never particularly cared for Campbell and made no effort to hide the fact. But since Campbell's separation from Dorothy Parker, Kaufman found him easier to take. Also, he was a friend of Leueen's. On May 9 Kaufman sailed on the *Elizabeth* to join Leueen; for company he took Anne with him, and he also took a draft of *The Lipstick War.* In the summer, Campbell also went to London, and the two settled to work.

Though Kaufman allowed himself to be drawn into the social life of theatrical London again this summer, he took small pleasure in it. Running through his mind were two questions: would he be active in the New York theater in the fall, and would Leueen come back to New York with him? The possibility that she might stay over in London to appear in a play was a summer-long threat to him; to Anne, who returned to New York in July, he confided by letter his dread of facing the winter alone. Yet he did not want Leueen to miss the opportunity of appearing on the stage in London if it arose.

The summer was lent some excitement when Kaufman and Leueen discovered that they were being systematically robbed by the Italian couple who worked for them. Missing a great many personal and household items, they searched through a trunk belonging to the servants and found all of them. They also found a revolver. Frightened, they called the police, but decided against pressing charges. Soon Leueen hired an Austrian couple to take the place of the Italians, and the household order was restored. But when Leueen went without him to Spain for a holiday, Kaufman was lonely in the house. Visits from his sisters Ruth and Helen were no compensation for the absence of Leueen.[21]

As for *The Lipstick War,* it came to nothing. The plot had to do with a young woman and a young man, each the owner of a cosmetics business, who at first are rivals but soon fall in love. This was a reasonable basis for the book of a musical, but was hardly of daring novelty. At first, Max Gordon was excited about its possibilities. To the astonishment of Kaufman, he went so far as to ask Rodgers and Hammerstein to compose the score. In a letter of this time to Moss and Kitty Hart, Kaufman expressed his feeling about not only the musical, but his state of being:

> I mean it when I say I think our show may be old-fashioned—it is hard to change one's style. On the theory that credit should be given where credit is deserved, I have prepared a credit list for the program, as follows:
>
> By George S. Kaufman, plus glucose, lecithin, Bemax, Serpisal, Anesolysene, neutrilite, lipsteine, Equanil, Veganin, Codeine, dramamine, Doctors E. B. Greenspan, L. S. Kubie, John Janvrin, S. L. Johnson, vitamins B1-2-3-4-5-6-7-8-9-10-11 and 12, Laboratory staff of Mt. Sinai Hospital, phenobarbital, seconal, numbutal, tuinol, and FUCKITALL
>
> —AND—
>
> Alan Campbell.[22]

When, as was inevitable, Max Gordon's proposition to Rodgers and Hammerstein was declined, the producer lost interest and returned the script. Though Kaufman talked of showing it to one or two other producers, he too decided to let it go.

Similarly, Leueen's prospect of remaining in London to appear in a play faded into nothing. She sailed with Kaufman on the *United States* on September 6. In the winter she was given a role in the Broadway production of Graham Greene's *The Potting Shed,* which opened on January 29, 1957. After the play had been running four weeks, Leueen told Kaufman that she was leaving him.

23

Last Scenes

It was natural that Leueen, then only forty-three, should feel restless under the constraint of her marriage to Kaufman. He was no less adoring than before, but because of his illnesses the marriage had become a union in the legal sense only. The eight years since her arrival in New York with *Edward, My Son* had made no marked change in Leueen's looks: she was still an alluring woman. The director and producer of her play, a young man some twelve years her junior, responded to her allure. It was not long before word spread that they had fallen in love. When Leueen came to Kaufman with the news that she wished to move out of the apartment at 1035 Park Avenue and into a place of her own, it was this young man with whom she thought of sharing her life.

Leueen was tactful and cautious in approaching Kaufman with her news. She hoped above all to avoid bringing about a further impairment of his health. Though not an invalid, he was gradually weakening; the slight cardiovascular episode of 1951 and that of 1955, precipitated by his anxiety over *Silk Stockings*, had taken their toll. He preferred to remain at home much of the time, cared for by his butler and cook, and seldom accepted invitations unless he was confident that he could break them without insulting his hosts or disturbing the dinner-table arrangements. He seemed to enjoy sitting with the cat, Adam, that he and Leueen had bought in London. When he did leave the apartment, he walked with a cane; it was one left to him by Harris, who had prized it because it had been a gift from Cohan. Kaufman did not limp or drag a foot, but the cane was useful for balance. Though in conversation and in his letters he was still the lightning-fast wit of old, he was fragile. He had to be handled with care.

Over the years Anne and Leueen had drawn very close. As two very different types of women, they sometimes irritated each other, but the irritations were an accepted part of the relationship, understood and tolerated and never lasting for long. Taking Anne into her confidence, Leueen told her that she had to begin a new chapter of her life, without Kaufman. But, deeply concerned lest she upset Kaufman's health, she suggested that together they ask his physician, Dr. Greenspan, for an opinion on the probable consequences to Kaufman if she left him.

The women met at Greenspan's office at 12:30 on February 27, and he told them that in his opinion Kaufman was strong enough to sustain the shock. They then proceeded to the apartment, and Leueen closeted herself with Kaufman to tell him what she felt she must do. Anne remained out of sight and earshot until their talk was over. She stayed on with her father as he wrote some notes to the Harts and other intimates to inform them of the break. That evening Anne had dinner at the apartment, and for some weeks thereafter she made a point of seeing her father every day.

Dr. Greenspan's prediction proved reasonably accurate: there was no obvious acceleration of the decline of Kaufman's physical health. However, he was deeply depressed by the loss of Leueen's presence, and to relieve the mental pain, he decided to undergo psychotherapy. In view of the special strength with which his relations with women had been invested for so long, it made good sense that at this difficult time he should choose a woman psychiatrist, Dr. Ruth Conkey. Though he did not continue treatment with Dr. Conkey for long, as much as he did receive from her was beneficial.

Leueen continued with *The Potting Shed* to the end of its run on June 1. Her plan, in which Kaufman concurred, was that she would go to Mexico for a quick divorce. She did not go at once, however. Remaining in New York, she saw Kaufman often, and the two even composed a two-character one-act play, *Amicable Parting*, about a couple who divide up their joint possessions before separating. The difference between the characters' circumstances and theirs was that at the close of the sketch the characters call off the separation. Kaufman's concern for Leueen abated not at all through this period in their lives. When she was ill, as she was toward the end of her run, he was alarmed; when in the summer he began to suspect that all was not well between her and her young man, he was troubled for her sake. Leueen put off the trip to Mexico until August; by that time her romance had indeed cooled.

Once it was determined that they would separate, the couple decided to give up the house in Blomfield Road. Kaufman's English secretary and general aide, Adza Vincent, began the packing and shipping of their effects in April, and also showed the house to persons interested in taking over the lease. Anne went abroad in April to assist with the final removal of possessions and then visited the Continent with a woman friend. Later in the year the house was bought by the Luce organization as the residence of the editor of the English edition of *Time*.[1]

Left alone in New York, Kaufman fought against despondency and loneliness by having friends in for dinner every few evenings. In the main, those whom he saw, in addition to the Harts, his favorite guests, were such old acquaintances as Natalie Schafer, Lillian Hellman, the Gordons, and, with a certain reluctance, Ferber. The intimate dinners were not always events that he looked forward to with pleasure; more often than not he undertook them out of a sense of duty, or because they kept his mind active. One friend who could not attend them was Augustus Goetz. Goetz was seriously ill with heart disease; Kaufman made repeated, anxious inquiries of Ruth Goetz about the state of his health.

As with many other elderly people, television proved increasingly to be a boon to Kaufman. He watched baseball games and developed an interest in the phenomenal progress of Charles Van Doren on the *Twenty-One* quiz show; later he was disillusioned and offended by Van Doren's revelation that the questions had been fed to him in advance and that he had been coached as to how to make a dramatic response to them on camera. Kaufman was marking time, but had no notion of the path his professional life might take in the future, if it took any at all.

Then in June, like a cooling rain after a parching heat wave, came an offer to direct a play. David Merrick, the most active producer on Broadway at the time, as well as the most controversial since Jed Harris, sought him out to stage Peter Ustinov's *Romanoff and Juliet*. The play had gathered good reviews in London; in the course of its long run Kaufman had seen it there and thought it not bad.[2] Like *The Love of Four Colonels*, it was a political comedy with elements of fantasy. Shaw and Giraudoux were its literary progenitors. Because the plot, a satiric comment on the Cold War, had to do with a love affair between an American girl and a young Russian, Merrick thought that on Broadway the play should have an American director. He felt that it required some cutting and altering for American tastes and believed that Kaufman, the legendary play doctor, was the only man for this task. Ustinov was to repeat his West End performance in the central role of the General who is also head of the government of the tiny European country where the action occurs, but most of the cast was to be American. Since

1953, when *The Love of Four Colonels* was produced on Broadway, Ustinov had known Kaufman; he and his wife had been guests at Blomfield Road. When Merrick proposed Kaufman as director, Ustinov was happy to have him. But on arriving in New York in August to begin rehearsals he regretted the choice, for the Kaufman he met at that time was not the Kaufman he had known. If not wraithlike, Kaufman was nearly so: he was a very tired, listless, elderly gentleman whose weight had fallen to 126 pounds.[3]

The problem of summoning strength to conduct rehearsals was exacerbated for Kaufman by his anxiety over the divorce. Anne was in Europe again, and Kaufman had been finding small ways of occupying himself, such as talking with a young writer, Helen Hunter, about a play she hoped to write with him and doing the correct thing by asking the voluble Ferber and Groucho, who was on a visit from California, to come for a meal. But much of his small store of energy he spent on fretting over the unsettled state of his relationship with Leueen. On August 17 he wrote to Anne: "I think I was divorced yesterday, but don't know. Leueen was planning to leave by plane for Mexico Thursday, but there was no two line squib in the paper this morning, so I'm not sure." On August 21, at last, the matter was settled; Leueen telephoned the news to him from Mexico. It was something of a relief to hear it, and rather glibly he passed it along to Anne: "Leueen phoned me yesterday—she found the divorce proceedings rather sordid and even comical—it takes three weeks before it is definite. She reports that she feels fine."[4]

Never a very physical director, Kaufman was not seriously handicapped in rehearsals of *Romanoff and Juliet* by the slowness of gait that his small strokes had caused. Apart from Ustinov, the actors did not feel let down by him. Though he believed that the work was good for him, at the same time he admitted that it was exhausting. Every evening at seven he came home and went to bed to conserve strength for the next day's work.[5] Ustinov, who could hardly be blamed for wanting to protect his play, told Merrick that he wanted Kaufman replaced. He was not distressed by Kaufman's lack of physical energy so much as by his suggestions for cutting and revising, which Ustinov steadfastly resisted. Merrick, however, stood up to Ustinov. He told the playwright that rather than dismiss Kaufman he would abandon the play.[6] To Elliot Norton of the Boston *Globe* Merrick reported that Kaufman had been reluctant, on the ground of ill health, to accept the assignment and had even said that he might not be able to finish what he began. But Merrick was pleased with the direction. "Just getting back to the theater," said the producer, "has made a new man of him." Still Ustinov remained in doubt; he was astonished to hear Kaufman say after the dress rehearsal that he had made some notes to give to the actors, but had lost them.[7]

Kaufman wanted Anne to be present at the Boston opening on September 9, and he asked her to plan to return from Europe in time for it. In that era before the use of jets on commercial flights, the trip to Boston from Nice, where Anne was then staying, took the better part of two days. Her schedule was tight; she arrived at the Ritz Hotel, where her father was awaiting her, before going to the theater. Annoyed that she had almost been late for the performance, he offered her no greeting at all. But afterward, when it was evident that the play was a success, he relaxed at the party given by Merrick and, a proud father, told the company that Anne had come to see them all the way from the south of France.

The production spent four weeks out of town. Though the notices were good, Ustinov was not entirely pleased with the cast and insisted on some changes. Both George Voskovec, as the Russian ambassador, and Alvin Epstein, as a Russian spy, were dismissed, as was a young, unknown actress whom Merrick had cast as Juliet. These changes required more rehearsals, which in turn added to Kaufman's tension. Fortunately, he had one good friend in the cast: Natalie Schafer, who played the wife of the American ambassador. For the New York *Herald Tribune* of September 29, Kaufman wrote a promotional piece that obliquely revealed how diminished he felt his authority to be: "Mr. Ustinov, to clear matters up, is the author and star of the play that I'm talking about—its name is *Romanoff and Juliet*. As for me, I am only the director, and very little of that."[8]

Despite whatever mental tortures he and Ustinov endured, the notices that greeted the play at its Broadway opening on October 10 were good. There were some complaints that it was thin and that at moments Kaufman's direction was slack, but these were too mild to keep the customers away. *Romanoff and Juliet* ran for 389 performances. Kaufman gave a party at his apartment after the opening and, gratified by the reviews as they came in, stayed up late with his guests to savor the experience of yet one more hit. Troubled still by the ebbing of his strength, he must have known that he would not direct another play. On the other hand, when, on November 14, *Amicable Parting* was given its first staging, at Columbia Teachers College, he did not suppose that this would be the last presentation of a new play of his writing. Until thought itself deserted him, he continued to invent new plots and set them down in dialogue.

He also kept up his practice of writing occasional magazine pieces. On November 3, 1957, in the *New York Times* Sunday magazine, he published an essay, "Musical Comedy—or Musical Serious?" on the new vogue of musicals with intense and even tragic plots, such as Leonard Bernstein's *West Side Story*. In January 1958 Bennett Cerf asked permission on behalf of Random House to bring out a volume of such essays as this and others by Kaufman that had appeared in papers and the *New Yorker* over the years. Kaufman vetoed the plan for the moment, but held out hope for the publication of such a book one day, provided he wrote enough new pieces of merit to flesh it out.[9] In the years remaining to him, he published some brief scraps in the *Saturday Review* and two of greater substance in the *New Yorker*: "When Your Honey's on the Telephone" (February 22, 1958) on the difficulty of wiping one's breakfast honey off any surface without getting it on another, and "Memoir" (June 11, 1960), on his summary rejection of the song "Always" when Berlin offered it to him for *The Cocoanuts*. But he never did authorize the publication of a collection.

One fellow playwright whom he saw frequently at the close of 1957 and through 1958 was Ruth Goetz. When her husband died on September 30, 1957, Kaufman shared her sorrow, and a gentle relationship developed between them. Ruth Goetz came to see him often, sometimes bringing her young daughter along. They would chat in his bedroom, where he stretched out his long legs, his head resting—but seldom easily—on a plumped-up pillow. Beside the bed was a night table, and on it Ruth Goetz saw more bottles of pills and medicines than she had ever seen in one place before. She could scarcely believe how many bottles stood there; they might have been the accumulated prescriptions of an elderly person's lifetime, not merely those gathered in only a few years. They were a reminder to her of the hypochondria from which, as she knew, he had always suffered. In the days of their work together on *Franklin Street*, he had dashed out of the room every few minutes to wash his hands, as though just by sitting and talking he had managed to coat them with germs. He could no longer leap up and wash; instead, he had his medicines.

His decline was made all the more evident on one evening when he ventured out to the theater with her and the Harts. During the second act of John Osborne's *The Entertainer*, at its Broadway opening on February 12, 1958, Kaufman felt uncomfortable, rose from his seat, and collapsed in the aisle. The performance continued without interruption, and he was assisted to the back of the house. An ambulance was summoned for him as he rested on the floor, unseen by the audience. When he rose he collapsed a second time, but on rising again he refused to enter the ambulance. Ruth Goetz and the Harts got him home in a taxi and called Dr. Greenspan, who later told the press that nothing serious was ailing his patient: "I've known George for twenty years and there's nothing to worry about. He'll be up and about tomorrow."[10]

But Greenspan's remarks were blather. Kaufman was far from well. Ruth Goetz continued to visit him. They talked of many subjects of mutual concern, among which was anti-Semitism. He told her that he had occasionally been subjected to anti-Semitic slurs, as a boy in Pittsburgh, and later as well, but that he had never let them interfere with his work. He recounted the incident of Frank Munsey and the Washington *Times*. Ruth Goetz had always known that her father detested Munsey, but had never heard him say what quality in Munsey's personality it was that so offended him. Now she knew. Kaufman spoke proudly of the fact that he and Hart had repeatedly refused to allow their plays to be produced in Germany and Austria. He asked her whether hers had been produced in either country. She replied that they had been, and felt a twinge of guilt.[11]

Then one day, as they were talking, Kaufman proposed that they write a play together. He suggested that B. S. Pully, who had been excellent as the tough-guy gambler Big Jule in *Guys and Dolls,* might make a fine comic dishonest labor leader. The news was full of accounts of the mishandling by union executives of their organizations' financial reserves; Kaufman thought that this might be a suitable topic for a play. Ruth Goetz, who was politically liberal, agreed, because she saw that the play could become a defense of honest unions and an attack on the leadership of those that robbed the rank and file.

For a few weeks in 1958 as winter turned to spring they worked on the project. As the plot developed, it included an internationally famous diva with whom the labor leader fell in love. "For many years," ran one of her lines, "I was so poor that I had to study from old scores that I picked out of garbage cans back of the opera house." Just when Ruth Goetz thought that the script was beginning to turn into something good, Kaufman told her that it would be better as a musical, not only because a singer was involved in it, but because musicals stood a chance of making much more money than non-musical plays. He suggested that they invite Howard Dietz and Arthur Schwartz to write the songs. Though she was not happy with this alteration of their plan, she agreed. Soon, however, she regretted giving her consent, because with the entrance of the songwriting pair the script changed its political direction and in her opinion became an antilabor tract. The writing dragged on to June, when finally Ruth Goetz decided that she could not continue it. Upset by her defection, Kaufman wrote her a letter that moved her profoundly as an appeal and as praise for her talent but that did not persuade her to change her mind. Dietz and Schwartz then also decided to withdraw. On July 1 Dietz informed Kaufman of this by letter, offering as an excuse a comment that the script did not provide an opportunity for a variety of songs, only songs about "graft and money." Though hurt and disappointed, Kaufman replied only that their decision was "perfectly understandable."[12]

Setting this piece of work aside for the time being, Kaufman started a new comedy with Leueen, who was living in New York and much concerned about his well-being. Their plot had to do with a romance that develops, improbably but quite happily, between a New York taxi driver and a woman poet from England. For the title they borrowed a line uttered by Dorothy Parker on seeing a newsapaper photograph of two orangutans costumed as bride and groom: "I give it six months." This cynicism was not reflected in the script, which ended with the driver and the poet lovingly paired. Max Gordon having gone into retirement, they circulated the script among other producers and were pleased when Gilbert Miller took an option on it.

But in the fall, before Kaufman's hope of a production could be realized, he fell ill again. Again suffering a stroke, he was taken to Mt. Sinai Hospital. Though the stroke neither crippled him nor distorted his speech, it was a chilling indication that not much time was left to him. On the afternoon of November 8, when Anne was at his bedside in the hospital, he asked her whether she knew what day it was. Realizing that he meant something more important than the day of the week, she said that she did not. "This is the fortieth birthday of my son John," he said, "who is not your brother." Not since her childhood had he ever alluded to the fact that she had been adopted. It was painful, but she held on and listened as he speculated about what sort of person his son might have been and what he might have made out of his life. Late in the evening, when he had talked himself out, she left the hospital.

Not long after that grim day Kaufman was home again, and casting the new comedy. He and Leueen decided that she should not take the leading role of Jessica Bolton, the poet, despite the fact it suited her. Nor in view of his physical state was it practical for him to plan on directing the play. These decisions about star and director were up in the air, but at least he knew that he wanted Mary Wickes for the role of secretary to the poet's American publisher. When the actress wrote that a prior commitment prevented her taking the part, he replied, somewhat belatedly, on November 27:

I haven't even the usual excuse for not writing sooner, which is that I don't know your address and I have to call up Anne and find out, and then I get all tangled up with other things and think she's given me Madame Pompadour's address by mistake, and I don't think I ought to be writing to Madame Pompadour—well, you understand—I'm making excuses.

I see by all the public prints that you're working all the time out there, but I still hope to make one more effort to lure you east, just to see one of those photographs with you getting off the train or plane with 4 dozen roses in your arms, and I shall be somewhere near-by with the air of a fellow who has given you the roses, and that takes some acting, because I'm a tight old bastard. Anyhow, I'm an *old* bastard—it's beginning to run into money.

But we'll get you here yet . . .

Ironically, just as Mary Wickes found herself free to accept the role after all, Gilbert Miller decided against producing the play. Kaufman tried to find someone else to put it on, but had no luck. He turned back to the romance of the labor leader and the diva, since to have no play in progress was unthinkable. Unwilling to try to complete it himself, Kaufman called Marc Connelly, even though they had not worked together in almost thirty years. Still in excellent health, Connelly was delighted at the prospect of writing with Kaufman again, and, as Ruth Goetz had done, he reported daily to 1035 Park Avenue. He realized that Kaufman was far from well, but worked patiently with him until the script was complete. At one point they had to decide on a birthday present that the protagonist would give his mother. Connelly suggested that they have him give her a union—the Brotherhood of Chinese Laundry Workers—and was delighted when Kaufman broke into laughter over this.[13] But as with *I Give It Six Months,* nothing came of the play. Though ideas came to his mind for still others, Kaufman was not able to get them down on paper.

There remained yet one more career for him.

Whiling away the late evening hours, he took pleasure in watching Jack Paar's talk show, which followed the eleven o'clock news on NBC. Thinking that it might be interesting to appear with Paar, he wrote the comedian a letter in March 1959. Paar was pleased to have him on the show. On the first evening, Paar astonished him by asking, "Mr. Kaufman, if I said that you were a very charming man, would that offend you?" "I wouldn't like it," he replied, drawing the expected laugh.[14]

On that evening, as on later ones, he arrived with a few stories to tell. One had to do with a plot for a musical that he thought might interest

Hollywood: at ten minutes to eight the understudy falls ill and the star has to go on. On another appearance he told Paar about an annual party held the evening of August 31, when the guests sit up to see the oyster season begin. Promptly at midnight waiters arrive with trays of oysters. But as for himself, he observed, "I wouldn't swallow one for $5000. Counting the hospital costs, I wouldn't make a nickel."

At Paar's invitation, Kaufman agreed to come on the show once a month. But his health did not permit him to come on so often, and he made only five appearances. Once when he was scheduled to appear, he was forced by illness to notify Paar that he could not keep the date. To Jean Dixon, whom he had asked to accompany him to the studio, he sent a message, "Just not up to Paar."[15] On his last appearance, in 1960, he was so weak that it was difficult for him to reach the platform where the guests sat and so cloudy of mind that he could not finish a story that he began. Paar's manner during this ordeal was smooth and correct. He remained helpful, and revealed no hint of alarm.

It was evident that arteriosclerosis had begun to impair Kaufman's mental powers. But long before his mind began to fail badly, he asked Leueen to marry him again. She now devoted much of her time to him, in the hope of compensating him for the unhappiness she had caused by leaving him in 1957. But she told him that to remarry him would only lead to embarrassment, since the public would think that she had done it for material gain. He did not press the point, but saw to it that she shared in his estate.

On April 7, 1960, occurred an event that Kaufman had long been expecting: the marriage of Anne and Irving Schneider. Kaufman was pleased about the marriage, but was too ill to attend the ceremony, which was held in the officiating rabbi's study. He asked Anne and Schneider, the Harts, and Leueen—his "family"—to have a drink in the apartment afterward.

Another important event of 1960 for Kaufman as well as for his circle was the publication of *Act One,* Moss Hart's memoir of his start in the theater, culminating in a description of the months of travail with Kaufman as they rewrote *Once in a Lifetime.* Hart dedicated the book to his wife, Kitty, but declared in it, "If it is possible for a book of this sort to have a hero, then that hero is George S. Kaufman."[16] His admiration and affection for the older man who was his mentor even before they met were allowed to shine out on every page of the long account of their first collaboration. The book was published in September, but as early as July Hart received copies from Random House. He sent one immediately to Kaufman and waited nervously for forty-eight hours before hearing from him.[17] When the message came, it was one of praise for Hart's achievement. A publishing triumph, the book was a best seller and was bought for the movies. Though Kaufman would have preferred that a film not be made, since he did not like the idea of being portrayed in it, he realized that it would be unfair to Hart if he were to withhold permission. When in 1963, after the death of both writers, the film was made and released, he was portrayed by Jason Robards, Jr.[18]

Kaufman's last moments formed a sad denouement to a life story that for most of its chapters had been more satisfying than is true of most lives. He became ever more nervous, easily distracted, and fearful about his condition, which made it all the worse. Rapidly his mind began to go. Once, when Ferber, four years older than he but mentally right as rain, came to call, he looked at her and told her she was dead. To Howard Teichmann he said that he had written some pages of dialogue that he wanted Teichmann to read, but which the younger man found to be a mass of indecipherable scribbling.[19] A male nurse was engaged to look after him. Both Anne and Leueen spent long hours at his bedside, but if the one who happened to be visiting left the room even briefly, he would say when she returned, "Why do you never come to see me any more? You don't care about me." Despite the supervision that he got from the nurse and the two women, he sometimes managed to leave the apartment house alone and would be spotted wandering on Park or Madison Avenue in his dressing gown and slippers, the tail of his nightshirt billowing around his white, spindly legs. One day Betsy, his granddaughter, then twelve years old, was walking along Madison Avenue. She saw a pair of legs in low stockings and looked up to discover that they belonged to her grandfather.[20]

Anne and Leueen were shaken by the reports of these adventures, since the possibility was always present that on one of them he would have a fatal accident. In fact, early in 1961 he had a near-fatal one when he fell against a hot steam-radiator in his own bathroom. Unattended and weak, he was slow to get up, and consequently was badly burned. The shock to his system was so great that seldom afterward did he leave his bed. Kaufman's nephew, Dr. Allan Friedlich, a cardiologist who practiced in Boston, was told about his uncle's condition and came to visit. Like Ruth Goetz a few years earlier, he was shocked to see the night table crowded with bottles. There were at least fifty medicines by Dr. Friedlich's hasty count, and Kaufman helped himself to them as he saw fit. His physician at that time was not Dr. Greenspan, but a specialist in geriatrics who had been recommended to him by the Rusk Institute in Manhattan. Dr. Friedlich went to see this man and found that he was too much in awe of his famous patient to treat him effectively.[21]

He then threw out the bottles and tried to limit his uncle's medications, but by that time the end was almost in sight.

Death came on June 2, 1961, at about 10:30 in the morning, only moments after he finished breakfast. It had not been the practice of Anne and Leueen to look in on him at this early hour; neither was with him at the time. Only his nurse was present. It was a peaceful end not preceded by a new medical crisis.

When his will was read, it was discovered that Kaufman had left his estate in equal shares to Anne and Leueen after making substantial bequests to his sisters and minor ones to the Actors' Fund and the Dramatists' Guild. In liquid assets, the estate came to well under a million dollars, and of this amount over a quarter of a million went in taxes. Thus, it was not a fortune of staggering dimensions that this celebrated playwright left behind. But augmenting it would be royalties from productions of the plays, which increased as the plays grew in popularity in the years after Kaufman's death.

Among the tributes to him, perhaps the most fitting was an editorial that appeared in the New York *Times*, where for thirteen years he had held down a job: "Mr. Kaufman was an enemy of cant and humbug, and his former colleagues . . . know how penetrating was his judgment and how healing his cauterizing wit."[22]

The funeral was held in New York on June 4 at the Frank E. Campbell Funeral Church. In charge of the service was Rabbi David A. Seligson, who had officiated at the wedding of Anne and Irving Schneider. Moss Hart, whose own death would come in December of that year, delivered the eulogy. After reminiscing about Kaufman the wit, the friend, and the writer, Hart said in closing,

> The people who worked with him in the theater and all of us, his friends, owe him a different kind of debt, a very special one. He was a unique and arresting man, and there are few enough unique people in anyone's time. Nature does not toss them up too often. And part of our loss is that we will not know again the uniqueness and the special taste and flavor that was George. But part of our solace is that we were lucky to have known him—that he lived in our time. Thank you, George, and farewell.

Notes

Some Notes on the Notes

The following abbreviations are used:

AK	Anne Kaufman [Schneider]
AW	Alexander Woollcott
BBK	Beatrice Bakrow Kaufman
EF	Edna Ferber
GSK	George S. Kaufman
LCL	Lincoln Center Library (New York Public Library Theater Collection)
LM	Leuecn MacGrath
MH	Moss Hart
NY	*New Yorker*
NYHT	New York *Herald Tribune*
NYT	*New York Times*
RKF	Ruth Kaufman Friedlich
WCTR	Wisconsin Center for Theater Research

When letters cited or quoted are in the collections of libraries, I have so indicated. Letters from George S. Kaufman to Beatrice Kaufman are in the possession of Anne Kaufman Schneider. All others not in libraries are in the possession of their recipients.

Many references are to clippings in the scrapbooks and folders in the New York Public Library Theater Collection. I have tried to make references as specific as possible to these materials, but with the exception of clippings from the *New York Times* and *Variety*, I have made no effort to track down missing dates.

Notes to Chapter 1   Beginnings

1. Max Gordon with Lewis Funke, *Max Gordon Presents* (New York: Bernard Geis Associates, 1963), p. 243; conversations with George Oppenheimer,

Kitty Carlisle Hart, Maurice Valency, Ruth Kaufman Friedlich, Lynn Fontanne, Edith Atwater.

2. GSK, Introd., "In Admiration," *Better Bridge for Better Players,* by Charles Goren (Garden City: Doubleday, Doran, 1942), p. xi.
3. Conversation with Burt Shevelove.
4. Elmer Rice, *Minority Report: An Autobiography* (New York: Simon & Schuster, 1963), p. 262.
5. Conversation with Natalie Schafer.
6. *Current Biography 1941,* ed. Maxine Block (New York: H. W. Wilson, 1941), p. 457.
7. *Vincent O'Connor vs. George S. Kaufman, Moss Hart,* et al., trial record, 1943, transcript in possession of Clinton Wilder.
8. Howard Teichmann, *George S. Kaufman: An Intimate Portrait* (New York: Atheneum, 1972), p. 40.
9. Clipping, source unidentified [interview, 1932], BBK scrapbook in possession of AK.
10. Scott Meredith, *George S. Kaufman and His Friends* (Garden City: Doubleday, 1974), p. 32.
11. Wilson, *The Twenties,* ed. Leon Edel (New York: Farrar, Straus and Giroux, 1975), p. 46.
12. Douglas Gilbert, "Town Wits," New York *World-Telegram,* undated clipping, BBK scrapbook.
13. AW, "The Deep, Tangled Kaufman," *NY,* May 18, 1929, p. 26.
14. "George S. Kaufman," *Living Authors,* ed. Dilly Tante [sic] (New York: H. W. Wilson, 1931), p. 204.
15. Conversation with Herbert J. Seligmann.
16. Conversations with Seligmann and RKF.

Notes to Chapter 2   Beatrice

1. BBK, autobiographical MS, in possession of AK.
2. BBK, autobiographical MS.
3. BBK, autobiographical MS.
4. Conversation with Leonard Bakrow.
5. Burns Mantle, *American Playwrights of Today* (New York: Dodd, Mead, 1929), pp. 90–91.
6. Mantle, *American Playwrights,* pp. 90–91.
7. BBK, autobiographical MS.
8. AW, "The Deep, Tangled Kaufman," *NY,* May 18, 1929, p. 29.
9. Conversation with Herbert J. Seligmann.
10. BBK, autobiographical MS.
11. On Broun's relations with Lopokova and Hale, see BBK, autobiographical MS.; Richard O'Connor, *Heywood Broun* (New York: Putnam, 1975), pp. 40–52.
12. Information on Kaufman's dates at *NYT* supplied by *NYT* Personnel Depart-

ment; Brooks Atkinson, *Broadway*, rev. ed. (New York: Macmillan, 1974), p. 236 (GSK's salary).

13. Atkinson, *Broadway*, rev. ed., pp. 234–36; conversation with Atkinson.
14. Brooks Atkinson, "Memoirs of a Sardonic Wit," *NYT*, June 11, 1961, Sec. 2, p. 1.
15. AW, "That Benign Demon, George S. Kaufman," *NYT*, Dec. 3, 1933, Sec. 9, p. 5.
16. Harpo Marx and Rowland Barber, *Harpo Speaks!* (New York: Bernard Geis Associates, 1961), p. 169.
17. Conversation with Lester Markel.
18. Pauline Kael, "Raising Kane," in *The Citizen Kane Book*, by Kael, Herman J. Mankiewicz, and Orson Welles (Boston: Little, Brown, 1971), pp. 10–12; conversation with Sara Mankiewicz.
19. Clipping, source unidentified, GSK scrapbooks, WCTR.
20. Burns Mantle, "The Co-Author Explains," column, *Evening Mail*, GSK scrapbooks, WCTR.
21. Conversation with RKF.
22. Conversation with Lynn Fontanne.
23. Clipping, date unidentified, GSK scrapbooks, WCTR.
24. "George S. Kaufman," *Current Biography 1941*, p. 457.
25. Conversation with Ruth Goodman Goetz.
26. AW, *Letters*, ed. Beatrice Kaufman and Joseph Hennessey (New York: Viking Press, 1944), p. 228 (AW to BBK, Jan. 28, 1940).

Notes to Chapter 3 *First Success*

1. On Debs, AK; on Moody, see GSK, "Lines upon Looking through a Pile of Old Checks," *NY*, May 1, 1937, p. 24: "Telephone and electric light, / *Unholy* amount of kale— / This check? . . . I heard a speech one night / (But Moody's still in jail)."
2. "George S. Kaufman and Marc Connelly, Who Wrote *Dulcy* and *To the Ladies*," clipping, source unidentified, GSK scrapbooks, WCTR.
3. Conversation with Marc Connelly.
4. *Variety*, Nov. 14, 1919, p. 18.
5. GSK scrapbooks, WCTR.
6. Conversation with Marc Connelly.
7. "George S. Kaufman and Marc Connelly, Who Wrote *Dulcy*."
8. George C. Tyler and J. C. Furnas, *Whatever Goes Up—* (Indianapolis: Bobbs-Merrill, 1934), p. 282.
9. Tyler and Furnas, *Whatever Goes Up—*, p. 298.
10. Conversation with Marc Connelly.
11. Marc Connelly, *Voices Offstage* (New York: Holt, Rinehart and Winston, 1968), pp. 59–60; AW, "Two-Eyed Connelly," *NY*, Apr. 12, 1930, p. 30; conversation with Connelly.
12. On this reason for the choice, see Connelly, *Voices Offstage*, p. 61.

13. Booth Tarkington, *On Plays, Playwrights, and Playgoers*, ed. Alan S. Downer (Princeton: Princeton University Library, 1959), p. 63.
14. Connelly, *Voices Offstage*, pp. 62–63.
15. Conversation with Marc Connelly (on GSK on opening night); conversation with Alfred Lunt and Lynn Fontanne.
16. Noel Coward, *Present Indicative* (Garden City: Doubleday, Doran, 1937), p. 137.

Notes to Chapter 4   Widening Circles

1. Conversation with Marc Connelly.
2. Margaret Case Harriman, *The Vicious Circle* (New York: Rinehart and Co., 1951), pp. 3–8.
3. AW, "The Captain's Memoirs," rpt. in *Vanity Fair: A Cavalcade of the 1920's and the 1930's*, ed. Cleveland Amory and Frederic Bradlee (New York: Viking Press, 1960), p. 128.
4. Anecdotes such as those in this and the following paragraph have been in circulation since the origin of the Round Table. See also Harriman, *Vicious Circle;* Frank Case, *Tales of a Wayward Inn* (New York: Frederick A. Stokes, 1938); and James R. Gaines, *Wit's End: Days and Nights of the Algonquin Round Table* (New York: Harcourt Brace Jovanovich, 1977).
5. Harriman, *Vicious Circle*, p. 14.
6. Franklin P. Adams, *Nods and Becks* (New York: Whittlesey House, 1944), pp. 60–61.
7. Harriman, *Vicious Circle*, p. 243.
8. Jane Grant, *Ross, the "New Yorker" and Me* (New York: Reynal and Co., 1968), p. 154.
9. AW, *Enchanted Aisles* (New York: G. P. Putnam's Sons, 1924), p. 249.
10. Harriman, *Vicious Circle*, p. 243.
11. Dale Kramer, *Heywood Broun* (New York: A. A. Wyn, 1949), p. 198.
12. Grant, *Ross*, pp. 187–88.
13. Grant, *Ross*, p. 210.
14. Peggy Wood, *How Young You Look* (New York: Farrar and Rinehart, 1941), p. 130.
15. Case, *Tales of a Wayward Inn*, p. 66.
16. Burton Bernstein, *Thurber: A Biography* (New York: Dodd, Mead, 1975), p. 181.
17. Harriman, *Vicious Circle*, p. 288.
18. Tyler and Furnas, *Whatever Goes Up—*, pp. 269–71.
19. Connelly, *Voices Offstage*, p. 74; Tracy Hammon Lewis, "Connelly and Kaufman Explain How and Why," *Morning Telegraph*, Mar. 12, 1922, *To the Ladies* scrapbook, LCL.
20. Lewis, "Connelly and Kaufman."
21. Tyler and Furnas, *Whatever Goes Up—*, p. 285.
22. Connelly, *Voices Offstage*, pp. 74–75; Catherine Hayes Brown, *Letters to*

Mary (New York: Random House, 1940), pp. 209–12; Lewis, "Connelly and Kaufman."

23. Connelly, *Voices Offstage*, p. 75.

Notes to Chapter 5   Ferber; Four Brothers

1. Franklin P. Adams, *The Diary of Our Own Samuel Pepys* (New York: Simon & Schuster, 1935), I, 412, 420, 439, 492–93.
2. See Coward's letter to Cole Lesley, written three years after the death of BBK, in Cole Lesley, *Remembered Laughter: The Life of Noel Coward* (New York: Alfred A. Knopf, 1976), p. 281.
3. Conversation with William W. Appleton, who as a boy overheard the remark.
4. Robert Benchley, *The Treasurer's Report* (New York: Harper & Brothers, 1930), pp. 334–45.
5. Ring Lardner, *Shut Up, He Explained,* ed. Babette Rosmond and Henry Morgan (New York: Charles Scribner's Sons, 1964), p. 126.
6. Broun, New York *World*, Nov. 7, 1922, *49ers* folder, LCL.
7. Connelly, *Voices Offstage*, pp. 92–93.
8. Connelly, *Voices Offstage*, pp. 79–80.
9. GSK and Connelly, "Let Authors Write Their Own Reviews," *Morning Telegraph*, Sept. 28, 1923 (rpt. from Indianapolis *Star*), *To the Ladies* scrapbook, LCL.
10. GSK and Connelly, "Revelations on the Making of 'Merton,'" New York *Herald*, Dec. 24, 1922, *Merton of the Movies* scrapbook, LCL; "Poor Old Plot Is Ruthlessly Tossed into the Discard," New York *Tribune*, Oct. 26, 1924, *Minick* scrapbook, LCL; conversation with Marc Connelly.
11. GSK and Connelly, "Revelations." In the novel, but not the play, it is stated that the girl's real name is Sierra Nevada Montague.
12. Harold Lloyd, *An American Comedy* (New York: Dover Books, 1971), p. 44.
13. *Variety*, Oct. 13, 1922, p. 16; *Variety*, Nov. 24, 1922, p. 14; *Bookman*, 56 (Jan. 1923), 665 (on Valentino).
14. Teichmann, *George S. Kaufman*, p. 277.
15. Connelly, *Voices Offstage*, pp. 76–77; Tyler and Furnas, *Whatever Goes Up—*, p. 286; letters to GSK from contributors, GSK Papers, WCTR.
16. Adams, *Diary*, I, 406.
17. Except where indicated, the information in this and the following paragraphs on *Helen of Troy, New York* is from Connelly, *Voices Offstage*, pp. 105–6; George Jessel, *So Help Me* (New York: Random House, 1943), pp. 61–69; Jessel, *The World I Lived In* (Chicago: Henry Regnery, 1975), pp. 48–53; conversation with Marc Connelly.
18. Groucho Marx, *The Groucho Letters* (New York: Simon & Schuster, 1967), p. 183.
19. Ruby to Marx, Marx, *Groucho Letters*, p. 183; Adams, *Diary*, I, 415.
20. *NYT*, Jan. 6, 1924, p. 25.

21. On the Guild's option, see Burns Mantle, *The Best Plays of 1923–24* (New York: Dodd, Mead, 1924), p. 160.
22. AW, Preface, *Beggar on Horseback*, by Kaufman and Connelly (New York: Boni & Liveright, 1924), p. 13.
23. John Corbin, *NYT*, Feb. 17, 1924, Sec. 7, p. 1.
24. *NYT*, June 6, 1925, p. 9; *Variety*, June 10, 1925, p. 35. Queried as to why Parker and not he collaborated with GSK on the play, Marc Connelly could not recall the reason.
25. EF, *A Peculiar Treasure* (New York: Doubleday, Doran, 1939), p. 283; on Kaufman in London, "Poor Old Plot Is Ruthlessly Discarded," *New York Tribune*, in *Minick* scrapbook, LCL.
26. EF, *A Peculiar Treasure*, pp. 283–84.
27. Conversations with Lynn Fontanne and Ruth Goodman Goetz. Williams, "Too Personal?" in *Small Craft Warnings* (New York: New Directions, 1972), p. 5, adds that he replied, "Madam, I can't even manage that."
28. EF, *A Peculiar Treasure*, pp. 311–12.
29. EF, *A Peculiar Treasure*, pp. 286–87; see also "Poor Old Plot."
30. Harpo Marx, *Harpo Speaks!*, p. 173.
31. Groucho Marx and Richard J. Anobile, *The Marx Bros. Scrapbook* (New York: Darien House, 1973), p. 113.
32. GSK, "How Minnie's Boys Made Their Marx" (review of Kyle Crichton, *The Marx Brothers*), *NYT Book Review*, June 18, 1950, p. 3.
33. On one occasion, in conversation with the present writer.
34. References to the game abound in the memoirs and biographies of the players. See Adams, *Diary*, I, 430; John Baragwanath, *A Good Time Was Had* (New York: Appleton-Century-Crofts, 1961), p. 109; Harpo Marx, *Harpo Speaks!*, pp. 228–35; Ring Lardner, Jr., *The Lardners: My Family Remembered* (New York: Harper & Row, 1976), p. 171; Howard Dietz, *Dancing in the Dark* (New York: Quadrangle, 1974), pp. 234–35; E. J. Kahn, Jr., *The World of Swope* (New York: Simon & Schuster, 1965) pp. 326–33. My understanding of what the game meant to the participants have been improved by conversations with Howard Dietz, AK, and LM, as well as GSK's letters of 1935 to BBK from Hollywood.

Notes to Chapter 6   Anne

1. Adams, *Diary*, I, 574.
2. Adams, *Diary*, II, 884.
3. Conversation with Marc Connelly.

Notes to Chapter 7   Hit after Hit

1. Connelly, *Voices Offstage*, p. 123, writes that he had no enthusiasm for Kaufman's new project. I am inclined to doubt that he was invited to participate in it.
2. Jessel, *So Help Me*, p. 70.

3. Crosby Gaige, *Footlights and Highlights* (New York: E. P. Dutton, 1948), p. 217.
4. Marx, *Harpo Speaks!*, pp. 186–87.
5. Conversation with Morrie Ryskind.
6. Conversation with Morrie Ryskind.
7. Mankiewicz, "Critique," *NY*, Dec. 19, 1925, pp. 17–18.
8. Conversation with Morrie Ryskind.
9. Conversation with Morrie Ryskind.
10. GSK, "Memoir," *NY*, June 11, 1960, p. 39. It is only fair to add that in an earlier essay, "Music to My Ears," *Stage*, Aug. 1938, n.p., GSK wrote that he liked the song and was puzzled when Berlin did not include it in the score.
11. Conversation with Sara Mankiewicz, who recalled that the collaboration took place in the summer months. She also stated firmly that her husband helped GSK with the writing of *The Butter and Egg Man* and was disappointed not to receive credit.
12. Conversation with Victor Killian, who took a minor role in the production.
13. Conversation with Sara Mankiewicz, Victor Killian, Marc Connelly; Connelly, *Voices Offstage*, pp. 131–32.
14. *NYT*, Nov. 2, 1930, Sec. 8, p. 4.
15. Edward Jablonski and Lawrence D. Stewart, *The Gershwin Years* (Garden City: Doubleday, 1973), p. 119.
16. Ira Gershwin, *Lyrics on Several Occasions* (New York: Alfred A. Knopf, 1959), pp. 224–25.
17. GSK, "Music to My Ears."
18. GSK, "Music to My Ears."
19. GSK, "Music to My Ears."
20. Hollis Alpert, *The Barrymores* (New York: Dial Press, 1964), p. 281.
21. EF, *A Peculiar Treasure*, p. 313; Ferber hints strongly that this ending was used at the suggestion of Jed Harris.
22. One reviewer said her "workmanlike performance . . . does not disturb the drama very much." Atkinson, *NYT*, Aug. 13, 1940, p. 15.
23. Behrman, *People in a Diary* (Boston: Little, Brown, 1972), p. 54; Harris, "The Royal Family," *Playbill*, April 1976, n.p.
24. EF, *A Peculiar Treasure*, p. 314; Harris, "The Royal Family."
25. This is according to William W. Appleton, who was so informed by Ethel Barrymore Colt.
26. Harris, "The Royal Family."

Notes to Chapter 8   *The Director*

1. This report on the organization of the Dramatists' Guild and earlier efforts at organization made by playwrights is based in part on the Guild's own publications and in part on reports in *NYT*, but chiefly on the account offered by George Middleton in *These Things Are Mine* (New York: Macmillan, 1947), pp. 298–332.
2. Sklar to Malcolm Goldstein, Oct. 7, 1967.

3. Ben Hecht, *Charlie: The Improbable Life and Times of Charles MacArthur* (New York: Harper & Brothers, 1957), p. 139.
4. Hecht, *Charlie,* p. 140.
5. Conversation with Max Gordon.
6. Conversation with Hiram Sherman.
7. Conversation with Natalie Schafer.
8. Conversation with George Oppenheimer.
9. Conversation with Jean Dixon Ely.
10. Conversation with Michael Wager.
11. Gordon, *Max Gordon Presents,* p. 178.
12. Conversation with Jean Dixon Ely.
13. AK.
14. Harpo Marx, *Harpo Speaks!,* pp. 263–64.

Notes to Chapter 9   With Ring Lardner

1. Marx and Anobile, *Marx Bros. Scrapbook,* p. 153.
2. Joe Adamson, *Groucho, Harpo, Chico, and Sometimes Zeppo* (New York: Simon & Schuster, 1973), p. 72.
3. Conversation with Groucho Marx.
4. Conversation with Groucho Marx; Marx and Anobile, *Marx Bros. Scrapbook,* pp. 153–54.
5. From a talk by Groucho Marx to the Academy of Motion Picture Arts and Sciences, quoted in Adamson, *Groucho,* pp. 73–74.
6. NY, July 17, 1928, p. 16.
7. Conversation with Jean Dixon Ely; Ring Lardner, Jr., *The Lardners,* p. 181.
8. Lardner, Jr., *The Lardners,* p. 182.
9. GSK, speech notes, 1940; GSK Papers, WCTR.
10. On Lardner's theatrical career, see Donald Elder, *Ring Lardner* (Garden City: Doubleday, 1956), pp. 243–76.
11. Conversation with Jean Dixon Ely.
12. Conversation with Jean Dixon Ely.
13. Elder, *Ring Lardner,* pp. 277–78.
14. Elder, *Ring Lardner,* pp. 374–76; Lardner, Jr., *The Lardners,* pp. 221–22; GSK, speech notes; conversation with Ring Lardner, Jr.
15. GSK, "Notes on an Infamous Collaboration," *Theatre Magazine,* Dec. 1929, p. 24.
16. Samuel Hopkins Adams, *A. Woollcott: His Life and His World* (New York: Reynal and Hitchcock, 1945), p. 155.
17. GSK, "Notes on an Infamous Collaboration," p. 24; Adams, *A. Woollcott,* pp. 83–84.
18. NYT, Feb. 13, 1930, p. 26.
19. Gordon, *Max Gordon Presents,* p. 246.

Notes to Chapter 10   Enter Moss Hart

1. Moss Hart, *Act One* (New York: Random House, 1959), p. 6. I have drawn heavily on this book for details of Hart's early years.
2. See clippings, *Once in a Lifetime* folder, LCL.
3. Clipping, source unidentified, *Once in a Lifetime*, scrapbook, LCL.
4. A copy of the original script is included in the Hart Papers, WCTR.
5. In an undated letter (1936) to BBK from Hollywood, GSK listed some of MH's mispronunciations, but with affection. One of the words, "xylophone," which MH pronounced "zollophone," GSK misspelled "zylophone."
6. Not, as MH has it in *Act One*, pp. 355–56, with Harpo, Woollcott, and Alice Duer Miller.
7. MH fails to mention the play in *Act One*.
8. Conversation with Jean Dixon Ely.
9. Atkinson, *Broadway*, rev. ed., pp. 237–38.
10. Conversation with Jean Dixon Ely.
11. *Theatre Magazine*, Dec. 1930, p. 46.
12. Conversation with Jean Dixon Ely.
13. Conversation with Edith Atwater.
14. Conversation with Jean Dixon Ely, to whom MH confided this doubt.
15. Clipping, source unidentified. *Once in a Lifetime*, scrapbook, LCL.

Notes to Chapter 11   Max

1. Conversation with Burt Shevelove. See also Shaw, *Our Theatres in the Nineties* (London: Constable, 1932), III, 386.
2. Conversation with Max Gordon.
3. Conversation with Margalo Gillmore.
4. Gordon, *Max Gordon Presents*, pp. 132–33.
5. Gordon, *Max Gordon Presents*, pp. 133–35.
6. Gordon, *Max Gordon Presents*, p. 133; conversations with Howard Dietz, Tilly Losch, Fred Astaire.
7. Gordon, *Max Gordon Presents*, p. 136.
8. NYT, June 14, 1931, Sec. 8, p. 2.

Notes to Chapter 12   Political Perspectives

1. GSK and Morrie Ryskind, "Socratic Dialogue," *Nation*, Apr. 12, 1933, p. 403.
2. Conversation with Morrie Ryskind; Irving Drutman, "'31 Musical Needed Few Changes," NYHT, May 4, 1952, Sec. 4, p. 1.
3. "Events Leading Up to a Congressional Record," NYT, Sec. 8, p. 2, Dec. 13, 1931.
4. "Events Leading Up."
5. Ira Gershwin, *Lyrics on Several Occasions*, pp. 331, 337.

6. "Events Leading Up"; "Harris Tells How He Came To Produce the Pulitzer Play," *NYHT*, May 8, 1932, *Of Thee I Sing* scrapbook, LCL.

7. "Events Leading Up"; Ira Gershwin, *Lyrics*, pp. 331–32. Ira Gershwin reports that the version of the title song composed in California was somewhat altered later.

8. The account in this and the following four paragraphs on the misfortunes of *Hot Pan* (*Eldorado*) is based on the following: accounts of Polisuk's suit in *Variety*, Jan. 27, 1937, pp. 52, 54, and *NYT*, Jan. 27, 1937, p. 23; miscellaneous clippings, *Hot Pan* and *Eldorado* folders, LCL; *Hot Pan* correspondence, Provincetown Playhouse folder, LCL; New Haven *Journal Courier*, Oct. 20, 1931, p. 8; New Haven *Register*, Oct. 20, 1931, p. 4; impressions of the production provided by George Sklar in conversation.

9. MH, *Act One*, p. 279.

10. "Events Leading Up"; AW, "The Ingenuous George [Gershwin]," *Cosmopolitan*, Nov. 1933, p. 122; conversation with Morrie Ryskind.

11. H. T. Parker, "Under Peril of Newfound Wisecrackery," Boston *Evening Transcript*, Dec. 22, 1931; "Fear Complex Clutches Four Laughing Men," *NYHT*, April 10, 1932, *Of Thee I Sing* scrapbook, LCL.

12. Conversation with Morrie Ryskind.

13. Atkinson, *NYT*, 1932, Sec. 8, p. 1; Heywood Broun, "It Seems to Me," New York *World-Telegram*, undated clipping, *Of Thee I Sing* scrapbook, LCL.

14. *NYT*, Dec. 29, 1932, p. 17.

15. Conversation with Allan Friedlich.

16. Conversation with Morrie Ryskind (on asking price).

17. GSK published a sketch, "Jimmy the Well-Dressed Man: A Vaudeville Act with Music," *Nation*, June 15, 1932, pp. 676–77, spoofing Walker's self-defense before Seabury. At the close Walker boasts that he will be re-elected and goes into a dance. "At this point the piper comes on the scene. The public pays him."

18. EF, *A Peculiar Treasure*, pp. 349–50.

19. According to MH, *Act One*, p. 364, he saw *Grand Hotel* in GSK's study during the period of rewriting *Once in a Lifetime*; "Dinner at Eight-Thirty," *NYT*, Oct. 30, 1932, Sec. 9, p. 3.

20. "Dinner at Eight-Thirty."

21. "Dinner at Eight-Thirty."

22. Conversations with George Oppenheimer and Ruth Goodman Goetz.

23. Conversation with George Oppenheimer.

24. Conversation with George Oppenheimer.

25. *NY*, Sept. 7, 1932, p. 14.

26. Conversation with George Oppenheimer.

27. *Variety*, Aug. 30, 1932, p. 45; *Variety*, Sept. 20, 1932, p. 46; Gordon, *Max Gordon Presents*, pp. 158–64.

28. EF, *A Peculiar Treasure*, p. 355.

Notes to Chapter 13
London Revisited; Miscalculations in New York

1. *NYT*, Nov. 20, 1932, Sec. 9, p. 1; GSK to BBK, undated letter.
2. GSK wrote five letters to BBK from London, of which only one is dated (Dec. 15). They form the principal source of this account of his London activities.
3. In New York, *Children in Uniform*, produced by Sidney Phillips and directed by Frank Gregory, played only twelve performances.
4. GSK, "With Gun and Camera in London," *NYT*, Jan. 22, 1933, Sec. 9, pp. 1, 3; EF, *A Peculiar Treasure*, p. 358; GSK to BBK, on EF's determination never to write with him again.
5. GSK to BBK (on Vanbrugh); A. J. Warner, "At Random," clipping, source unidentified, BBK scrapbook; "How Kaufman Put Galluses on a London Bridge," *NYHT*, Jan. 1, 1934, *Dinner at Eight* scrapbook, LCL.
6. Conversation with Morrie Ryskind.
7. *Nation*, Apr. 12, 1933, p. 403.
8. *NYT*, Feb. 18, 1933, p. 13.
9. "Authors Pick Their Favorite Critics," New York *Journal-American*, June 3, 1933, *Let 'Em Eat Cake* folder, LCL.
10. *Variety*, Nov. 28, 1933, p. 56.
11. Conversation with Morrie Ryskind; Lois Moran Young to Malcolm Goldstein, July 30, 1977.
12. *Variety*, Nov. 28, 1933, p. 56; Ward Morehouse, "Broadway after Dark," New York *Sun*, Dec. 9, 1933, *Dark Tower* scrapbook, LCL; AW, "That Benign Demon, George S. Kaufman," *NYT*, Dec. 3, 1933, Sec. 9, p. 5.
13. Samuel Hopkins Adams, *A. Woollcott*, p. 208.
14. Morehouse, "Broadway after Dark."
15. George Oppenheimer, *The View from the Sixties* (New York: David McKay, 1966), p. 91; conversation with George Oppenheimer.
16. *NYHT*, Feb. 15, 1933, *Roman Scandals* folder, LCL. Goldwyn's biographers and Cantor in his memoirs are silent on this point.
17. John Mason Brown, *The Worlds of Robert E. Sherwood: Mirror to His Times* (New York: Charles Scribner's Sons, 1965), p. 297. Brown does not mention this film.
18. *Variety*, June 1, 1938, p. 6, and June 14, 1939, p. 6.
19. Katharine Dayton, "It Must Be Fun To Work with Kaufman," *NYT*, Dec. 8, 1935, Sec. 10, p. 3; Lucius Beebe, "Washington Comedy as Seen by Katharine Dayton," *NYHT*, Dec. 1, 1935, *First Lady* scrapbook, LCL.
20. Dayton, "It Must Be Fun."
21. "On a Hart and Its Beat," *NYT*, Oct. 14, 1934, Sec. 10, p. 3; Allene Tallmey, "Biography of a Play," *Stage*, Nov. 1934, pp. 18–22.
22. GSK to BBK, undated letter from Palm Springs.
23. Conversation with Murial Williams.
24. Tallmey, "Biography of a Play."

25. Wilella Waldorf, "Forecasts and Postscripts," New York *Post*, Oct. 8, 1935, *Merrily We Roll Along* scrapbook, LCL.
26. Quoted in Atkinson, *Broadway*, rev. ed., p. 239. GSK made a note to himself to quote this comment in his speech of 1940.
27. *Variety*, Nov. 27, 1934, p. 55 (review of *Bring On the Girls*).
28. Conversation with Morrie Ryskind.
29. Conversation with Jean Dixon Ely.
30. "Panorama of the Fortnight," *Town and Country*, Sept. 1, 1934, p. 21.
31. Hedda Hopper, *From Under My Hat* (Garden City: Doubleday, 1952), p. 239.
32. *Nation*, Oct. 17, 1934, p. 462.

Notes to Chapter 14   Hollywood

1. Mary Astor, *My Story* (Garden City: Doubleday, 1959), p. 59.
2. Astor, *My Story*, p. 161.
3. *Time*, Aug. 17, 1936, p. 30.
4. Los Angeles *Times*, Aug. 13, 1936, p. 4.
5. Conversation with Jean Dixon Ely.
6. Los Angeles *Times*, Aug. 13, 1936, p. 4.
7. Clippings, GSK folder, LCL.
8. Astor, *My Story*, p. 136.
9. Marx and Anobile, *Marx Bros. Scrapbook*, p. 203.
10. Adamson, *Groucho*, p. 264.
11. Marx and Anobile, *Marx Bros. Scrapbook*, pp. 203, 211.
12. Conversation with Morrie Ryskind; GSK to Tyler, in Tyler Papers, Princeton University Library (one of GSK's few dated letters); GSK, notes for speech, 1940.
13. In the 1940 speech notes, GSK includes this anecdote.
14. S. N. Behrman, "They Left 'Em Laughing," *NYT*, Nov. 21, 1965, Sec. 2, p. 1.
15. BBK preserved a typed copy of this item, dated Feb. 12, 1935, in her scrapbook.
16. Bob Thomas, *Thalberg: Life and Legend* (Garden City: Doubleday, 1969), p. 183.
17. Marx and Anobile, *Marx Bros. Scrapbook*, p. 203.
18. Marx and Anobile, *Scrapbook*, p. 214.
19. Los Angeles *Examiner*, Aug. 13, 1936, p. 4.
20. Marx and Anobile, *Scrapbook*, p. 81.
21. Both were published in one volume by Viking Press in 1969.
22. Marx and Anobile, *Scrapbook*, p. 206. Wood's reactionary political views, and McGuinness's, were a source of vast displeasure to the Marxes.
23. Conversation with Kitty Carlisle Hart.
24. Conversation with Kitty Carlisle Hart.
25. BBK to AW, undated letter, AW Papers, Harvard University Library.
26. Conversation with Frances McFadden.

27. Letters to BBK from GSK in 1937 reveal this concern.
28. *NYHT,* Jack Curtis scrapbook, LCL, undated clipping.
29. Coward to BBK, Nov. 15, 1935.
30. Conversation with Frances McFadden.
31. Samuel Marx to Malcolm Goldstein, July 5, 1977.
32. Conversation with George Seaton.
33. GSK to BBK, undated letter.
34. GSK to BBK, undated letter.
35. GSK to BBK, undated letter.
36. Conversations with Tilly Losch and Sara Mankiewicz.
37. Carmel Snow with Mary Louise Aswell, *The World of Carmel Snow* (New York: McGraw-Hill, 1962), p. 114.
38. *Time,* Aug. 17, 1936, p. 30 (a summary, with excerpts).
39. Astor, *My Story,* p. 131.
40. Conversation with Kitty Carlisle Hart.
41. New York *Daily News,* Aug. 13, 1936, p. 4.
42. Astor, *My Story,* p. 170.
43. *NYT,* Aug. 16, 1936, p. 23; *Time,* Aug. 24, 1936, p. 30.
44. *Time,* Aug. 17, 1936, p. 31.
45. Brooklyn *Eagle,* Aug. 27, 1936, BBK folder, LCL.
46. New York *Daily News,* Aug. 28, 1936, p. 3; *NYT,* Aug. 29, 1936, p. 6.

Notes to Chapter 15   Birth of a Classic

1. *NY,* May 25, 1935, p. 20.
2. Atkinson, *NYT,* Nov. 27, 1935, p. 17.
3. EF writes that it was *Dinner at Eight* that the collaborators began on New Year's Eve. EF, *A Peculiar Treasure,* pp. 351–52. But see "Origins of *Stage Door,*" *NYT,* Oct. 25, 1936, Sec. 10, p. 3.
4. Clipping, source unidentified, *Stage Door* scrapbook, LCL.
5. "Origins of *Stage Door*"; clippings, *Stage Door* scrapbook, LCL.
6. "Origins of *Stage Door.*"
7. Harold Clurman, *The Fervent Years* (New York: Alfred A. Knopf, 1945), pp. 37–38, 154.
8. Conversations with Mary Wickes and Janet Fox.
9. *Variety,* Sept. 30, 1936, p. 56.
10. *NYT,* Nov. 22, 1936, Sec. 11, p. 3; GSK to Atkinson, undated letter, Atkinson Papers, LCL.
11. EF, *A Peculiar Treasure,* p. 387; GSK to BBK, letters from Hollywood, 1937, 1938; Brooke Hayward, *Haywire* (New York: Alfred A. Knopf, 1977), p. 68.
12. GSK, speech notes, 1940.
13. Bruce Cook, *Dalton Trumbo* (New York: Charles Scribner's Sons, 1977), pp. 95–96.
14. *You Can't Take It with You,* souvenir program [1937], p. 4.
15. *You Can't Take It with You,* souvenir program, pp. 3–4. William G. B. Car-

son, *Dear Josephine* (Norman: U. of Oklahoma Press, 1963), p. 224, offers the following excerpt from Josephine Hull's diary: "June 29 [1936]. To Sam Harris office for appointment. Kaufman-Hart play, new."

16. GSK to BBK, undated letter. The date of writing can be ascertained by GSK's reference to Katharine Cornell's opening performance in *Saint Joan* in Los Angeles the preceding evening.

17. Miscellaneous clippings, *You Can't Take It with You* scrapbook, LCL.

18. Miscellaneous clippings, *You Can't Take It with You* scrapbook, LCL.

19. "It Started as a Funny Play, but Now It's a Mass Industry," source unidentified, *You Can't Take It with You* scrapbook, LCL.

20. *Variety*, Dec. 7, 1938, p. 48.

21. *NYT*, Nov. 14, 1938, p. 48.

22. GSK to BBK, undated letter, spring 1937.

23. Gordon, *Max Gordon Presents*, p. 205.

24. Ilka Chase, *Past Imperfect* (Garden City: Doubleday, Doran, 1942), p. 185.

25. Conversation with Margalo Gillmore.

26. Conversation with Max Gordon.

Notes to Chapter 16   The Farm

1. Conversation with Clinton Wilder.

2. GSK to BBK, undated letter, 1937.

3. Conversation with Clinton Wilder.

4. Margaret Case Harriman, *Take Them Up Tenderly* (New York: Alfred A. Knopf, 1944), p. 81.

5. Miscellaneous clippings, *I'd Rather Be Right* scrapbook, LCL.

6. In *Steinbeck: A Life in Letters*, eds. Elaine Steinbeck and Robert Wallsten (New York: Viking Press, 1975), p. 136.

7. E. Steinbeck and Wallsten (eds.), *Life in Letters*, p. 136; GSK to BBK, undated letter.

8. GSK to BBK, undated letter.

9. E. Steinbeck and Wallsten (eds.), *Life in Letters*, p. 141.

10. John Peter Toohey, "Regarding Three Men Who Would Rather Be Right," *NYT*, Nov. 3, 1937, Sec. 9, p. 2; Herbert Drake, "The Playbill," *NYHT*, Feb. 28, 1937, *I'd Rather Be Right* scrapbook, LCL; GSK to BBK, undated letter (on Webb).

11. Toohey, "Regarding Three Men."

12. Clipping, source unidentified, *I'd Rather Be Right* scrapbook, LCL.

13. Toohey, "Regarding Three Men"; GSK to BBK, undated letters Richard Rodgers, *Musical Stages* (New York: Random House, 1975), pp. 184–85.

14. Charles Schwartz, *Gershwin: His Life and His Music* (Indianapolis: Bobbs-Merrill, 1973), pp. 281–82; S. N. Behrman, *People in a Diary*, p. 255; Rodgers, *Musical Stages*, p. 183; RKF.

15. GSK to BBK, undated letter.

16. Rodgers, *Musical Stages*, p. 185.

17. Rodgers, *Musical Stages,* pp. 186–87; conversation with Irving Schneider (on Cohan's demand for character-building songs).
18. Conversation with Henry Ephron.
19. Rodgers, *Musical Stages,* pp. 181–86; miscellaneous clippings, *I'd Rather Be Right* scrapbook, LCL; conversation with Henry Ephron.
20. *Life,* Oct. 25, 1937, p. 27.
21. Hallie Flanagan, *Arena* (New York: Duell, Sloan and Pearce, 1940), p. 436. Flanagan points out that this was the equivalent of the cost of one battleship and that on it 10,000 persons had employment, each of whom, on average, supported four others.
22. *Variety,* Nov. 3, 1937, p. 55.
23. Henry Haller, "This Busy Playwright Business," Baltimore *Sun,* Oct. 31, 1937, *I'd Rather Be Right* scrapbook, LCL; S. N. Behrman, "They Left 'Em Laughing," *NYT,* Nov. 21, 1965, Sec. 2, p. 1.
24. Steinbeck to GSK, GSK Papers, WCTR.
25. Steinbeck to Critics' Circle, Apr. 23, 1938; to Elizabeth Olds, May 1938, in E. Steinbeck and Wallsten (eds.), *Life in Letters,* pp. 164–65.
26. Conversation with Janet Fox (on EF); GSK to BBK, undated letter.
27. "The Fabulous Invalid," *NYT,* Oct. 30, 1938, Sec. 9, p. 2.
28. George Seaton to Malcolm Goldstein, June 27, 1977.
29. Conversation with George Seaton.
30. Conversation with Irving Schneider.
31. Conversation with Harold Rome.
32. Conversation with Harold Rome. Which of the sketches were the contributions of GSK and MH is no longer clear. Conversation with Hiram Sherman, who recalled that GSK and MH rewrote the material while rehearsals were in progress.
33. Conversations with Rome and Sherman; New York *Daily News,* Aug. 30, 1938, *Sing Out the News* scrapbook, LCL. An earlier report (*World-Telegram,* Aug. 11) had it that not only would GSK take over the direction, but that he and MH were writing sketches for the show.
34. "Hart-Kaufman Novelty Does a G.W.T.W.," source unidentified, *I'd Rather Be Right* folder, LCL.
35. Conversation with Henry Ephron.
36. Leonard Maltin (ed.), *The Real Stars,* Vol. II (New York: Curtis Books, 1973), p. 10.
37. "The Fabulous Invalid."

Notes to Chapter 17   End of an Era

1. This occurred in 1943, conversation with Clinton Wilder.
2. *Variety,* May 17, 1939, p. 41.
3. *Time,* Nov. 20, 1939, p. 69.
4. AW, *Letters,* p. 239 (AW to Frode Jensen, Apr. 15, 1940).
5. As with *The Women,* it was rumored that GSK had a hand in the writing of this play.

6. John Mason Brown, *The Worlds of Robert E. Sherwood: Mirror to His Times*, p. 373.
7. Conversation with Jean Dixon Ely.
8. GSK to BBK, undated letter, Feb. 1939.
9. MH, "How A. W. Came to Dinner, and Other Stories," *NYT*, Oct. 29, 1939, Sec. 9, pp. 1, 3; *Vincent O'Connor vs. George S. Kaufman, Moss Hart, et al.*, p. 104.
10. MH, "How A. W. Came to Dinner."
11. GSK to BBK, undated letter, c. Feb. 16, 1939.
12. GSK to BBK, undated letter, c. Feb. 20, 1939.
13. MH, "How A. W. Came to Dinner."
14. *Vincent O'Connor vs. George S. Kaufman, Moss Hart, et al.*, p. 107.
15. George Oppenheimer, *The View from the Sixties*, pp. 79–80.
16. *Time*, Nov. 20, 1939, p. 69.
17. Morton Eustis, "The Man Who Came to Dinner," *Theatre Arts*, Nov. 1939, pp. 798–89.
18. Conversation with Edith Atwater.
19. Conversation with Mary Wickes.
20. Exchanges of letters between Kaufman and Cerf, Cerf Papers, Columbia University Library.
21. Cerf to GSK, Aug. 17, 1939; GSK to Cerf, "Monday," Cerf Papers, Columbia University Library.
22. AW, *Letters*, p. 223.
23. GSK to BBK, undated letter, Jan. 1940.
24. Irwin Shaw to Malcolm Goldstein, July 1, 1977; conversation with Edith Atwater.
25. "How To Write a Play: Forget Your Big Idea," *NYHT*, Nov. 3, 1940, *George Washington Slept Here* scrapbook, LCL.
26. Hart dedicated the published text of *Lady in the Dark* to "L.S.K.," and Dr. Kubie, signing himself "Dr. Brooks," the name of the analyst in the play, wrote an appreciative foreword to it.
27. MH, "The Saga of Gertie," *NYT*, Mar. 2, 1941, Sec. 9, p. 2.
28. MH, "Saga of Gertie."
29. Noel Coward, *Future Indefinite* (Garden City: Doubleday, 1954), p. 134.
30. Martin to Scott Meredith, Mar. 4, 1941, Meredith Papers, WCTR.
31. AK, on offer to Broderick; conversation with Jean Dixon Ely; "She Hates the Country," *New York Post*, Oct. 26, 1940, *George Washington Slept Here* scrapbook, LCL.
32. Conversation with Jean Dixon Ely.
33. *Variety*, Sept. 25, 1940, p. 58.
34. Conversation with Jean Dixon Ely.
35. Robert Rice, "Rice and Old Shoes," undated clipping, *PM*, *George Washington Slept Here* scrapbook, LCL.
36. Conversation with Henry Ephron.
37. Miscellaneous clippings, *George Washington Slept Here* scrapbook, LCL.
38. Broun, New York *World-Telegram*, undated clipping, *George Washington*

Slept Here scrapbook, LCL; Atkinson, "Country Matters," *NYT*, Oct. 27, 1940, Sec. 9, p. 1.

39. Burns Mantle, "*Washington* Leads 80 Summer Shows," New York *Daily News,* June 30, 1941, *George Washington Slept Here* scrapbook, LCL.
40. Conversations with Henry Ephron, Jean Dixon Ely, Jerome Chodorov.
41. *Variety,* Oct. 30, 1940, p. 56.
42. Undated letter, AW Papers, Harvard University Library.
43. Gordon, *Max Gordon Presents,* pp. 224–25; conversation with Jerome Chodorov.
44. Conversation with Jerome Chodorov.
45. Conversation with Jerome Chodorov; Gordon, *Max Gordon Presents,* pp. 239–40; Jay Martin, *Nathanael West: The Art of His Life* (New York: Farrar, Straus & Giroux, 1970), pp. 3–7.
46. Conversation with Natalie Schafer.
47. Conversation with Kitty Carlisle Hart.
48. Robert Rice, "Rice and Old Shoes," *PM*, Feb. 3, 1941, p. 22.

Notes to Chapter 18 *Wartime*

1. *NYT,* Feb. 22, 1941, p. 10.
2. *NYT,* Feb. 24, 1941, p. 6; Sillman, *Here Lies Leonard Sillman* (New York: Citadel Press, 1959), pp. 308–10.
3. "Authors of 'Mr. Big' Had Luck To Meet the Big Mr. Kaufman," clipping, source unidentifiable, *Mr. Big* folder, LCL.
4. *Variety,* Oct. 8, 1941, p. 44.
5. GSK, "Notes of a Co-Author," *NYT,* Nov. 2, 1941, Sec. 9, p. 1.
6. Undated letter, AW Papers, Harvard University Library.
7. Robert O. Foote, "A Summer of George S. Kaufman," *NYT,* July 29, 1941, Sec. 9, p. 2.
8. Conversation with William Walton.
9. Conversation with William Walton.
10. Gordon, *Max Gordon Presents,* pp. 242–43.
11. BBK to AW, undated letter, AW Papers, Harvard University Library.
12. Julie Goldsmith Gilbert, *Ferber* (Garden City: Doubleday, 1978), p. 277.
13. Conversation with Clinton Wilder.
14. Conversations with Edith Atwater and Clinton Wilder.
15. *NYT,* Oct. 8, 1941, p. 52.
16. Gordon, *Max Gordon Presents,* p. 258.
17. Conversation with William Walton; AK.
18. GSK to BBK, undated letters, Dec. 1941.
19. Groucho Marx, *The Groucho Letters,* p. 33 (letter to Arthur Sheekman, Jan. 26, 1943).
20. GSK to BBK, undated letter.
21. Hilton to GSK, Dec. 15, 1941, GSK Papers, WCTR.
22. GSK to BBK, undated letter.
23. Miscellaneous clippings, GSK folder, LCL.

24. Conversation with George Oppenheimer.
25. BBK to AW, undated letter, AW Papers, Harvard University Library.
26. Richard Meryman, *Mank: The Wit, World, and Life of Herman Mankiewicz* (New York: William Morrow, 1978), p. 281.
27. Groucho Marx to GSK, undated letter, GSK Papers, WCTR.
28. Conversation with Ruth Goodman Goetz.
29. Conversation with Ruth Goodman Goetz.
30. Conversation with William Walton.
31. Conversation with Ruth Goodman Goetz.
32. AK to Clinton Wilder, undated letter.
33. Misdated 1942 in Marx, *Groucho Letters,* p. 31.
34. Miscellaneous clippings, *Doughgirls* scrapbook, LCL.
35. Conversation with Max Gordon.
36. Thus Fields reported to Chodorov; conversation with Jerome Chodorov.
37. Gordon, *Max Gordon Presents,* pp. 260–61.
38. BBK to AK, undated letter.
39. BBK to AW, undated letter, AW Papers, Harvard University Library.
40. BBK to AK, undated letter.
41. BBK, autobiographical MS.

Notes to Chapter 19   Sorrow

1. GSK to AW, undated letter, AW Papers, Harvard University Library.
2. GSK to AK, undated letter, spring 1942.
3. Conversation with Cecelia Ager; BBK to AW, undated letter, May 1943, AW Papers, Harvard University Library; GSK to AK, undated letter, May 1943.
4. John Chapman, New York *Journal-American,* undated clipping, *Naked Genius* folder, LCL.
5. Maurice Zolotow, "Genius with Its Clothes On," *NYT,* Oct. 31, Sec. 2, p. 1.
6. Zolotow, "Genius"; *Variety,* Nov. 17, 1943, p. 50.
7. Max Gordon, *Max Gordon Presents,* pp. 270–72; Ruth Gordon, *My Side* (New York: Harper & Row, 1976), pp. 443–45.
8. Ruth Gordon, *My Side,* p. 447.
9. Max Gordon, *Max Gordon Presents,* pp. 272–73; Ruth Gordon, *My Side,* p. 450; GSK to MH, undated letter, MH Papers, WCTR.
10. GSK to MH, undated letter, MH Papers, WCTR.
11. Max Gordon, *Max Gordon Presents,* p. 245; GSK, "On Getting Mr. Apley Straight," *NYT,* Nov. 26, 1944, Sec. 2, p. 1.
12. Lucius Beebe, "Stage Asides: It Happened in Boston," *NYHT,* undated clipping, *Late George Apley* folder, LCL.
13. GSK, "On Getting Mr. Apley Straight."
14. Leo G. Carroll to Jane Douglass, July 1966, Harvard University Library.
15. BBK to John Booth, Nov. 5, 1944.
16. MS in possession of AK.
17. MH to BBK, undated letter; conversation with William Walton.
18. BBK to John Booth, Apr. 1, 1945.

19. GSK, "Now It Can Be Told; Author of Latest 'Pinafore' Obliges," *NYHT*, *Hollywood Pinafore* scrapbook, LCL.
20. GSK, "Now It Can Be Told."
21. Conversation with Jerome Chodorov.
22. GSK, "By the Way," *Saturday Review of Literature*, Aug. 11, 1945, p. 22.
23. Conversation with Phyllis Cerf Wagner; *Variety*, Oct. 10, 1945, p. 54; AK.
24. Conversation with Cecelia Ager.

Notes to Chapter 20   Leueen

1. GSK to AK, undated letter, Feb. 1946.
2. Teichmann, *George S. Kaufman*, pp. 112–13.
3. *Variety*, Dec. 26, 1945, p. 42.
4. Undated clipping, *Park Avenue* folder, LCL.
5. Conversation with John Booth.
6. GSK to AK, undated letter, Feb. 1946.
7. GSK Papers, WCTR.
8. GSK to AK, undated letters, Feb.–Mar., 1946; conversation with Natalie Schafer.
9. Nunnally Johnson, "Kaufman Collaborator Pleads for More Play," Philadelphia *Daily Record*, undated clipping, *Park Avenue* folder, LCL (on writing the musical at GSK's suggestion).
10. Conversation with Burt Shevelove.
11. Undated letter from London, 1956, MH Papers, WCTR.
12. Conversation with Max Gordon.
13. GSK to AK, undated letter, Feb. 1946.
14. Conversation with Goodman Ace; Michael Singer, "Goody," NY, Apr. 4, 1977, p. 62.
15. Conversation with Bruce Colen.
16. J. D. Spiro, "Touring the Hollywood Studios," *NYT*, July 13, 1947, Sec. 2, p. 3.
17. Nunnally Johnson to Malcolm Goldstein, July 27, 1976.
18. GSK to MH, undated letter from London, early 1950s, MH Papers, WCTR.
19. Ring Lardner, Jr., *The Lardners*, p. 172; *Senator* script, Charles MacArthur Papers, WCTR.
20. Conversation with Beatrice Colen.
21. Conversation with Alfred Lunt.
22. *NYHT*, Nov. 20, 1948, *Bravo!* folder, LCL.
23. Conversation with Bruce Colen.
24. Conversations with Mary Wickes and Hiram Sherman.
25. Conversation with Mary Wickes.
26. Conversations with Max Gordon and Kitty Carlisle Hart.
27. Undated clipping, LM folder, LCL.
28. Conversations with Jerome Chodorov, Harold Rome, Kitty Carlisle Hart.
29. *NYT*, July 20, 1949, p. 21; *NYT*, July 21, 1949, p. 21.
30. *Variety*, Feb. 22, 1950, p. 56.

31. *NYT*, Dec. 7, 1949, p. 43; *Variety*, Feb. 22, 1950, p. 56.
32. Conversations with LM and Maurice Valency.
33. Conversations with Maurice Valency and with Alfred Lunt and Lynn Fontanne.
34. Undated clipping, *Enchanted* folder, LCL.
35. *Variety*, Apr. 19, 1950, p. 56.
36. GSK, "Gothamite in London," *NYT*, Aug. 6, 1950, Sec. 2, p. 1.
37. This and the following two paragraphs are based on GSK's letters to AK, May–July 1950.
38. Burrows, "Runyon 'Characters' Come to Broadway," *NYHT* Nov. 19, 1950, Sec. 5, p. 1; Marx, *Groucho Letters*, p. 195 (Kurnitz to Marx, Feb. 17, 1951).
39. Undated clipping, *Guys and Dolls* scrapbook, LCL.

Notes to Chapter 21
New Collaborators; Causes for Alarm

1. GSK, "Amazing Anecdotes," *NYT*, Feb. 11, 1951, Sec. 2, p. 1.
2. Conversation with Michael Wager.
3. Conversation with LM.
4. Miscellaneous clippings, *Of Thee I Sing* (1952) scrapbook, LCL.
5. Lewis Funke, "The Kaufman Team," *NYT*, Jan. 13, 1952, Sec. 2, p. 1; miscellaneous clippings, *Fancy Meeting You Again* folder, LCL; *Of Thee I Sing* (1952) scrapbook, LCL.
6. Undated clippings, *Fancy Meeting You Again* folder, LCL.
7. *Variety*, Dec. 5, 1951, p. 70.
8. *NYT*, Jan. 15, 1952. p. 23.
9. Sidney Fields, "Only Human," *Daily Mirror*, Feb. 27, 1953, LM folder, LCL.
10. *Variety*, Feb. 13, 1952, p. 67.
11. *Of Thee I Sing* (1952) folder, LCL.
12. Gordon, *Max Gordon Presents*, pp. 298–99; Teichmann, *George S. Kaufman*, pp. 1–4; conversation with Howard Teichmann.
13. Conversation with Howard Teichmann.
14. Conversation with Howard Teichmann.
15. John Crosby, Earl Wilson, clippings, GSK folder, LCL.
16. *Time*, Jan. 12, 1953, p. 68; *NYT*, Dec. 30, 1952, p. 21; *NYT*, Jan. 4, 1953, p. 65.
17. Conversation with Howard Teichmann.

Notes to Chapter 22   Tests of Endurance

1. Conversation with Howard Teichmann.
2. Clipping, source unidentifiable, *Solid Gold Cadillac* scrapbook, LCL.
3. Teichmann, *George S. Kaufman*, p. 13.
4. *Solid Gold Cadillac* scrapbook, LCL.
5. *NYT*, Oct. 19, 1953, p. 23.

6. Gilbert Milstein, "The Playwright's Ordeal by Fire, Etc.," *NYT Magazine,* Dec. 12, 1954, p. 12.
7. Conversation with Howard Teichmann.
8. GSK to AK, undated letter, May 1954.
9. Conversation with Howard Teichmann; GSK to Max Gordon, undated letter, 1954, Gordon Papers, Princeton University Library; GSK to AK, undated letter [1954].
10. GSK to AK, undated letter [July 1954].
11. *Silk Stockings* scrapbook, LCL; Hildegard Knef, *The Gift Horse* (New York: McGraw-Hill, 1971), p. 285.
12. Conversation with George Eells, Porter's biographer.
13. Knef, *Gift Horse,* pp. 303–5.
14. Conversation with Howard Teichmann.
15. *Silk Stockings* scrapbook, LCL.
16. Conversation with Lucinda Ballard Dietz.
17. Elliot Norton, "Kaufman Was Replaced in Philly," Boston *Globe,* Jan. 28, 1955, *Silk Stockings* scrapbook, LCL; Knef, *Gift Horse,* pp. 306–7.
18. Conversation with Howard Teichmann.
19. Excerpted from two undated (1955) letters from GSK to AK, in one of which GSK quotes the remark written to MH.
20. Undated letter, MH papers, WCTR.
21. GSK to AK, undated letters, summer 1956.
22. June 28, 1956, MH papers, WCTR.

Notes to Chapter 23   Last Scenes

1. Adza Vincent to Malcolm Goldstein, Oct. 10, 1978.
2. GSK to AK, undated letter [1956].
3. GSK to AK, Aug. 22, 1957 (on weight).
4. GSK to AK, Aug. 17, Aug. 22, 1957.
5. GSK to AK, Aug. 17, 1957.
6. Conversation with Natalie Schafer.
7. Norton, "Kaufman and 'Romanoff' Raise First Curtain," Boston *Globe,* Aug. 30, 1957, *Romanoff and Juliet* folder, LCL; Peter Ustinov, *Dear Me* (Boston: Little, Brown, 1977), pp. 293–94.
8. GSK, "The Tryout Blues (or Coos)," *Romanoff and Juliet* folder, LCL.
9. GSK to Cerf, Jan. 8, 1958, Cerf Papers, Columbia University Library.
10. Conversation with Ruth Goodman Goetz; GSK folder, LCL.
11. Conversation with Ruth Goodman Goetz.
12. Exchange of letters, Theater Collection of the Museum of the City of New York.
13. Conversation with Marc Connelly.
14. From an audio tape of excerpts of the broadcasts in the possession of AK.
15. Conversation with Jean Dixon.
16. Hart, *Act One,* p. 281.
17. Conversation with Kitty Carlisle Hart.

18. George Hamilton played Hart. The film, which was produced and directed by Hart's friend Dore Schary, was not a success.
19. Conversation with Howard Teichmann.
20. Conversation with Beatrice Colen.
21. Conversation with Allan Friedlich.
22. Editorial, *NYT*, June 3, 1961, p. 22.

Index